MW01092320

Essentials of Statistics for Criminology and Criminal Justice

This book is dedicated to our son, John Bachman-Paternoster, and John would like to dedicate this book to our wonder-dog, Mickey.

Sara Miller McCune founded SAGE Publishing in 1965 to support the dissemination of usable knowledge and educate a global community. SAGE publishes more than 1000 journals and over 800 new books each year, spanning a wide range of subject areas. Our growing selection of library products includes archives, data, case studies and video. SAGE remains majority owned by our founder and after her lifetime will become owned by a charitable trust that secures the company's continued independence.

Los Angeles | London | New Delhi | Singapore | Washington DC | Melbourne

Essentials of Statistics for Criminology and Criminal Justice

Raymond Paternoster
University of Maryland

Ronet D. Bachman
University of Delaware

Los Angeles | London | New Delhi
Singapore | Washington DC | Melbourne

FOR INFORMATION:

SAGE Publications, Inc.
2455 Teller Road
Thousand Oaks, California 91320
E-mail: order@sagepub.com

SAGE Publications Ltd.
1 Oliver's Yard
55 City Road
London EC1Y 1SP
United Kingdom

SAGE Publications India Pvt. Ltd.
B 1/I 1 Mohan Cooperative Industrial Area
Mathura Road, New Delhi 110 044
India

SAGE Publications Asia-Pacific Pte. Ltd.
3 Church Street
#10-04 Samsung Hub
Singapore 049483

Copyright © 2018 by SAGE Publications, Inc.

All rights reserved. No part of this book may be reproduced or utilized in any form or by any means, electronic or mechanical, including photocopying, recording, or by any information storage and retrieval system, without permission in writing from the publisher.

All trademarks depicted within this book, including trademarks appearing as part of a screenshot, figure, or other image are included solely for the purpose of illustration and are the property of their respective holders. The use of the trademarks in no way indicates any relationship with, or endorsement by, the holders of said trademarks. SPSS is a registered trademark of International Business Machines Corporation.

Printed in the United States of America

ISBN 978-1-5063-6547-3

Acquisitions Editor: Jessica Miller
Editorial Assistant: Jennifer Rubio
eLearning Editor: Laura Kirkhuff
Production Editor: Kelly DeRosa
Copy Editor: D. J. Peck
Typesetter: Hurix Systems Pvt. Ltd.
Proofreader: Theresa Kay
Indexer: Jeanne Busemeyer
Cover Designer: Michael Dubowe
Marketing Manager: Amy Lammers

This book is printed on acid-free paper.

17 18 19 20 21 10 9 8 7 6 5 4 3 2 1

Brief Contents

Detailed Contents

Preface

One of the most important aspects of teaching a statistics course is conveying to students the vital role that research and statistics play in the study of criminology and criminal justice. After years of teaching statistics courses, we have found that the best avenue for achieving this goal has been to link the teaching of "how to calculate and interpret statistics" with contemporary research examples from the field. By combining discussions of the "how to" in statistics with real data and research examples, students not only learn how to perform and understand statistical analyses but also learn how to make the connection between how they are used and why they are so important.

In this text, *Essentials of Statistics for Criminology and Criminal Justice* published by SAGE, we have retained our unique method of "instruction by example" that is used in our more comprehensive text, *Statistics for Criminology and Criminal Justice* (fourth edition). Our goal in this text is to describe the basic statistical procedures used in our discipline that is more accessible and readable for students. In view of this general goal, we have chosen to emphasize a practical approach to the use of statistics in research. We continue to stress the interpretation and understanding of statistical operations in answering research questions, be they theoretical or policy oriented in nature. Of course, this approach is at the expense of a detailed theoretical or mathematical treatment of statistics. Accordingly, we do not provide derivations of formulas, nor do we offer proofs of the underlying statistical theory behind the operations we present in this text. As you will see, however, we have not sacrificed statistical rigor.

Given the title, it is clear that we had the student majoring in criminology and criminal justice particularly in mind as a reader of this text. This can easily be seen in the nature of the research examples presented throughout the book. What are the causes of violence? What is the nature of hate crimes in the United States? Do different types of police patrolling activities affect rates of crime? Is crime increasing or decreasing? These and many other research questions are examined in the examples provided in the book, which we believe not only makes the book more interesting to criminal justice students but also makes the statistical material easier to understand and apply. If this book communicates the excitement of research and the importance of careful statistical analysis in research, then our endeavor has succeeded. We hope that students will enjoy learning how to investigate research questions related to criminal justice and criminology with statistics and that many will learn how to do some research of their own along the way.

In *Essentials of Statistics for Criminology and Criminal Justice*, we continue to use our basic approach of describing each statistic's purpose and origins as we go. To facilitate learning, we present statistical formulas along with step-by-step instructions for calculation. The primary emphasis in our coverage of each statistical operation is on its interpretation and understanding. This edition updates all crime data and includes many new research examples. Each chapter sets up case studies from the research literature to highlight the concepts and statistical techniques under discussion. There are hand calculation practice problems at the end of each chapter that include examples from contemporary research in the field. There are also SPSS exercises on the student study site that correspond to the chapter material; these exercises use real data, including subsets of data from the National Crime Victimization Survey, Monitoring the Future, the Youth Risk Behavior Survey, state-level crime data from the Uniform Crime Reports (UCR), and opinion data from the General Social Survey. In addition, answers to all practice problems and computer output for all IBM® SPSS® Statistics* exercises are available on the instructor's website, and the answers to odd-numbered practice problems are available to students in the back of the book.

---

*IBM® SPSS® Statistics was formerly called PASW® Statistics. SPSS is a registered trademark of International Business Machines Corporation.

▣ Organization of the Book

The first chapter of the text sets the stage for statistical inquiry by highlighting the important role that understanding this material plays in our discipline. This chapter also describes the important concepts of populations and samples, variables, and the different ways of measuring and presenting variables. Chapter 2 offers an overview of interpreting data through the use of such graphical techniques as frequency distributions, pie charts, and bar graphs for qualitative data as well as histograms, frequency polygons, and time plots for quantitative data. Chapter 3 provides an overview of measures of central tendency, and Chapter 4 discusses the various statistical techniques for measuring the variability of a variable, including the standard deviation.

From this discussion of descriptive statistics, Chapter 5 outlines the foundation of inferential statistics, probability theory, and sampling distributions (the normal distribution). In this chapter, the concept of hypothesis testing using the binomial distribution is also introduced. The remainder of the book concerns issues related to hypothesis testing and the search for a relationship between one or more independent variables and a dependent variable. Chapter 6 begins the journey into inferential statistics with confidence intervals. The steps to formal hypothesis testing are systematically repeated in each of the subsequent chapters.

Chapter 7 introduces hypothesis testing using one independent variable to predict one dependent variable by focusing on hypothesis tests for one population mean. Chapter 8 is concerned with hypothesis testing when both independent and dependent variables are categorical using cross-tabulation and chi-square. Chapter 9 examines hypothesis tests involving two population means or proportions, including tests for independent and matched groups. Chapter 10 discusses hypothesis testing involving three or more means using analysis of variance techniques. In Chapter 11, bivariate correlation and ordinary least-squares (OLS) regression analysis are both introduced. This chapter discusses the essential framework of linear regression, including the notion of "least squares," the importance of scatterplots, the regression line, and hypothesis tests with slopes and correlation coefficients. The book concludes with Chapter 12, which extends OLS regression to two independent variables and one dependent variable.

▣ Learning Aids

Working together, the authors and editors have developed a format that makes *Essentials of Statistics for Criminology and Criminal Justice* a readable, user-friendly text. In addition to all of the changes we have already mentioned, the text also features the following student learning aids:

- Step-by-step lists and marginal key term and key formula boxes are included in every chapter to make mastery of statistical concepts and procedures easier.

- Each chapter closes with traditional practice problems to give students plenty of hands-on experience with important techniques, incorporating research questions from contemporary published research from the discipline. Solutions to all end-of-chapter problems are also provided to instructors.

▣ Digital Resources

study.sagepub.com/paternoster

As a full-service publisher of quality educational products, SAGE does much more than just sell textbooks. It also creates and publishes supplements for use with those textbooks.

Calling all instructors!

It's easy to log on to SAGE's password-protected Instructor Teaching Site for complete and protected access to all text-specific Instructor Resources. Simply provide your institutional information for verification and within 72 hours you'll be able to use your login information for any SAGE title! Password-protected Instructor Resources include the following:

- **Test banks** provide a diverse range of pre-written options as well as the opportunity to edit any question and/or insert personalized questions to effectively assess students' progress and understanding

- **Sample course syllabi** for semester and quarter courses provide suggested models for structuring one's course

- Editable, chapter-specific **PowerPoint® slides** offer complete flexibility for creating a multimedia presentation for the course

- EXCLUSIVE! Access to full-text **SAGE journal articles** have been carefully selected to support and expand on the concepts presented in each chapter to encourage students to think critically

- **Web resources** include links that appeal to students with different learning styles

- **Extra practice tests and solutions** to allow students to test their knowledge of the material

- **Discussion group problems and solutions** provide sample chapter test questions, final exam questions, and solutions

- **Extra practice exercises** for all chapters to encourage class discussions and activities focused on chapter content

- **Downloadable Data from real data sets:** (1) a subset of the 2013 Monitoring the Future Survey, (2) a state-level data set that includes rates of homicide, burglary, and violent crime along with demographic and social indicators such as poverty and social disorganization, (3) a subset of the 2013 Youth Risk Behavior Survey, and (4) a sample of violent victimizations from the National Crime Victimization Survey

Use the Student Study Site to get the most out of your course! Our Student Study Site is completely open-access and offers a wide range of additional features. The open-access Student Study Site includes the following:

- Mobile-friendly **eFlashcards** strengthen understanding of key terms and concepts

- Mobile-friendly practice **quizzes** allow for independent assessment by students of their mastery of course material

- **Web resources** include links that appeal to students with different learning styles

- **SPSS Student Datasets** to enhance student learning and provide more integration with the content

- **SPSS exercises** provide the opportunity to apply the statistics covered in each chapter using a computer software program

- **Practice problems and solutions**

- **Practice tests and solutions**

- **Discussion group problems and solutions**

- **Learning objectives** reinforce the most important material

- EXCLUSIVE! Access to full-text **SAGE journal articles** that have been carefully selected to support and expand on the concepts presented in each chapter

▣ Acknowledgments

Many authors have good editors, but not many have good editors who also turn out to be good friends. We are very lucky in having both with Jerry Westby, an editor extraordinaire and one of the most decent persons either of us have bumped into. We have cherished his sage (☺) advice on editorial matters, but even more the close bond of friendship that we share. We are also indebted to others on the SAGE team, including our developmental editor (and SAGE's new acquisitions editor, taking over for Jerry), Jessica Miller, who provided invaluable pedagogical advice along with a very critical eye while shepherding the text through the publication process, D. J. Peck for his meticulous and most excellent copyediting (a.k.a. "eagle eye Peck"), and Laura Kirkhuff and Kelly DeRosa for their attention to the numerous issues related to the ancillaries and the production process that seemed to never end!

We owe a huge debt of gratitude to those who provided meticulous reviews and sage advice for this text:

Joe Young, American University

Gary Vause II, University of Illinois at Chicago

Emmanuel N. Amadi, Mississippi Valley State University

Shaila Khan, Tougaloo College

Stephen Holmes, University of Central Florida

Shawn Morrow, Angelo State University

Dennis Mares, Southern Illinois University Edwardsville

Gina Erickson, Hamline University

Don Hummer, Penn State Harrisburg

Christopher Salvatore, Montclair State University

In addition, our hats are off to two PhD students: Theodore (Teddy) Wilson for his meticulous proofreading under pressure and for the end-of-chapter practice problems and Matthew (Matt) Manierre for the creative end-of-chapter SPSS exercises. Teddy and Matt are both amazing methodologists and statisticians in their own right and put forth Herculean efforts for this text!

Of course, we continue to be indebted to the many students we have had an opportunity to teach and mentor over the years at both the undergraduate and graduate levels. In many respects, this book could not have been written without these ongoing and reciprocal teaching and learning experiences. To all of our students, past and future: You inspire us to become better teachers! And finally, to whom this book is dedicated, our son, John, thank you for being you—our "beautiful boy"!

—Ronet Bachman and Ray Paternoster,
Newark, Delaware

About the Authors

Raymond Paternoster, PhD is a professor in the Department of Criminology and Criminal Justice at the University of Maryland. He received his B.A. in sociology at the University of Delaware, where he was introduced to criminology by Frank Scarpitti, and obtained his PhD at Florida State University under the careful and dedicated tutelage of Gordon Waldo and Ted Chiricos. He is coauthor of *The Death Penalty: America's Experience With Capital Punishment* (with Robert Brame and Sarah Bacon). In addition to his interest in statistics, he also pursues questions related to offender decision making and rational choice theory, desistance from crime, and capital punishment. With funding from the National Institute of Justice, he is currently working on research comparing the decision-making patterns and characteristics of a sample of serious adult offenders and a comparable group of community members.

Ronet D. Bachman, PhD is a professor in the Department of Sociology and Criminal Justice at the University of Delaware. She is coauthor of *The Practice of Research in Criminology and Criminal Justice* (sixth edition, with Russell Schutt), coauthor of *Violence: The Enduring Problem* and *Murder American Style* (with Alexander Alvarez), coeditor of *Explaining Crime and Criminology: Essays in Contemporary Criminal Theory* (with Raymond Paternoster), and author of *Death and Violence on the Reservation: Homicide, Suicide and Family Violence in Contemporary American Indian Communities* as well as author/coauthor of numerous articles that examine the epidemiology and etiology of violence, with a particular emphasis on women, the elderly, and minority populations. Her most recent federally funded research was a mixed methods study that investigated the long-term trajectories of offending behavior using official data of a prison cohort released during the early 1990s and then interviewed in 2011.

CHAPTER 1

Setting the Stage: Why Learning This Stuff Is Important!

" Do not worry about your difficulties in Mathematics. I can assure you mine are still greater. "

—Albert Einstein

LEARNING OBJECTIVES

1. Describe the role statistical analyses play in criminological and criminal justice research.

2. Identify the difference between a sample and a population and explain the difference between probability and nonprobability sampling techniques.

3. State the difference between descriptive and inferential statistics.

4. Identify the four levels of measurement that variables can have.

5. Describe the difference between variables that identify qualities and variables that identify quantities.

6. Explain the differences among raw frequencies, proportions, percentages, and rates.

🔲 Introduction

Most of you reading this book are probably taking a course in statistics because it is required to graduate, not because you were seeking a little adventure and thought it would be fun. Nor are you taking the course because there is something missing in your life and, thus, you think the study of statistics is necessary to make you intellectually "well rounded." At least this has been our experience when teaching statistics courses. Everyone who has taught a statistics course has probably heard the litany of sorrows expressed by their students at the beginning of the course—the "wailing and gnashing of teeth." "Oh, I have been putting this off for so long—I dreaded having to take this." "I have a mental block when it comes to math—I haven't had any math courses since high school." "Why do I have to learn this? I'm never going to use it."

Although it is impossible for us to allay all of the fear and apprehension you may be experiencing right now, it may help to know that virtually everyone can and will make it through this course, even those of you who have trouble counting change. We have found that persistence and tenacity can overcome even the most extreme mathematical handicaps. Those of you who are particularly rusty with your math, and those of you who just want a quick confidence builder, should refer to Appendix A at the back of this book, which reviews some basic math lessons. Our book also includes practice problems and, more important, the answers to those problems. After teaching this course for more than two decades, we have found that every student who puts forth effort and time can pass the course! Our chapters are designed to provide step-by-step instructions for calculating the statistics with real criminal justice data and case studies so you will learn not only about statistics but also a little about research going on in our discipline.

We hope that after this course you will be able to understand and manipulate statistics for yourself and that you will be a knowledgeable consumer of the statistical material you are confronted with daily and, believe it or not, you will confront in your criminal justice career. Understanding how to manipulate data and interpret statistics will be a tremendous asset to you, no matter what direction you plan to take in your career. Virtually every job application, as well as every application to graduate school and law school, now asks you about your data analysis skills. We now exist in a world where programs to organize and manipulate data are everywhere. Many police academies now have training for data analysis because virtually every police department now uses crime mapping programs to monitor high crime areas known as "hot spots" for special prevention efforts.

In addition to the mathematical skills required to compute statistics, we also hope to leave you with an understanding of what different statistical tests or operations can and cannot do and what they do and do not tell us about a given problem. The foundations for the statistics presented in this book are derived from complicated mathematical theory. You will be glad to know, however, that it is *not* the purpose of this book to provide you with the proofs necessary to substantiate this body of theory. In this book, we provide you with two basic types of knowledge: (1) knowledge about the basic mathematical foundations of each statistic, as well as the ability to manipulate and conduct statistical analysis for your own research, and (2) an ability to interpret the results of statistical analysis and to apply these results to the real world. We want you, then, to have the skills to both calculate and comprehend social statistics. These two purposes are not mutually exclusive but are related. We think that the ability to carry out the mathematical manipulations of a formula and come up with a statistical result is almost worthless unless you can interpret this result and give it meaning. Therefore, information about the mechanics of conducting statistical tests and information about interpreting the results of these tests will be emphasized equally throughout this text.

Student Study Site

Visit the open-access Student Study Site at study.sagepub.com/paternoster to access additional study tools including mobile-friendly eFlashcards, web quizzes, links to SAGE journal articles, additional data sets, SPSS exercises, and more!

🔲 Setting the Stage for Statistical Inquiry

Before we become more familiar with statistics in the upcoming chapters, we first want to set the stage for statistical inquiry. The data we use in criminology are derived from many different sources:

from official government agency data such as the Federal Bureau of Investigation's (FBI) Uniform Crime Reports; from social surveys conducted by the government (the Bureau of Justice Statistics' National Crime Victimization Survey), ourselves, or other researchers; from experiments; from direct observation, as either a participant observer or an unobtrusive observer; or from a content analysis of existing images (historical or contemporary) such as newspaper articles or films. As you can see, the research methods we employ are very diverse.

Criminological researchers often conduct "secondary data analysis" (Riedel, 2012), which, simply put, means re-analyzing data that already exist. These data usually come from one of two places; either they are official data collected by local, state, and federal agencies (e.g., rates of crime reported to police, information on incarcerated offenders from state correctional authorities, or adjudication data from the courts), or they are data collected from surveys sponsored by government agencies or conducted by other researchers. Virtually all of these data collected by government agencies and a great deal of survey data collected by independent researchers are made available to the public through the Inter-University Consortium for Political and Social Research (ICPSR), which is located at the University of Michigan.

The ICPSR maintains and provides access to a vast archive of criminological data for research and instruction, and it offers training in quantitative methods to facilitate effective data use. For example, data available online at the ICPSR include the Supplementary Homicide Reports (SHR) provided by the U.S. Department of Justice, which contain information for each homicide from police reports, including such details as the relationship between victims and offenders, use of weapons, and other characteristics of victims and offenders; survey data from the National Crime Victimization Survey (NCVS), which interviews a sample of U.S. household residents to determine their experiences with both property and violent crime, regardless of whether the crimes were reported to police or anyone else; and survey data from the National Opinion Survey of Crime and Justice, which asked adults for their opinion about a wide range of criminal justice issues. These are just a few examples of the immense archive of data made available at the ICPSR. Take a look at what is available by going on its website (www.icpsr.umich.edu).

▣ The Role of Statistical Methods in Criminology and Criminal Justice

Research and statistics are important in our discipline because they enable us to monitor phenomena over time and across geographic locations, and they allow us to determine relationships between phenomena. Of course, we make conclusions about the relationships between phenomena every day, but these conclusions are most often based on biased perceptions and selective personal experiences.

In criminological research, we rely on scientific methods, including statistics, to help us perform these tasks. Science relies on logical and systematic methods to answer questions, and it does so in a way that allows others to inspect and evaluate its methods. In the realm of criminological research, these methods are not so unusual. They involve asking questions, observing behavior, and counting people, all of which we often do in our everyday lives. The difference is that researchers develop, refine, apply, and report their understanding of the social world more systematically.

Descriptive Research

Defining and describing social phenomena of interest is a part of almost any research investigation, but descriptive research is the primary focus of many studies of youth crime and violence. Some of the central questions used in descriptive studies are as follows: "How many people are victims of youth violence?" "How many youths are offenders?" "What are the most common crimes committed by youthful offenders?" and "How many youths are arrested and incarcerated each year for crime?"

Science: A set of logical, systematic, documented methods for investigating nature and natural processes; the knowledge produced by these investigations.

Descriptive research: Research in which phenomena are defined and described.

Case Study

Youth Violence

The population of the United States all too frequently mourns the deaths of young innocent lives taken in school shootings. The deadliest elementary school shooting to date took place on December 14, 2012, when a 20-year-old man named Adam Lanza walked into an elementary school in Newtown, Connecticut, armed with several semiautomatic weapons and killed 20 children and 6 adults. On April 16, 2007, Cho Seung-Hui perpetrated the deadliest college mass shooting by killing 32 students, faculty, and staff and left more than 30 others injured on the campus of Virginia Tech in Blacksburg, Virginia. Cho was armed with two semiautomatic handguns that he had legally purchased and a vest filled with ammunition. As police were closing in on the scene, he killed himself. The deadliest high school shooting occurred on April 20, 1999, when Eric Harris and Dylan Klebold killed 12 students and a teacher before killing themselves at Columbine High School in suburban Colorado.

None of these mass murderers was a typical terrorist, and each of these incidents caused a media frenzy. Headlines such as "The School Violence Crisis" and "School Crime Epidemic" were plastered across national newspapers and weekly news journals. Unfortunately, the media play a large role in how we perceive both problems and solutions. What are your perceptions of violence committed by youths, and how did you acquire them? What do you believe are the causes of youth violence? Many (frequently conflicting) factors have been blamed for youth violence in American society, including the easy availability of guns, the lack of guns in classrooms for protection, the use of weapons in movies and television, the moral decay of our nation, poor parenting, unaware teachers, school and class size, racial prejudice, teenage alienation, the Internet and World Wide Web, anti-Semitism, violent video games, rap and rock music, and the list goes on.

Of course, youth violence is not a new phenomenon in the United States. It has always been a popular topic of social science research and the popular press. Predictably, whenever a phenomenon is perceived as an epidemic, numerous explanations emerge to explain it. Unfortunately, most of these explanations are based on the media and popular culture, not on empirical research. Unlike the anecdotal information floating around in the mass media, social scientists interested in this phenomenon have amassed a substantial body of findings that have refined knowledge about the factors related to the problem of gun violence, and some of this knowledge is being used to shape social policy. Research that relies on statistical analysis generally falls into three categories of purposes for social scientific research: descriptive, explanatory, and evaluation.

Police reports: Data used to measure crime based on incidents that become known to police departments.

Uniform Crime Reports (UCR): Official reports about crime incidents that are reported to police departments across the United States and then voluntarily reported to the Federal Bureau of Investigation (FBI), which compiles them for statistics purposes.

National Incident-Based Reporting System (NIBRS): Official reports about crime incidents that are reported to police departments across the United States and then voluntarily reported to the Federal Bureau of Investigation (FBI), which compiles them for statistics purposes. This system is slowly replacing the older UCR program.

Case Study

How Prevalent Is Youth Violence?

Police reports: One of the most enduring sources of information on lethal violence in the United States is the FBI's SHR. Data measuring the prevalence of nonlethal forms of violence such as robbery and assaults are a bit more complicated. How do we know how many young people assault victims each year? People who report their victimizations to police represent one avenue for these calculations. The FBI compiles these numbers in its **Uniform Crime Reports (UCR)** system, which is slowly being replaced by the **National Incident-Based Reporting System (NIBRS)**. Both of these data sources rely on state, county, and city law enforcement agencies across the United States to participate voluntarily in the reporting program. Can you imagine why relying on these data sources may be problematic for estimating prevalence rates of violent victimizations? If victimizations are never reported to police, they are not counted. This is especially problematic for victimizations between people who know each other and other offenses like rape in which only a fraction of incidents are ever reported to police.

Surveys: Many, if not most, social scientists believe the best way to determine the magnitude of violent victimization is through random sample surveys. This basically means randomly selecting individuals in the population of interest and asking them about their victimization experiences via a mailed or Internet, telephone, or in-person questionnaire. The only ongoing survey to do this on an annual basis is the NCVS, which is sponsored by the U.S. Department of Justice's Bureau of Justice Statistics. Among other questions, the NCVS asks questions like "Has anyone attacked or threatened you with a weapon, for instance, a gun or knife; by something thrown, such as a rock or bottle; include any grabbing, punching, or choking?" Estimates indicate that youths aged 12 to 24 years all have the highest rates of violent victimization, which have been declining steadily since the highs witnessed in the early 1990s despite the recent increases observed in homicide rates for this age group in some locations.

Another large research survey that estimates the magnitude of youth violence (along with other risk-taking behavior such as taking drugs and smoking) is called the Youth Risk Behavior Survey (YRBS), which has been conducted every 2 years in the United States since 1990. Respondents to this survey are a national sample of approximately 16,000 high school students in grades 9 through 12. To measure the extent of youth violence, students are asked a number of questions, including the following: "During the past 12 months, how many times were you in a physical fight?" "During the past 12 months, how many times were you in a physical fight in which you were injured and had to be seen by a doctor or nurse?" "During the past 12 months, how many times were you in a physical fight on school property?" and "During the past 12 months, how many times did someone threaten or injure you with a gun, knife, or club on school property?"

Of course, another way to measure violence would be to ask respondents about their offending behaviors. Some surveys do this, including the Rochester Youth Development Study (RYDS). The RYDS sample consists of 1,000 students who were in the seventh and eighth grades in the Rochester, New York, public schools during the spring semester of the 1988 school year. This project has interviewed the original respondents at 12 different times, including the last interview that took place in 1997 when respondents were in their early 20s (Thornberry, Krohn, Lizotte, & Bushway, 2008). As you can imagine, respondents are typically more reluctant to reveal offending behavior compared with their victimization experiences. However, these surveys have been a useful tool for examining the factors related to violent offending and other delinquency. We should also point out that although this discussion has been specific to violence, the measures we have discussed in this section, along with their strengths and weaknesses, apply to measuring all crime in general.

Explanatory Research

Many people consider explanation to be the premier goal of any science. **Explanatory research** seeks to identify the causes and effects of social phenomena, to predict how one phenomenon will change or vary in response to variation in some other phenomenon. Researchers adopted explanation as a goal when they began to ask such questions as "Are kids who participate in after-school activities less likely to engage in delinquency?" and "Does the unemployment rate influence the frequency of youth crime?" In explanatory research, studies are often interested in explaining relationships between variables. A **variable** is any element to which different values can be attributed. In surveys, respondents' gender is usually a variable with two values, male and female. Race/ethnicity is a variable with many values such as American Indian, African American, Asian, Hispanic, Caucasian, and mixed-race. Age is another variable that can take on different values such as 2, 16, and 55 years.

Surveys: Research method used to measure the prevalence of behavior, attitudes, or any other phenomenon by asking a sample of people to fill out a questionnaire either in person, through the mail or Internet, or on the telephone.

Explanatory research: Research that seeks to identify causes and/or effects of social phenomena.

Variable: Any element to which different values can be attributed.

When we are interested in relationships between variables, we call that which we are attempting to explain a dependent variable. In research, the dependent variable is expected to vary or change depending on variation or change in the independent variable. In this causal type of explanation, the independent variable is the cause and the dependent variable is the effect.

Case Study

What Factors Are Related to Youth Delinquency and Violence?

When we move from description to explanation, we want to understand the direct relationship between two or more things. Does x explain y, or if x happens, is y also likely to occur? What are some of the factors related to youth violence? Using the South Carolina YRBS (described earlier), John MacDonald and colleagues (MacDonald, Piquero, Valois, & Zullig, 2005) examined whether constructs from general strain theory (GST) (Agnew, 1992) and Michael R. Gottfredson and Travis Hirschi's (1990) general theory of crime could predict youth violence. Testing hypotheses generated from theory is often a goal of explanatory research. A theory is a logically interrelated set of propositions about empirical reality. Examples of criminological theories include social learning theory, general strain theory, social disorganization theory, and routine activities theory. A hypothesis is simply a tentative statement about empirical reality involving a relationship between two or more variables.

GST generally contends that strain, such as a disjunction or misfit between expectations and aspirations (e.g., wanting a good job but not being able to get one), increases the likelihood that individuals will experience negative emotions (e.g., anger and anxiety), which in turn increases the likelihood of antisocial or violent behavior. The general theory of crime claims that self-control, which is primarily formed by the relationship children have with their parents and/or guardians, is the motivating factor for all crime. Individuals with low self-control, the theory predicts, will be more likely to pursue immediate gratification, be impulsive, prefer simple tasks, engage in risky behavior, have volatile tempers, and so on.

Earlier we described how the YRBS measures violent offending. To measure life satisfaction, MacDonald et al. (2005) used six questions from the YRBS that asked respondents to report on general satisfaction or the degree to which they felt "terrible" or "delighted" about family life, friendships, school, self, residential location, and overall life. To measure self-control, the authors used the indicators of smoking and sexual behavior to represent risky behaviors that are not illegal since they "reflect impulsivity and short-run hedonism" (p. 1502). When predicting violent behavior, they also controlled for a number of other factors like employment, drug use, family structure, and religious participation, along with age, race, and gender.

Consistent with the general theory of crime, MacDonald et al. (2005) found that high school students who reported more impulsive behaviors, indicative of low self-control, also reported greater participation in violent behavior. In addition, results indicated that students who were more satisfied with life were significantly less likely to have engaged in violence compared with their less satisfied peers. In this way, MacDonald and his colleagues were conducting explanatory research.

Dependent variable: Variable that is expected to change or vary depending on the variation in the independent variable.

Independent variable: Variable that is expected to cause or lead to variation or change in the dependent variable.

Theory: Logically interrelated set of propositions about empirical reality that can be tested.

Hypothesis: Tentative statement about empirical reality involving the relationship between two or more variables.

Evaluation research: Research about social programs or interventions.

Evaluation Research

Evaluation research seeks to determine the effects of a social program or other types of intervention. It is a type of explanatory research because it deals with cause and effect. However, evaluation research differs from other forms of explanatory research because evaluation research considers the implementation and effects of social policies and programs. These issues may not be relevant in other types of explanatory research.

Evaluation research is a type of explanatory research, but instead of testing theory, it is most often used to determine whether an implemented program or policy had the intended outcome. To reduce violence and create a safer atmosphere at schools across the country, literally thousands of schools have adopted some form of violence prevention training. These programs generally provide cognitive–behavioral and social skills training on various topics using a variety of methods. Such programs are commonly referred to as conflict resolution and peer mediation training. Many of these prevention programs are designed to improve interpersonal problem-solving skills among children and adolescents by training children in cognitive processing such as identifying interpersonal problems and generating nonaggressive solutions. There is limited evidence, however, that such programs are actually effective in reducing violence.

Case Study

How Effective Are Violence Prevention Programs in Schools?

As many school administrators will tell you, there are direct mail, e-mail, and in-person direct sales efforts to sell them programs that reduce violence, increase empathy among students, promote a positive school environment, promote other forms of mental well-being, and on and on. Unfortunately, not many of these programs have been rigorously evaluated to ensure they actually do what they promise. One program that has been the target of rigorous evaluation is Gang Resistance Education and Training (G.R.E.A.T.), which is a school-based gang and violence prevention program. This cognitive-based program was intended to, among other things, teach students about crime and its effects on victims, how to resolve conflicts without violence, and how to improve individual responsibility through goal setting. The G.R.E.A.T. program addresses multiple risk factors for violent offending among three domains: school, peer, and individual. Because it is curriculum based in the school, it does not address risk factors present in the family or neighborhood. It is a 13-week program taught in sixth or seventh grade and attempts to affect several risk factors, including school commitment and performance, association with conventional or delinquent peers, empathy, and self-control, among others.

Finn-Aage Esbensen and his colleagues (Esbensen, Osgood, Peterson, Taylor, & Carson, 2013) evaluated the long-term effects of the G.R.E.A.T. program in seven cities across the United States. Schools selected for the program randomly assigned some seventh-grade classrooms to get the treatment (experimental groups), while the other classrooms did not (control groups). This is called a true experimental design. It is an extremely strong research method for determining the effects of programs or policies because if groups are truly randomly assigned, there is a strong reason to believe that differences between the groups after program implementation, such as reduced violent offending, are because of the program and not some other factor that existed before the introduction of the treatment.

Both experimental and control group students in Esbensen and colleagues' (2013) study completed four follow-up surveys annually for 4 years. The statistical methods employed by Esbensen and his colleagues are very complicated and beyond the scope of this text, so we will simply highlight the general findings. When the data for all seven sites were combined, there were no differences in violent offending between experimental and control group students over the 4-year period. Those students who participated in the G.R.E.A.T. program were, however, less likely to become members of gangs, had higher levels of altruism, had less anger and risk taking, and had more favorable attitudes toward the police, among other things.

With these results, would you deem the G.R.E.A.T. program a success? These are the important questions evaluation research must address. Esbensen et al. (2013) agree that the program did not reduce general delinquency or violent offending but note that it was effective in reducing gang membership, which is also a risk factor for violent offending. Can these findings be generalized to all the seventh-grade students? That is the question to which we now turn.

▣ Populations and Samples

The words "population" and "sample" should already have some meaning to you. When you think of a population, you probably think of the population of some locality such as the United States, or the city or state in which you reside, or the university or college you attend. As with most social science research, samples in criminology consist of samples at different units of analysis, including countries, states, cities, neighborhoods, prisons, schools, and individuals. Since it is too difficult, too costly, and sometimes impossible to get information on the entire population of interest, we must often solicit the information of interest from samples. Samples are simply subsets of a larger population.

Most official statistics collected by the U.S. government are derived from information obtained from samples, not from the entire population (the U.S. Census taken every 10 years is an exception). For example, the NCVS is a survey used to obtain information on the incidence and characteristics of criminal victimization in the United States based on a sample of the U.S. population. Every year, the NCVS interviews more than 100,000 individuals aged 12 years or older to solicit information on their experiences with victimization that were both reported and unreported to the police. Essentially, professional interviewers ask persons who are selected into the sample if they were the victim of a crime during the past 6 months regardless of whether this victimization was reported to police.

You may be thinking right now, "Well, what if I am only interested in a small population?" Good question! Let's say we were interested in finding out about job-related stress experienced by law enforcement officers in your state. Although it would be easier to contact every individual in this population compared with every U.S. citizen, it would still be extremely difficult and costly to obtain information from every law enforcement officer, even within one state. In fact, in almost all instances, we have to settle for a sample derived from the population of interest rather than study the full population. For this reason, the "population" usually remains an unknown entity whose characteristics we can only estimate. The generalizability of a study is the extent to which it can be used to inform us about persons, places, or events that were *not* studied.

We usually make a generalization about the characteristics of a population by using information we have from a sample; that is, we make inferences from our sample data to the population. Because the purpose of sampling is to make these generalizations, we must be very meticulous when selecting our sample. The primary goal of sampling is to make sure that the sample we select is actually *representative* of the population we are estimating and want to generalize to. Think about this for a minute. What is representative? Generally, if the characteristics of a sample (e.g., age, race/ethnicity, gender) look similar to the characteristics of the population, the sample is said to be representative. For example, if you were interested in estimating the proportion of the population that favors the death penalty, then to be representative your sample should contain about 50% men and 50% women because that is the makeup of the U.S. population. It should also contain about 15% of individuals age 65 years or older. If your sample included a disproportionately high number of males or less than 15% age 65 or older, it would be unrepresentative.

In sum, the primary question of interest in sample generalizability is as follows: *Can findings from a sample be generalized to the population from which the sample was drawn?* Sample generalizability depends on sample quality, which is determined by the amount of sampling error present in your sample. Sampling error can generally be defined as the difference between the sample estimate and the population value that you are estimating. The larger the sampling error, the less representative the sample and, as a result, the less generalizable the findings are to the population.

With a few special exceptions, a good sample should be representative of the larger population from which it was drawn. A representative sample looks like the population from which it was selected in all respects that are relevant to a particular study. In an unrepresentative sample, some characteristics are overrepresented and/or some characteristics may be underrepresented. Various procedures can be used to obtain a sample; these range from the simple to the complex, as we will see next.

Sample: Subset of the population that a researcher must often use to make generalizations about the larger population.

Population: Larger set of cases or aggregate number of people that a researcher is actually interested in or wishes to know something about.

Generalizability: Extent to which information from a sample can be used to inform us about persons, places, or events that were not studied in the entire population from which the sample was taken.

Sampling error: The difference between a sample estimate (called a sample statistic) and the population value it is estimating (called a population parameter).

One of the primary problems we face when generalizing information obtained from a sample to a population is accuracy. How accurately does our sample reflect the true population? This question is inherent in any inquiry because with any sample we represent only a part—and sometimes only a small part—of the entire population. The goal in obtaining or selecting a sample, then, is to select it in a way that increases the chances of this sample being representative of the entire population.

One of the most important distinctions made about samples is whether they are based on a probability or nonprobability sampling method. Sampling methods that allow us to know in advance how likely it is that any element of a population will be selected for the sample are **probability sampling methods**. Sampling methods that do not let us know the likelihood in advance are **nonprobability sampling methods**.

The fundamental aspect of probability sampling is **random selection**. When a sample is selected in this way, it is typically called a **random sample**. These include all samples obtained through a random process like random digit dialing or randomly selecting students from a school directory using a random numbers table like the one provided in Table B.1. When a sample is randomly selected from the population, this means every element of the population (e.g., individual, school, city) has a known and independent chance of being selected for the sample. All probability sampling methods rely on a random selection procedure.

Probability sampling techniques not only serve to minimize any potential bias we may have when selecting a sample, but also they allow us to gain access to probability theory in our data analysis, which you will learn more about later in this text. This body of mathematical theory allows us to estimate more accurately the degree of error we have when generalizing results obtained from known sample statistics to unknown population parameters. You will learn more about probability theory later in the book. For now, we simply want you to understand that random samples are more likely to be representative of the entire population because they have no systematic bias. When the goal is to generalize your findings to a larger population, it is this characteristic that makes probability samples more desirable than nonprobability samples. In fact, we must have a random sample to use inferential statistics. What are those, you ask? We will talk about them next.

Descriptive and Inferential Statistics

Traditionally, the discipline of statistics has been divided into descriptive and inferential statistics. In large part, this distinction relies on whether one is interested in simply describing some phenomenon or in "inferring" characteristics of some phenomenon from a sample to the entire population. See? An understanding of sampling issues is already necessary.

Descriptive statistics can be used to describe characteristics or some phenomenon from either a sample or a population. The key point here is that you are using the statistics for "description" only. For example, if we wanted to describe the number of parking tickets given out by university police or the amount of revenues these parking tickets generated, we could use various statistics, including simple counts and averages.

If, however, we wanted to generalize this information to university police departments across the country, we would need to move into the realm of **inferential statistics**. Inferential statistics are mathematical tools for estimating how likely it is that a statistical result based on data from a random sample is representative of the population from which the sample was selected. If our interest is in making inferences, a **sample statistic** is really only an estimate of the population statistic, called a **population parameter**,

---

Probability sampling methods: These methods rely on random selection or chance and allow us to know in advance how likely it is that any element of a population is selected for the sample.

Nonprobability sampling methods: These methods are not based on random selection and do not allow us to know in advance the likelihood of any element of a population being selected for the sample.

Random selection: The fundamental aspect of probability sampling. The essential characteristic of random selection is that every element of the population has a known and independent chance of being selected for the sample.

Random sample: A sample that was obtained through probability sampling methods.

Descriptive statistics: Statistics used to describe the distribution of a sample or population.

Inferential statistics: Mathematical tools for estimating how likely it is that a statistical result based on data from a random sample is representative of the population from which the sample was selected.

Sample statistic: Statistic (i.e., mean, proportion, etc.) obtained from a sample of the population.

Population parameter: Statistic (i.e., mean, proportion, etc.) obtained from a population. Since we rarely have entire population data, we typically estimate population parameters using sample statistics.

which we want to estimate. Because this sample statistic is only an estimate of the population parameter, there will always be some amount of error present. Inferential statistics are the tools used for calculating the magnitude of this sampling error. As we noted earlier, the larger the sampling error, the less accurate the sample statistic will be as an estimate of the population parameter. Of course, before we can use inferential statistics, we must be able to assume that our sample is actually representative of the population. And to do this, we must obtain our sample using appropriate probability sampling techniques. We hope the larger picture is beginning to come into focus! We next want to talk more specifically about how variables are measured.

▣ Levels of Measurement

As we noted above, data generally come from one of three places: They are gathered by us personally, gathered by another researcher, or gathered by a government agency. No matter how they were collected, data sets are by definition simply a collection of many variables. For illustrative purposes, imagine that we were interested in the relationship between levels of student drinking and drug use and student demographic characteristics such as gender, age, religion, and year in college (first year, sophomore, junior, or senior). Table 1.1 displays the small data set we might have obtained had we investigated this issue by collecting surveys from 20 college students (a random sample, of course).

To measure the extent to which each student used alcohol and other drugs, let's say we asked the students these questions: "How many drinks do you consume in an average month? By 'drinks' we mean a beer, a mixed drink, or a glass of wine." "How many times during an average month do you take drugs such as ecstasy, marijuana, cocaine, or any other illegal drug?" Each of the other variables in Table 1.1 relates to other information about each student in the sample. Everything listed in this table, including the respondent's identification number, is a variable. All of these variables combined represent our data set. The first thing you may notice about these variables is that some are represented by categories and some are represented by actual numbers. Gender, for example, is divided into two categories, female and male. This type of variable is often referred to as a **qualitative** or **categorical variable**, implying that the values represent qualities or categories only. The values of this variable have no numeric or quantitative meaning. Other examples in the data set of qualitative variables include college year and religion.

The rest of the variables in our data set, however, have values that do represent numeric values that can be quantified—hence the name **quantitative or continuous variables**. The values of quantitative variables can be compared in a numerically meaningful way. Respondent's identification number, age, grade point average (GPA), number of drinks, and number of times drugs were used are all quantitative variables. We can compare the values of these variables in a numerically meaningful way. For example, from Table 1.1, we can see that respondent 1 has a lower grade point average than respondent 19. We can also see that respondents 7 and 16 have the highest levels of alcohol consumption in the sample.

In Table 1.1, it is relatively easy to identify which variables are qualitative and which are quantitative simply because the qualitative variables are represented by **alphanumeric data** (by letters rather than by numbers). Data that are represented by numbers are called **numeric data**. A good way to remember the distinction between these two types of data is to note that alphanumeric data consist of letters of the alphabet, whereas numeric data consist of numbers.

It is certainly possible to include alphanumeric data in a data set, as we have done in Table 1.1, but when stored in a computer, as most data are, alphanumeric data take up a great deal of space, and alphanumeric data are difficult to statistically analyze. For this reason, these data are usually converted to or represented by numeric data. For example, females may arbitrarily be identified with the number 1, rather than with the word "female," and males with the number 2. Assigning numbers to the categorical values of qualitative variables is called "coding" the data. Of course, which numbers get assigned to qualitative variables (e.g., 1 for females and 2 for males) is arbitrary because the numeric

Qualitative or categorical variables: Values that refer to qualities or categories. They tell us what kind, what group, or what type a value is referring to.

Quantitative or continuous variables: Values that refer to quantities or different measurements. They tell us how much or how many.

Alphanumeric data: Values of a variable that are represented by letters rather than by numbers.

Numeric data: Values of a variable that represent numerical qualities.

| Table 1.1 | Example of the Format of a Data Set From a Survey of 20 College Students |

| ID Number | Gender | Age | College Year | GPA | Average Month | | Religion |
					# Drinks	# Times Drugs Used	
1	Female	19	Sophomore	2.3	45	22	Catholic
2	Male	22	Senior	3.1	30	10	Other
3	Female	22	Senior	3.8	0	0	Protestant
4	Female	18	Freshman	2.9	35	5	Jewish
5	Male	20	Junior	2.5	20	20	Catholic
6	Female	23	Senior	3.0	10	0	Catholic
7	Male	18	Freshman	1.9	45	25	Not religious
8	Female	19	Sophomore	2.8	28	3	Protestant
9	Male	28	Junior	3.3	9	0	Protestant
10	Female	21	Junior	2.7	0	0	Muslim
11	Female	18	Freshman	3.1	19	2	Jewish
12	Male	19	Sophomore	2.5	25	20	Catholic
13	Female	21	Senior	3.5	2	0	Other
14	Male	21	Junior	1.8	19	33	Protestant
15	Female	42	Sophomore	3.9	10	0	Protestant
16	Female	19	Sophomore	2.3	45	0	Catholic
17	Male	21	Junior	2.8	29	10	Not religious
18	Male	25	Sophomore	3.1	14	0	Other
19	Female	21	Junior	3.5	5	0	Catholic
20	Female	17	Freshman	3.5	28	0	Jewish

code (number) assigned has no real quantitative meaning. Males could be given either a 1 or a 2, or a 0, with females coded either a 2 or a 1; it makes no difference.

Table 1.2 redisplays the data in Table 1.1 numerically as they would normally be stored in a computer data set. Because values of each variable are represented by numbers, it is a little more difficult to distinguish the qualitative variables from the quantitative variables. You have to ask yourself what each of the values really means. For example, for the variable gender, what does the "1" really represent? It represents the code for a female student and, therefore, is not numerically meaningful; it is a random code number given to all female students who filled out the questionnaire. Similarly, the number "1" coded for the religion variable represents those students who said they were Catholic, and the code "3" represents those students who said they were Jewish. There is nothing

| Table 1.2 | **Example of the Data Presented in Table 1.1 as They Would Be Stored in a Computer Data File** |

ID Number	Gender	Age	College Year	GPA	Average Month # Drinks	Average Month # Times Drugs Used	Religion
1	1	19	2	2.3	45	22	1
2	2	22	4	3.1	30	10	6
3	1	22	4	3.8	0	0	2
4	1	18	1	2.9	35	5	3
5	2	20	3	2.5	20	20	1
6	1	23	4	3.0	10	0	1
7	2	18	1	1.9	45	25	5
8	1	19	2	2.8	28	3	2
9	2	28	3	3.3	9	0	2
10	1	21	3	2.7	0	0	4
11	1	18	1	3.1	19	2	3
12	2	19	2	2.5	25	20	1
13	1	21	4	3.5	2	0	6
14	2	21	3	1.8	19	33	2
15	1	42	2	3.9	10	0	2
16	1	19	2	2.3	45	0	1
17	2	21	3	2.8	29	10	5
18	2	25	2	3.1	14	0	6
19	1	21	3	3.5	5	0	1
20	1	17	1	3.5	28	0	3

inherently meaningful about the numbers 1 and 3. They simply represent categories for the religion variable, and we changed the letters of the alphabet for numbers. For the variable age, what does the number 19 represent? This is actually a meaningful value—it tells us that this respondent was 19 years of age and, therefore, it is a quantitative variable.

In addition to distinguishing between qualitative and quantitative, we can differenti-ate among variables in terms of what is called their **level of measurement**. The four levels of measurement are (1) nominal, (2) ordinal, (3) interval, and (4) ratio. Figure 1.1 depicts the difference among these four levels of measurement.

Level of measurement: Mathematical nature of the values for a variable.

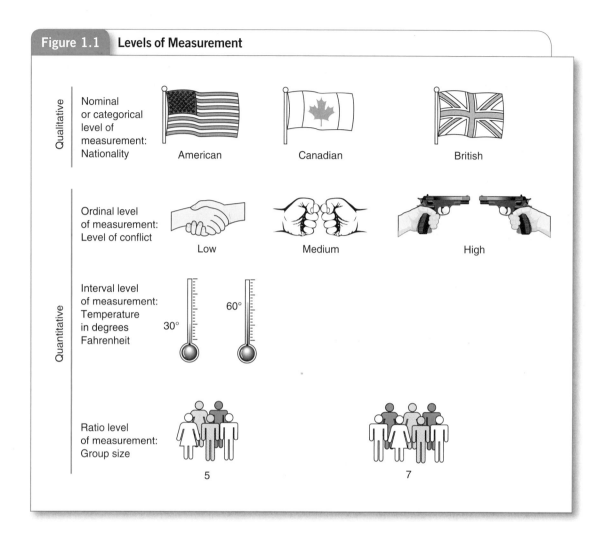

| Figure 1.1 | Levels of Measurement |

Nominal Level of Measurement

Variables measured at the nominal level are exclusively qualitative in nature. The values of **nominal-level variables** convey classification or categorization information *only*. Therefore, the only thing we can say about two or more nominal-level values of a variable is that they are different. We cannot say that one value reflects more or less of the variable than the other. The most common types of nominal-level variables are gender (male and female), religion (Protestant, Catholic, Jewish, Muslim, etc.), and political party (Democrat, Republican, Independent, etc.). The values of these variables are distinct from one another and can give us only descriptive information about the type or label attached to a value. Notice we can say that males are different from females but not that they have more "gender." We can say that Protestants have a different religion than Catholics or Jews but, again, not that they have more "religion." The only distinction we can make with nominal-level variables is that their values are different.

Because they represent distinctions only of kind (one is merely different from the other), the categories of a nominal-level variable are not related to one another in any meaningful numeric way. This is true even if the alphanumeric values are converted or coded into numbers. For example, in Table 1.2, the values assigned to the variables gender and religion are given numeric values. Remember, however, that these numbers

> **Nominal-level variables:** Values that represent categories or qualities of a case only.

were simply assigned for convenience and have no numeric meaning. The fact that Catholics are assigned the code of 1 and Protestants are assigned the code of 2 does not mean that Protestants have twice as much religion as Catholics or that the Protestant religion is "more than" the Catholic religion. The only thing that the codes of 1 and 2 mean is that they refer to different religions. Because we cannot make distinctions of "less than" or "more than" with them, then, nominal-level variables do not allow us to rank-order the values of a given variable. In other words, nominal-level measurement does not have the property of order. It merely reflects the fact that some values are different from others. Consequently, mathematical operations cannot be performed with nominal-level data. With our religion variable, for example, we cannot subtract a 2 (Protestant) from a 3 (Jewish) to get a 1 (Catholic). Do you see how meaningless mathematical operations are with variables measured at the nominal level?

Ordinal Level of Measurement

The values of **ordinal-level variables** are not only categorical in nature, but the categories also have some type of relationship to each other. This relationship is one of order or transitivity. That is, categories on an ordinal variable can be rank-ordered from high (more of the variable) to low (less of the variable) even though they still cannot be exactly quantified. As a result, although we can know whether a value is more or less than another value, we do not know exactly *how much* more or less. The properties of ordinal-level measurement are clearer with an example.

Let's say that on a survey, we have measured income in such a way that respondents simply checked the income category that best reflected their annual income. The categories the survey provided are as follows:

1. Less than $20,000
2. $20,001 to $40,000
3. $40,001 to $60,000
4. More than $60,000

Now suppose that one of our respondents (respondent 1) checked the first category and that another respondent (respondent 2) checked the third category. We don't know the exact annual income of each respondent, but we do know that the second respondent makes more than the first. Thus, in addition to knowing that our respondents have different annual incomes (nominal level), we also know that one income is more than the other. In reality, respondent 1 may make anywhere between no money and $20,000, but because income was measured using ordinal categories, we will never know. Had we measured income in terms of actual dollars earned per year, we would be able to make more precise mathematical distinctions. Suppose we had a third person (respondent 3) who checked the response more than $60,000. The property of transitivity says that if respondent 1 makes less than respondent 2, and if respondent 2 makes less than respondent 3, then respondent 1 also makes less than respondent 3. The rank order, thus, is as follows:

1. Less than $20,000 respondent 1
2. $20,001 to $40,000
3. $40,001 to $60,000 respondent 2
4. More than $60,000 respondent 3

Other examples of ordinal-level variables include the "Likert-type" response questions found on surveys that solicit an individual's attitudes or perceptions. You are probably familiar with this type of survey question. The following is a typical one: "Please respond to the following statement by circling the appropriate number: '1' Strongly Agree, '2' Agree, '3' Disagree, '4' Strongly Disagree." The answers to these questions represent the ordinal level of measurement. Often these categories are displayed like this:

Ordinal-level variables: Values that not only represent categories but also have a logical order.

1	2	3	4
Strongly Agree	Agree	Disagree	Strongly Disagree

Response categories that rank-order attitudes in this way are often called *Likert* responses after Rensis Likert, who is believed to have developed them back in the 1930s. There are other ways to measure judgments using a Likert-type response. For example, the aggression questionnaires (AQs) in the literature are designed to measure an individual's propensity to feel anger and hostility (Buss & Warren, 2000). It consists of 34 items such as "Given enough provocation, I may hit another person," "When people annoy me, I may tell them what I think of them," and "I have trouble controlling my temper." Individuals taking the AQ are asked to respond to the statements using a five-point Likert-type scale from "not at all like me," which is coded 0, to "completely like me," which is coded 5.

Interval Level of Measurement

In addition to enabling us to rank-order values, interval-level variables allow us to quantify the numeric relationship among them. To be classified as an interval-level variable, the difference between adjacent values along the measurement scale must be the same at every two points. For example, the difference in temperature on the Fahrenheit scale between 40 degrees and 41 degrees is the same as the difference between 89 degrees and 90 degrees: one degree. Another characteristic of interval-level measurement is that the zero point is arbitrary. An arbitrary zero means that, although a value of zero is possible, zero does not mean the absence of the phenomenon. A meaningless zero is an arbitrary zero. For example, a temperature on the Fahrenheit scale of 0 degrees does not mean that there is no temperature outside, it simply means that it is cold! Zero degrees on the Fahrenheit scale is arbitrary. These characteristics allow scores on an interval scale to be added and subtracted, but meaningful multiplication and division cannot be performed. This level of measurement is represented in Figure 1.1 by the difference between two Fahrenheit temperatures. Although 60 degrees is 30 degrees hotter than 30 degrees, 60 in this case is not twice as hot as 30. Why not? Because heat does not begin at 0 degrees on the Fahrenheit scale.

Social scientists often treat indices (see the AQ earlier) that were created by combining responses to a series of variables measured at the ordinal level as interval-level measures. One example of an index like this could be created with responses to the Core Institute's (2015) questions about friends' disapproval of substance use (see Table 1.3). The survey has 13 questions on the topic, each of which has the same three response choices. If Do Not Disapprove is valued at 1, Disapprove is valued at 2, and Strongly Disapprove is valued at 3, then the summed index of disapproval would range from 12 to 36. The average could then be treated as a fixed unit of measurement. So a score of 20 could be treated as if it were 4 more units than a score of 16 and so on.

Ratio Level of Measurement

Ratio-level variables have all the qualities of interval-level variables, and the numeric difference between values is based on a natural, or true-zero, point. A true-zero point means that a score of zero indicates that the phenomenon is absent. For example, if people were asked how many hours they worked last month and they replied "zero hours," it would mean that there was a complete absence of work—they were unemployed that month. Ratio measurement allows meaningful use of multiplication and division as well as addition and subtraction. Therefore, we can divide one number by another to form a ratio—hence the name of this level of measurement. Suppose we were conducting a survey of the victimization experiences of residents in rural areas and asked them to provide their annual income in dollars. This variable would be an example of the ratio level of measurement because it has both a true-zero point and equal and known distances between adjacent values. For example, a value of no income, "zero dollars," has inherent meaning to all of us, and the difference between $10 and $11 is the same as that between $55,200 and $55,201.

Interval-level variable: In addition to an inherent rank order, a value's relationship to other values is known. There is an equal and constant distance between adjacent values. Therefore, the values can be added and subtracted.

Ratio-level variables: Variables that we assume can be added and subtracted, as well as multiplied and divided, and that have true-zero points.

Table 1.3	Ordinal-Level Variables Can Be Added to Create an Index With Interval-Level Properties: Core Alcohol and Drug Survey		
How Do You Think Your Close Friends Feel (or Would Feel) About You? (mark one for each line)	Do Not Disapprove	Disapprove	Strongly Disapprove
a. Trying marijuana once or twice			
b. Smoking marijuana occasionally			
c. Smoking marijuana regularly			
d. Trying cocaine once or twice			
e. Taking cocaine regularly			
f. Trying LSD once or twice			
g. Taking LSD regularly			
h. Trying amphetamines once or twice			
i. Taking amphetamines regularly			
j. Taking one or two drinks of an alcoholic beverage (e.g., beer, wine, liquor) nearly every day			
k. Taking four or five drinks nearly every day			
l. Having five or more drinks in one sitting			
m. Taking steroids for bodybuilding or improved athletic performance			

Source: Adapted from Core Alcohol and Drug Survey: Long Form © 2015 from the Core Institute.

Four Levels of Measurement

Nominal: Values represent categories or qualities of a case only.

Ordinal: Values not only represent categories but also have a logical order.

Interval: In addition to an inherent rank order, a value's relationship to other values is known. There is an equal and constant distance between adjacent values.

Ratio: Not only can distances be determined between values, but these distances are based on a true-zero point.

There are a few variables in Table 1.2 that are measured at the ratio level. One is the number of drinks respondents had in an average month. Notice that there were a few respondents who had "0" drinks—this is an absolute zero! And a college student who drinks an average of 20 drinks a month has 10 more drinks than someone who has 10 drinks a month and 10 fewer drinks than someone who has an average of 30 drinks a month. We have not shown you how to calculate the mean yet, but imagine that we calculate the average number of drinks a senior in college has from this table and find that it is 10.5 drinks. We then calculate the average number of drinks a first-year student has as 31.75. Because this is a ratio-level variable with an absolute zero, we could now take the ratio of drinks consumed by a first-year student compared with a senior to be (31.75 / 10.5 = 3.02) and say that first-year students consume about three times as much alcohol as seniors! Does this seem accurate to you? Because we can do this, the level of measurement is called "ratio."

For most statistical analyses in social science research, the interval and ratio levels of measurement can be treated as equivalent. In addition to having numerical values, both the interval and ratio levels also involve **continuous measures**; the numbers indicating the values of variables are points on a continuum, not discrete categories. Because of this,

Table 1.4 **Properties of Measurement Levels**

Examples of Comparison Statements	Appropriate Math Operations	Relevant Level of Measurement			
		Nominal	Ordinal	Interval	Ratio
A is equal to (not equal to) B	= (≠)	√	√	√	√
A is greater than (less than) B	> (<)		√	√	√
A is three more than (less than) B	+ (−)			√	√
A is twice (half) as large as B	× (÷)				√

researchers often treat variables measured at the interval and ratio levels as comparable. They then refer to this as the **interval–ratio level of measurement**. In this text, we generally rely on this distinction.

The Case of Dichotomies

Dichotomies are variables having only two values and are a special case from the standpoint of levels of measurement. Although variables with only two categories are generally thought of as nominally measured, we can also think of a dichotomy as indicating the presence or absence of an attribute. Suppose, for example, we were interested in differences between individuals who had never used illegal drugs in the last year and those who had used at least one illegal drug in the last year. We could create a variable that indicated this dichotomous distinction by coding those individuals who said they did not use any of the substances listed as 0 and all others as 1. Viewed in this way, there is an inherent order to the two values; in one group the attribute of consuming illegal substances is absent (those coded 0), and in another group it is present (those coded 1). When we code variables like this as 0 or 1, they are often called **binary variables**.

Comparing Levels of Measurement

Table 1.4 summarizes the types of comparisons that can be made with different levels of measurement as well as the mathematical operations that are legitimate. All four levels of measurement allow researchers to assign different values to different cases. All three quantitative measures allow researchers to rank cases in order.

🔲 Ways of Presenting Variables

In this section, we examine some of the most commonly used pieces of information you will confront in criminology: counts, rates, ratios, proportions, and percentages. These are simply different ways in which to present, describe, and compare variables.

Counts and Rates

The most elementary way of presenting information is to present the counts or frequencies of the variable you are interested in. A **count** or **frequency** is simply the number of times that an event occurs in your data. The numbers of violent victimizations recorded by the NCVS, which includes rapes, robberies, and assaults, by age for 2013 are presented here:

Continuous measure: Measure with numbers indicating the values of variables as points on a continuum.

Interval-ratio level of measurement: Variables that we assume can be added and subtracted as well as multiplied and divided regardless of whether they have true-zero points.

Dichotomy: Variable having only two values.

Binary variable: Dichotomous variable that has been coded 0 or 1.

Count or frequency: Number of units in the sample that has a particular value in a variable distribution.

Age Group	Number of Victims (f)
12–17	545,370
18–24	527,410
24–34	604,500
35–49	684,150
50–64	566,990
65 and older	112,760

These numbers tell us exactly how many victims of violent crime there were in the United States in 2013 in each of the six age groups. Violent crimes include rapes, robberies, and assaults. We can see from these data that there were fewer victims in the age 65 and older group than in any other age group. The highest number of victims of violent crime appeared in the 35 to 49 age group (684,150 victims). Based on these counts, who has the greatest vulnerability to becoming a victim? Do those who are aged 35 to 49 have a greater risk of becoming the victim of violence compared with those aged 18 to 24, or those aged 12 to 17? The short answer is no. The long answer is that if we want to make comparisons across different categories, whether they be age categories, gender, race/ethnicity, city, year, or any other aggregation, it is not possible to produce conclusions of relative risk. Why? Because simple counts and frequencies do not take into consideration the size of the total at-risk population within each category. Although we may sometimes come to the same conclusion, using simple frequencies to make these comparisons most often leads to misleading conclusions.

To make comparisons accurately across units with different population sizes, it is important to control for the size of the populations you are comparing. To do this, it is necessary to calculate the **rate** of an occurrence.

Case Study

The Importance of Rates for Victimization Data

Let's assume we want to assess how much risk a person across each age group has of experiencing a violent victimization. Table 1.5 presents the same violent victimization data along with the population counts for each age group. Rates are derived by dividing the observed number of occurrences or phenomena by the total number that could theoretically have been observed within the population of interest. In addition, rates are usually standardized according to some population base such as a rate per 1,000, 10,000, or 100,000 people:

$$\text{Rate} = \frac{\text{Number in subset}}{\text{Total number}} \times \text{Constant (e.g., 1,000)} \qquad \text{(Formula 1-1)}$$

As formula 1-1 shows, to derive the victim rate of violence within age categories, we must first divide the number of victims of violent crimes observed within an age group by the total number of potential victims within this age group. This latter number would be the entire population for this age group because, theoretically, everyone in the age group could have become a victim of a violent crime. We then multiply that by some population standard to get a rate per 1,000 population or a rate per 10,000 or 100,000 population. What population standard you choose should be what is most meaningful.

Rate: Number of a phenomenon divided by the total possible, which is then multiplied by a constant such as 1,000, 10,000, or 100,000.

Let's calculate the rate of violent crime for those aged 18 to 24 years using the population standard of 1,000:

$$\left(\frac{527,410}{27,143,454} \right) = .0194 \times 1,000 = 19.4$$

We obtain a rate of violent crime for those aged 18 to 24 of 19.4 per 1,000 of those aged 18 to 24. When we calculate the victimization rates for each age category displayed in Table 1.5, a very different picture of vulnerability emerges. After standardizing for the size of the at-risk population, we see that those between the ages of 12 and 17 have the highest risk of violent victimization compared with all other age categories. In fact, the risk of victimization for those in this age group is more than twice as great as for those who are 35 to 49 years of age.

Let's look at another dramatic example of how a frequency count can mislead you because of differences in population size, whereas a rate will not. In 2013, there were 99 murders and non-negligent manslaughters in Kansas City, Missouri. In that same year, there were 49 of these same crimes in Baton Rouge, Louisiana. From the numbers, Kansas City is more dangerous to live in compared with Baton Rouge; in fact, there were more than twice as many murders there. But before you pack your bags and move to Baton Rouge, stop and think about it. Can you compare these raw frequency counts? No. You can't compare relative risk by using simple frequency counts in this case! In fact, the population of Baton Rouge at the time was only 230,212, whereas the population in Kansas City was nearly a half-million (465,514). Now let's calculate the rate of homicide per 100,000 people in each city:

$$\text{Rate for Kansas City} = \left(\frac{99}{465,514} \right) = .000212 \times 100,000 = 21.2$$

$$\text{Rate for Baton Rouge} = \left(\frac{49}{230,212} \right) = .000212 \times 100,000 = 21.2$$

Amazing! The relative risk for becoming a murder victim in both Kansas City and Baton Rouge was the same in 2013. A final analogy that is often used to underscore the notion of relative risk will help to cement this point. If you are like us, every time we are about to take off in an airplane, we get a bit nervous. In fact, when our son was very young, we occasionally took separate flights to ensure that if the airplane crashed, one of us would be alive to take care of him. Unfortunately, we weren't thinking very clearly because we both took the same taxi to the airport even when we were on different flights. The problem in this scenario is that we had a greater risk of being in an accident in the taxi on the

Table 1.5	Violent Crime Victims, Total Population, and Violent Crime Rates per 1,000 by Age Group, 2013		
Age Group	Number of Victims	Total Population	Rate per 1,000
12–17	545,370	24,633,684	22.1
18–24	527,410	27,143,454	19.4
24–34	604,500	39,891,724	15.2
35–49	684,150	65,240,931	10.5
50–64	566,990	41,860,232	13.5
65 and older	112,760	34,991,753	3.2

Source: Adapted from *Criminal Victimization, 2013* by Truman and Langton, 2014, from the Bureau of Justice Statistics, U.S. Department of Justice.

way to and from the airport than we did on the flight. On average, flying kills about 200 people a year in the United States, whereas driving kills about 32,300 people (Motavalli, 2012). Let's assume a 2010 U.S. population of 308,745,538 and plug this number into a rate per 100,000 as we have done here:

$$\text{Rate of Death for Flying} = \left(\frac{200}{308,745,538}\right) = .00000064 \times 100,000 = .064$$

$$\text{Rate of Death for Driving} = \left(\frac{32,300}{308,745,538}\right) = .0001046 \times 100,000 = 104.6$$

Our thinking about taking separate flights but the same taxi to the airport was really flawed! Remember that a **ratio** is a number that expresses the relationship between two numbers and indicates their relative size. As you saw earlier, the ratio of x to y is determined by dividing x by y. A ratio for the relative risk of dying while driving compared with flying is 104.6 / .064 = 1,634. Wow! This tells us that the risk of dying while driving is 1,634 times greater compared with flying. Think about that the next time you get behind the wheel of your car. Buckle up!

Proportions and Percentages

Two other common techniques used to present information about variables are **proportions** and **percentages**. These measures are really special kinds of ratios obtained by dividing the number of observations from a subset of your sample by the total number in your sample. In other words, a proportion is obtained by dividing the number of counts for a given event (f) by the total number of events (n). More specifically, proportions are obtained using the following formula:

$$\text{Proportion} = \frac{\text{Number in subset of sample}}{\text{Total number in sample}} = \frac{f}{n} \qquad \text{(Formula 1-2)}$$

A proportion may also be called a **relative frequency** because it expresses the number of cases in a given subset (f) relative to the total number of cases (n). In this text, we use the terms "proportion" and "relative frequency" interchangeably.

Percentages are obtained simply by multiplying a proportion by 100. This standardizes the numbers to a base of 100, which is generally easier for an audience to interpret:

$$\text{Percentage} = \frac{f}{n} \times 100 = \text{Proportion} \times 100 \qquad \text{(Formula 1-3)}$$

Ratio: Expresses the relationship between two numbers and indicates their relative size.

Proportion: Number of some value in a variable distribution that is divided by total possible scores.

Percentage: Number of some value in a variable distribution that is divided by total possible scores and then is multiplied by 100.

Relative frequency: See Proportion.

Let's go through an example. Using data from the NCVS for 2013, Table 1.6 presents the total number of each type of victimization, the total number of each that was reported to police, the proportion reported, and the percent reported to police. If we were attempting to understand the differences in reporting behavior across different types of crimes, comparing the number of crimes reported would not tell us anything about which crime was most likely to be reported. However, examining either the proportion or percentage column tells us a great deal. We can easily see that rapes and sexual assaults (.35) are the least likely violent crimes to be reported to police. The crime most likely to be reported to police is motor vehicle theft. Still, it is quite interesting that almost one fourth (100% – 76% = 24%) of motor vehicle thefts are never reported to police.

	Total Number			
Type of Crime	(n)	Number Reported (f)	Proportion (f / n)	Percent (f / n) × 100
Violent crime	**3,041,170**	**1,398,938**	**.46**	**46**
Rape/Sexual assault	173,610	60,073	.35	35
Robbery	369,070	250,967	.68	68
Assault	2,600,920	1,118,395	.43	43
Aggravated assault	633,090	405,177	.64	64
Simple assault	2,046,600	777,708	.38	38
Domestic violence	589,140	335,809	.57	57
Intimate partner violence	369,310	210,506	.57	57
Stranger violence	1,244,560	609,834	.49	49
Violence with injury	849,240	305,726	.56	56
Property crime	**11,531,420**	**4,151,311**	**.36**	**36**
Burglary	2,458,360	1,401,265	.57	57
Motor vehicle theft	555,660	422,301	.76	76
Personal theft	9,070,680	2,630,497	.29	29

Table 1.6 Total Number, Number Reported, Proportion, and Percentage of Crimes Reported to Police by Type of Crime (NCVS, 2013)

Source: Adapted from Tables 4 and 6 of *Criminal Victimization, 2013* by Truman and Langton, 2014, from the Bureau of Justice Statistics, U.S. Department of Justice.

Units of Analysis

The final issue we discuss in this chapter is often referred to as the unit of analysis. The **unit of analysis** is the particular unit or object we have gathered our data about and to which we apply our statistical methods. Stated differently, our unit of analysis is whatever constitutes an observation in our data set. For example, are our observations or data points made up of persons? Prisons? Court cases? States? Nations? In social research, we employ many different levels of aggregation for research. Sometimes we use questionnaires or interviews to obtain data from individuals. The NCVS, for example, interviews individuals in households from around the United States and asks them about their experiences with criminal victimization. In this particular research, the unit of analysis is the individual or person because the data are obtained from individual respondents, but these data can also be aggregated to the household level.

In other instances, the unit of analysis is a group or collectivity. Often, these data originally were collected from individuals and then combined, or aggregated, to form a collectivity. For example, the FBI collects information about the number of crimes reported by individuals to local police departments. However, the FBI aggregates this information, identifying what state the report came from and, in some cases, what city and/or county. Depending on what data you use, then, the unit of analysis may be states, counties, or cities.

As an example of data at the state level of analysis, Table 1.7 presents the homicide rate per 100,000 population for each state. This information is collected by each local law enforcement agency within a state, and then this information is aggregated to reflect the total number of people killed during this time period. Even though the information is based on small levels of aggregation (e.g., law enforcement agencies), the units of analysis in this case are the individual states, not the individual agencies.

This concept is important when making statistical interpretations from data, as you will see in the next chapter. We can only make generalizations about the units of analysis for which our data are represented. For example, if we have state-level data and we find

> **Units of analysis:** Particular units or aggregations (e.g., people and cities) that constitute an observation in a data set.

Table 1.7	Murder Rates by State per 100,000 Population		
Alabama	7.2	Montana	2.2
Alaska	4.6	Nebraska	3.1
Arizona	5.4	Nevada	5.8
Arkansas	5.4	New Hampshire	1.7
California	4.6	New Jersey	4.5
Colorado	3.4	New Mexico	6.0
Connecticut	2.4	New York	3.3
Delaware	4.2	North Carolina	4.8
Florida	5.0	North Dakota	2.2
Georgia	5.6	Ohio	3.9
Hawaii	1.5	Oklahoma	5.1
Idaho	1.7	Oregon	2.0
Illinois	5.5	Pennsylvania	4.7
Indiana	5.4	Rhode Island	2.9
Iowa	1.4	South Carolina	6.2
Kansas	3.9	South Dakota	2.4
Kentucky	3.8	Tennessee	5.0
Louisiana	10.8	Texas	4.3
Maine	1.8	Utah	1.7
Maryland	6.4	Vermont	1.6
Massachusetts	2.0	Virginia	3.8
Michigan	6.4	Washington	2.3
Minnesota	2.1	West Virginia	3.3
Mississippi	6.5	Wisconsin	2.8
Missouri	6.1	Wyoming	2.9

Source: Adapted from Table 4 of *Crime In the United States* from the Federal Bureau of Investigation (2013a).

that states that have higher rates of poverty also tend to have higher rates of murder, we can generalize this finding to the states only, not to counties or cities. Nor can we say that individuals who live under conditions of poverty are more likely to experience a homicide. Only if we were analyzing individual victims and offenders could we make statements about individual factors related to lethal violence. We will remind you of this throughout the book!

▣ Summary

Our goal in this introductory chapter was to underscore the nature of the importance of statistics in criminology and criminal justice along with several fundamental aspects of the research process. We have set the stage for us to begin our exploration into the realm of statistics. Can't wait!

We have seen that, unlike observations we make in everyday life, criminological research relies on scientific methods. Statistical methods play a role in three types of research we conduct in our field: descriptive research, explanatory research, and evaluation research.

Because it is almost never possible to obtain information on every individual or element in the population of interest, our investigations usually rely on data taken from samples of the population. Generalizability exists when we can assume that results obtained from a sample can be generalized to the population. Typically, only samples selected using probability sampling techniques can be assumed to be representative of the population.

After a brief discussion of descriptive and inferential statistics, we described the different levels of measurement for variables along with their units of analysis. The remainder of the chapter examined the differences between simple counts of a phenomenon (referred to as frequencies) and rates, ratios, proportions, and percentages. The final section discussed the units of analysis used in research.

Key Terms

> Review key terms with eFlashcards. Visit study.sagepub.com/paternoster.

alphanumeric data   10
binary variable   17
continuous measure   16
count or frequency   17
dependent variable   6
descriptive research   3
descriptive statistics   9
dichotomy   17
evaluation research   6
explanatory research   5
generalizability   8
hypothesis   6
independent variable   6
inferential statistics   9
interval-level variable   15
interval-ratio level of measurement   17
level of measurement   12

National Incident-Based Reporting System
   (NIBRS)   4
nominal-level variables   13
nonprobability sampling methods   9
numeric data   10
ordinal-level variables   14
percentage   20
police reports   4
population   8
population parameter   9
probability sampling methods   9
proportion   20
qualitative variable or categorical
   variables   10
quantitative or continuous variables   10
random sample   9
random selection   9

rate   18
ratio   20
ratio-level variables   15
relative frequency   20
sample   8
sample statistic   9
sampling error   8
science   3
survey   5
theory   6
Uniform Crime Reports
   (UCR)   4
units of analysis   21
variable   5

Key Formulas

Rate (formula 1-1):

$$\text{Rate} = \frac{\text{Number in subset}}{\text{Total number}} \times \text{Constant (e.g., 1,000)}$$

Percentages (formula 1-3):

$$\text{Percentage} = \frac{f}{n} \times 100 = \text{Proportion} \times 100$$

Proportions (formula 1-2):

$$\text{Proportion} = \frac{\text{Number in subset of sample}}{\text{Total number in sample}} = \frac{f}{n}$$

Practice Problems

> Test your understanding of chapter content.
> Take the practice quiz at study.sagepub.com/paternoster.

1. Describe the difference between descriptive research and explanatory research.

2. Discuss the importance of probability sampling techniques.

3. For each of the following variables, define the level of measurement as either qualitative or quantitative and, furthermore, as one of the four more distinct levels: nominal, ordinal, interval, or ratio:

   a. A convicted felon's age in years

   b. A driver's score on the breathalyzer exam

   c. The fine for a parking ticket

   d. The specific offense code of a felony

   e. A defendant's gender

   f. Fines levied on industrial companies convicted of violating the Clean Air Act

4. What distinguishes a variable measured at the ordinal level from a variable measured at the interval level of measurement? What more does the ratio level of measurement add to this?

5. In a study examining the effects of arrest on convicted drunk drivers' future drunk-driving behavior, which is the independent variable and which is the dependent variable?

6. If we are interested in determining the extent to which males and females are more or less afraid to walk outside alone at night, which variable would we designate as our independent variable and which as our dependent variable?

7. To compute a rate of violent crime victimizations against people 14 to 18 years old, what would we use as the numerator and what as the denominator?

8. What are the advantages of rates over frequency counts? Give an example.

9. From the following table, compute the proportions and percentages of the household crime victimizations that were reported to the police by the lost value of the victimization:

	f	Proportion	%
Less than $10	16		
$10–$49	39		
$50–$99	48		
$100–$249	86		
$250–$999	102		
$1,000 or more	251		
	n = 542		

10. Patrick Schnapp (2015) examined the effect of immigration on homicide rates in 146 U.S. cities. He found that rates of immigration in cities did not affect the homicide rates. In this study, what were the units of analysis? Another study by Jason Rydberg and Jesenia Pizarro (2014) examined the factors related to homicide clearance rates. They found that homicide cases in which the victims were more involved in deviant lifestyles took longer to be cleared by arrest compared with victims who were not engaged in deviance. In this study, what were the units of analysis?

11. To test the existence of a relationship between unemployment and crime, we use data from 50 states of the United States. What are the units of analysis? What would you select to be the independent variable? What would you deem to be the dependent variable?

12. Suppose we are interested in the amount of time police departments took to respond to reports of crime. We track response times for several police departments within large metropolitan areas to see whether there are any differences based on the location of the jurisdiction. In this study, what are the units of analysis?

STUDENT STUDY SITE

WANT A BETTER GRADE?

Get the tools you need to sharpen your study skills. Access practice quizzes, eFlashcards, data sets, and SPSS exercises at **study.sagepub.com/paternoster.**

CHAPTER 2

Understanding Data Distributions With Tables and Graphs

Often the most effective ways to describe, explore, and summarize a set of numbers—even a large set—is to look at pictures of those numbers.

—Edward Tufte

LEARNING OBJECTIVES

1. Describe the purpose of frequency distributions to examine a variable.

2. Identify bar charts and pie charts and the types of variables for which they are used.

3. Explain the usefulness of a grouped frequency distribution for a quantitative variable.

4. Describe the difference between a histogram and a bar chart.

5. Describe the difference between a histogram and line graph.

6. Discuss the concept of cumulative frequencies and cumulative percentages.

7. Identify the shape of a distribution and determine types of skewness.

8. Create time plots of variables.

▣ Introduction

In general, the rate of gun violence in the United States has been decreasing steadily during the past two decades. In fact, the rate of both fatal and nonfatal gun violence has been *decreasing* (Truman & Langton, 2014). Despite this fact, most Americans believe that gun violence has *increased* during recent years (Cohn et al., 2013). With one glance, we can capture these two facts with a chart displaying gun violence rates along with attitudes toward gun violence, as done in Figure 2.1. From this figure, you can clearly see the difference between empirical reality and perceptions. Of course, we could have also displayed this information in table form with the actual numbers, but sometimes a picture is worth a thousand words, to borrow a cliché!

The first step (and one of the most important steps) in any statistical analysis is having a clear understanding of the general characteristics or appearance of your data. Understanding the distributions of your variables is referred to as univariate analysis because it is examining the distribution of one variable. One theme that we emphasize throughout this text is that no matter how simple or complex your statistical analysis is, there is no substitute for first knowing the shape and characteristics of your variables: the number of different values each variable has, the frequency or number of cases for each value, whether your observations "bunch up" at a few values of a variable or are more evenly distributed across the different values, and whether your data are skewed or have outliers. All of this very valuable information should be known *before* you do any additional statistical analyses.

The purpose of this chapter is to provide you with some tabular and graphical tools for examining and describing the characteristics and patterns of your data. A tabular display of your data can show you exactly how many values your variable has, how many cases or observations you have for each value (and the percentage or proportion of the total that the frequency represents), how extreme your values are, and the extent to which the cases cluster around a few values or are more evenly spread across the different values. The graphical presentation of the distribution of a variable can display much of the same information in picture form, although usually with much less detail. One advantage that a graphical display of your data has over a tabular presentation, however, is that it immediately and vividly shows you what your data look like. A glance at a graphical presentation of data can reveal some very important features of your data. As you will see, we strongly recommend using both tabular and graphical displays to get the complete picture of your data. You will also learn that preparing and communicating to others about the characteristics of your data is as much art as it is science and that the key question to ask when constructing tables and graphs from your data is, "Is this format effectively communicating the important characteristics of these variables?" In this chapter, we will treat nominal-level variables as qualitative and ordinal and treat interval/ratio-level variables as quantitative.

Student Study Site

Visit the open-access Student Study Site at study.sagepub.com/paternoster to access additional study tools including mobile-friendly eFlashcards, web quizzes, links to SAGE journal articles, additional data sets, SPSS exercises, and more!

▣ The Tabular and Graphical Display of Qualitative Data

Recall from Chapter 1 that qualitative variables—those measured at the nominal level—capture differences *in kind* among the values only. That is, the values of a nominal-level variable differ in quality and not quantity, which is why they are referred to as qualitative data. To refresh your memory, gender is a qualitative variable with two values, male and female, that differ only in kind. Males are only different from females; they do not have more "gender" (even if we add a third value like "transgender," it is still a nominal-level variable). The only sort of comparative statement we can make about different values of a nominal-level variable is simply that they are not the same. One of the easiest ways to show a nominal-level variable is to report some descriptive information about the variable's values such as the frequency of each value and the percentage or proportion of the total for each value. This is done in a descriptive table of the variable.

Univariate analysis: Examining the distribution of one variable.

| Figure 2.1 | Rate of Firearm-Related Violent Victimization per 1,000 People 12 Years or Older: National Crime Victimization Survey |

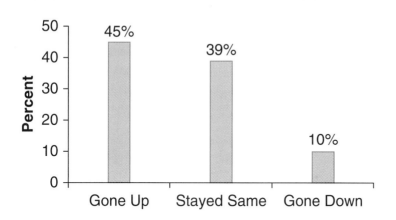

In recent years, have gun crimes in America gone up or down?

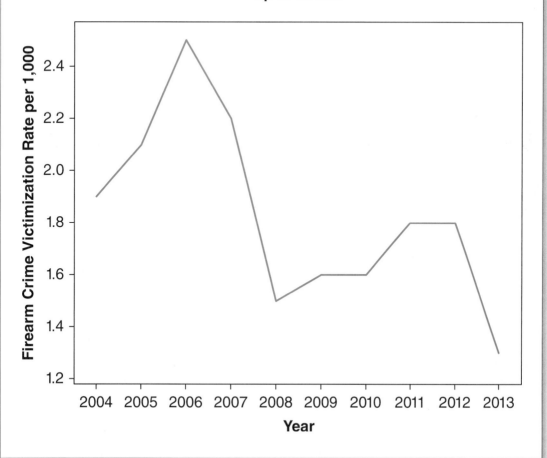

Frequency Tables

Case Study

An Analysis of Hate Crimes Using Tables

In Table 2.1, we report descriptive information for a nominal-level variable, the types of hate crime incidents reported by law enforcement agencies in the year 2013. Hate crimes are criminal acts that are perpetrated in part or entirely by personal prejudice or animosity against others because of their race, religion, sexual preference, ethnicity or national background, or some real or perceived disability.

In the *Hate Crime Statistics Act of 1990,* the U.S. Congress required the collection of nationwide information about criminal acts that were motivated by hate or prejudice. To comply with this act, the Federal Bureau of Investigation (FBI) began to compile data about crimes across the United States that were motivated by racial, religious, sexual, or ethnic/national origin as well as by disability hatred. This information is collected in a yearly report, *Hate Crime Statistics.*

Table 2.1 provides four pieces of information for this nominal-level variable: the different values of the variable hate crime (the basis of hate), the frequency of each value for the variable, the relative frequency or the proportion of the total number of cases for each value, and the percentage of the total for each value. Recall from the previous chapter that a frequency (f) is just a count of the number of times each value appears or occurs, the proportion is a relative frequency found by dividing the frequency of each value by the total number of values or observations (proportion $= f / n$), and the percentage is found by multiplying the proportion by 100 (percentage $= f / n \times 100$) to create a frequency standardized by 100. This tabular presentation of descriptive data, then, describes a variable by displaying the frequency, proportion, and percentage for each of its values.

According to Table 2.1, in the year 2013 there were a total of 5,922 reported incidents of single-bias hate crimes motivated by racial, religious, sexual, or ethnic/national origin as well as by disability bias. A single-bias hate crime is one that is motivated by one source of bias (bias against someone's religion or race but not both). Table 2.1 breaks these 5,922 incidents down by the specific basis or nature of the bias (the different values of the variable "hate crime"). The

Table 2.1	Types of Hate Crime Incidents Reported to Police in 2013		
Basis of Hate	*f*	*Proportion*	*%*
Race	2,871	.485	48.5
Religion	1,031	.174	17.4
Sexual orientation	1,233	.208	20.8
Ethnicity/National origin	655	.111	11.1
Disability	83	.014	1.4
Gender	18	.003	0.3
Gender identity	31	.005	0.5
Total	5,922	1.000	100.0

Source: Adapted from *Hate Crime Statistics—2013* from the Federal Bureau of Investigation (2013b).

qualitative variable we are interested in for this example is "hate crime," which takes on seven different nominal-level values: racial hatred, religious hatred, sexual orientation hatred, hatred directed at the victim's race/national origin, hatred because of the victim's disability, hatred because of the victim's gender, and hatred directed at the victim's gender identity. You should be able to determine that this is a nominal or qualitative variable because these values differ only in kind or quality. We can only say that one value of the hate crime variable is simply different from another value, not that one such crime is "more" or "less" of a hate crime than the other. For example, a racially motivated hate crime differs from a sexually motivated hate crime but is not "more" of a hate crime or more hateful than one motivated by a victim's sexual orientation.

We can see from this table that of the 5,922 hate crimes that were reported by law enforcement agencies in 2013, 2,871 of them were motivated by racial hatred. In other words, there was a frequency of 2,871 incidents of racially motivated hate crimes. This is the frequency or count of racial hate crimes for that year. We can also see that dividing this frequency by 5,922 (2,871 / 5,922), the total number of hate crime incidents for that year, we conclude that the proportion of hate crimes that were racially motivated was .485, or just under one half of the total number of hate crime incidents that year. Multiplying this by 100 to obtain the percentage, we see that racial hate crimes constituted 48.5% of the total number of hate crimes in 2013.

Looking at Table 2.1, we can see that there were 1,031 hate crimes that were motivated by religious bias in 2013. This is the frequency of religiously motivated hate crimes for that year, and the proportion of hate crimes that were religiously motivated was .174, or 17.4% of the total. A total of 1,233 hate crimes were motivated by hatred against another's sexual preference, and the corresponding proportion of the total number of hate crimes is .208, or 20.8%. The frequency of hate crimes motivated by bias against the victim's ethnicity or national origin was 655 with a corresponding proportion of .111, or 11.1%, of the total number of hate crimes. There were only 83 hate crimes motivated by the victim's disability in 2013, comprising .014, or a little more than 1%, of the total number of hate crimes reported in 2013. We will let you figure out the proportion and percentage of the total for the other two hate crimes—those resulting from gender and gender identity—and compare these with the figures in the table. Finally, you should note that the frequency column will sum to the total number of observations (5,922 hate crimes), the column of proportions will sum to 1.0 (unless there is some rounding error), and the column of percentages will sum to 100.0 (again, unless there is some rounding error).

Pie and Bar Charts

Although this tabular presentation of frequency, proportion, and percentage information is helpful in seeing the makeup of the different sources of hate crimes, we would now like to provide a graphical representation of this descriptive data, which may be more illustrative. When we have qualitative data, such as we have here with "hate crimes," we can graphically present the frequency, proportion, and percentage data in either a pie chart or a bar chart. A **pie chart** is exactly what the term implies. It consists of a round "pie" shape divided into parts, or "slices," where each slice represents a separate value of the variable. The size of each slice of the pie is proportionate to the frequency (or proportion or percentage of the total) for each value; that is, the greater the contribution that a given value makes to the total number of observations, the larger the slice of the pie for that value. The total area of the pie chart should equal the number of observations if you are graphing the frequencies, 1.0 if you are graphing proportions and 100 if you are graphing percentages. Figure 2.2 shows what a pie chart would look like for the frequency distribution reported in Table 2.1.

This pie chart of the frequency data does a very nice job of clearly showing the characteristics of the hate crime data. First, it reports the frequency of each value, as did Table 2.1. It shows that there were 2,871 racially motivated hate crimes reported in 2013, which is the largest slice of the pie. It shows about equally sized slices for crimes motivated by religious hatred (1,031) and by sexual orientation (1,233); a much smaller slice for hate crimes committed because of the victim's ethnicity or national origin (655);

Pie chart and bar chart: Graphical ways to display nominal- or ordinal-level variables. These charts can include frequencies, proportions, or percentages. Pie charts represent quantities as slices, and bar charts represent quantities as bars.

and a very small, almost indiscernible slice of the pie for disability-based hate crimes (83) and hate crimes motivated by gender (18) or gender identity (31). The size of each pie slice vividly shows the relative contribution of each value to the total number of observations. The relative sizes of the slices clearly indicate that almost one half of the hate crimes reported by the police in 2013 were racially motivated, about an equal proportion were motivated by either religious or sexual prejudice, and relatively few were motivated by disability or gender-based bias.

Figure 2.3 provides the same frequency data in the form of a pie chart but adds the percentage for each value along with the frequency count. There is no reason why we could not have reported the proportion rather than the percentage in Figure 2.3, but it is more conventional to report percentages rather than proportions since they make more intuitive sense to most people. We do, however, think that it is very important to report both the frequency for each value in a pie chart and its corresponding percentage (or proportion), as we have done in Figure 2.3.

We will go through one final example of tabular data with a corresponding pie chart. Table 2.1 reveals that 1,031 hate crimes motivated by religious hatred were reported in 2013. Table 2.2 breaks these hate crimes down into more specific subtypes. As shown, most of these hate-related crimes were directed against those of perceived Jewish faith ($f = 625$; 60.6%). These incidents greatly surpassed anti-Catholic ($f = 70$; 6.8%), anti-Protestant ($f = 35$; 3.4%), and anti-Islamic hate crimes ($f = 135$; 13.1%).

We take these frequency and percentage data and create a pie chart for graphical illustration, as shown in Figure 2.4. Unlike the previous pie chart, this one appears a bit cluttered, and although it is clear that most hate crimes motivated by religious bias are anti-Jewish, the other details are hard to discern.

When your pie chart of qualitative data looks a little messy and you think you are losing your ability to communicate the characteristics of your data, it is time to consider using a second graphical form to display the descriptive data at the nominal or ordinal level that we have been discussing: frequency counts, proportions, and percentages. Like the pie chart, the **bar chart** is appropriate for the graphical display of qualitative data only (nominal and ordinal). A bar chart represents the frequency, proportion, or percentage of each value by a vertical or horizontal bar. The width of the bar is equal to 1.0, and the height (or length for a horizontal bar chart) is equal to the value's frequency, proportion, or percentage (it does not matter which because the shape will be the same regardless). When we make the width of the

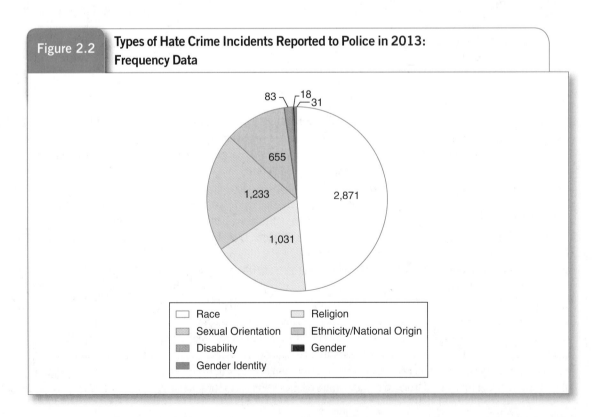

Figure 2.2   **Types of Hate Crime Incidents Reported to Police in 2013: Frequency Data**

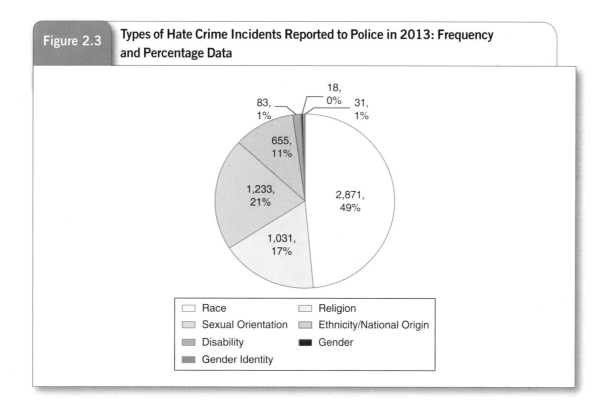

Figure 2.3 Types of Hate Crime Incidents Reported to Police in 2013: Frequency and Percentage Data

Table 2.2 Hate Crime Incidents Reported to Police in 2013 That Were Motivated by Bias Against the Victim's Religion

Type of Religious Hate	f	Proportion	%
Anti-Jewish	625	.606	60.6
Anti-Catholic	70	.068	6.8
Anti-Protestant	35	.034	3.4
Anti-Islamic	135	.131	13.1
Anti-other religions	117	.113	11.3
Anti-multireligious group	42	.041	4.1
Anti-agnostic/atheist	7	.007	0.7
Total	1,031	1.00	100.0

Source: Adapted from *Hate Crime Statistics—2013* from the Federal Bureau of Investigation (2013b).

bar equal to 1 and the height (or length) equal to the value's frequency (or proportion or percentage), the total area of a bar in a bar chart corresponds to the area represented by the frequency (or proportion or percentage) of that value.

Figure 2.5 shows a bar chart for the frequency data reported in Table 2.2. This is a vertical bar chart because the variable's different values are represented along the *x* (horizontal) axis and the frequency scale is represented along the *y* (vertical) axis. Note that the height of each bar can be followed to the *y* axis to determine the frequency count, but

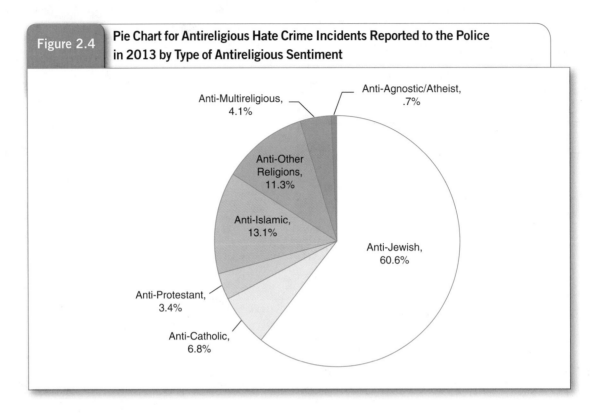

Figure 2.4 Pie Chart for Antireligious Hate Crime Incidents Reported to the Police in 2013 by Type of Antireligious Sentiment

in this bar chart the frequencies are provided above each bar for easy reading. Note also that the bars in a bar chart are not connected to each other but rather are separated along the *x* axis by a space or gap. This is intentional. It reminds us that the measurement for this variable is not continuous, with one value moving meaningfully along the continuum of numeric measurement to the next, but rather is discrete and qualitative. Anti-Catholic sentiment in a hate crime is not "more" of a hate crime than anti-Jewish sentiment; it is simply different. We could just as easily and meaningfully have these bars switched in our table, with anti-Catholic sentiment coming before anti-Jewish sentiment. The placements of the values of this and other qualitative variables are simply distinctions in quality or kind, and their location along the *x* axis is arbitrary, which is why we can move their location around on the graph.

The bar chart in Figure 2.5 is more effective than the pie chart in communicating the distribution of these data because it appears less cluttered. We could just as easily have created a bar chart with the proportion data in Table 2.2 or the percentage data. Both pie charts and bar charts can be used for the graphical display of frequency counts, proportions, or percentages (or combinations of the three).

One advantage of a bar chart over a pie chart for graphing qualitative data is that you can create overlapping or double bar charts that employ more than one variable. Table 2.3 reports the percentage of arrests for violent, property, and total index offenses for both males and females for the year 2013. This simple tabular presentation of descriptive data reports only percentages and not raw frequencies or proportions, but a graph may help to illustrate its features. The table shows that in the year 2013, males represented slightly less than 80% of the arrests for violent crimes in the United States, more than 60% of the property crimes, and almost 75% of the total index arrests.

These data are shown in a vertical bar chart in Figure 2.6. Note that in this figure, we are graphing the percentage of the total for each value, not its frequency count. As you can see from this figure, the height of each bar corresponds to the percentage for that value. By tracing the height of each bar over to the *y* axis, you can determine the approximate percentage. Note, for example, that by following the height of the bar for violent crimes, you can easily see that nearly 80% of the arrests for violent index crimes in 2013 were of men, 62% of all index property crimes were of men, and approximately 74% of the arrests for all index crimes were of men. The data in Figure 2.6 are exactly the same as those in Table 2.3, but sometimes a figure is easier to interpret than a table.

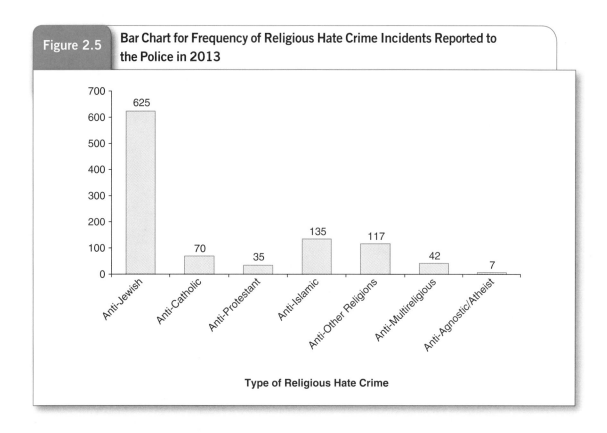

Figure 2.5   Bar Chart for Frequency of Religious Hate Crime Incidents Reported to the Police in 2013

Table 2.3   Percentage of Arrests for Violent Crimes, Property Crimes, and Total Index Crimes by Gender, 2013

Crime Type	% Male	% Female
Violent crimes	79.9	20.1
Property crimes	62.2	37.8
Total index crimes	73.5	26.5

Source: Adapted from table 42 of *Crime In the United States* from the Federal Bureau of Investigation (2013a).

🔲 The Tabular and Graphical Display of Quantitative Data

Ungrouped Distributions

Quantitative data are data measured at the ordinal, interval, or ratio level. The values of a quantitative variable express how much of the variable exists. As we learned in the previous chapter, ordinal-level variables consist of rank-ordered categories, whereas interval-level and ratio-level variables have values that consist of equidistant intervals that are continuous with either an arbitrary zero (interval scales) or an absolute zero (ratio scales). As with nominal-level data, we can present descriptive information for quantitative data in both tabular and graphical form.

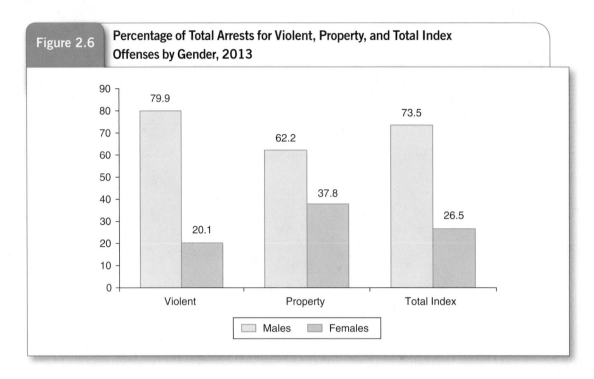

Figure 2.6 Percentage of Total Arrests for Violent, Property, and Total Index Offenses by Gender, 2013

Case Study

Police Response Time

We will start with a simple example consisting of ratio-level data. Table 2.4 shows the response time for a sample of 50 "911" calls (requests for police service) made to a local police department. The measurement unit is minutes, and each call time was rounded to the nearest minute. There is no ordering to these data; they simply appear in the order in which they occurred in the dispatcher's log sheet. Looking at these data does not provide much information about these response times because the information is disorganized and chaotic. This table is simply too difficult to read and comprehend. For example, it is not easy to locate the quickest and slowest response times, and we cannot easily determine whether the data tend to cluster around some typical response time.

We need to impose some order on these data so we can better understand them and know exactly what they suggest about police response times. The easiest way to organize these data is to create a table that includes descriptive

Table 2.4 Hypothetical Response Times of the Police to a 911 Call (in Minutes)

7	4	3	1	3	2	6	10	7	2
5	3	5	9	2	4	9	3	1	4
4	4	6	6	5	6	11	5	3	8
3	2	1	4	8	5	6	3	3	2
1	2	6	7	5	3	1	4	4	6

Table 2.5	Ungrouped Frequency Distribution for 50 Police Response Times to a 911 Call for Service					

Minutes	f	cf	p	cp	%	c%
1	5	5	.10	.10	10	10
2	6	11	.12	.22	12	22
3	9	20	.18	.40	18	40
4	8	28	.16	.56	16	56
5	6	34	.12	.68	12	68
6	7	41	.14	.82	14	82
7	3	44	.06	.88	6	88
8	2	46	.04	.92	4	92
9	2	48	.04	.96	4	96
10	1	49	.02	.98	2	98
11	1	50	.02	1.00	2	100
Total	50		1.00		100	

information such as the frequency of each value, its proportion, and its percentage—just as we did with the qualitative data in the previous section. With quantitative data, however, we can provide even more information.

We begin the process of describing these data by first listing all values in the data in some meaningful order, either from lowest to highest (ascending order) or from highest to lowest (descending order). We list all values of the "911 response time" variable in ascending order in the first column of Table 2.5. In the second column, we report the frequency of each value (f), which is a count of the number of times each response time or value occurs in the data. In this case, each value represents the time it took the police to respond to a 911 call for police assistance. Table 2.5 is referred to as an **ungrouped frequency distribution**. It is an ungrouped distribution because we have recorded all values or the entire range of scores from the lowest to the highest with no score left out. The data values go from the lowest of 1 minute to the highest of 11 minutes, and all recorded times in between appear in the frequency distribution. An ungrouped frequency distribution, therefore, lists all of the values of the variable that exist in the data along with how many times each value occurs.

We can see from Table 2.5 that the fastest the police responded to a 911 call was within 1 minute and that they did this 5 out of 50 times. The slowest police response time was 11 minutes, which occurred only once. You will note from the frequency column that the response times appear to cluster in the 2- to 6-minute range. It seems that most often the police responded to a 911 call in somewhere between 2 and 6 minutes. There are only a handful of very quick response times (a minute or less), and there were only a few responses of 7 minutes or more, with a diminished frequency at the longest response times. Finally, you can also see that the sum of the frequency column equals the number of scores or observations ($\Sigma f = n$). In these data, there were 50 recorded response times to 911 calls, so the total number of cases is 50. As you can see, a frequency distribution for these data was relatively simple to create, but it provides much more useful information, clarity, and organization than the data in Table 2.4. A simple frequency distribution has much to offer in helping you to understand and communicate the important features of a quantitative variable.

Ungrouped frequency distribution:
Every value of a variable is displayed, in contrast to a grouped frequency distribution, which displays intervals that correspond to the data values.

In addition to a frequency distribution, Table 2.5 provides, in the third column, something called a **cumulative frequency distribution** (*cf*). The cumulative frequency distribution indicates how many scores were at or lower than a given value, or at a given value or higher, depending on how you tally the cumulative frequencies. You may have noticed that we did not report cumulative frequencies in the table from the previous section of this chapter on qualitative data (Table 2.1). This is because qualitative data differ only in kind, not in degree. We cannot, therefore, speak of "more than" or "less than" or "lower than" with qualitative data.

The column of cumulative frequencies reported in Table 2.5 begins at the lowest value and cumulates until the highest value, and it is created in the following manner. In the first entry of the cumulative frequency column, enter the frequency for the first or lowest value. In this example, the first entry is 5, indicating that there were five instances where the police responded to a 911 call within 1 minute. Note that by subtracting this frequency of 5 from our total number of observations (50), we could also observe that there were 45 instances where the police took more than 1 minute in responding to a call. To continue with the cumulative frequency column, we add the frequency for the next value (2 minutes) to the first frequency. Thus, the second entry in the cumulative frequency column becomes 11. This tells us that there were 11 times when the police responded to a 911 call in 2 minutes or less (the five times they responded to a call in a minute or less and the six times they responded in between 1 and 2 minutes). We then proceed to the next value and note that there were nine instances when the police responded in between 2 and 3 minutes. Adding this to the cumulative frequency accumulated so far, we find that the next entry in the cumulative frequency column is 20 (5 + 6 + 9), indicating that the police responded to a 911 call within 3 minutes 20 times. We continue summing the frequencies for each value in succession. When we get to the last value of 11 minutes, the cumulative frequency is 50, telling us that the police responded to a 911 call in 11 minutes or less all 50 times. This should make intuitive sense because no call was responded to in more than 11 minutes and there were only 50 calls in our sample. The final entry in a cumulative frequency column should always equal the total number of observations, or *n*.

Cumulative frequencies like the one we just did where we start at the lowest value tell us how many observations were at or less than a given value (and by implication, how many were more than a given value). For example, Table 2.5 shows that 28 of the 50 calls for police assistance (more than one half) were responded to in 4 minutes or less. Therefore, slightly less than one half took more than 4 minutes to respond to. We also know that 44 of the 50 calls were responded to in 7 minutes or less. This implies that six calls took more than 7 minutes to respond to. We could also just as easily have

Cumulative frequency distribution: Frequency distribution reserved for ordinal or interval/ratio-level data made by starting with the lowest value of the variable (or the highest value) and cumulating (keeping a running tally or sum) the frequencies in each adjacent value until the highest value is reached (or the lowest value is reached). The sum of a cumulative frequency distribution should be equal to the total number of cases (*n*).

Cumulative proportions: Identical to a cumulative frequency distribution except that what is cumulated is the proportion at each value. The cumulative summing of proportions can go either from the lowest to the highest score or from the highest to the lowest score. The sum of a cumulative percentage distribution should be 1.0.

calculated our cumulated frequency distribution in the opposite direction, starting with the highest value and cumulative frequencies in each adjacent lower value. Doing it this way is perfectly acceptable and would give us at any point the number of observations that were at a given value or greater.

Table 2.5 also reports other descriptive information about the variable "police response time," including the familiar column of proportions and percentages. We can determine from Table 2.5 that .10 of the response times were within 1 minute, .12 of them were responded to in between 1 and 2 minutes, .18 of them were responded to in between 2 and 3 minutes, and .02 of them took 11 minutes to respond to. The column next to the proportion column consists of the **cumulative proportions** (*cp*). These cumulative proportions are calculated in the same manner as the cumulative frequencies.

Begin with the proportion of the first value, .10, which indicates that .10 (about 1 in 10) of the 911 calls were responded to in 1 minute or less. Since .12 of the calls were responded to in between 1 and 2 minutes, we add this to the .10 and note that .22 (the second entry in the *cp* column) of the calls were responded to in 2 minutes or less. We continue summing the proportions for each successive value until we reach the last value of 11 minutes. Here we see that 1.0, or all, of the 911 calls were responded to within 11 minutes. The last entry in a column of cumulative proportions should be 1.0 (or close to that in the presence of rounding error). Cumulative proportions are useful in revealing the proportion of cases at a given value or less. For example, we can quickly see from Table 2.5 that slightly more than one half (.56) of the 911 calls were responded to within 4 minutes and more than 9 out of 10 (.92) within 8 minutes (implying that only .08, or 1 – .92, of the 911 calls took more than 8 minutes to respond to). As with our cumulative frequency column, we could have started at the highest value and cumulated proportions toward the lowest value.

The next column of numbers in Table 2.5 shows the percentage for each value. We can determine from Table 2.5 that 10% of the 911 calls were responded to within 1 minute, 12% were responded to in between 1 and 2 minutes, nearly 20% (18%) were responded to in between 2 and 3 minutes, and only 4% took between 8 and 9 minutes to respond to.

The final column in Table 2.5 is a column of cumulative percentages (c%). These are generally more useful than cumulative proportions because they are easier for most people to comprehend. The cumulative percentages are calculated in exactly the same manner as the cumulative frequencies and cumulative proportions. For example, take the percentage of the first value, 10% of the calls were responded to within 1 minute, and add that to the percentage for the second value (12%). This reveals that 22% of the 50 911 calls were responded to in 2 minutes or less. Now add the percentage for the third value, response times between 2 and 3 minutes, and we can see that 4 in 10 (40%) of the calls were responded to within 3 minutes. By subtraction, 60% of the calls took longer than 3 minutes to respond to. Finally, we can see that more than 9 in 10 of the 911 calls (92%) were responded to in 8 minutes or less. The final entry in a column of cumulative percentages should be 100%, or close to that if there is rounding error. Cumulative percentages can also be calculated in either direction. Table 2.5, then, provides a great deal of information about our sample of 50 911 calls to the police. You will not be surprised, however, to learn that we can also display this information in a graphical display. The first we will examine is called a histogram.

Histograms

A histogram is very much like a bar chart. It is a graph of bars where the width of each bar on the x axis is equal to 1.0 and the height of the bar on the y axis is equal to the value's frequency, percentage, or proportion. However, there are two important differences between a bar chart and a histogram. The first is that in the histogram, the bars are connected to one another, indicating that the underlying measurement continuum is continuous and quantitative. Recall that in a bar chart, the bars are separated by a space or gap to indicate that the underlying measurement is discrete and qualitative rather than quantitative. Second, the bars on a histogram are placed on the graph from lowest score to highest score. In the bar chart, the placement of the values along the x axis is arbitrary.

Figure 2.7 shows a histogram for the ungrouped frequency distribution reported in Table 2.5. In graphical form, it shows that the most frequent response time was 3 minutes and that the data cluster around the 3- to 6-minute response time values. You can also see that the reported response times fall off fairly substantially after 6 minutes. At least in this sample, the police do seem to respond to a 911 call within 6 minutes.

Line Graphs or Polygons

If we have continuous data, we can also use other graphs to illustrate the frequency, proportion, or percentage distribution. One of these graphs is a line graph or polygon (frequency polygon, proportion polygon, or percentage polygon). The difference between a histogram and a polygon is that in a polygon, the frequency (or percentage or proportion) is represented by a point or dot above each score, rather than by a rectangular bar, where the height of the point corresponds to the magnitude of the frequency. The points or dots are then connected by a series of straight lines. Figure 2.8 illustrates the use of a frequency polygon for the 911 response call data in Table 2.5.

Like the histogram, this frequency polygon clearly shows that the response times to 911 calls in this sample cluster in the range of 3 to 6 minutes. It also clearly shows that

Cumulative percentages: Identical to a cumulative frequency distribution except that what is cumulated is the percentage at each value. The cumulative summing of percentages can go either from the lowest to the highest score or from the highest to the lowest score. The sum of a cumulative percentage distribution should be 100%.

Histogram: Method of graphing the distribution of an interval/ratio-level variable. It consists of a series of bars at each value of a variable where the height of the bar reflects the frequency of a value, its proportion, or its percentage.

Line graph (polygon): Method of graphing interval/ratio-level data.

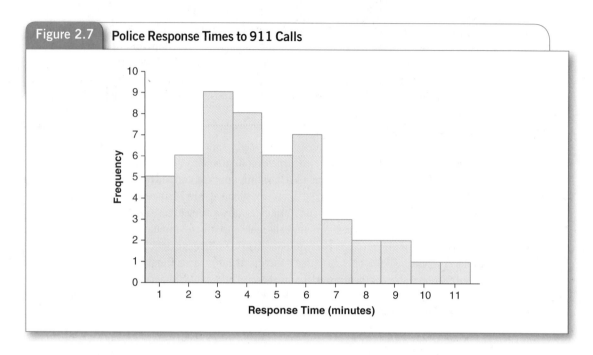

Figure 2.7 — Police Response Times to 911 Calls

there are far fewer response times that are 7 minutes or more. In other words, although there are some response times that are 8, 9, 10, and 11 minutes, there are not very many of them. Figure 2.9 illustrates that you could also create a polygon with the percentage data (or even the proportion data), and the story would be the same. The most likely response time (18% of the time) was 3 minutes, followed by 4 minutes, with a clustering of cases in the response time range of 3 to 6 minutes.

Finally, it is possible to graph the cumulative data as well—cumulative frequencies, cumulative percentages, and cumulative proportions—in the form of a line graph or polygon. Figure 2.10 shows a cumulative percentage polygon, but keep in mind that we could just as easily have graphed the cumulative frequencies or cumulative proportions. In the cumulative percentage polygon, the entry for each value of the variable corresponds to the percentage of cases or scores at that value or less. To interpret this cumulative percentage graph, simply move up from a value on the *x* axis until you hit the line and then move over to the *y* axis to find the percentage of the cases that are at that value or less. For example, start at the value of 3 minutes, move up to hit the line and then over to the *y* axis, and you will discover that 40% of the response times for the police were in 3 minutes or less. Approximately 80% of the response times were within 6 minutes, and 90% were within 8 minutes. Of course, 100% of the calls were responded to in 11 minutes or less. You should know that since cumulative percentages are calculated by summing the successive percentages for each value, the line on a cumulative percentage polygon should never fall; it should always be either rising or flat. This holds true for graphs of cumulative frequencies and cumulative proportions as well.

Grouped Frequency Distributions

Case Study

Recidivism

From prison release data, we know that nearly two out of three people released from prison will be rearrested within 1 year. Table 2.6 presents hypothetical data from a sample of 120 male offenders released from a penitentiary and followed until they were arrested for a new offense. For each person, we have recorded the number of days he was free

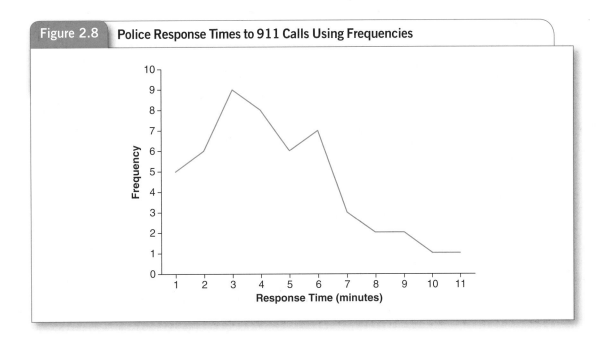

Figure 2.8 Police Response Times to 911 Calls Using Frequencies

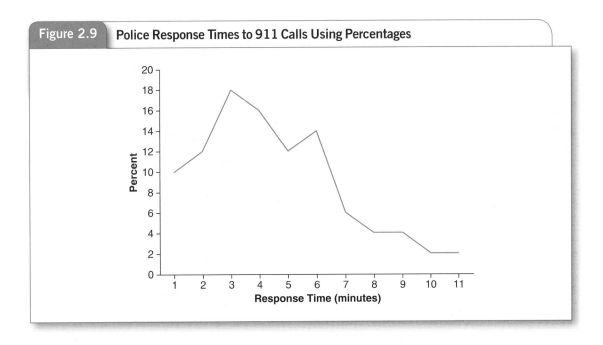

Figure 2.9 Police Response Times to 911 Calls Using Percentages

before he committed a new offense. The first value in the table, 25, implies that someone was out in the community for 25 days before he committed a new offense or was arrested for a parole violation, the second value shows that another person was free for 37 days before he was rearrested, and the last person in Table 2.6 was free for 34 days before he was rearrested.

This variable is measured at the ratio level. Notice that all 120 released offenders were rearrested at some time. Criminologists sometimes refer to this variable as a "time until failure" variable (because a rearrest is considered a "failure" for corrections). Since our interest here is the time until failure, all 120 of the hypothetical offenders are rearrested.

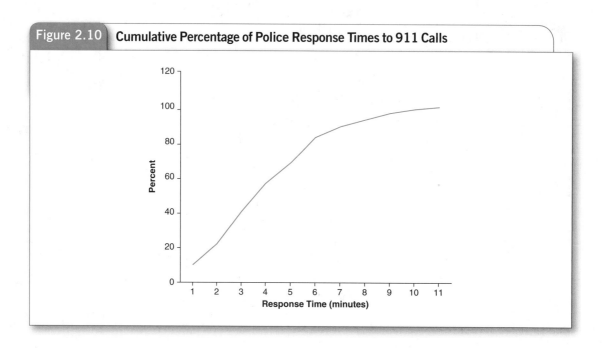

Figure 2.10 Cumulative Percentage of Police Response Times to 911 Calls

As you can see, it is hard to comprehend a pattern with the data in Table 2.6. We cannot easily tell much about the time it took for the typical person to be rearrested. It is even difficult to determine very simple information such as how quickly the first person was arrested and how long it was before the last offender was rearrested. The first thing we would like to do with our data, therefore, is to organize them. So far, we have learned how to organize data into an ungrouped frequency distribution.

Table 2.7 shows the ungrouped frequency distribution for these data. This ungrouped frequency distribution gives us some clarity but not very much. We can now see, for example, that one person was rearrested in 17 days, whereas four offenders lasted 40 days before they were rearrested. From the cumulative percentage column, we can also see that about one half (50.8%) of the 120 offenders were rearrested within 31 days. Although this ungrouped frequency distribution is somewhat helpful in organizing the data, it still looks a little cluttered. This is because we have so many different values to report—there are 24 different values reported for the variable—and with few exceptions the frequency for each value is fairly low. We provide a histogram of these ungrouped data in Figure 2.11. This histogram is also not especially helpful for us to visualize the variable's patterns or features. There is simply too much information. We need to reorganize these data to make the picture a little clearer.

We will first create a **grouped frequency distribution**. Unlike an ungrouped distribution, which reports all scores in a distribution, a grouped distribution organizes the data by grouping scores into groups of values or class intervals. Then it lists the frequency, proportion, and percentages associated with each class interval rather than with each separate value. A **class interval** is simply a range of values for a variable. For example, rather than reporting the individual values 17, 18, 19, 20, ... days until rearrest, in a grouped distribution we may have a class interval that goes from 17 to 20 days. We would then determine the number or frequency of cases that fell within this interval and report that. What we are going to do is take the ungrouped distribution reported in Table 2.7 and construct a grouped distribution. Before we do this, however, we need to discuss some rules and guidelines for the construction of grouped frequency distributions.

But first, one general point needs to be made. The construction of a grouped frequency distribution is as much art as it is science. By this we mean you must keep in mind that your goal in creating a grouped distribution is to organize your data and communicate their important characteristics and features. A good grouped frequency distribution

Grouped frequency distribution: Reports the values of a quantitative continuous variable in intervals or a range of values rather than reporting every distinct value.

Class interval: In creating a grouped frequency distribution, the class interval defines the range of values that are included in each interval.

| Table 2.6 | Number of Days Until Rearrest for Sample of 120 Released Offenders |

25	30	31	33	19	36
37	34	39	32	33	37
20	27	38	29	23	36
29	39	30	28	33	35
27	27	25	24	29	38
28	26	34	23	36	17
40	31	29	28	33	38
26	31	32	35	37	32
30	29	37	33	33	25
18	19	33	40	31	29
27	23	40	24	36	38
24	27	35	33	32	32
34	30	31	31	36	36
24	25	25	26	27	28
34	32	28	35	33	29
35	29	35	31	28	27
31	34	37	36	36	35
40	29	31	34	34	33
30	32	30	29	29	30
31	33	33	34	35	34

does this, and a poor one does not. Unfortunately, there is often not a single or "correct" way to organize data into a grouped distribution. What you have to do is make some tentative decisions about how to construct your grouped distributions, make the distribution in accordance with those decisions, and then look at the distribution you have made. You must then determine whether this distribution adequately conveys the features of your data (e.g., their shape or most typical score) or obscures them. If you think the grouped distribution you have made is inadequate or fails to show the features of your data, simply construct another one and go through the same process. Keep the grouped frequency distribution that you are convinced appropriately reveals the features of your data.

Several "hard-and-fast" rules apply to the creation of a grouped frequency distribution. These rules should never be broken:

1. Make your class intervals **mutually exclusive.** That is, be certain that each value falls into one and only one interval. Do not have overlapping intervals like, for example, 17–20 days and 20–24 days. Under this incorrect scheme, someone who was rearrested in 20 days could be placed in either the first or the second interval.

Mutually exclusive intervals: Class intervals must not overlap.

Table 2.7	Time Until Rearrest: Ungrouped Frequency and Percentage Distribution		
Days Until Rearrest	f	%	c%
17	1	0.8	0.8
18	1	0.8	1.6
19	2	1.7	3.3
20	1	0.8	4.1
21	0	0.0	4.1
22	0	0.0	4.1
23	3	2.5	6.6
24	4	3.3	9.9
25	5	4.2	14.1
26	3	2.5	16.6
27	7	5.8	22.4
28	6	5.0	27.4
29	11	9.2	36.6
30	7	5.8	42.4
31	10	8.3	50.7
32	7	5.8	56.5
33	12	10.0	66.5
34	8	6.7	73.2
35	8	6.7	79.9
36	8	6.7	86.6
37	6	5.0	91.6
38	4	3.3	94.9
39	2	1.7	96.6
40	4	3.3	99.9*
Total	n = 120	99.9*	

*Does not sum to 100% because of rounding.

Exhaustive intervals: Class intervals must provide a place to count all original values of the variable distribution.

2. Make your class intervals **exhaustive.** In other words, make sure that each value falls into an interval. Do not make intervals that leave some values off. For example, in our time until rearrest data, do not have your first two intervals be 18–21 days and 22–25 days. Although these intervals are mutually exclusive, they are not exhaustive because you have a value of 17 days in your data, and it is not included in either interval.

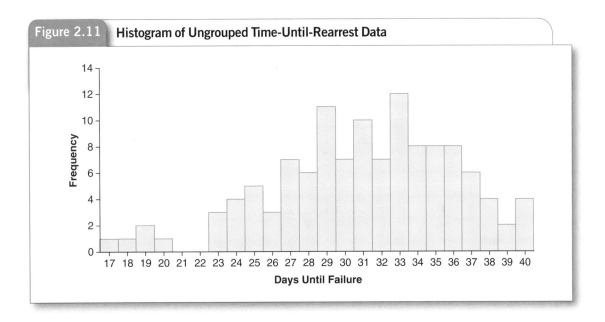

Figure 2.11 **Histogram of Ungrouped Time-Until-Rearrest Data**

3. Make all your intervals the same width. The **interval width,** symbolized as w_i, is the number of values that the class interval contains. For example, a class interval of 17–20 days has an interval width of 4 because it includes four values: 17, 18, 19, and 20 days until rearrest. The class interval 21–29 days has an interval width of 9. You would not want to have a grouped distribution that has the two intervals 17–20 days and 21–29 days because these class intervals do not have the same width. Class intervals of different widths would distort the appearance of your distribution.

4. Make sure that your first class interval contains your lowest value and that your last class interval contains your highest value. In other words, do not make your first or last interval such that no cases fall into it. In the time-until-rearrest data, we would not want to make our first class interval 13–16 days and our second class interval 17–20 days. Although both class intervals have a width of 4 and they are mutually exclusive, with the data we have the first interval would have a frequency of 0 since the earliest rearrest time was in 17 days. For the same reason, we would not want to have 41–44 days as our last class interval since it too would have a frequency of 0.

These rules for the construction of a grouped frequency distribution should be followed at all times and never violated. This is the science part, but beyond this it becomes art.

Let's try to make a grouped frequency distribution from the rearrest time data shown in Table 2.7. There are really only three steps to follow in making a grouped frequency distribution. These three steps are as follows. As you perform them, keep the hard-and-fast rules in mind and follow them carefully.

Step 1: Determine the Number of Class Intervals You Want. Here we directly confront the "art" of creating grouped frequency distributions. There is no hard-and-fast rule about how many class intervals you should have; it depends entirely on your data. But there are some things you avoid as you decide how many intervals you want to have. You should not have so few intervals that you lose most of the information in your data. And you should not have too many intervals because you are trying to simplify, organize, and make sense of your data. A reasonable guide to follow is that at least at first you should have somewhere between 7 and 14 class intervals. After examining your data, determine what you think might be a good number of class intervals to begin the process. For our time-until-rearrest data, then, we will start with the decision to have 10 class intervals.

> **Interval width:** Number of different values that are contained within the class interval. For example, for the given interval 0–5 arrests, the width is 6 because the interval contains the values 0, 1, 2, 3, 4, and 5 arrests.

Step 2: Determine the *Width* of the Class Interval. Once you have determined the number of class intervals you want, you have to decide what your interval width should be. Keep in mind the hard-and-fast rule that each class interval must be the same width. To estimate an approximate interval width, the following simple routine is useful. First, find the range in your data where the range is simply the arithmetic difference between your highest and lowest scores. In our time-until-rearrest data, the range is 23 days since the longest time until rearrest was 40 days and the shortest time was 17 days (range = 40 − 17 = 23 days). With this, an estimate of the interval width can be obtained by taking the ratio of the range to the number of class intervals you selected in Step 1. The formula for the estimated interval width is

$$w_i = \frac{\text{Range}}{\text{Number of intervals}}$$ (Formula 2-1)

In this example,

$$w_i = \frac{23}{10}$$
$$w_i = 2.3$$

Given the fact that our data consist of whole numbers, we would not really want to have an interval width with a decimal place. We could round down and have a class interval width of 2 or round up and have an interval width of 3. Again, this is the "art" part where there are no hard-and-fast rules to guide you. Because this is not mathematical precision and partly art, let's decide to round up. We now have two critical pieces of information to make our grouped frequency distribution. We know we would like to have approximately 10 class intervals, and we want each interval width to be 3.

Step 3: Make Your Class Intervals. Now we are ready to make our class intervals. With the understanding that they must be mutually exclusive, must be exhaustive, and must include the lowest score in the first interval and the highest score in the last interval, we want to approximate 10 class intervals, and each class interval will have a width of 3. In making our grouped frequency distribution with the time-until-rearrest data, we have to make sure that our first interval contains the value 17 days because that is our lowest score. One way we can ensure this is to have the first interval begin with 17. The score that defines the beginning of any class interval is called the *lower limit* of the interval. If the first interval begins with 17 days, what should the last value of this interval be? The last value of any class interval is the *upper limit* of the interval. Many students make the mistake of adding the interval width to the lower limit to determine what the upper limit of the interval should be. For example, if we did this, we would obtain an interval of 17–20 since 17 + 3 (the interval width) = 20. Unfortunately, this would give us an interval width of 4 rather than 3 since it contains the values 17, 18, 19, and 20 days until rearrest.

A helpful hint in making your class intervals is to do the following. First, select the lower limit of your first class interval. In this case, it is 17. Instead of figuring out what the upper limit is, leave it unknown for the moment.

Add your interval width to this lower limit, and this value becomes the lower limit of the next interval. In our case, the lower limit of the second class interval should be 20 (lower limit of first class interval + interval width = 17 + 3):

17 – ?
20 – ?

Since the lower limit of the second interval is 20 days, the upper limit of the first interval must be 19 days. The first class interval, then, is 17–19 days, and it contains three values: 17, 18, and 19 days. This is as it should be with an interval width of 3. You can complete your class intervals very easily now by adding the interval width to the lower limit of each class interval to find out what the lower limit of the next class interval should be. Repeat this procedure until you have a class interval that includes your highest score, and then you can stop.

Table 2.8	Grouped Distribution for Time-Until-Rearrest Data					

Stated Class Limits (days)	f	cf	p	cp	%	c%
17–19	4	4	.0333	.0333	3.33	3.33
20–22	1	5	.0083	.0416	0.83	4.16
23–25	12	17	.1000	.1416	10.00	14.16
26–28	16	33	.1333	.2749	13.33	27.49
29–31	28	61	.2333	.5082	23.33	50.82
32–34	28	89	.2333	.7415	23.33	74.15
35–37	21	110	.1750	.9165	17.50	91.65
38–40	10	120	.0833	.9998	8.33	99.98
Total	120		.9998*		99.98*	

*Does not sum to 1.0, or 100%, because of rounding.

For our time-until-rearrest data, the class intervals are shown for you in the first column of Table 2.8 under the heading "Stated Class Limits." The **stated class limits** define the range of values for each class interval in the grouped frequency distribution. As we mentioned, there are two components to any stated class interval, a lower class limit and an upper class limit. Remember that the first score in any class interval is the lower limit of the interval (LL), and the last score of the class interval is the upper limit of the interval (UL). For the first class interval, then, the lower limit is 17 days and the upper limit is 19 days. The lower limit of the second class interval is 20 days and the upper limit is 22 days.

Note that because we rounded up our estimated interval width from 2.3 to 3.0, we have 8 class intervals rather than the 10 we thought we were going to have according to Step 1. Had we rounded the estimated interval width down to 2.0, we would have had 12 class intervals rather than 10. Stay calm! This is the art part. For now, we will work with the 8 intervals and see if we like it. We have abided by our hard-and-fast rule that that each class interval has the same width—ours is 3—and that the intervals are mutually exclusive and exhaustive. The first interval contains the lowest score (17), and the last interval contains the highest score (40). Everything looks good so far.

Now that we have our class intervals created, we can make a frequency distribution by counting the number of cases that fall into each class interval. For example, by looking at the data in Table 2.8, you can determine that there are 4 offenders who were rearrested between 17 and 19 days, only 1 who was rearrested between 20 and 22 days, 12 who were rearrested between 23 and 25 days, and so on until you find that there are 10 people who were rearrested between 38 and 40 days. As was true with an ungrouped frequency distribution, the sum of the frequency column in a grouped frequency distribution should equal the total number of cases ($\sum f = n$)—in this example, 120. We can use these frequencies now to determine the proportions (p) and percentage of the total for each class interval where $p = f / n$ and percentage $= p \times 100$. Since there were 4 offenders out of 120 who were rearrested between 17 and 19 days, they comprise .0333 of the total (4/120 = .0333), or 3.33%. Similarly, since there were 28 offenders who were rearrested between 29 and 31 days, they comprise .2333 of the total (28/120 = .2333), or 23.33%. We can also meaningfully calculate the cumulative frequencies, cumulative proportions, and cumulative percentages for each class interval.

One thing you should immediately notice about our grouped frequency distribution is that while our ungrouped data were measured at the interval/ratio level, by creating class intervals we now have ordinal-level data. Our data values now consist of rank-ordered categories rather than of equally distanced values. In a sense, then, we "dumbed down" our data from interval/ratio to ordinal level.

Stated class limits: Lowest value that is included in an interval and the highest value that is included in an interval.

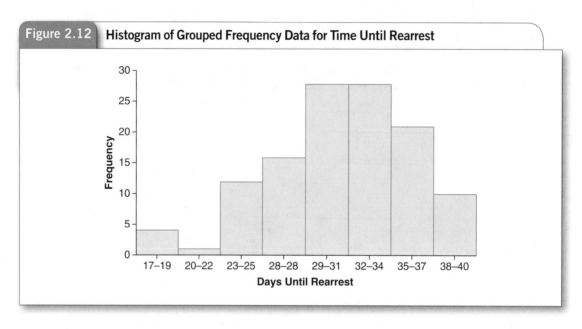

Figure 2.12 Histogram of Grouped Frequency Data for Time Until Rearrest

To see this clearly, assume we take one hypothetical person from each of the first two class intervals. What we now know is that the person who falls into the first class interval (17–19 days) was rearrested sooner than the person who is in the second class interval (20–22 days)—"sooner" implies a rank order of time (sooner rather than at the same time or later). What we do not know, however, is *how much* sooner the first person was rearrested. Since we know only that he falls into the first interval and not the precise number of days until rearrest, we can use only words like "rearrested sooner" and "rearrested later" and not more precise words like "rearrested 2 days sooner" and "arrested twice as fast." With our original continuous data that measured the exact number of days until rearrest, we could calculate precise things like "how much more than" and "how much less than"—statements we cannot make with ordinal-level data. In creating a grouped frequency distribution from continuous data, then, we lose some precision in our measurement. What we will have to determine is how large a price we have to pay for creating a grouped frequency distribution. In other words, how much precision did we lose in going from interval/ratio to ordinal-level measurement? We will address this issue in later chapters.

Even though there is some loss of precision because we have created categories or class intervals rather than reporting every value, Table 2.8 shows the distribution of the data much better than the ungrouped distribution shown in Table 2.7. We can see here that not many people were immediately rearrested. There were no rearrests for 16 days and then only a handful until 23 days after release (5 rearrests, or less than 5% of the total). There were, however, a large number of people rearrested between 29 and 37 days; in fact, 77 cases, or nearly two thirds (64.17%) of the total, were rearrested within that range. By the 37th day after their release, 110 offenders of the 120 had been rearrested, and this consisted of more than 9 out of 10 released offenders, or greater than 90% of the total. By having constructed this grouped distribution, we will now construct a histogram of the grouped frequency data, shown for you in Figure 2.12.

This histogram of the grouped frequency distribution is a little more informative than that for the ungrouped data in Figure 2.11. We clearly see that few persons were rearrested very soon after release, that it was not until approximately 29 days after release when most offenders began to be rearrested, and that they then were rearrested at a fairly steady level until the 37th day. One is immediately struck by the fact that a large proportion of rearrests occurred between 29 and 34 days—approximately a month after release.

In case we were not satisfied with the grouped frequency distribution that has 8 class intervals and an interval width of 3, we might want to try constructing a different set of intervals. Rather than rounding the interval width up from 2.3 to 3.0, we will now round down and have class intervals with a width of 2. We go through the same procedures as before, and as practice you should stop reading any further and attempt to create this grouped frequency distribution on your own. Then check it with what we have done.

Table 2.9	Grouped Distribution for Time-Until-Rearrest Data Using Interval Width of 2

Stated Class Limits	f	%
17–18	2	1.7
19–20	3	2.5
21–22	0	0.0
23–24	7	5.8
25–26	8	6.7
27–28	13	10.8
29–30	18	15.0
31–32	17	14.2
33–34	20	16.7
35–36	16	13.3
37–38	10	8.3
39–40	6	5.0
Total	120	100.0

The grouped frequency distribution where the width of each class interval is 2 is shown in Table 2.9 along with the percentage distribution. The corresponding histogram for the grouped frequency distribution is given in Figure 2.13. Because the interval width is 2.0 rather than 3.0, there are now 12 rather than 8 class intervals. But the story provided by the table and graph are virtually the same as when the interval width was 3.0, and both sets of tables and graphs are very easy to read, interpret, and understand. One would be hard-pressed to say that one set of tables/graphs is any better than the other. It looks as if they both are effective in showing the distribution of these time-until-rearrest data. You now have clear evidence that making a grouped frequency distribution does not have a clearly defined single answer and that making such distributions is "as much art as it is science."

Refinements to a Grouped Frequency Distribution

Recall that we created our grouped frequency distribution in the previous section with data that were initially quantitative and continuous. The variable, time until rearrest, was measured at the interval/ratio level as the number of days a released offender was out in the community before he was rearrested. We then collapsed this data into ordinal-level categories. We see this categorization in our stated class limits. We would like to show you the difference between continuous data and the ordinal-level categories of the class intervals. First the interval/ratio-level data measure time until rearrest in continuous increments of 1 day:

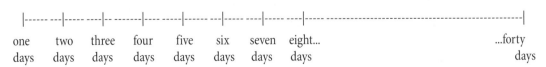

This measurement of time until rearrest is continuous, and this continuity is seen in the gradual evolution of 1 day into 2 days, into 3 days, and so on. When we collapsed the data into the ordinal categories of stated class intervals as in Table 2.8, however, our class intervals became discrete categories:

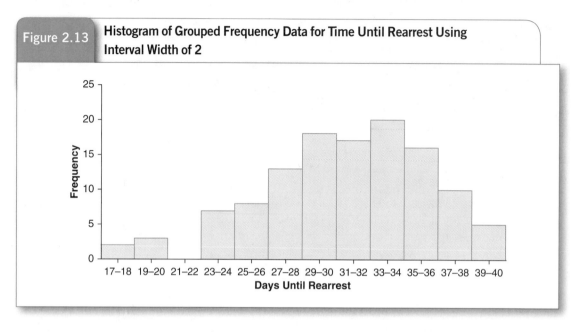

Figure 2.13 Histogram of Grouped Frequency Data for Time Until Rearrest Using Interval Width of 2

```
|----------|  |-----------|  |----------|  |-----------|  |-----------|  |-----------|  |----------|  |----------|
 17–19 days   20–22 days    23–25 days    26–28 days    29–31 days    32–34 days    35–37 days    38–40 days
```

There will be times, however, when we will want to maintain the continuous nature of our original interval/ratio measurement even though we have created ordinal-level categories. We do this by constructing something called **real class limits**. The creation of real class limits will both remind us that our underlying measurement is truly continuous and enable us to perform certain statistical operations on the data (discussed in later chapters), which we could not do if the data were truly ordinal.

Constructing real class limits is very simple. Let's take as an illustration the first and second class intervals in Table 2.8. First, note that there is a 1-unit "gap" between the upper limit of a given class interval and the lower limit of the next. For example, there is a 1-unit (1-day) "gap" between the upper limit of the first stated class interval (19 days) and the lower limit of the next stated class interval (20 days). Note that this 1-unit "gap" exists for each stated class limit, even the first class interval (the stated class interval 14–16 exists; we simply didn't use it because our first observed value is 17 days). What we are now going to do is extend the upper limit of the first stated class interval one half of the distance of this "gap." Since the "gap" is 1 unit, this means we will increase the upper limit of the first stated class limit by one half or .5 unit. Now the upper limit of the first stated class interval will be .5 unit closer to the lower limit of the next stated class interval. The real upper limit for the first class interval would then be 19.5 days.

Similarly, we need to decrease the lower limit of the second stated class interval one half of the distance of the "gap," or .5 unit, so that now it is .5 unit closer to the upper limit of the previous stated class interval. The real lower limit for the second class interval would then be 19.5 days. We continue by decreasing the lower limit of each stated class interval by .5 (half the distance of the "gap" between the stated class limits) and by increasing the upper limit of each state class interval by .5 (also half the distance of the "gap"). The lower real limit for our first class interval would be 16.5 because we are decreasing the lower stated limit of 17 by .5 unit, and the upper real limit would be 19.5 because we are increasing the upper stated limit of 19 by .5 unit. We do this for all class intervals, including the first and the last. When we complete this, our real class limits are as follows.

Real class limits: Real limits in a grouped distribution take into account the space between the adjacent intervals. For example, for an interval with stated limits of 0–5 and 6–11 prior arrests, the real limits are 0.5–5.5 and 5.5–11.5.

Real Class Limits

16.5–19.5 days

19.5–22.5 days

22.5–25.5 days

25.5–28.5 days

28.5–31.5 days

31.5–34.5 days

34.5–37.5 days

37.5–40.5 days

Note that the upper real limit of each class interval is equal to the lower real limit of the next class interval. The intervals now merge together, reflecting the continuous nature of the underlying data. There are no "gaps" in these continuous data. Essentially, we have tried to recapture some of the measurement properties we lost when we created a grouped frequency distribution and made the originally continuous data categorical. What we are trying to remind ourselves, therefore, is that despite the fact that we created ordinal categories with our grouped frequency distribution, the underlying measurement of the original data was continuous. We illustrate this in the following diagram. With real class limits, we now have

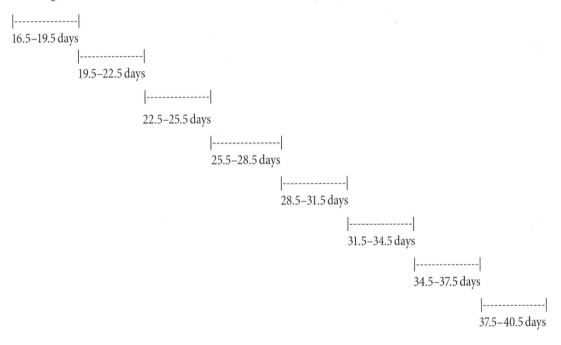

We will use these real limits in later chapters to do some simple statistical calculations that normally would require us to have interval/ratio-level data. You should note that we cannot use these real class limits to calculate our frequency, proportion, or percentage distributions for grouped data. Why not? Recall that one of the hard-and-fast rules in making a grouped frequency distribution is that the class intervals must be mutually exclusive. This means that a given score must fall in one and only one class interval. Real class limits violate this rule because the intervals overlap. Where, for example, would we place a score of 19 days? Would it go in the first or second class interval?

Another piece of information we are now going to add to our grouped frequency distribution is something called the midpoint of the interval (the midpoint of a given class interval i is given by m_i). We will use the interval midpoints in the next two chapters when we discuss measures of central tendency and dispersion. The **midpoint** of a class interval is exactly what the term implies; it is a score that lies exactly at the midpoint of the class interval, exactly one half of the distance between the lower limit and the upper limit of a given class interval. Each class interval, therefore, has its own midpoint. The midpoint of

Midpoint: Exact middle value in an interval of a grouped frequency distribution. The midpoint is found by summing the lower and upper limits (stated or real) and dividing by 2.

a class interval is very easy to calculate. Simply take the sum of the lower limit and the upper limit of the interval and divide by 2. It does not matter whether you use the lower and upper limits of the stated class limits or of the real class limits; the result will be the same:

$$m_i = \frac{\text{Lower limit} + \text{Upper limit}}{2}$$ (Formula 2-2)

For example, with our grouped frequency distribution in Table 2.8, we can calculate the midpoint of the first interval as $(17 + 19) / 2 = 36 / 2 = 18$ using the stated limits or as $(16.5 + 19.5) / 2 = 36 / 2 = 18$ using the real class limits. Midpoints are always calculated for every class interval in a grouped frequency distribution. Table 2.10 shows the real limit and midpoint of each class interval for the grouped frequency distribution data in Table 2.8 where the width of each stated class interval was 3.0.

| Table 2.10 | Stated Class Limits, Real Class Limits, and Midpoints for Grouped Frequency Distribution in Table 2.8 |

Stated Class Limits	Real Class Limits	m_i	f
17–19	16.5–19.5	18	4
20–22	19.5–22.5	21	1
23–25	22.5–25.5	24	12
26–28	25.5–28.5	27	16
29–31	28.5–31.5	30	28
32–34	31.5–34.5	33	28
35–37	34.5–37.5	36	21
38–40	37.5–40.5	39	10
			Total = 120

▣ The Shape of a Distribution

One important piece of information that a graph of continuous data can give you at a glance is the shape of your distribution. For statistical purposes, one important shape of a continuous distribution is normal. A **normal distribution** is a distribution that is symmetrical, which means that if you drew a line down the center of the distribution, the left half would look exactly like the right half. A normal distribution has a single peak in the middle of the distribution, with fewer and fewer cases as you move away from this middle. The ends of a distribution of continuous scores are often called the "tails" of the distribution. A distribution has both a left or negative tail and a right or positive tail.

A normal distribution is often referred to as a "bell-shaped curve" because it is shaped a bit like a bell. An example of a normal distribution is shown in Figure 2.14. We will discuss the normal distribution in great detail in Chapter 5 because many variables of interest in criminology and criminal justice are normally or approximately normally distributed, and many of the statistics we apply to our data depend on the assumption that they are normally distributed.

Normal distribution: Symmetrical distribution that has the greatest frequency of its cases in the middle of the distribution with fewer cases at each end or "tail" of the distribution. A normal distribution looks like a bell when drawn, and it is often referred to as a "bell-shaped" distribution.

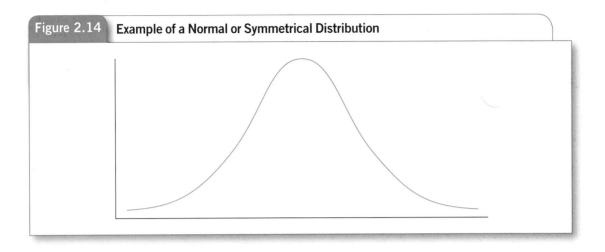

Figure 2.14 **Example of a Normal or Symmetrical Distribution**

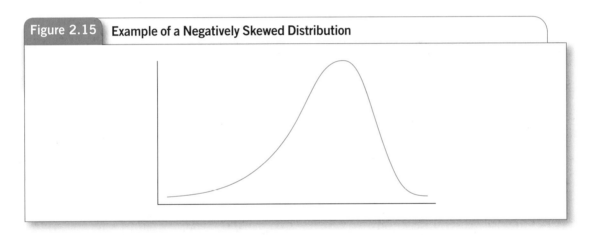

Figure 2.15 **Example of a Negatively Skewed Distribution**

When a distribution departs, or *deviates,* from normality, it is said to be a **skewed distribution.** There are two forms of skewed distributions. Figure 2.15 shows a distribution where there is a long series of low scores with most of the scores at the high end of the distribution. Note that this distribution has a long left or negative tail. This type of skew is called a **negative skew** because the long tail of the distribution is to the left, and the left side of the number line moves toward negative numbers. In a distribution with a negative skew, then, most of the scores cluster at higher values of the variable and there is a long left tail, indicating that there are low values with few cases at each value. Figure 2.16 shows a distribution where there are series of low-frequency high scores with most of the scores clustered at the low end of the distribution. Note that this distribution has a long right or positive tail. This type of skew is called a **positive skew** because the long tail of the distribution is to the right, and the right side of the number line moves toward positive numbers. In a distribution with a positive skew, therefore, most of the scores cluster at lower values of the variable and there is a long right tail, indicating that there are a lot of high values with few cases at each value. Remember that the skew is indicated by the direction where the tail is being pulled by a few low frequency scores, not by where the bulk of the data lie.

If you think of a very high or very low score as an **outlier,** then a negatively skewed distribution has outliers at the left tail of the distribution (the long tail), whereas a positively skewed distribution has outliers at the right tail of the distribution.

Skewed distribution: Non-normal (nonsymmetrical) distribution.

Negatively skewed distribution: Long "tail" is found on the left side of the distribution (toward the negative numbers).

Positively skewed distribution: Long "tail" is found on the right side of the distribution (toward the positive numbers).

Outlier: Unusually high or low value or score for a variable.

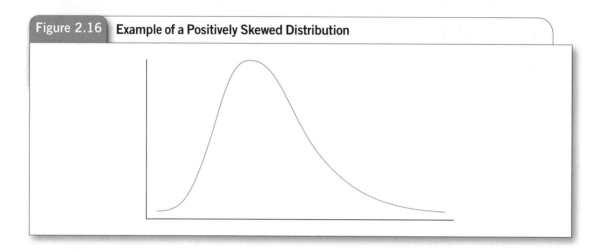

Figure 2.16 **Example of a Positively Skewed Distribution**

▣ Time Plots

Frequently in criminology and other social sciences, we are interested in the extent to which events change or remain stable over time. In other words, the values of some of our variables may change over time, and we would like to have a convenient way to show this. We can do this in a table where we report the value of a variable at different time points—for example, every 6 months or every year. In addition to the tabular presentation of the value of a variable over time, we can graph the change in a time plot. A time plot is simply a graphical display of a variable's values over some unit of time (year, month, week, etc.). It is actually a type of line graph where the height of the line on the *y* axis reflects some attribute of the value (a frequency or a percentage) and its length is marked off in units of time on the *x* axis. In such a time plot, we can easily determine the value of the variable at any given point in time.

Table 2.11	Annual Rates (per 100,000) of Rape, Robbery, and Aggravated Assault Known to the Police and Reported to the FBI's Uniform Crime Reports Program, 1972–2013		
Year	Rape Rate	Robbery Rate	Aggravated Assault Rate
1972	22.5	180.7	188.8
1973	24.5	183.1	200.5
1974	26.2	209.3	215.8
1975	26.3	220.8	227.4
1976	26.6	199.3	233.2
1977	29.4	190.7	247.0
1978	31.0	195.8	262.1
1979	34.7	218.4	286.0
1980	36.8	251.1	298.5

Year	Rape Rate	Robbery Rate	Aggravated Assault Rate
1981	36.0	258.7	289.3
1982	34.0	238.9	289.0
1983	33.7	216.5	279.4
1984	35.7	205.4	290.6
1985	37.1	208.5	304.0
1986	37.9	225.1	347.4
1987	37.4	212.7	352.9
1988	37.6	220.9	372.2
1989	38.1	233.0	385.6
1990	41.2	257.0	422.9
1991	42.3	272.7	433.4
1992	42.8	263.7	441.9
1993	41.1	256.0	440.5
1994	39.3	237.8	427.6
1995	37.1	220.9	418.3
1996	36.3	201.9	391.0
1997	35.9	186.2	382.1
1998	34.5	165.5	361.4
1999	32.8	150.1	334.3
2000	32.0	144.9	323.6
2001	31.8	148.5	318.6
2002	33.1	146.1	309.5
2003	32.3	142.5	295.4
2004	32.4	136.7	288.6
2005	31.8	140.8	290.8
2006	30.9	149.4	287.5
2007	30.1	155.7	292.6
2008	29.4	154.0	281.6
2009	28.9	139.6	268.3
2010	27.8	122.7	255.5
2011	26.8	117.1	243.5
2012	26.7	116.3	246.5
2013	23.1	112.9	233.7

Source: Adapted from *Uniform Crime Reports* from the Federal Bureau of Investigation (1990, 1995, 2000, 2005–2013).

Case Study

A Trend Analysis of Crime Rates

Table 2.11 reports annual rates of crimes reported to the police for three "index offenses"—forcible rape, robbery, and aggravated assault—in the United States over the time period 1972–2013. There are, then, three variables—rape rates, robbery rates, and aggravated assault rates—that are reported over more than a 40-year-period. We reproduce these rates for each of the three crimes as a time plot in Figure 2.17. Note that we have graphed all three crimes in one plot. The rates for robbery and aggravated assault use the y axis on the left side of the chart, but because the level of rape rates is so much lower, these rates rely on the y axis on the right side of the chart. You can see that the rates for the three violent index crimes trend closely together over time, although the level of their values is different. If we had plotted rape rates with the same axis values as the other two index crimes, the rates for rape would have appeared very flat over time and you would not be able to see the variation over time. Not that there was no variation over time, but you would not be able to see it. We plot the crime rates for the three index crimes using the same y axis in Figure 2.18 to illustrate. Unlike Figure 2.17, notice that in this figure the time trend line for forcible rape is flat. Again, this is not because there is no variation over time in rape arrest rates, but it is lost because its absolute rate is much lower than the other two crimes. This example serves as a reminder to be aware of your measurements when making graphs and, more important, when examining graphs made by others!

Notice that the graphical display of the arrest rates allows us to see the variation over time much more quickly and clearly. As shown in Figure 2.17, crime rates for all three crimes started at a moderate level in the early 1970s, and there was a consistent increase in the rates of all three crimes until around 1980. After this increase, there was a slight decline in the rates of robbery and a fairly flat rate for aggravated assault and rape until the middle to late 1980s, and then a fairly steady increase until the early 1990s, when all three crime rates reached a peak (rape and armed robbery in 1991 and aggravated assault in 1992). After the peak, there was a gradual decline over the next 25 years. A useful statistic that allows us to quantify the change in trends is called a percent change score. Let's examine some percent change scores over different parts of the time trend. To calculate percent change scores, we perform the following calculations:

$$\% \text{ Change} = \left(\frac{\text{End value} - \text{Start value}}{\text{Start value}} \right) \times 100 \qquad \text{(Formula 2-3)}$$

If we calculate the percent change in the crime rate from 1972 until the peak rate for each crime in the early 1990s, we can determine that rates of forcible rape increased 90% [(42.8 – 22.5) / 22.5 × 100 = 90.22%], while rates of robbery increased by only about 51% [(272.7 – 180.7) / 180.7 × 100 = 50.9%] and rates of aggravated assault increased by 134% [(441.9 – 188.8) / 188.8 × 100 = 134.1%]. Thus, over the period from the early 1970s to the early 1990s, rates of forcible rape increased almost twice as much as rates of armed robbery. Now let's calculate the percent change in crime rates for each offense from its peak in the early 1990s until the end of the time period in 2013. When we do this, we see that rape rates declined by 46% [(23.1 – 42.8) / 42.8 × 100 = –46.0%], about the same as the decline in aggravated assault rates [(233.7 – 441.9) / 441.9 × 100 = –47.1%] but less than the decline in armed robbery rates [(112.9 – 272.7) / 272.7 × 100 = –58.6%].

Percent change score: Score that quantifies the percent change of a score between two different time periods or other units.

Figure 2.17

Time Plot of Forcible Rape, Armed Robbery, and Aggravated Assault Rates Using Both y Axes, 1972–2013

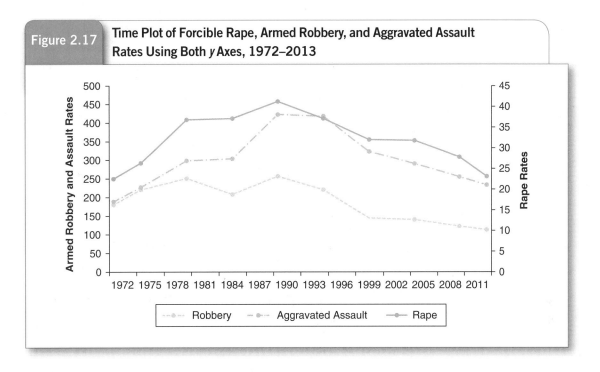

Figure 2.18

Time Plot of Forcible Rape, Armed Robbery, and Aggravated Assault Rates Using Only One y Axis, 1972–2013

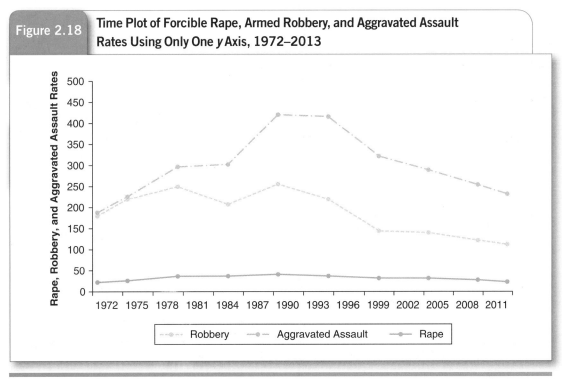

▣ Summary

In this chapter, we covered some ways to present qualitative and quantitative data in tabular (or numeric) form and in graphs. An important point to take away from this chapter is that it is always a good idea to look at the appearance or distribution of your data before conducting any further statistical analyses. Qualitative data can be examined in both tabular and graphical form along with the calculation of some very simple descriptive information such as the distribution of frequencies, proportions, and percentages. A frequency distribution displays the values that the qualitative variable takes and how many cases fall into each value. The proportions and percentages show the relative frequencies. Qualitative data can be graphed with either a pie chart or a bar chart.

Quantitative or continuous data can also be viewed in tabular or graphical form. With quantitative data, there is a greater variety of descriptive information to report. With quantitative data, we can meaningfully calculate relative and cumulative frequencies, proportions, and percentages. If every value of a quantitative variable is reported, along with its frequency, proportion, and/or percentage, the distribution is called an ungrouped frequency distribution. If the data are collapsed into ranges/intervals of values, the corresponding distribution is referred to as a grouped frequency distribution. Continuous data can be graphed with a histogram or one of several different kinds of line graphs or polygons. Frequently in criminology and criminal justice, we are interested in reporting the values of a variable over time. This information can also be displayed in a table or with a graph called a time plot. When there are sharp fluctuations in the data over a short period of time, it is often helpful to smooth the data before graphing the trend.

Key Terms

> ➤ Review key terms with eFlashcards. Visit study.sagepub.com/paternoster.

class interval   40
cumulative frequency
    distribution   36
cumulative percentages   37
cumulative proportions   36
exhaustive intervals   42
grouped frequency distribution   40
histogram   37

interval width   43
line graph (polygon)   37
midpoint   49
mutually exclusive intervals   41
negatively skewed distribution   51
normal distribution   50
outlier   51
percent change score   54

pie chart and bar chart   29
positively skewed distribution   51
real class limits   48
skewed distribution   51
stated class limits   45
ungrouped frequency
    distribution   35
univariate analysis   26

Key Formulas

Estimated interval width (formula 2-1):

$$w_i = \frac{\text{Range}}{\text{Number of intervals}}$$

Midpoint of class limit (formula 2-2):

$$m_i = \frac{\text{Lower limit} + \text{Upper limit}}{2}$$

Percent change scores (formula 2-3):

$$\% \text{Change} = \left(\frac{\text{Finish value} - \text{Start value}}{\text{Start value}} \right) \times 100$$

Practice Problems

➤ Test your understanding of chapter content.
Take the practice quiz at study.sagepub.com/paternoster.

1. Which of the following two grouped frequency distributions is more effective in displaying the data on the number of prior offenses? Why?

Number of Prior Offenses for a Sample of Convicted Offenders

Stated Class Limits	f
0–7	0
7–10	35
10–15	40
16–30	50
Total	125

Number of Prior Offenses for a Sample of Convicted Offenders

Stated Class Limits	f
7–9	35
10–12	25
13–15	15
16–18	20
19–21	10
22–24	5
25–27	10
28–30	5
Total	125

2. If you had data on a variable called "the number of offenders sentenced to death in the United States from 1977 to 2014" and wanted to graph the frequency distribution, which type of graph would you use?

3. Imagine that you took a sample of 150 persons in a large lecture class from your university and asked each student the following question: "During the past 12 months, how many times did you use marijuana, cocaine, or some other illegal drug?" The possible response options were "never," "a few times," "more than a few times but not a lot," and "a lot." You found that 30 people reported "never" using drugs during the past year, 75 reported that they had used drugs "a few times," 35 said they had used drugs "more than a few times but not a lot," and 10 reported using drugs "a lot."

a. What is the level of measurement for your variable "self-reported drug use"?

b. What is the ratio of "users" to "nonusers"?

c. What is the ratio of users who reported using drugs "more than a few times but not a lot" to those reporting "a lot"?

d. Construct an ungrouped frequency distribution from your data, and include both the proportion and percentage.

e. What percentage of your sample reported using drugs?

f. What proportion of your sample reported using drugs "a lot"?

4. You are the director of a state's department of corrections. You have 20,751 inmates currently confined in five types of institutions: community correctional facilities ($n = 5,428$), minimum security institutions ($n = 3,285$), medium security institutions ($n = 1,733$), maximum security institutions ($n = 875$), and pretrial detention centers ($n = 9,430$).

a. Construct a frequency distribution with these data, and include the percentage and proportion.

b. What percentage of your inmates are housed in minimum security institutions?

c. What proportion of your inmates are housed in maximum security institutions?

d. What percentage of your inmates are housed in pretrial detention facilities?

e. Graph these data with the appropriate graph.

5. As the head of a state's police academy, you give a final examination to each class of recruits. This 20-question examination covers things that a rookie police officer should know such as safety rules, constitutional requirements in arrests, and other matters. The following table shows the scores received on this exam by the last class of recruits, which included 25 people. It also shows the gender of each recruit.

Scores on the Police Officer Recruit Test

Number Correct	Gender
15	Male
16	Female
11	Male

(Continued)

(Continued)

Number Correct	Gender
10	Male
14	Male
15	Male
15	Female
11	Female
10	Male
10	Male
20	Female
15	Female
14	Male
16	Male
15	Male
19	Female
11	Male
13	Male
15	Female
13	Female
10	Male
20	Male
15	Male
16	Female
10	Male

a. Construct an ungrouped frequency distribution of the test scores. In the table, also include the proportions, percentages, cumulative frequencies, cumulative proportions, and cumulative percentages.

b. Construct a frequency distribution of the variable "gender," including both proportions and percentages.

c. If a score of 14 or higher constituted a "pass" on the exam, how many and what percentage of the recruits passed the test?

d. If a score of 18 or higher earned a rookie the distinction of "passing with honors," how many and what proportion of the class passed with honors?

e. If those who had a score of 13 or lower have to repeat their training, how many in this class will have to repeat it?

f. What were the proportions of males and females in this class?

g. Graph the frequency data for the test scores and the percentage data (with a pie chart) for the gender data.

h. Graph the cumulative frequency data for the test scores.

6. You have a sample of 75 adults and have asked them all to report the age at which they committed their first delinquent or criminal act. The responses are shown in the following table. With these data, construct a grouped frequency distribution. Make the lower limit of your first class interval be 6 and have an interval width of 5. Then make a frequency distribution that includes the proportions, percentages, cumulative frequencies, cumulative proportions, and cumulative percentages.

Age at First Offense

17	22	13	24	15
12	30	17	27	16
21	14	12	13	18
18	27	19	18	25
11	19	11	26	30
28	28	23	14	35
8	13	26	22	21
17	20	15	39	15
26	24	16	30	31
31	25	24	23	6
15	32	29	38	36
34	16	12	34	12
20	12	33	35	34
7	21	11	37	19
11	21	20	43	35

Then answer the following questions:

a. What are the real limits of these class intervals?

b. What is the midpoint of each class interval?

c. How many of these persons committed their first offense before the age of 31?

d. What proportion committed their first offense between the ages of 11 and 15?

e. What percentage committed their first offense after age 20?

f. What percentage committed their first offense before the age of 16?

7. The data in the following table show the total property crime victimization rate from the National Crime Victimization Survey for the time period 1993–2013. Graph these data with a time plot. What time trend or trends do you detect in these data?

National Crime Victimization Survey Property Crime Trends, 1993–2013

Victimization Year	Rate per 1,000 Households	Victimization Year	Rate per 1,000 Households
1993	351.8	2004	167.5
1994	341.2	2005	159.5
1995	315.5	2006	169.0
1996	289.3	2007	154.9
1997	267.1	2008	142.6
1998	237.1	2009	132.6
1999	210.6	2010	125.4
2000	190.4	2011	138.7
2001	177.7	2012	155.8
2002	168.2	2013	131.4
2003	173.4		

Source: Data taken from the Bureau of Justice Statistics at www.ojp.usdoj.gov/bjs/.

8. The following data represent the estimated number of arrests over the time period 1994–2012 for robberies among adults as determined by the FBI's Uniform Crime Reports. With these data, construct a time plot of the number of arrests.

Year	Number of Arrests	Year	Number of Arrests
1994	117,300	2004	83,700
1995	116,200	2005	85,600
1996	106,400	2006	90,800
1997	92,300	2007	92,400
1998	86,900	2008	94,200
1999	79,200	2009	95,000
2000	78,600	2010	85,100
2001	81,900	2011	82,900
2002	81,200	2012	82,200
2003	82,300		

Source: Data taken from Easy Access to FBI Arrest Statistics at www.ojjdp.gov/ojstatbb/ezaucr/asp/ucr_display.asp.

STUDENT STUDY SITE

WANT A BETTER GRADE?

Get the tools you need to sharpen your study skills. Access practice quizzes, eFlashcards, data sets, and SPSS exercises at **study.sagepub.com/paternoster.**

CHAPTER 3

Measures of Central Tendency

> " *Welcome to Lake Wobegon, where all the women are strong, all the men are good-looking, and all the children are above average.*
>
> —Garrison Keillor "

LEARNING OBJECTIVES

1. Describe the only measure of center appropriate for a nominal-level variable.

2. Identify the difference between the median and the mean.

3. Describe when the median may be a better measure of center compared with the mean.

4. Explain how to calculate and interpret all measures of center from both grouped and ungrouped data.

Introduction

What do you think about when you think about the average or typical prisoner released from state prisons today? Well, the most recent data available tell us that the typical state prisoner released is more likely to be a male who is 40 years of age or older and has an average of 4.9 prior convictions (Durose, Cooper, & Snyder, 2014). We have conveyed a lot of information with concepts such as "typical" and "average" in this sentence, but in this chapter you are going to learn more precise statistical concepts used to describe the most typical quality or value of a variable. In Chapter 2, we learned to describe our data using frequency distributions and graphical displays. These pieces of information are important, but they should be combined with summary statistics that also help to describe our variable distribution. In this chapter, you will learn about summary statistics called **measures of central tendency**. Think of the two key words in this term and what they connote—central tendency—a tendency to be at the center of something, in this case the center of data. Measures of central tendency capture the "typical," "average," or "most likely" score or value in a distribution of scores like the 40-year-old male with 4.9 prior convictions typical state prisoner above.

We will discuss three different measures of central tendency in this chapter: the mode, the median, and the mean. Each measure captures a somewhat different notion of "central tendency," and you should not be surprised to learn that each requires a certain level of measurement.

Student Study Site

Visit the open-access Student Study Site at **study.sagepub.com/paternoster** to access additional study tools including mobile-friendly eFlashcards, web quizzes, links to SAGE journal articles, additional data sets, SPSS exercises, and more!

The Mode

The **mode** is one measure of central tendency. The mode conceptualizes "central tendency" in terms of what is the *most likely, most common,* or *most frequent* score in a distribution of scores. The mode can be calculated with data measured at the nominal, ordinal, or interval/ratio level. However, if you have nominal- or purely ordinal-level data (purely ordinal in the sense that the data are not continuous data that you have made ordinal by making class intervals or grouping your data), then the mode is the *only* appropriate measure of central tendency that you may legitimately use. If the data are in numerical or tabular form, the mode can be easily identified by finding the score or value in a distribution that has (a) the greatest frequency, (b) the largest proportion, or (c) the highest percentage. If the data are in graphical form, the mode can be identified by finding the score or value in the graph that has (a) the largest slice in a pie chart, (b) the longest bar in a bar chart, or (c) the highest bar in a histogram. Thus, the way the mode "interprets" central tendency is that it is the most likely or probable or the most frequent score or value in a distribution of values.

Case Study

The Modal Category of Hate Crime

Let's go through a couple of examples. In Chapter 2, we presented data that showed the distribution of different kinds of hate crimes that were reported to the police in the year 2013 (Table 2.1); these data are reproduced in Table 3.1. A hate crime is defined as one that is intended to hurt and intimidate someone because of his or her race, ethnicity, national origin, religion, sexual preference, or disability. As you can see, there were 5,922 single-bias hate crime incidents reported to the Federal Bureau of Investigation (FBI) Uniform Crime Reports program that year that fell into one of five distinct types based on the motivation or the type of hate that precipitated the crime. The variable "reported hate crime" is measured at the nominal level because the only distinction among the values of this variable are qualitative distinctions of "kind"—a hate crime driven by racial hatred is simply different from one driven by religious hatred.

Looking at the distribution of scores in this table, we can discern that the most frequent type of hate crime in 2013, or the modal hate crime, was one motivated by racial hostility. We would conclude, therefore, that the mode for this variable is "racially motivated hate crime." There are a number of different ways we could come to this conclusion, each of which would converge on the same answer. First, we could look at the reported frequencies and note that the frequency of racial hate crimes is clearly greater than the frequency for all other kinds of reported hate crimes. Second, we could look

Measures of central tendency: Summary statistics that capture the "typical," "average," or "most likely" scores or values in variable distributions.

Mode: Value of a variable that occurs more often than any other value.

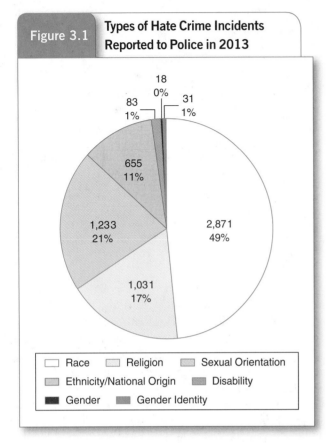

Figure 3.1 Types of Hate Crime Incidents Reported to Police in 2013

18
0%
83
1%
31
1%
655
11%
1,233
21%
2,871
49%
1,031
17%

☐ Race   ☐ Religion   ☐ Sexual Orientation
☐ Ethnicity/National Origin   ☐ Disability
■ Gender   ▨ Gender Identity

Table 3.1 Types of Hate Crime Incidents Reported to Police in 2013

Basis of Hate	f	Proportion	%
Race	2,871	.485	48.5
Religion	1,031	.174	17.4
Sexual orientation	1,233	.208	20.8
Ethnicity/National origin	655	.111	11.1
Disability	83	.014	1.4
Gender	18	.003	0.3
Gender identity	31	.005	0.5
Total	5,922	1.000	100.0

Source: Adapted from *Hate Crimes Statistics—2013* from the Federal Bureau of Investigation (2013b).

at the column of proportions, find that nearly one half (.485) of all hate crimes that were reported were racially motivated, and note that this proportion is greater than the proportion for any other kind of hate crime. Third, we could examine the row of percentages, find that 48.5% of all hate crimes in 2013 were racially motivated hate crimes, and note that this percentage is greater than the percentage for any other type of hate crime. Finally, we could use the information we have about proportions to determine the probability of each type of hate crime and then draw a conclusion about what the mode is. Since the proportion or relative frequency of a value/score can also be understood as its probability of occurring, we can see that if we were to select randomly 1 out of the 5,922 hate crimes in 2013, the probability that it would be a racially motivated hate crime would be .485, the probability that it would be motivated by religious prejudice would be .174, the probability of a sexually motivated hate crime would be .208, and so on. The greatest probability event, therefore, is a racial hate crime, a probability that exceeds those of all other possible outcomes. All of our different ways to capture the mode tell us that the modal type of hate crime was racially motivated hate crime.

Another way to determine what the mode is for a nominal- or ordinal-level variable is to examine the graph of the frequency data (or the graphed proportions or percentages). In Figure 3.1, we show the pie chart of the data in Table 3.1 with both the frequency and the percentage of each value. Note that the largest slice in the pie is for the value "race hate crime." This is the modal hate crime for 2013.

The modal type of hate crime reported in 2013, then, is a racially motivated hate crime. Note that the mode is the *value* or *score* that is most frequent or most likely, not the actual numerical value of the frequency, proportion, or percentage. The mode for the variable "reported hate crime in the year 2013" is "racially motivated hate crime." The mode is not 2,871 or .485 or even 48.5%. The mistake that students most frequently make when they are first learning statistics is that they conclude that the mode is some frequency, proportion, or percentage rather than the value of a given variable. To avoid making this mistake, just remember that the mode is the *value, score,* or *outcome* of a variable that is most likely or frequent, not the actual frequency of that value.

Case Study

The Modal Number of Prior Arrests

In Table 3.2, we report the frequency distribution (and percentages) of the number of prior arrests for a hypothetical sample of 150 armed robbery suspects. The data are in the form of an ungrouped frequency distribution, and the variable "number of prior arrests" is measured at the interval/ratio level. The histogram for the frequency data is shown in Figure 3.2. Note in the table that there are two values that are more frequent than all of the others: "0 prior arrests" and "1 prior arrest." The frequencies for these values are very comparable and much greater than any of the other values. This corresponds to the height of the two largest rectangular bars in the histogram (Figure 3.3) for 0 and 1 prior arrest. Even though the frequencies for 0 and 1 prior arrests are not exactly equal, they are very comparable, and their frequencies are much greater than those of any other value. They are comparable enough that it might be misleading to say that there is one and only one distinct mode in these data. It would appear more appropriate, then, that for this variable there are two distinct modes: a mode of 0 prior arrests and a mode of 1 prior arrest. Because there are two modes in the data, this distribution has a bimodal distribution. A **bimodal distribution** is a distribution that has two distinct values with the greatest frequency or the largest probability of occurring even if their frequencies are not

Table 3.2	Number of Prior Arrests for a Sample of Armed Robbery Suspects	
Number	f	%
0	38	25.33
1	35	23.33
2	10	6.67
3	9	6.00
4	14	9.33
5	7	4.67
6	11	7.33
7	8	5.33
8	10	6.67
9	5	3.33
10 or more	3	2.00
Total	n = 150	99.99*

*Percentages may not sum to 100% due to rounding.

Figure 3.2 Number of Prior Arrests Among 150 Suspected Armed Robbers

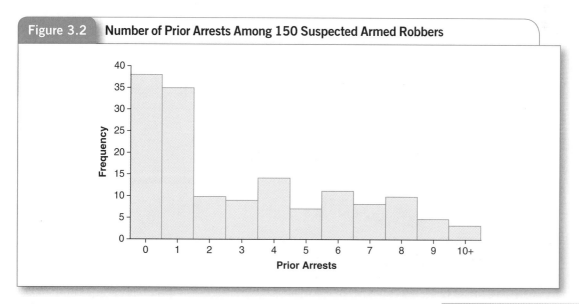

exactly equal. It tells us that there are two scores that are roughly the most typical or most likely scores in the distribution.

The strategy for identifying the mode when the data are in the form of a grouped frequency distribution is pretty much the same as what we have just discussed. Table 3.3

Bimodal distribution: Distribution that contains two distinct modes with the greatest frequency even if the frequencies are not exactly equal.

Table 3.3	Grouped Frequency Distribution for Time-Until-Rearrest Data for 120 Released Offenders		
Stated Limits (Days)		f	Midpoint
17–19		4	18
20–22		1	21
23–25		12	24
26–28		16	27
29–31		28	30
32–34		28	33
35–37		21	36
38–40		10	39
		n = 120	

provides the grouped frequency distribution for the variable "time until rearrest" for a sample of 120 male inmates who were released from prison and who were rearrested at some point after release. We first presented these data in the previous chapter. Recall that each person's "score" reflects the number of days he was out in the community after being released before he committed a new offense. The histogram for these data is shown in Figure 3.3, where the class intervals are shown on the x axis. When we look at this frequency distribution, it is apparent that these are bimodal data. The two modes are represented by the class intervals 29–31 days and 32–34 days. For both of these class intervals, the frequency is higher than for any other class interval. Exactly 28 persons were arrested between 19 and 31 days after release and 28 persons were rearrested between 32 and 34 days (very close to 1 month) after their release from prison. The two modes also can be seen from the histogram as the two highest peaks in Figure 3.3.

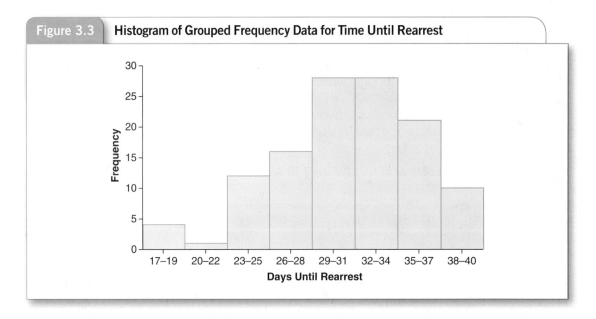

Figure 3.3 Histogram of Grouped Frequency Data for Time Until Rearrest

Advantages and Disadvantages of the Mode

As a measure of central tendency, the mode has both advantages and disadvantages relative to other measures. One advantage of the mode is that it is very simple to determine and is appealing conceptually. It is the score or value that is the most frequent and that has the greatest probability of occurring in a distribution of scores. This simple elegance means that the mode is very easy for readers to comprehend and understand, which is a key quality that statistical measures should have. The mode is also very simple to "calculate." In fact, there is no real arithmetic calculation to determine the mode—nothing to add or subtract. We just identify the score with the greatest frequency (or proportion or percentage) in either a tabular presentation of data or a graph (find the tallest or longest bar or the largest slice of pie). Finally, the mode is a very general measure of central tendency since it can be determined for variables measured at any level. The mode is an appropriate measure of central tendency for data measured at the nominal, ordinal, and interval/ratio levels.

The simplicity of understanding and determining the mode is offset by its disadvantage. Since the mode is based only on the most frequent score or scores, it does not take into account all or even most of the information available in a distribution. One thing statisticians do not like to do is ignore data or information, but that is exactly what the mode does; it ignores all information in the data except the values/scores with the highest frequency. By ignoring or throwing out information, the mode may at times give us a very misleading notion of the central tendency of our data. For example, Table 3.4 shows the number of subsequent charges of domestic violence accumulated over a 1-year period by a sample of 60 men who had been arrested for intimate partner assault. According to the table, the mode would be "0 new charges since arrest" since this value has the greatest frequency. Note, however, that the ease of identifying "0 new charges" as the mode comes at the price of ignoring the fact that many of the men in this sample *did* have numerous new charges of being abusive toward their partner after they were first arrested. Although it is technically correct that the modal number of new charges is zero, this is somewhat misleading and does not represent the entire distribution of values. Because of this deficiency with the mode, when we have interval/ratio-level data, we most often use an alternative measure of central tendency such as the median or the mean.

Table 3.4	Number of New Charges for Domestic Violence for 60 Men Arrested for Domestic Abuse

Number of New Charges	f
0	14
1	7
2	5
3	8
4	6
5	4
6	3
7	3
8	5
9	3
10 or more	2
	n = 60

The Median

The **median** is an appropriate measure of central tendency for quantitative data measured at the interval/ratio level or for data that may have originally been measured at the interval/ratio level but now consist of grouped data (class intervals for grouped frequency distributions that have real limits). The easiest way to think of the median is that it is the value that is at the 50th percentile in a rank-ordered distribution of scores. The 50th percentile is also known as the second quartile when the data are divided into four quartiles (one quartile is equal to 25 percentiles). The median score, in other words, is the score in the exact middle of a rank-ordered distribution of quantitative scores such that the median is the point above which one half of the scores are and below which the other one half of the scores fall.

> **Median:** Score at the 50th percentile in a rank-ordered distribution of scores. Thus, one half of a variable's values are less than the median and one half are greater than the median.

When the data are continuous (not grouped), the median value is very easy to find by following these two steps:

> ***Steps to Find the Median***
>
> **Step 1:** Rank-order all scores from lowest score to highest score.
>
> **Step 2:** Find the position of the score (*x*) that is the median score by the following formula: Median position = $(n + 1) / 2$. This formula says that the *position* of the median score is found by adding 1 to the total number of scores and then dividing by 2. *This formula will not give you the value of the median but will give you the position of the median score.* To find the value of the median, find the score in the position indicated by the formula in the rank-ordered array of scores.

When there are an odd number of scores, this formula is very easy to use.

Case Study

The Median Police Response Time and Vandalism Offending

Rank	Score
1	1 minute
2	2 minutes
3	3 minutes
4	6 minutes
5	9 minutes
6	12 minutes
7	15 minutes

Rank	Score
1	1 minute
2	2 minutes
3	3 minutes
4	6 minutes
5	9 minutes
6	12 minutes
7	15 minutes
8	18 minutes

Let's say that we have seven scores that represent the number of minutes it takes the police to respond to a "911" call for service: 9, 1, 3, 6, 12, 2, and 15. To find the median number of minutes it takes the police to respond, step 1 instructs us first to rank-order the scores from low to high (see top left table).

Then we find the position of the median with our positional locator, $(n + 1) / 2$, which in this case is $(7 + 1) / 2 = 8 / 2 = $ 4th position. The median score is in the fourth position in our rank-ordered scores. Again, we emphasize that the median is not 4, but it falls in the fourth position of our rank-ordered scores. The scores, therefore, must all be put in rank order before you can find the median. To find the value of the median, find the score in the fourth position. We can do this either by starting at the top of the rank-ordered scores (the lowest score) and counting down until we find the fourth score or by starting at the bottom (the highest score) and counting up until we find the fourth score. The result is the same; the score in the fourth position of our rank-ordered scores is 6 minutes. The median amount of time it took to respond to a 911 call for service, therefore, is 6 minutes. Note that exactly one half of the scores in this distribution are lower (1, 2, and 3 minutes) and exactly one half are higher (9, 12, and 15 minutes). The median score, then, sits in the exact middle of the distribution of rank-ordered scores. This is the way the median "interprets" central tendency—it is a positional measure. We can say that 50% of the scores in the distribution of police response time fall below 6 minutes and 50% fall above this value.

Now let's add one more call for service to these data. In this case, it took the police 18 minutes to respond—the longest time so far. We now have a total of eight scores, and the rank order of these eight scores is as shown in the bottom left table.

When we use our positional locator formula for the median, we find that the position of the median is $(8 + 1) / 2 = 9 / 2 = $ 4.5th score (notice that we now have eight data points, so the numerator in our formula is 8). What does a position of 4.5 mean? It means that the median score is the score that is at the midpoint between the fourth and fifth scores in our rank-ordered distribution of scores. Since our fourth score (starting from the lowest score) is 6 minutes and our fifth score (again from the lowest score) is 9 minutes, the median score is the midpoint between these scores. Had we found the fourth and fifth scores by starting at the bottom or highest score and counted up, the two scores would still have been 9 and 6. To find the midpoint between our two scores, we have to add the two scores and then divide by 2. The midpoint between 6 minutes and 9 minutes is $(6 + 9) / 2 = 15 / 2 = 7.5$ minutes. The median number of minutes it took the police to respond in this second set of scores, then, is 7.5 minutes. Note that one half of the scores are greater than this time and one half are less. The median measures central tendency as the score in the middle in a set of rank-ordered scores, or 50th percentile. That is what the median means.

Another way to identify the median in a set of continuous scores is to find the 50th percentile in a cumulative percentage distribution (you already learned how to make a cumulative percentage distribution, so this should be good practice). Table 3.5 reports the distribution of scores for a variable called "number of times committing vandalism" for a sample of 77 boys; the values range from 0 times to 10 or more times. The first column in Table 3.5 reports the value or score (the number of times a boy reported committing an act of vandalism), the second column shows the frequency for each value, the third column reports the cumulative frequency, the fourth column is the percentage for each value, and the fifth and final column compiles the cumulative percentages.

There are two ways to find the median number of acts of vandalism in this distribution. One is to use the formula for the position of the median we just learned. Since we have $n = 77$ total scores, the median is in the $(77 + 1) / 2 = 78 / 2 = $ 39th position. To find the score at the 39th position, all we have to do is use the column of cumulative frequencies. We can see from this column that 30 scores are at the value of 2 or lower and that 41 scores are at the value of 3 or lower. If the 30th score is a 2, and that is the last 2 in the distribution, we have to go to the next value to find the next scores. This means that the 31st score is a 3, the 32nd score is a 3, …, the 39th score is a 3, and the 40th and 41st scores as well (the 42nd score is a 4). Since the median score is the 39th score, the median must be "3 acts of vandalism." We could also have discovered this by looking at the column of cumulative percentages. Since the median is the 50th percentile, all we have to do is find the score at the 50th percentile. We can see that values of "2 acts of vandalism" are at the 39th percentile and that values of "3 acts of vandalism" go from the 40th to the 53rd percentile—the 50th percentile is contained here. The 50th percentile, then, is at the score of "3 acts of vandalism." In words, then, 50% of the boys in the sample committed 3 or fewer acts of vandalism and 50% of the boys committed 3 or more acts of vandalism.

Table 3.5 Reported Number of Times Committing Vandalism for 77 Boys

# of Times	f	cf	%	c%
0	15	15	19	19
1	10	25	13	32
2	5	30	7	39
3	11	41	14	53
4	7	48	9	62
5	8	56	10	72
6	5	61	7	79
7	4	65	5	84
8	5	70	7	91
9	4	74	5	96
10 or more	3	77	4	100
Total	n = 77		100	

The Median for Grouped Data

What do we do when we have grouped data and want to find the median score? Things get a little more complicated, but with a formula and a little work, we can determine the median with grouped data as well. Table 3.6 reports the grouped frequency distribution for the example of 120 prison inmates who had served their sentences and were released into the community for whom we have the number of days they were "free" before they were rearrested. Note that this table reports the real limits of the class intervals. As you will see, you need to know the real limits when calculating the median for grouped data. The presence of real limits tells us that these ordinal-level data were once measured at the interval or ratio level, permitting us to calculate a median. The procedure for determining the value of the median for these grouped data is comparable to that for ungrouped data.

First, we have to rank-order the values of the variable. In Table 3.6, the values of the variable "time until rearrest" consist of class intervals, and they are already rank-ordered from low to high. Now that the class intervals are rank-ordered, we need to find the interval that contains the median. We can use our positional locator $(n + 1) / 2$ and the column of cumulative frequencies to find the interval that contains the median. Since $n = 120$, the median is in the $(120 + 1) / 2 = 121 / 2 = 60.5$th position, or the score that is at the midpoint between the 60th and 61st scores. We now have to locate the class interval that has the median. The class interval 26–28 days contains the 18th score to the 33rd score, according to the column of cumulative frequencies. The 34th score to the 61st score, then, can be found in the class interval

Table 3.6 Grouped Frequency Distribution for Time-Until-Rearrest Data for 120 Inmates

Stated Limits	Real Limits	f	cf
17–19 days	16.5–19.5 days	4	4
20–22 days	19.5–22.5 days	1	5
23–25 days	22.5–25.5 days	12	17
26–28 days	25.5–28.5 days	16	33
29–31 days	28.5–31.5 days	28	61
32–34 days	31.5–34.5 days	28	89
35–37 days	34.5–37.5 days	21	110
38–40 days	37.5–40.5 days	10	120
		n = 120	

29–31 days (see the column of cumulative frequencies). This is the interval that contains the median since the median score is the midpoint between the 60th and 61st scores and the 60th and 61st scores are at the end of that interval. With this information, we are now ready to calculate the actual value of the median. We can determine the value of the median (and not just the location in this case) with the following formula:

$$X_{median} = L + \left(\frac{\left(\frac{n+1}{2} \right) - cf}{f} \right) w_i$$

(Formula 3-1)

where

X_{median} = the value of the median
L = the lower real limit of the class interval that contains the median
cf = the cumulative frequency of the class interval just before the class interval that contains the median
f = the frequency of the interval that contains the median
w_i = the width of the class interval
n = the total number of observations in the sample

Now let's calculate what the median number of days until rearrest is in these data:

$$X_{median} = L + \left(\frac{\left(\frac{n+1}{2} \right) - cf}{f} \right) w_i$$

$$X_{median} = 28.5 + \left(\frac{\left(\frac{120+1}{2} \right) - 33}{28} \right) 3$$

$$X_{median} = 28.5 + \left(\frac{60.5 - 33}{28} \right) 3$$

$$X_{median} = 28.5 + (.98)3$$

$$X_{median} = 28.5 + 2.94$$

$$X_{median} = 31.44 \text{ days until rearrest}$$

The median number of days until rearrest, then, is 31.44 days. In this distribution of grouped data, we can say that one half of the inmates were rearrested within 31.44 days, or about 1 month, and one half were arrested at 31.44 days or later. Remember that all of the people in this sample were eventually arrested.

Advantages and Disadvantages of the Median

The median has a number of advantages as a measure of central tendency. First, unlike the mode that can have more than one value, there will always be only one median. Second, as the score in the exact middle of a rank-ordered distribution of scores, the median value has intuitive appeal—it is easy to understand. For example, if when you took the ACT or SAT before college you found out that you scored at the 50th percentile on the test, you knew that you were in the middle of the rank-ordered scores, that one half of the students taking the test at the same time you did scored higher than you and one half scored lower than you. Third, the median is a useful measure of central tendency that is used in some graphical displays of data. Finally, because the median does not use all of the scores in our data, it is not influenced by extremely high or extremely low scores. As we learned in the last chapter, extremely high or low scores in a distribution are referred to as outliers. Since the median locates the score in the middle of the distribution, or at the 50th percentile, it does not matter whether there are outliers in the data. Let's explain.

Table 3.7 records three columns of data. Each column represents the rate of forcible rape per 100,000 people for a sample of U.S. cities in 2013. There are seven cities in the first column, and the rape rates have already been rank-ordered. The position of the median in these data is the 4th score, starting at either the lowest or highest score:

$$\left(\frac{7+1}{2} = 4 \right)$$

The median rape rate for these seven cities is 28.1 rapes per 100.000. In the next column of cities, we simply add one more city, Anchorage, Alaska, with a rape rate of 133.2 per 100,000. This is an extremely high rape rate, and adding it to this list of seven cities makes it a high outlier. What happens to the value of the median? Well, with eight cases now in the distribution, the median score is the midpoint between the 4th and 5th scores:

$$\left(\frac{8+1}{2} = 4.5 \right)$$

As such, we have to take the average of the scores in the 4th and 5th positions, which gives us:

$$\left(\frac{28.1+28.4}{2} = 28.25 \right) \text{rapes per } 100,000$$

As you can clearly see, adding this very high outlier did not change the median rape rate much at all, only from 28.1 rapes per 100,000 to 28.25 rapes per 100,000. Despite the outlier, the median still gives a very accurate assessment of the central tendency of rape rates in these data. The median is sturdy or robust in the presence of a high outlier.

In the next set of cities, we remove Anchorage and substitute Goldsboro, North Carolina, which in 2013 had a rate of forcible rape of only 4.0 per 100,000, one of the lowest rape rates of all major U.S. cities (since these are rape rates, or the number of rapes per population, it does not matter that Goldsboro is a small town; Goldsboro has a population that is greater than that of Redmond, Oregon). The rape rate for Goldsboro is an example of a low outlier. We once again find the median for these eight scores as the midpoint between the 4th and 5th scores:

$$\frac{28.0+28.1}{2} = 28.05 \text{ rapes per } 100,000$$

By comparing the three medians we calculated with seven cities, the median rape rate was 28.1 per 100,000. When we added Anchorage with a high outlier, the median rate was 28.25. And when we added Goldsboro with a low outlier, the median rape rate was 28.05. In each case, the measure of central tendency tells us that the median rape rate is around 28 per 100,000 population. Even when there are outlying scores, then, the median is a very stable measure of central tendency because it is defined as the 50th percentile and does not take the value of each and every score into account. This is an important advantage of the median as a measure of central tendency. One disadvantage of the median is that, like the mode, it uses only one or two pieces of information. The next measure of central tendency we will discuss, the mean, uses all the information in the data to determine its central tendency.

Table 3.7   **Rape Rates (per 100,000 People) for Selected U.S. Cities in 2013**

Rank	City	Rate	Rank	City	Rate	Rank	City	Rate
1	Binghamton, NY	22.2	1	Binghamton, NY	22.2	1	Goldsboro, NC	4.0
2	Albany, GA	23.5	2	Albany, GA	23.5	2	Binghamton, NY	22.2
3	Redmond, OR	28.0	3	Redmond, OR	28.0	3	Albany, GA	23.5
4	Cedar Rapids, IA	28.1	4	Cedar Rapids, IA	28.1	4	Redmond, OR	28.0
5	Charleston, SC	28.4	5	Charleston, SC	28.4	5	Cedar Rapids, IA	28.1
6	Boston, MA	33.8	6	Boston, MA	33.8	6	Charleston, SC	28.4
7	Akron, OH	38.4	7	Akron, OH	38.4	7	Boston, MA	33.8
			8	Anchorage, AK	133.2	8	Akron, OH	38.4

Source: Adapted from *Crime In the United States* from the Federal Bureau of Investigation (2013a).

The Mean

The third and final measure of central tendency that we will examine is the mean. Like the median, the mean requires that the data be measured at the interval/ratio level. However, it too can be calculated if you have ordinal data in the form of a grouped frequency distribution where you have taken continuous data and created class intervals.

Case Study

Calculating the Mean Time Until Rearrest

The **mean** is defined as the arithmetic average of a group of scores and is calculated by summing all of the scores and then dividing by the total number of scores. You are already very familiar with the mean. Your college grade point average (GPA) is a mean. For example, suppose you took five classes last semester and earned two A's, a B, a C, and one D (in math, of course). Let's assume that your college assigns 4.0 for an A grade, 3.0 for a B grade, 2.0 for a C grade, and 1.0 for a D grade. Your GPA for last semester, then, would be (4 + 4 + 3 + 2 + 1) / 5 = 14 / 5 = 2.8. This is the mean grade you received in all five of your classes. Your average would be almost a B, reflecting the fact that you did get two A's but also received a C and a D.

Before we get some practice in calculating the mean, we need to distinguish between the mean of a population and the mean of a sample. Recall from our discussion in Chapter 1 that a population consists of the universe of cases we are interested in. For example, if we are interested in the relationship between IQ scores and delinquency among male youths between the ages of 12 and 18 years in the United States, then our population would consist of all male youths between the ages of 12 and 18 who reside in the United States. The population we are interested in, then, is generally very large and both difficult and costly to study directly. Our population of male adolescents, for example, would number in the millions. A sample, you will remember, is a subset of the population. We select a sample from the population and study the sample with the intention of making an inference to the population based on what we know about the sample. The sample is much smaller than the population.

It would be possible (although it would involve a great deal of work and money) to calculate the mean of a population. The mean of a population, therefore, is unknown but knowable. In statistics, the mean of a population is denoted by the symbol μ (the Greek letter mu) and is defined as the sum of all scores in the population divided by the total number of observations in the population:

Mean: Arithmetic average of a group of scores calculated as the sum of the scores divided by the total number of scores. The mean is an appropriate measure of central tendency for interval/ratio-level data.

$$\mu = \frac{\sum\limits_{i=1}^{N} X_i}{N}$$

(Formula 3-2)

where

X_i = each X score in the population
N = the total number of observations in the population

To calculate the population mean, therefore, sum all scores in the population, starting with the first and ending with the last or Nth, and then divide by the total number of observations (N). Note that the mean takes all scores into account since we have to sum all scores before calculating the mean.

When we have a sample and wish to calculate the mean of the sample, the formula we use is slightly different:

$$\bar{X} = \frac{\sum\limits_{i=1}^{n} x_i}{n}$$

(Formula 3-3)

where

$\bar{X}$ = the symbol used for the sample mean and is pronounced "x bar"
x_i = the ith raw score in a distribution of sample scores
$\sum_{i=1}^{n} x_i$ = the instruction to sum all x_i scores, starting with the first score
($i = 1$) and continuing until the last score ($i = n$)
n = the total number of scores

This formula is telling you that to calculate the sample mean, you begin by summing all of the scores in your sample, starting with the first score and ending with the last or nth score, and then divide this sum by the total number of scores in your sample. For example, if you had a distribution of 10 scores, you would calculate the mean of those scores by taking the sum of all 10 scores and then dividing by 10: $\bar{X} = (x_1 + x_2 + x_3 + \ldots + x_{10}) / 10$. Unlike the median, the mean is not a positional measure of central tendency. Since the mean takes into account all of your scores, you do not need to rank-order them beforehand; you can simply start summing numbers from the very first score.

As an example of calculating the mean, let's begin by calculating the mean rape rate for the seven cities that make up the first column of Table 3.7. The mean rate of forcible rape would be as follows:

$$\bar{X} = \frac{\sum_{n-1}^{n} X1}{n}$$

$$\bar{X} = \frac{X_1 + X_2 + X_3 + X_4 + X_5 + X_6 + X_7}{7}$$

$$\bar{X} = \frac{22.2 + 23.5 + 28 + 28.1 + 28.4 + 33.8 + 38.4}{7}$$

$$\bar{X} = \frac{202.4}{7}$$

$$\bar{X} = 28.91 \text{ rapes per 100,000}$$

As practice, let's also calculate the mean rape rate per 100,000 for the second column of cities in Table 3.7:

$$\bar{X} = \frac{22.2 + 23.5 + 28 + 28.1 + 28.4 + 33.8 + 38.4 + 133.2}{8}$$

$$\bar{X} = \frac{335.6}{8}$$

$$\bar{X} = 41.95 \text{ rapes per 100,000}$$

Like the median, the mean also is a sort of balancing score. The mean exactly balances the distance of each score from the mean. If we were to subtract the mean of a sample from each score in the sample, the negative differences from the mean would exactly equal the positive differences. Let's take a simple example. We have a set of five scores (2, 4, 6, 8, and 10). We calculate the mean and find the following:

$$\bar{X} = \frac{(2+4+6+8+10)}{5} = \frac{30}{5} = 6$$

We then subtract this mean from each score:

2 − 6 = −4
4 − 6 = −2
6 − 6 = 0
8 − 6 = 2
10 − 6 = 4

Subtracting the mean from each score yields what is called the *mean deviation*. Note that the sum of the negative differences is −6 and the sum of the positive differences is +6, so the sum of all differences from the mean is equal to zero. This will always be true. It is in this sense that the mean is a balancing score of the differences. The mean is the only measure of central tendency that has this characteristic. The sum of the differences of each score from the mean, then, will always be zero. In mathematical terms, this means that $\Sigma(x_i - \bar{X}) = 0$.

Formula 3-3 for calculating the sample mean is very simple and easy to use when there are only a few scores. When there are a large number of scores, however, this formula is a bit cumbersome. To calculate the sample mean when there are many scores in a frequency distribution, the following formula is easier to use:

$$\bar{X} = \frac{\Sigma X_i f_i}{n}$$

(Formula 3-4)

where

$\bar{X}$ = the sample mean
x_i = the *i*th score
f_i = the frequency for the *i*th score
$X_i f_i$ = the *x*th score multiplied by its frequency
n = the total number of scores

Formula 3-4 may seem a bit complicated, so let's illustrate its use step by step with an example.

Case Study

Calculating the Mean Police Response Time

Table 3.8 shows an ungrouped frequency distribution of response times to 911 calls to the police for assistance. Each response time was rounded to the nearest minute. Just so there is no confusion here, note that there were five occasions when the police responded to a 911 call within 1 minute, six times when they responded within 2 minutes, nine times when they responded within 3 minutes, and so on, concluding with one time when they responded to a call for assistance within 11 minutes. You may recall that we used these data in the last chapter. The first step in calculating the mean is to create a new column of scores where each entry in the column is the product of each.

The x score is multiplied by its frequency f (this column is labeled $x_i f_i$). For example, the first entry in the $x_i f_i$ column is 5, which represents the fact that the police responded to a 911 call within 1 minute five times. Normally, to calculate the mean, we would add these five scores of 1 by doing $1 + 1 + 1 + 1 + 1 = 5$. By taking the product of the score and its frequency $(x_i f_i)$ instead, we are simply taking advantage of the fact that $1 + 1 + 1 + 1 + 1 = 1 \times 5 = 5$. For the second entry of the third column we are taking advantage of the fact that $2 + 2 + 2 + 2 + 2 + 2 = 2 \times 6 = 12$. We take each x_i score and multiply it by its frequency to form the column of $x_i f_i$. The second step in calculating the mean is to sum all of these products. The sum of the column of $x_i f_i$ in Table 3.8 is 224. This is what we would have obtained had we taken the first approach and summed all x_i scores $(1 + 1 + 1 + 1 + 1 + \ldots + 7 + 7 + 7 + \ldots + 10 + 11 = 224)$. The third step in calculating the mean is to divide the sum of the product $x_i f_i$ by the total number of sample scores. In this case, since there were 50 911 calls, we can calculate the mean or average response time to a 911 call as $\overline{X} = 224 / 50 = 4.48$ minutes. Since .48 minute is equal to 28.8 seconds ($.48 \times 60$ seconds), the average response time was 4 minutes and 28.8 seconds, or about 4.5 minutes.

Remember that the total number of sample scores is n and is the sum of the number of frequencies. Very often, students will use the number of different scores in the frequency distribution, rather than the total number of scores, as the denominator for the mean. For example, rather than using 50 as the denominator in the earlier problem since there were 50 response times recorded, many students are tempted to use 11 because there are 11 different values. There may be only 11 values for the variable "police response time," but there were a total of 50 calls for police services, and this is the total number of observations.

Table 3.8	Response Times to 911 Calls for Police Assistance	
Minutes	f_i	xf_i
1	5	5
2	6	12
3	9	27
4	8	32
5	6	30
6	7	42
7	3	21
8	2	16
9	2	18
10	1	10
11	1	11
	$n = 50$	$\Sigma = 224$

Steps to Calculate the Mean From an Ungrouped Frequency Distribution

Step 1: Multiply each x_i score by its frequency (f_i). This will give you a column of products $(x_i f_i)$.

Step 2: Sum the obtained products from Step 1:

$$\Sigma(x_i f_i)$$

Step 3: Divide this by the total number of scores (n):

$$\overline{X} = \frac{\Sigma(x_i f_i)}{n}$$

The Mean for Grouped Data

The procedures for calculating the mean when the data are in a grouped frequency distribution are very similar to those used when the data are in an ungrouped frequency distribution. The first thing you have to determine is that the underlying measurement of the data is continuous even though the data are grouped. If you are satisfied that the data are continuous and have been put into a grouped frequency distribution for convenience and clarification, then you may proceed. Keep in mind that since the data are in the form of a grouped frequency distribution, there are no individual x_i scores. Rather, the data are now in the form of class intervals, and although we know which class interval a score falls into, we do not know the exact score. To calculate a mean with grouped data, then, we are going to have to make a simplifying assumption. We must make the assumption that *each score within a class interval is located exactly at its midpoint.* Once we make this assumption, we do not exactly have a distribution of x_i scores, but we have a distribution of *mi* scores, where the *mi* refers to the midpoint of the *i*th class interval.

Earlier in this chapter, Table 3.3 provided the grouped frequency distribution data for the time until arrest for a sample of 120 offenders released into the community. Recall that these data are a count of the number of days a released offender was in the community until he was rearrested. These are grouped data that were originally continuous, so we can legitimately calculate a mean. Our simplifying assumption is that each score within a class interval lies at its midpoint. So, for purposes of calculating the mean, we are going to assume that all four cases in the first class interval are at the midpoint of 18 days, the one score in the second class interval is at the midpoint of 21, the 12 scores in the third class interval are at the midpoint of 24, and so on. Recall that we need to make this assumption because to calculate a mean, we need to have a specific score (e.g., 18 days) rather than an interval within which a score lies (17–19 days). Since we are making this assumption, we are getting only an estimate of the mean for these data. This estimate is probably not going to be exactly what the value of the mean would be if we calculated it from the original continuous data. In a moment, we will check and see how accurate we are in making this assumption.

Once we have made this assumption, we are ready to calculate our mean. Recall that when we have data in the form of a frequency distribution, we can use formula 3-4 to calculate the mean by taking the product of each *x* score and its frequency $(x_i f_i)$, summing these products over all x_i scores, and then dividing by the total number of scores. We are going to modify this formula only slightly and use it to calculate a mean from grouped data. With grouped data, we do not have an individual x_i score, but we do have *mi* scores since we are assuming that each score within its class interval lies at its midpoint (m_i). To calculate the mean from grouped data, then, we just substitute m_i for x_i in formula 3-4 and take the product of each midpoint and the number of scores that are assumed to lie at that midpoint:

$$\bar{X} = \frac{\sum m_i f_i}{n}$$

(Formula 3-5)

where

$\bar{X}$ = the mean
m_i = the midpoint for the *i*th class interval
f_i = the frequency for the *i*th class interval
$m_i f_i$ = the m_i midpoint multiplied by its frequency
n = the total number of scores

In other words, to calculate the mean, we multiply the midpoint of each class interval by the frequency of that class interval. Once we have done this for each class interval, we sum these products over all intervals and then divide by the total number of scores. We will illustrate the use of the mean formula for grouped data with the time-until-rearrest data. Table 3.9 provides the information we need.

The sum of each midpoint multiplied by its frequency is 3,723. Now, to calculate the mean, all we have to do is divide this sum by the total number of scores or observations. The mean number of days free until rearrest, therefore, is

$$\bar{X} = \frac{3,723}{120} = 31.02 \text{ days}$$

On average, then, these offenders were free for 31.02 days before being rearrested and returned to prison. When you calculate the mean from grouped data using this method, make sure that you use the correct sample size for the denominator. The *n* in the formula is the total number of sample observations or scores you have. In this example, our data consist of 120 observations.

Recall that these time-until-rearrest data were originally measured at the interval/ratio level from which we created class intervals. In the previous example, we estimated the mean number of days an offender was free in the community based on the class interval scores. The question to answer now is whether we were accurate in our estimation of the mean using this grouped data. To determine our precision, let's calculate the mean number of days until rearrest from the original variable measured at the interval/ratio level and compare it with our estimate with formula 3-5. Table 3.10 gives the frequency distribution for the time-until-rearrest data in their original form, and we provide the necessary $(f_i x_i)$ column. Using the ungrouped data, then, we can calculate the mean as 3,729 / 120 = 31.075 days. Our estimate of the mean with the grouped data was 31.02 days, so we were pretty close to the value of the mean had the data remained in its original interval/ratio form. In general, you will find that you will not lose much accuracy in estimating the mean when you use grouped data rather than ungrouped data if the grouping was carefully done.

Advantages and Disadvantages of the Mean

The mean has a number of advantages as a measure of central tendency. First, it is intuitively appealing. Everyone is familiar with an average. The mean also uses all of the information in a data set, and this is an advantage as long as there are no outliers in the data. The mean is also an efficient measure of central tendency. In other words, if we had a population of scores (with a mean and a median), and from this population we took many samples and calculated both the mean and the median for each sample, the medians of these samples would differ more from each other and the population median than the means would differ from each other and the population mean.

Because we usually draw only one sample from a population, we want to have the measure of central tendency that is the most precise. This is the mean. The one disadvantage of the mean is a by-product of one of its strengths; because it takes every score into account, the mean may be distorted by high or low outliers. When we sum every score to calculate

| Table 3.9 | Calculating a Mean Using Grouped Data: Time Until Rearrest for 120 Inmates |

Stated Limits (Days)	F	Midpoint	mf_i
17–19	4	18	72
20–22	1	21	21
23–25	12	24	288
26–28	16	27	432
29–31	28	30	840
32–34	28	33	924
35–37	21	36	756
38–40	10	39	390
	$n = 120$		$\Sigma = 3{,}723$

Steps to Calculate the Mean From a Grouped Frequency Distribution

Step 1: Multiply each midpoint (m_i) by its frequency (f_i). This will give you a column of products $(m_i f_i)$.

Step 2: Sum the obtained products from Step 1:

$$\Sigma(m_i f_i)$$

Step 3: Divide this by the total number of scores (n):

$$\overline{X} = \frac{\Sigma m_i f_i}{n}$$

the mean, we may at times be adding uncharacteristically high or uncharacteristically low scores. When this happens, the value of the mean will give us a distorted sense of the central tendency of the data. To illustrate this point, let's return to Table 3.7, which provided three columns of rape rates per 100,000 people for selected U.S. cities. The first column consists of seven cities. Calculate the mean rape rate for these cities. You should have obtained a value of $\overline{X} = 202.4 / 7 = 28.91$ rapes per 100,000. What happens to the mean when we include the high outlier of Anchorage from the second column? The mean now is $\overline{X} = 335.6 / 8 = 41.95$ rapes per 100,000. Note what happened to the value of the mean when we included this high outlier. The magnitude of the mean increased dramatically, and it is now more than 64 rapes per 100,000. The inclusion of a high outlier, then, had the effect of inflating our mean.

Now look at the third column of cities in Table 3.7. What happens to the mean when we drop the high outlier of Anchorage and add the low outlier of Goldsboro, with a rape rate of 4.0 per 100,000? The value of the mean is now $\overline{X} = 202.4 / 8 = 25.3$ rapes per 100,000. The mean has now declined slightly, although it does not distort the central tendency as much as our high outlier did. As you can see, however, the effect of a low outlier is to lessen the magnitude of the mean.

Table 3.10	Calculating a Mean Using Ungrouped Data: Time Until Rearrest for 120 Inmates	
x_i	f_i	$x_i f_i$
17	1	17
18	1	18
19	2	38
20	1	20
21	0	0
22	0	0
23	3	69
24	4	96
25	5	125
26	3	78
27	7	189
28	6	168
29	11	319
30	7	210
31	10	310
32	7	224
33	12	396
34	8	272
35	8	280
36	8	288
37	6	222
38	4	152
39	2	78
40	4	160
	$n = 120$	$\Sigma = 3,729$

The purpose of this exercise is to show that sometimes the mean can provide a distorted sense of the central tendency in our data. Since the mean uses every score in our distribution, high outliers can inflate the mean, and low outliers can deflate the mean, relative to what the value of the mean would be without the outliers. For this reason, it is generally a good idea to report *both* the mean and the median when you are discussing the central tendency in your data. With respect to Table 3.7, we saw how the mean increases or decreases with the inclusion of outliers in the data.

Reporting both the mean and the median can also tell us something important about the shape of our data. In Chapter 2, we illustrated the difference between symmetrical and skewed distributions. In Chapter 5, we will be discussing the normal or "bell-shaped" distribution, which is a very important theoretical probability distribution in statistics. A normal distribution has one mode (it has a single peak), and it is symmetrical. If a line were drawn down the center of the distribution, the left half would be a mirror image of the right half. In a symmetrical or normal distribution, the mean, median, and mode are all the same, located right at the center of the distribution. If a distribution is not normal, recall that it is said to be a skewed distribution. In a negatively skewed distribution, the mean is less than the median. This is because there are low outlying scores on the left of the distribution pulling the value of the mean down. Stated differently, in a negatively skewed distribution, the mean is lower in magnitude than the median because low outliers are deflating the mean. This is what we saw in the third column of Table 3.7. Thus, knowing that in a distribution of scores the mean is much lower than the median, we might suspect that the distribution has a negative skew. The greater the difference there is between the mean and the median, the greater the negative skew. Conversely, in a positively skewed distribution, the mean is greater than the median because high outliers are inflating the magnitude of the mean relative to the median, as we saw in the second column of Table 3.7.

▣ Summary

In this chapter, we focused on measures of central tendency. These measures of central tendency are used as summary indicators of the typical, usual, most frequent, or average score in a distribution of scores. There are three measures of central tendency: the mode, the median, and the mean.

The mode is the score or value with the highest frequency. Therefore, it is the score or value that has the greatest probability or likelihood of occurring. There may be more than one mode in a given distribution of scores. As a measure of central tendency, the mode is probably the easiest to obtain since it requires no real calculations and is an appropriate measure of central tendency for nominal, ordinal, or interval/ratio-level data.

The median is the score at the 50th percentile. Thus, it is the score or value that divides a rank-ordered distribution of scores into two equal halves. A characteristic of the median, then, is that one half of the scores will be greater than the median and one half will be less than it. The median requires continuous-level data (interval/ratio) or continuous-level data that have been made ordinal through the creation of a grouped frequency distribution. Since the median locates the score at the 50th percentile, it is not affected by outlying scores in a distribution. For this reason, it is a very good measure of central tendency when the data are skewed.

The mean is the arithmetic average of all scores. It is calculated by summing all scores and dividing by the total number of scores. Calculation of the mean requires the same level of measurement as does the median. Because the mean uses all of the scores, it can be substantially affected by the presence of outliers in the data. In a normal distribution, the mode, median, and mean are the same. In a negatively skewed distribution, the mean is less than the median, and in a positively skewed distribution, the mean is greater than the median. Because the presence of outliers may distort the mean as a measure of central tendency, it is generally a good policy to report both the median and the mean.

Key Terms

➤ Review key terms with eFlashcards. Visit study.sagepub.com/paternoster.

bimodal distribution   63
mean   70

measures of central tendency   61
median   65

mode   61

Key Formulas

Sample median for grouped data (formula 3-1):

$$X_{\text{median}} = L + \left(\frac{\left(\frac{n+1}{2}\right) - cf}{f} \right) w_i$$

where

X_{median} = the value of the median

L = the lower real limit of the class interval that contains the median

cf = the cumulative frequency of the class interval just before the class interval that contains the median

f = the frequency of the interval that contains the median

w_i = the width of the class interval

n = the total number of observations in the sample

Sample mean of a population (formula 3-2):

$$\mu = \frac{\sum_{i=1}^{N} X_i}{N}$$

where

X_i = each X score in the population

N = the total number of observations in the population

Sample mean (formula 3-3):

$$\bar{X} = \frac{\sum_{i=1}^{n} x_i}{n}$$

where

$\bar{X}$ = the symbol used for the sample mean (pronounced "x bar")

x_i = the ith raw score in a distribution of scores

$\sum_{i=1}^{n} x_i$ = the instruction to sum all x_i scores, starting with the first score ($i = 1$) and continuing until the last score ($i = n$)

n = the total number of scores

Sample mean for data in a frequency distribution (formula 3-4):

$$\bar{X} = \frac{\sum m_i f_i}{n}$$

where

$\bar{X}$ = the mean

x_i = the ith score

f_i = the frequency for the ith score

$x_i f_i$ = the xth score multiplied by its frequency

n = the total number of scores

Sample mean for grouped data (formula 3-5):

$$\bar{X} = \frac{\sum m_i f_i}{n}$$

where

$\bar{X}$ = the mean

m_i = the midpoint for the ith class interval

f = the frequency for the ith class interval

$m_i f_i$ = the m_i midpoint multiplied by its frequency

n = the total number of scores

Practice Problems

> Test your understanding of chapter content.
> Take the practice quiz at study.sagepub.com/paternoster.

1. As a measure of central tendency, the mode is the most common score. Consider the following information on a variable called "the number of delinquent friends that someone has." What is the mode for these data, and what does it tell you? Why can't you calculate the "mean number of delinquent friends"?

Number of Delinquent Friends

X	f
None	20
Some	85
Most	30
All	10

2. Say you asked a random sample of seven correctional officers what their annual salary was, and their responses were as follows:

$25,900

$32,100

$28,400

$31,000

$29,500

$27,800

$26,100

What is the median salary, and what is the mean salary, for this sample?

3. The following data show the homicide rate per 100,000 people for 10 American cities. Given these data, which measure of central tendency would you use and why?

City	Homicide Rate
Boston, MA	6.8
Cincinnati, OH	4.5
Denver, CO	6.0
Las Vegas, NV	8.8
New Orleans, LA	43.3
New York, NY	8.7
Pittsburgh, PA	10.5
Salt Lake City, UT	5.6
San Diego, CA	4.3
San Francisco, CA	7.7

4. Rachel Sutherland and her colleagues (2015) have investigated the relationship between injection drug use and criminal activity. The hypothetical data that follow represent the number of crimes committed during a 2-year period by 20 heroin addicts. Using ungrouped data, calculate the mean and the median for these 20 persons. Which measure of central tendency do you think best summarizes the central tendency of these data and why?

Person Number	Number of Crimes Committed	Person Number	Number of Crimes Committed
1	4	11	4
2	16	12	11
3	10	13	10
4	7	14	88
5	3	15	9
6	112	16	12
7	5	17	8
8	10	18	5
9	6	19	7
10	2	20	10

5. In a study of police interventions and mental illness in a large Canadian city, Yannick Charette, Anne Crocker, and Isabelle Billette (2014, p. 513) reported the following distribution of the reasons for police intervention when the subject was without mental illness:

Request	Frequency
Offense against person	213
Offense against property	496
Other criminal offense	238
Potential offense	3,784
Individual in distress	139
Noncriminal incident	986

What is the measure of central tendency most appropriate for these data? Why? What does this measure of central tendency tell you about the "most typical" reason for a police intervention when the subject was without mental illness?

6. The following hypothetical data show the distribution of the percentage of total police officers who do narcotics investigation in 100 American cities. Determine the mode, median, and mean.

Percentage of Force Doing Investigation

Narcotics Investigation (%)	Frequency
0–9	5
10–19	13
20–29	26
30–39	38
40–49	14
50–59	2
60–69	2

7. The following data represent the number of persons executed in the United States from 2007 to 2014.

Year	# of Executions
2007	42
2008	37
2009	52
2010	46
2011	43
2012	43
2013	39
2014	35

What were the mean number and median number of executions over this time period? What happens to the median and mean when we add the year 2006, in which there were 53 executions? Which measure of central tendency would you use to describe the 2007–2014 distribution?

8. One seemingly inconsistent finding in criminological research is that women have a greater subjective fear of crime than men even though their objective risk of being the victim of a crime is lower. In one study, Jodi Lane and Kathleen Fox (2013) tried to explain this fact in part through the shadow of sexual assault thesis by suggesting that women are more afraid of crime because of their fear of sexual assault and the intense physical and emotional consequences they would face if raped. They suggest that women transfer this fear of sexual assault to a fear of crime generally. The hypothetical data that follow represent the responses of a sample of 200 women who were asked to report to an interviewer the number of times that they had been sexually assaulted during the previous 5 years. Using these data, calculate the mean, median, and mode.

Number of Times Assaulted	Frequency
0–1	85
2–3	70
4–5	30
6–7	15

9. Research reported by Adrian Raine, Annis Lai Chu Fung, Jill Portnoy, Olivia Choy, and Victoria Spring (2014) suggests that there is a link between low resting heart rates and aggression and psychopathic traits. They define those with resting heart rates below 67 beats per minute as having low resting heart rates. In a random sample of 20 violent offenders currently incarcerated in a state penitentiary, the prison doctor finds the following resting heart rates. Calculate the mean and median for these data. Are the mean and median the same or different? Why do you think this is so?

Person	Resting Heart Rate	Person	Resting Heart Rate
1	59	11	60
2	62	12	55
3	69	13	52
4	62	14	70
5	64	15	52
6	70	16	57
7	54	17	53
8	66	18	61
9	51	19	64
10	56	20	63

STUDENT STUDY SITE

WANT A BETTER GRADE?

Get the tools you need to sharpen your study skills. Access practice quizzes, eFlashcards, data sets, and SPSS exercises at **study.sagepub.com/paternoster.**

CHAPTER 4

Measures of Dispersion

"
Resemblances are the shadows of differences.

Different people see different similarities and similar differences.

—Vladimir Nabokov
"

LEARNING OBJECTIVES

1. Explain what measures of dispersion tell us about a variable distribution compared with measures of center.

2. Identify a measure of dispersion appropriate for nominal- or ordinal-level data.

3. Describe the difference between the range and the interquartile range.

4. Discuss the relationship between the variance and the standard deviation.

5. Calculate and interpret the standard deviation with both grouped and ungrouped data.

▣ Introduction

At the beginning of Chapter 3, we told you that the average age of inmates in state correctional facilities across the United States was 40 years. What if we told you that the age range of individuals housed in state prisons was from 17 to 82 years? These last numbers convey a different type of information about the age of state prisoners. The range of ages captures the differences among scores within a group of scores. Unless all of the scores in a distribution are the same (i.e., unless what we have is a constant and not a variable), the scores will be different from one another, and the magnitude of this difference is important to know. Measures that capture differences within a variable are called measures of dispersion or variability. Like the measures of central tendency we discussed in Chapter 3, measures of dispersion are summary measures that in one number reflect the differences among the values of a variable. In this chapter, you will learn that there are different measures of dispersion and, like the case of measures of central tendency, which one we use depends on the level of measurement of our variable. For nominal- and purely ordinal-level data, we will discuss a measure of dispersion called the variation ratio. With interval- and ratio-level variables, we can use four different measures: the range, the interquartile range, the variance, and the standard deviation. The latter two measures of dispersion are particularly important, and we will use them frequently in later chapters. You will learn how to calculate and interpret the variance and standard deviation with both grouped and ungrouped data.

> **Measures of dispersion:** Capture how different the values of a variable are. The more dispersion there is in a variable, the more different the values are from each other or from some central tendency and the more heterogeneity in the data.

Measures of dispersion tell us about the heterogeneity in the data. Heterogeneity exists whenever scores are dissimilar. The opposite is homogeneity, which exists when all scores are very similar. Take the following group of five scores that are the number of crimes reported in five different neighborhoods over a 2-year period:

$$103, 104, 102, 103, 103$$

You can see that these scores are very similar to each other and are not very different from the mean of 103 crimes (calculate this mean for yourself), so the homogeneity in the scores is high and the heterogeneity is low. Now consider the following five different neighborhood crime totals over 2 years:

$$74, 130, 80, 120, 111$$

The scores from these neighborhoods have the same mean number of crimes as the first group (103 crimes), but compared with the first group, these neighborhood crime levels are very different both from each other and from the mean of the scores. In this second group of scores, the homogeneity of these crime levels is low and the heterogeneity is high. Measures of dispersion capture this notion of the heterogeneity of scores.

As a more detailed illustration of the importance and kind of information a measure of dispersion provides, let's look at Table 4.1. This table reports the sentence length in years given by two different judges to 20 defendants convicted of armed robbery. The data have been rank-ordered and put into a frequency distribution, so it is pretty easy to calculate the mean and the median of the sentence lengths given by these two judges. Each judge sentenced 20 different convicted armed robbers. The median sentence length for both judges is 8.5 years, and they have the same mean sentence length of 9.0 years. As far as these two measures of central tendency are concerned, therefore, the two judges are similar in how they sentence armed robbery defendants. But does this convey all we need to know about the behavior of these two judges? No. Judge 1's sentencing behavior is clustered narrowly around the mean of 9 years and median of 8.5 years—her lowest sentence length is 5 years, and her highest sentence length is 14 years. Judge 2, however, seems "all over the map" when it comes to sentencing. Her sentences are not so tightly clustered around the mean and the median. Judge 2's sentences for armed robbery are as low as 1 year and as high as 20 years! You can see this very clearly in Figure 4.1, which shows the sentence lengths given by the two judges along with their common mean (solid line) and median (dashed line) sentence lengths. Note that the line showing the sentences given by Judge 1 is much closer to the mean and median lines than is the line showing the sentences given by Judge 2. What the table and figure both show is that even though these judges have the same median and mean sentence length, Judge 2 exhibits much more flexible and diverse sentencing behavior than Judge 1.

What we need to do is indicate the amount of heterogeneity or dispersion in a variable in addition to a measure of central tendency. This is what measures of dispersion do; they are summary measures that capture the amount of dispersion or heterogeneity in a variable. Offering a measure of dispersion, then, in addition to a measure of central tendency, will help us to understand our variables better. Just as there is more than one measure of central tendency, there is more than one measure of dispersion, and the appropriate measure of dispersion depends on the level of measurement of your variable.

> **Student Study Site**
>
> Visit the open-access Student Study Site at **study.sagepub.com/paternoster** to access additional study tools including mobile-friendly eFlashcards, web quizzes, links to SAGE journal articles, additional data sets, SPSS exercises, and more!

	Table 4.1	Number of Years of Prison Time for Convicted Armed Robbery Defendants	

	Judge 1	Judge 2
Defendant	Sentence Given	Sentence Given
1	5	1
2	7	2
3	7	2
4	7	3
5	7	3
6	7	3
7	8	4
8	8	4
9	8	5
10	8	8
11	9	9
12	9	10
13	9	11
14	10	14
15	11	15
16	11	15
17	11	16
18	12	17
19	12	18
20	14	20
$n = 20$	$\Sigma = 180$ $\overline{X} = 9$	$\Sigma = 180$ $\overline{X} = 9$

Measuring Dispersion for Nominal- and Ordinal-Level Variables

The Variation Ratio

The variation ratio is a very simple measure of dispersion that you can use whenever you have data measured at the nominal or ordinal level. Recall from Chapter 3 that when we employ nominal or ordinal measurement, the only measure of central tendency we can use is the mode, which is the score or value with the greatest frequency. The measure of dispersion for this type of data, the variation ratio, is based on the mode. The variation ratio (VR) simply measures the extent to which the observations are *not* concentrated in the modal category of the variable. More specifically, it is the proportion of cases not in the modal category of the variable. The smaller the proportion of cases that are in the modal category, the larger the variation ratio will be. The greater the value of the variation ratio is, the more variation or heterogeneity that will be found in the data. The formula for the variation ratio is

Variation ratio: Appropriate measure of dispersion to use when variables are measured at the nominal or purely ordinal level. It measures the proportion of cases of a variable that are not in the modal value.

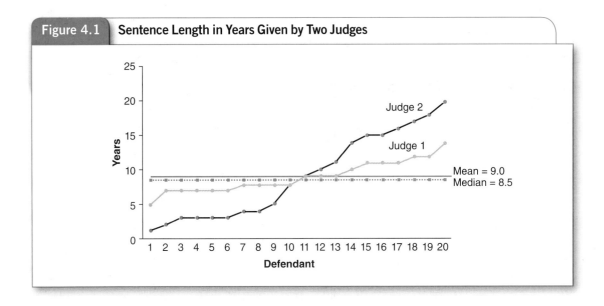

Figure 4.1 Sentence Length in Years Given by Two Judges

$$VR = 1 - \frac{f_{\text{modal}}}{n}$$

(Formula 4-1)

where

f_{modal} = the frequency of cases in the modal category

n = the total number of cases

The numerator of the fraction in equation 4-1, then, is the frequency in the modal category, and the denominator is the number of cases in the sample. Since the frequency of the modal category divided by n is just a proportion—the proportion in the mode—1 is the proportion not in the mode.

Note that if all of the cases in the variable fell into one value or category, two things would be true: (1) There would be no variation or dispersion in the data since the "variable" would actually be a constant (all cases fall into only one value), and (2) the magnitude of the variation ratio would be zero since f_{modal} would equal n, so f_{modal} / n would be equal to 1.0 and, thus, $1 - f_{\text{modal}}$ / n would be zero. So the lower limit of the variation ratio occurs when all cases fall into one and only one category of the nominal or ordinal variable and there is no variability at all—the variation ratio is equal to 0 (no variation). We will show you later in this section that the upper limit for the variation ratio is not so easily determined.

Case Study

Types of Patrolling Practices

Let's start with a simple example. In Table 4.2, we report the number of shifts in a given week for each of three types of patrolling practices used by a city police department. A shift is simply a block of time when officers are working— sometimes the shifts last 8 or 10 hours, and sometimes they last 12 hours. So, for example, the first shift of the day might last from 7 am to 5 pm, a 10-hour shift. The variable "type of patrolling practice" is a nominal-level variable because its values differ only in kind or quality—patrolling on foot is different from police car patrolling; it is not more patrolling. We can see that there were 45 shifts where the police were doing neighborhood patrols, and in 5 of these

Table 4.2	**Type and Frequency of Patrolling Used in Police Shifts in One U.S. City**

	f
Foot patrol only	5
Car patrol only	30
Foot and car patrol	10
Total number of shifts	45

they did foot patrol only, in 30 they patrolled only by police car, and 10 shifts involved a mixture of foot and car patrols. The modal type of police patrolling is car patrol since it has the greatest frequency. The variation ratio is

$$VR = 1 - \frac{30}{45}$$
$$VR = 1 - .67$$
$$VR = .33$$

The value of the variation ratio, then, is .33. About a third (33%) of all police patrols are not in the modal category of car patrol.

As another example, in Table 4.3, we present a nominal-level variable that we used in Chapters 2 and 3. The variable "type of hate crime" is a nominal-level variable because the values represent only qualitative distinctions; one type of hate crime is simply different from another, not "more" of a hate crime. We learned in the last chapter that the mode for this variable is "racial hate crime" since there were more of this kind of hate crime reported in 2013 than of any other kind. More specifically, .485 of the total number of hate crimes were racially motivated hate crimes. We can calculate the value of the variation ratio for this variable as

$$VR = 1 - \frac{2,871}{5,922}$$
$$VR = 1 - .485$$
$$VR = .515$$

The variation ratio, then, is .515, which tells us that slightly more than one half of the cases (51.5% to be exact) are not in the modal category of racial hate crimes.

Table 4.3	**Type of Hate Crime Incident Reported to Police in 2013**

Basis of Hate	*f*	Proportion	%
Race	2,871	.485	48.5
Religion	1,031	.174	17.4
Sexual orientation	1,233	.208	20.8
Ethnicity/National origin	655	.111	11.1
Disability	83	.014	1.4
Gender	18	.003	0.3
Gender identity	31	.005	0.5
Total	5,922	1.0	100.0

Source: Adapted from *Hate Crime Statistics—2013* from the Federal Bureau of Investigation (2013b).

Table 4.4 lists some hypothetical data on hate crimes. There are still 5,922 reported hate crimes, but in this example there are 4,975 cases in the category "racial hate crimes." Note that there is less dispersion or heterogeneity in these data than in Table 4.3 because there is a greater concentration of cases in one category (the mode, racially motivated hate crimes). Now when we calculate the variation ratio, we get

$$VR = 1 - \frac{4,975}{5,922}$$
$$VR = 1 - .840$$
$$VR = .160$$

There are now only .160, or 16%, of the total number of cases not in the modal category. This means that 84% of the cases fall into the modal category, more than in our previous example with real data, indicating that there is *less* heterogeneity in these data than in those found in Table 4.3. This is reflected in a lower magnitude of the variation ratio for Table 4.4.

Now look at Table 4.5, which gives another set of hypothetical data. In this example, we still have 5,922 reported hate crimes, but now the cases are evenly distributed across the four values. In fact, there is no mode because every category has the same frequency. For Table 4.5, when we calculate the magnitude of the variation ratio, we find it to be

$$VR = 1 - \frac{846}{5,922}$$
$$VR = 1 - .143$$
$$VR = .857$$

Now .857, or about 86%, of the cases are not in the modal category, indicating that this distribution of hate crimes has more dispersion than the other two examples.

One problem with the variation ratio is that the maximum value it can attain is not some fixed value. The maximum amount of heterogeneity or the maximum value for the variation ratio for any table will be obtained when there is no mode and the cases, therefore, are equally distributed in each of the values, but it also depends on the *number of categories* the variable has. The maximum value of the VR will always be

$$1 - \left(\frac{\left(\frac{n}{k} \right)}{n} \right)$$

where k is equal to the number of values or categories a variable has and n is the total number of cases. For the data we used in Tables 4.3 to 4.5, the maximum magnitude of the VR is .857, the value we calculated from the data in Table 4.5:

$$VR = 1 - \frac{\left(\frac{5,922}{7} \right)}{5,922}$$
$$VR = 1 - \frac{846}{5,922}$$
$$VR = 1 - .143$$
$$VR = .857$$

Another way to understand what the VR is telling us about the dispersion in a set of nominal/ordinal data is to take the ratio of the variation we observe over the maximum possible variation and then multiply by 100 to get the percentage of the maximum variation observed. For example, in Table 4.3, which is the real hate crime data from the Federal

Table 4.4   Hypothetical Hate Crime Data

Type of Hate	f	Proportion
Racial	4,975	.840
Religious	414	.070
Sexual orientation	272	.046
Ethnicity/National origin	148	.025
Disability	53	.009
Gender	30	.005
Gender identity	30	.005
Total	5,922	1.000

Table 4.5   Hypothetical Hate Crime Data

Type of Hate	f	Proportion
Racial	846	.143
Religious	846	.143
Sexual orientation	846	.143
Ethnicity/National origin	846	.143
Disability	846	.143
Gender	846	.143
Gender identity	846	.143
Total	5,922	1.001*

*Greater than 1.0 due to rounding.

Bureau of Investigation's (FBI) Uniform Crime Reports, the variation ratio was .515. Since we just calculated the maximum amount of variation we could possibly have in these data from Table 4.5 and we found that to be equal to .857, we can take the ratio of VR we observe to the maximum VR (.515 /.857), which is .60, and then multiply by 100 to get 60%. Now what we can conclude is that in Table 4.3 we have about 60% of the total possible amount of variation that could be observed. The important thing to keep in mind is that higher values of the variation ratio imply greater dispersion in the distribution of a nominal/ordinal-level variable or more heterogeneity in the data. If you think that the variation ratio is a very crude measure of dispersion since it captures only the proportion of cases not in the modal category, you are right. It is pretty crude and not greatly informative. But recall that the mode is a very simple and crude measure of central tendency, reflecting simply the value with the greatest number of cases.

🔲 Measuring Dispersion for Interval- and Ratio-Level Variables

The Range and Interquartile Range

Let's now consider the case where we have data measured at the interval/ratio level—in other words, data that can be considered continuous (continuous data that have been grouped). When we have continuous data, there are other, more precise, ways that we can characterize. The simplest measure of dispersion with continuous data is called the range. For ungrouped data, the range is the difference between the highest score and the lowest score in the distribution:

$$\text{Range} = \text{Highest value} - \text{Lowest value}$$

When we have data in a grouped frequency distribution, the range is the difference between the midpoint of the last class interval and the midpoint of the first class interval, or the difference between the highest and lowest midpoints.

Case Study

Calculating the Range of Sentence Lengths

In Table 4.1, the range for Judge 1's sentences for convicted armed robbery defendants is 9 years because the longest sentence she imposed was 14 years and the shortest sentence she imposed was 5 years (14 – 5 = 9 years). The range for Judge 2 is 19 years because her longest sentence was 20 years and her shortest sentence was 1 year (20 – 1 = 19 years). Based on the calculation of the range, there is more dispersion or heterogeneity in the sentencing of Judge 2 than in that of Judge 1. Sometimes the range is expressed as the lowest and highest values rather than as the difference between these values. In these terms, the range for Judge 1 would be "between 5 and 14 years," and for Judge 2 it would be "between 1 and 20 years." No matter how it is expressed, the range in sentencing is greater for Judge 2 than it is for Judge 1—a fact expressed by the greater magnitude of the range for Judge 2.

Table 4.6 shows the grouped frequency distribution for the "time-until-rearrest" data of our 120 offenders released into the community—the same data that we have used in previous chapters. These were originally interval- and ratio-level data, which we made ordinal by creating a grouped frequency distribution. We have midpoints for our class intervals, so we can calculate a range for the data. Since the midpoint of the last class interval is 39 days and the midpoint for the first class interval is 18 days, the range for these time-until-rearrest ordinal data is 39 – 18 = 21 days. We can also say that the range in the time-until-rearrest data is between 18 and 39 days.

Range: Measure of dispersion appropriate for interval/ratio-level data. It is calculated as the difference between the highest value or score and the lowest value or score: Range = Highest value – Lowest value.

The range is a very simple measure of dispersion to calculate and is very easy to understand. The ease of calculating the range, however, may come at a high price; with some data, the range may distort the amount of dispersion that exists in the data. Since the range includes only two scores in our data, the highest and the lowest, it completely ignores the dispersion that may lie between these two values. If either or both of these two scores are unusual or extreme (in other words, an outlier), using the range as our only measure of dispersion may be misleading.

For example, let's look at Table 4.7, which shows the sentencing data of two different judges. In both cases, the judges sentenced 20 convicted armed robbery defendants, and just as in Table 4.1, the range in sentencing is 9 years for Judge 1 and 19 years for Judge 2. Using the range, then, we would get the impression that there is a great deal more dispersion or heterogeneity in the sentencing behavior of Judge 2 compared with Judge 1. Although the ranges of 9 and 19 years are technically correct, would it really be accurate to conclude that Judge 2 has a lot more dispersion in her sentencing than Judge 1? Fortunately, we have other measures of dispersion for continuous variables that take more information into account than just the highest and lowest scores.

One alternative to the range as a measure of dispersion is something called the **interquartile range** (IQR). In calculating the interquartile range, we still take the difference between two scores, but rather than taking the difference between the highest and lowest scores, in the IQR we take the difference between the score at the 75th percentile (the third quartile or Q_3) and the score at the 25th percentile (the first quartile or Q_1). Note that since we are taking the range of scores between the 75th and 25th percentiles, this range covers the dispersion at the middle 50% of our distribution. In other words, one half of all our scores can be found between the 75th and 25th percentiles, and the IQR measures the dispersion within those two boundaries.

Recall that we can divide our distribution in many different ways. One of these ways we already know. For example, we can divide our scores into percentiles, or units of 100, as we do in Table 4.8. We can then take these percentiles and group them into intervals of 10, or deciles. There are 10 deciles for 100 percentiles. The first 10 percentiles make up the first decile, the second 10 percentiles make up the second decile, and so on. We can also group our percentiles into intervals of 25%, or quartiles. Since the 100 percentiles are equally distributed into four quartiles, each quartile comprises 25 percentiles, or 25% of the data. The first 25 percentiles make up the first quartile (Q_1), and the second 25 percentiles make up the second quartile (Q_2). Recall that

Table 4.6	Grouped Frequency Distribution for Time-Until-Failure Data for 120 Inmates		
Stated Limits (Days)		f	Midpoint
17–19		4	18
20–22		1	21
23–25		12	24
26–28		16	27
29–31		28	30
32–34		28	33
35–37		21	36
38–40		10	39
		n = 120	

Table 4.7	Number of Years of Prison Time for Convicted Armed Robbery Defendants		
Judge 1		Judge 2	
Years Sentenced	f	Years Sentenced	f
5	1	1	10
6	1	20	10
7	3		
8	4		
9	3		
10	1		
11	3		
12	2		
13	1		
14	1		
	n = 20		n = 20

Interquartile range: Measure of dispersion appropriate for interval/ratio-level data. It measures the range of scores in the middle 50% of a distribution of continuous scores and is calculated as the difference between the score at the third quartile (the 75th percentile) and the score at the first quartile (the 25th percentile).

Q_1, Q_2, Q_3, **and** Q_4: The interquartile range depends on finding the values for Q_1 and Q_3. Q_1 is the 25th percentile, and Q_3 is the 75th percentile. When a percentage distribution is divided into quartiles, there are four of them: Q_1, the 25th percentile; Q_2, the 50th percentile or median; Q_3, the 75th percentile; and Q_4, the 100th percentile. See Table 4.8.

the median is the second quartile. The next 25 percentiles, from the 51st to the 75th percentiles, are contained in the third quartile (Q_3), and the last 25% of the cases are in the fourth quartile (Q_4). This information on percentiles, deciles, and quartiles is shown in Table 4.8.

With this information, we can see that the 25th percentile is the first quartile (Q_1) and that the 75th percentile is the third quartile (Q_3). To find the interquartile range, then, we are going to have to locate the score that lies at the 75th percentile (x_{Q3}), locate the score that lies at the 25th percentile (x_{Q1}), and then take the difference between these two scores:

$$IQR = x_{Q_3} - x_{Q_1} \qquad \text{(Formula 4-2)}$$

As you can see, the interquartile range reflects the range in the data in between the 75th and 25th percentiles, or the middle 50% of the distribution, thereby ignoring the highest and lowest scores. The calculation of the IQR is pretty straightforward, and we will show you two different ways to calculate the IQR in the following case study.

Case Study

Calculating the Interquartile Range of the Number of Escapes by Prison

For this example, let's use the data in Table 4.9, which shows the hypothetical number of escapes from 20 correctional institutions in the prison system of two states, State A and State B. We can easily calculate the range in the number of escapes for the prisons in these two states. For State A, the range is 23 because the highest number of escapes was 23 and the lowest was 0. For State B, the range is 9 because there was a high of 10 escapes and a low of 1. Judging by the range, there seems to be substantially more dispersion in the number of escapes in State A. However, the range is greater for State A only because there was one prison that had an unusually high number of escapes (23 of them), and this outlier is distorting the true dispersion in the data. Given this outlier, we should calculate the interquartile range. There are two different ways to calculate the IQR.

One way is first to rank-order the data in ascending order (lowest to highest). After the data are rank-ordered, we need to identify something called the *truncated median position* or TMP. The truncated median position is simply the position of the median in the data with the decimal place in the calculation truncated (*truncated* means that the decimal place is dropped or rounded down to the nearest integer). For example, we have 20 observations for each state in Table 4.9. Using our positional formula for the location of the median, we find that the median is in the (20 + 1) / 2 = 10.5th position. The truncated median position is 10, which was found by dropping the .5. With the value of the TMP, we can now identify where the third and first quartiles can be found, or the quartile positions (QPs):

$$QP = (TMP + 1) / 2$$

With a truncated median position of 10, we can determine that the position of the two quartiles (Q_1 and Q_3 or the 25th and 75th percentiles) is (10 + 1) / 2 = 5.5th position (the truncated median position plus 1 divided by 2). The third and first quartiles, then, are at the midpoint of the 5th and 6th scores in the rank order of scores. More specifically, *in a rank-ordered distribution of scores,* the first quartile is the midpoint between the 5th and 6th *lowest* scores, and the third quartile is the midpoint between the 5th and 6th *highest* scores. In Table 4.10, we provide the number of escapes from each state in rank order along with the positions of the first (Q_1) and third (Q_3) quartiles. To find the first quartile, we start from the lowest score, identify what the 5th and 6th scores are, and find the average of those two scores. To find the third quartile, we start from the highest score, identify what the 5th and 6th scores are, and find the average.

The first quartile for State A is 2 because the scores at both the 5th and 6th positons are equal to 2 ([2 + 2] / 2 = 2), and the first quartile for State B is 3 ([3 + 3] / 2 = 3). The third quartile for both states is 6 because both states have 6 escapes at the 5th and 6th values down from the highest score ([6 + 6] / 2 = 6).

With this information, we can now calculate the interquartile range for both states:

$$\text{IQR State A} = 6 - 2 = 4 \text{ escapes}$$

$$\text{IQR State B} = 6 - 3 = 3 \text{ escapes}$$

Thus, the interquartile ranges for the two states are fairly comparable, indicating that in the middle 50% of the distributions of the number of escapes there is about an equal amount of variation in the two states. This is a different picture of the dispersion in the data from the one we got when we calculated the range, which was influenced by the fact that one institution in State A experienced 23 escapes.

Another way to find the interquartile range without having to identify the truncated median position is to use cumulative percentages. Recall that the first quartile is the score at the 25th percentile, and the third quartile is the score at the 75th percentile. We can find the scores at the 25th and 75th percentiles by simply calculating a column of cumulative percentages. Table 4.11 provides the frequency, percentage, and cumulative percentage distribution of escapes for the two states. For State A, the score at the 25th percentile is 2 escapes. How do we know this? Note that 15% of the scores are either 0 or 1 and that 30% of the scores are 0, 1, or 2. This indicates that the scores at the 16th percentile, the 17th percentile, and all the way to the 30th percentile are all 2s. The score at the 25th percentile, then, is a 2, or 2 escapes. For State A, the score at the 75th percentile is 6 escapes because 70% of the scores are 5 or lower, and 80% of the scores are 6 escapes or lower, so this must mean that the scores at the 71st percentile, the 72nd percentile, and all the way to the 80th percentile are 6 escapes. The 75th percentile, then, is 6 escapes. For State A, the IQR is 6 − 2 = 4 escapes. For State B, the score at the 25th percentile is 3 escapes because 20% of the scores are 2 escapes or lower and 40% of the scores are 3 escapes or lower. The score at the 25th percentile, then, is a 3. The score at the 75th percentile is 6 escapes since 70% of the scores are 5 escapes or lower and 80% of them are 6 escapes or lower. The score at the 75th percentile, then, is 6 escapes. The IQR

Table 4.8 The Relationship Among Percentiles, Deciles, and Quartiles

Percentile	Decile	Quartile
100th	10th	4th (Q_4)
99th		
98th		
90th	9th	
.		
80th	8th	
.		
.		
75th		3rd (Q_3)
.		
.		
60th	6th	
.		
.		
50th	5th	2nd (Q_2)
.		
.		
.		
30th	3rd	
29th		
28th		
25th		1st (Q_1)
.		
.		
20th	2nd	
.		
3rd		
2nd		
1st		

| Table 4.9 | Number of Escapes From 20 Correctional Institutions in Two States |

Institution	State A	State B
1	3	3
2	2	4
3	4	1
4	9	2
5	2	3
6	5	6
7	6	5
8	4	3
9	1	4
10	3	4
11	4	5
12	5	2
13	2	3
14	0	5
15	7	8
16	1	1
17	7	6
18	6	8
19	9	9
20	23	10

| Table 4.10 | Rank-Ordered Number of Escapes From 20 Correctional Institutions in Two States From Table 4.9 |

Institution	State A	State B
1	0	1
2	1	1
3	1	2
4	2	2
5	2	3
6	2	3
7	3	3
8	3	3
9	3	4
10	4	4
11	4	4
12	4	5
13	5	5
14	5	5
15	6	6
16	6	6
17	7	8
18	7	8
19	9	9
20	23	10

| Table 4.11 | Frequency Counts, Percentages, and Cumulative Percentages for Escape Data From Two States |

State A # of Escapes	f	%	Cum %	State B # of Escapes	f	%	Cum %
0	1	5	5	1	2	10	10
1	2	10	15	2	2	10	20
2	3	15	30	3	4	20	40
3	3	15	45	4	3	15	55

State A # of Escapes	f	%	Cum %	State B # of Escapes	f	%	Cum %
4	3	15	60	5	3	15	70
5	2	10	70	6	2	10	80
6	2	10	80	8	2	10	90
7	2	10	90	9	1	5	95
9	1	5	95	10	1	5	100
23	1	5	100				
	$n = 20$	100			$n = 20$	100	

for State B is 6 – 3 = 3 escapes. These are the same answers we got using the truncated median position formula and finding our quartiles that way. The next measures of dispersion we will cover provide yet a different way to measure a variable's dispersion!

The Standard Deviation and Variance

Recall that with interval- and ratio-level data, we can calculate a mean or arithmetic average as a measure of central tendency. Not surprisingly, there are measures of dispersion that use the mean as the reference point to measure dispersion. These measures are based on the notion that measuring how much heterogeneity there is for a quantitative variable is to determine how different a value is from the mean. The most common of these mean-based measures of dispersion are the variance and standard deviation.

Both the standard deviation and the variance measure dispersion by taking the difference, or deviation, of each score from the mean of a variable. Scores that are clustered very close to the mean are less disperse, or more homogeneous, than scores that are very far from the mean. The *distance from the mean or the deviation from the mean,* therefore, is another way to capture the amount of dispersion in a variable. The simple formula for taking the distance of a score from a sample mean is $x_i - \overline{X}$ where x_i is the score for the ith score and $\overline{X}$ is the mean of the sample.

As we will see, using the distance or deviation from the mean as the basis for a measure of dispersion for continuous data will give us two pieces of information. First, the sign of the distance or deviation will tell us whether the score is less than or greater than the mean. Second, the magnitude of the deviation will tell us how far the score is—its distance from the mean. Let's use this simple formula $(x_i - \overline{X})$ for the distance of a score from the sample mean, referred to as a **mean deviation score**, and determine how it applies to the notion of dispersion.

Figure 4.2 shows two distributions of one variable. The mean of both distributions is 25. In the first distribution, shown in Figure 4.2(a), you can see that most of the values or scores are close to the mean. The farthest a score is away from the mean is 2 units (a score of 23 is –2 units from the mean, whereas a score of 27 is +2 units away). In other words, for this variable, the distance of each score from the mean is not great, indicating that the scores are not very different from the mean (or, by implication, from each other). There does not seem to be much dispersion or heterogeneity in this distribution, and this fact is reflected in the short distance of each score from the mean. However, in the second distribution shown in Figure 4.2(b), the scores are much more different from the mean than those in Figure 4.2(a), and this is indicated by the fact that there is a greater distance between each of these scores and the mean. Without doing any math, you should be able to determine that the distribution shown in Figure 4.2(b)

Mean deviation score: Distance between a score and the mean of the group of scores.

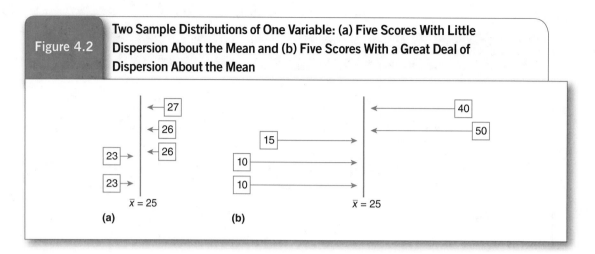

Figure 4.2 Two Sample Distributions of One Variable: (a) Five Scores With Little Dispersion About the Mean and (b) Five Scores With a Great Deal of Dispersion About the Mean

For the scores in Figure 4.2(a)

Score	Mean	Deviation From Mean	Squared Deviation
23	25	23 − 25 = −2	4
26	25	26 − 25 = +1	1
23	25	23 − 25 = −2	4
27	25	27 − 25 = +2	4
26	25	26 − 25 = +1	1

For the scores in Figure 4.2(b)

Score	Mean	Deviation From Mean
10	25	10 − 25 = −15
50	25	50 − 25 = +25
15	25	15 − 25 = −10
40	25	40 − 25 = +15
10	25	10 − 25 = −15

has more dispersion (the scores are more different from the mean, or more heterogeneous) than the distribution of scores in Figure 4.2(a). In sum, the notion of distance from the mean, or mean deviation scores, is another way to capture the dispersion of a variable measured at the interval/ratio level.

Let's take this example one step further and calculate, for each score in Figure 4.2, the distance from the mean. We mentioned earlier that the distance of each score from the mean is also called a *deviation* from the mean.

As we mentioned, the deviation from the mean contains two pieces of information. Let's take the first x score, 23, where the deviation from the mean is −2. The negative sign of the deviation tells us that a score of 23 is less than the mean, and the magnitude of 2 tells us that it is 2 units away from the mean. A negative mean deviation, then, indicates that the x score is less than the mean, whereas a positive mean deviation indicates that the score is greater than the mean. Moreover, the greater the magnitude of the mean deviation, the greater the distance the x score is from the mean. Finally, the greater the overall distance a distribution of scores is from the mean, the more dispersion or variability there is in the data. Knowing this, it's pretty easy to see that there is more dispersion in the second set of scores, and this is reflected in the fact that when we take all of the scores into account, the magnitude of the deviations, regardless of their sign, is much greater in the second set of scores than in the first set.

Rather than having all of these deviation scores (imagine how messy things would look if we had 50 or 100 scores!), it might be nice to create a summary measure or one number that captures the *average distance* or deviation from the mean. That is, since we know that the mean is a good measure of central tendency, let's calculate the mean deviation score that would provide us with one number that indicates the average distance of each score from the mean. This number would then give us the average, or mean, of the deviations. This would be easy to do. Again, we know that the formula for the mean is

$$\bar{X} = \frac{\sum\limits_{i=1}^{n} x_i}{n}$$

and that it is calculated by adding up all the scores in the sample and dividing by the total number of scores. We can use this same formula for the mean here; the only difference is that our "score" is not an x_i but rather a difference score: $(x_i - \overline{X})$. All we have to do is say $x_i = (x_i - \overline{X})$ and calculate our mean distance or mean deviation score as

$$\overline{D} = \frac{\sum_{i=1}^{n}(x_i - \overline{X})}{n}$$

(just for now, let's let $\overline{D}$ be the symbol for the average deviation or distance score). This formula simply tells us to subtract scores from the mean and then sum up these deviation scores and divide by the total number of scores. For the scores in Figure 4.2(a), the average deviation would be

$$\overline{D} = \frac{-2+1-2+2+1}{5}$$

$$\overline{D} = \frac{0}{5}$$

For the scores in Figure 4.2(b), the average deviation would be

$$\overline{D} = \frac{-15+25-10+15-15}{5}$$

$$\overline{D} = \frac{0}{5}$$

We've hit a snag! The numerator of our formula for the average distance from the mean is zero; in fact, *it will always be zero*. The essence of the mean as a measure of central tendency is that it is a score that perfectly balances the negative and positive differences from it. In other words, the sum of the negative deviations from the mean is exactly equal to the sum of the positive deviations from the mean. As a result, when we add the negative deviations from the mean to the positive deviations from the mean, we are always left with a sum of zero. The way to state this property in words is to say that "the sum of the deviations around the mean is always zero" or in formula:

$$\sum_{i=1}^{n}(x_i - \overline{X}) = 0$$

Because of this property of the mean, we are stuck. One way to get unstuck would be to get rid of the negative signs for the scores. An easy way to do this would be to square the deviation scores, which would give us $(x_i - \overline{X})^2$. This squaring of deviations will ensure all positive values (since the square of a negative number is a positive number) in the numerator. Then we can take the mean of these squared deviations. Now, our formula for measuring dispersion looks like this:

$$\frac{\sum_{i=1}^{n}(x_i - \overline{X})^2}{n}$$

In words, this formula says to subtract each score from the mean (the "mean deviation score"), square this deviation for each score, sum all of these squared deviations, and finally divide by the total number of scores. Let's use this formula with our data in Figures 4.2(a) and 4.2(b).

For the scores in Figure 4.2(a):

Score	Mean	Deviation From Mean
23	25	23 – 25 = –2
26	25	26 – 25 = +1
23	25	23 – 25 = –2
27	25	27 – 25 = +2
26	25	26 – 25 = +1

For the scores in Figure 4.2(b):

Score	Mean	Deviation From Mean	Squared Deviation
10	25	10 − 25 = −15	225
50	25	50 − 25 = 25	625
15	25	15 − 25 = −10	100
40	25	40 − 25 = 15	225
10	25	10 − 25 = −15	225

The average squared deviation from the mean in Figure 4.2(a) would be

$$\bar{D} = \frac{4+1+4+4+1}{5} = \frac{14}{5} = 2.8$$

The average squared deviation from the mean in Figure 4.2(b) would be

$$\bar{D} = \frac{225+625+100+225+225}{5} = \frac{1,400}{5} = 280$$

Now we have one number for each set of scores that measures the amount of dispersion in the data by taking the average squared deviation from the mean. By using this, we can see clearly that there is substantially more dispersion in the second set of scores than in the first set, and that is exactly the impression we got from Figure 4.2.

Congratulations! What you have actually just done is to calculate the **variance**. The variance is the average squared difference of each score in a set of scores from the mean of those scores. The greater the magnitude of the variance, the more dispersion there is in the data. We now need to complicate things a little because we must distinguish between the variance of a population and the variance of a sample.

Recall from our discussion in Chapter 1 that a population consists of the universe of cases that we are interested in. For example, if we are interested in the relationship between IQ scores and delinquency among male youths between the ages of 12 and 18 years in the United States, our population consists of all male youths between the ages of 12 and 18 who reside in the United States. The population we are interested in, then, is generally very large and both difficult and costly to study directly. Our population of male adolescents, for example, would number in the millions. A sample, you will remember, is a subset of the population. We select a sample from the population and study the sample with the intention of making an inference to the population based on what we know about the sample. The sample is much smaller than the population, and it is the group that we actually study. We might, for example, first take a sample of states, then a sample of cities, and finally a sample of youths between the ages of 12 and 18 from those cities.

As was true for the mean, it would be entirely possible (although it would require a great deal of work and a considerable amount of money) to calculate the variance of most populations. As such, its value generally remains unknown. In statistics, the variance of a population is noted by the term σ^2 (the Greek letter sigma squared) and is defined as the averaged squared deviation of each score in a population from the mean of that population:

$$\sigma^2 = \frac{\sum_{i=1}^{N}(x_i - \mu)^2}{N} \qquad \text{(Formula 4-3)}$$

where μ is the population mean and N is the total number of scores in the population.

If we do not have the entire population and have, instead, drawn a sample from that population, we have to estimate the unknown population value with our sample data. Recall that for the mean, we estimated μ, the unknown population mean, with $\bar{X}$, the mean of the sample. Similarly, when we have sample data, we will estimate the variance of the population (σ) with the variance of our sample data. The formula for the variance of the sample is

$$s^2 = \frac{\sum_{i=1}^{n}(x_i - \bar{X})^2}{n-1} \qquad \text{(Formula 4-4)}$$

Variance: Measures the average squared deviations from the mean for an interval/ratio variable.

There are two differences between the formula for the variance of a population (equation 4-3) and the formula for the variance of a sample (equation 4-4). In the variance of a population, we take the sum of the squared deviations of each score from the population mean (μ) and divide by the population size (N). In the variance of a sample, we take the sum of the squared deviations of each score from the sample mean ($\overline{X}$) and divide by the number of scores in the sample (n) minus 1. The reason we use $n-1$ in the denominator of the sample variance s^2 is that it is a biased estimator of the population value σ^2. To correct for that bias, we divide by $n-1$ rather than by n in our sample formula. Note that the practical effect of using $n-1$ is that we have a smaller denominator. This means that the estimate of the sample variance will be larger than if we simply used the sample size. It also means that the difference between $n-1$ and n will be more substantial when the sample size is small. This should make sense to you because it means the bias is larger in smaller samples. Note also that to get rid of the negative signs in calculating the variance, we took the *squared* deviation of each score from the mean. The variance, therefore, measures dispersion in the awkward terminology of "average squared deviation from the mean."

The other measure of dispersion for interval- and ratio-level data that we will discuss, the standard deviation, adjusts for the squaring of the deviations about the mean. It does this by taking the square root of the variance (taking the square root of a value is the "opposite" operation to squaring it; e.g., 2 squared is 4, and the square root of 4 is 2). The symbol σ is used to denote the population standard deviation, which has the formula

$$\sigma = \sqrt{\frac{\sum_{i=1}^{N}(x_i-\mu)^2}{N}}$$

(Formula 4-5)

The symbol s is used to denote the sample **standard deviation**, which has the formula

$$s = \sqrt{\frac{\sum_{i=1}^{n}(x_i-\overline{X})^2}{n-1}}$$

(Formula 4-6)

Notice that

$$\text{Variance} = \text{Standard deviation}^2$$

$$\text{Standard deviation} = \sqrt{\text{Variance}}$$

The variance is the standard deviation squared, whereas the standard deviation is the square root of the variance. So if you calculate the sample variance, all you have to do to get the standard deviation is take the square root of that value. The variance and standard deviation are the two most frequently used measures of dispersion for interval- and ratio-level data. To summarize what we have covered in this section, Table 4.12 shows the population and sample formulas for the variance and the standard deviation.

Standard deviation: Square root of the squared deviations about the mean.

Case Study

Calculating the Variance and Standard Deviation of Judges' Sentences

Let's practice using these sample formulas by calculating the variance and standard deviation for our two judges' sentencing data from Table 4.1. Since these are samples of 20 sentences from the population of sentences that these judges handed down to convicted defendants, we will use the sample formulas for the variance

Table 4.12	Definitional Formulas for Population and Sample Variance and Standard Deviation

Population	
Variance (σ^2)	$\sigma^2 = \dfrac{\Sigma(xi - \mu)^2}{N}$
Standard deviation (σ)	$\sigma = \sqrt{\dfrac{\Sigma(x_i - \mu)^2}{N}}$
Sample	
Variance (s^2)	$s^2 = \dfrac{\Sigma(x_i - \bar{X})^2}{n-1}$
Standard deviation (s)	$s = \sqrt{\dfrac{\Sigma(x_i - \bar{X})^2}{n-1}}$

Table 4.13	Calculations for the Variance and Standard Deviation in Judge 1's Sentencing ($n = 20$)

x	$x_i - \bar{x}$	$(x_i - \bar{x})^2$
5	$5 - 9 = -4$	16
7	$7 - 9 = -2$	4
7	$7 - 9 = -2$	4
7	$7 - 9 = -2$	4
7	$7 - 9 = -2$	4
7	$7 - 9 = -2$	4
8	$8 - 9 = -1$	1
8	$8 - 9 = -1$	1
8	$8 - 9 = -1$	1
8	$8 - 9 = -1$	1
9	$9 - 9 = 0$	0
9	$9 - 9 = 0$	0
9	$9 - 9 = 0$	0
10	$10 - 9 = 1$	1
11	$11 - 9 = 2$	4
11	$11 - 9 = 2$	4
11	$11 - 9 = 2$	4
12	$12 - 9 = 3$	9
12	$12 - 9 = 3$	9
14	$14 - 9 = 5$	25
		$\Sigma = 96$

(equation 4-4) and standard deviation (equation 4-6). Let's calculate the variance first by using the following steps:

Steps in Calculating the Sample Variance

Step 1: Calculate the mean.

Step 2: Subtract the mean from each score: $x_i - \bar{X}$.

Step 3: Square the deviation of each score from the mean: $(x_i - \bar{X})^2$.

Step 4: Sum the squared deviations for all scores, starting with the first score and continuing to the last score:

$$\sum_{i=1}^{n}(x_i - \bar{X})^2$$

This is called the sum of the squared deviations from the mean.

Step 5: Divide by the number of scores minus 1:

$$\frac{\sum_{i=1}^{n}(x_i - \bar{X})^2}{n-1}$$

This is the sample variance.

Now we will calculate the variance separately for each judge. First, the calculations for Judge 1 are shown in Table 4.13. We can see from this table that the sum of the squared deviations is 96. To find the variance, we divide this by the number of scores (n) minus 1. The variance for Judge 1, therefore, is

$$s^2 = \frac{96}{20-1}$$

$$s^2 = \frac{96}{19}$$

$$s^2 = 5.05$$

The calculations necessary to find the variance for Judge 2 are shown in Table 4.14. We can see from this table that the sum of the squared deviations about the mean for Judge 2 is 754. Again, to find the variance, we divide this by the number of scores (n) minus 1. The variance for Judge 2, therefore, is

$$s^2 = \frac{754}{20-1}$$

$$s^2 = \frac{754}{19}$$

$$s^2 = 39.68$$

When we calculate the variances for Judge 1 and Judge 2, then, we find that the magnitude is much higher for Judge 2, confirming our suspicion that there is more dispersion, or heterogeneity, in this judge's sentencing behavior than in that of Judge 1. The interpretation of a sample variance is really only useful with reference to the sample mean. The interpretation for these sample variances would be as follows: For Judge 1 the sample of 20 sentences varied 5.05 squared deviation units around their mean of 9, and for Judge 2 the sample of 20 sentences varied 39.68 squared deviation units around their mean of 9. The problem, of course, is who can imagine what these squared deviation units actually mean? That's why the standard deviation is most often utilized to describe the variability in sample data, and we can easily calculate that now!

If you look at the formula for the sample standard deviation, you can see that all we have to do is take the square root of the variance. Thus, there is only one more step involved in calculating the standard deviation. Since this is our first time calculating the standard deviation, however, we will give you each of the necessary steps:

| Table 4.14 | Calculations for the Variance and Standard Deviation in Judge 2's Sentencing ($n = 20$) |

x	$x_i - \bar{x}$	$(x_i - \bar{x})^2$
1	$1 - 9 = -8$	64
2	$2 - 9 = -7$	49
2	$2 - 9 = -7$	49
3	$3 - 9 = -6$	36
3	$3 - 9 = -6$	36
3	$3 - 9 = -6$	36
4	$4 - 9 = -5$	25
4	$4 - 9 = -5$	25
5	$5 - 9 = -4$	16
8	$8 - 9 = -1$	1
9	$9 - 9 = 0$	0
10	$10 - 9 = 1$	1
11	$11 - 9 = 2$	4
14	$14 - 9 = 5$	25
15	$15 - 9 = 6$	36
15	$15 - 9 = 6$	36
16	$16 - 9 = 7$	49
17	$17 - 9 = 8$	64
18	$18 - 9 = 9$	81
20	$20 - 9 = 11$	121
		$\Sigma = 754$

Steps in Calculating the Sample Standard Deviation

Step 1: Calculate the mean.

Step 2: Subtract the mean from each score: $x_i - \bar{X}$. This is called taking the deviation from the mean.

Step 3: Square the deviation of each score from the mean: $(x_i - \bar{X})^2$.

(Continued)

(Continued)

Step 4: Sum the squared deviations for all scores, starting with the first score and continuing to the last score:

$$\sum_{i=1}^{n}(x_i - \bar{X})^2$$

This is called the sum of the squared deviations from the mean.

Step 5: Divide the number of scores by n minus 1:

$$\frac{\sum_{i=1}^{n}(x_i - \bar{X})^2}{n-1}$$

$$\sqrt{\frac{\sum_{i=1}^{n}(x_i - \bar{X})^2}{n-1}}$$

This is the sample standard deviation.

Since we already have the variances, let's quickly calculate the two standard deviations. First, for Judge 1:

$$s = \sqrt{s^2}$$
$$s = \sqrt{5.05}$$
$$s = 2.25$$

This value is measured in units that are consistent with the measurement units of the variable, in this case years sentenced. So we can interpret this by saying that the average variation around the sentences handed down by Judge 1 for this sample of 20 robbery defendants was 2.25 units (years) around the mean sentence length of 9 years. The standard deviation for Judge 2 is

$$s = \sqrt{s^2}$$
$$s = \sqrt{39.68}$$
$$s = 6.30$$

For Judge 2, the average variation around the sentences handed down is 6.30 units (years) around the mean of 9 years. It should be noted that you should never compare standard deviation values across variables that are measuring the same thing. In this case, we have the same variables, so the comparison makes sense. Because the standard deviation is much larger for Judge 2's sentences compared with those of Judge 1, we can say there is more dispersion or heterogeneity for Judge 2's sentencing practices.

Case Study

Self-Control for Delinquent Youths

Let's go through one more example of calculating the variance and standard deviation with ungrouped data before moving on to the grouped case. Michael Gottfredson and Travis Hirschi (1990) theorized that those individuals who had low self-control would be at greater risk for engaging in crime, delinquency, and other self-destructive behaviors. Studies have indicated consistent support for this theory (Meldrum, Barnes, & Hay, 2015). In Table 4.15, we have a sample of males from a juvenile correctional facility. To measure their self-reported self-control, suppose we asked them a number of questions about risk-taking behavior and their ability to delay gratification along with other questions intended to measure individual levels of self-control. The self-control scale has a low of 65, indicating very low self-control, and a high of 150, indicating very high levels of self-control. We find in this sample of 25 youths that the mean self-control score is 91.00.

The second column of Table 4.15 presents the deviations from the mean, and the third column presents the squared deviations from the mean. If you were to sum the second column (the deviations from the mean), you should obtain

$$\sum_{i=1}^{n}(x_i - \bar{X}) = 0$$

The sum of the third column gives us the numerator for the sample variance, the sum of the squared deviations from the mean. In this example, the sum of the squared deviations is equal to 2,052. We can very easily obtain the sample variance by dividing this by $n - 1$. The variance of these self-control scores, then, is equal to

$$s^2 = \frac{2,052}{24}$$
$$s^2 = 85.50$$

The average squared distance of each self-control score from the mean of 91 is equal to 85.5. The standard deviation is equal to

$$s = \sqrt{\frac{2,052}{24}}$$
$$s = \sqrt{85.50}$$
$$s = 9.25$$

The interpretation of this is more understandable: For this sample of incarcerated male adolescents, the average self-control score is 91 with an average variability around this mean of 9.25 units. In this case, we can only refer to the scores as units since they are not measured in any more understandable units such as years, dollars, convictions, and so on. Let's move on to calculate the variance and standard deviation from grouped data.

Table 4.15	Self-Control Scores for a Sample of 25 Incarcerated Youths	
x	$x_i - \bar{x}$	$(x_i - \bar{x})^2$
85	85 − 91 = −6	36
100	100 − 91 = 9	81
87	87 − 91 = −4	16
93	93 − 91 = 2	4
78	78 − 91 = −13	169
103	103 − 91 = −12	144
88	88 − 91 = −3	9
94	94 − 91 = 3	9
94	94 − 91 = 3	9
101	101 − 91 = 10	100
94	94 − 91 = 3	9
92	92 − 91 = 1	1
83	83 − 91 = −8	64
70	70 − 91 = −21	441
110	110 − 91 = 19	361
87	87 − 91 = −4	16
91	91 − 91 = 0	0
79	79 − 91 = −12	144
84	84 − 91 = −7	49
88	88 − 91 = −3	9
90	90 − 91 = −1	1
104	104 − 91 = 13	169
100	100 − 91 = 9	81
98	98 − 91 = 7	49
82	82 − 91 = −9	81
		$\Sigma = 2,052$

Calculating the Variance and Standard Deviation With Grouped Data

In previous chapters, we have used continuous (interval/ratio)-level data to create class intervals that transformed our variable into the ordinal level of measurement. As we did in the last chapter, we will make the assumption that each score in any given class interval falls at the midpoint of the interval so that we can calculate a mean and a deviation from the mean score. Once we calculate the deviation from the mean, we can easily calculate a variance and standard deviation. To calculate a variance and standard deviation with grouped data, we need to make only two minor modifications to our formulas. Here is the formula to calculate a sample variance with grouped data:

$$S^2 = \frac{\sum\limits_{i=1}^{k} f_i(m_i - \bar{X})^2}{n-1}$$

(Formula 4-7)

where

k = the number of class intervals or categories

m_i = the midpoint of the ith interval

f_i = the frequency of the ith interval

$\bar{X}$ = the mean of the grouped frequency distribution

In words, here is what equation 4-7 is telling you to do. Start with the first class interval ($k = 1$) and subtract the mean from the midpoint of this interval. Square this difference or deviation, multiply that squared difference by the number of scores that are in that class interval, and then go to the next class interval and do the same thing, continuing until you do the last class interval. Finally, sum these values and divide by the total number of scores minus 1.

There are two differences between this equation for the variance of grouped sample data and the equation for the variance of ungrouped sample data (equation 4-4). The first difference is that we do not have an x_i score but rather have an m_i score since we use the midpoint of each class interval (m_i) as the score from which we subtract the mean. Second, we have to take into account that there may be more than one score in a given class interval—that, in fact, there are f_i scores in each class interval, all of which are assumed to lie at the midpoint. Hence, rather than taking $(m_i - \bar{X})^2 f$ number of times (one for each case in the interval), we multiply $(m_i - \bar{X})^2$ by the number of scores in the interval. Once we have the variance of a sample of grouped data, we can very easily find the sample standard deviation by taking the square root of the variance just as we did with ungrouped data:

$$s = \sqrt{\frac{\sum\limits_{i=1}^{k} f_i(m_i - \bar{X})^2}{n-1}}$$

(Formula 4-8)

Case Study

Time Until Rearrest for a Sample of Released Inmates

Let's do an example of calculating the variance and standard deviation with grouped data.

Table 4.16 shows a very familiar data set. It is the time-until-rearrest data for our sample of 120 inmates released from a correctional institution and followed up until they were rearrested. Remember that this is a sample in which all were eventually rearrested. Table 4.16 gives the stated class limits for each interval, the midpoint of the interval, and the frequency for each interval. In Chapter 3, we learned that the mean of these grouped data was 31.02 days. To make our calculations a little easier, let's calculate the variance and standard deviation with a mean of 31 days. You can refer back to Chapter 3 for the steps involved in calculating the mean with grouped data.

Steps in Calculating the Sample Variance and Standard Deviation With Grouped Data

Step 1: Determine the midpoint of each class interval (m_i).

Step 2: Calculate the mean $(\overline{X})$ from the grouped data.

Step 3: Subtract the mean from the midpoint $(m_i - \overline{X})$ of the first interval.

Step 4: Square the deviation of the midpoint from the mean: $(m_i - \overline{X})^2$.

Step 5: Multiply the squared deviation of the midpoint from the mean by the frequency for the class interval: $f_i(m_i - \overline{X})^2$.

Step 6: Repeat Steps 2 to 4 for each class interval, starting with the first and ending with the last.

Step 7: Sum the $f_i(m_i - \overline{X})^2$ for all class intervals.

Step 8: Divide the result in Step 7 by the number of scores minus 1:

$$\frac{\left(\sum\limits_{i=1}^{k} f_i \left(m_i - \overline{X} \right)^2 \right)}{n-1}$$

This is the variance for grouped data.

Step 9: Take the square root of this:

$$\sqrt{\frac{\left(\sum\limits_{i=1}^{k} f_i \left(m_i - \overline{X} \right)^2 \right)}{n-1}}$$

This is the sample standard deviation for grouped data.

We show the necessary calculations to calculate the variance for these grouped data in Table 4.17. The sum of the squared deviations about the mean for these grouped data is equal to 2,925. Now we are ready to calculate the variance:

$$s^2 = \frac{\left(\sum\limits_{i=1}^{k} f_i (m_i - \overline{X})^2 \right)}{n-1}$$

$$s^2 = \frac{2,925}{119}$$

$$s^2 = 24.58$$

The average squared distance of each score from the mean, then, is 24.58 days. Since we have the variance, the standard deviation would be

Table 4.16 Stated Class Limits, Midpoints, and Frequencies for Grouped Frequency Distribution of Time-Until-Rearrest Data ($n = 120$)

Stated Class Limits	Midpoints (m_i)	f
17–19	18	4
20–22	21	1
23–25	24	12
26–28	27	16
29–31	30	28
32–34	33	28
35–37	36	21
38–40	39	10

Table 4.17	Calculations for Variance and Standard Deviation for Time-Until-Rearrest Data ($n = 120$)

Midpoint of Class Interval	$m_i - \bar{X}$	$(m_i - \bar{X})^2$	f_i	$f_i(m_i - \bar{X})^2$
18	$18 - 31 = -13$	169	4	$4(169) = 676$
21	$21 - 31 = -10$	100	1	$1(100) = 100$
24	$24 - 31 = -7$	49	12	$12(49) = 588$
27	$27 - 31 = -4$	16	16	$16(16) = 256$
30	$30 - 31 = -1$	1	28	$28(1) = 28$
33	$33 - 31 = 2$	4	28	$28(4) = 112$
36	$36 - 31 = 5$	25	21	$21(25) = 525$
39	$39 - 31 = 8$	64	10	$10(64) = 640$
				$\Sigma = 2{,}925$

$$s^2 = \sqrt{\frac{\left(\sum_{i=1}^{k} f_i(m_i - \bar{X})^2\right)}{n-1}}$$

$$s^2 = \sqrt{\frac{2{,}925}{119}}$$

$$s^2 = 4.96$$

In words, the average time until rearrest for this sample of offenders is 31 days with an average variability around this mean of 4.96 units (about 5 days).

You may be wondering how much precision we lost by categorizing the original interval- and ratio-level time-until-rearrest data into ordinal-level class intervals. Recall from Chapter 3 that the mean with the time-until-rearrest data when measured at the interval/ratio level was 31.075 days (and 31.025 days when the data were grouped). For the grouped data, we learned in the previous paragraph that the variance was 24.58 days and the standard deviation was 4.96. When these 120 observations were kept at their original interval/ratio level of measurement, the variance was 24.81 and the standard deviation was 4.98. Clearly, in this case we have not lost much precision in our data by grouping the values into class intervals.

Computational Formulas for Variance and Standard Deviation

In the last two sections, we provided you with what are called definitional formulas for the variance and standard deviation because they clearly show what these measures of dispersion capture. By taking the term $(x_i - \bar{X})^2$ (or m_i for grouped data), you can quickly see that they are based on the squared distance of each score from the mean of the scores. Although these formulas are useful because we can see exactly how dispersion is being measured, some students find them a little difficult to use, and all the calculations provide opportunities for error. In this section, we will provide several computational formulas that you might find easier to use in calculating the variance and standard deviation. We will then use these formulas with data from earlier in the chapter to show that we get the same result no matter which formula we use.

When we have ungrouped data, the computational formulas for the sample variance and standard deviation are

$$\text{Variance} = s^2 = \frac{\Sigma(x_i^2) - \frac{(\Sigma x_i)^2}{n}}{n-1} \qquad \text{(Formula 4-9)}$$

$$\text{Standard deviation} = s = \sqrt{\frac{\Sigma(x_i^2) - \frac{(\Sigma x_i)^2}{n}}{n-1}} \qquad \text{(Formula 4-10)}$$

where

$\Sigma x_i^2 =$ the sum of each squared x score

$\Sigma(x_i)^2 =$ the sum of the x scores squared

$n =$ the total number of scores

These computational formulas for ungrouped data require that we obtain three quantities. The first of these quantities is the sum of the squared x_i scores [$\Sigma(x_i^2)$]. To get this, we take each x_i score, square it (x_i^2), and then sum across all scores ($x_1^2 + x_2^2 + x_3^2 + \ldots + x_n^2$). The second quantity is the sum of the x_i scores squared. This is obtained by first summing across all x scores and then squaring that sum ($x_1 + x_2 + x_3 + \ldots + x_n$)^2. The third quantity is simply the number of scores or n. As measures of dispersion, these computational formulas may not make as much intuitive sense to you as the definitional formulas, but they may be easier to use because they involve fewer calculations. Rather than taking the square of each score from the mean, all you have to do with the computational formula is to take the squares of the raw scores and the sum of the raw scores squared.

Let's practice one problem with these computational formulas before moving on to the computational formulas for grouped data. Let's use the sentencing data from the two judges we reported in Table 4.1. We reproduce these data along with the squared x scores in Table 4.18. Using the computational formula for Judge 1, we have the following estimates of the variance and standard deviation:

$$s^2 = \frac{\Sigma(x_i^2) - \frac{(\Sigma x_i)^2}{n}}{n-1}$$

$$s^2 = \frac{1,716 - \frac{(180)^2}{20}}{19}$$

$$s^2 = \frac{1,716 - 1,620}{19}$$

$$s^2 = 5.05 \text{ this is the variance}$$

$$s = \sqrt{5.05}$$

$$s = 2.25 \text{ this is the standard deviation}$$

Steps for Using Computational Formulas for Variance and Standard Deviation With Ungrouped Data

Step 1: Square each of the x_i scores and sum these squared values: $\Sigma(x_i^2)$.

Step 2: Add all of the x scores, square this sum, and divide by the number of scores:

$$\frac{(\Sigma x_i)^2}{n}$$

Step 3: Subtract the results in Step 2 from the value in Step 1:

$$\Sigma(x_i^2) - \frac{(\Sigma x_i)^2}{n}$$

Step 4: Divide this by the number of scores minus 1:

$$\frac{\Sigma(x_i^2) - \dfrac{(\Sigma x_i)^2}{n}}{n-1}$$

This is the variance.

Step 5: Take the square root of Step 4:

$$\sqrt{\frac{\Sigma(x_i^2) - \dfrac{(\Sigma x_i)^2}{n}}{n-1}}$$

This is the standard deviation.

Table 4.18 Data and Calculations for Variance and Standard Deviation: Judge Sentencing Data From Table 4.1

Judge 1		Judge 2	
x	x²	x	x²
5	25	1	1
7	49	2	4
7	49	2	4
7	49	3	9
7	49	3	9
7	49	3	9
8	64	4	16
8	64	4	16
8	64	5	25
8	64	8	64
9	81	9	81
9	81	10	100
9	81	11	121
10	100	14	196
11	121	15	225
11	121	15	225
11	121	16	256
12	144	17	289
12	144	18	324
14	196	20	400
$\Sigma = 180$	$\Sigma = 1{,}716$	$\Sigma = 180$	$\Sigma = 2{,}374$

For Judge 2, the variance and standard deviation are

$$s^2 = \frac{\Sigma(x_i^2) - \dfrac{(\Sigma x_i)^2}{n}}{n-1}$$

$$s^2 = \frac{2{,}374 - \dfrac{(180)^2}{20}}{19}$$

$s^2 = 39.68$ this is the variance

$s = \sqrt{s^2}$

$s = 6.30$ this is the standard deviation

These results with the computational formula are exactly the same as the estimated variance and standard deviation we got when we used the definitional formulas earlier in the chapter. We also have computational formulas to use when we have grouped data. With grouped data, the computational formula for the variance and standard deviation are

$$\text{Variance} = s^2 = \frac{\Sigma(m_i^2 f_i) - \dfrac{\left(\Sigma m_i f_i\right)^2}{n}}{n=1} \qquad \text{(Formula 4-11)}$$

$$\text{Standard deviation} = s = \sqrt{\frac{\Sigma(m_i^2 f_i) - \dfrac{\left(\Sigma m_i f_i\right)^2}{n}}{n-1}} \qquad \text{(Formula 4-12)}$$

where

$(\Sigma m_i^2 f_i)$ = the sum of each squared midpoint (m_i) times the frequency of the class interval (f_i)

$(\Sigma m_i f_i)^2$ = the sum of the product of each midpoint (m_i) multiplied by the frequency of the class interval (f_i), with the sum then squared

n = the total number of scores

These computational formulas for ungrouped data require that we obtain three quantities. The first of these quantities requires us to square the midpoint of each class interval (m_i^2), multiply each squared midpoint by the frequency of that class interval $[f_i(m_i^2)]$, and then sum across all intervals $(\Sigma\, m_i^2 f)$. The second quantity is obtained by multiplying the midpoint of each class interval by the frequency of that interval $[f_i(m_i)]$, summing across all class intervals, and then squaring this sum $[(\Sigma\, m_i f_i)^2]$. The third quantity is simply the number of scores or n.

Table 4.19	Calculations for Variance and Standard Deviation for Grouped Time-Until-Rearrest Data				
Midpoint	mf	f_i	$m_i^2 f_i$	$m_i f_i$
18	324	4	1,296	72
21	441	1	441	21
24	576	12	6,912	288
27	729	16	11,664	432
30	900	28	25,200	840
33	1,089	28	30,492	924
36	1,296	21	27,216	756
39	1,521	10	15,210	390
			$\Sigma = 118,431$	3,723

Steps for Using Computational Formulas for Variance and Standard Deviation With Grouped Data

Step 1: Square each of the midpoints of the class intervals (m_i), multiply each of these squared midpoints by the frequency of its class interval (f_i), and then sum across all class intervals: $\left[\Sigma f_i(m_i^2)\right]$.

Step 2: Multiply each midpoint by the frequency of its class interval $(f_i m_i)$, sum across all class intervals, and square this sum:

$$\left[\Sigma(m_i f_i)\right]^2$$

Step 3: Subtract the results in Step 2 from the value in Step 1:

$$\Sigma(m_i^2 f_i) - \frac{\left(\Sigma m_i f_i\right)^2}{n}$$

(Continued)

(Continued)

Step 4: Divide this by the number of scores minus 1:

$$\frac{\Sigma(m_i^2 f_i)\dfrac{\left(\Sigma m_i f_i\right)^2}{n}}{n-1}$$

This is the variance.

Step 5: Take the square root of Step 4:

$$\frac{\Sigma(m_i^2 f_i)\dfrac{\left(\Sigma m_i f_i\right)^2}{n}}{n-1}$$

This is the standard deviation.

Let's use these computational formulas for grouped data to calculate the variance and standard deviation of our time-until-rearrest data that appeared in Table 4.6. We reproduce those data and all the necessary calculations for the variance and standard deviation in Table 4.19. The variance and standard deviation are

$$s^2 = \frac{\Sigma(m_i^2 f_i) - \dfrac{\left(\Sigma m_i f_i\right)^2}{n}}{n-1}$$

$$s^2 = \frac{118,431 - \dfrac{(3,723)^2}{120}}{119}$$

$$s^2 = \frac{118,431 - 115,506.075}{119}$$

$$s^2 = 24.58$$

$$s = \sqrt{s^2}$$

$$s = 4.96$$

These are exactly the same values for the variance and standard deviation that we obtained when we used the definitional formulas.

Summary

In this chapter, we learned about measures of dispersion that capture how different the values of a variable are from some reference point. Just as there are different measures of central tendency, and which one is appropriate depends on the level of measurement of a variable, different measures of dispersion also correspond to the levels of measurement.

For variables measured at the nominal or ordinal level, a common measure of dispersion is the variation ratio. The variation ratio measures dispersion with reference to the mode and reflects the extent to which the observations do not cluster in the modal category. When we have data measured at the interval/ratio level (or can assume we have this level of measurement), there are more measures of dispersion to employ. The simplest is the range, which is merely the difference between the highest and lowest values of a variable. The interquartile range is the difference between the score at the third quartile (the 75th percentile) and the first quartile (the 25th percentile). Thus, the interquartile range captures the dispersion present in the middle 50% of a distribution of continuous scores. By far the most common measures of dispersion for continuous (interval/ratio)-level data are the variance and standard deviation. The variance and standard deviation use the mean as the reference point for measuring the amount of dispersion in a variable. Both are based on the deviation from the mean, which is the difference between a given score and the mean of its distribution.

Key Terms

> Review key terms with eFlashcards. Visit study.sagepub.com/paternoster.

interquartile range (IQR)   88
mean deviation score   91
measures of dispersion   81

$Q_1, Q_2, Q_3,$ and Q_4 88
range   86
standard deviation   95

variance   94
variation ratio   82

Key Formulas

We also learned that the boxplot, a technique under the rubric of exploratory data analysis, is a useful tool for displaying the dispersion of a variable. With one glance at a boxplot, you can determine the shape of a distribution, along with that distribution's center, its variability, and any abnormalities that may exist.

Variation ratio (formula 4-1):

$$VR = 1 - \frac{f_{\text{modal}}}{n}$$

Range:

$$\text{Highest } x_i \text{ score} - \text{Lowest } x_i \text{ score}$$

Interquartile range (formula 4-2):

$$IQR = XQ_3 - XQ_1$$

Variance of a population (formula 4-3):

$$\sigma^2 = \frac{\sum_{i-1}^{N}(x_i - \bar{X})^2}{N}$$

Variance of a sample (formula 4-4):

$$s^2 = \frac{\sum_{i=1}^{n}(x - \bar{X})^2}{n-1}$$

Standard deviation of a population (formula 4-5):

$$\sigma = \sqrt{\frac{\sum_{i=1}^{N}(x - \bar{X})^2}{N}}$$

Standard deviation of a sample (formula 4-6):

$$s = \sqrt{\frac{\sum_{i=1}^{n}(x - \bar{X})^2}{n-1}}$$

Variance of a sample with grouped data (formula 4-7):

$$s^2 = \frac{\sum_{i=1}^{n} f_i(m_i - \bar{X})^2}{n-1}$$

Standard deviation of a sample with grouped data (formula 4-8):

$$s = \sqrt{\frac{\sum_{i=1}^{n} f_i(m_i - \bar{X})^2}{n-1}}$$

Computational formula for sample variance with ungrouped data (formula 4-9):

$$s^2 = \frac{\sum(x_i^2) - \frac{(\sum x_i)^2}{n}}{n-1}$$

Computational formula for sample standard deviation with ungrouped data (formula 4-10):

$$s = \sqrt{\frac{\sum(x_i^2) - \frac{(\sum x_i)^2}{n}}{n-1}}$$

Computational formula for sample variance with grouped data (formula 4-11):

$$s^2 = \frac{\sum(m_i^2 f_i) - \frac{(\sum m_i f_i)^2}{n}}{n-1}$$

Computational formula for sample standard deviation with grouped data (formula 4-12):

$$s = \sqrt{\frac{\sum(m_i f_i^2) - \frac{(\sum m_i f_i)^2}{n}}{n-1}}$$

Practice Problems

➤ Test your understanding of chapter content. Take the practice quiz at study.sagepub.com/paternoster.

1. What is the difference between the central tendency and the dispersion in a group of scores, and why is it important to know about and report both the central tendency and the dispersion of our variables?

2. A sample of 1,090 youths who had been arrested for one of four offenses (property, violent, drug, or status offense) were asked what type of crime they committed previous to this one. Below are the data. As you can see, of the 125 current property offenders, 75 of them last committed a property offense; of the 110 current violent offenders, 30 of them last committed a violent offense; of the 230 drug offenders, 110 of them last committed a drug offense; and of the 575 status offenders, 320 of them last committed a status offense. With these data, calculate the variation ratio for each type of current offense. Which type of current offense has the most variation/dispersion and which has the least?

		Current Offense Is:			
		Property	Violent	Drug	Status
Previous offense was:	Property	75	50	40	120
	Violent	10	30	30	20
	Drug	20	10	110	115
	Status	20	20	50	320
Total		125	110	230	575

3. A sample of 205 high school males were asked to report the number of times during the past year that they had stolen something that was worth at least $25 in value. Their responses are shown in the following grouped frequency distribution. With these data, calculate the variance and standard deviation.

Number of Thefts	f
0–4	76
5–9	52
10–14	38
15–19	21
20–24	10
25–29	8

4. You take a random sample of 20 females from the population of female offenders incarcerated in a state prison system and find out how many years of school they have completed. The data are shown as follows. Calculate the following:

a. The range
b. The interquartile range
c. The variance
d. The standard deviation

Person	Years of Education	Person	Years of Education
1	11	11	9
2	8	12	9
3	12	13	5
4	9	14	9
5	9	15	7
6	9	16	6
7	10	17	10
8	10	18	12
9	10	19	9
10	11	20	5

5. You have data on the race of the new inmates committed to a state's penitentiary for 4 years: 1980, 1990, 2000, and 2010. Is there a trend in the dispersion found in these data?

Year	Race	f
1980	White	852
	Black	675
	Hispanic	112
	Asian	25
	Other	59
1990	White	979
	Black	756
	Hispanic	262
	Asian	86
	Other	78
2000	White	1,211
	Black	925
	Hispanic	636
	Asian	310
	Other	120
2010	White	1,300
	Black	1,017
	Hispanic	750
	Asian	400
	Other	145

6. The data at right show the 2012 arrest rates for robbery (per 100,000 persons) for a sample of 18 states. For these data, determine the following:

   a. The range
   b. The interquartile range
   c. The variance
   d. The standard deviation

State	Robbery Arrest Rate	State	Robbery Arrest Rate
Arizona	29	New York	70
Arkansas	22	North Carolina	41
Colorado	17	North Dakota	7
Georgia	32	Oregon	30
Idaho	6	Pennsylvania	51
Kentucky	29	South Carolina	32
Maine	17	Texas	25
Maryland	56	Utah	13
Missouri	33	Wyoming	5

Source: Adapted from Puzzanchera and Kang © 2014 from the Office of Juvenile Justice and Delinquency Prevention.

STUDENT STUDY SITE

WANT A BETTER GRADE?

Get the tools you need to sharpen your study skills. Access practice quizzes, eFlashcards, data sets, and SPSS exercises at **study.sagepub.com/paternoster.**

CHAPTER 5

Moving Beyond Description

Introducing Inferential Statistics—Probability Distributions and an Introduction to Hypothesis Testing

> *[A]s we know, there are known knowns; there are things we know we know. We also know there are known unknowns; that is to say we know there are some things we do not know. But there are also unknown unknowns—the ones we don't know we don't know.*
>
> —Donald Rumsfeld
>
> *What did he just say?*
>
> —John Bachman-Paternoster

LEARNING OBJECTIVES

1. Explain the basic notion of probability of being in "the long run" compared with predictions of single cases.

2. Describe the notion of independence between variables.

3. Summarize the difference between probability distributions and empirical distributions.

4. Identify the rules of probability.

5. Describe how probability distributions are used to test hypotheses.

6. State the difference between a null hypothesis and a research hypothesis.

7. Identify areas under the normal curve and how we can transform values from a variable distribution to z scores and determine the probability of their occurrence.

8. Describe why probability theory is important for criminological and criminal-justice-related research.

▣ Introduction

Imagine you are a probation officer in charge of a new program called Honest Opportunity Probation and Enforcement (HOPE). This program was first implemented in Hawaii and is based on regular random drug testing and swift and certain sanctions to positive drug tests. In contrast to traditional probation where multiple violations of parole may be tolerated, probationers in the HOPE program know that if they commit another crime or fail a drug test, they will immediately be sent to jail. This may sound severe, but the difference is that instead of being sent to prison for an extended sentence, the sentence is short. As such, the sanction is swift but not severe. Although it may be swift and certain, the sanction is typically only a few days in jail. Although early evaluations of the HOPE program in Hawaii seemed to be successful in reducing parole violations, results of replication studies in other locations have not been consistent (Zajac, Lattimore, Dawes, & Winger, 2015). If you were a probation officer who wanted to determine whether your implementation of the HOPE program worked, you would need to conduct inferential statistics to do so. And to conduct inferential statistics, you would need a solid understanding of probability theory!

So far in this book, we have discussed the differences between samples and populations along with how to organize, display, and summarize important features of your data. Statistical tools like frequency and percentage distributions, graphs and charts, measures of central tendency and dispersion, and the techniques of exploratory data analysis are all useful ways to describe variables. As you learned in Chapter 1, this collection of statistical tools is often referred to as descriptive statistics. Descriptive statistics are useful in helping us to understand what our data look like and in communicating the properties and characteristics of our data to others. Descriptive statistics do exactly what they say—they usually describe characteristics of our sample. In addition to describing our variables, however, we often wish to do other things such as use the information we have collected from our sample to make an inference about some unknown population value or to make a decision about the relationship between two variables in a population based on the relationship we find in our sample data. A very important part of statistical work in criminology and criminal justice, therefore, does not consist of describing information gathered from a sample but rather consists of using the sample data to make inferences about some unknown population value. Recall from Chapter 1 that these statistics are called inferential statistics, and they will be the focus of our attention for the remainder of this book.

Descriptive statistics: Statistics used to describe the distribution of a sample or population.

Inferential statistics: Statistical tools for estimating how likely it is that a statistical result based on data from a random sample is representative of the population from which the sample has been selected.

Student Study Site

Visit the open-access Student Study Site at **study.sagepub.com/paternoster** to access additional study tools including mobile-friendly eFlashcards, web quizzes, links to SAGE journal articles, additional data sets, SPSS exercises, and more!

An important set of tools you will learn in this book are the tools of inferential statistics. In inferential statistics, we have information that we observed from our sample data, and with it we wish to make an inference to a larger population. The foundation of inferential statistics, the link between our sample data and the population, is probability theory. You do not need to be an expert in probability theory to understand the statistical procedures in this book, but the background provided in this chapter should prove helpful. In this chapter, we will discuss two notions of probability: the chance that an event occurs in one trial and the chance that an event occurs "over the long run." We will learn how to calculate the probability of events, including unconditional, conditional, and joint probabilities. To calculate these probabilities, you will learn some basic probability rules. With this basic knowledge of probability, we will apply these rules and learn about probability distributions, which are extremely important because we use these theoretical distributions to conduct hypothesis tests. There are two probability distributions that you will learn in this chapter: a distribution for events that have only two outcomes (binomial) and a continuous distribution (the standard normal distribution). The standard normal distribution is one of the most useful probability distributions because of a theorem in statistics called the central limit theorem, which is the foundation for many statistical tests you will learn in the remainder of the book.

▣ Probability—What Is It Good for? Absolutely Everything!

The foundation of inferential statistics is probability theory. Probability theory can be a very difficult foundation to understand, but in this chapter we will break it down into its most basic elements and rules. You no doubt already have some idea of what probability is because you have likely asked yourself questions like the following: "What is the chance that I will pass a test if I go out partying the night before rather than studying?" "What is the likelihood that I will win the lottery if I buy one ticket today?" "How likely is it that I will get stopped for running this kind of a yellowish-red traffic light?" Questions like these are all about the probability of an event. The answers you had to these typical questions are typically along the lines of "not likely but I will try anyway" or "a snowball's chance in hell." In this chapter, we will teach you to be a little more precise about how you speak about probabilities. To consider more precisely the concept of probability and how it applies to research problems in our field, we must first discuss the mathematical notion of probability.

In mathematical terms, the probability of an event has a definite meaning. The probability of an event is defined as the number of times that a specific event can occur relative to the total number of times that any event can occur. The probability of an event (say event A) is often written as $P(A)$, and the total number of times that any event can occur is often referred to as the number of trials. For simplicity's sake, let's think about the simple case of drawing an ace from a deck of cards. There are four aces in a standard deck of 52 cards. The probability of selecting one ace from the deck, then, is

$$P(\text{Ace}) = \frac{4\,(\text{aces})}{52\,(\text{cards})} = .0769$$

since there are four possible ways of an ace occurring (an ace of hearts, diamonds, clubs, or spades) and there are 52 possible cards (52 possible outcomes) in the deck. Similarly, if we were to flip a coin, what is the probability that it would land on heads? Since there are two and only two possible outcomes in one flip of a coin (either heads or tails), and we want to know the probability of one possible outcome (a heads), the probability would be

$$P(\text{Heads}) = \frac{1(\text{heads})}{2(\text{possible outcomes in one flip})} = .50$$

We need to maintain a distinction in this book between two related but different notions of the concept of the probability of an event. The first conception of probability is the one we have just discussed. The probability of an event is the number of times an event can occur in a given number of trials. In our coin-flipping example, the probability of getting a heads in one flip of a coin is .5. This does not mean, however, that if we flip a coin 10 times, we will always get 5 heads and 5 tails even though the probability of a heads (and that of a tails, of course) is .5.

The second notion of probability—let's refer to this as the sampling notion of probability—tells us, however, that *in the long run, the most likely or most probable* outcome when you flip a coin 10 times is that you will get 5 heads and 5 tails. Sometimes, but rarely, you will observe 0 heads or 0 tails in 10 flips. Sometimes, but less rarely, you will observe 1 heads or 1 tails, but the most likely or most probable outcome if you flip a coin 10 times will be 5 heads and 5 tails. If you were to repeat the coin flip experiment a large number of times (say 10,000 times), the outcome with the greatest frequency (and, therefore, the one with the greatest probability) would be 5 heads and 5 tails. To understand probability better, we need to learn some basic rules.

🔲 The Rules of Probability

The first probability rule is called the bounding rule (Rule 1). Recall that the formula for determining a probability is

$$P(A) = \frac{\text{Number of times event } A \text{ can occur}}{\text{Total number of possible events or trials}}$$

Let's designate the denominator, the total number of events, as n. Note that we can have no fewer than 0 events of A out of n trials and no more than n events of A out of n trials. This means that the minimum value of a probability is $0/n$, or zero, and the maximum value is n/n, or 1.0. The minimum probability occurs when event A occurs 0 times out of n, and the maximum probability occurs when event A occurs n times out of n. This expresses the **bounding rule of probabilities**—the probability that any event is bounded by 0 and 1.0. Any probability can never be less than 0 or greater than 1.0. A probability of 0 means that event A is impossible, probabilities close to 0 imply that event A is unlikely to occur, probabilities close to 1.0 imply that there is a good chance that event A will occur, and a probability of 1.0 implies that event A will always occur.

The probability of an event *not* occurring is called the **complement of an event**. We have defined the probability of event A occurring as $P(A)$. The probability of event A not occurring, $P(\text{not-}A)$, is referred to as the complement of event A. Based on the bounding rule (since the maximum probability can only be 1.0), if the probability of event A is $P(A)$, then the probability that A will not occur, or the probability of its complement, must be $1 - P(A)$. For example, the probability of drawing one ace from a deck of cards is $4 / 52 = .0769$ because there are four aces in the deck of 52 cards. The probability of not drawing an ace, therefore (the probability of drawing any card but an ace), must be $48 / 52 = .9231$, or $1 - .0769$. The bounding rule tells us, therefore, that the sum of an event and its complement is 1.0.

Notice one thing about the probability of an event and its complement—they cannot both occur at the same time. If the complement of event A consists of all occurrences that are not A, then we cannot have both A occurring and not-A occurring. For example, we cannot both select an ace from a deck of cards (event A) and select a card other than an ace (event not-A) in a single draw from the deck. In other words, an event and its complement are **mutually exclusive events**. The probability of two mutually exclusive events occurring at the same time, therefore, is zero.

Figure 5.1 shows a Venn diagram that illustrates the notion of mutually exclusive events. Note that the areas covered by the probability of event A and event B never overlap or intersect. This means that their joint occurrence is impossible. They cannot both occur at the same time, so they are mutually exclusive events.

Bounding rule of probabilities: Probability of any event can never be less than zero or greater than $0 \le P(A) \le 1.0$.

Complement of an event: Complement of event A is the set of all outcomes of a sample space that are not A. It is calculated as $1 - P(A)$.

Mutually exclusive events: Events that cannot occur at the same time. In other words, there is no intersection of mutually exclusive events, so their joint probability is equal to zero.

With our knowledge of mutually exclusive events, we can now discuss the second rule of probabilities—the addition rule of probabilities. The addition rule will help us to answer the question, "What is the probability *of either event A or event B occurring*?" This rule is also known as the "or" rule because it allows us to calculate the probability of one event *or* the other event occurring. There are two forms of the addition rule for probabilities: a general version and a more restricted or limited version. The restricted version covers instances where we can assume that all events are mutually exclusive. In the general version, we cannot maintain this assumption. We call this the *general form* of the addition rule because you can also use this rule when events are or are not mutually exclusive. The restricted rule is a little simpler, so we will discuss it first.

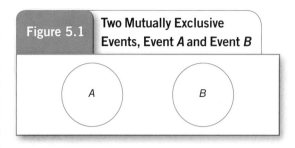

Figure 5.1 Two Mutually Exclusive Events, Event *A* and Event *B*

The **restricted addition rule of probabilities (Rule 2a)** states that the probability of either of two mutually exclusive events occurring is equal to the sum of their separate probabilities. In other words, if event *A* and event *B* are mutually exclusive events, then the probability of event *A* or *B* occurring, which is written $P(A$ or $B)$, is equal to $P(A) + P(B)$.

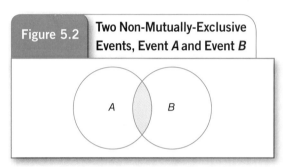

Figure 5.2 Two Non-Mutually-Exclusive Events, Event *A* and Event *B*

What if we can't assume the events are mutually exclusive? Figure 5.2 shows a Venn diagram of two events, event *A* and event *B*, which are not mutually exclusive. Recall that non-mutually-exclusive events can occur at the same time. The possibility of their joint occurrence is illustrated in the Venn diagram by the intersection of the two events. The intersection of the two events shows the area where both event *A* and event *B* are occurring. The greater the area of the intersection of the two events is, the greater the probability of their joint occurrence.

When two events are not mutually exclusive, we cannot use the restricted version of the addition rule and must apply the **general addition rule of probabilities (Rule 2b)**. We will see why in a moment. This form of the addition rule states that, for two non-mutually-exclusive events, events *A* and *B*, the probability of event *A* or event *B* occurring is equal to the sum of their separate probabilities minus the probability of their joint occurrence: $P(A$ or $B) = P(A) + P(B) - P(A$ and $B)$. The new part of the addition rule is the last term, $P(A$ and $B)$, and is the probability of events *A* and *B* occurring at the same time or simultaneously—that is, their *joint probability*. For example, the probability of drawing a heart from a deck of cards is 13 out of 52, and the probability of drawing a king is 4 out of 52. The joint probability of a heart and a king is the probability of drawing the king of hearts, or 1 out of 52. The probability of the king of hearts is the joint probability of a king and a heart occurring at the same time. When two events are not mutually exclusive, this joint probability must be subtracted from the sum of the two separate probabilities because, as we will see, it is counted twice: once in determining the probability of event *A* and again in determining the probability of event *B*.

Let's answer some probability questions that require the use of this general addition rule and find out why it is more general than the restricted rule. One prominent theory in criminology, *general strain theory,* maintains that participation in delinquent behavior is more likely when youths experience strain in the form of stressful or unpleasant stimuli. In Table 5.1, we show some data pertaining to two variables: whether a youth's parents were separated or divorced during the past year (a stressful event) and whether one of the children committed a delinquent act during the subsequent year.

What is the probability that parents were divorced/separated or the child did not commit a delinquent act? Note that these events are not mutually exclusive. How do we

Restricted addition rule of probabilities (Rule 2a): If two events are mutually exclusive, the probability of event *A* occurring or event *B* occurring is equal to the sum of their separate probabilities: $P(A$ or $B) = P(A) + P(B)$.

General addition rule of probabilities (Rule 2b): If two events are not mutually exclusive, the probability of event *A* occurring or event *B* occurring is equal to the sum of their separate probabilities minus their joint probability: $P(A$ or $B) = P(A) + P(B) - P(A$ and $B)$.

Table 5.1	Adolescents' Delinquent Conduct by Family Status			
	Number of Delinquent Acts Committed			
Parents Are Divorced/ Separated	0	1–4	5 or More	Total
No	125	60	15	200
Yes	10	35	65	110
Total	135	95	80	310

know this? To determine whether two events are mutually exclusive, ask yourself if it is possible for both events to occur simultaneously. In this case, is it possible that the parents could have experienced a separation or divorce and have a child who did not commit delinquent acts? By looking at Table 5.1, you should be able to see that the answer to that question is "yes"; in fact, there were 10 instances when there was both a separation/divorce and a non-delinquent child. There are instances, therefore, of separation/divorce and a child with no delinquent offenses. Since there is an intersection of the two events, separation/divorce and delinquency are not mutually exclusive. Thus, we cannot use the restricted form of the addition rule but must instead appeal to its general form. The probability of having separated/divorced parents and a non-delinquent child is equal to the probability of separated/divorced parents plus the probability of a non-delinquent child minus the probability of both separated/divorced parents and a non-delinquent child:

$$P(\text{divorced / separated or no delinquent acts}) = \frac{110}{310} + \frac{135}{310} - \frac{10}{310} = \frac{235}{310} = .76$$

Why do we have to subtract the joint occurrence of divorced/separated parents and no delinquent acts from the sum of the separate probabilities? Note that we included these 10 cases when we counted the number of divorced/separated parents and then again when we counted those with no delinquent acts. Since these 10 non-mutually-exclusive cases include those with both a divorced/separated parent and no delinquent acts, they are counted twice. The final term removes these cases that were counted twice.

In our discussion of the addition rule of probabilities for events that are not mutually exclusive, we introduced the concept of joint probability, or the simultaneous occurrence of two events. Recall that non-mutually-exclusive events are two or more events that can occur at the same time (see Figure 5.2) such as having divorced/separated parents (event A) and committing five or more delinquent acts (event B). We had to subtract the joint occurrence of two events from the sum of the separate probabilities in applying the general form of the addition rule (the "or rule"). What we did not discuss, however, was exactly how one calculates the joint probability of two or more events—that is, the probability of event A and event B both occurring.

The joint probability of two or more events is determined by applying the *multiplication rule of probabilities*. The multiplication rule of probabilities is often referred to as the "*and* rule" because with it we can determine the probability of both one event *and* another (or others) occurring. The application of the multiplication rule to two events is written as $P(A \text{ and } B)$. There are also two forms of the multiplication rule; one is more general in its application, and the other is used under more restricted conditions.

The restricted multiplication rule of probabilities (Rule 3a) concerns the case where the events are independent of one another. Two events are independent of each other when the occurrence of one event has no effect on (does not influence) the occurrence of another event. In other words, there is no relationship between independent events. For example, in two flips of a coin, the fact that the first flip resulted in a heads does not affect the outcome of the second flip—a heads is no more likely to follow a tails than to follow another heads. Later in this section, we will examine a more formal test for the independence of two events. If two or more events are independent, then the probability of their joint occurrence is equal to the product of their separate probabilities. For

Restricted multiplication rule of probabilities (Rule 3a): If two events are independent of each other, the probability of event A occurring and event B occurring is equal to the product of their separate probabilities: $P(A \text{ and } B) = P(A) \times P(B)$.

example, assuming that event *A* and event *B* are independent, the probability of both event *A* and event *B* occurring is equal to $P(A \text{ and } B) = P(A) \times P(B)$.

Let's take as our first example a coin toss. The probability of a heads (or of a tails) on any given flip of a fair coin is .5. In two flips of a coin, the probability of getting two heads is $.5 \times .5 = .25$. In three flips of a coin, the probability of getting three heads is $.5 \times .5 \times .5 = .125$.

What do we do when we cannot assume events are independent? In this case, we cannot use the restricted form of the multiplication rule but instead must use a more *general form*. The **general multiplication rule of probabilities (Rule 3b)** states that the probability of two non-independent events, events *A* and *B*, occurring is equal to the probability of event *A* times the **conditional probability** of event *B*: $P(A \text{ and } B) = P(A) \times P(B|A)$. The last term of this formula, the conditional probability, is something new and is read, "the conditional probability of event *B* given event *A*." We will learn about this and about the general multiplication rule by revisiting Table 5.1.

Previously, when we were interested in calculating a probability, we used as our denominator the total number of events. For example, in Table 5.1, the probability that any child will have committed 1–4 delinquent acts was found by dividing the number of children who committed 1–4 delinquent acts (95) by the total number of children (310), the number who theoretically could have committed 1–4 delinquent acts in our sample. This probability is called an unconditional probability. When we are interested in conditional probabilities, however, we are saying that some other event occurs first. The conditional probability of *B* given *A* asks, "What is the probability of event *B* occurring given that event *A* has already occurred?" In other words, the probability of *B* is now conditioned on *A*. In a conditional probability, the denominator is the number of events for event *A*, not the total number of events.

For example, in Table 5.1, the unconditional probability of 1–4 delinquent acts is .31, P(1–4 delinquent acts = 95 / 310). Now, what is the conditional probability of 1–4 delinquent acts *given that* there are divorced or separated parents [P(1–4 acts| divorced/separated parents)]? Before we calculate the probability of *B* (1–4 delinquent acts), event *A* (divorced/separated parents) has to occur first. So now let's look only at the subgroup of observations involving divorced/separated parents. There are 110 divorced/separated parents, and since we are conditioning on this event, this becomes the denominator of our probability. Of these 110 divorced/separated parents, 35 have children who committed 1–4 delinquent acts. The conditional probability of 1–4 delinquent acts given divorced/separated parents, therefore, is 35 / 110 = .32. In this case, the conditional probability is not that much different from the unconditional probability, but this will not always be the case.

What Is Independence?

We needed to learn about conditional probabilities in order to use the general version of the multiplication rule. Before we move on to this, however, we would like to discuss the notion of independence and its relationship to the multiplication rule. We have said that if we can assume that two events are independent of each other, then we can determine their joint probability, $P(A \text{ and } B)$, with the simpler restricted version of the multiplication rule, $P(A \text{ and } B) = P(A) \times P(B)$. If, however, our events are not independent, then we have to use the more restricted (and more complicated) general rule, $P(A \text{ and } B) = P(A) \times P(B|A)$. How do we know if two events are independent?

Remember that two events are **independent events** if one event occurring has no effect on the probability of the other event occurring. Our example of two independent events was flipping a coin two times—a heads on the second flip of a coin is no more or less likely to occur just because the first flip lands on heads. When two events are not independent, however, the outcome of one event influences the outcome of the other. If two events are independent, then knowing about the first event will help us to predict the second event better. A more formal way to state this is to say that *if two events*

General multiplication rule of probabilities (Rule 3b): If two events are not independent of each other, the probability of event *A* occurring and event *B* occurring is equal to the product of the unconditional probability of event *A* and the conditional probability of event *B* given *A*: $P(A \text{ and } B) = P(A) \times P(B|A)$.

Conditional probability: Probability of one event occurring (*A*) given that another event has occurred (*B*), written as $P(A|B)$.

Independent events: Two events, *A* and *B*, are independent when the unconditional probability of A is equal to the conditional probability of A given B: $P(A) = P(A|B)$. When two events are independent, knowledge of one event does not help to predict the probability of the other event occurring.

Table 5.2	Joint Frequency Distribution for Right- and Left-Handedness and Delinquency		

Handedness	Committed Delinquent Act Last Year?		Total
	No	Yes	
Left-handed	25	25	50
Right-handed	25	25	50
Total	50	50	100

(A *and* B) *are independent, then the unconditional probability of* A *will be equal to the conditional probability of* A *given* B: P(A) = P(A|B). In this instance, knowing that event B has occurred does not change the probability of event A. If two events (A and B) are not independent, however, the unconditional probability of A will not be equal to the conditional probability of A given B: $P(A) \neq P(A|B)$. In this case, knowing that event B has occurred does alter the probability of A occurring.

Table 5.2 presents the joint distribution of two variables or events based on information collected from 100 youths. Variable or event A is whether the youth was right- or left-handed, and variable or event B is whether the youth committed a delinquent act during the previous year. Let's find out what the probability is that a youth will have committed a delinquent act. Since 50 of the 100 youths committed at least one delinquent act, this unconditional probability of delinquency is equal to .50.

Now let's find out if knowing whether someone is right- or left-handed helps to predict whether he or she will engage in delinquency. What is the conditional probability of at least one delinquent act given that a youth was left-handed? Since there were 50 left-handed youths, and 25 of them had committed a delinquent offense during the past year, the conditional probability of delinquency given left-handedness is .50 (25 / 50). Now, what is the conditional probability of at least one delinquent act given that a youth was right-handed? Since there were 50 right-handed youths, and 25 of them had committed a delinquent offense during the past year, the conditional probability of delinquency given right-handedness is .50 (25 / 50). What we have discovered is that the unconditional probability of delinquency is equal to the conditional probability of delinquency given that the person is left-handed (and given the fact that the person is right-handed). Does knowing whether someone is left-handed help us to predict the probability that this person will be delinquent? No, because the conditional probability of delinquency given left-handedness (.5) is the same as the unconditional probability of delinquency (.5).

Now let's look at Table 5.3, where we have the joint distribution of two events for the same 100 youths. As before, 50 youths committed a delinquent act during the past year and 50 did not. Instead of handedness, however, the other event is whether the youth was impulsive according to a psychological test. In this instance, 50 of them were deemed to be impulsive and 50 were not. As in Table 5.2, the unconditional probability that a youth committed a delinquent act is .50 since 50 out of 100 youths committed a delinquent act.

Now, does knowing whether a youth was not impulsive affect this probability of a delinquent act? The conditional probability of a delinquent act given the fact that a youth was not impulsive is P(delinquency|not impulsive) = 10 / 50 = .20. The conditional probability of delinquency for those who were not impulsive is much less than the unconditional probability of delinquency (.20 vs. .50). Does knowing whether a youth was impulsive affect the probability of a delinquent act? The conditional probability of a delinquent act given the fact that a youth was impulsive is P(delinquency|impulsive) = 40 / 50 = .80. The unconditional probability of delinquency is not equal to the conditional probability of delinquency given being impulsive (.50 vs. .80). It seems that a youth who is impulsive has a much greater risk of being delinquent, and one who is not impulsive has a much lower risk. Does knowing the level of a youth's impulsivity affect the probability that the youth will be delinquent? The answer is yes; they youth is at a greatly reduced risk of delinquency if he or she is not impulsive and is at a greatly elevated risk of delinquency if he or she is impulsive. As such, knowing whether someone is impulsive *does* affect the outcome of delinquency, so we can say that the two events (delinquency and impulsivity) are not independent.

Now that we know about conditional probability and the independence of two events, we are ready to apply the more general form of the multiplication rule, which states that if two events, A and B, are not independent, then the probability of A and B occurring is equal to the probability of A times the probability of B given A: $P(A \text{ and } B) = P(A) \times P(B|A)$. Let's use this version of the multiplication rule to answer a few probability questions about Table 5.3. We already know that impulsivity and the commission of delinquent acts are not independent.

What is the probability that a youth has been rated not impulsive and has committed no delinquent acts? The answer is found by determining the unconditional probability of being not impulsive times the conditional probability of having no delinquent acts given the fact that a youth was not rated impulsive: P(not impulsive) = 50 / 100 = .50, P (not delinquent|not impulsive) = 40 / 50 = .80. Therefore, P(not impulsive and not delinquent) = .50 × .80 = .40.

What is the probability that a youth has been rated impulsive but has not committed a delinquent act? The unconditional probability that a youth has been rated impulsive is P(impulsive) = 50 / 100 = .50, and the conditional probability that a youth has not committed a delinquent offense given that

Table 5.3	Joint Frequency Distribution for Impulsivity and Delinquency		
	Committed Delinquent Act Last Year?		
Youth Impulsive?	No	Yes	Total
No	40	10	50
Yes	10	40	50
Total	50	50	100

the youth has been rated impulsive is P(not delinquent|impulsive) = 10 / 50 = .20. Therefore, P(impulsive and not delinquent) = .50 × .20 = .10.

We have summarized all of the probability rules we have discussed so far in Table 5.4.

Probability Distributions

We can now apply our knowledge about probability to understanding a critically important concept in inferential statistics—a probability distribution. We already know from our study of descriptive statistics what a frequency distribution is. A frequency distribution is a tally of the number of times *that we observe* the different values of a variable. A frequency distribution, then, captures what we actually have observed or measured. A **probability distribution** is not something we actually observe; rather, it is a theoretical distribution of what we *should* observe over the long run. In other words, in a probability distribution, we do not have the probability that each outcome actually occurred; rather, we have the theoretical probability that it will occur over the long term. This may sound a bit confusing, and a quick example might help before we go on.

Let's say we are interested in the number of times we get a heads when we flip a coin two times. To calculate a probability distribution, we first determine what the possible outcomes are. If we flip a coin two times, we could get the following:

1. A heads followed by another heads {H,H}—two heads

2. A heads followed by a tails {H,T}—one heads

3. A tails followed by a heads {T,H}—one heads

4. A tails followed by another tails {T,T}—no heads

So, on two flips of a coin, we could get zero, one, or two heads. Since flipping a coin once and then flipping it a second time are independent events, we can use the restricted multiplication rule to determine the probability of each of the four outcomes:

1. P(heads and heads) = .5 × .5 = .25

2. P(heads and tails) = .5 × .5 = .25

3. P(tails and heads) = .5 × .5 = .25

4. P(tails and tails) = .5 × .5 = .25

Probability distribution: Distribution of all possible outcomes of a trial and the associated probability of each outcome.

Table 5.4	Probability Rules

Rule 1: The Bounding Rule

The probability of an event (event *A*) must always be greater than or equal to zero or less than or equal to 1.0.

$0 \leq P(A) \leq 1$

Rule 2: The Addition Rule

Rule 2a: The Restricted Addition Rule for Mutually Exclusive Events

If two events (events *A* and *B*) are mutually exclusive, the probability of either event *A* or event *B* occurring is equal to the sum of their separate probabilities.

$P(A \text{ or } B) = P(A) + P(B)$

Rule 2b: The General Addition Rule

If two events (events *A* and *B*) are not mutually exclusive, the probability of either event *A* or event *B* occurring is equal to the sum of their separate probabilities minus their joint probability.

$P(A \text{ or } B) = P(A) + P(B) - P(A \text{ and } B)$

Rule 3: The Multiplication Rule

Rule 3a: The Restricted Multiplication Rule for Independent Events

If two events (events *A* and *B*) are independent, the probability of event *A* and event *B* occurring simultaneously is equal to the product of their separate probabilities.

$P(A \text{ and } B) = P(A) \times P(B)$

Rule 3b: The General Multiplication Rule

If two events (events *A* and *B*) are not independent, the probability of event *A* and event *B* occurring simultaneously is equal to the product of the unconditional probability of *A* and the conditional probability of *B* given *A*.

$P(A \text{ and } B) = P(A) \times P(B|A)$

In Table 5.5, we show you the number of heads possible from flipping a coin twice and the probability of each outcome. Note that we had to use our addition rule to find the probability of getting one heads since we could obtain one heads by getting a heads on the first flip and then a tails on the second flip *or* by getting a tails on the first flip and a heads on the second: *P*(heads and tails) or *P*(tails and heads) = .25 + .25 = .5.

Table 5.5 is a probability distribution. This probability distribution is a theoretical distribution based on probability theory, and it shows us what we should expect to see over the long run if we flip a coin twice. The sum of the probabilities is equal to 1.0, indicating that we have listed all possible outcomes and correctly calculated their probabilities. It is important to understand that this distribution is completely theoretical, based on probability theory, and is not what we observe. If we actually flipped a coin twice and recorded the number of times we got a heads, we

Table 5.5	Probability Distribution of the Number of Heads From Flipping a Coin Two Times

Number of Heads	p
0	.25
1	.50
2	.25

would have a frequency distribution. We would like to do an experiment now. Take a coin and flip it twice, recording the number of heads you get. Then repeat this 10 times (for 10 trials). We did, and Table 5.6 shows what we obtained.

We observed zero heads five times, one heads three times, and two heads twice. What we observed from 10 trials of flipping a coin twice was a greater proportion of no heads than what we saw in Table 5.5. Based on probability theory, the probability of getting zero heads is .25, but one half, or .50, of our actual coin flips resulted in getting no heads. This shows you the difference between a frequency distribution (Table 5.6), which is observed, and a theoretical probability distribution (Table 5.5), which is based on probability theory.

There are different kinds of probability distributions for different kinds of events or outcomes. In the remainder of this chapter, we will discuss two important kinds of probability distributions. In the first, the event we are interested in has only two outcomes (e.g., heads or tails, guilty or innocent, rearrested or not rearrested). In the second, the event has a large number of possible outcomes (e.g., IQ scores, criminal propensity) and is a continuous probability distribution. These are not all of the possible probability distributions, but they do have wide applicability in criminology and criminal justice and they will help us to transition to hypothesis testing in the upcoming chapters.

Table 5.6	Observed Results From the Flipping of a Coin Twice 10	
Number of Heads	*f*	*p*
0	5	.50
1	3	.30
2	2	.20
Total	10	1.00

🔲 A Discrete Probability Distribution—The Binomial Distribution

There are many instances in criminology and criminal justice research when we are interested in events that have only two outcomes. Examples include whether a defendant appears for trial, whether an accused gets a public defender or retains his or her own lawyer, and whether someone who is arrested tests positive or negative for the presence of drugs. In statistics, a process that generates only two outcomes is called a Bernoulli process. The probability distribution based on a Bernoulli process is referred to as the **binomial distribution**. Let's examine the binomial probability distribution in some detail.

As our example, let's examine defendants who pay a cash bail after being arrested pending trial, and we are interested in the event that they appear (or fail to appear) for their trial. The event we are looking at, therefore, has two outcomes: The defendant either shows up for trial or fails to show up. The probability that the defendant appears for trial is denoted as p, and the probability that he or she fails to show up for trial is $1 - p$, or q. Let's assume that, based on past research, we know that the probability of showing up for trial if the defendant has been released on a cash bail is .80 and the probability of failing to show up, therefore, is .20. Let's say that we have five persons recently released on cash bail, and we want to calculate the probability distribution of the number of times that they would appear for trial. Let's use the term "success" for any defendant who shows up for trial and designate that with the letter r; we'll use the term "failure" for any defendant who fails to show up.

With five defendants, it is possible that either none, one, two, three, four, or all five of them would show up for trial. We will assume that the event of one defendant showing up for trial is independent of the others, so that we have independent events. By applying the restricted version of the multiplication rule, using knowledge that the probability of a success is .80 and the probability of a failure is .20, and letting r be the number of successes (showing up for trial) and n be the total number of trials (therefore, $n - r$ is the number of failures or those who do not show up), we can use the following

Binomial distribution: Probability distribution for events where there are just two possible outcomes with fixed probabilities that sum to 1.0.

formula to calculate the probability of each outcome: $p^r q^{n-r}$. Let's use this formula to determine the probability that zero defendants will show up for trial (this means that we have no successes and five failures out of five defendants):

$$P(0 \text{ successes}) = (.8^0)(.2^5) = .2 \times .2 \times .2 \times .2 \times .2 = .0003$$

The probability that one defendant would show up for trial would be

$$P(1 \text{ success}) = (.8^1)(.2^4) = .8 \times .2 \times .2 \times .2 \times .2 = .00128$$

Now we need to stop and point something out. The probability we calculated above is the probability of one success followed by four failures. In other words, in this instance the first person out on cash bail showed up for trial, but the next four did not. But there are other ways that we could observe one success in five trials, aren't there? The first case could fail, the second one could be a success, and the next three could be failures (F,S,F,F,F). Or the first two could fail, the next one could show up for trial (be a success), and the two after that could fail (F,F,S,F,F).

What we need to do is to figure out how to count all the different ways of having one success out of five trials. Fortunately, there is a very simple counting rule in probability that we can use to determine this. This is the counting rule for combinations, and the formula is

$$\binom{n}{r} = \left(\frac{n!}{r!(n-r)!} \right)$$

The first expression

$$\binom{n}{r}$$

is read as "n choose r" and is the number of ways in which r objects can be ordered out of n objects without regard to order. The expression that it is equal to

$$\left(\frac{n!}{r!(n-r)!} \right)$$

is read as "n factorial" over "r factorial times $n - r$ factorial." A *factorial* is just an operation where the number we are taking the factorial of is multiplied by every whole number less than itself and greater than zero. Thus, 5! is equal to $5 \times 4 \times 3 \times 2 \times 1 = 120$. By convention, 0! = 1.

Let's use this combination formula to calculate the number of ways in which we could get one success (defendant showing up for trial) out of five trials:

$$\frac{5!}{1!(5-1)!} = \frac{5!}{1!4!} = \frac{5 \times 4 \times 3 \times 2 \times 1}{1 \times 4 \times 3 \times 2 \times 1} = \frac{120}{24} = 5$$

We can verify this by noting that the success could appear in the 1st, 2nd, 3rd, 4th, or 5th case (the probability of each outcome is written next to it):

$$(S,F,F,F,F) \ P = (.8 \times .2 \times .2 \times .2 \times .2) = .8^1 \times .2^4 = .00128$$

$$(F,S,F,F,F)\ P = (.2 \times .8 \times .2 \times .2 \times .2) = .8^1 \times .2^4 = .00128$$

$$(F,F,S,F,F)\ P = (.2 \times .2 \times .8 \times .2 \times .2) = .8^1 \times .2^4 = .00128$$

$$(F,F,F,S,F)\ P = (.2 \times .2 \times .2 \times .8 \times .2) = .8^1 \times .2^4 = .00128$$

$$(F,F,F,F,S)\ P = (.2 \times .2 \times .2 \times .2 \times .8) = .8^1 \times .2^4 = .00128$$

Now, if we want to know the probability of getting one success out of five failures, we can do one of two things. We can use our addition rule and determine the probability of (S,F,F,F,F) or (F,S,F,F,F) or (F,F,S,F,F) or (F,F,F,S,F) or (F,F,F,F,S), which would be .00128 + .00128 + .00128 + .00128 + .00128 = .0064. Or we could use our counting rule that we can get one success out of five trials five different ways. The probability of getting one success out of five trials in any order is.00128; multiplying the two together, we get $5 \times .00128 = .0064$. No matter which way we do it, we get the same result.

If we use the counting rule, we now have a general formula to determine the probability of getting r successes out of n trials where the probability of a success is p and the probability of failure is $q(1 - p)$:

$$P(r) = \binom{n}{r} p^r q^{n-r}$$

$$P(r) = \left(\frac{n!}{r!(n-r)!} \right) p^r q^{n-r}$$

(Formula 5–1)

Equation 5-1 is known as the *binomial theorem*. The binomial theorem can be used to determine the probability of any number of successes, r, so long as there are only two outcomes—success (p) and failure (q).

We will use the binomial coefficient to calculate the probability of zero, one, two, three, four, and five successes where success is defined as a defendant who posted a cash bail and who shows up for trial. We show both the calculations and the probabilities in Table 5.7, and we graph the probability distribution in Figure 5.3.

From Table 5.7, we can see that the probability of no defendant showing up for trial is quite small, as is the probability of only one or two of them appearing at their trial. Based on probability theory, we would expect to see three out of five appear for trial about 20% of the time, and four defendants would appear about 40% of the time. Finally, if the probability of appearing at trial for a defendant released on ROR (release on recognizance) is .80, we would expect all five to show up about one third of the time ($p = .3277$).

Just like a frequency distribution, a probability distribution has both a mean and a standard deviation. For a binomial probability distribution, the mean is given by np (the number of trials or observations multiplied by the probability of a success). The mean of a theoretical probability distribution is generally referred to as the expected value $E(x)$, so for a binominal distribution $E(x) = np$. The formula for the variance of a binomial distribution is $\sigma^2 = npq$, and for the standard deviation we simply take the square root of the variance, $\sigma = \sqrt{npq}$. The mean of the probability distribution in Table 5.7 is $5(.8) = 4.0$. This means that if the probability of a success is .8, and we have five observations, the expected value of the number of observed successes is 4. Out of five persons who post cash bail, then, the average number who would be expected to appear at trial would be four. Note from both the probability distribution and the histogram in Figure 5.3 that the greatest expected probability corresponds to four successes. This means that "over the long run" we would expect to see, on average, four people out of five show up for their trials if they posted a cash bail. You can use these formulas to find that the variance of the probability distribution is .8 ($5 \times .8 \times .2$) and the standard deviation is .89 ($\sqrt{.8}$). Remember that this does *not* mean

Table 5.7	Probability Distribution of Appearance at Trial Where p (Success) = .8, q (Failure) = .2, and $n = 5$	

Number of Successes	Calculation	p
0	$\left(\dfrac{5!}{0!(5-0)!}\right).8^0.2^5$	.0003
1	$\left(\dfrac{5!}{1!(5-1)!}\right).8^1.2^4$	.0064
2	$\left(\dfrac{5!}{2!(5-2)!}\right).8^2.2^3$	.0512
3	$\left(\dfrac{5!}{3!(5-3)!}\right).8^3.2^2$	.2048
4	$\left(\dfrac{5!}{4!(5-4)!}\right).8^4.2^1$	.4096
5	$\left(\dfrac{5!}{5!(5-5)!}\right).8^5.2^0$	.3277
		Total = 1.00

that we will obtain this result every time, but we should be more likely to obtain it *over the long run* compared with any other outcome.

Hypothesis Testing With the Binomial Distribution

So why is all this important? One important use of probability distributions is that they enable us to make decisions under a situation of uncertainty. That is, they are critical in the testing of hypotheses. As we noted in Chapter 1, a *hypothesis* is simply a scientific "hunch" or assumption about the relationship between two variables that is tested empirically. In explanatory research, we start with a hypothesis, collect data or information that pertains to that hypothesis from a sample, and then, with the help of a known probability distribution, come to some decision about the hypothesis. In hypothesis testing, we want to make an inference about what is going on the population from knowledge about our sample, and what allows us to make this inference is a probability distribution. Let's go through a brief example.

Figure 5.3   Histogram of Probability Distribution From Table 5.7

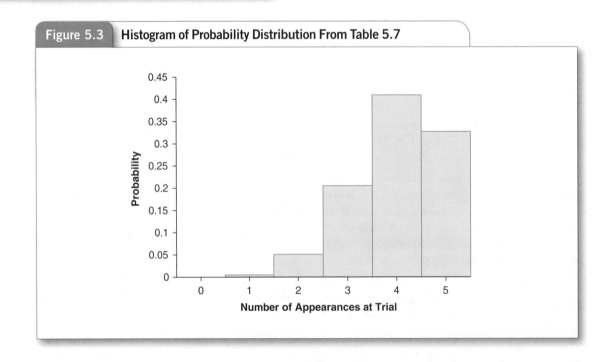

Case Study

Predicting the Probability of a Stolen Car Being Recovered

Let's say we recently purchased a car and we are concerned about the possibility of car theft. We hear from commercials that the car theft device "LoJack" is effective in helping the police to recover your car should it get stolen. The LoJack device is a hidden transformer in your car that you activate when the car is stolen. The transformer sends out an electronic transmission that the police are able to monitor in order to locate your car. The company claims that with LoJack, the police are better able to find and quickly recover stolen cars. You talk to the local police chief, and she claims that, based on 10 years' worth of evidence, the police department recovers about 40% of the stolen cars reported and returns them undamaged to the owner. You have a hunch that LoJack might produce a recovery rate better than 40%. But you do not know that for a fact, and before you spend money installing LoJack in your new car, you want to make sure that it will give you more protection from auto theft than the police working without the assistance of LoJack. Here's what you do.

First, you collect information from people (your sample) who have LoJack in their car and ask them (a) if they have ever had it stolen and, (b) if so, whether it was returned undamaged. You find 10 people who have had their cars stolen and who had LoJack, and you learn that 8 of those cars were returned undamaged within 24 hours. What you observe, therefore, is an 80% recovery rate. But this is just what you found in your sample, and you still do not know the recovery rate for all cars with LoJack (your population). You wonder whether this means that LoJack does result in a greater probability of recovery. Maybe the 8 people who had their cars returned quickly happened to be very lucky and are not typical of most car owners with LoJack. Perhaps if you selected a different 10 people who had cars stolen with LoJack you would find that only 2 had their cars returned undamaged. In other words, the 80% recovery rate you observed from your sample of 10 people may have been due to random sampling variation, not to the superiority of LoJack in the overall population.

How do you decide whether LoJack is better than the police alone for all LoJack users (the population) and not just within your sample? One way to be more confident that you made the correct decision is to conduct a formal hypothesis test. There are a number of steps involved in a hypothesis test, and the basic framework of these steps will be the same throughout this book. In the remainder of this section, we will discuss these steps of a hypothesis test, but do not be alarmed if you do not understand them right away. We will be conducting hypothesis tests under different situations in every chapter, so you will have a chance to review this material regularly. For now, it is important to understand the basic process of hypothesis testing!

The first step in a hypothesis test is to make a few assumptions. In science, we always test an assumption that states there is no relationship between our variables. In this case, having LoJack would be the independent variable (have it or not) and vehicle recovery is the dependent variable (recovered or not). The assumption that we test, therefore, states that LoJack is no better than not having LoJack in recovering stolen cars. Practically, this means that our starting assumption is that 40% of the stolen cars equipped with LoJack will be recovered undamaged. In other words, we presume that LoJack does not work, and our hypothesis test will involve disproving this assumption. Researchers call this assumption the **null hypothesis** because of the implication that there is no relationship—or, in our specific case, that LoJack does not work any better than the police. The null hypothesis is usually designated by H_0. Since our null hypothesis involves the assumption that LoJack's recovery rate is no better than that without it, this means that the expected probability of recovering a stolen LoJack-equipped car is .40. Here, then, is our null hypothesis:

H_0: The probability of recovering a stolen car that has LoJack is .40: $P(\text{recovery}) =$ .40. In other words, LoJack does not work.

In addition to making an assumption in the null hypothesis (assume LoJack does not work), we also make an assumption about an alternative outcome. This assumption asks the question, "If the null hypothesis is not true, then what do we think is really going on?" This hypothesis is called the research or alternative hypothesis and is designated by H_1.

> **Null hypothesis:** In a hypothesis test, the null hypothesis is the hypothesis that is initially assumed to be true. It is called the null hypothesis because it presumes that there is no relationship (null) between the variables being tested.

It is called the alternative hypothesis because this is the alternative to the null hypothesis, and it's sometimes called the research hypothesis because it is usually based on the question motivating our research—in this case, does LoJack work? There are two general ways of stating the alternative hypothesis. It can be stated as a directional (one-tailed) alternative hypothesis or as what is called a non-directional (two-tailed) alternative hypothesis.

In our example with LoJack, the null hypothesis states that the probability of recovering a stolen car with LoJack is no greater than that without LoJack. Now, let's say we think that LoJack is likely to increase the probability of recovering a stolen car undamaged because the company claims that the transmitting device will enable the police to find the stolen car easier. With this a priori knowledge (knowledge we have before we make our hypothesis), we can make the assumption in the alternative hypothesis that the probability of recovering a stolen car undamaged with LoJack is greater than .40. We do not have to say exactly how much greater in our alternative hypothesis, just that we think it is greater than that assumed in the null hypothesis:

H_1: The probability of recovering a stolen car that has LoJack is greater than .40: $P(\text{recovery}) > .40$.

This alternative hypothesis is basically saying that LoJack works—if you have it in your car and it gets stolen, the chances are greater that you will get your car back than if you did not have it. This is a *directional alternative hypothesis* because we have assumed that the recovery rate with LoJack is greater than what it would be if you did not have LoJack (.40) and, therefore, have stated a specific direction (greater than) for LoJack's recovery probability.

Alternatively, we could have stated that the probability of recovery with LoJack will be less than .40: $P(\text{recovery} < .40)$. This too is a directional alternative hypothesis because we have stated a specific direction in our alternative with respect to the null hypothesis (it is less than that assumed in the null). To support this alternative assumption, we might have created a theory that the police might be insulted when someone reports that they have LoJack in their car and might be less than enthusiastic in recovering it. This seems very unlikely, however, and our alternative hypothesis of a greater probability of recovery seems more plausible.

And finally, we also could have created a *non-directional alternative hypothesis*. In a non-directional alternative hypothesis, we simply state that the expected outcome is different from that assumed in the null hypothesis—not that it is greater or less, just that it is different. So, for example, our non-directional alternative would have been that the rate of recovery for cars with LoJack is not equal to .40: $P(\text{recovery}) \neq .40$. As we will see, there are implications if we select a one-tailed versus two-tailed hypothesis test. For our example, we are satisfied with our alternative hypothesis that the probability of recovery for cars with LoJack is greater than .40, so let's continue with that. We now have two hypotheses, a null hypothesis and a directional alternative hypothesis:

H_0: The probability of recovering a stolen car that has LoJack is .40: $P(\text{recovery}) = .40$.

H_1: The probability of recovering a stolen car that has LoJack is greater than .40: $P(\text{recovery}) > .40$.

It is very important to understand that in the process of hypothesis testing, *only the null hypothesis is tested*. We never directly test the alternative hypothesis. We are really asking how likely it is that the null hypothesis is true—that is, that there is no relationship—given what our sample data tell us. Because we test only the null hypothesis, we make our decision by either rejecting the null hypothesis or failing to reject the null hypothesis. For example, if we discover that what is stated in the null hypothesis is "very unlikely" or is a "rare event" given our data (and we will discuss in a moment what we mean by "very likely" or a "rare event"), we will reject the null hypothesis. When we reject the null hypothesis, we no longer believe that the assumption it contains is true, and our faith in the truthfulness of the alternative hypothesis is strengthened (not proven, but strengthened). Therefore, although the alternative hypothesis is never directly tested, in rejecting the null hypothesis we gain confidence in the alternative hypothesis.

A useful analogy for the idea of hypothesis testing is the task given to a jury in a criminal trial. The jury starts with the assumption or hypothesis that the defendant is innocent; the alternative hypothesis is that the defendant is guilty. It then tests this assumption of innocence (the null hypothesis) by looking at the data—in this case, the evidence presented by the prosecution and the defense. After examining this evidence, the jury makes a determination about how likely it is that the defendant is innocent in the face of the evidence. If it thinks that the evidence is consistent with the defendant's innocence, then it acquits (it fails to reject the hypothesis of innocence). If, however, the jury thinks that the evidence raises grave suspicions about the defendant's innocence (meaning that it surpasses the burden of proof of "beyond a reasonable doubt"), then it rejects the null hypothesis, and the assumption of innocence is abandoned in favor of the alternative. The jury essentially says, "The person cannot be so unlucky that he is innocent and yet has all this evidence indicating guilt." The standard of "beyond a reasonable doubt," then, is like an implicit probability level. If the probability is very great that the person did the crime based on the evidence, then the jury should reject its "null hypothesis" of innocence. If, however, the probability is not great, not "beyond a reasonable doubt," then the jury should not reject its null hypothesis and continue to assume that the defendant is innocent.

Notice one very important thing about the jury's decision (and our own decisions about null hypotheses). In making its decision, the jury almost never knows with absolute certainty that it is correct. That is, the jury will have a notion about how likely it is that the defendant is innocent, but it has no way of knowing for sure (only the defendant knows that). This means that the jury is making a decision under uncertainty, so it might have been the wrong decision.

There are two types of wrong decisions or errors a jury may make. First, it could reject the null hypothesis of innocence when in fact the defendant is innocent. In this error, the jury convicts an innocent person. The jury could also continue to accept the null hypothesis of innocence and acquit the defendant when, in fact, the accused is guilty. In this error, the jury lets a guilty person go free. In our legal system, we generally think the first error is worse than the second. That is, we think it is worse to convict an innocent person than to acquit a guilty person. In an effort to ensure that we do not convict innocent people, the legal system makes the requirement of proof very great in criminal cases—the jury must believe "beyond a reasonable doubt" that the defendant is guilty before it may reject the null hypothesis of innocence. The phrase "beyond a reasonable doubt" means that the jury must determine that the null hypothesis of innocence is very, very unlikely before it may reject it.

In trying to answer our research question about car theft protection, we are very much like the jury. We will not know for sure whether LoJack produces a higher recovery rate of stolen cars because we have information from only 10 owners of LoJack, not from everyone who has installed it (our population). In other words, we have a sample of LoJack owners, not the entire population, and the success rate we observed might be unique to our sample. When we make a decision about the null hypothesis, therefore, we (like the jury) are making it under uncertainty. Since we have incomplete information, we might err in making our decision about the null hypothesis. We could reject a null hypothesis that happens to be true, or we could fail to reject a null hypothesis that is false. These errors have names, as shown in Table 5.8. Rejecting a null hypothesis that is true is referred to as a Type I error, and failing to reject a false null hypothesis is referred to as a Type II error.

It would be nice if we could minimize the risk of making both kinds of errors, but unfortunately that is not possible. As we will learn, as we reduce the risk of making a Type I error, we simultaneously increase our risk of making a Type II error. Think about this for a moment with respect to the jury's decision. One way that it can minimize the risk of a Type I error (convicting an innocent person) would be to make the burden of proof even greater than beyond a reasonable doubt. Such a standard might be something like, "Do not convict someone unless you are 99.999% sure that they are guilty—way beyond a reasonable doubt." Although this will decrease the risk of convicting an innocent person, it will increase the risk that a truly guilty person will be found innocent (a Type II error). Similarly, minimizing the risk of making a Type II error (acquitting a truly guilty person) by lessening the standard of proof in criminal proceedings, say, to the standard that applies in civil court ("a preponderance of the evidence") increases the risk of convicting an innocent person. What we have to do, therefore, is carefully balance the risks of making each type of error.

In research, we establish beforehand some level of risk we are willing to take that we will make a Type I error. This level of risk is called a level of **significance** or **alpha level** (*a*). Alpha and significance are interchangeable terms in research, and alpha is symbolized as the Greek letter α. For example, if we set $\alpha = .05$, we are saying that we are willing to risk rejecting a true null hypothesis 5 times out of 100, or 5% of the time. If we wanted to reduce that risk, we could adopt a significance level of .01 or even .001.

> **Significance or alpha level (α):** Risk we are willing to take in rejecting a true null hypothesis. For example, if we select an alpha level of .05, we are willing to be incorrect .05 or 5% of the time.

Table 5.8	Decision Making in Hypothesis Tests	

True State of Affairs	Decision Regarding Null Hypothesis	
	Fail to Reject	Reject
Null hypothesis is true	Correct decision	Type I error
Null hypothesis is false	Type II error	Correct decision

Recall that we begin our hypothesis test by assuming that the null hypothesis is true (that having LoJack is no better than not having it). We then say that we are going to continue to assume this is true unless our data (what we observe) tell us that the outcome we actually observed is "very unlikely" or "a rare event" given the null hypothesis. What we do, then, is maintain our belief in the null hypothesis until we are informed by the data that this belief is improbable given what we have observed. What we mean by "very unlikely" or "a rare event" is determined by the significance level. *What the significance level actually tells us is the probability of observing our data if the null hypothesis is true.* If this probability is very great, then we have no reason to think our null hypothesis is false, and we continue to assume it is true and fail to reject it.

However, if the probability of observing what we did given that the null hypothesis is true is very low (where low is defined as less than or equal to our level of significance), or if what we observe is a "rare event" (where how rare is defined by our significance level), then it seems to us more probable that the null hypothesis is false and we can reject it. This does not mean that we know the null hypothesis is wrong. It means only that the observed outcome is so unlikely that it's more likely that the null hypothesis is wrong or false than that it is correct. We are making a decision based on what we think is "most probable or likely," but we will never know for sure what is actually true. Before moving on, we also want to underscore why we can *never* accept a null hypothesis, we can only reject or fail to reject it. Why? Because we are dealing in the world of probability, and since we can never be 100% certain that our sample data reflect the population, we can only make generalizations with less than 100% certainty.

Let's say that with respect to our LoJack example, we are willing to accept a 5% risk of making a Type I error, giving us a .05 level of significance or alpha. What we are saying is that we are assuming that the null hypothesis is true unless the outcome that we observe is unlikely where "unlikely" now specifically means that it has a probability of occurring of .05 or less. If what we observe has a probability of occurring greater than .05, we continue to assume that the null hypothesis is true. If, however, what we observe has a probability of occurring less than or equal to .05, we reject the null hypothesis and conclude that it is false.

How, you may ask, do we know what the probability observing our actual data is? More specifically, what is the probability of having 8 out of 10 stolen cars with LoJack recovered undamaged if the true probability of recovery is .40? This is an excellent question. This is where probability distributions enter, and we have the tools in our toolbox now to calculate that probability distribution.

In our null hypothesis, we are assuming that the probability of recovering a stolen car with LoJack is no better than that with not having it. Specifically, the information from the chief of police tells us this probability is .40. So we assume that P(recovery with LoJack) = .40. We now ask the following question: "If the probability of recovering a stolen car with LoJack is .40, what is the probability that we would have observed 8 people out of 10 who have LoJack recovering their stolen car undamaged (this is what you observed, so these are your data)?" Actually, what we really want to know is this: Given a level of significance of .05, what are all the outcomes with a probability of .05 or less because those are the outcomes that would lead us to reject the null hypothesis? If 8 recovered cars is included among those outcomes, we reject the null hypothesis. If it is not included among those outcomes, we fail to reject the null hypothesis.

Note that the event of recovering a stolen car can be considered a Bernoulli event—the car either is recovered undamaged or it is not. With our binomial formula in equation 5-1, we can determine the probability of 0, 1, 2, ..., 10 undamaged recoveries. Here is the binomial formula as it translates for this particular problem where $n = 10$ (the number of trials or the number of people in our sample who had LoJack when their cars were stolen), $p = .40$ (the probability of recovery), and $q = .60$ ($1 - p$, or the probability of not getting the car recovered undamaged):

$$P(r) = \left(\frac{10!}{r!(10-r)!} \right)(4^r)(6^{10-r})$$

where r = the number of successful recoveries of a stolen car. You should use this formula to calculate on your own the probability of 0 to 10 successful recoveries. We report the results for you in Table 5.9 and graph the probability distribution in Figure 5.4.

Note that if the null hypothesis is true, P(recovery) = .40, the probability of observing exactly 8 successfully recovered cars out of 10 is .0106. By using our addition rule of probabilities, we can determine that the probability of 8, 9, or 10 recoveries, P(8, 9, or 10) is equal to .0123 (.0106 + .0016 + .0001). Understand what this means. It says that if the true probability of undamaged recovery is .40 (what we are assuming under the null hypothesis), then the probability that we would observe 8, 9, or 10 successful recoveries is .0123 or less—that is, 1% of the time or less.

Earlier we adopted a level of significance of .05. We said that we would reject the null hypothesis if what we observed was "very unlikely," which we defined as an event with a probability of .05 or less. We have just determined that the event of 8 or more undamaged recoveries out of 10 given a recovery probability of .40 has a probability of .0123. What we have observed, then, fits our definition of "very unlikely." We now have information that leads us to conclude that 8 out of 10 recoveries is very unlikely given a true recovery probability of .40, so we can reject the null hypothesis that P(recovery) = .40. In rejecting this, we can conclude that we believe the alternative hypothesis is more likely to be true in the population. As such, we can conclude that having a LoJack will make it more likely that our car, if stolen, will be recovered by police compared with not having LoJack. Keep in mind, however, that we might be wrong in rejecting the null hypothesis—that is, we might be committing a Type I error!

Note from Table 5.9 that with a significance level of .05, we would have rejected the null hypothesis had we observed 10 successful recoveries out of 10, 9 successful recoveries out of 10, or 8 successful recoveries out of 10. We know that the cumulative probability of each of these events is equal to .0123, which is less than .05. In research, we have a special name for these events. This is called the **critical region of a probability distribution** for any given test. The critical region defines *all outcomes* that will lead us to reject the null hypothesis. In our case, the three outcomes of 8, 9, and 10 successful recoveries will lead us to reject the null hypothesis because their cumulative probability is less than our .05 level of significance. Since the event that we observed (8 out of 10 undamaged car recoveries) falls into this critical region, our decision is to reject the null hypothesis. We show you the critical region for this specific problem in Figure 5.4.

Suppose we had observed 7 out of 10 successful recoveries; what would our decision have been at the same significance level? By using our addition rule and the information in Table 5.9, we can determine that the probability of 7, 8, 9, or 10 successful recoveries is equal to .0548 (.0425 + .0106 + .0016 + .0001 = .0548). Since our definition of a "very unlikely" or "rare" event is an event with a probability of .05 or less, the event

| Table 5.9 | Probability Distribution of Recovering a Stolen Car With LoJack Where p (Success) = .4, q (Failure) = .6, and n = 10 |

Number of Successes	Calculation	P
0	$\left(\dfrac{10!}{0!(10-0)!}\right).4^0.6^{10}$	.0060
1	$\left(\dfrac{10!}{1!(10-1)!}\right).4^1.6^9$	.0403
2	$\left(\dfrac{10!}{2!(10-2)!}\right).4^2.6^8$	.1209
3	$\left(\dfrac{10!}{3!(10-3)!}\right).4^3.6^7$	.2150
4	$\left(\dfrac{10!}{4!(10-4)!}\right).4^4.6^6$	.2508
5	$\left(\dfrac{10!}{5!(10-5)!}\right).4^5.6^5$	.2007
6	$\left(\dfrac{10!}{6!(10-6)!}\right).4^6.6^4$	.1115
7	$\left(\dfrac{10!}{7!(10-7)!}\right).4^7.6^3$	.0425
8	$\left(\dfrac{10!}{8!(10-8)!}\right).4^8.6^2$	.0106
9	$\left(\dfrac{10!}{9!(10-9)!}\right).4^9.6^1$	.0016
10	$\left(\dfrac{10!}{10!(10-10)!}\right).4^{10}.6^0$	.0001 Total = 1.00

Critical region of a probability distribution: Defines the entire class of outcomes that will lead us to reject the null hypothesis. If the event we observe falls into the critical region, our decision will be to reject the null hypothesis.

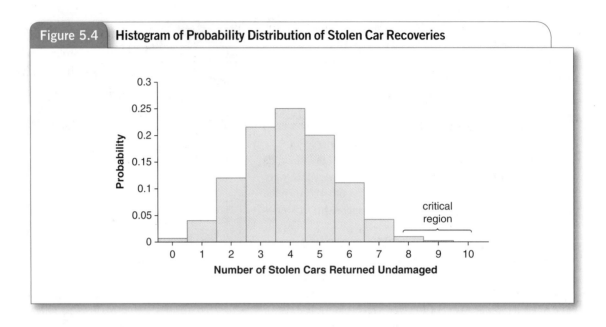

Figure 5.4 | Histogram of Probability Distribution of Stolen Car Recoveries

of 7 or more successful recoveries just misses being unlikely enough to lead us to reject the null hypothesis. Had we observed 7 out of 10 successful car recoveries, therefore, we would continue to assume that the null hypothesis is true and would not reject it because the event of 7 successful car recoveries does not fall into our critical region.

Now suppose that we had observed 8 out of 10 successful recoveries, but instead of a significance level of .05, we had decided earlier to adopt a significance level of .01. The selection of a significance level is adopted *before* the hypothesis test is conducted, but we are changing the rules of the game to make a point here. By lowering the level of significance, we are saying that what is to be considered a "very unlikely" event must now have an even less likely probability of occurring before we are willing to reject the null hypothesis. In other words, we are reducing the risk we are willing to take that we will make a Type I error from 5% to 1%. We know that the probability of observing 8, 9, or 10 successful car recoveries if P(recovery) = .40 is .0123. Since .0123 is greater than .01, our decision would have been to fail to reject the null hypothesis at a .01 level of significance. Note that by lowering our level of significance, we are making it more difficult to reject the null hypothesis. With a .01 level of significance the critical region becomes 9 or 10 successful recoveries out of 10, whereas with a .05 alpha level the critical region becomes 8, 9, or 10 successful recoveries.

The following list reviews all the steps in that process. Make sure you understand each step because you will be seeing them again and again throughout this book.

Steps of a Hypothesis Test

Step 1: Formally state your null and alternative hypotheses.

Step 2: Determine what probability distribution you will use for your test.

Step 3: Define what you mean by a "very unlikely" event by selecting a level of significance (the alpha level).

Step 4: Calculate the probability of observing your sample data under the null hypothesis.

Step 5: Make a decision about the null hypothesis (reject or fail to reject) and interpret your results.

In this section of the chapter, we have been concerned with events (called Bernoulli events) that have only two possible outcomes. The binomial probability distribution that characterizes these events is very useful because many interesting events in criminology and criminal justice have only two outcomes. But other interesting events are continuous, are measured at the interval/ratio level, and have many more than two possible outcomes. For example, we might be interested in continuous variables like the number of years convicted homicide defendants are sentenced to prison. Unfortunately, we cannot use the binomial distribution to characterize continuous variables. We must learn another type of probability distribution—a continuous probability distribution.

A Continuous Probability Distribution—The Standard Normal Probability Distribution

In this section, we are going to investigate another kind of probability distribution that has wide applicability in criminology and criminal justice research—the normal probability distribution. The normal distribution is a probability distribution for continuous events and looks like a smooth curve (unlike the binomial probability distribution, which looks like a series of "steps"). Figure 5.5 is an example of what a normal probability distribution might look like. Note that the probability of an event occurring is greater in the center of the curve and declines for events at each of the two ends, or "tails," of the distribution. A characteristic of the tails of the distribution is that they never touch the x axis, meaning that they go to both positive and negative infinity. It makes sense that the tails extend to infinity if we keep in mind that the normal distribution is a theoretical probability distribution. Like the binomial, the normal distribution is defined by a mathematical equation, and although many characteristics can be assumed to be distributed as normal, the normal distribution is not an empirical distribution. There are some common features of any normal distribution. The normal distribution is a unimodal, symmetrical distribution and assumes the appearance of a bell-shaped curve. By a "symmetrical distribution," we mean that if we drew a line down the center of the curve, the left and right halves would be mirror images of each other. Compare this smooth curve with the histogram for a binomial probability distribution in Figure 5.4.

The mathematical formula for the normal distribution, or the normal probability density function, is

$$f(x) = \frac{1}{\sigma\sqrt{2\pi}} e^{\frac{-(x-\mu)^2}{2\sigma^2}}$$

(Formula 5-2)

where

μ = the mean (expected value) of the continuous variable x

σ^2 = the variance of x

π and e = constants equal to 3.14 and 2.72, respectively

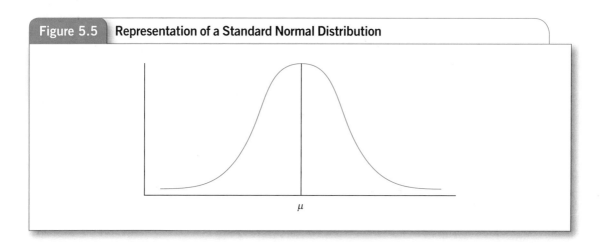

| Figure 5.5 | Representation of a Standard Normal Distribution |

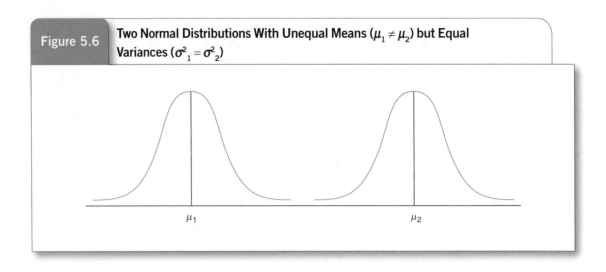

Figure 5.6 **Two Normal Distributions With Unequal Means ($\mu_1 \neq \mu_2$) but Equal Variances ($\sigma^2_1 = \sigma^2_2$)**

μ_1 μ_2

Any normal distribution is defined by its two parameters, its mean (μ) or expected value and its variance (σ^2). The mean defines the location of each normal distribution on the number line, and the variance defines its general shape. What this means is that there is not just one but many normal distributions, which vary in terms of their mean, their variance, or both. Figure 5.6 shows two normal distributions, each with a mean different from the other but the same variance. Figure 5.7 shows two normal distributions with equal means but different variances, and Figure 5.8 shows two normal distributions with different means and different variances. All of these curves are normal curves, illustrating that there is not one but rather a family of normal curves defined by μ and σ^2.

We could employ equation 5-2 and determine the probability distribution for any continuous variable. There is, however, one significant difference between determining the probability of a discrete variable and determining that of a continuous one. When we calculated the probability of a discrete variable by using the binomial probability distribution, we could employ the binomial formula to calculate the probability of a given event (i.e., the probability of recovering 8 or more stolen cars out of 10). A continuous distribution, however, comprises events that are theoretically infinite. For example, response time to a "911" call could theoretically be measured in millionths of a second or in even finer gradations. Continuous events by their very nature are not discrete events, and this is reflected in the fact that the continuous probability distribution is a smooth curve. What we are interested in, therefore, is a point on a smooth curve. Recall from your high school or college geometry that the area of a point on a curve is zero—there is no area to a point; it is theoretically undefined. What we must do with continuous events, therefore, is determine the area between two points on a curve. For example, what we must do is calculate the probability that a 911 response time will be between 2 and 4 minutes, $P(2 \leq x \leq 4)$, or the probability that it will be more than 6 minutes, $P(x > 6)$.

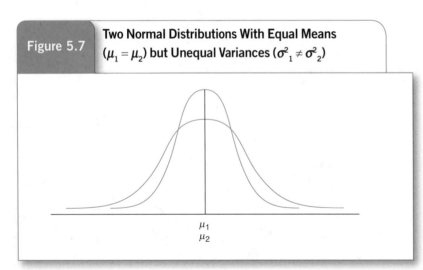

Figure 5.7 **Two Normal Distributions With Equal Means ($\mu_1 = \mu_2$) but Unequal Variances ($\sigma^2_1 \neq \sigma^2_2$)**

μ_1
μ_2

The Area Under the Normal Curve

Since the normal distribution is a probability distribution, the area under the curve is 1.0. In other words, all possible outcomes are included in the area under a normal curve.

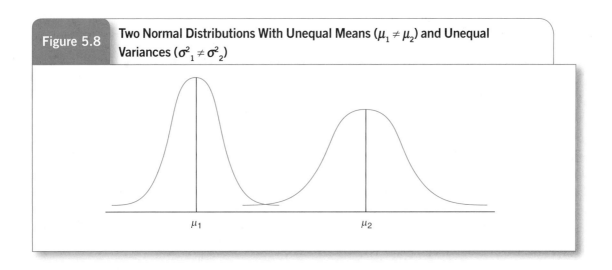

Figure 5.8 Two Normal Distributions With Unequal Means ($\mu_1 \neq \mu_2$) and Unequal Variances ($\sigma^2_1 \neq \sigma^2_2$)

One of the most important properties of a normal probability distribution is that there is a fixed area or a fixed proportion of cases that lie between the mean and any number of standard deviations to the left or right of that mean. Moreover, based on mathematical theory, we can determine the exact proportion of cases between the mean and any point at a given number of standard deviations away from the mean. For example, we know that for every normal distribution, .3413 (34.13%) of the area of the curve lies between the mean and a point that is 1.0 standard deviation to the right of that mean ($\mu + 1\sigma$). In other words, if we drew a line through any normal curve at its mean and another line through the curve at 1.0 standard deviation to the right of the mean, the area between those two lines would be .3413 of the total area under the curve. This means that .3413 of the events in a normal probability distribution lie within 1.0 standard deviation to the right of the mean. We also know from mathematical theory that .4772 (or 47.72%) of the events of a normal probability distribution lie in an area from the mean to a point 2.0 standard deviations to the right of the mean and that .4987 (or 49.87%) of the cases lie within 3.0 standard deviations to the right of the mean. This property of the normal distribution is illustrated in Figure 5.9.

Combining this information with the fact that any normal distribution is symmetrical enables us to make some additional conclusions. If there is .3413 of the area of the normal curve from the mean to a point 1.0 standard deviation to the right of the mean, then since a normal distribution is symmetrical, .3413 of the area of the curve must also lie from the mean to a point 1.0 standard deviation to the *left* of the mean. We can conclude from this that .6826 (.3413 + .3413) of the area (or 68.26%) of any normal distribution must lie within ±1 standard deviation of the mean. Similarly, if .4772 of the area of any normal curve lies between the mean and a point 2.0 standard deviations to the right of the mean, then .4772 also lies between the mean and a point 2.0 standard deviations to the left of the mean. We can conclude from this that .9544 (.4772 + .4772) of the area (or 95.44%) of any normal curve lies within ± 2 standard deviations from the mean. Finally, .9974 (or 99.74%) of the area under any normal curve will lie within ± 3 standard deviations away from the mean. See Figure 5.10.

By using these properties of normal distributions, we have some way of determining and understanding

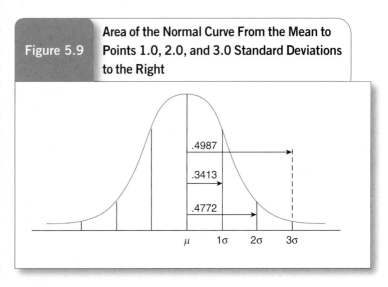

Figure 5.9 Area of the Normal Curve From the Mean to Points 1.0, 2.0, and 3.0 Standard Deviations to the Right

.4987

.3413

.4772

μ 1σ 2σ 3σ

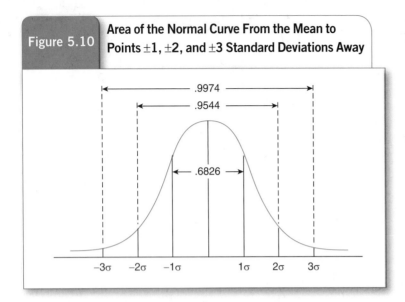

Figure 5.10 Area of the Normal Curve From the Mean to Points ±1, ±2, and ±3 Standard Deviations Away

the probability of continuous events. With our knowledge of normal distributions and standard deviations, we can define a "very unlikely" or "rare" continuous event. For example, suppose we were told that a given continuous x score was 2.4 standard deviations to the right of the mean. What would we conclude about its probability? Since we know that about 95% of all scores in a normal probability distribution lie within ±2 standard deviations of the mean, an x score that is more than 2.0 standard deviations from the mean occurs with a probability less than .05 (less than 5% of the time). This can be considered a "very unlikely" or "rare" event. An x score that is 3.0 standard deviations to the left of the mean is also a "very unlikely" event since we know that approximately 99% of all scores lie within ±3 standard deviations of the mean. An x score that is only 1.0 standard deviation to the right of the mean would *not* be considered "very unlikely" because we now know that approximately 68% of the area of the normal curve lies within 1.0 standard deviation from the mean.

With our knowledge about the relationship between the area under any normal curve and standard deviations, we can use equation 5-2 to calculate probabilities with any continuous variable x. There is one practical difficulty with this, however. In addition to some complex mathematics we would have to do, since normal distributions differ depending on the value of their two parameters (μ and σ), we would have to calculate new probabilities for virtually every problem we confronted. (The mean and standard deviation of response times, e.g., would be different from the mean and standard deviations of sentence length, IQ, the number of self-reported offenses committed, etc. because each of these distributions would have a different mean and a different standard deviation.) It would be easier if we had only one normal probability distribution with known values of μ and σ to use, wouldn't it? Luckily for us there is, and it is known as the *standard normal probability distribution* or the *z* distribution. Remember how having one normal distribution like this is making our work easier as we move along!

The Standard Normal Distribution and Standard Scores

The standard normal distribution is a normal probability distribution that has a mean of 0 and a standard deviation of 1.0. To use the standard normal probability distribution, however, we need to convert the scores of a continuous variable x into what is called a **standard score** or z score. A z score is simply a score for a continuous x variable that has been converted into standard units—in this case, into standard deviation units—rather than how the original variable was measured (e.g., months, years, dollars). The formula for converting a raw x score into a standard z score is

$$z = \frac{x - \overline{X}}{s}$$

(Formula 5-3)

Standard score (z score): Score from the standard normal probability distribution that indicates how many standard deviation units a score is from the mean of zero.

where

x = a raw score for a continuous variable

$\overline{X}$ = the sample mean of the empirical distribution

s = the standard deviation of the empirical distribution

Let's go through an example.

Suppose we have an empirical distribution of 10 scores. These 10 scores represent the number of prior offenses committed by a sample we took of persons arrested by our local police department during the past year. The level of measurement for this variable is interval/ratio, and the exact metric of measurement here is "number of arrests." This variable distribution is displayed in Table 5.10. The mean number of prior arrests for this sample is 5.1, and the standard deviation is 4.25. Let's convert the first raw score, 3 (which is measured in units of "arrests"), into a standardized z score measured in terms of standard deviation units:

$$z = \frac{3 - 5.1}{4.25}$$

$$z = -.49$$

There are two pieces of information we can get from any z score: its sign and its magnitude. The sign of our z score of $-.49$ is negative, telling us that it lies to the left of the mean of the standard normal distribution (remember that the mean of the standard normal distribution is 0). The magnitude of this z score is .49, telling us that it is approximately one half of a standard deviation away from the mean (remember that the mean of the standard normal distribution is 1). The sign of a z score, then, tells us whether it is to the left of (less than) or to the right of (greater than) the mean, and the magnitude tells us how many standard deviation units away from the mean the score is. The greater the absolute value of the magnitude of a z score, the farther out on the tail of the probability distribution it is and the lower its probability. For this distribution, then, a raw score of 3 tells us that it is equivalent to having a score that is .49 standard deviation unit below the mean of 5.1. Note also that the difference between 3 and 5 prior arrests is 2, and this is approximately one half of the standard deviation of 4.25. So, a raw score of 3 arrests when converted into a z score is equal to a score that is almost one half a standard deviation (.49) to the left (in the negative direction) of the mean of the z distribution of 0.

What is the corresponding z score for 13 prior arrests?

$$z = \frac{3 - 5.1}{4.25}$$

$$z = 1.86$$

This tells us that a raw score of 13 prior arrests corresponds to a z score that is 1.86 standard deviation units above or to the right of the mean. In essence, what we are saying is that a raw score of 13 prior arrests corresponds to a score of 1.86 on the z scale.

Once we have converted our raw scores into z scores, we can begin to answer probability questions. Like the binomial distribution, the standard normal distribution is a known probability distribution. To answer probability questions, we need to refer to what is called a standard normal or z table. Table B.2 in Appendix B is such a z table, and we need to become very familiar with it because we will be using it a few more times in this book. Table B.2 provides you with the area or proportion of the standard normal curve that lies between the mean and some given z score. The z scores in this table are always reported to two decimal places. The z score can be located by using the first column of the table to the far left side, which lists the value of the one's digit and the first decimal place. The value of the second decimal

Table 5.10	Number of Prior Arrests for Sample of 10 Persons Arrested During Past Year
Person	*Number of Prior Arrests*
1	3
2	2
3	0
4	8
5	0
6	6
7	13
8	4
9	10
10	5

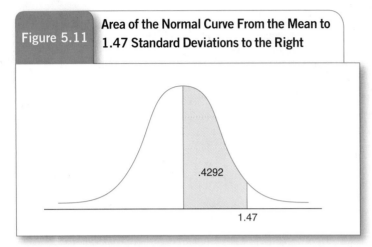

Figure 5.11 Area of the Normal Curve From the Mean to 1.47 Standard Deviations to the Right

.4292

1.47

place can be found in the row at the top of the table. The values reported in the body of the table are the proportions of the standard normal distribution (also called the z distribution) that lie between the mean and that z score. This is probably a little confusing, so let's do a couple of examples.

Suppose we had a z score of 1.47. The question then becomes, "How much of the standard normal curve lies between the mean and this z score?" To find out, we go down the first column of numbers until we reach the value 1.4 (1 is our units digit, and .4 is our first decimal place). Then we use the row of z scores at the top of the table until we find the value of the second decimal place, .07. Where the row of 1.4 intersects the column of .07 (our z score of 1.47), we see the table entry .4292. What this tells us is that .4292 (or 42.92%) of the area of the normal curve lies from the mean to a point 1.47 standard deviation units to the right. We show this for you in Figure 5.11. This means that the probability that a z score is greater than or equal to zero and less than or equal to 1.47 is .4292: $P(0 \leq z \leq 1.47) = .4292$. Since the z distribution is symmetrical, we also know that .4292 of the normal curve lies between the mean and a z score of −1.47. By using this information, we can calculate that .8584 (or 85.84%) of the normal curve lies between a z score of −1.47 and a z score of +1.47.

What proportion of the normal curve lies between the mean and a z score of −1.96? To find this, we follow the same procedure as earlier. Since the z distribution is symmetrical, we can ignore the minus sign. We go down the first column until we find the value 1.9, and then we use the z column at the top of the page until we find .06. At the convergence of the 1.9 row and the .06 column, we see the entry .4750, telling us that .4750 (or 47.50%) of the area of the normal curve lies between the mean and a z score of -1.96. Therefore, the probability that a z score is less than or equal to zero and greater than or equal to −1.96 is .4750: $P(−1.96 \leq z \leq 0) = .4750$.

What is the probability that a z score will be less than −1.96, that is, will fall below it? We know that .50 of the normal curve lies to the right of the mean. We also know that .4750 of the curve lies from the mean to a z score that is 1.96 standard deviation units to the left of the mean. By combining this knowledge, we know that .9750 (.50 + .4750) of the curve lies to the right of a z score of −1.96. Since the total area of the normal curve is 1.0, we can determine that 1 − .9750, or .025, of the curve lies to the left of $z = −1.96$. The probability that a z score is less than or equal to −1.96, therefore, is .025 (see Figure 5.12). A z score that is less than −1.96, then, can be considered a "rare" or low-probability event since it occurs less than 3% of the time. Because the z distribution is symmetrical, a z score greater than or equal to 1.96 is also a low-probability event because it occurs less than 3% of the time. Combining these two probabilities (.025 + .025) tells us that a z score that is less than −1.96 or greater than +1.96 is a low-probability event because it occurs 5% of the time or less (see Figure 5.13).

Now let's answer the following probability question: "What z scores are so unlikely that they fall into the top 1% of the standard normal probability distribution?" We show you the approximate top 1% of the z distribution in Figure 5.14. Let's use what we know about the z distribution to solve this problem. First, we know that .50 of the curve lies to the left of the mean, telling us that the probability is .50 that a z score will be less than or equal to 0 (the mean). Since .50 of the normal curve lies to the left of

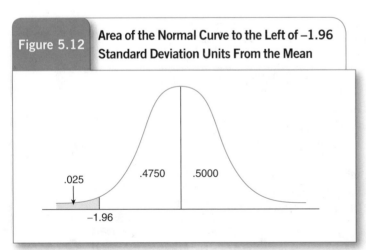

Figure 5.12 Area of the Normal Curve to the Left of −1.96 Standard Deviation Units From the Mean

.025

.4750   .5000

−1.96

the mean, we know we have to find .49 of the area to the right of the mean (which, with .50 to the left of the mean, will sum to .99). Go into the body of the *z* table (Table B.2) and try to find .4900.

You don't see .4900, but you should see. 4901, which will be close enough. What we need, though, is not the area but rather the *z* score that corresponds to this area. To find the *z* score that corresponds to this area, work backward. First find the *z* score for this row (this will identify the digit and the first decimal place of your *z* score, and it will be 2.3). Then find the second decimal place by finding the column you are in (column .03). You now have a *z* score of 2.33. By combining all this information, you know that the probability that a *z* score will be less than 2.33 is .9901 (.50 + .4901). The probability that a *z* score will be greater than or equal to 2.33, therefore, is .009, or almost .01 (1%). Another way to state this is to say that a *z* score greater than 2.33 will fall in the upper 1% of the standard normal distribution, and as such it is a low-probability or "rare" event.

We will not show you here how to conduct hypothesis tests using the standard normal distribution because we will be doing that in several later chapters. We do, however, hope you see how we would conduct such a hypothesis test by defining in probability terms what a "very unlikely" or low-probability event is based on our selected level of alpha and then finding exactly what that means in terms of *z* scores. In the last section of this chapter, we want to discuss why the standard normal distribution is so important for our statistical work.

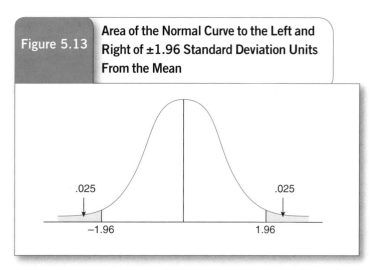

Figure 5.13 Area of the Normal Curve to the Left and Right of ±1.96 Standard Deviation Units From the Mean

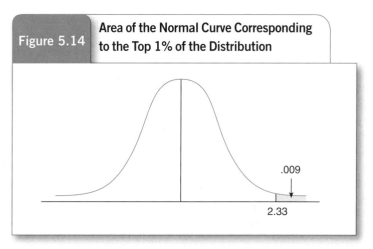

Figure 5.14 Area of the Normal Curve Corresponding to the Top 1% of the Distribution

Samples, Populations, Sampling Distributions, and the Central Limit Theorem

A good understanding of the properties of the normal distribution is very important for statistical analysis. At some point in your reading of this chapter, though, you may have wondered just why the normal distribution is so important. You may have thought that although there certainly are some variables that are normally distributed in the population, many others are not really normal. For example, population characteristics such as the number of crimes committed or convictions experienced by persons are not likely to be normally distributed (most people commit zero or only a few crimes, and there is a long right tail of the distribution where few offenders commit many crimes). If only a few variables are normally distributed in the population, the utility of the normal distribution surely must be rather restricted. Not so!

The normal distribution has wide applicability that makes it invaluable for research. The reason behind the generality of the normal distribution is based on one of the most important and remarkable theorems of statistics: the *central limit theorem*. It is because of the central limit theorem that we can employ the standard normal distribution in so much of our statistical work even if we do not have normal populations. Before we examine this theorem and its implications, however, we need to discuss some preliminary issues.

Recall that in conducting research, we typically draw a sample from a large population rather than studying the entire population. We draw a sample from our population and collect data on characteristics of the sample with the intention of making an *inference* about the corresponding, but unknown, characteristics in the population. Thus, although we know a great deal about the characteristics of our sample (we know its mean, its standard deviation, the skew of the distribution, etc.), we know virtually nothing about the characteristics of the population. This is a problem because it is to the population that we want to generalize. Fortunately, through inferential statistics, we can make some estimate about the characteristics of populations from our knowledge of sample characteristics. The connection between sample information and population characteristics involves something called a sampling distribution.

As an example, let's assume that we are interested in the variable of height, and we want to know the mean height of persons in some population (the students at a university). In this problem, we collect data on the height of those selected into our random sample from which to estimate the height of our larger population. Let's also assume for the moment that the distribution of height in the population is normal. We draw a random sample of 100 persons, so our sample size is 100 ($n = 100$). Both our sample of 100 persons and the larger population from which it was drawn have a mean value. Recall that for our sample, the mean height is symbolized by our *sample statistic*. The corresponding population value is called the *parameter* and is symbolized by μ.

In our sample of 100 persons, some people are taller than the sample mean height, some are shorter, and some may actually be equal to the mean. We have, then, variation around our sample mean, which we measure with the sample standard deviation (s). Similarly, in our population, not everyone is the same height as the population mean, and this variation around the mean is measured in terms of the population standard deviation (σ). Keep in mind that although the population is normally distributed (we have assumed that this is true), our sample of 100 heights may not be normally distributed. The distribution of height from our sample may in fact be very skewed.

Now, instead of taking just one random sample of 100 people from our population, let's imagine taking 10,000 random samples of 100 people ($n = 100$). For each one of these 10,000 samples of 100, we can determine the mean ($\overline{X}$) This would involve a huge amount of time and effort. We would draw a sample of 100 people and then calculate the mean of that sample ($\overline{X}_1$). We draw a second random sample of size 100 and determine the mean of that sample ($\overline{X}_2$). We continue drawing a random sample from a population 10,000 times, each of size 100, and calculate the mean of each sample ($\overline{X}_{10,000}$). This would give us 10,000 sample means. Since these 10,000 sample means are not all alike (i.e., the value of the mean will vary from sample to sample because different people are in each sample), there is a corresponding distribution of means and a corresponding mean and standard deviation of this distribution of means. The fact that we are referring to a very large number (10,000) of sample means should alert you to the fact that we are speaking about a theoretical distribution, not an empirical distribution that is based on real information. The distribution of these 10,000 sample means with a sample size of 100 is called a sampling distribution of means in this case, but more generally it is just a sampling distribution.

In this sampling distribution of 10,000 sample means, although the value of each mean will vary from sample to sample, these values will still cluster around the mean of the population from which we sampled (μ). The standard deviation of this distribution of 10,000 sample means will be equal to

$$\frac{\sigma}{\sqrt{n}}$$

Sampling distribution: Probability distribution of a sample statistic (e.g., mean or proportion) drawn from a very large number of samples from some given population.

Based on this formula, you can see that the larger the size of the random sample we select from this normal population (n), the smaller the standard deviation of the sampling distribution will be because the larger n becomes, the larger the denominator becomes, which decreases the value of s. As our sample size increases, then, variation around the mean of the sampling distribution decreases and, therefore, is more likely to cluster around the true population mean (μ). Stated another way, the means will have less variation from sample to sample with a large sample size (n). *Therefore, we will have more faith that any given sample represents the population mean if we have a large sample size.* Since the mean of the sample is our best estimate of the unknown mean of the population, we can draw two conclusions: (1) There is a certain amount of error in using a known sample mean to estimate an unknown population mean since there is variation in the means from sample to sample, and (2) the amount of this error or imprecision decreases as the size of the sample (n) increases. Since it reflects the amount of error due to sampling variation, the standard deviation of the sampling distribution

$$\left(\frac{\sigma}{\sqrt{n}}\right)$$

is generally referred to as the standard error; in this case, it is the *standard error of the mean.*

Figure 5.15 shows what happens to the standard deviation of the sampling distribution or the standard error when sample size is increased. Note that the distribution of the sample means is narrower than the population distribution (except, of course, when $n = 1$; then it is the same), and the larger the sample size (n), the more narrow that sampling distribution will be. As you can see, then, the larger the sample size, the more likely it will be that any particular randomly drawn sample of size n will be close to the population mean (μ). In other words, the larger the sample size, the less error there is in using our known sample statistic ($\bar{X}$) to estimate our unknown population parameter (μ). *The general rule to remember is that larger samples are always better than smaller ones because they give more precise estimates.* This should make intuitive sense; larger samples will more likely represent the population better compared with smaller samples.

In addition to having a known mean and standard deviation (μ and $\sigma/\sqrt{n}$, respectively), according to one probability theorem, the distribution of these 10,000 sample means drawn from a normal population (the sampling distribution) will also be normal. We will state this theorem explicitly:

If an infinite number of random samples of size n are drawn from a normal population, with a mean equal to μ and a standard deviation equal to σ, the sampling distribution of the sample means will itself be normally distributed with a mean equal to μ and a standard deviation equal to $\sigma/\sqrt{n}$.

In other words, the theoretical sampling distribution of the means of a very large number of random samples drawn from a normal population will have a normal distribution.

Before we introduce an even more useful and important statistical theorem, the central limit theorem, you need to remember that in the discussion earlier we referred to *three distinct distributions,* only two of which were normal. First, we have an empirical distribution of raw scores from a single random sample that we actually obtain. These scores are empirically observed and represent the heights of the individual persons in our random sample. The scores within our sample differ, so there is a distribution of sample scores with a mean ($\bar{X}$) and standard deviation (s). The distribution of our sample values is *not* presumed to be normal. The characteristic of interest (mean height) is referred to as a sample statistic. The second distribution is the distribution of our population characteristic (height). The scores in this distribution vary one from the other and are presumed to be normally distributed with mean (μ) and standard deviation (σ). The characteristic of

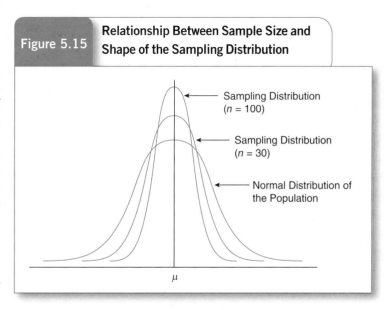

Figure 5.15 Relationship Between Sample Size and Shape of the Sampling Distribution

Table 5.11	Characteristics of Three Types of Distributions		
	Mean	Standard Deviation	Distribution
Sample	$\bar{X}$	s	Empirical and known
Population	μ	σ	Empirical but not known
Sampling distribution	μ	$\dfrac{\sigma}{\sqrt{n}}$	Theoretical

interest in this distribution (mean height) is called the population parameter. The third distribution discussed is the sampling distribution, which is a theoretical distribution of a sample of means obtained from a very large number of random samples drawn from our normally distributed population. Based on the theorem provided earlier, this distribution is also assumed to be normally distributed, with a mean equal to the population parameter (μ) and a standard deviation equal to $\sigma / \sqrt{n}$. These three distributions and their associated characteristics are summarized in Table 5.11.

You should keep in mind that these are three distinct distributions. The first is a distribution of sample scores (empirical), and the second is a distribution of population scores (empirical but not known). What connects these two is the third (theoretical) distribution, which in this case is a distribution of sample means. With our sampling distribution, we can determine the probability of obtaining our sample statistic. Since the sampling distribution of means is normal and the population is assumed to be normal, we can make use of the standard normal distribution to determine this probability regardless of whether our empirical sample data are normally distributed. This can be represented in the following flow diagram:

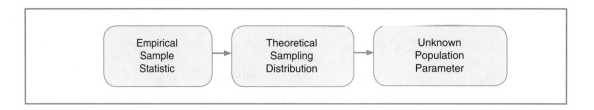

You may be thinking to yourself right now, "What if we can't assume that the population distribution is normally distributed? Does this mean that the normal distribution is inapplicable?" No. We can employ the normal distribution even if our population is not normally distributed (so long as we take a large sample). This is because of the remarkable nature of the **central limit theorem**:

> If an infinite number of random samples of size n are drawn from any population with mean μ and standard deviation σ, then as the sample size (n) becomes large, the sampling distribution of sample means will approach normality, with mean μ and standard deviation $\sigma / \sqrt{n}$, even if the population distribution is not normally distributed.

The importance of this theorem is that the sampling distribution does not depend on normality in the population. No matter what the shape of the distribution in the population, the theoretical probability distribution of sample means will approximate a normal distribution as the sample size becomes large. The sampling distribution not only will be normal but also will have a mean equal to the population mean (μ) and a standard deviation equal to $\sigma / \sqrt{n}$. This is a very important theorem because it suggests that even if our population distribution is quite skewed (like the number of arrests in the population), we can still assume that our sampling distribution of means will be normal as the size of the sample becomes large. Since it is the sampling distribution that links our sample estimate to

Central limit theorem: Statistical theorem that states that the sampling distribution of any statistic will approximate normality as the sample size increases.

the population parameter, we can employ the normal probability distribution in instances where our population is not normal.

Three Characteristics of the Sampling Distribution of the Mean Based on the Central Limit Theorem

Whenever the sample size is large:

1. We can assume that the mean of the sampling distribution is equal to the population mean, μ.

2. We can assume that the standard deviation of the sampling distribution is equal to $\sigma / \sqrt{n}$.

3. We can assume the sampling distribution is normally distributed even if the population from which the sample was drawn is not.

The important and practical question to ask now is, "How large is large enough so we can relax the normality assumption and appeal to the central limit theorem?" A rough rule of thumb (although it is only a rule of thumb) is that the assumption of normality can almost always be relaxed when the sample size is 30 or more ($n \geq 30$). With sample sizes of less than 30, the normality assumption should not be made. In the case of small samples, statistics that do not appeal to the central limit theorem and normal distribution must be employed.

▣ Summary

We have covered a lot of important ground in this chapter, a discussion that will serve as the foundation for our discussion of inferential statistics, which makes up the remainder of this book. At the core of this foundation is the notion of probability. We have discussed two types of the probability: (1) the chance or likelihood that a single event will occur in a given trial and (2) the chance that an event will occur over the long run with an infinite number of trials. We introduced the notion of the probability distribution—a theoretical distribution of outcomes determined by the laws of probability. One of these probability distributions is the binomial probability distribution, which governs events that have only two possible outcomes, called Bernoulli events. The binomial probability distribution is an important one for us since many of the events we are interested in have only two outcomes.

We then discussed a probability distribution that describes continuous events, the normal distribution. This unimodal, symmetrical distribution looks like a bell-shaped curve. We learned that there is a large family of normal distributions, which would make for some cumbersome probability calculations were it not for the standard normal distribution. The standard normal distribution is a normal distribution with a mean of 0 and a standard deviation of 1.0. To use the normal distribution to figure out the probability of continuous events, we must convert our raw x scores into what are called standard normal z scores. The z score is measured in standard deviation units. Once we have a z score, the determination of probabilities is relatively simple with the use of a z table.

Finally, we considered how a sample, a sampling distribution, and a population differ along with the relationship between them. We usually take one sample of size n from a single population and use the information from a sample to make an inference about some unknown population value using theoretical sampling distributions. Like any other distribution, a sampling distribution has a mean and a standard deviation. We also learned the important central limit theorem, which says that as our sample size increases, the sampling distribution will begin to approximate normality no matter what the shape of the population looks like.

Key Terms

➤ Review key terms with eFlashcards. Visit study.sagepub.com/paternoster.

binomial distribution   121
bounding rule of probabilities   114
central limit theorem   140
complement of an event   114
conditional probability   117
critical region of a probability
   distribution   129
descriptive statistics   112

general addition rule of probabilities
   (Rule 2b)   115
general multiplication rule of
   probabilities (Rule 3b)   117
independent events   117
inferential statistics   112
mutually exclusive events   114
null hypothesis   125

probability distribution   119
restricted addition rule of probabilities
   (Rule 2a)   115
restricted multiplication rule of
   probabilities (Rule 3a)   116
sampling distribution   138
significance or alpha level (α)   127
standard score (z score)   134

Key Formulas

The probability of success—the binomial theorem
(formula 5-1):

$$P(r) = \binom{n}{r} p^r q^{n-r}$$

$$P(r) = \left(\frac{n!}{r!(n-r)!} \right) p^r q^{n-r}$$

The mathematical formula for the normal distribution
(formula 5-2):

$$f(x) = \frac{1}{s\sqrt{2\pi}} e^{\frac{-(x-\mu)^2}{2s^2}}$$

Formula for converting a raw score into a z score
(formula 5-3):

$$z = \frac{x - \overline{X}}{s}$$

Practice Problems

➤ Test your understanding of chapter content.
Take the practice quiz at study.sagepub.com/paternoster.

1. The following data are the starting salaries for police officers in 110 police departments in a northeastern state:

Salary	f
$25,000	6
$26,000	8
$27,500	9
$28,000	10
$30,000	16
$31,500	19
$32,000	12
$32,500	15
$34,000	8
$35,000	7
Total	110

With this information, calculate the following:

a. The probability that a starting salary will be exactly $30,000.

b. The probability that a starting salary will be exactly $35,000.

c. Whether a starting salary of $30,000 and a starting salary of $35,000 are mutually exclusive events. Explain.

d. The probability that a starting salary will be at least $31,000.

e. The probability that a starting salary will be $30,000 or less.

f. The probability that a starting salary will be between $27,800 and $33,000.

g. The probability that a starting salary will be less than $25,000.

h. The probability that a starting salary will be $28,000, $32,000, or $35,000.

2. The probability of being acquitted in criminal court in Baltimore, Maryland, is .40. You take a random sample of the past 10 criminal cases where the defendant had a public defender and find that there were seven acquittals and three convictions. What is the probability of observing seven or more acquittals out of 10 cases if the true probability of an acquittal is .40? By using an alpha of .05, test the null hypothesis (that the probability of an acquittal is .40 for defendants with public defenders) against the alternative hypothesis that it is greater than .40.

3. Assume that you have a normal distribution of IQ scores with a mean of 100 and a standard deviation of 10.

   a. What is the z score for a raw score of 115?

   b. What is the z score for a raw score of 83?

   c. What is the z score for a raw score of 70?

   d. What proportion of the cases have an IQ score above 115?

   e. What proportion of the cases have an IQ score between 90 and 110?

   f. What is the probability that you would find an IQ score of 70 or below?

   g. What is the probability that you would find an IQ score of 125 or above?

4. In a recent article, Thomas Loughran, Greg Pogarsky, Alex R. Piquero, and Raymond Paternoster (2012) examined the relationship between perceived certainty of punishment and self-reported offending. They found that the certainty of punishment deterred the criminal behavior only for those who believed the likelihood of getting caught for committing a crime was medium to great. Let's say you are interested in the same idea with the concept of impulsivity. That is, you think the impulsive cannot be deterred. You do some research and find the following joint distribution between impulsivity and whether someone was deterred by the certainty of punishment:

| Impulsivity | Was the Person Deterred? | | |
	Deterred	Not Deterred	Total
Not impulsive	75	15	90
Impulsive	5	25	30
Total	80	40	120

   a. What is the probability that someone was deterred?

   b. Is this a conditional probability or an unconditional probability? Explain.

   c. What is the probability that someone was not deterred?

   d. What is the probability that someone was impulsive?

   e. What is the probability that someone was impulsive or not deterred by punishment? Are these mutually exclusive events? Explain.

   f. What is the conditional probability that someone was not deterred given that the person was impulsive?

   g. What is the conditional probability that someone was deterred by punishment given that the person was not impulsive?

   h. Are impulsivity and being deterred by punishment independent events? Explain.

   i. What is the probability that someone was impulsive and not deterred?

   j. What is the probability that someone was not impulsive and deterred?

5. The department of corrections in the state where you live has a policy whereby it accepts as correctional officers only those who score in the top 5% of a qualifying exam. The mean of this test is 80, and the standard deviation is 10.

   a. Would a person with a raw score of 95 be accepted?

   b. Would a person with a raw score of 110 be accepted?

   c. What is the minimum score you would need to have on the test in order to be accepted?

6. Explain how a sample, a sampling distribution, and a population differ. What is the mean and standard deviation for each of these?

7. Draw a picture indicating what proportion (area) of the normal curve lies (a–d):

   a. To the right of a z score of 1.65

   b. To the left of a z score of –1.65

   c. Either to the left of a z score of –1.96 or to the right of a z score of 1.96

   d. To the right of a z score of 2.33

   e. Is a z score of –2.56 a rare or low-probability score? Explain.

8. There has been some controversy about school violence and how to prevent it. To study measures that might prevent school violence, you take a random sample of 250 schools that differ in what they do to prevent school violence. You also collect information on the number of violent acts that were committed in each school during the previous school year. The information you have collected is shown as follows:

Number of Violent Acts	Type of Preventive Measure				Total
	No Measures	Metal Detectors Only	Guards Only	Guards and Metal Detectors	
None	5	10	15	30	60
1–4 acts	25	20	15	15	75
5 or more acts	50	30	25	10	115
Total	80	60	55	55	250

With these data, answer the following probability questions:

a. What is the probability that a school had no violent acts last year?

b. What is the probability that a school had guards only as part of its violence prevention measures?

c. What is the probability that either metal detectors or guards, but not both, were used?

d. What is the probability that no measures were used?

e. What is the probability that a school used both guards and metal detectors together or had one to four violent acts committed last year?

f. What is the probability that a school used metal detectors only or had five or more violent acts committed last year?

g. What is the conditional probability of no violent acts in a school given that there were no preventive measures used?

h. What is the conditional probability of no violent acts in a school given that some type of preventive measure was used?

i. What is the conditional probability of five or more violent acts given that metal detectors only were used?

j. What is the conditional probability of five or more violent acts given that both guards and metal detectors were used?

k. Are the two events, type of preventive measure used and number of violent acts in the school, independent events? Explain.

l. What is the probability of no violent acts and the presence of guards only as a preventive measure?

m. What is the probability of no preventive measures and five or more violent acts?

n. What is the probability of both guards and metal detectors together and one to four violent acts in the school?

9. A jail has an inmate population where the mean number of prior arrests is 6 and the standard deviation is 2.

a. Would a new inmate with 9 prior arrests have an unusually high number where unusual is in the top 5%?

b. Would a new inmate with 11 prior arrests have an unusually high number where unusual is in the top 5%?

c. Would an inmate with 2 prior arrests have an unusually low number where unusual is in the bottom 5%?

10. What is the central limit theorem? What does it enable us to assume about sampling distributions if we have a large enough sample?

STUDENT STUDY SITE

WANT A BETTER GRADE?

Get the tools you need to sharpen your study skills. Access practice quizzes, eFlashcards, data sets, and SPSS exercises at **study.sagepub.com/paternoster.**

CHAPTER 6

Point Estimation and Confidence Intervals

"Confidence, like art, never comes from having all the answers; it comes from being open to all the questions.

—Earl Gray Stevens *"*

LEARNING OBJECTIVES

1. State the difference between a point estimate and a confidence interval.

2. Describe how probability theory allows us to make generalizations from a point estimate to a population parameter.

3. Identify the relationship between levels of confidence and the precision of an interval at a given sample size.

4. Explain why different sampling distributions to make inferences from point estimates are necessary when using small versus large samples.

回 Introduction

On June 17, 2015, 21-year-old Dylann Roof opened fire at a Bible study meeting at the Emanuel African Methodist Episcopal Church in Charleston, South Carolina, using an illegally obtained semi-automatic handgun. Nine people were killed at short range, all with multiple bullet wounds (Harlan, Brown, & Fisher, 2015). The British newspaper *The Guardian* notes that after mass shootings in the United States, the reaction is virtually always the same—"Gun control groups diagnose an epidemic, the president declares a crisis, and gun advocates prescribe more guns" (McCarthy & Gambino, 2015, p. 1)—and this mass shooting resulted in little variation to this script. In addition to politicians making statements, television reports and newspaper articles frequently feature "person on the street" interviews that ask passersby to voice their opinions about the tragedy. These opinions are usually presented as if they are representative of something larger.

In Chapter 1, you learned that we cannot make generalizations from a sample to the population of interest unless we have collected a random sample that is representative of that population. Clearly, these "person on the street" interviews are not representative of any population. In research, if we want to have confidence in findings, including findings about attitudes, we have to examine the sample and data very systematically. For example, we know from professional opinion polls that have been conducted with random samples (of about 1,000 respondents) of the U.S. population (Pew Research Center, 2015) that a majority of Americans are in favor of certain forms of gun control, including the following:

	Favor (%)
Background checks for private and gun show sales	85
Preventing people with mental illness from purchasing guns	80
Federal database to track gun sales	67
Ban on semi-automatic weapons	58
Ban on high-capacity ammunition clips	54

Sample statistic: Statistic obtained from a sample.

Point estimates: Sample statistics such as the mean and proportion that are sample estimates of the same values in the population.

Population parameter: Statistic obtained from the population.

Student Study Site

Visit the open-access Student Study Site at study .sagepub.com/paternoster to access additional study tools including mobile-friendly eFlashcards, web quizzes, links to SAGE journal articles, additional data sets, SPSS exercises, and more!

The purpose in taking the sample was to estimate what the opinions are of the entire adult U.S. population, with the reported percentages being that sample estimate. The estimation of the population percent from the sample value, however, contains error, and the margins of error that Pew calculated around these percentages were about plus or minus 4%. Therefore, the percentages displayed here are really just our best estimates of public sentiment about gun control legislation. Before we can make generalizations from these estimates to the population, we have to provide some level of statistical accuracy in our results. These statements of accuracy are usually made with regard to a "margin of error" or "sampling error," and they are usually found in the fine print of a story or in the final paragraph, but they must be provided if the results are to be believed. These estimates of error are created using inferential statistics.

In this chapter, we take our first step into the world of inferential statistics. We concentrate on two sample statistics in this chapter, the *mean* $(\bar{X})$ and the *proportion* (p). The estimates of the mean and proportion that we obtain from a sample are referred to as point estimates of the same values in the population. Think of these point estimates as our best guess, based on sample information, as to what the unknown population parameters are.

Since our sample only gives us estimates, these estimates contain error and we have to construct what are called confidence intervals around them. These intervals enable us to make generalizations to the population with a known degree of certainty (i.e., confidence), and they are frequently used in the media as well as in scientific research. By the end of the chapter, you will be able to construct and interpret confidence intervals on your own. In addition, you will become more informed consumers of the point estimates that are presented in the media on a daily basis.

Making Inferences From Point Estimates: Confidence Intervals

To reiterate, the objective of the chapter is to show you how to make inferences about an unknown population characteristic based on information we obtain from a sample. In this chapter, we will examine different ways of estimating a population parameter based on a sample statistic. A population parameter is some unknown characteristic of a population. An example would be the mean reading level of inmates in all the prisons of a state correctional system. We do not know what this mean reading level is—that is our unknown population parameter (μ)—but we would like to estimate what it is without giving reading tests to every single inmate. So let's say we select a random sample of 500 inmates from a state prison with a population of 6,500, give them a reading test, and determine that the mean grade level at which this sample can read is 8.3. This is our known sample statistic ($\bar{X}$). We use the sample statistic from our sample of 500 as our point estimate of the unknown population parameter.

Our general goal is to evaluate how accurate our sample statistic (mean or proportion) is as an estimate of the true population parameter. To generalize these estimates to the entire population, we have to construct a margin of error around the point estimate that consists of a range of values or an interval into which we believe, with some established degree of confidence, the population value falls. This interval is called a **confidence interval**. Think of a confidence interval as an estimated interval that we are reasonably confident contains the true population value "over the long run." The confidence interval gives formal mathematical expression to the uncertainty we have in capturing the true population parameter with our sample statistic. To see this, think of a confidence interval as made up of two parts, a point estimate and a margin of error: confidence interval = point estimate ± margin of error.

Table 6.1 displays the results of a Gallup poll conducted in October 2014, asking respondents about the crimes they worry about the most (Gallup, 2014a). Typically, most news outlets, such as television reports and newspapers, focus primarily on the point estimates for each question. For example, they would typically report that 69% of Americans state that the crime they fear the most is identity theft of a credit card, whereas only 45% report that the crime they worry about the most is burglary of their home when they are not there, and only 31% say that it is being mugged. However, to be scientific, the confidence interval around this point estimate must also be noted somehow, usually at the end of a story. On its website, Gallup says the following about the sample and the confidence interval around the point estimates: "For results based on the total sample of national adults, the margin of sampling error is ±4 percentage points at the 95% confidence level." What this is really telling readers is that, to be 95% confident that the true population parameter (percent) is included in the estimate, you must add 4% to, and subtract 4% from, any point estimate to create an interval, which would then become a 95% confidence interval. For example, 42% reported that the crime they worried about the most was having their car broken into. This 42% is the point estimate of our unknown population parameter. To make a generalization about how worried the population is of getting their car broken into, we have to create a margin of error around this estimate. Gallup did this and concluded that to be 95% confident in the estimation, it would be 42% ± 4%.

Confidence interval: Statistical interval around a point estimate (e.g., mean) that we can provide a level of confidence to for capturing the true population parameter.

Table 6.1	Top Crime Worries of Americans

Crime Worries in United States
How often do you, yourself, worry about the following things—frequently, occasionally, rarely, or never? How about …

	% Frequently or Occasionally Worry
Having the credit card information you have used at stores stolen by computer hackers	69
Having your computer or smartphone hacked and the information stolen by unauthorized persons	62
Having your home being burglarized when you are not there	45
Having your car stolen or broken into	42
Having a school-aged child physically harmed attending school	31
Getting mugged	31
Having your home being burglarized when you are there	30
Being the victim of terrorism	28
Being attacked while driving your car	20
Being a victim of a hate crime	18
Being sexually assaulted	18
Getting murdered	18
Being assaulted/killed by a coworker/employee where you work	7

Source: Copyright ©2014 Gallup, Inc. All rights reserved. The content is used with permission; however, Gallup retains all rights of republication.

What does this tell us? Well, it says that we can be 95% confident that the true percentage of adults in the United States who worry most about having their car broken into is between 38% and 46%. What is important about this statement is that a level of confidence, 95%, accompanies it. Without creating a confidence interval around the point estimate of 42%, researchers would not be able to provide any confidence claims in their inferences. Also note that researchers had to start with a probability sample to do this in the first place! In addition, the correct technical interpretation of a 95% confidence interval is that if we repeated our sampling and point estimation an infinite number of times (or a very large number of times) and created a 95% confidence interval around each point estimate, 95% of those intervals would contain the true population parameter, whereas the other 5% would not. In other words, we have confidence in our procedure of sample selection and estimation, not in our one sample statistic.

Figure 6.1 illustrates the concept of a 95% confidence interval graphically. It shows a hypothetical example in which 20 samples ($n = 100$) are drawn from the same population. From each sample, the mean number of times individuals from that sample ran a stop sign per month was calculated, and a 95% confidence interval was drawn around each mean. The horizontal lines across the figure represent these 95% confidence intervals, and the vertical line running down the middle of the figure represents the true population mean of stop sign violations. From Figure 6.1, you can see that 95% (19) of these confidence intervals actually contain the true population mean, whereas 5% (1) do not. Even

| Figure 6.1 | A Hypothetical Example of 95% Confidence Intervals Computed From 20 Different Samples of the Same Size Drawn From the Same Population |

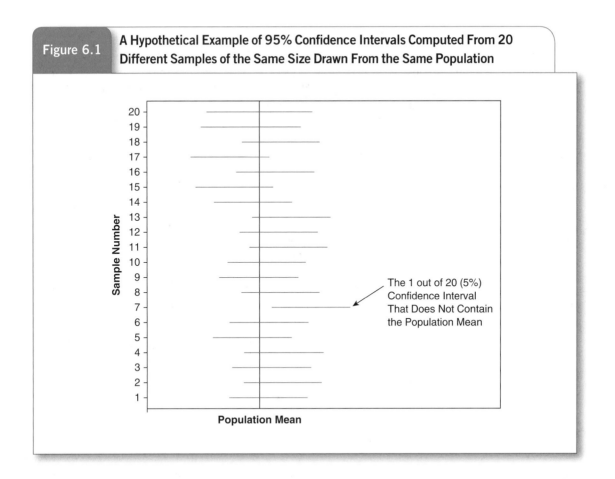

The 1 out of 20 (5%) Confidence Interval That Does Not Contain the Population Mean

Sample Number (vertical axis, 1–20)

Population Mean

though each of these confidence intervals varies from sample to sample, 95% of them nevertheless contain the true population parameter. You should also note that the true population parameter does not change but that the estimated interval does vary from sample to sample. This illustrates that what we are 95% confident about is the procedure, not the particular confidence interval we estimate with our sample data. That is, we should interpret our confidence interval as saying that over the long run, 95% of the confidence intervals we would estimate using this sample size and sampling procedure would include the true population parameter. This is the goal of inferential statistics: to make inferences to the target population with some degree of confidence.

Of course, in the real world, we never take repeated samples from the population and we never really know for sure whether we have contained the "true" population parameter within our confidence interval. However, if we have drawn our sample using probability sampling techniques (e.g., a simple random sample), we can use both probability theory and what we know about probability distributions to estimate a population parameter from only one sample. And probability theory enables us to make numerical statements about the accuracy or the confidence we have in our estimates.

In the sections that follow, we begin by examining the properties that any good estimate should have. We then examine confidence interval estimation procedures for sample means based on large samples ($n \geq 30$). We use the z distribution to do this. Next, we will introduce the t distribution, which is used for estimating means from small samples ($n < 30$). We will conclude the chapter by examining estimation procedures used for proportions and percentages.

z Distribution: Statistical sampling distribution used in many statistical tests, including for constructing confidence intervals, for determining the difference between two means, and for calculating the number of standard deviations an observation is above or below the mean.

t Distribution (Student's t distribution): Statistical sampling distribution used in many statistical tests, including for constructing confidence intervals and determining the difference between two means.

▣ Properties of Good Estimates

The first parameter we are going to estimate is a population mean, which is symbolized by the Greek letter μ. We are going to use the sample mean $(\bar{X})$ as our point estimate of the population mean. Why use the sample mean? Why not use the sample median or the average of the mean and the median value as our point estimator? The sample mean is chosen as our estimator because it is an *unbiased estimate* of the population mean. Any given estimate of a population parameter is unbiased if the mean of its sampling distribution is equal to the parameter being estimated. In the last chapter, we learned that the mean of the sampling distribution of means (the mean of a distribution of a large number of sample means) is the population mean (μ). Of course, one cannot conclude from this that any given sample mean $(\bar{X})$ will be equal to the population mean. Think of bias in the long run. With an infinite (or very large number) number of samples of size n within which we calculate a mean for each sample, the mean of all the sample means will be equal to the population mean. We know this is probably a bit confusing, but it will become clear, we promise. What is important to know is that our estimate must be unbiased. The sample mean and proportion are unbiased estimates of their respective population values. In addition to being unbiased, a second important property of an estimate is that it must be efficient.

The efficiency of an estimate is the degree to which the sampling distribution is clustered about the true population value. In this case, an efficient estimate for the mean is one where the sampling distribution of means is clustered close to the population mean. The more the sample means cluster about the population mean, the greater the efficiency of the estimate. Recall from Chapter 5 that sampling distributions are simply theoretical distributions that we would obtain if we were to draw many random samples of the same size from the same population and calculate the statistic of interest. In this case, we are talking about the mean. As with any theoretical distribution such as the normal distribution, there are theoretical properties of the sampling distribution of the mean. These properties are displayed in Table 6.2.

You will remember from the previous chapter that the standard deviation of the sampling distribution of means is equal to

$$\frac{\sigma}{\sqrt{n}}$$

where n is the size of your sample. The standard deviation of the sampling distribution, therefore, is in proportion to n, the sample size. As sample size increases, the standard deviation of the sampling distribution decreases. This tells us that the sample means themselves differ less from one another and cluster more tightly about the population mean. As we learned in the last chapter, as sample size increases, the sampling distribution of means becomes narrower. The practical implication of this is that our sample estimate of the true population parameter becomes more efficient as sample size increases. We will reiterate this important point throughout this and other chapters.

Standard error of the mean: Standard deviation of the sampling distribution of the mean.

Table 6.2	Properties of the Sampling Distribution of $\bar{X}$

1. The mean of this sampling distribution of $\bar{X}$ is μ.
2. The standard deviation of the sampling distribution of $\bar{X}$ is

$$\sigma_{\bar{X}} = \frac{\sigma}{\sqrt{n}}$$

where σ is the standard deviation of the original population, n is the sample size, and $\sigma_{\bar{x}}$ is used to denote the standard deviation of the sampling distribution. This entire term is called the **standard error of the mean**.

3. Because of the central limit theorem, when n is large (safely, when $n \geq 30$), the sampling distribution is normally distributed regardless of the distribution of the population from which the sample was drawn.
4. As the sample size increases, the standard deviation of the sampling distribution (the standard error of the mean) decreases.

🔲 Estimating a Population Mean From Large Samples

We just learned that a sample mean is an unbiased estimate of the population mean and that the efficiency of the sample mean as an estimate is increased by increasing sample size. We are now ready to get down to the business of constructing confidence intervals. Based on the properties of the sampling distribution of the mean and on what we know about the normal distribution and probability theory, we can use the following formula to construct a confidence interval around a sample mean $(\bar{X})$ where we will assume that we have taken a large sample $(n \geq 30)$ so we can invoke the central limit theorem and use the standard normal probability distribution or the z distribution:

$$\bar{X} \pm z_{\alpha}(\hat{\sigma}_{\bar{X}}) = \bar{X} \pm z_{\alpha}\left(\frac{s}{\sqrt{n}}\right)$$

(Formula 6-1)

where

$\bar{X}$ = the mean of our sample

z_{α} = the z score corresponding to the level of alpha we are using to construct our interval (i.e., the level of confidence we will have in our estimate)

$\hat{\sigma}_{x}$ = the standard deviation of the sampling distribution (i.e., the standard error), which is estimated with $\dfrac{s}{\sqrt{n}}$

The confidence interval, then, is determined by going out in both a positive and a negative direction from the point estimate (the mean in equation 6-1) a specified multiple of standard errors $\left(\dfrac{s}{\sqrt{n}}\right)$ of the z or standard normal distribution. How many standard errors we go out from the point estimate is a function of the **confidence level** we select.

The first order of business, then, is to select the degree of confidence we desire for our interval. Typically, researchers choose an alpha level of .05 or .01, which correspond to a 95% or 99% confidence interval, respectively. In fact, most of the poll data you hear about in the media virtually use a 95% confidence level. If $\alpha = .05$, we have a 95% confidence level. If $\alpha = .01$, we have a 99% confidence level. A 95% confidence level means that over the long run, we are willing to be wrong only 5% of the time. A 99% confidence level means that over the long run, we are willing to be wrong only 1% of the time. Being wrong in this case means that the population mean will not fall within the boundaries established by the confidence interval. We will later see that the size of the confidence interval is a function of how confident we want to be *and* how large our sample is.

Let's begin with a 95% confidence interval. After we have selected our level of confidence, we must next determine the corresponding z score from the z distribution for that level of confidence. The z score corresponding to an alpha of .05 (95% confidence) is 1.96 (see Table B.2 in Appendix B). Why is it 1.96? With a 95% confidence interval, we are concerned with 5% of the tail of the standard normal distribution. Since, however, we do not know whether our sample statistic $(\bar{X})$ is less than or greater than the true population value (μ), we are really concerned about both the left and right tails of the distribution. Hence, we divide our 5% into two equal halves (2.5%) and place them at each tail of the z distribution. The proportion of the standard normal curve that corresponds to an area under the curve of 2.5% is .025. Remember that in the standard normal curve, .50 of the area lies to the left of the mean and .50 of the area lies to the right of the mean. Since we have .025 in each tail where our alpha is, we find the area of the curve and then our z score by taking the difference .50 – .025 = .4750. So we must go into the body of the z table and find the area .4750 or as close as we can to .4750. The z score that corresponds to .4750 of the normal curve (.50 – .025) is 1.96 (from Table B.2). To repeat, to find this z score, simply go into the body of the table until you see the proportion .4750; the z score for this proportion is 1.96. Since we are interested in both tails of the distribution, our z score is ±1.96. In Table 6.3, we provide a list of some common confidence intervals and their corresponding z scores.

> **Confidence level:** Level of confidence (e.g., 95% or 99%) that is set for a statistical inference from the sample to the population.

| Table 6.3 | Common Confidence Intervals and Their Corresponding Critical Values of z From the Sampling Distribution of z |

Confidence Level (%)	Significance (α)	z Score
90	.10	1.65
95	.05	1.96
99	.01	2.58
99.9	.001	3.27

Let's go through an example.

Case Study

Estimating Alcohol Consumption for College Students

Suppose that we conducted a survey from a random sample of 140 undergraduate university students from a state university, asking them about the number of drinks of alcohol they consumed during the last month. One objective of the study was to estimate (make an inference about) the average number of drinks per month that undergraduate students attending this university ingest. The population we are interested in making an inference about is all undergraduate students at that university, but since that population is too large for us to study, we took a simple random sample of 140 students. The sample statistics we obtained were as follows:

$$\bar{X} = 12.4$$

$$s = 8.2$$

$$n = 140$$

The sample mean tells us that, on average, the students from our sample have an average of 12.4 alcoholic drinks per month. To remind you, this sample statistic $(\bar{X})$ is referred to as our point estimate of the true population parameter (μ). What does our sample mean tell us about the mean of the entire population of university students? This is the question we are really trying to answer. We don't think that the average number of alcoholic drinks an undergraduate has is exactly equal to 12.4, but it is our best guess, or our point estimate. We can't simply report that our best guess is 12.4 drinks per month without formally stating our level of confidence with a margin of error. To do this, we use formula 6-1 to construct a 95% confidence interval around the sample mean estimate of 12.4 using the critical value of z of 1.96 obtained from Table 6.3 as follows:

95% Confidence Interval (c.i.) of Drinks per Month for University Students

$$95\% \text{ c.i.} = 12.4 \pm 1.96\left(\frac{8.2}{\sqrt{140}}\right)$$

$$95\% \text{ c.i.} = 12.4 \pm 1.96 \left(\frac{8.2}{11.83} \right)$$

$$95\% \text{ c.i.} = 12.4 \pm 1.96(.69)$$

$$95\% \text{ c.i.} = 12.4 \pm 1.35$$

To find the confidence interval for our mean, we simply subtract 1.35 from the mean of 12.4 to get what is called the lower limit of our confidence interval and then add 1.35 to the mean of 12.4 to get our upper limit:

$$12.4 - 1.35 = 11.05$$

$$12.4 + 1.35 = 13.75$$

$$95\% \text{ c.i.} = 11.05 \text{ to } 13.75 \text{ alcoholic drinks per month}$$

What does this interval tell us? First of all, it tells us that our point estimate of the number of monthly drinks that undergraduate students in the population imbibe is 12.4 and the 1.35 drinks per month is our margin of error. Second, it tells us that, based on our sample data, we can be 95% confident that the mean number of drinks that university students in the population consume per month lies between 11.05 and 13.75. The correct interpretation is that if we had taken a large number of random samples from this same population (undergraduate students at this university) and calculated a 95% confidence interval around the mean obtained from each sample, approximately 95% of these intervals would include the true population mean (μ) and 5% would not (this 5% of the intervals that would not contain our population parameter is our margin of error). Another way to express this confidence interval would be as follows:

$11.05 \leq \mu \leq 13.75$ drinks per month

Or, simply, (11.05, 13.75)

We are 95% confident that the mean number of monthly drinks in the undergraduate university population is greater than or equal to 11.05 and less than or equal to 13.75.

To illustrate how levels of confidence affect the size of the confidence interval, let's create a 90% confidence interval around the same sample mean rather than a 95% confidence interval. From Table 6.3 we see that the z score corresponding to an alpha level (α) of .10, or a 90% confidence interval, is 1.65. As before, using formula 6-1 and the same sample mean, standard deviation, and n, we construct our confidence interval as follows:

$$90\% \text{ c.i.} = 12.4 \pm 1.65 \left(\frac{8.2}{\sqrt{140}} \right)$$

$$90\% \text{ c.i.} = 12.4 \pm 1.65(.69)$$

$$90\% \text{ c.i.} = 12.4 \pm 1.14$$

$$90\% \text{ c.i.} = 12.4 \text{ to } 13.54 \text{ drinks per month}$$

$11.26 \leq \mu \leq 13.54$

This interval indicates that we are 90% confident that the true mean number of drinks per month in the population of undergraduate university students falls between 11.26 and 13.54 drinks. Note that the 90% confidence interval is slightly narrower than the 95% confidence interval, but the trade-off of this narrower interval is that we are less confident (90% compared with 95% confident) that our true population mean falls into this interval. By lowering our level of confidence, we gained some precision in our estimate. We could reduce the width of our confidence interval even more, but we would have to pay the price in a lower level of confidence. Similarly, if we wanted to increase our confidence, say using a 99% confidence level, how would our confidence interval change? If you thought it would have increased, you would be correct!

One way to decrease the width of our interval without compromising our level of confidence would be to increase our sample size. Why? Remember that a large standard error (like a large standard deviation) indicates that the mean varies a great deal from sample to sample, whereas a small standard error indicates that there is little variation from sample to sample. Intuitively, then, as the size of the standard error decreases, the level of confidence we have in any one sample estimate typically increases. The larger the sample size (n), the smaller the standard error will be (or our estimate of the standard error). If you look at the estimate we use of the standard error of the mean $\left(\frac{s}{\sqrt{n}} \right)$, you can see that as the sample size increases (n), the magnitude of the standard error decreases.

Case Study

Probation Officer Behavior

Let's go through another example from the criminal justice literature. In an article in the journal *Justice Quarterly,* Joel Miller (2015) examined the role of community corrections officers who perform probation officer duties. More than 1,700 probation officers were sampled from the population of members of the American Probation and Parole Association and completed a questionnaire. One item on the questionnaire asked how much they relied on reminding probationers of the legal consequences of their behavior. This item was designed to measure a component of the law enforcement duties that probation officers have, that is, to remind those under their supervision about the legal consequences of their behavior. The response options provided for the probation officers ranged on a seven-point continuum from 0 (never) to 6 (always). The mean response for this item was 4.69 (much closer to "always" than to "never") with a standard deviation of 1.34. Let's construct a 95% confidence interval around this sample mean but assume that the sample size was 200 ($n = 200$):

$$95\% \text{ c.i.} = 4.69 \pm 1.96 \left(\frac{1.34}{\sqrt{200}} \right)$$

$$95\% \text{ c.i.} = 4.69 \pm 1.96 \left(\frac{1.34}{14.14} \right)$$

$$95\% \text{ c.i.} = 4.69 \pm 1.96(.095)$$

$$95\% \text{ c.i.} = 4.69 \pm .186$$

$$95\% \text{ c.i.} = 4.504 \text{ to } 4.876$$

$$4.504 \leq \mu \leq 4.876$$

How would you interpret this interval? This 95% confidence interval indicates that we can be 95% confident, based on our sample statistics, that in the population of all probation officers who are members of this professional organization, the mean number of times they remind those under their supervision about the legal consequences of their behavior is between 4.504 and 4.876 on a scale where 0 equals never and 6 equals always. This suggests that reminding their clients of the possible legal consequences of their actions is a fairly common strategy used by probation officers in their practice. Now let's take the same data, and instead of constructing a 95% confidence interval, let's increase the confidence we have in our interval estimate by calculating a 99% interval. The only change that is necessary in the formula is the critical value of z. Because we have increased the level of confidence we wish to have about our point estimate ($\overline{X}$), the critical value of z increases from 1.96 to 2.58 (Table 6.3). Using formula 6-1, the calculation of the 99% interval is

$$99\% \text{ c.i.} = 4.69 \pm 2.58 \left(\frac{1.34}{\sqrt{200}} \right)$$

$$99\% \text{ c.i.} = 4.69 \pm 2.58\left(\frac{1.34}{14.14}\right)$$

$$99\% \text{ c.i.} = 4.69 \pm 2.58(.095)$$

$$99\% \text{ c.i.} = 4.69 \pm .245$$

$$99\% \text{ c.i.} = 4.445 \text{ to } 4.925$$

$$4.445 \leq \mu \leq 4.925$$

This 99% confidence interval indicates that we can be 99% confident, based on our sample statistic, that in the population of all probation officers who are members of this professional organization, the mean number of times they remind those under their supervision about the legal consequences of their behavior is between 4.445 and 4.925. Note that this 99% confidence interval is wider than that from the same data with only a 95% confidence interval. We wanted to be more confident that our interval contains the population mean with the 99% confidence interval, and this increased confidence comes at the price of a wider confidence interval. By now, this should be making sense to you. It suggests that if we want to be more confident that the true population mean falls in our estimated interval, we have to make the interval wider (everything else staying equal). To reiterate, greater confidence comes at a price, and the price we pay is the precision (width) of the confidence interval.

Think for a minute about this question: "If we want to be more confident without increasing the size of the interval, what can we do?" If your answer was to increase our sample size, you were right! A confidence interval will be smaller with a larger sample size because when the standard deviation of the sampling distribution (standard error) is reduced, the sample value is a more accurate estimate of the true population mean.

After all of this discussion of different confidence levels, you may be asking yourself, "When do we want to use a 99% confidence interval compared with a 95% interval or even a 90% interval? What guides us in selecting a level of confidence?" Unfortunately, there are no "hard-and-fast" rules for this. The decision you make is in part a judgment call that depends on the nature of your research and on the importance of having high confidence weighed against having a slightly larger confidence interval. Just remember that there is usually a trade-off between confidence and precision.

Estimating Confidence Intervals for a Mean With a Small Sample

In constructing confidence intervals with formula 6-1, we used the sample standard deviation to estimate the population standard deviation. When our sample size is large (recall from Chapter 5 that when the sample size is at least 30, the assumption of a normal population can generally be relaxed), the sample standard deviation is a fairly good estimate of σ. This is not true, however, when our sample size is small. In the case of small sample sizes ($n < 30$), the sample standard deviation shows substantial variation from sample to sample. For small samples, therefore, the standard deviation of the sampling distribution (standard error) is greater than that for large samples. The practical implication of this is that the z distribution cannot be used for constructing confidence intervals when the sample size is small because the sampling distribution cannot be assumed to be approximately normal.

There are many times, however, when we must rely on small samples. In such instances, the assumptions we make about the normal distribution do not apply. Why? Well, recall that the properties of the central limit theorem (described in the last chapter) applied only to large samples. Therefore, if our sample is small, we must use statistics that do not invoke this "large sample" assumption. When our research dictates that we have no choice and must use

> **Figure 6.2** **The z Distribution and the t Distribution**
>
>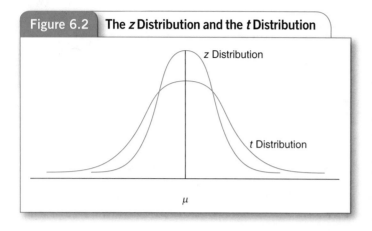
>
> z Distribution
>
> t Distribution
>
> μ

a small sample, Student's t distribution is typically used to make inferences from the sample mean, $\bar{X}$, to the population mean, μ, instead of the z distribution.

The theoretical sampling distribution called Student's t was calculated by W. S. Gosset and published in 1908. Gosset was a statistician for the Guinness brewing company. Although Guinness did not usually allow its employees to publish their own work, Gosset was permitted to do so under the pen name of "Student." Hence, his distribution has been called Student's t distribution.

The t distribution is flatter and has a greater spread (fatter at the tails) than the z distribution, which indicates that there is more sample-to-sample variability in the former. The two sampling distributions are shown in Figure 6.2. There is a different t distribution for each sample size, and the smaller the sample size, the flatter the t distribution is, compared with the normal distribution. Just like the standard normal distribution (z), the t distribution has several known properties, which are listed in Table 6.4.

As noted in Table 6.4, there are actually many t distributions, depending on the **degrees of freedom (df)** present in the sample. As the sample size (and df) becomes larger, the t distribution more closely approximates the standard normal distribution (z distribution). When $n > 120$, the two distributions are virtually identical, but the t distribution will always be flatter and fatter at the tails than the z distribution. The values of t associated with these degrees of freedom at different levels of alpha (α) and for one- and two-tailed hypothesis tests are displayed in Table B.3 in Appendix B. Remember that by definition, confidence intervals are two-tailed tests because we do not know whether our sample statistic is greater than or less than the true population value. For confidence intervals, then, we always use values of t associated with a two-tailed test (see Table B.3) since we are creating an interval by going around a sample statistic and, therefore, using both tails of the sampling distribution.

Let's say we had a sample size of $n = 10$ and wanted to make an inference to the population mean at the 95% level. With this, we would go into the t table using $\alpha = .05$ for a two-tailed test. We next have to find the degrees of freedom associated with our sample size, which in the case of confidence intervals is $n - 1$, giving us a df equal to 9 ($10 - 1 = 9$). Going down the alpha column of $\alpha = .05$ for a two-tailed test to the row that lists 9 degrees of freedom, we would obtain a critical value of $t = 2.262$. That is the value that we would plug into the formula for our t-based confidence interval.

In Table B.3, note that when the sample size is greater than 100, the critical values of t are about the same as those for z, and that when the sample size is greater than 120 (at the infinity symbol sign), the critical values of t and z are identical. This reflects the fourth property listed in Table 6.4, which states that as the sample size approximates 120, the t distribution begins to look more and more like the z distribution. This should make intuitive sense to you based on our discussion in the last chapter.

The formula for calculating a confidence interval around a mean using the t distribution is shown as follows. It looks almost exactly like that employed when calculating confidence intervals using the z distribution, doesn't it? That's because it is the same except that we use the t value from the t table rather than the z value from the z table:

> **Degrees of freedom (df):** Value necessary, along with a given alpha value, to determine the critical value and region for a null hypothesis test or for a confidence interval.

$$\bar{X} \pm z_\alpha(\hat{\sigma}_{\bar{X}}) = \bar{X} \pm z_\alpha\left(\frac{s}{\sqrt{n}}\right)$$

(Formula 6-2)

Table 6.4	**Properties of the Sampling Distribution of *t***

1. The *t* distribution is bell-shaped and symmetrical and centers around $t = 0$.
2. The *t* distribution is flatter and has fatter tails than the *z* distribution.
3. There are many different *t* distributions based on the sample size. More specifically, the distribution of *t* that we use for our statistical test is based on a parameter called the degrees of freedom (*df*). The number of degrees of freedom is different for different kinds of statistical problems. For confidence intervals, there are $n - 1$ degrees of freedom where *n* is the sample size.
4. With sample sizes of 120 or more, the *t* distribution becomes virtually identical to the *z* distribution.

Case Study

Work-Role Overload in Policing

Let's go through an example of making inferences about μ with a small sample using the *t* distribution. Linda Duxbury, Chris Higgins, and Michael Halinski (2015) developed a study to measure what they called "work-role overload" in policing. Work-role overload occurs when police officers experience stress and anxieties because of the demands of the different duties, obstacles, and organizational demands they face in their policing job. For example, police feel stress and overwhelmed because of the emotional demands of the job, excessive paperwork, unpredictable work schedules, financial limitations, and demands made by supervisors. The ultimate objective of the study was to design an instrument to measure this role overload.

Suppose we were interested in using this work-role overload data collection instrument in our own study of police in a large urban police department. The department has thousands of police officers (this is our population), and we take a random sample of 14 officers for our study. The mean score on the overload measure for our officers was 31 with a standard deviation of 3. Let's assume the actual overload measure has a low of 0, indicating no perceived overload, and a high of 50, indicating the maximum score possible on the overload scale. The point estimate for the average work overload from our sample of officers was 31, and to generalize this point estimate to the entire department, we want to build a 95% confidence interval around that estimate. Since we have such a small sample, we cannot invoke the central limit theorem and must use the *t* distribution for our confidence interval.

Police Officers' Overload Score in Our Sample
$\bar{X} = 31$
$s = 3$
$n = 14$

The first step involves calculating the degrees of freedom and finding the critical value of *t*. With a sample size of 14, our degrees of freedom are equal to 13 ($n - 1$). We first note that we look for a two-tailed *t* because all confidence intervals are two-tailed tests (we use a two-tailed test for the *t*, which is the same as dividing our alpha level by 2 as we did with the *z* table doing confidence intervals with a large sample), then we find our alpha level of .05 (since we have a 95% confidence interval), and then we go down the rows until we find our degrees of freedom (13). Going down the appropriate column and across the appropriate row in the *t* table (Table B.3), you find the critical value needed is 2.160. Remember that the selection of the confidence level (and the corresponding critical value) is up to you. Once you have this, you can construct your confidence interval with formula 6-2:

$$95\% \text{ c.i.} = 31 \pm 2.160 \left(\frac{3}{\sqrt{14}} \right)$$

$$95\% \text{ c.i.} = 31 \pm 2.160 \left(\frac{3}{3.74} \right)$$

Female Police Officers' Scores on Work Overload Test	Male Police Officers' Scores on Work Overload Test
$\bar{X} = 41.9$	$\bar{X} = 32.5$
$s = 7.8$	$s = 9.3$
$n = 15$	$n = 15$

95% c.i. = $31 \pm 2.160(.80)$

95% c.i. = 31 ± 1.73

95% c.i. = 29.27 to 32.73

$29.27 \leq \mu \leq 32.73$ overload score

As before, to find the lower and upper **confidence limits**, we subtract 1.73 from and add 1.73 to our sample mean of 31, respectively. This interval tells us that based on our sample data, we can be 95% confident that the mean work overload of police officers in the city police department is between 29.27 and 32.73. If we had taken a large number of random same-sized samples from this same population of police officers and calculated 95% confidence intervals around the means obtained from each sample, approximately 95% of these intervals would include the true population mean, μ, and 5% would not.

Note the difference between the critical value in this confidence interval for small samples and that for the same 95% confidence interval we calculated earlier for large samples. If we had a larger sample in this case, we could have used the critical z value of 1.96 instead of the larger t value of 2.160 that was necessary here. To reiterate the reasoning behind this, remember that since the t distribution is flatter than the z distribution and fatter at the tails, we have to go farther out in the tail to find our critical region. At the same alpha level, with small sample sizes, the critical value of t will be larger than the large sample z.

For the t distribution, the relationships among confidence levels, sample sizes, and confidence intervals are still the same. At a fixed sample size, decreasing the confidence level will narrow the confidence interval, and increasing the confidence level will widen the confidence interval. The confidence interval can be narrowed (even when increasing the confidence level) by increasing the sample size.

Let's work with two more examples using Duxbury and colleagues' (2015) study. Let's assume that the police work overload test they developed ranged from a low of 0, meaning absolutely no work overload stress, to a maximum of 50, meaning that the different demands of police work are completely overwhelming. Let's also assume that we drew a sample of 15 male officers and 15 female officers from the same city police department and gave them the work overload instrument. It turned out that the mean score for the males was 32.5 with a standard deviation of 9.3, and the mean score of the females was 41.9 with a standard deviation of 7.8. Let's build a 99% confidence interval around each of these two estimates. First, the information for males and females is in the box above.

The first step in this procedure is to find our t value. We go to the t table in Table B.3 knowing that this is a two-tailed test; then we find our alpha level of .01, and we go down the row to find our degrees of freedom. With a sample size of 15, our degrees of freedom are equal to 14 ($n-1$). Going down the appropriate column and across the appropriate row in the t table (Table B.3), you find that the critical value needed is 2.977. The 99% confidence interval for female officers is

$$99\% \text{ c.i.} = 41.9 \pm 2.977\left(\frac{7.8}{\sqrt{15}}\right)$$

$$99\% \text{ c.i.} = 41.9 \pm 2.977\left(\frac{7.8}{3.87}\right)$$

$$99\% \text{ c.i.} = 41.9 \pm 2.977(2.02)$$

$$99\% \text{ c.i.} = 41.9 \pm 6.01$$

$$99\% \text{ c.i.} = 35.89 \text{ to } 47.91$$

$$35.89 \leq \mu_{females} \leq 47.91$$

Confidence limits: Numerical lower and upper values that correspond to any given confidence interval around a point estimate from the sample.

This interval tells us that based on our sample data, we can be 99% confident that the mean score for the females on the work overload scale is between 35.89 and 47.91. The female population mean is, therefore, estimated to be at the upper or overwhelmed end of the scale.

The 99% confidence interval for the male officers is

$$99\% \text{ c.i.} = 32.5 \pm 2.977\left(\frac{9.3}{\sqrt{15}}\right)$$

$$99\% \text{ c.i.} = 32.5 \pm 2.977\left(\frac{9.3}{3.87}\right)$$

$$99\% \text{ c.i.} = 32.5 \pm 2.977(2.40)$$

$$99\% \text{ c.i.} = 32.5 \pm 7.14$$

$$99\% \text{ c.i.} = 25.36 \text{ to } 39.64$$

$$25.36 \leq \mu_{males} \leq 39.64$$

This confidence interval tells us that based on our sample data, we can be 99% confident that the mean score for the males on the work overload scale is between 25.36 and 39.64. For both females and males, if we had taken a large number of random same-size samples from this same population of police officers and calculated 99% confidence intervals around the means obtained from each sample, approximately 99% of these intervals would include the true population mean and 1% would not.

Suppose we wanted to decrease our interval but did not want to gather more data. We would have to decrease our level of confidence to 95%. The degrees of freedom necessary to find the critical value of t for a 95% confidence interval would still be 14 ($n - 1$), but we would select an alpha (α) level of .05 instead of the .01 level we used for the 99% confidence interval earlier. From Table B.3, we see that the critical value of t for this interval becomes 2.145 and the computation of the confidence interval for the female officers is as follows:

$$95\% \text{ c.i.} = 41.9 \pm 2.145\left(\frac{7.8}{\sqrt{15}}\right)$$

$$95\% \text{ c.i.} = 41.9 \pm 2.145\left(\frac{7.8}{3.87}\right)\left(\frac{7}{8}\right)$$

$$95\% \text{ c.i.} = 41.9 \pm 2.145(2.02)$$

$$95\% \text{ c.i.} = 41.9 \pm 4.33$$

$$95\% \text{ c.i.} = 37.57 \text{ to } 46.23$$

$$37.57 \leq \mu_{females} \leq 46.23$$

Note that the interval got narrower with this change from the 99% to the 95% level of confidence. The advantage of being less confident is to have more precision in our point estimate. Now we can say, however, that we are 95% confident that the population mean of female police officers on the work overload scale is between 37.57 and 46.23. We now have a 5% probability ($\alpha = .05$) of not including the true population mean female workload scale in our confidence interval.

Let's now estimate this same 95% confidence level for the female officers and assume that we had a sample size of 30 rather than 15. To find the necessary critical value of t, we now enter Table B.3 with 29 degrees of freedom (30 − 1 = 29). The critical value necessary for this confidence interval is 2.045 ($df = 29$, $\alpha = .05$). The confidence interval in this case would be

$$95\% \text{ c.i.} = 41.9 \pm 2.045\left(\frac{7.8}{\sqrt{30}}\right)$$

$$95\% \text{ c.i.} = 41.9 \pm 2.045\left(\frac{7.8}{5.48}\right)$$

$$95\% \text{ c.i.} = 41.9 \pm 2.045(1.42)$$

$$95\% \text{ c.i.} = 41.9 \pm 2.90$$

$$95\% \text{ c.i.} = 39.00 \text{ to } 44.80$$

$$39.00 \leq \mu_{females} \leq 44.80$$

As shown, with a 95% confidence level and a sample size of 30, our confidence interval is 39.00 to 44.80. This interval is narrower than the interval at the same confidence level for an n of 15. This is because the estimated standard deviation of the sampling distribution

$$\frac{s}{\sqrt{n}}$$

gets smaller when the sample size is increased, and our value of t from the t table gets smaller. In the example with $n = 15$, the standard error was 2.02. When we increased our sample size to 30, the standard error was reduced to 1.42. The value of t in our calculations went from 2.145 to 2.045. The confidence intervals for our female officers at each level of confidence and sample size were as follows:

$$n = 15, 95\% \text{ confidence interval} = 37.57{-}46.23$$
$$n = 15, 99\% \text{ confidence interval} = 35.89{-}47.91$$
$$n = 30, 95\% \text{ confidence interval} = 39.00{-}44.80$$

As you can see, when the sample size is the same, confidence intervals for 99% will be larger compared with those for 95%. To decrease the size of the interval at any level of confidence, you can increase your sample size!

🔲 Estimating Confidence Intervals for Proportions and Percentages With a Large Sample

Compared with the confidence intervals around means that we have just examined, you are perhaps more familiar with confidence intervals constructed around proportions and percentages. The media bombard us with examples of these all the time. Results of opinion polls are usually quickly followed by a phrase such as "plus or minus 3%." This is one way of presenting a confidence interval to the public in a way people will better understand. The calculation of a confidence interval around a proportion when you have a large sample is done by using the z distribution and the following formula:

$$\text{Confidence interval} = \hat{p} \pm z_\alpha \left[\sqrt{\frac{p(1-p)}{n}} \right] \qquad \text{(Formula 6-3)}$$

where

$$\hat{p} = \text{sample proportion}$$

It is fairly easy to determine whether you have a large enough sample to use the z probability distribution. If $\hat{P}$ is the sample proportion estimated from the data, and $\hat{q} = 1 - \hat{p}$, and n is your sample size, then the following two conditions must both be true for you to use the z probability distribution: $n\hat{p} > 5$ and $n\hat{q} > 5$.

The term to the right of the z score in equation 6-3 is referred to as the **standard error of the proportion.**

In formula 6-3, the value of $\hat{p}$ in the confidence interval formula is the sample proportion. It is the sample point estimate $(\hat{q})$ of the unknown population parameter (P). As with the confidence interval for the mean with large samples, z is the critical value of z we obtain from the standard normal table. As before, the precise value of z depends on the particular confidence level we select.

Standard error of the proportion: Standard deviation of the sampling distribution of the proportion.

Case Study

Estimating the Effects of Community Policing

Many police departments across the United States have adopted a policing innovation called "community-oriented policing," or (naturally) COP for short. Community policing is designed to increase the frequency of police–citizen encounters, which is then expected to improve relationships between the police and community residents. Jihong Zhao and Ling Ren (2015) conducted a study of public attitudes toward the police with telephone surveys in Houston, Texas. Let's assume we conduct a similar study in a small midwestern city and find that 33% of our 100 sample respondents ($n = 100$) are not satisfied with the police. The sample proportion of .33, then, would be our point estimate. Let's construct 95% and 99% confidence intervals around this sample estimate. First, let's verify we can use the z probability distribution here and our large sample formula. Since $\hat{P} = .33$, $.33 \times 100 = 33$, which is greater than 5, and since $\hat{P} = .67$, $.67 \times 100$ is also greater than 5, we can use the large sample formula for proportions. Since we have large samples, we can use the critical value of z at the $\alpha = .05$ and .01 levels. First, the calculations for the 95% confidence interval:

$$95\% \text{ c.i.} = \hat{p} \pm z_\alpha \left(\sqrt{\frac{\hat{p}(1-\hat{p})}{n}} \right)$$

$$95\% \text{ c.i.} = .33 \pm 1.96 \left(\sqrt{\frac{.33(.67)}{100}} \right)$$

$$95\% \text{ c.i.} = .33 \pm 1.96 \left(\sqrt{.002} \right)$$

$$95\% \text{ c.i.} = .33 \pm 1.96 (.045)$$

$$95\% \text{ c.i.} = .33 \pm .09$$

$$95\% \text{ c.i.} = .24 \text{ to } .42$$

$$.24 \leq P \leq .42$$

To find the lower limit of our confidence interval, we subtracted the margin of error (.09) from our point estimate of .33, and to find the upper limit, we added .09 to our point estimate. We then converted these proportions to percentages by multiplying each limit by 100. We have 95% confidence that the true proportion of the population in our city who are not satisfied with the police is between .24 and .42, or between 24% and 42%.

Now the calculations for a 99% confidence interval:

$$99\% \text{ c.i.} = \hat{p} \pm z_\alpha \left(\sqrt{\frac{\hat{p}(1-\hat{p})}{n}} \right)$$

$$99\% \text{ c.i.} = .33 \pm 2.58 \left(\sqrt{\frac{.33(.67)}{100}} \right)$$

$$99\% \text{ c.i.} = .33 \pm 2.58 \left(\sqrt{.002} \right)$$

$$99\% \text{ c.i.} = .33 \pm 2.58 (.045)$$

$$99\% \text{ c.i.} = .33 \pm .12$$

$$99\% \text{ c.i.} = .21 \text{ to } .45$$

$$.21 \leq P \leq .45$$

By interpreting this interval, we can say we have 99% confidence that the true proportion of citizens who are not satisfied with the police is between .21 and .45, or between 21% and 45%. Again, notice that when we went from a 95% confidence interval to a 99% confidence interval with the same sample size, the width of our interval increased. The price to be paid for greater confidence is less precision.

Case Study

Clearing Homicides

Let's go through another quick example. Jason Rydberg and Jesenia M. Pizarro (2014) were interested in explaining the time it takes police to clear a homicide by an arrest. They had a theory, lifestyle theory, which hypothesized that if the victim was involved in a "deviant lifestyle," it would take the police longer to solve the homicide. The connection between being involved in a deviant lifestyle and a longer clearance rate for homicides was the expectation that law enforcement would in essence be more indifferent to solving the murder of a victim who may also have been less than lawful. This lifestyle theory had been used in the past to explain who is likely to become a homicide victim, but Rydberg and Pizarro were the first to use the theory to explain homicide clearances. By using data from the Newark, New Jersey, police department's homicide unit, they found that the more indicators of a deviant lifestyle for a victim (the victim was a gang member, was a drug dealer, had a criminal history, etc.), the longer it took for the police to solve the homicide.

Let's assume we did a related study by examining a sample of gang-related homicides and finding the proportion of them that were cleared by an arrest within 1 year in a northeastern city. From our sample of 150 gang-related homicides, we find that 58% were cleared within 1 year. Our point estimate of the proportion of gang-related homicides in the northeastern city that were cleared by an arrest, then, would be .58. Let's build a 95% confidence interval around that point estimate:

$$95\% \text{ c.i.} = .58 \pm 1.96\sqrt{\frac{.58(1-.58)}{150}}$$

$$95\% \text{ c.i.} = .58 \pm 1.96\sqrt{\frac{.58(.42)}{150}}$$

$$95\% \text{ c.i.} = .58 \pm 1.96\sqrt{\frac{.24}{150}}$$

$$95\% \text{ c.i.} = .58 \pm 1.96\sqrt{.0016}$$

$$95\% \text{ c.i.} = .58 \pm 1.96(.04)$$

$$95\% \text{ c.i.} = .58 \pm .078$$

$$95\% \text{ c.i.} = .502 \text{ to } .658, \text{ or } 50.2\% \text{ to } 65.8\%$$

$$.502 \leq P \leq .658$$

To determine the lower limit of our confidence interval, we simply subtract the margin of error (.078) from the sample point estimate of .58, and to determine the upper limit, we add .078 to our point estimate of .58. Our 95% confidence interval of the proportion of gang-related homicides in this city cleared by an arrest is between .502 and .658, or between 50.2% and 65.8%. This is quite a large interval. How could we make our confidence interval narrower without losing any confidence? We hope your immediate answer was, "*Increase the sample size!*"

🔲 Summary

In this chapter, we have examined the procedures for estimating population parameters using confidence intervals. To estimate confidence intervals around a $\bar{X}$ obtained from a large sample, we examined estimation procedures based on the z distribution. We also examined the formula based on the t distribution used to construct confidence intervals around means obtained from small samples. We concluded the chapter by examining the estimation procedures used to construct confidence intervals around proportions and percentages with a large sample.

Each type of interval could have been constructed using any level of confidence (e.g., 75%, 88%, 95%). However, we focused on confidence levels of 95% and 99% since these are the levels typically used in all disciplines, including criminology and criminal justice. We discussed the trade-offs made when adopting particular levels of confidence; at the same sample size, higher levels of confidence (e.g., 99% compared with 95%) produce wider intervals. So while you gain confidence in your estimation, you also lose precision. Smaller samples always inflate the standard error of the sampling distribution you are working with, thereby increasing the width of a confidence interval. Thus, larger samples are more desirable than smaller ones because whether we are estimating a population mean or proportion, the larger the sample, the more precise our sample statistic is.

Key Terms

➤ Review key terms with eFlashcards. Visit study.sagepub.com/paternoster.

confidence interval   147
confidence level   151
confidence limits   158
degrees of freedom (*df*)   156

point estimates   146
population parameter   146
sample statistic   146
standard error of the mean   150

standard error of the proportion   160
t distribution (Student's *t* distribution)   149
z distribution   149

Key Formulas

Confidence interval around a sample mean with large samples (formula 6-1):

$$\bar{X} \pm z_\alpha \left(\frac{s}{\sqrt{n}} \right)$$

Confidence interval around a sample mean with small samples (formula 6-2):

$$\bar{X} \pm t_\alpha \left(\frac{s}{\sqrt{n}} \right)$$

Confidence interval around a sample proportion with large samples (formula 6-3):

$$\hat{p} \pm z_a \sqrt{\frac{\hat{p}(1-\hat{p})}{n}}$$

Practice Problems

> Test your understanding of chapter content.
> Take the practice quiz at study.sagepub.com/paternoster.

1. What is the purpose of confidence intervals?

2. Describe the differences between the z distribution and the t distribution. When is it appropriate to use the z distribution for estimation procedures?

3. A hypothetical study concerned with estimating the amount of marijuana use per year among a teenage population obtained a sample of 110 high school students. With the following sample statistics, construct a 95% confidence interval around the mean number of times this sample uses marijuana during a given 6-month period:

   $$\bar{X} = 4.5 \text{ times per year}$$

   $$s = 3.2$$

   $$n = 110$$

   What does the interval you constructed tell us about marijuana use in the population? Interpret these results.

4. By using the same mean and standard deviations as in problem 3, change the sample size to 25 and construct a confidence interval around the mean using the appropriate procedures. How does the interval change? Provide an interpretation for your interval.

5. What does the standard deviation of the sampling distribution of the mean tell us? What affects the size of the standard error?

6. In a 2014 article, Evan McCuish, Raymond Corrado, Patrick Lussier, and Stephen D. Hart investigated the role of psychopathic traits in determining patterns of offending from adolescence into adulthood. They found those with psychopathic traits were far more likely to have more serious offending trajectories. Let's say you have a sample of 20 young males who have been in juvenile institutions at least twice. The mean psychopathic trait score for these 20 males was 18 with a standard deviation of 4. Build a 99% confidence interval around this point estimate.

7. A mayor of a large city wants to know how long it takes the police in his city to respond to a call for service. In a random sample of 15 citizens who called the police for service, the mayor's research director found that the average response time was 560 seconds with a standard deviation of 45 seconds. Construct a 95% confidence interval around your point estimate. What would you say to the mayor?

8. Wayne N. Welsh, Gary Zajac, and Kristofer Bucklen (2014) investigated the extent to which recidivism rates differed between convicted offenders who were assigned to a therapeutic community (TC) drug treatment and those who were assigned to outpatient (OP) group counseling. Treatment was randomly assigned to the offenders toward understanding which treatment modality was more effective at curbing recidivism. Recidivism in this study was operationalized by computing the percentage of youths who had been reincarcerated for any crime within 36 months of their release from the programs. About .44 of the offenders assigned to TC ($n = 286$) were reincarcerated within 36 months compared with .38 of the offenders assigned to the OP group ($n = 318$). Construct a 95% confidence interval around each of these sample proportions.

9. If you constructed a 99% confidence interval around the proportions in problem 8, how would this change the intervals? Why?

STUDENT STUDY SITE

WANT A BETTER GRADE?

Get the tools you need to sharpen your study skills. Access practice quizzes, eFlashcards, data sets, and SPSS exercises at **study.sagepub.com/paternoster.**

CHAPTER 7

Hypothesis Testing for One Population Mean and Proportion

> " *It is, in fact, nothing short of a miracle that the modern methods of instruction have not entirely strangled the holy curiosity of inquiry.*
>
> —Albert Einstein

LEARNING OBJECTIVES

1. Explain the purpose of hypothesis testing to determine the difference between a population mean and proportion and a sample mean and proportion.

2. Conduct and interpret the results of hypothesis tests for a sample mean and proportion.

3. Describe the difference between a directional (one-tailed) and non-directional (two-tailed) null hypothesis test.

4. Evaluate the advantage of conducting a directional (one-tailed) hypothesis test compared with a non-directional test.

5. Identify the appropriate sampling distribution to use for a one-sample hypothesis test when the sample size is small.

🔲 Introduction

Although research has examined sentence disparities between white collar crime and street crime, there is still a paucity of research that has investigated the sentencing disparities between types of white collar crime, especially for different subgroups of the population (e.g., by gender and race). Kristy Holtfreter (2013) recently examined survey data collected by the Association of Certified Fraud Examiners (ACFE), which asked respondents to provide details about their most recently investigated closed case. She found that the mean sentence length in months given to the entire sample was 41.4. Suppose you wanted to determine whether white collar criminals convicted of fraud in your state received sentences that were similar to this national estimate, which you assume represents the population estimate of sentence length for people convicted of fraud. How would you answer this question? Luckily for you, this chapter will provide you with all you need to investigate these types of questions.

In this chapter, we are going to make an assumption or hypothesis about what the value of the unknown population parameter is and ask whether this assumption is realistic given a particular sample statistic we observed from our data. Our question in this chapter is, then, "Is it likely that the unknown population parameter (mean or proportion) is equal to what we have assumed or hypothesized it to be, given what we know about our sample value (our sample mean or proportion)?"

As we did in Chapter 5, when we performed a hypothesis test using the binomial distribution, in this chapter we again will compare information we have from our sample with what we assume to be true about our population. We use probability theory to help us decide the reasonableness of our assumption. The decision we make, however, is not without some risk of error. Recall the LoJack car security issue from Chapter 5—no matter what we decide, there is always a chance that we have made the wrong decision. Probability theory permits us to understand in advance the probability of making the wrong decision. It lets us make our decision with some level of confidence.

Let's use a hypothetical thought exercise. Suppose you have been hired by the warden of a correctional institution to evaluate a literacy program in the prison. After reviewing all the records at the state department of corrections, you know that the average reading level for the population of incarcerated inmates in the state who have not been in a literacy program is 7.5 years. You take a random sample of 100 "graduates" of the literacy program and find that their mean reading level is 9.3 years, with a standard deviation of 2.2 years. You want to know whether the mean reading level for the sample of literacy program graduates is equal to the general population mean—that is, whether the population mean of literacy program graduates is equal to 7.5 years, the same as for the general population. The question you must ask yourself is, "Is it reasonable to assume that the population mean for program graduates is 7.5 years, given that my sample mean is 9.3 years?" Note that if you assume that the mean population reading level of your sample of graduates is no different from the mean reading level of incarcerated inmates of 7.5 years, you are assuming that your literacy program has no effect on increasing the reading level of those who complete the program. In other words, there is no "treatment effect" for being in a literacy program while in prison.

If, instead of a sample of 100 graduates, you had information about every graduate who had ever completed the program (the population of program graduates), you would be better able to answer your question. In this case, you could simply compute the average reading level for your population of program graduates and see whether it was equal to 7.5 years. Either it would be equal or not. You would have no doubt, and there would be no risk of error about your conclusion because you would have the information about the entire population. In the real world, however, we rarely have information about the entire population; instead, we must make inferences about the population from information we acquire from a sample of the population.

Of course, with sample information, we can never be 100% positive about whatever decision we make. Even if your sample mean is very different from the presumed value of the population mean, you cannot automatically conclude that your assumption about the value of that population mean was wrong. The difference between

Student Study Site

Visit the open-access Student Study Site at
study.sagepub.com/paternoster to access additional study tools including mobile-friendly eFlashcards, web quizzes, links to SAGE journal articles, additional data sets, SPSS exercises, and more!

> | Figure 7.1 | **Formal Steps for Hypothesis Testing** |
>
> **Step 1:** Formally state your null (H_0) and research (H_1) hypotheses.
>
> **Step 2:** Select an appropriate test statistic and the sampling distribution of that test statistic.
>
> **Step 3:** Select a level of significance (alpha = α) and determine the critical value and rejection region of the test statistic based on the selected level of alpha.
>
> **Step 4:** Conduct the test; calculate the obtained value of the test statistic and compare it with the critical value.
>
> **Step 5:** Make a decision about your null hypothesis and interpret this decision in a meaningful way based on the research question, sample, and population.

your sample mean and the presumed population mean might be due simply to **sampling variation** or chance. This is because the means of repeated samples taken from the same population are invariably different from the true population value. Enter probability theory! With the information provided by your sample and the presumed value of the population mean, you can determine the likelihood or probability of obtaining the sample mean if, in fact, the **null hypothesis** is true. We do this through the formal procedures of conducting a hypothesis test. Something to remember: We will not know with 100% certainty that we are correct no matter what we decide, only the probability that we are correct!

The remainder of this chapter examines the ways to test a hypothesis about a single population mean using both large and small samples and about a population proportion using a large sample. We also examine the difference between **hypothesis testing** using **non-directional (so-called two-tailed) tests** versus directional (one-tailed) tests. Before we begin this new section, however, let's refresh our memory from Chapter 6 about the steps involved in any hypothesis test by examining Figure 7.1. In the following sections, we consistently apply these five steps to the problem of testing first a hypothesis about a sample mean and then a hypothesis about sample proportion.

Hypothesis Testing for Population Means Using a Large Sample: The z Test

Case Study

Testing the Mean Reading Level From a Prison Literacy Program

Let's begin our discussion of hypothesis testing using the example about reading levels for the sample of prison literacy program graduates and the general population of incarcerated inmates discussed earlier. We can summarize what we know about the two groups as follows:

	Population	*Sample*
Mean reading level	$\mu = 7.5$	$\bar{x} = 9.3$
Standard deviation	σ = unknown	$s = 2.2$
	N = unknown	$n = 100$

Sampling variation: Differences between the sample and the population that are due to chance or sample variation.

Null hypothesis: Hypothesis that is tested; it always assumes there is no relationship between the independent and dependent variables.

Non-directional hypothesis test: When a research/alternative hypothesis does not state the direction of difference; it states only that there is a relationship between the independent and dependent variables.

What we know for sure, then, is that the mean reading level of our sample of 100 literacy program graduates ($\bar{X} = 9.3$) is different from the mean for the entire population of incarcerated inmates ($\mu = 7.5$). But is the mean reading level of the literacy program graduates really different from the population mean? In statistical terms, are the means *statistically significantly* different, or are they different merely because of sampling variation or chance? To conduct a formal hypothesis test to answer this question, we will initially assume that the population of literacy program graduates has the same mean reading level as the rest of the inmates—that is, 7.5 years. Remember, science is not about proving research hypotheses but rather about disproving null hypotheses. How valid is this assumption given the fact that our sample mean, 9.3 years, appears quite different from the presumed population mean of 7.5 years? Because we have only a *sample* of literacy program graduates, we can account for this apparent difference in one of two ways.

One explanation for the difference between our sample mean of 9.3 years and the population mean of 7.5 years is that the mean population reading level of literacy graduates is not really 7.5 years. This means that our initial assumption about the value of the population mean of 7.5 years is incorrect and that the true population mean for the literacy program graduates is actually different from this. The implication of this is that literacy program graduates come from a different population with a different mean than non-program inmates. By this, we mean that our sample did not come from the population of all other incarcerated offenders but rather came from another population, the population of literacy program graduates, which has a different mean reading level (hopefully a mean reading level that is higher than the general population's).

Figure 7.2 illustrates this explanation by showing the distribution of reading levels for the two populations. In Figure 7.2, the curve on the left is the population of incarcerated offenders with a mean reading level of 7.5 years ($\mu = 7.5$). The one on the right is a different population with a higher population mean ($\mu = 10$). One explanation for the difference between our sample mean (9.3 years) and what we have assumed is the true population mean (7.5 years) is that our sample was actually drawn from a different population. Perhaps our sample was drawn from the population on the right where the population mean is 10 years rather than 7.5 years. If this is true, our assumption that the population mean reading level for literacy program graduates is 7.5 years is not correct and we would like to reject that assumption.

A second explanation for the difference between the presumed population mean (7.5 years) and the observed sample mean (9.3 years) is based on sampling variation—that the difference in means is simply due to the fact that we just happened to select a sample with a high mean reading level even though the true population mean is really equal to 7.5 years. Figure 7.3 illustrates this possibility. If we assume that this explanation is true, we conclude that the population mean for both program graduates of the literacy program and non-graduates is, in fact, 7.5 years. We then conclude that there is only one population and that population has a mean reading level of 7.5 years. If this is true, our assumption that the population mean for literacy program graduates is 7.5 years is correct. Well, you may wonder, "If the true population mean is 7.5 years, why is our sample mean different?" The explanation is that the only reason the

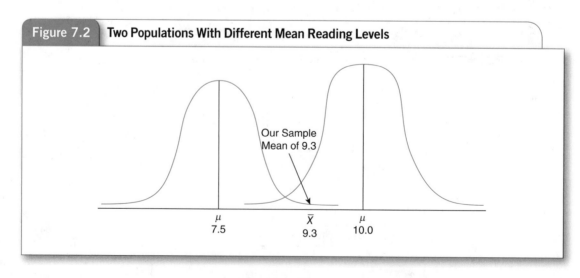

Figure 7.2   Two Populations With Different Mean Reading Levels

sample mean (9.3 years) is different from the presumed population mean (7.5 years) is that not every sample selected from a population will have a mean equal to that population's mean. Based on chance alone, we may have selected a sample that has a different mean than the true population mean has. It was just the "luck of the draw," so to speak, just like it is entirely possible to get 8 heads in 10 flips of a coin. There will always be variation in the proximity of the many sample means to the true population mean. In other words, simple sampling variation can account for the difference between a sample mean and the mean of the population from which that sample was drawn.

Recall from our discussion of the sampling distribution of the mean in Chapter 6 that if we take a very large or infinite number of samples of size n from a population whose mean is μ, the individual sample means will differ from one another and from the true population value (μ), but the mean of the infinite number of

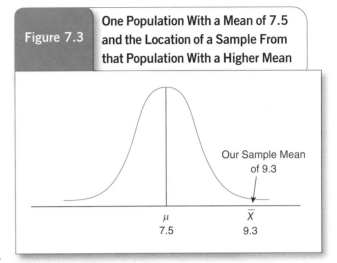

Figure 7.3 One Population With a Mean of 7.5 and the Location of a Sample From that Population With a Higher Mean

sample means will still be μ. Well, according to this second explanation, we have simply selected one of those samples from the population in which the sample mean just happens to be quite different from the population mean. In this case, the sample we have was drawn from a population with a mean reading level of 7.5 years, but the sample mean just happens to be quite different from that (9.3 years). The reason it is different, then, is not that the population means are actually different; rather, the reason is sampling variation—chance alone.

As you can perhaps imagine, the implications of these two explanations are quite different. The first explanation implies that there are two different populations with two different population means. In this scenario, our sample mean differs from the presumed population mean because the sample was drawn from an entirely different population. If this explanation is correct, we would conclude that the observed difference between the sample and population means is "statistically significant." In other words, it is a difference due to a difference in population means, not to chance factors such as sampling variation. In drawing this conclusion, we would be saying that our initial assumption that the population mean is equal to 7.5 years was incorrect. In a word, we would *reject* this assumption.

If the second explanation is correct, however, the observed difference between our sample and population means is probably attributable to our just happening to pick a sample whose mean reading level was different from the population mean, but the sample still came from this same population. Thus, there is really no significant difference between the sample mean and the population mean. In this case, the observed difference is not "statistically significant"—it is due not to a real difference between the two groups but instead simply to sampling variation. In drawing this conclusion, we have not rejected our initial assumption that the population mean is 7.5 years. Stated in statistical terms, we have *failed to reject* our initial assumption or hypothesis. We would continue to assume that the prison literacy program is not related to reading levels.

In sum, we have two possible and equally compelling explanations for the difference between our sample mean and population mean—but two explanations with very different implications. Which explanation is correct? Unfortunately, because we have sample data, not information from a population, we cannot know for certain which explanation is correct. Remember that we did not know what the mean reading level was in the population for the literacy program graduates; we know only the mean of a sample. We assumed that it was a given value, and we wondered how safe an assumption that was given what we observed our sample mean to be. Although we cannot know for certain which explanation is true, what we can do is set up a decision-making rule that will help us to decide whether one of the two explanations described earlier is more likely than the other. The basis of this decision rule is the subject matter of hypothesis testing.

In making a hypothesis test about our two explanations, we begin by assuming that the second explanation is correct—that is, that the sample actually was drawn from the population in question. We are assuming, then, that the population mean is a particular value—in our example, that the mean reading level in the population is equal to 7.5 years. We have suggested that this assumption implies that the literacy program graduates come from the same population as do non-program inmates. In essence, we assume that the two groups come from the same population. We want to be very conservative in our decision making and not jump to any conclusion that the two groups are different. We proceed, then, by initially assuming that they are not different and seeing whether that assumption can be maintained given the sample information. The one-population explanation is the one we assume at first because it is more parsimonious than the two-population explanation. The assumption that there is one population with a mean of 7.5 years constitutes our null hypothesis. The word "null" implies that there is nothing going on, that things are null, and that any difference you see between sample and population characteristics is due to chance. We stated that the null hypothesis is the hypothesis of no difference between our sample mean and the assumed but unknown population mean. Our hypothesis that the population mean is 7.5 years is a null hypothesis because we are assuming that there is no "real" difference between the observed sample mean of 9.3 years and the population mean of 7.5 years. The difference is null or of no consequence because it is due simply to sampling variation or chance, not to any real difference between the sample and the population. "Real difference" in this case means that the treatment of having inmates in a literacy program "works" and increases the level at which they can read such that their population mean reading level is higher than that of those not in such a program. The starting point of the process of hypothesis testing, then, is an assumption of no differences—a null hypothesis. In a hypothesis test, we determine whether this assumption is reasonable given the evidence we have from our sample data.

In our research example, the null hypothesis is the hypothesis that the true population mean reading level for the population of literacy program graduates is equal to 7.5 years. It specifically refers to the fact that the sample mean and the population mean are not really (significantly) different. So our initial assumption or null hypothesis is

H_0: The population mean is equal to 7.5 years. The sample mean is not significantly different from this population mean.

Since the null hypothesis is symbolized by a capital H with a subscript of zero (the zero symbolizes the null condition or no difference), there are actually two ways to state this symbolically:

H_0: $\mu = 7.5$ years

and

H_0: $\overline{X} - \mu = 0$

After stating this null hypothesis, we ask ourselves, "If this null hypothesis is not true, what is the alternative state?" We formally express this by stating the alternative hypothesis (sometimes called the research hypothesis because it is often our belief in this hypothesis that motivates us to do the research in the first place). The *alternative hypothesis* is the likely true state of affairs if the null hypothesis is not true. In the case at hand, one of three alternative states may be true:

H_1: The sample was drawn from a population whose mean reading level is less than 7.5 years:

$$\mu < 7.5 \text{ years}$$

Substantively, this means that the literacy program made things worse and that those who completed the course read at a lower mean level than those who did not take the program.

OR

H_1: The sample was drawn from a population whose mean reading level is more than 7.5 years:

$$\mu > 7.5 \text{ years}$$

Substantively, this means that the literacy program improved reading and that those who completed the course read at a higher mean level than those who did not take the program.

OR

H_1: The sample was drawn from a population whose mean reading level is different from 7.5 years:

$$\mu \neq 7.5 \text{ years}$$

Substantively, this means that the literacy program made some difference, but we are not willing to say in advance whether the program made things worse or better. The alternative hypothesis is stated with a capital "H" and subscript of 1.

For reasons that should now be easy to remember, the first two alternatives are called directional alternative hypotheses and involve a one-tailed hypothesis test, and the third alternative is called a non-directional alternative hypothesis and involves a two-tailed hypothesis test.

Having stated our null hypothesis ($\mu = 7.5$ years), then, we ask whether the assumption made in the null hypothesis is likely to be true. We ask, "What is the probability of getting the particular sample mean ($\bar{X} = 9.3$ years) if the sample was, in fact, drawn from a population whose mean is stated in the null hypothesis ($\mu = 7.5$ years)?" In other words, we want to know how likely it is that we would observe the value of our sample mean if the population mean is 7.5 years. In our specific example, we determine the probability of selecting a sample with a mean reading level of 9.3 years from a population whose mean is 7.5 years. If the null hypothesis is true, we can determine the probability of observing the given value of our sample mean. Moreover, we can state in advance that if this probability is very small (say 5 chances out of 100, which translates to an alpha level of .05 [$\alpha = .05$], or 1 chance out of 100, which translates to an alpha level of .01 [$\alpha = .01$]), we will conclude that the assumption behind the null hypothesis must be false. In other words, if our sample data would be very unlikely (where "very unlikely" is defined by our alpha level) to occur under the assumption of the null hypothesis, we would reject the null hypothesis. So we will continue to assume that the null hypothesis is true unless the probability of our observing the sample data under this assumption is such a "rare event," an event with a probability of .05 or less or .01 or less, that it is more likely that the alternative hypothesis is true, and we must reject the null hypothesis. This is exactly the procedure we used in Chapter 5 with our hypothesis involving LoJack. There we determined that if the probability of getting your stolen car returned 8 out of 10 times was very unlikely or rare, we would reject the assumption that the return rate of stolen cars with LoJack was different from that of stolen cars without LoJack. Although we have previously suggested that .05 and .01 are commonly selected levels of alpha, this is just conventional practice. There are at times compelling reasons to use a larger (.10) or much smaller (.001) alpha level. Recall that in choosing a particular alpha level, we are selecting the risk we are willing to take of making a Type I error—that is, of rejecting a null hypothesis that is actually true. Sometimes the cost of a Type I error may be very great and we may want to be very, very sure before we reject the null hypothesis (say with a probability of 1 out of 1,000). This is the situation in criminal trials where the cost of a Type I error, convicting a person who in fact is innocent, is thought to be extraordinarily high. To avoid making this mistake, we set the bar of evidence very high, "beyond a reasonable doubt"—a probability that must be very, very low. In civil proceedings, there is much less at stake since the defendant who loses usually forfeits only money rather than liberty. In this case, the cost of a Type I error of convicting an innocent person is lower, so the burden of proof required is also lower: "a preponderance of the evidence."

As scientists, we have to do the same kind of balancing act and weigh the cost of making a Type I error against the cost of making a Type II error (failing to reject a null hypothesis that is in fact not true). There are some cases where the cost of a Type I error is very high and that of a Type II error is low. Suppose, for instance, that we have two treatment programs for those convicted of drunk driving. One of these programs is exceptionally expensive and involves a great deal of intrusion into a person's life (it involves random drug tests and surprise home visits), whereas the other treatment is very inexpensive and involves little in the way of intrusion. Before we decide to make convicted drunk drivers take the first treatment, we want to make sure that it is more effective than the second treatment. In this instance, we might set the risk of a Type I error at .001. If, however, we are comparing two treatments that cost about the same and involve the same loss of liberty, then we might want to increase our risk of a Type I error to .05 or even .10. The point you should remember is that *you need to think carefully about the cost of making a Type I error and of making a Type II error before deciding what your alpha level is going to be.* In addition, you must remember that you cannot reduce the probability of both types of errors simultaneously. If you decrease the risk of making a Type I error (the probability of rejecting a null hypothesis that is in fact true) by setting alpha very low, you are increasing the risk of making a Type II error (the probability of failing to reject a null hypothesis that is in fact wrong). There is no such thing as a free lunch!

Let's get back to our literacy program example. There are a few remaining questions we must address before we begin the nitty-gritty work of hypothesis testing with one sample mean. One question concerns how we determine the likelihood or probability of observing a particular sample mean $\bar{X}$ given an observed population with mean μ. For example, how do we know the likelihood of obtaining a sample mean of 9.3 if the true population mean is 7.5? We can determine this likelihood or probability based on what we know about the theoretical sampling distribution of means, the central limit theorem, and the standard normal distribution (the z distribution). From the central limit theorem, we know that with a large enough sample ($n \geq 30$), the sampling distribution of an infinite number of sample means from a population with mean μ and standard deviation σ will be normally distributed and have a mean of μ and a standard deviation of $\sigma_{\bar{X}}$ where

$$\sigma_{\bar{X}} = \frac{\sigma}{\sqrt{n}}$$

We also know that if the sampling distribution of means is normally distributed with a known mean and standard deviation, we can convert our sample mean into a standard normal score called a z score. With our given sample mean expressed as a z score, we can then use our knowledge of the standard normal distribution (the z distribution) and determine the probability of observing a mean of this value given the known population mean. If this probability is less than or equal to our selected alpha level, we will reject the null hypothesis. If the probability is greater than our selected alpha level, we will fail to reject the null hypothesis.

The only piece of information we lack now is how to translate our sample mean $\bar{X}$ into a z score. We transformed a raw score into a z score in Chapter 5 with the formula

$$z = \frac{x - \bar{X}}{s}$$ (Formula 7-1)

where

x = our raw score

$\bar{X}$ = the mean for the sample

s = the sample standard deviation

To transform our sample mean into a z score, we need to slightly modify equation 7-1:

$$z = \frac{\bar{X} - \mu}{s/\sqrt{n}}$$ (Formula 7-2)

In this equation, our raw score (x) is replaced by the sample mean $\bar{X}$, the sample mean in equation 7-1 is replaced by the mean of the sampling distribution (which is μ, the population mean), and the standard deviation of the sample (s) is replaced by the estimated standard deviation of the sampling distribution of means, which is called the standard error:

$$\frac{s}{\sqrt{n}}$$

The formula for the *z test* when the population standard deviation is not known and our sample size is large enough, then, becomes

z Test: Statistical test used to test several null hypotheses, including the difference between two means.

$$z_{obt} = \frac{\bar{X} - \mu}{s/\sqrt{n}}$$ (Formula 7-3)

We are now ready to conduct our hypothesis test with our hypothetical data about mean reading levels.

To refresh your memory, we have a sample of 100 graduates from a prison literacy program where the sample mean reading level was 9.3 years. The mean reading level for the population of incarcerated inmates was 7.5 years. We want to know whether our sample came from a population whose mean reading level is 7.5 years.

Step 1: We begin our hypothesis test by stating the null hypothesis and the research, or alternative, hypothesis.

H_0: The two means are equal, $\overline{X} = \mu$. We could also state this null hypothesis by giving the value of the population parameter ($\mu = 7.5$). Our hypothesis test is whether the sample, whose mean we have observed, comes from a population with a mean of 7.5.

H_1: The two means are not equal, $\overline{X} \neq \mu$.

Note that the alternative hypothesis (H_1) simply states that the two means are not equal. Remember that this is called a *non-directional* (or two-tailed) *alternative hypothesis* because it does not state the directional difference between the means. It simply assumes that they are different. We will have more to say about directional and non-directional tests later in this chapter.

Step 2: The next step in hypothesis testing is to select an appropriate test statistic and obtain the sampling distribution for that statistic. Because the population standard deviation is not known, we use the z score formula in equation 7-3. Because we have a large sample, we use the standard normal distribution (z distribution) as our sampling distribution. By calculating the test statistic z with equation 7-3, what we are actually doing is obtaining a measurement of the distance in *standard error units* between the sample statistic (the sample mean, $\overline{X}$) and the hypothesized population parameter (the population mean, μ). If, for example, we obtained a z score of 1.5, this would indicate that our sample mean was 1.5 standard deviations above the population mean μ. An obtained z score of -2.3 would indicate that our sample mean was 2.3 standard deviations below μ and so on.

Step 3: The next step in formal hypothesis testing is to select a level of significance, termed our alpha level (α), and identify the critical region. Remember that the alpha level we set determines our risk of making a Type I error—that is, of rejecting a null hypothesis that is really true. Also remember that the selection of an alpha level is a judgment call. By tradition, the usual alpha levels in criminology and most other social sciences are .05, .01, and .001, but there is nothing sacred about these values. Based on our selected level of alpha, we must then find the critical value of our z statistic, which we refer to as z_{crit}. This critical value determines the rejection region for our hypothesis test.

For the sake of illustration, let's opt for an alpha level of .05 ($\alpha = .05$). Because we are testing a non-directional hypothesis, we have to divide our selected alpha level into two equal halves and place one half in each tail of the distribution (hence, it is referred to as a two-tailed test). With an alpha level of .05, we are interested in identifying the z score that corresponds to .05 / 2 = .025 of the area at each tail of the normal curve. This .025 of the area at each tail of the normal distribution defines our *critical region*. Since in the normal distribution .50 of the curve lies on each side of the mean, it will be easy to calculate the area that we need by subtraction. With a critical region of .025 in each tail of the curve, the remaining area up to the mean is equal to .50 – .025 = .4750, so we need to find the z score that corresponds to .4750 of the curve (an area equal to .025 lies to the right and left of this area, and these are our critical regions). We find this from the z table in Table B.2 in Appendix B. Going into the body of the table until we find .4750, we can determine that the corresponding z score is 1.96. Because the normal curve is symmetrical, we do the same thing for the other tail of the distribution where the corresponding z score is -1.96. The critical value of z for a two-tailed test with an alpha level of .05, then, is ± 1.96 ($z_{crit} = \pm 1.96$). This means that for us to reject the null hypothesis at the .05 level based on our sample data, the value of z we obtain from our test (z_{obt}) must fall 1.96 standard errors or more either above or below the population mean. Stated another way, our decision rule is to reject the null hypothesis if $z_{obt} \leq -1.96$ or $z_{obt} \geq +1.96$ and to fail to reject the null hypothesis if $-1.96 < z_{obt} < 1.96$. For future reference, the critical values of z that are used most often are provided in Table 7.1.

Now that we have our critical value of z, we can define the critical region in the sampling distribution. The critical region is the area of the sampling distribution that contains all unlikely or improbable sample outcomes (think of it as containing "rare events" where a rare event is defined by our alpha level) based on the selected alpha level. We use the word "region" because *the critical value of our test statistic defines the class of all obtained values that would lead us to reject the null hypothesis.* For example, if we defined our critical value of z as ±1.96, one critical region would consist of all obtained z scores equal to or less than −1.96. The second critical region would consist of all obtained z scores equal to or greater than +1.96. The critical value of z at ±1.96 and the corresponding rejection regions are shown in Figure 7.4.

Because we selected an alpha level equal to .05 and are conducting a two-tailed hypothesis test, the critical region is equal to .025 (.05 / 2) of the area of the normal curve at each tail. If you are getting a little lost (and even a bit hysterical), no worries, just remain calm and continue through the entire example. The small pieces of the picture often become clear when we observe the picture in its entirety!

Table 7.1	Alpha (α) Levels and Critical Values of *z* for One- and Two-Tailed Hypothesis Tests			
Type of Hypothesis Test	*Significance/Alpha Level*	*Critical Area in Each Tail*	*Critical z*
Two-tailed	.10	.05	1.65
One-tailed	.10	.10	1.29
Two-tailed	.05	.025	1.96
One-tailed	.05	.05	1.65
Two-tailed	.01	.005	2.58
One-tailed	.01	.01	2.33
Two-tailed	.001	.0005	3.27
One-tailed	.001	.001	3.08

Figure 7.4	Critical *z* and Critical Region for Two-Tailed Test and Alpha = .05

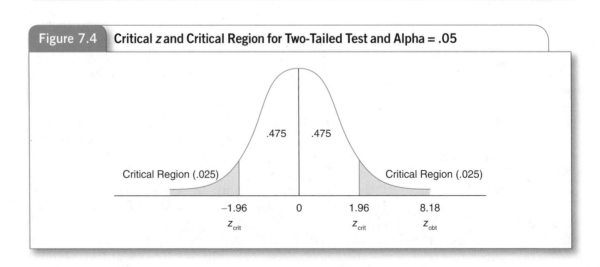

Step 4: The fourth step is to calculate the obtained test statistic, in this case z_{obt}, using the data we obtained from our sample. We have the sample size ($n = 100$), sample mean ($\overline{X} = 9.3$), and sample standard deviation ($s = 2.2$), so we can simply plug them into equation 7-3. The value of μ that is used in our calculations is always the value of μ we are testing in the null hypothesis; in this case, it is 7.5. The calculation of the z_{obt} statistic follows:

$$z_{obt} = \frac{\overline{X} - \mu}{s/\sqrt{n}}$$

$$z_{obt} = \frac{9.3 - 7.5}{2.2/\sqrt{100}}$$

$$z_{obt} = \frac{1.8}{2.2/10}$$

$$z_{obt} = \frac{1.8}{.22}$$

$$z_{obt} = 8018$$

Step 5: The obtained value of z, then, is 8.18. The final step of our hypothesis-testing enterprise involves making a decision about the validity of the null hypothesis based on the results of our statistical test. We do this by comparing our critical value of z ($z_{crit} = \pm1.96$) with the value we obtain from our statistical test ($z_{obt} = 8.18$), or by seeing whether our obtained statistic falls into one of our defined critical regions (see Figure 7.4). We see that the obtained z value of 8.18 is greater than 1.96. In fact, it falls well into the critical region, more than 8 standard deviation units above the hypothesized μ. Because $z_{obt} > 1.96$, we will reject the null hypothesis that the population mean is equal to 7.5. This observed sample outcome is highly unlikely if the null hypothesis is really true. Since our sample value of 9.3 years is very unlikely given our hypothesized population value, we are going to reject the null hypothesis; that is, we reject the assumption that our sample comes from a population whose mean reading level is 7.5 years. We will conclude instead that the sample of literacy program graduates comes from a population where the mean reading level is not equal to 7.5 years.

Case Study

Testing the Mean Sentence Length for Robbery

Let's do another example. Suppose we were interested in the mean length of the sentences given to convicted armed robbers in a state after the passage of a new firearms law. This new legislation provides for an automatic 3-year additional prison term for those convicted offenders sentenced for any felony in which a gun was used during the commission of a crime. What we really want to know is whether this new law has actually changed sentencing practices for armed robbery. We know that the mean sentence length given to convicted armed robbers during the 10 years before the new legislation was passed was 52.5 months. We will assume that this is our population mean μ. We take a random sample of 110 armed robbers who were convicted under the new law and sentenced to prison. The mean sentence length given to these 110 offenders was 53.2 months with a standard deviation of 6 months. The information we know, then, is as follows:

Population Parameters for Armed Robberies Before New Legislation	Sample Statistics for Armed Robberies After New Legislation
μ = 52.5 months	$\bar{x}$ = 53.2 months
σ = unknown	s = 6
N = unknown	n = 110

We want to know whether our observed sample mean of 53.2 months is significantly different from the population mean assumed under the null hypothesis. Of course, we know that it is different since 53.2 months is not 52.5 months, but this difference can be due to sampling variation, not to the fact that sentences imposed after the law was passed are greater than those imposed before the law was passed. In other words, we want to know if we can reject chance and assume that the observed difference is *significantly* different. To find out, we must conduct a formal hypothesis test. Again, let's state each step along the way.

Step 1: The first step is to state our null and alternative hypotheses. Our null hypothesis in this example is that the mean sentence length for our sample of armed robbers sentenced under the new law is the same as the mean from the population of previously sentenced armed robbers. This is the same thing as saying that the new law has had no effect on sentence lengths. Formally, the null hypothesis is that our sample is drawn from a population with a mean of 52.5 months:

$$H_0: \mu = 52.5$$

For our research or alternative hypothesis, we will state the non-directional alternative that the population from which our sample was drawn has a mean that is not equal to 52.5. We are not stating direction in this research hypothesis because we do not know for sure whether the mean sentence length under the new law will be more than or less than the previous mean sentence. We are hesitant to predict direction because other things are working to affect the mean sentence length of armed robbers in addition to the new legislation. For example, the state may be experiencing tremendous prison overcrowding, and judges might respond to this by decreasing the average prison sentence they impose in all cases despite the new law. In addition, judges might not like the fact that the state legislators are "meddling" in their sentencing domain. They might respond to the automatic 3-year addition to a sentence length by taking off 3 years from what they normally would have imposed. Because of these countervailing effects, the only alternative hypothesis we feel comfortable asserting is that the mean sentence length for newly convicted armed robbers is not 52.5.

$$H_1: \mu \neq 52.5$$

Step 2: The second step requires that we select our test statistic and the sampling distribution of that statistic. In this example, our test statistic is the z test and the sampling distribution is the standard normal (z) distribution. The population standard deviation (σ) is not known, so we will use equation 7-3.

Step 3: Our third step in hypothesis testing is to select a level of significance (alpha level, α) and determine the critical value and critical region(s) of our test statistic. We select a .01 alpha level for this example. As we have stated, for a non-directional research hypothesis, we place half of our selected alpha level (.01 / 2 = .005) in each tail of the z distribution. With .005 in each tail, we look in the z table for the area corresponding to .495. We find that the z score for this area is 2.58 (actually ±2.58). You can also find this critical value in Table 7.1 These areas constitute our critical regions, and they are marked in Figure 7.5.

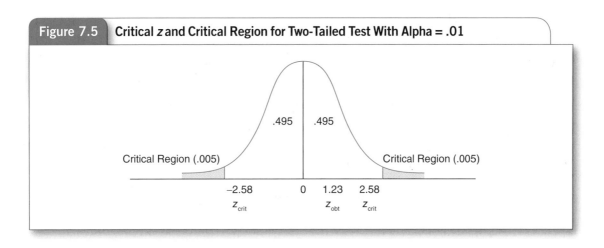

Figure 7.5 Critical z and Critical Region for Two-Tailed Test With Alpha = .01

Any obtained z score that falls into either of these two critical regions will lead us to reject the null hypothesis. Thus, our decision rule is to reject the null hypothesis if either $z_{obt} \leq -2.58$ or $z_{obt} \geq +2.58$ or to fail to reject the null hypothesis if $-2.58 < z_{obt} < 2.58$.

Step 4: Now that we have our critical value of z ($z_{crit} = \pm 2.58$), we need to compute our test statistic (z_{obt}). Using equation 7-3, we can transform our sample mean into a z score as follows:

$$z_{obt} = \frac{\overline{X} - \mu}{s/\sqrt{n}}$$

$$z_{obt} = \frac{53.2 - 52.5}{6/\sqrt{110}}$$

$$z_{obt} = \frac{.7}{6/10.49}$$

$$z_{obt} = \frac{.7}{.57}$$

$$z_{obt} = 1.23$$

Step 5: With our sample data, we have an obtained z score of 1.23. Using this obtained value of z, our fifth and final step is to make a decision about our null hypothesis. Because our obtained z score of 1.23 is less than our critical z score of 2.58 and more than our critical value of –2.58, and it does not fall into either critical region, we must fail to reject the null hypothesis. We conclude that the sample mean does, in fact, come from a population where the mean sentence length is 52.5 months. Thus, it appears that the sentencing enhancement (an additional 3 years for using a gun during a felony) stipulated by the new law has not significantly increased the length of sentences for those convicted of armed robbery compared with the population mean sentence length before the law was implemented. Remember, it is necessary not only to make a decision about your null hypothesis but also to interpret this decision based on the data and your research question.

▣ Directional and Non-Directional Hypothesis Tests

The choice between a *directional hypothesis test* and a *non-directional hypothesis test* depends on the researcher's beliefs about the population from which the sample was drawn and how much a priori information (from either theory or prior research) the researcher has about the question. Directional hypothesis tests are referred to as "one-tailed" statistical tests, and non-directional hypothesis tests are called "two-tailed" statistical tests. In our one-sample-mean problems earlier, the null hypothesis stated that the observed sample mean came from a population with a known mean (μ). The possibility that our sample came from the population whose mean is known and is expressed in the null hypothesis is one possible state of affairs. But there is another possibility—that the sample we drew came from a different population with a different mean. This other possible state of affairs is expressed in the alternative hypothesis. There are three possible versions of the alternative state of affairs:

1. The sample was drawn from a population with a different mean ($\bar{X} \neq \mu$).

2. The sample was drawn from a population with a higher mean ($\bar{X} > \mu$).

3. The sample was drawn from a population with a lower mean ($\bar{X} < \mu$).

The first possibility simply states a difference, but the latter two state a more specific direction of difference.

The first possibility is a non-directional hypothesis. As we have seen, non-directional hypotheses are tested by a two-tailed hypothesis test. The second two possibilities are variations of a directional research hypothesis. Directional hypotheses are tested with a one-tailed hypothesis test.

In the preceding two examples, the alternative hypothesis was stated as a non-directional alternative. In both cases, although we did not think that our sample came from the null hypothesis population, we did not know whether the population from which the sample was drawn had a mean higher or lower than that stated in the null hypothesis. For example, in the most recent example, maybe the population of convicted armed robbers from which we drew our sample had a mean sentence length that was higher than 52.5 months, or maybe it had a mean sentence length that was lower than that. These two possibilities are shown in Figure 7.6. You can perhaps see from this figure why we are interested in both tails of a sampling distribution when we have a non-directional research hypothesis—we have to cover both possibilities.

Unlike this scenario, directional research hypotheses state a more precise relationship between the sample and the null hypothesis parameter (in this case, population mean). When we use directional hypotheses, we believe not only that the sample and population means are different but also that we can define the exact direction of that difference. For example, in the previous problem, if we had been more confident in our belief

> **Directional hypothesis test:** When a research/alternative hypothesis states the directional difference expected.

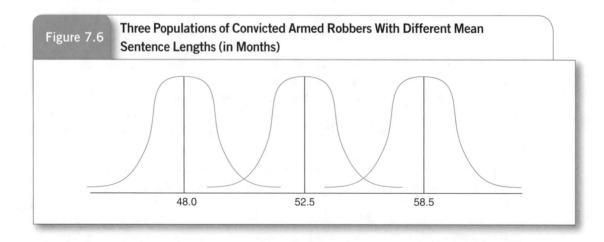

Figure 7.6 Three Populations of Convicted Armed Robbers With Different Mean Sentence Lengths (in Months)

that the effect of the firearm law would be unequivocally to increase the prison term of those convicted of a felony involving a weapon, we could have stated our alternative hypothesis more specifically as $H_1: \mu > 52.5$. This is a directional alternative hypothesis because we are specifically stating what type of difference the population mean has from our sample mean. In this case, we are saying that our sample was drawn from a population whose mean is greater than the population mean expressed in the null hypothesis. This is illustrated in Figure 7.7, which shows two curves. The curve on the left is the curve for the population defined by the null hypothesis with a mean of 52.5. The curve to the right is an example of a possible population defined by the directional alternative hypothesis ($H_1: \mu > 52.5$). In this population, the mean is hypothesized to be greater than that for the population of the null hypothesis. Had our directional alternative hypothesis stated that the sample mean came from a population whose mean was less than 52.5 ($H_1: \mu < 52.5$), our two curves would look like those in Figure 7.8. Thus, when stating a directional alternative or research hypothesis, we are stating the direction in which, we believe, the population from which our sample was drawn lies: either above (Figure 7.7) or below (Figure 7.8) the mean specified by the null hypothesis.

You may be wondering what possible difference it makes whether we state our research hypothesis as non-directional or directional. It does make a difference. If you can, it is to your advantage as a researcher to specify a direction for your alternative hypothesis. This does not mean that in the absence of prior knowledge or sound theory, you should always make a directional research hypothesis—only that if you can, it is to your advantage to do so. Of course, this answer leads to another question: "Why is testing a directional hypothesis rather than a non-directional hypothesis to my advantage?" Well, let's think about this for a minute. When we state a non-directional research hypothesis, we hypothesize that our sample was drawn from a population with a mean that is different from that specified in the null

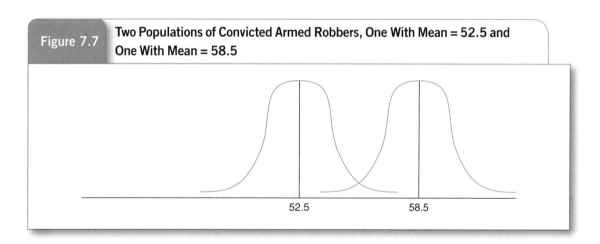

Figure 7.7 Two Populations of Convicted Armed Robbers, One With Mean = 52.5 and One With Mean = 58.5

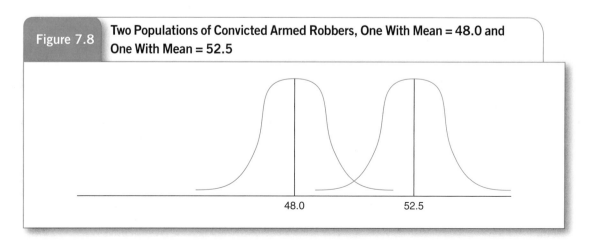

Figure 7.8 Two Populations of Convicted Armed Robbers, One With Mean = 48.0 and One With Mean = 52.5

hypothesis. We do not know, then, whether the population from which our sample was drawn has a mean that is larger or smaller than that stated in the null hypothesis. These two possibilities, and the null hypothesis, are illustrated in Figure 7.6. As you can see, in the non-directional case, we are interested in both tails of the distribution for the null hypothesis. That is why we divide our alpha level into two equal halves and place one half in the right tail and one half in the left tail of the distribution. Note that when we divide our alpha level in half, we are also cutting the area of the critical region in the tail of the sampling distribution in half and going out farther on the tail of the probability distribution. Instead of .05 of the area of the curve in one tail of the sampling distribution, we have .025 (.05 / 2) of the area in each tail. As we just said, because we are interested in a smaller area of the curve, the effect of this is to push the critical region farther out into the tail of the distribution. As you can see, it is not that our critical region is smaller in the two-tailed (non-directional) research hypothesis; our critical area (alpha level) is still .05 of the curve. But this total area is now divided into two equal halves.

When we state a directional research hypothesis, however, we make the much more specific statement that we believe the population from which our sample was drawn has a mean that is higher (or lower) than that stated in the null hypothesis. Examples of a directional research hypothesis are shown in Figures 7.7 and 7.8. In these directional hypotheses, we are interested in only one tail of the sampling distribution. Figure 7.7 illustrates the case when we hypothesize that the sample comes from a population with a higher mean than that stated in the null hypothesis. Because we suspect a higher population mean, our attention is directed at the right tail. Figure 7.8 illustrates the case when we hypothesize that the sample comes from a population with a lower mean than that stated in the null hypothesis. Now the critical region is only in the left tail of the distribution. Both instances are examples of one-tailed hypothesis tests. Unlike the case with the non-directional hypothesis, we do not have to divide our alpha level into two equal halves. In the one-tailed case, all of our alpha level is in one tail of the distribution. When using a two-tailed hypothesis test, then, we are pushed out farther into the tail of the sampling distribution, which increases our critical value of z. As a result, to reject the null hypothesis, our obtained z will have to be greater than that required in a directional (one-tailed) alternative hypothesis at the same alpha level; therefore, it will be more difficult to reject the null hypothesis.

Figures 7.9 and 7.10 illustrate this point. In Figure 7.9, we show the critical region for a two-tailed hypothesis test with an alpha of .05. Each critical region is equal to .025 of the area under the normal curve, and the critical value of z is ±1.96. Thus, to reject the null hypothesis, we would need to obtain a z score less than or equal to –1.96 or greater than or equal to +1.96. This two-tailed hypothesis test would correspond to the situation in Figure 7.6. In Figure 7.10, we have a one-tailed hypothesis test at the same alpha level (α = .05). In this test, all .05 of our critical region is in one tail of the sampling distribution. You can see that the critical region in the right tail of Figure 7.10 is larger than that in Figure 7.9; in fact, it is twice as large. Because we do not have to go so far out into the right tail, our critical value of z is only 1.65 compared with the 1.96 z value for the non-directional two-tailed test in Figure 7.9. The greater the absolute value of the critical value, the more difficult it is to reject the null hypothesis. The same principle applies when moving from a .05 alpha to a .01 alpha (for either a one- or two-tailed test); our critical value increases because we are going

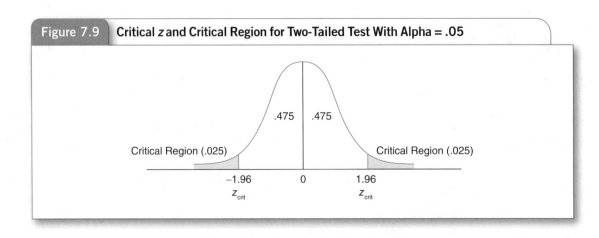

Figure 7.9 Critical *z* and Critical Region for Two-Tailed Test With Alpha = .05

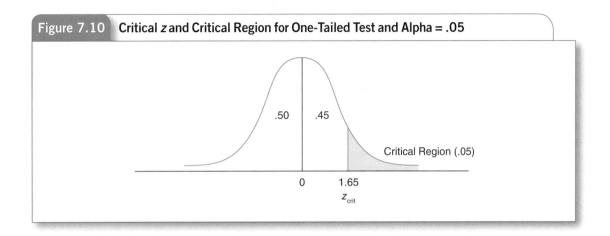

Figure 7.10 Critical *z* and Critical Region for One-Tailed Test and Alpha = .05

farther out into the tail of the probability distribution, and our critical alpha will be greater for the .01 alpha than for an alpha of .05.

As you can see, at any given level of alpha, we will need a smaller z_{obt} to reject the null hypothesis in the one-tailed (directional) hypothesis test. Now you can see more clearly why it is to your advantage to specify a directional alternative hypothesis *if you can*. The critical *z* values reported in Table 7.1 confirm that at each level of alpha, you will need a smaller value of z_{obt} to reject the null hypothesis using a one-tailed test than using a two-tailed test. Remember, though, that, no matter which type of test you are conducting, directional or non-directional, the steps necessary to conduct a hypothesis test remain the same. Let's go through another example.

Case Study

Mean Socialization Levels of Violent Offenders

Some criminologists and psychologists have long contended that there are important and stable personality differences between criminal offenders and the non-offending population. One of these supposed personality differences between offenders and non-offenders is psychopathy—the degree to which persons act antisocially or lack any regard for the feelings of others. A frequently used psychological test that has been assumed to measure the trait of psychopathy is the Socialization (SO) scale of the California Psychological Inventory. The SO scale measures such things as one's ability to form close social relationships, the extent to which one is concerned with the rights and feelings of others, and one's tendency for deliberately planned rather than impulsive behavior. As a measure of healthy socialization, then, we would expect that adult criminal offenders might score lower on the SO scale than non-offenders. When the scale was first designed, Edwin Megargee (1972) reported a mean SO scale score of 35.99 for a large group of working-class male adults. We will take this as our population value. Let's suppose that we collected a sample of 177 male prison inmates convicted of violence in California who had a mean SO scale score of 27.76 and a standard deviation of 6.03. We want to know whether our sample of California prison inmates came from the non-incarcerated population with a mean of 35.99. Because we expect the mean for the prisoners to be less than that for the non-incarcerated population, we can state a directional research hypothesis. We now explicitly go through our formal hypothesis test.

Step 1: Our null and alternative hypotheses are as follows:

$H_0: \mu = 35.99$

$H_1: \mu < 35.99$

Remember that the null hypothesis is always the same whether you state a directional or a non-directional alternative hypothesis. In the directional research hypothesis, we are specifically stating that the true population mean for the incarcerated sample is less than 35.99, so we will conduct a one-tailed test. It is important to remember our substantive question of whether those who are incarcerated have lower socialization scores (or more psychopathy) than those who are not incarcerated.

Step 2: Our test statistic will be the z statistic, and our sampling distribution will be the standard normal distribution (z distribution).

Step 3: We will select .01 as our alpha level. The critical value of z for $\alpha = .01$ with a one-tailed test in this direction is –2.33 ($z_{crit} = -2.33$). The critical value of z is negative because in our research hypothesis we have predicted that the true population mean is less than the mean stated in the null hypothesis. We are, therefore, interested in the left tail of the sampling distribution. If it helps, think of the numerator of formula 7-3. When the sample mean $\bar{X}$ is less than the hypothesized population mean μ, the value of the numerator will be negative. If you are making a directional hypothesis test stating this difference $\bar{X} < \mu$ the critical value of your test statistic should also be negative. For this example, then, the critical region will consist of all z_{obt} scores less than or equal to –2.33. Our decision rule, therefore, is to reject H_0 if $z_{obt} \leq -2.33$.

Step 4: The value of z_{obt} is

$$z_{obt} = \frac{\bar{X} - \mu}{s/\sqrt{n}}$$

$$z_{obt} = \frac{27.76 - 35.99}{6.03/\sqrt{177}}$$

$$z_{obt} = \frac{-8.23}{.45}$$

$$z_{obt} = -18.29$$

Step 5: Because the obtained value of z falls inside the critical region and $-z_{obt} < -z_{crit}$, we would reject the null hypothesis. This is illustrated in Figure 7.11. We would, therefore, conclude that the population of incarcerated offenders has a mean SO scale score that is less than 35.99. Based on this test, then, we can also conclude that incarcerated violent offenders demonstrate greater psychopathy than non-offenders in the population.

Because hypothesis testing involves probabilities and not certainties, let us acknowledge yet another time that there is some known risk of error in rejecting the null hypothesis. Our alpha level of .01 serves notice that, in the long run, there is 1 chance in 100, or a 1% chance, that we could have observed a sample mean of 27.76 even if the true

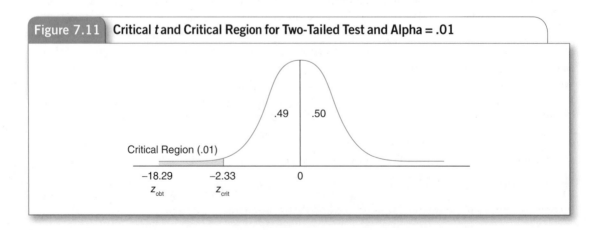

Figure 7.11 Critical t and Critical Region for Two-Tailed Test and Alpha = .01

.49   .50

Critical Region (.01)

–18.29   –2.33   0

z_{obt} z_{crit}

population mean was 35.99. Because the probability of that occurring is very small, however (it is what we have come to know as a "rare event"), we have opted to reject the null hypothesis in favor of the alternative. Nevertheless, there is no way of knowing for sure whether we are correct. Keep in mind that the risk of rejecting a true null hypothesis is always present and is equal to alpha.

▣ Hypothesis Testing for Population Means Using a Small Sample: The *t* Test

In the previous section, we discussed hypothesis testing about one sample mean when our sample size was large enough so that we could invoke the central limit theorem, which states that when the sample size gets large (generally $n \geq 30$), the distribution of an infinite number of sample means drawn from any population is approximately normal. This theorem enables us to use the *z* test and the *z* distribution as our probability distribution in order to conduct our hypothesis test. When we have small samples ($n < 30$), however, we cannot take advantage of the central limit theorem in this manner. As with the differences we observed between calculating confidence intervals when we have large and small samples, the techniques we use when testing a hypothesis about a population mean also are a little bit different when we are using a small sample. With small samples, the appropriate test statistic is the *t* test we used in Chapter 6 with confidence intervals. Our sampling distribution, then, is the Student's *t* distribution.

As we discussed in Chapter 6, the *t* distribution is somewhat different from the *z* distribution. The *t* distribution is flatter than the *z* distribution, and it is much flatter when the sample size is small and is fatter at the tails. This means that the critical value of *t* at a given alpha level will be greater than the comparable critical value of *z* and can be much greater when *n* is very small. As an example, you know that the critical value of *z* for a one-tailed test at $\alpha = .05$ is 1.65. Let's take the same alpha level and find the critical value of *t* with an *n* of 10. As before, to find the critical value of *t*, go to the table of *t* values in Table B.3 of Appendix B. You first locate the appropriate alpha (significance) level and type of test (one- or two-tailed) at the top of the table. Then you must determine the correct degrees of freedom (*df*) where *df* is equal to $n - 1$ in this problem. With a sample size of 10, therefore, we have 9 degrees of freedom. Keep in mind that, unlike the *z* table, the numbers in the body of the *t* table correspond to critical values of *t*, not to areas under the curve. We can see from the *t* table that the critical value of *t* for a one-tailed test and an alpha of .05 with 9 degrees of freedom is 1.833. This is greater than the critical value of *z* at the same alpha level (1.65).

As an exercise, stay in the same column of *t* and move down the page. Note what happens when the size of the sample increases. The size of critical *t* decreases. At a sample size of 121 (120 degrees of freedom), the critical value of *t* (1.658) is almost the same as the critical value of *z* (1.65). Therefore, you can see that the more the sample size increases, the more the *t* distribution more closely approximates the shape of the *z* distribution. When our sample size has reached about 100, the two distributions are virtually identical.

The formula for the *t* test used to conduct a hypothesis test about a population mean using small samples is identical to the formula used for the *z* test when the population standard deviation is unknown:

$$t_{\text{obt}} = \frac{\bar{X} - \mu}{s/\sqrt{n}}$$

(Formula 7-4)

The steps involved in conducting a hypothesis test with *t* are the same as in the previous section with the *z* test; the only difference is that we use the *t* probability distribution and the *t* table rather than the standard normal (*z*) probability distribution and table. We first state the null and alternative hypotheses. We then determine our test statistic and sampling distribution. We next select an alpha level, and based on this we determine the

***t* Test:** Statistical test used to test several null hypotheses, including the difference between two means.

critical value of our test statistic (t_{crit}) and the critical region of our sampling distribution. We calculate our test statistic (t_{obt}) and compare it with the critical value. Finally, we make a decision about our null hypothesis and interpret this decision in a way that is meaningful to the research question at hand. The main difference between hypothesis testing using the t test and that using the z test lies in these statistics' respective sampling distributions and, consequently, in the critical values and rejection regions for a given level of alpha. Let's go through an example.

Case Study

Assets Seized by ATF

The Federal Bureau of Alcohol, Tobacco, Firearms, and Explosives (ATF) routinely seizes the assets of arrested drug dealers. In a given year with thousands of cases, the average dollar amount seized by the ATF is $75,200 per case. We are going to assume that this is our population value as the average dollar amount of asset seizures in drug cases for that year. In the state in which we live, our local police department began seizing the assets of the drug dealers it arrested, and in one year with 14 cases it seized an average dollar amount of $71,500 with a standard deviation of $3,900. Our research question is, "Does our state seize more or less than the average dollar amount in the population?" The statistical information we have, then, is as follows:

National Sample of Asset Seizures in Dollars from ATF	Sample of 14 Asset Seizures in Our State in Dollars
μ = $75,200	$\bar{x}$ = $71,500
σ = unknown	s = $3,900
N = unknown	n = 14

Step 1: With these data, we want to test the null hypothesis that the population mean dollar amount seized by our police department is equal to the average compiled by the ATF ($75,200). In other words, we want to test the hypothesis that our sample of 14 asset seizures came from the overall ATF population. Our alternative hypothesis states that μ is not equal to $75,200. Since we are not stating the direction of this difference, our alternative hypothesis is non-directional or a two-tailed test. Formally, these hypotheses would be stated like this:

H_0: μ = $75,200

H_1: $\mu \neq$ $75,200

Step 2: Because we have a small sample ($n = 14$), we will use the t statistic and the sampling distribution of the t to perform the hypothesis test.

Step 3: We decide to adopt an alpha level of .01 to test the null hypothesis. The next step is to find the critical value of t and map out our critical regions. We know that we are conducting a non-directional test using $\alpha = .01$, but we also need to calculate how many degrees of freedom we have in our sample. Remember that in this problem the degrees of freedom is equal to $n - 1$ (14 − 1), which gives us 13 degrees of freedom. From Table B.3 of Appendix B, we find that for a two-tailed test with an alpha of .01 and 13 degrees of freedom, our critical value of t is 3.012. Recall that when doing a non-directional test, we are interested in both tails of our sampling distribution. In a non-directional test, then, the critical value corresponds to both positive and negative values. Our critical value of t, therefore, is $t_{crit} = \pm 3.012$. Our decision rule will be to reject the null hypothesis if t_{obt} is less than or equal to −3.012 or greater than or equal to +3.012. Stated differently, we must fail to reject the null hypothesis if −3.012 < t_{obt} < 3.012.

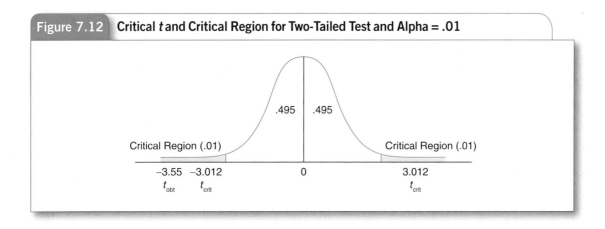

Figure 7.12 Critical *t* and Critical Region for Two-Tailed Test and Alpha = .01

Step 4: We are now ready to compute our test statistic:

$$t_{obt} = \frac{\overline{X} - \mu}{s/\sqrt{n}}$$

$$t_{obt} = \frac{71,500 - 75,200}{3,900/\sqrt{14}}$$

$$t_{obt} = \frac{-3,700}{3,900/3.74}$$

$$t_{obt} = \frac{-3,700}{1,042.78}$$

$$t_{obt} = -3.55$$

Step 5: The value of *t* we obtained from our statistical test was −3.55. Figure 7.12 shows the obtained value of *t* relative to the critical regions of the sampling distribution. Because our obtained test statistic falls into the critical region on the left side of the sampling distribution (negative end), and because $t_{obt} < t_{crit}$, we must reject the null hypothesis that the dollar amount seized from drug dealers in our state is the same as the ATF average. It seems that there is a significant difference between our sample mean and the population mean. From our sample data, we can conclude that our state seizes significantly less compared with the national average.

Case Study

Rate of Law Enforcement Personnel

Let's go through another quick example. You should have the steps down fairly well now, so we will not go into any great detail, but make a mental note as we take each step. The Federal Bureau of Investigation (FBI) has reported that the average number of law enforcement officers per 1,000 inhabitants during recent years was generally around 3.3. That is, there were an average of 3.3 police officers for every 1,000 inhabitants in cities and townships. We are going to assume this is our population mean. Let's suppose that we represent a group of small-town mayors who want to challenge this figure to demonstrate that rural towns have a lower number of officers to serve their population compared with the United States as a whole. To investigate this, we collect information about the number of sworn officers from a sample of 9 rural communities ($n = 9$). From this sample of rural police departments, we find that the average number of police officers per 1,000 inhabitants is 2.9 with a standard deviation of .8.

To determine whether this mean is significantly different from the population mean, we must conduct a formal hypothesis test. The null and alternative hypotheses are

$$H_0: \mu = 3.3$$

$$H_1: \mu < 3.3$$

For this test, we decide that an alpha level of .05 is sufficient. Because we are stating a directional research hypothesis, we will be conducting a one-tailed test, and our concern is with the left tail of the probability distribution (the negative end). Given this information, along with our sample statistics, we next define our critical value of t to be equal to -1.86 ($df = 8$, $\alpha = .05$, one-tailed test). The critical region is any t value equal to or less than -1.86. Our decision rule is to reject H_0 if $t_{obt} \leq -1.86$. Our critical value of t is -1.86 because in our alternative hypothesis we have specifically hypothesized that the sample comes from a population with a lower mean than that expressed in the null hypothesis. Stated differently, we are hypothesizing that our sample was drawn from a population with a mean that is less than 3.3 officers per 1,000 population. If this is correct, we should obtain a negative value of t. If t_{obt} is positive, we will fail to reject the null hypothesis even if it is greater than the absolute value of t_{crit} because it is in the wrong direction from that stated in the alternative hypothesis. Next we calculate the test statistic as follows:

$$t_{obt} = \frac{2.9 - 3.3}{.8/\sqrt{9}}$$

$$t_{obt} = \frac{-.4}{.8/3}$$

$$t_{obt} = \frac{-.4}{.267}$$

$$t_{obt} = -1.50$$

Since we stated a directional alternative hypothesis, we are interested only in the left tail of the t distribution and in negative values of t_{obt}. The obtained t value of -1.50 does not fall within our stated critical region, $t_{obt} > t_{crit}$. In Figure 7.13, we illustrate the critical value of t and the rejection region relative to the value of t we obtained in our test. We must, therefore, fail to reject the null hypothesis and conclude that the mean number of law enforcement officers per 1,000 persons in rural areas (2.9) is not significantly different from 3.3, the population mean number of police officers per capita for the United States as a whole. Contrary to the mayors' contention, then, there is no statistical evidence that rural communities have lower levels of police protection per capita than other areas of the country.

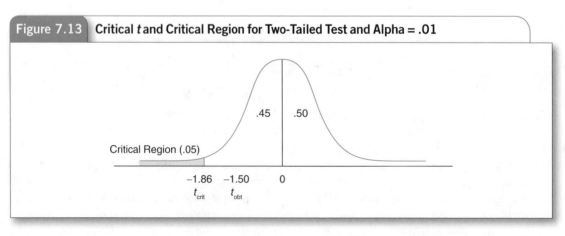

Figure 7.13 Critical t and Critical Region for Two-Tailed Test and Alpha = .01

So far, we have talked about hypothesis tests for population means only. We have conducted hypothesis tests for a population mean μ using data from both large samples (z test) and small samples (t test). Before we move on to hypothesis tests for proportions, let us summarize the types of tests that we can use when conducting hypothesis tests about a single population mean μ. The accompanying text box displays the three combinations of hypothesis tests that can be conducted when making an inference from a sample to the population about μ.

Formal Statements of the Null and Research/Alternative Hypotheses for Both Non-Directional (Two-Tailed) and Directional (One-Tailed) Tests With a Hypothetical Population Mean of 5

Non-directional hypotheses for a population mean:

$H_0: \mu = 5$

$H_1: \mu \neq 5$

Directional hypotheses for a larger population mean:

$H_0: \mu = 5$

$H_1: \mu > 5$

Directional hypotheses for a smaller population mean:

$H_0: \mu = 5$

$H_1: \mu < 5$

Hypothesis Testing for Population Proportions and Percentages Using Large Samples

Very frequently, we find that our data consist of a proportion or percentage rather than a mean. These data include such things as the percentage of the American public who support the death penalty, the percentage of the public who own firearms, the proportion of arrested defendants who test positive for drugs, and the proportion of arrested defendants who plead guilty in exchange for a lesser charge. Even though we have percentage and proportion data, we still may be interested in the kind of problem we have been examining thus far in the chapter: testing the difference between a sample statistic and an unknown population parameter. In this case, however, our sample statistic is a proportion or percentage, as is the unknown population parameter. The question is, "Can we still conduct a hypothesis test about a population parameter if that parameter is a proportion or percentage?" The answer to that question is yes, and it is very simple to do.

The general procedure used to conduct a hypothesis test about a single population proportion is virtually identical to that used for a population mean, so we will not need to go into great detail here. As in the last chapter, we use $\hat{p}$ to denote the proportion obtained from our sample data and P to denote the population proportion. In this chapter, we focus exclusively on tests used for proportions obtained from a large sample. With a large sample, we can invoke the central limit theorem and use our familiar z test. The general rule regarding sample size in tests of proportions is that the normal approximation (standard normal or z distribution) can be used when both $n(\hat{p}) \geq 5$ and $n(\hat{p} - 1) \geq 5$. For example, if $\hat{p} = .5$, we would need a sample size of at least 10 to conduct a z test because $10(.5) \geq 5$. If $\hat{p} = .10$, we would need a sample size of at least 50 because $50(.10) \geq 5$.

To perform a hypothesis test about a population proportion using large samples, we again use the *z* test as our test statistic and the *z* distribution as our sampling probability distribution. The formula used to conduct a *z* test for proportions is comparable to the formula for hypothesis tests with a mean:

$$z = \frac{\hat{p} - P}{\sigma_{\hat{p}}}$$

(Formula 7-5)

where

$$\sigma_{\hat{p}} = \sqrt{\frac{PQ}{n}}$$

$\hat{p}$ = the sample proportion
P = the population proportion assumed under the null hypothesis
$Q = 1 - P$

The numerator of this formula simply is the difference between the sample proportion and the assumed population proportion. This represents the distance between the sample statistic and the hypothesized population parameter. The denominator of

$$\sigma_{\hat{p}} = \sqrt{\frac{PQ}{n}}$$

is an estimate of the standard deviation of the sampling distribution, which is called the standard error of the proportion and should be very familiar to you by now. This is the standard deviation of the distribution of an infinite or very large number of samples of size *n* where we have calculated the sample proportion ($\hat{p}$) for each sample. Notice that in the formula for the estimated standard error of the proportion we have the population parameter for the proportion P and $Q(1 - P)$. Normally, we do not know the value of a population parameter, and here we do not know what it is, but *we are assuming a value of P in the null hypothesis,* and that is the value we use.

Case Study

Attitudes Toward Gun Control

Let's go through the procedures of conducting a hypothesis test for a population proportion. Since 1990, the Gallup Polling Organization has included in one of its polls this question: "In general, do you feel that the laws covering the sale of firearms should be made more strict, less strict, or kept as they are now?" In 2014, the proportion of the total population who believed that the sale of firearms should be made "more strict" was .47 (Gallup, 2014b). This will be used as the population parameter in this example. Let's say that we believe that such attitudes regarding a law like this vary significantly by community. For example, we believe that individuals residing in communities such as Newtown, Connecticut, who have experienced traumatic mass murders (such as the killings at the Sandy Hook Elementary School where 20 children lost their lives) will be much more likely on average to favor such a law.

Step 1: To test our hypothesis, we collect a random sample of 107 individuals from communities that have experienced some form of mass murder where the killings were perpetrated with a gun. As all good researchers do, we formally state our hypotheses (we use a directional or one-tailed research hypothesis in this case) before conducting the statistical test. Our hypotheses are as follows:

$$H_0: P = .47$$

$$H_1: P > .47$$

Step 2: Since we have an appropriately large number in our sample, we will use the z test along with the corresponding z sampling distribution.

Step 3: We next specify the level of alpha at .05 and determine the critical region. The critical value of z with $\alpha = .05$ using a directional hypothesis is equal to 1.65 (Table 7.1). The critical value is positive in this case because we believe the proportion of residents who live in a community that has experienced a firearm-related traumatic incident will be much more likely to favor a gun control law. What we are saying is that our sample was drawn from a population where the proportion of those who favor restrictive gun laws is greater than .47. The critical region includes all values of z_{obt} that are equal to or greater than 1.65. We will reject the null hypothesis, then, if $z_{obt} \geq 1.65$.

Step 4: The results of our sample indicate that 66 of the 107 individuals from our sample believe that the sale of firearms should be made stricter. Remember that to obtain the proportion, we simply divide the frequency of interest—in this case those in favor of the law—by the total number in the sample ($f / n = 66 / 107$), which gives us a sample proportion of $\hat{p} = .62$. With this information, we calculate the obtained test statistic of z:

$$Z_{obt} = \frac{\hat{P} - P}{\sqrt{\dfrac{P(1-P)}{N}}}$$

$$Z_{obt} = \frac{.62 - .47}{\sqrt{\dfrac{.47(1-4.7)}{107}}}$$

$$Z_{obt} = \frac{.15}{\sqrt{\dfrac{.47(.53)}{107}}}$$

$$Z_{obt} = \frac{.15}{\sqrt{\dfrac{.249}{107}}}$$

$$Z_{obt} = \frac{.15}{\sqrt{.0023}}$$

$$Z_{obt} = \frac{.15}{.48}$$

$$Z_{obt} = 3.12$$

The value of z we obtain from our statistical test indicates, just as all z scores do, that if the null hypothesis were true, the sample proportion $\hat{p} = .62$ would fall about 3.12 standard errors above the hypothesized population proportion P of .47. Since the obtained z of 3.12 is greater than the critical value of 1.65, it falls within the rejection region. The obtained value of z relative to the critical value of z is displayed in Figure 7.14. Because $z_{obt} > z_{crit}$, we can reject the null

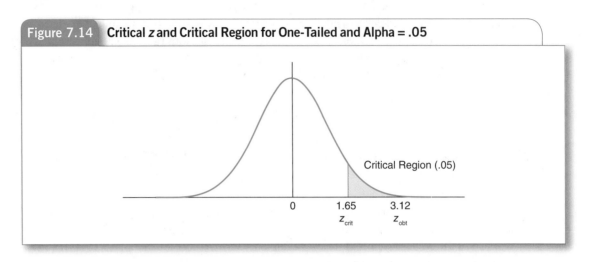

Figure 7.14 Critical *z* and Critical Region for One-Tailed and Alpha = .05

hypothesis and conclude that among residents of communities who have experienced gun trauma, the true proportion who favor stricter regulation of the sale of guns is significantly greater than .47. We can state this in terms of percentages by simply multiplying the proportions by 100. Based on our hypothesis test, then, we can conclude that among people who reside in communities that have experienced a mass shooting, the percentage of residents favoring stricter gun sales is higher than the national percentage.

Case Study

Random Drug Testing of Inmates

Let's do another example, this time using percentages. Imagine that you have passed your statistics course with flying colors, have received your degree, and are now the research specialist for a municipal jail. During the course of your duties, you notice that in a random drug test of 100 new pretrial detainees, 36 of them (36%) tested positive for some form of cocaine. You begin to wonder whether the population of pretrial detainees contains a higher than normal percentage of cocaine users. You do a little background research and discover that, according to the National Survey on Drug Use and Health conducted in 2013, approximately 12% of young adults (aged 18–25 years) have used cocaine at some time in their lives. By using this as your population parameter, you decide to test the hypothesis that the percentage of cocaine use among your pretrial detainees is significantly higher than the 12% found in the general population.

You have the following information:

Population	Sample
$P = 12\%$	$\hat{p} = 36\%$
	$n = 100$

With your well-honed statistical skills, you identify this as a call for a hypothesis test of a one-sample proportion and go through the following steps in order.

Step 1: You state the null and research hypothesis:

$$H_0: P = .12, \text{ or } 12\%$$

$$H_1: P > .12, \text{ or } 12\%$$

Because you suspect that the sample of pretrial detainees comes from a population where the percentage of cocaine use is greater than 12%, you state a directional research hypothesis.

Step 2: Because you have a large sample ($n = 100$), you select the z test for proportions as your statistical test and the z distribution as your sampling distribution.

Step 3: You select an alpha level of .01. With a one-tailed test, the critical level of z at this level of alpha is 2.33. The critical region is composed of all z_{obt} values greater than or equal to 2.33. Your decision rule, therefore, is to reject the null hypothesis if $z_{obt} > 2.33$.

Step 4: For ease of calculation, you convert the percentages back into proportions by simply dividing them by 100. You calculate the obtained value of your test statistic, z_{obt}:

$$Z_{obt} = \frac{.36 - .12}{\sqrt{\frac{.19(1-.19)}{100}}}$$

$$Z_{obt} = \frac{.24}{\sqrt{\frac{.19(.81)}{100}}}$$

$$Z_{obt} = \frac{.24}{\sqrt{\frac{.15}{100}}}$$

$$Z_{obt} = \frac{.24}{\sqrt{.0015}}$$

$$Z_{obt} = \frac{.24}{.04}$$

$$Z_{obt} = 6.00$$

Step 5: The location of the obtained value of z relative to the critical value and the critical region are illustrated in Figure 7.15. Because $z_{obt} > 2.33$ and falls into the critical region, you would reject the null hypothesis, knowing that there is 1 chance in 100 that you are making the wrong decision (Type I error). From this hypothesis test, you can conclude that the percentage of your pretrial detainees who have ever used cocaine is significantly greater than the percentage who have used cocaine in the general population of young adults.

Figure 7.15 **Critical *z* and Critical Region for a One-Tailed Test With Alpha = .05**

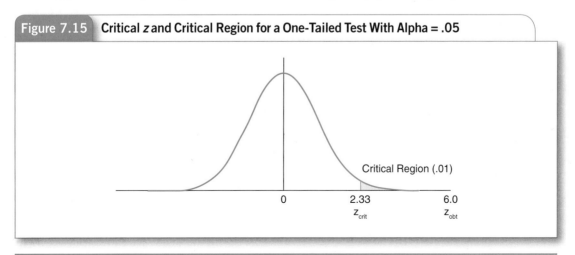

▣ Summary

In this chapter, we have examined the procedures used to make inferences about two population parameters: inferences from an observed sample mean ($\overline{X}$) about an unknown population mean (μ), and inferences from an observed sample proportion ($\hat{p}$) to an unknown population proportion (P). We used a z test when making inferences about both sample means and sample proportions when we had large samples. When working with small samples, we demonstrated the steps necessary for hypothesis testing involving a mean using a t test. Each of these hypothesis tests involved a series of decisions. The first one is whether to state a directional or non-directional alternative hypothesis. If there are sound reasons to state your research hypothesis as a directional one, you should do so. The second decision to make concerns which test statistic and which corresponding sampling distribution to use. The third decision pertains to which level of significance (the alpha level) to use in conducting your hypothesis test. This is one of the most important decisions you will make in hypothesis testing because the alpha level determines the risk you accept of rejecting a null hypothesis that is really true (i.e., the risk of making a Type I error). Finally, the last and easiest decision you have to make is whether to fail to reject or to reject your null hypothesis. This is the easiest decision because if you have properly conducted the hypothesis test and followed the steps in order, this last decision will have essentially been made for you. Once you have chosen your alpha level and found the critical value and critical region, all you need to do is determine whether the obtained value of your test statistic falls in the critical region. If it does, you reject the null hypothesis; if it does not, you fail to reject the null hypothesis. What could be easier?

Key Terms

> ➤ Review key terms with eFlashcards. Visit study.sagepub.com/paternoster.

directional hypothesis test 178	null hypothesis 167	t test 183
non-directional hypothesis test 167	sampling variation 167	z test 172

Key Formulas

To find a z score (formula 7-3):

$$z_{obt} = \frac{\overline{X} - \mu}{s/\sqrt{n}}$$

To find a t score (formula 7-4):

$$t_{obt} = \frac{\overline{X} - \mu}{s/\sqrt{n}}$$

To conduct a hypothesis test for proportions (formula 7-5):

$$z = \frac{\hat{p} - P}{\sigma_{\hat{p}}}$$

where

$$\sigma_{\hat{p}} = \sqrt{\frac{PQ}{n}}$$

$\hat{p}$ = the sample proportion

P = the population proportion under the null hypothesis

$Q = 1 - P$

1. When is it appropriate to use a *t* test for hypothesis testing instead of a *z* test?

2. We are interested in the average dollar amount lost by victims by burglary. The National Insurance Association has reported that the mean dollar amount lost by victims of burglary is $2,222. Assume that this is the population mean. We believe that the true population mean loss is different from this. Formally state the null and research hypotheses we would test to investigate this question. What if we believed the dollar amount to be higher?

3. The Internal Revenue Service has claimed that the mean number of times the average U.S. citizen has cheated on his or her taxes during the last 10 years is 4.6 times. Assume that this is your population value. We believe the actual population mean (μ) of the number of times individuals cheat on their taxes is higher than this. We collect a random sample of 61 tax-paying citizens and find the following sample statistics: $\bar{X} = 6.3, s = 1.9$. Perform all of the procedures necessary for conducting a hypothesis test based on our assumption. Set your alpha level at .01. What do you conclude?

4. A major research study concluded that the mean number of times that adolescents had engaged in vandalism during the previous 12 months was 3.5. We believe the true population mean to be less than this. After collecting our own sample of 29 adolescents, we find that the mean number of times they have vandalized property during a 1-year period was $\bar{X} = 2.9$ with a standard deviation equal to .7. Perform all of the procedures necessary for conducting a hypothesis test based on our assumption. What do you conclude? Set your alpha level at .05.

5. Over a 20-year period, the average sentence given to defendants convicted of aggravated assault in the United States was 25.9 months. Assume this to be your population mean. Because you think it might be different in your home state, you conduct a little study to examine this question. You take a random sample of 175 jurisdictions in your home state and find that the mean sentence for aggravated assault is 27.3 months with a standard deviation of 6.5. Test the null hypothesis that the mean sentence length in your state is 25.9 months against the alternative hypothesis that it is different from that. Set your alpha level at .01.

6. A study conducted by the Research Institute of America has concluded that the average number of hours that inmates at state correctional facilities spend in their cells during a day is 15. We believe the population mean number of hours to be different from this. We contacted a sample of 15 state correctional facilities and inquired about the mean number of hours that inmates housed in these facilities spent in their cells. We came up with the following sample data:

Facility Number	Hours Spent in Cells
1	16.3
2	21.1
3	14.9
4	13.5
5	22.2
6	15.3
7	18.1
8	19.0
9	14.2
10	9.3
11	10.1
12	21.1
13	22.3
14	15.4
15	13.2

Calculate the mean number of hours inmates spend in their cells from the sample data. Test the null hypothesis that the mean number of hours inmates spend in their cells is 15 against the null hypothesis that it is different from that. Set your alpha level at .05. *Hint:* You will also have to calculate the standard deviation. Remember, practice makes perfect! What do you conclude?

7. You are on the police force in a small town. During an election year, a candidate for mayor claims that fewer police are needed because the average police officer makes only 4 arrests per year. You think the population mean is much higher than that, so you conduct a small research project. You ask 12 other officers how many arrests they made during the past year. The average for this sample of 12 is 6.3 with a standard deviation of 1.5. With your sample

evidence, test the null hypothesis that the population mean is 4 arrests against the alternative that it is greater than 4. Set your alpha level at .01.

8. The American Bar Association reports that the mean length of time for a hearing in juvenile court is 25 minutes. Assume that this is your population mean. As a lawyer who practices in the juvenile court, you think that the average hearing is much shorter than this. You take a sample of 20 other lawyers who do juvenile work and ask them how long their last case in juvenile court was. The mean hearing length for this sample of 20 was 23 minutes with a standard deviation of 6. Test the null hypothesis that the population mean is 25 minutes against the alternative that it is less than 25. Set your alpha level at .05.

9. A spokesperson for the National Rifle Association (NRA) states that 45% of the households in the United States contain at least one firearm. Assume that this is your population value. You take a random sample of 200 homes and find that about 23% of them contain a firearm. Test the null hypothesis that the population proportion is 45%

against the alternative that it is less than that. Set your alpha level at .01.

10. A friend of yours claims that 20% of the people in your neighborhood have been the victim of a crime during the past year. Take this as your population value. You take a random sample of 60 homes and find that about 31% of the homes reported some kind of crime. Test the null hypothesis that the population proportion is 20% against the alternative that it is different from 20%. Set your alpha level at .05.

11. A public opinion study concluded that the proportion of Americans agreeing with the statement, "Prisons should be for punishment, not rehabilitation" was .31. You believe the true population proportion agreeing with this statement is actually higher than that. After collecting your own sample of 110 individuals and asking them the same question, you find that .46 agree with the statement. Test the null hypothesis that the population proportion is .31 against the alternative that it is more than this. Set your alpha level at .05.

STUDENT STUDY SITE

WANT A BETTER GRADE?

Get the tools you need to sharpen your study skills. Access practice quizzes, eFlashcards, data sets, and SPSS exercises at **study.sagepub.com/paternoster.**

CHAPTER 8

Testing Hypotheses With Categorical Data

The TV scientist who mutters sadly, "The experiment is a failure; we have failed to achieve what we had hoped for," is suffering mainly from a bad script writer. An experiment is never a failure solely because it fails to achieve predicted results.

—Robert M. Pirsig

LEARNING OBJECTIVES

1. Identify the appropriate sampling distribution to use for a hypothesis test when both the independent and dependent variables are measured at the nominal or ordinal levels.

2. Identify the components of a cross-tabulation table.

3. Explain how to calculate and interpret the appropriate cell percentages in a cross-tabulation table when you want to determine whether the independent variable affects the dependent variable.

4. Conduct and interpret the results of a hypothesis test for the bivariate relationship between a nominal/ordinal independent variable and a nominal/ordinal dependent variable.

5. Describe what a measure of association tells us compared with the chi-square hypothesis test.

6. Calculate and interpret measures of association appropriate for both nominal- and ordinal-level variables.

▣ Introduction

This first step in all research is identifying bivariate relationships, that is, identifying a relationship between one independent variable and one dependent variable. You will later learn that this does not allow us to establish causal relationships between variables, only associations. Why did the homicide rate drop substantially during the past two decades, and why has it significantly increased in the past year in some cities? Do tougher gun control policies reduce gun-related crimes? All of these are research questions that begin understanding bivariate relationships. In this chapter, you will learn about the chi-square statistic and how it is used to test whether there is a relationship between two categorical variables—variables measured at the nominal or ordinal level. When we have two categorical variables, the chi-square statistic enables us to test the null hypothesis that the two variables are independent. This assumption of independence implies that there is no relationship between the variables. Whether a relationship exists between two categorical variables can be seen by inspecting a contingency table, which may also be referred to as a cross-tabulation table. A contingency table shows the joint distribution of two categorical variables. With a contingency table, we can look for the presence of a relationship between the two variables by comparing percentage differences on the dependent variable and by looking at relative risks. Finally, we will examine measures of association for the relationship between two variables. Although the chi-square statistic can tell us whether there is a relationship between two categorical variables in the population, it tells us nothing about the possible strength of the relationship. Telling us about the strength of a relationship is the job of a measure of association.

In this chapter, we will be concerned with testing hypotheses and exploring relationships with categorical variables. Categorical variables are measured at either the nominal level or the ordinal level, and the values of these variables consist of distinct categories. One example of a categorical nominal-level variable would be whether a teenager most frequently plays violent video games or sports video games. An example of a categorical ordinal-level variable would be "number of delinquent acts committed in the past year," with the values "none," "1–5 delinquent acts," "6–10 delinquent acts," and "11 or more delinquent acts." Using a chi-square (χ^2) test (pronounced "ki" as in *kite*) where χ is the Greek letter chi, we can test the null hypothesis that two variables are independent or that they are not statistically related to each other (*test of independence*). If we determine that the two variables are not independent but that, in fact, there is a relationship or an association between them, we then ask how strongly they are related to each other.

▣ Contingency Tables and the Two-Variable Chi-Square Test of Independence

When we are examining the relationship between two variables, we can usually distinguish between the independent variable and the dependent variable. Recall that an independent variable is a variable that we think has an influence on another variable, called the dependent variable. When we use causal language, we refer to the independent variable as the "cause" and to the dependent variable as the "effect." In the rest of this chapter, we will be interested in determining two things: (1) whether the independent and dependent variables are related to one another when both of the variables are nominal or ordinal, and (2) if so, how strongly they are related. You may remember from Chapter 5 that two events (the values of two variables) are independent if the outcome of one variable has no effect or influence on the outcome of the other. With categorical variables, the tool we use to determine this is the chi-square test of independence. Before we get to the chi-square test, however, we need to examine what the two-categorical-variable problem looks like and exactly how we are going to attack it.

Chi-square test of independence: Tests the null hypothesis that two nominal- or ordinal-level variables are independent.

Student Study Site

Visit the open-access Student Study Site at study .sagepub.com/paternoster to access additional study tools including mobile-friendly eFlashcards, web quizzes, links to SAGE journal articles, additional data sets, SPSS exercises, and more!

Case Study

Gender, Emotions, and Delinquency

One of the most persistent facts in criminology is that males are more antisocial and engage in more violence than females. The question is why. There are several theoretical explanations for this, but one that has received a great deal of attention is general strain theory (GST) (Agnew, 1992). The main idea with GST is that when people experience strain, they then experience negative emotions such as anger and depression. These negative emotions may be alleviated through particular coping measures like substance abuse and aggressive outbursts. The ways in which males and females process these emotional reactions to strain may be one reason why males are more aggressive compared with females. The empirical evidence is mixed, with some research finding that males and females respond similarly to strain (Jennings, Piquero, Gover, & Perez, 2009; Piquero, Fox, Piquero, Capowich, & Mazerolle, 2010), whereas others find that males are more likely to experience anger in response to strain while females are more likely to experience depression (DeCoster & Zito, 2010; Francis, 2014).

Let's assume we are conducting research to examine the relationship between gender and emotions among a sample of adolescents. Our independent variable is gender (male or female), and our dependent variable is how the individuals experience negative emotions (high vs. low negative emotions). The first step in exploring the relationship between these two categorical variables is to examine their **joint frequency distribution**. The joint frequency distribution of two variables is simply a distribution that shows how the values of the two variables occur simultaneously or jointly. In Table 8.1, we show the frequency distribution of these two variables for a sample of 120 adolescents. Of the 120 adolescents, the frequency distribution for gender shows that there are 60 males and 60 females. The 120 persons in Table 8.1 were given a personality test, and the frequency distribution for that variable shows that 90 of them were found to have "low" negative emotions and 30 were found to have "high" negative emotions. Both of these variables are categorical variables; gender is a nominal-level variable, and negative emotions is an ordinal-level variable. Note also that each variable has two values (male and female; low and high negative emotions).

The third distribution (the contingency table) is actually the joint frequency distribution of the two variables—gender and negative emotions. A joint frequency distribution of two variables shows the number of cases for each value of one variable at each value of the second variable. For example, there are 46 females who have low negative emotions. This is the joint distribution of the value "female" for the variable "gender" and the value "low negative emotions" for the variable "negative emotions." There are 14 females who have high negative emotions. This is the joint distribution of the value "female" and the value "high negative emotions." There are also 44 males with low negative emotions and 16 males with high negative emotions. Since there are two values of gender and two values of negative emotions, their joint distribution will result in four possible outcomes: (1) female and low negative emotions, (2) female and high negative emotions, (3) male and low negative emotions, and (4) male and high negative emotions. All four of these joint outcomes and the frequency of each are shown in Table 8.1.

A joint frequency distribution of categorical variables like that in Table 8.1 is called a contingency table, sometimes referred to as a cross-tabulation table. **Contingency tables** are generally defined by the number of rows and columns that they have. Table 8.1 is called a 2 × 2 (read 2 by 2) contingency table because there are two rows (female and male) and two columns (low and high negative emotions). In general, contingency tables are referred to as $R \times C$ tables where R is the number of rows and C is the number of columns. A contingency table with three rows and two columns, then, would be a 3 × 2 contingency table. The rows and columns refer to the number of levels or values of each categorical variable. The product of the number of rows in a contingency table and the number of columns is equal to the number of "cells." The number of cells corresponds to the total number of possible outcomes of the joint distribution of the two variables.

Joint frequency distribution: For two categorical variables, the intersection of two values or categories.

Contingency table: Shows the joint distribution of two categorical variables. A contingency table is defined by the number of rows and the number of columns it has. A contingency table with three rows and two columns is a "3 by 2" contingency table. It is also called a cross-tabulation table.

Table 8.1	Distribution of Gender and Negative Emotionality and Joint Distribution of Gender and Negative Emotionality in Contingency Table

Gender	f
Female	60
Male	60

Negative Emotionality	f
Low	90
High	30

Contingency Table of Observed Joint Frequency Distribution

Gender	Negative Emotionality		Total
	Low	High	
Female	46	14	60
Male	44	16	60
Total	90	30	120

Table 8.2	Labeling a 2 × 2 Contingency Table

Number of Rows	Number of Columns		Row Marginals
	1	2	
1	A*	B*	R_1
2	C*	D*	R_2
Column marginals	C_1	C_2	N

*Cell frequencies.

Row marginal or row frequency: Total frequencies for the categories of a variable displayed in the rows of a cross-tabulation table.

Column marginal or column frequency: Total frequencies for the variable displayed on the column of a cross-tabulation table.

For example, in Table 8.1, there are two rows and two columns, for a total of four ($2 \times 2 = 4$) cells. These four cells of the contingency table correspond to the four possible outcomes of the joint distribution of the two variables. Table 8.2 provides important information that is contained in a contingency table. First, there are the row marginals (R_1 and R_2) and column marginals (C_1 and C_2). The **row marginals** correspond to the number of cases in each row of the table, and the **column marginals** correspond to the number of cases in each column of the table. In the contingency table in Table 8.1, for example, the row marginals are 60 females and 60 males. The column marginals are 90 persons low in negative emotions and 30 persons high in negative emotions. The sum of the row marginals should equal the sum of the column marginals, and these should equal the total number of cases ($R_1 + R_2 = C_1 + C_2 = n$). For example, in Table 8.1, the sum of the two row marginals (60 + 60) is equal to the sum of the two column marginals (90 + 30), which is equal to the total number of cases (120).

One reason for looking at a joint frequency distribution is that it can provide us with information about the relationship between the two variables. Recall that our research question is, "Are males more likely to experience negative emotions than females?" In hypothesizing that there is a relationship between gender and negative emotions, we presume that gender is the independent variable and the experience of negative emotions is the dependent variable. Our null hypothesis would be that there is no relationship between gender and negative emotions, and our alternative hypothesis would be that males are more likely than females to experience such negative emotional states. Later in this chapter, we will learn about the chi-square test for independence, which is a formal hypothesis test, but first we will learn what a reading of the contingency table alone can tell us about the relationship between two variables.

Because our hypothesis is that one's gender has an impact or influence on the kinds of emotional experiences one is likely to have, what we would like to know is the extent to which males are more likely than females to have negative emotions. In other words, if gender varies, does the tendency to have negative emotions vary? One way to answer this question is to examine the percentage of males who have negative emotions and compare that with the percentage of females who have them. This implies that in examining percentages in contingency tables, we look at the percentage of cases for *different levels* of the independent variable at *the same level* of the dependent variable. This means that we calculate our percentages using the marginal frequencies of the independent variable (IV) and compare percentages on the dependent variable (DV). That is, the marginal frequencies for our independent variable are the denominator we use in calculating these percentages, and this is true whether the independent variable is the row variable or the column variable. Because you never know where someone will

Table 8.3	Relationship Between Gender and Negative Emotionality: Comparing Percentages Across the IV Categories Within a DV Category		

Gender (IV)	Negative Emotionality (DV)		Row Total
	Low	High	
Female	A	B	60
	46	14	100%
	77%	23%	
Male	C	D	60
	44	16	100%
	73%	27%	
Column total	90	30	$n = 120$

> Calculate percentages based on the marginals of the independent variable

> Compare on a category of the dependent variable across categories of the independent variable

place the independent variable on a contingency table, we think it is extremely important that you understand how to calculate the appropriate percentages wherever the independent variable happens to be! Let's go through an example.

In the contingency table shown in Table 8.1, gender is our IV. To calculate the appropriate cell percentages, we use the row marginals as the denominators for our percentage calculations because gender is on the row of the table. In this way, the percentages should sum to 100% at the end of each row or each value of the independent variable. After calculating these, we find that 77% of females are low in negative emotions [(46 / 60) × 100] and 23% of females are high in negative emotions [(14 / 60) × 100]. Next, in calculating the percentage of males who are low in negative emotions, we find that 73% of males are low in negative emotions [(44 / 60) × 100] and 27% of males are high in negative emotions [(16 / 60) × 100]. Again, it is important to use the marginals for the independent variable to calculate our percentages. The relevant percentages for this contingency table are reported in Table 8.3.

Having calculated our percentages on the independent variable, we will now compare them at a fixed level of the dependent variable. Notice that we have labeled the cells A through D for ease of discussion. We want to know whether gender affects negative emotions, so we must make comparisons *across* gender categories *within* a category of emotions. In cell C, we find that 23% of the females have high negative emotions *compared with* 27% of the males (cell D). We could have compared gender percentages *across* the low negativity cells just as easily. The rule is that we must compare **percentage differences** found in different categories of the independent variable (female and male) at the same category level of the dependent variable (high negative emotions) because in doing this notice that we are varying the independent variable (female vs. male) and seeing if there is variation between females and males on the dependent variable. Instead of using percentages, you could have left your calculations as proportions. Some people call this (the percentage or proportion) the relative risk of the dependent variable occurring. For example, the relative risk of having high negative emotions is .23 for females and .27 for males; the relative risk of having low negative emotions is .77 for females and .73 for males. Regardless of which category of the dependent variable you use (high or low negative emotions), you will come to the same conclusion. It seems that males are only slightly more likely to have high negative emotions than females.

What can we conclude as to whether males are more likely to have higher negative emotions than females? Well, a percentage difference of 4% is not very impressive. Is a 4-percentage-point difference enough for us to conclude that a relationship exists between gender and negative emotions? How large should the percentage difference be before we could conclude with confidence that there is a relationship—5%? 10%? What if

Percentage differences: One way to examine the bivariate relationship in a contingency table. The rule is to calculate the percentages based on the marginals of the independent variable and compare different levels of the independent variable at the same level or category of the dependent variable.

the 4% difference we observed is due only to random sampling variation, and the true difference is 0%? What if the 4% difference was actually a real difference between males and females, but the relationship was just very weak? What we need is a formal hypothesis test of this difference of percentages with a known sampling distribution and a measure of association to tell us about the strength of the relationship. First, we will work on the formal hypothesis test. The chi-square test gives us that formal hypothesis test. Before we discuss this two-variable chi-square test, however, let's look at another example of a contingency table.

Case Study

Liking School and Delinquency

Social control theory predicts that adolescents who are more committed to school and who like school will be less likely to engage in delinquency (Hirschi, 1969). Table 8.4 shows the joint distribution between two variables: whether the respondent said that he or she "liked school" and the number of delinquent acts he or she reported committing during the past year. This information was collected from a sample of 450 youths. We are interested in this joint distribution because we think that adolescents who like school are less likely to commit delinquent acts than those who dislike school. A positive attitude toward school, we hypothesize, is a positive social bond that we think will inhibit an inclination to commit delinquency. In this example, attitude toward school is our independent variable, and the number of delinquent acts is the dependent variable. Note that in this contingency table, our independent variable is the column variable, not the row variable. In determining whether there is a relationship between attitude toward school and number of delinquent acts committed, we will look at percentage differences and relative risks.

Why is it necessary to compute percentages before we examine the relationship between the variables? In Table 8.4, attitude toward school is our independent variable, so we want to compare information at different categories of this variable at a fixed category of the dependent variable. Let's fix the category of the dependent variable at "2+ delinquent acts." If we were to compare raw frequencies, we would say that 70 youths who liked school committed 2 or more delinquent acts during the past year and 60 youths who disliked school committed 2+ delinquent acts during that time. It would seem, therefore, that those who disliked school were less likely to commit a lot of delinquent acts than those who were neutral and those who liked school—a finding counter to our hypothesis. But note that there are only 135 students out of 450 who disliked school. Because the marginal frequencies for attitude toward school are so different ($C_1 = 315$, $C_2 = 135$), we can't simply compare raw frequencies. We must standardize these column marginals by calculating percentages. Remember that percentages are standardized frequencies that show the frequency per 100 observations.

Remember that we must calculate our percentages *based on the marginal frequencies of the independent variable* regardless of whether it is the column or the row. Since the independent variable (liking school) in Table 8.5 is the column variable, we will use the column marginals to calculate the percentages (calculate down). Our percentages, then, should sum to 100% at the end of each column. Table 8.5 reports both the cell frequencies and the cell percentages for Table 8.4. When we compare percentages, we now come to a different conclusion. Of those who reported that they liked school, only 22% committed two or more delinquent offenses during the

| Table 8.4 | Relationship Between Attitudes Toward School and Self-Reported Delinquency: Observed Frequencies |

DV: Number of Self-Reported Delinquent Acts	IV: Do You Like School?		Total
	Like	Dislike	Total
0	140	25	165
1	105	50	155
2+	70	60	130
Total	315	135	450

past year compared with 44% of those who disliked school. If you dislike school, then, you are twice as likely to have committed two or more delinquent acts. Note that we compared percentages for different values of the independent variable at one category of the dependent variable (2+ delinquent offenses).

This should make intuitive sense to you because what we are doing is examining the variation in the independent variable to determine whether this variation is related to different percentages on the dependent variable. If there is a relationship between our two variables, there will be variation; if there is no relationship, the percentage differences will be small or close to zero. This table seems to indicate that there is a relationship between attitude toward school and number of delinquent acts committed. More specifically, it looks like there is a negative relationship between liking school and delinquency. Having a positive attitude toward school does seem to restrain the commission of delinquent acts.

Although we have a larger percentage difference across different values of the independent variable in Table 8.5 than we did in Table 8.3, we still cannot be confident that this difference is a "real" one and not due to sampling variation or chance. To dismiss the probability of random sampling variation producing our observed results, we need to perform a formal hypothesis test involving a test statistic that has a known sampling distribution. Fortunately, we have one, and it is called the chi-square test of independence.

Table 8.5	Relationship Between Attitudes Toward School and Self-Reported Delinquency: Observed Frequencies With Percentages and Making Comparisons Across the IV Categories

| DV: Number of Self-Reported Delinquent Acts | IV: Do You Like School? | | Total |
	Like	Dislike	
0	140 45%	25 19%	165
1	105 33%	50 37%	155
2+	70 22%	60 44%	130
Total	315 100%	135 100%	450

The Chi-Square Test of Independence

The chi-square test of independence tests the null hypothesis that two categorical variables are independent of each other. In hypothesizing that they are independent, we are making the assumption that they are not related to one another—in causal terms, that the independent variable does not affect or influence the dependent variable. Recall from Chapter 5 that events are independent when they do not influence or affect the outcome of each other. If we can reject this null hypothesis, we can presume that they are related at least at our stated level of confidence. If, however, we fail to reject the null hypothesis of independence, we must assume that they are not related to each other.

The definitional formula for the chi-square test of independence is the following:

$$\chi^2 = \sum_{i=1}^{k} \frac{(f_o - f_e)^2}{f_e}$$

(Formula 8-1)

where

f_o = the observed cell frequencies from our sample data

f_e = the expected cell frequencies we should get under the null hypothesis

k = the number of cells in the table

Note that in describing this formula, we are referring to the cells of a contingency table. More specifically, the chi-square test of independence is based on the cell frequencies. The frequencies we must calculate ourselves are the "expected" where "expected" means the frequency we would expect to find in each cell if the two variables were, in fact, independent or not related to each other (which is the assumption of our null hypothesis). What we have, then, is a contingency table of observed cell frequencies and another contingency table of expected cell frequencies. For each cell, we take the difference between the observed and expected cell frequencies, square that difference, divide this squared difference by the **expected frequency**, and sum across all cells. What we do not know yet is where the values of expected cell frequencies come from. We need to explore this in a little detail before proceeding to our hypothesis test.

Let's return to our example involving gender and negative emotions. In the contingency table in Table 8.1, we have two categorical variables, a person's gender and whether that person scored "low" or "high" on a measure of negative emotionality. The easiest way to calculate the expected cell frequencies is using the following formula:

$$\text{Expected cell frequency of cell } f_e = \frac{RM_i \times CM_j}{n}$$ (Formula 8-2)

where

RM_i = the row marginal frequency for row i

CM_j = the column marginal frequency for column j

n = the total number of cases

In words, to find the expected frequency of a given cell, multiply the frequency at the end of the row for this cell times the frequency at the bottom of the column for this cell, divide this product by the total number of cases, and then do this for each cell in the table. By applying this simple formula to our **observed frequencies** in Table 8.1, we can calculate the expected cell frequencies (expected under the null hypothesis of independence) as follows:

$$\text{Female and low negative emotions} = \frac{60 \times 90}{120} = 45$$

$$\text{Female and high negative emotions} = \frac{60 \times 30}{120} = 15$$

$$\text{Male and low negative emotions} = \frac{60 \times 90}{120} = 45$$

$$\text{Male and high negative emotions} = \frac{60 \times 30}{120} = 15$$

Expected frequencies: Joint frequency distribution we would expect to see if the two categorical variables were independent of each other. The expected frequencies, therefore, are calculated under the assumption of the null hypothesis—or no relationship between the two variables.

Observed frequencies: Joint distribution of two categorical variables that we actually observed in our sample data.

We now have two tables of frequencies for gender and negative emotions. Table 8.6 displays both the original observed frequencies and these calculated expected frequencies. We have also labeled the cells A through D for easier reference. The *expected frequencies* tell us what the joint frequency distribution of gender and negative emotions should look like if, in fact, the two variables were independent. This is what we should see if our two categorical variables are not related to each other. Notice that the row and column marginals and the total number of cases are the same in both the observed and expected tables; the only thing that differs is their joint distribution, which is found in the cells of the table.

The chi-square test of independence answers this question: "Are the observed frequencies significantly different from the expected frequencies?" More specifically, the chi-square test takes the difference between the observed and expected cell frequencies for each cell in the table. If the observed frequencies are equal to the expected frequencies (i.e., if the difference between them is zero), we would be confident in concluding that the two variables are independent and not related. In fact, if the difference between the observed and expected cell frequencies is zero, the chi-square test will also be zero. As the difference between the observed and expected cell frequencies increases, the value of chi-square increases and our assumption of independence becomes less likely. Of course, the difference between the expected and observed cell frequencies is generally not going to be exactly zero even when the two variables are independent. In other words, even if the two variables are independent, we would still expect to find a nonzero value of the chi-square statistic. What we have to determine, therefore, is how large a difference we must find between the observed and expected cell frequencies, or how large a chi-square we demand before we are willing to reject the null hypothesis of independence. How large the difference must be is determined by the chi-square probability distribution.

The answer to this question is that the observed value of the chi-square statistic must be equal to or greater than the critical value of chi-square we obtain from our chi-square table at a given alpha level (our selected level of significance) and degrees of freedom. We need to set our alpha level, determine our degrees of freedom, and then go to the chi-square table and identify our critical value and the critical region of the chi-square probability distribution.

To determine our level of significance, we simply weigh the costs of making a Type I error and a Type II error. Let's say we have done this and decided that an alpha level of .05 is reasonable for our current problem. The determination of the number of degrees of freedom in a chi-square test of independence is based on the following formula:

$$\text{Degrees of freedom} = (\# \text{ of rows} - 1) \times (\# \text{ of columns} - 1)$$

$$\text{Degrees of freedom} = (R - 1) \times (C - 1)$$

In the chi-square test of independence, then, the degrees of freedom are equal to the number of rows minus 1 times the number of columns minus 1. In Table 8.6, we have two rows and two columns, so there is $(2-1)(2-1) = 1$ degree of freedom. As you will see in the next chapters, degrees of freedom are usually based on the sample size. However, for chi-square they are based on the table size for a good reason. Recall that a degree of freedom refers to a value that is free to vary, which means that it is not fixed and can assume any number. In Table 8.7, we have question marks in each cell of our contingency table, with the row and column marginals provided. Which cell frequencies are free to vary given the observed row and column marginals?

In determining how many degrees of freedom we have, the row and column marginals or frequencies are given; they are not free to vary. What are free to vary are the four cell frequencies that correspond to the joint distribution of the two variables. Let's start in cell A of Table 8.8 (female and low negative emotions) and ask what value this frequency can be, restricted only by the row and column marginals. Theoretically, this cell can have any frequency as long as we can still get sums of 60 for the row and 90 for the column. Although we could use any number, let's use the number 46 in that cell. Let's now move to cell B. What value can this cell frequency be and still have a row total of 60 and a column total of 30? There is only one number that this cell frequency can be, and that is 14. A cell frequency of 14 and only 14 will make the row marginal equal to 60. As such, this cell frequency is not free to vary because it can only equal 14. How about cell C? Is this cell frequency free to vary? No. The column marginal must sum to 90, and the row marginal must sum to 60. The only way that this can happen is if the cell frequency was 44. It is fixed, then, and not free to vary, as is the cell just to the right of this one (male and high negative emotions). It is not free to vary because the row marginal must sum to 60 and the column marginal must sum to 30. The only value this frequency can be is 16. In sum, in a 2 × 2 table, there is only

Table 8.6 Observed Cell Frequencies and Expected Cell Frequencies for Relationship Between Gender and Negative Emotionality

Gender	Negative Emotionality Low	High	Row Total
Female	A 46 $f_e = 45$	B 14 $f_e = 15$	60
Male	C 44 $f_e = 45$	D 16 $f_e = 15$	60
Column total	90	30	$n = 120$

| Table 8.7 | Row and Column Marginals for Gender and Negative Emotions Data Found in Table 8.6 | | |

	Negative Emotionality		
Gender	Low	High	Total
Female	?	?	60
Male	?	?	60
Total	90	30	120

| Table 8.8 | Determining Degrees of Freedom in a 2 × 2 Table: Fixing the Frequencies for the First Cell | | |

	Negative Emotionality		
Gender	Low	High	Total
Female	A	B	60
	46	?	
Male	C	D	60
	?	?	
Total	90	30	120

one cell frequency that is free to vary, and once that cell frequency is determined, all the other cell frequencies are fixed (i.e., they can be only one value). That is what the concept of degrees of freedom means with respect to contingency tables.

We now have all the information we need to conduct our formal hypothesis test. The null hypothesis is that the two variables are independent, and the alternative hypothesis is that they are not independent and there is a relationship between them. We will test this hypothesis with an alpha of .05.

With an alpha of .05 and 1 degree of freedom, we can go to our chi-square probability distribution table (Table B.4 in Appendix B) and find our critical value of the chi-square statistic. By looking at the table, we see that the critical value of chi-square is 3.841, and since all values of chi-square are positive, the critical region is any chi-square value that is greater than or equal to 3.841. We are now ready to conduct our formal hypothesis test one step at a time.

Step 1: H_0: Gender and negative emotions are independent of each other. If they are independent, we would expect the value of our obtained chi-square statistic to be zero: $\chi^2 = 0$.

H_1: Gender and negative emotions are not independent of each other. If they are not independent, we would expect the value of our obtained chi-square statistic to not be equal to zero: $\chi^2 > 0$.

The chi-square distribution is a positive distribution in that we will never have an obtained value that is less than zero. That is because we square the difference between the observed and expected frequencies. The chi-square test of independence, therefore, will always be a directional or one-tailed test with the alternative stated as $\chi^2 > 0$.

Step 2: Our test statistic is the chi-square test of independence. The chi-square test has a chi-square distribution with $(R-1) \times (C-1)$ degrees of freedom.

Step 3: We selected an alpha level of .05 and have 1 degree of freedom in our 2 × 2 table. We discovered that the critical value of chi-square is 3.841. The critical region is defined as any chi-square greater than or equal to 3.841 (a chi-square is always positive, so the hypothesis test will be whether the obtained chi-square is greater than or equal to the critical chi-square).

Step 4: We have our table of observed and expected frequencies in Table 8.6. The definitional formula for the chi-square test of independence is

$$\chi^2 = \sum_{i=1}^{k} \frac{(f_o - f_e)^2}{f_e}$$

where $k =$ the number of cells. What this formula tells us to do is subtract the expected cell frequency from the observed cell frequency, square this difference, divide this squared difference by the expected cell frequency, repeat the procedure for every cell in the table, and sum the results over all cells. This is our obtained value of the chi-square statistic. The calculations for the independence of gender and negative emotions are shown in Table 8.9, and we have an obtained chi-square of .178.

Step 5: Since our obtained chi-square ($\chi^2_{\text{obt}} = .178$) is less than our critical chi-square ($\chi^2_{\text{crit}} = 3.841$) and does not fall into the critical region, our decision is to fail to reject the null hypothesis. Our conclusion, therefore, is that gender and negative emotions are independent; that is, there is no relationship between them in the population. Our data do not support the hypothesis that males are more likely than females to experience high negative emotions.

A Simple-to-Use Computational Formula for the Chi-Square Test of Independence

Table 8.9	Calculation of the Chi-Square Statistic for the Null Hypothesis That Gender and Negative Emotions Are Independent

f_o	f_e	$f_o - f_e$	$(f_o - f_e)^2$	$\dfrac{(f_o - f_e)^2}{f_e}$
46	45	1	1	.022
14	15	−1	1	.067
44	45	−1	1	.022
16	15	1	1	.067
				$\chi^2_{\text{obt}} = .178$

You may find the definitional formula for the chi-square statistic in equation 8-2 somewhat cumbersome. There is an alternative computational formula you can use to calculate your observed chi-square statistic that you might find easier to use since it involves fewer computations. The computational formula for the chi-square test of independence is

$$\chi^2 = \sum_{i=1}^{k} \left(\frac{f_o^2}{f_e} \right) - n \qquad \text{(Formula 8-3)}$$

In this computational formula, the observed frequency for each cell is first squared, and then each squared observed frequency is divided by the expected cell frequency. This is done for each cell in the contingency table. Next these values are summed, and the total number of cases is subtracted from that sum. In steps:

Step 1: Square the observed frequency for each cell in your table.

Step 2: Divide each squared observed frequency by its expected frequency.

Step 3: Perform this operation on each cell in your contingency table, and then sum over all cells.

Step 4: Subtract the sample size from this sum. This is your obtained chi-square statistic.

Let's use this computational formula to calculate the chi-square statistic for our gender and negative emotions data in Table 8.6. We show the necessary calculations in Table 8.10. The value of our obtained chi-square statistic is .178, which is exactly the same as what we obtained when we used the definitional formula.

Table 8.10	Calculations for Chi-Square Statistic on Gender and Negative Emotions Data Using the Computational Formula

f_o	f_o^2	f_e	$\dfrac{f_o^2}{f_e}$
46	2,116	45	(2,116 / 45) = 47.022
14	196	15	(196 / 15) = 13.067
44	1,936	45	(1,936 / 45) = 43.022
16	256	15	(256 / 15) = 17.067
			$\Sigma = 120.178$
			$\chi^2 = 120.178 - 120 = .178$

Case Study

Socioeconomic Status of Neighborhoods and Police Response Time

Table 8.11 gives the joint distribution for two categorical variables: (1) the socioeconomic status of a neighborhood and (2) the speed of police response time to a "911" call for assistance. Both variables are measured at the ordinal level. Based on the literature, we think that the affluence of the neighborhood influences police response time and that the police respond faster to calls for assistance made from higher status neighborhoods. In this case study, therefore, neighborhood socioeconomic status is the independent variable and police response time is the dependent variable.

Our independent variable, neighborhood socioeconomic status, has three levels or categories ("low status," "medium status," and "high status"), and the dependent variable, police response time, is also a three-category, ordinal-level variable ("less than 3 minutes," "between 3 and 7 minutes," and "more than 7 minutes"). Table 8.11 is a 3 × 3 contingency table because there are three rows and three columns. Each cell in this table represents the joint occurrence of neighborhood status and police response time. With three rows and three columns, there are a total of nine cells, with each cell constituting one possible outcome of the joint occurrence of the two variables. Again, we have labeled the cells A through I for ease of discussion.

We are now going to test the hypothesis that neighborhood status and police response time are independent events. In other words, the null hypothesis we are testing assumes that the socioeconomic status of the neighborhood is not related to how quickly the police respond to a 911 call for assistance. Before we conduct a formal hypothesis test, however, let's examine the appropriate percentages across values of the independent variable for a fixed value of the dependent variable. Recall that we need to examine how variation in the independent variable affects variation in the dependent variable. Since the socioeconomic status of the neighborhood is the independent variable, we will use the row marginals as the denominator for our percentages. Practically, this means that our percentages will sum to 100% at the end of the rows. We calculate these percentages in Table 8.12.

Let's examine the value of the dependent variable at a response time of more than 7 minutes. From Table 8.12, we can see that 56% of the time the police responded to a 911 call for assistance in a low-status neighborhood in more than 7 minutes. This drops to 25% of the time in medium-status neighborhoods, and it drops still further to only 9% of the time in high-status neighborhoods. As the social status of the neighborhood varies from low to high, then, it becomes less likely that the police will take longer than 7 minutes to respond to a 911 call. In other words, police respond faster in high-status neighborhoods than either medium- or low-status neighborhoods. We reach the same substantive conclusion when we examine the value of the dependent variable at a quick police response time—less than 3 minutes. Police responded quickly only 17% of the time in a low-status neighborhood, 30% of the time in a medium-status neighborhood, and 64% of the time in a high-status neighborhood. From these percentage differences, it looks like there is a relationship between the socioeconomic status of the neighborhood and how quickly the police respond to a 911 call; they are more likely to respond quickly, and less likely to respond slowly, in more affluent neighborhoods.

Examining how these two variables covary is only the first indicator, however, in determining whether a relationship exists between the two variables. The problem with using the calculation of percentage differences is that there is no probability distribution associated with these statistics. Without a known probability distribution, there is no way to determine whether the difference in percentages we observed in our sample data is due to a relationship between the two variables in our population or to random sampling variability. A formal hypothesis test avoids this ambiguity, and that is why we use the chi-square test for independence.

Table 8.11	Joint Distribution of Neighborhood Socioeconomic Status and Police Response Time to a 911 Call for Assistance

Neighborhood Socioeconomic Status	Police Response Time			Total
	Less Than 3 Minutes	3–7 Minutes	More Than 7 Minutes	
Low	A 11	B 17	C 35	63
Medium	D 16	E 24	F 13	53
High	G 48	H 20	I 7	75
Total	75	61	55	191

Table 8.12	Relationship Between Neighborhood Socioeconomic Status and Police Response Time to a 911 Call for Assistance: Examining Percentages

Neighborhood Socioeconomic Status	Police Response Time			Total
	Less Than 3 Minutes	3–7 Minutes	More Than 7 Minutes	
Low	11 17%	17 27%	35 56%	63 100%
Medium	16 30%	24 45%	13 25%	53 100%
High	48 64%	20 27%	7 9%	75 100%
Total	75	61	55	191

The first step in conducting a chi-square test of independence is to determine what the expected frequencies would be if the two variables were in fact independent. Let's use the formula to calculate the expected frequencies:

$$\left(\frac{RM_i \times CM_j}{n} \right)$$

Here is what you should obtain:

Low status and less than 3 minutes response time: $\dfrac{63 \times 75}{191} = 25$

Low status and 3–7 minutes response time: $\dfrac{63 \times 61}{191} = 20$

Low status and more than 7 minutes response time: $\dfrac{63 \times 55}{191} = 18$

Medium status and less than 3 minutes response time: $\dfrac{53 \times 75}{191} = 21$

Medium status and 3–7 minutes response time: $\dfrac{53 \times 61}{191} = 17$

Medium status and more than 7 minutes response time: $\dfrac{53 \times 55}{191} = 15$

High status and less than 3 minutes response time: $\dfrac{75 \times 75}{191} = 29$

High status and 3–7 minutes response time: $\dfrac{75 \times 61}{191} = 24$

High status and more than 7 minutes response time: $\dfrac{75 \times 55}{191} = 22$

The expected cell frequencies under the null hypothesis that neighborhood socioeconomic status and police response time are independent of each other are given along with the original observed cell frequencies in Table 8.13. Remember that the expected cell frequencies tell us the joint distribution of neighborhood status and police response time we would *expect to see* if these two variables were not related to each other, that is, if they were independent.

We next need to select an alpha level and calculate our degrees of freedom. Let's use an alpha of .01 for this hypothesis test. By using our formula for the correct degrees of freedom in a contingency table $[df = (R - 1) \times (C - 1)]$, we can see that we have $(3 - 1) \times (3 - 1)$ or 4 degrees of freedom. With an alpha level of .01 and 4 degrees of freedom, we can now go to our chi-square probability distribution table (Table B.4 in Appendix B) and find our critical value of the chi-square statistic. By looking at the table, we see that the critical value of chi-square is 13.277. The critical region for rejecting the null hypothesis, then, is any chi-square value that is greater than or equal to 13.277. We are now ready to conduct our formal hypothesis test one step at a time:

Table 8.13	Observed and Expected Cell Frequencies Under the Null Hypothesis of Independence

	Police Response Time			
Neighborhood Socioeconomic Status	Less Than 3 Minutes	3–7 Minutes	More Than 7 Minutes	Total
Low	11 $f_e = 25$	17 $f_e = 20$	35 $f_e = 18$	63
Medium	16 $f_e = 21$	24 $f_e = 17$	13 $f_e = 15$	53
High	48 $f_e = 29$	20 $f_e = 24$	7 $f_e = 22$	75
Total	75	61	55	191

Table 8.14	Computational Formula: Calculation of the Chi-Square Statistic for the Null Hypothesis That Neighborhood Socioeconomic Status and Police Response Time Are Independent

f_o	f_o^2	f_e	$\dfrac{f_o^2}{f_e}$
11	121	25	4.84
17	289	20	14.45
35	1,225	18	68.06
16	256	21	12.19
24	576	17	33.88
13	169	15	11.27
48	2,304	29	79.45
20	400	24	16.67
7	49	22	2.23
			$\Sigma = 243.04$
			$\chi^2_{obt} = 243.04 - 191$
			$\chi^2_{obt} = 52.04$

Step 1:

H_0: Neighborhood socioeconomic status and police response time are independent of each other. Our obtained value of chi-square should not be significantly different from zero: $\chi^2 = 0$.

H_1: Neighborhood socioeconomic status and police response time are not independent of each other; neighborhood status and police response time are related to each other. Our obtained value of chi-square should be significantly greater than zero: $\chi^2 > 0$.

Step 2: Our test statistic is the chi-square test of independence. The chi-square test has a chi-square distribution.

Step 3: We selected an alpha level of .01 and have 4 degrees of freedom in our 3×3 table $[(3-1)(3-1)=4]$. The critical value of chi-square is 13.277. The critical region is defined as any chi-square greater than or equal to 13.277.

Step 4: We have both our observed and expected cell frequencies in Table 8.13, and we will use the computational formula to calculate the chi-square statistic:

$$\chi^2 = \sum_{i=1}^{k} \left(\frac{f_o^2}{f_e} \right) - n$$

The calculations for this problem are shown for you in Table 8.14, and our obtained chi-square is 52.04.

Step 5: Since our obtained chi-square, $\chi^2_{obt} = 52.04$, is greater than our critical chi-square $\left(\chi^2_{crit} = 13.277 \right)$ and falls into the critical region, our decision is to reject the null hypothesis. Our conclusion, therefore, is that neighborhood socioeconomic status and police response time are not independent; they are related to one another in the population. We can also conclude the direction of this relationship. We can generalize that in the population, neighborhoods with higher socioeconomic status are more likely to get quicker police response times than neighborhoods with lower socioeconomic status.

Although the chi-square statistic enables us to reject the null hypothesis of independence in favor of the alternative hypothesis, it does not tell us anything about the magnitude or strength of the relationship. Two variables may be related to each other in the population, but the relationship may be very weak, it may be of moderate strength, or it may be very strong. To determine the strength of the relationship between two categorical variables, we need to learn about something called measures of association. We will do this in the next section.

▣ Measures of Association: Determining the Strength of the Relationship Between Two Categorical Variables

The chi-square statistic enables us to determine whether two categorical variables (nominal or ordinal) are independent or are related to each other in the population, but it tells us nothing about the strength of the relationship if in fact one exists. Throughout this text, you will continually be reminded that a significant relationship does not always indicate that two variables have a strong relationship. In fact, with a large enough sample size, many relationships can attain significance but be only weakly related. When we are interested in understanding the strength of the relationship between our variables, we need to be acquainted with something called measures of association. A **measure of association** is a summary measure that captures the magnitude or strength of the relationship between two variables. There are different kinds of measures of association, depending on the level of measurement for our variables.

Measures of association: Statistics that inform us about the strength, or magnitude, as well as the direction of the relationship between two variables.

Nominal-Level Variables

Case Study

Gender and Police Officer Work

Let's start with a very simple problem. In this problem, we have a 2 × 2 contingency table with nominal-level data. For example, in Table 8.15, we have the joint distribution of two nominal-level variables, the gender of a police officer (male/female) and the type of job that officer does (desk job/patrol). We believe that male and female police officers may be given very different assignments. In this scenario, gender is our independent variable, and work assignment is the dependent variable. When we calculate the percentages in the table, by using the row marginals as the denominators because the independent variable is on the row, we see that 67% of female police officers work in desk jobs compared with only 36% of male officers. If we were to conduct a hypothesis test of the independence of these two variables, we would obtain a chi-square of 12.25. With 1 degree of freedom, we would reject the null hypothesis of independence at either a .05 or .01 level of significance. We would conclude that in the population, female police officers are more likely to be in desk jobs compared with patrol jobs.

A measure of association we could use in this problem to gauge the strength of the relationship is the phi coefficient. The **phi coefficient** (ϕ) is appropriate when we have nominal-level variables and a 2 × 2 table. The phi coefficient is very simple to calculate and uses the obtained value of our chi-square coefficient along with the sample size:

$$\phi = \sqrt{\frac{\chi^2_{obt}}{n}}$$

(Formula 8-4)

The formula tells us to take the ratio of the obtained chi-square statistic to the number of cases in the sample and then take the square root. The phi coefficient has a finite range between 0 and 1; it will equal 0 when there is no relationship and will attain a maximum value of 1.0 with a perfect relationship. The phi coefficient will always be positive, and the magnitude of the relationship will tell us how strongly the two nominal-level variables are related. Magnitudes of phi near zero indicate a very weak relationship, and those near 1.0 indicate a very strong relationship. A helpful rule of thumb to follow with the phi coefficient (and with any other measure of association) is that relationships between 0 and ±29 can be considered "weak," relationships between ±.30 and ±.59 can be considered "moderate," and relationships between ±.60 and ±1.00 can be considered "strong." However, this is only an informal guide. For the data in Table 8.15, we would have a phi coefficient of

Table 8.15	Joint Distribution of Gender of Police Officer and Type of Work Performed		
Gender	Desk Job	Patrol	Total
Low	45	80	125
	36%	64%	100%
Medium	30	15	45
	67%	33%	100%
Total	75	95	170

$$\phi = \sqrt{\frac{12.25}{170}}$$

$$\phi = .27$$

A phi coefficient of .27 tells us that there is only a weak relationship between gender and type of assignment on the police force.

Phi coefficient: A measure of association used to measure the strength of the relationship between two nominal-level variables in a 2 × 2 contingency table.

Case Study

Type of Counsel and Sentence

Table 8.16 shows you the joint distribution of two nominal-level variables: (1) the type of lawyer a criminal defendant had and (2) the type of sentence the criminal defendant received after conviction. We think that the type of lawyer a defendant has affects the kind of sentence received, so type of lawyer is the independent variable and type of sentence is the dependent variable. When we examine the joint percentage distributions within the dependent variable category "receiving a fine and jail time," we see that 73% of those who had a court-appointed lawyer received this sanction compared with only 46% of those who had a public defender and only 12% of those who had a private attorney. It seems that having a private attorney gives you an advantage at sentencing. By looking at the least severe sanction of probation, we see that 63% of those who had a private attorney received a probation-only sentence compared with 9% of those who had a court-appointed lawyer and 23% of those who had a public defender. When we conduct a chi-square test of independence at an alpha level of .01 and with 4 df, we can reject the null hypothesis because $\left(\chi^2_{crit} = 13.277\right)$ and $\chi^2_{obt} = 44.94$. We conclude from this that there is a relationship in the population between these two variables, although we do not know the strength of the relationship. Another measure of association for nominal-level variables is known as **Cramer's V**. can also be used with tables that are larger than 2×2. Like the phi coefficient, it is based on chi-square and ranges in magnitude from 0 to 1.0. The formula for calculating V is

$$V = \sqrt{\frac{\chi^2_{obt}}{n(k-1)}}$$

(Formula 8-5)

where k = the number of rows or the number of columns, whichever is smaller. For Table 8.16, the value of V would be

Cramer's V: Statistical measure of association that quantifies the strength or magnitude of a relationship between two nominal-level variables.

$$V = \sqrt{\frac{44.94}{160(3-1)}}$$

$$V = .37$$

We would conclude from this that there is a moderately strong association between type of lawyer and type of sentence.

Table 8.16 Joint Distribution for Type of Lawyer and Type of Sentence Received

Type of Lawyer	Type of Sentence Received			Total
	Probation	Fine Only	Fine and Jail Time	
Court-appointed	5 9%	10 18%	40 73%	55 100%
Public defender	15 23%	20 31%	30 46%	65 100%
Private	25 63%	10 25%	5 12%	40 100%
Total	45	40	75	160

🔲 Ordinal-Level Variables

When our variables are measured at the ordinal level, phi and Cramer's *V* are no longer appropriate measures of association. With ordinal-level variables, one of the most popular measures of association in the literature is **Goodman and Kruskal's gamma**. Gamma (γ) is referred to as a proportionate reduction in error measure, which takes on a minimum value of 0 (when there is no relationship between the two ordinal-level variables) and a maximum value of ± 1.0 (for a perfect positive relationship or a perfect negative relationship). As we noted with respect to the phi coefficient, a helpful rule of thumb to follow with any measure of association—although it is only an informal guide—is that relationships between 0 and $\pm .29$ can be considered "weak," relationships between $\pm .30$ and $\pm .59$ can be considered "moderate," and relationships between $\pm .60$ and ± 1.00 can be considered "strong." Gamma is also a symmetric measure of association, which means that it does not matter which variable we designate as the independent variable and which one we designate as the dependent variable.

In the special case of a 2 × 2 table (a table with two rows and two columns), gamma is often referred to as Yule's *Q*. With the four cells labeled as follows:

A	B
C	D

Yule's *Q* or gamma for a 2 × 2 table is defined as

$$Q = \frac{(f_{\text{cell A}} \times f_{\text{cell D}}) - (f_{\text{cell B}} \times f_{\text{cell C}})}{(f_{\text{cell A}} \times f_{\text{cell D}}) + (f_{\text{cell B}} \times f_{\text{cell C}})}$$

(Formula 8-6)

To calculate the *Q* coefficient, then, all you do is take the product of the frequency in cell A and the frequency in cell D (called the cross-product) and the product of the frequency in cell B and the frequency in cell C (the other cross-product). In the numerator of *Q* we take the difference between these two values, and in the denominator we take the sum.

Let's use this formula to calculate the value of *Q* for our two variables in Table 8.3, which showed the joint distribution of gender and negative emotions. Recall that we failed to reject the null hypothesis when we conducted our chi-square test of independence. The value of *Q* for these data is

$$Q = \frac{(46 \times 16) - (44 \times 14)}{(46 \times 16) + (44 \times 14)}$$

$$Q = \frac{120}{1,352}$$

$$Q = .09$$

The value of Yule's *Q* here is very small—not that much different from zero.

> **Goodman and Kruskal's gamma:** Statistical measure of association that quantifies the strength or magnitude of a relationship between two ordinal-level variables. It is also called Yule's *Q* with a 2 × 2 table.

Case Study

Adolescents' Employment and Drug and Alcohol Use

Let's try another example. Table 8.17 shows the joint distribution of two variables. One variable is the number of hours that a youth spends working during the school year, and the second variable is the number of times during the year that the youth reports using drugs or alcohol. In this example, we will take the number of working hours as the independent variable and the level of drug/alcohol use as the dependent variable. Since the independent variable is located on the rows, that is how the percentages are calculated. We can see that 80% of those adolescents who work 20 hours or less per week have used alcohol or drugs on two or more occasions compared with only 33% of those who work more than 20 hours per week. When we conduct a chi-square test of independence, we obtain a chi-square value of 31.85, which with 1 degree of freedom is significant at either a .05 or .01 level. Therefore, we reject the null hypothesis of independence and conclude that there is a relationship between the two variables. In the population, we can conclude that students who work more are less likely to engage in drug and alcohol use compared with those who work less. We can then determine the strength of the relationship with Yule's Q:

$$Q = \frac{(15 \times 20) - (40 \times 60)}{(15 \times 20) - (40 \times 60)}$$

$$Q = \frac{-2,100}{2,700}$$

$$Q = -.78$$

Table 8.17	Joint Distribution of Number of Hours Worked per Week During the School Year and Number of Times a Youth Has Used Drugs or Alcohol		

| Number of Hours Worked per Week | Number of Times Used Drugs/Alcohol | | |
	0	1 or More	Total
Court-appointed	15	60	75
	20%	80%	100%
Public defender	40	20	60
	67%	33%	100%
Total	55	80	135

We have a Yule's Q of $-.78$, implying that there is a fairly strong negative relationship between working while in school and substance use. What does a negative relationship imply here?

In a **negative relationship**, increasing the level of one variable has the effect of decreasing the level of the other, whereas in a **positive relationship**, increasing the level of one variable has the effect of increasing the level of the other. Note that in Table 8.17, the two variables are arranged in increasing order in the sense that drug/alcohol use increases from left to right (from no use to using it one or more times), and working increases from less than 20 hours per week in the top row to 20 or more hours per week in the lower row (we can talk about more than or less than because we have an ordinal level variable). A negative relationship between two ordinal-level variables means that increasing the independent variable decreases the dependent variable. In this case, increasing the level of working from less than 20 to 20 or more hours per week has the effect of decreasing the level of the dependent variable from one or more times using drugs/alcohol to not using. Had we obtained a Q coefficient of $+.78$, we would have concluded that increasing the level of working from less than 20 hours to more than 20 hours per week increases the risk of drug/alcohol use from zero times to one or more times.

In contingency tables that are larger than 2×2, we cannot use Yule's Q but instead must use a more general formula for Goodman and Kruskal's gamma. The formula for gamma is

$$\gamma = \frac{CP - DP}{CP + DP} \qquad \text{(Formula 8-7)}$$

Negative relationship: An increase in one variable is related to a decrease in the other variable.

Positive relationship between two variables: An increase in one variable is related to an increase in the other.

where

CP = the number of concordant pairs of observations

DP = the number of discordant pairs of observations

Before we get to the application of the gamma coefficient, we need to understand exactly what a concordant pair and a discordant pair of observations are. We are not going to calculate the value of gamma by hand, but it is important for you to understand what it is actually measuring.

Case Study

Age of Onset for Delinquency and Future Offending

Let's begin with two variables measured from a sample of adult offenders. Both variables are measured at the ordinal level and have three levels or categories. The independent variable is the age at which adults first engaged in delinquent offending:

Variable 1 (V_1): Age of First Delinquent Act

Level 1: 8–10 years old

Level 2: 11–13 years old

Level 3: 14–16 years old

The dependent variable is the number of years into adulthood that the person offends:

Variable 2 (V_2): Years of "Criminal Career"

Level 1: 1–4 years

Level 2: 5–8 years

Level 3: 9 years or more

Person Number	Level on V_1	Level on V_2
1	1	2
2	2	3
3	3	2
4	3	3
5	3	2

Since these two variables are measured at the ordinal level, those at a higher level or category have more of the variable than those at a lower level. Let's now take five people from our sample who fall into different categories of the two ordinal variables. The following table shows the level, or "score," on both variables for each of these five people.

Two pairs of observations are said to be *concordant* when the scores on the two variables are consistently higher or consistently lower. For example, let's take person 1 and person 2. In comparing person 1 and person 2 on the two variables, we see that the second person scores higher on both V_1 and V_2 (2 vs. 1 on V_1 and 3 vs. 2 on V_2). This pair of persons or pair of observations, then, is concordant because person 2 scores consistently higher on both variables compared with person 1. Person 4 is concordant with person 1 also because that person also scores higher on both variables (3 vs. 1 on V_1 and 3 vs. 2 on V_2). Now let's compare person 2 and person 3. Person 2 is lower on V_1 compared with person 3 (2 vs. 3) but is higher on V_2 (3 vs. 2). Person 2 is not, therefore, consistently higher (or lower) on both variables than person 3 but, rather, is higher on one variable and lower on another. Pairs of observations like these, where one case is higher on one variable but lower on another, are called *discordant pairs*. Think of discordant pairs of cases as those where the scores on the two variables are dissimilar. A person is higher than the other person on one variable but lower than that person on the other. Person 5 is also discordant with person 2. Now let's compare person 3 with person 4. In this pair of observations, persons 3 and 4 are tied on V_1 and person 4 is higher than person 3 on V_2. Person 4 is also tied with person 2 on the second variable (V_2). Person 3 is tied with person 5 on both variables. These three comparisons are neither concordant nor discordant; they are referred to as *tied* pairs of observations because they have the same score on at least one variable.

Table 8.18 Grades in School and Self-Reported Acts of Petty Theft

Grades in School	Self-Reported Thefts			
	0	1 to 5	6 or More	Total
Mostly Ds and Fs	23	19	20	62
Mostly Cs	307	157	123	587
Mostly Bs	762	345	155	1,262
Mostly As	418	166	56	640
Total	1,510	687	354	2,551

In comparing a pair of cases, then, there are three possible outcomes: concordant, discordant, or tied pairs. In a given contingency table, if concordant pairs outnumber discordant pairs, we will find a positive relationship because the predominance of concordant pairs implies that as one variable increases, so does the other. If we have instead a predominance of discordant pairs, we will find a negative relationship between the two variables because this implies that as one variable increases, the other decreases. If there are approximately the same number of concordant pairs as discordant pairs, our variables are not related to one another or are not related very strongly. Now that we know what concordant and discordant pairs are, we can reintroduce the gamma coefficient and apply it to a few of our problems.

Recall that the formula for gamma is

$$\gamma = \frac{CP - DP}{CP + DP}$$

Gamma, therefore, simply takes the ratio of the difference between the number of concordant pairs of cases (CP) and the number of discordant pairs (DP) to the sum of the concordant and discordant pairs.

Like Yule's Q, gamma ranges in magnitude from 0 to ± 1.0, with 0 indicating no relationship between our ordinal-level variables, -1.0 indicating a perfect negative relationship, and $+1.0$ indicating a perfect positive relationship. As you can perhaps see from the formula, gamma takes into account only concordant and discordant pairs of cases; it ignores all those pairs that are tied on one or both of the variables. Note also that when $CP < DP$, gamma will be positive, and when $CP > DP$, gamma will be negative. Finally, note that the magnitude of gamma will increase as the number of CP or DP cases increases relative to the other. Now, the only issue remaining is how we go about calculating gamma. As you might imagine, calculating the value of gamma by hand can be quite time-consuming. Those of you interested can go to the website to find out how to calculate the value of gamma by hand for the data in Table 8.18. This table shows the joint distribution for a high school sample of 2,551 students and the independent variable of grades in school and the dependent variable of self-reported thefts during the past year. For the rest of you, we are simply going to give you the number of concordant and discordant pairs! The number of concordant pairs is 472,657, and the number of discordant pairs is 699,336. This results in the value of gamma for Table 8.18 as follows:

$$\gamma = \frac{472,657 - 699,336}{472,657 + 699,336}$$

$$\gamma = -.19$$

If we calculated the value of chi-square for these data, we would have been able to reject the null hypothesis and would have concluded that in the population, students with higher grades were less likely to engage in property crime. The gamma coefficient of $-.19$ tells us that there is only a weak negative relationship between school grades and self-reported thefts. This should be a reminder that just because we reject the null hypothesis and conclude that there is a relationship between two variables in the population does not necessarily mean that the relationship is a strong one. Here, we reject the null hypothesis, but the relationship happens to be weak. Recall that the presence of a negative relationship means that an increase in the independent variable is associated with a decrease in the dependent variable. By looking at Table 8.18, this means that as a student's grades "increase" (e.g., improve by going from Ds and Fs to As), the student is less likely to commit acts of theft. In other words, having good grades decreases the probability that high school students will engage in property crime.

🖳 Summary

In this chapter, we learned how to test a null hypothesis when both the independent and dependent variables are measured at the nominal or ordinal level using a chi-square (x^2) test. Because testing the significance of a relationship is different from determining the strength of a relationship, we also examined measures of association, which capture information about the strength of the relationship between two categorical variables. The appropriate measure of association depends on the level of measurement of our variables.

Key Terms

▸ Review key terms with eFlashcards. Visit study.sagepub.com/paternoster.

chi-square test of independence   196
column marginal or column
   frequency   198
contingency table   197
Cramer's V 212

expected frequencies   202
Goodman and Kruskal's gamma   213
joint frequency distribution   197
measures of association   210
negative relationship   214

observed frequencies   202
percentage differences   199
phi coefficient   211
positive relationship   214
row marginal or row frequency   198

Key Formulas

Definitional formula for chi-square statistic (formula 8-1):

$$\chi^2 = \sum_{i=1}^{k} \frac{(f_o - f_e)^2}{f_e}$$

Computational formula for expected cell frequencies (formula 8-2):

$$\left(\frac{RM_i \times CM_j}{n} \right)$$

Computational formula for chi-square statistic (formula 8-3):

$$\chi^2 = \sum_{i=1}^{k} \left(\frac{f_o^2}{f_e} \right) - n$$

Phi coefficient (formula 8-4):

$$\phi = \sqrt{\frac{\chi^2_{obt}}{n}}$$

Cramer's V (formula 8-5):

$$V = \sqrt{\frac{\chi^2_{obt}}{n(k-1)}}$$

Yule's Q (formula 8-6):

$$Q = \frac{(f_{cell\,A} \times f_{cell\,D}) - (f_{cell\,B} \times f_{cell\,C})}{(f_{cell\,A} \times f_{cell\,D}) + (f_{cell\,B} \times f_{cell\,C})}$$

Gamma (formula 8-7):

$$\gamma = \frac{CP - DP}{CP + DP}$$

Practice Problems

> Test your understanding of chapter content.
> Take the practice quiz at study.sagepub.com/paternoster.

1. The following contingency table describes the joint distribution of two variables: (1) the type of institution a correctional officer works in and (2) whether the officer reports being satisfied with the job. Your hypothesis is that those who work in medium-security facilities will be more satisfied with their job:

Type of Institution	Satisfied With Job?		Total
	No	Yes	
Medium security	15	30	45
Maximum security	100	40	140
Total	115	70	185

a. What is the independent variable, and what is the dependent variable?

b. How many observations or cases are there?

c. What are the column marginals?

d. What are the row marginals?

e. What is the size of this contingency table?

f. How many correctional officers are in medium-security facilities and are satisfied with their jobs?

g. How many correctional officers are in maximum-security facilities and are not satisfied with their jobs?

h. How many degrees of freedom are there in this table?

i. Calculate the relative risk of not being satisfied with one's job for each of the two types of facilities. What does this suggest?

j. Test the null hypothesis that the two variables are independent. Use an alpha level of .05 and state each step of your hypothesis test. If you reject the null hypothesis, how strongly are the two variables related?

2. Social disorganization theorists have argued that neighborhoods that lack the capacity to solve their own problems (i.e., are socially disorganized) have higher rates of crime and other social problems than neighborhoods that are organized. To test this hypothesis, you take a random sample of 250 communities and determine whether they are socially organized or disorganized and whether they have low or high crime rates. Here are your data:

Type of Institution	Social Organization		Total
	Socially Organized	Socially Disorganized	
Low crime rate	90	98	188
High crime rate	10	52	62
Total	100	150	250

a. What is the independent variable, and what is the dependent variable?

b. How many observations or cases are there?

c. What are the column marginals?

d. What are the row marginals?

e. What is the size of this contingency table?

f. How many socially disorganized neighborhoods have a high crime rate?

g. How many socially organized neighborhoods have a high crime rate?

h. How many degrees of freedom are there in this table?

i. Calculate the relative risk of a high neighborhood crime rate for both socially organized and socially disorganized communities. What does this suggest?

j. Test the null hypothesis that the two variables are independent. Use an alpha level of .01 and state each step of your hypothesis test.

3. You think that there is a relationship between where a defendant's case is tried and the type of sentence the defendant receives. To test this hypothesis, you collect data on 425 defendants convicted in rural, suburban, and urban courts in your state. Here are your data:

Type of Sentence Received	Where Defendant Was Tried			Total
	Rural Court	Suburban Court	Urban Court	
Jail only	18	30	94	142
Fine and jail	22	37	36	95
Less than 60 days of jail time	24	38	50	112

Type of Sentence Received	Where Defendant Was Tried			
	Rural Court	Suburban Court	Urban Court	Total
60 or more days of jail time	16	20	40	76
Total	80	125	220	425

a. What is the independent variable, and what is the dependent variable?

b. How many observations or cases are there?

c. What are the column marginals?

d. What are the row marginals?

e. What is the size of this contingency table?

f. How many defendants from suburban courts received a sentence of less than 60 days of jail time?

g. How many defendants from rural courts received a sentence of a fine and jail time?

h. How many degrees of freedom are there in this table?

i. Calculate the relative risk of getting a sentence of 60 or more days of jail time for defendants from different court jurisdictions. What does this suggest?

j. Test the null hypothesis that the two variables are independent. Use an alpha level of .05 and state each step of your hypothesis test. If you reject the null hypothesis, how strongly are the two variables related?

4. You think that there might be a relationship between race and the number of property crimes a defendant has committed. To test this hypothesis, you take a random sample of 360 defendants convicted of a crime, examine their criminal records, and count the number of property crimes they have committed. Here are your data:

Race	Number of property Crimes		Total
	0–4	5 or More	
Non-White	77	33	110
White	180	70	250
Total	257	103	360

a. What is the independent variable, and what is the dependent variable?

b. How many observations or cases are there?

c. What are the column marginals?

d. What are the row marginals?

e. What is the size of this contingency table?

f. How many non-White offenders have committed 5 or more property offenses?

g. How many White offenders have committed 0-4 property offenses?

h. How many degrees of freedom are there in this table?

i. Calculate the relative risk of having 5 or more property crime arrests for each race. What does this suggest?

j. Test the null hypothesis that the two variables are independent. Use an alpha level of .05 and state each step of your hypothesis test. If you reject the null hypothesis, how strongly are the two variables related?

5. Daniel Mears, Xia Wang, and William Bales (2014) argued that employment and labor market conditions influence reentry experiences and the likelihood of recidivism. Let's say you were interested in this notion and studied the post-release behavior of random samples of three groups of formerly incarcerated offenders: those who had a stable and satisfying job, those who had intermittent or sporadic employment, and those who were unable to find a job. For each group, you were able to determine how many had been rearrested within 3 years of their release from prison. Here is what you found:

Number of Arrests Within 3 Years	Stable Employment	Sporadic Employment	Unemployed	Total
None	30	14	10	54
One or more	15	16	30	61
Total	45	30	40	115

a. What is the independent variable, and what is the dependent variable?

b. How many observations or cases are there?

c. What are the column marginals?

d. What are the row marginals?

e. What is the size of this contingency table?

f. How many persons with sporadic employment had one or more arrests within 3 years?

g. How many persons who were unemployed had no arrests within 3 years?

h. How many degrees of freedom are there in this table?

i. Calculate the relative risk of having one or more

arrests for those with different types of post-release employment. What does this suggest?

j. Test the null hypothesis that the two variables are independent. Use an alpha level of .05 and state each step of your hypothesis test. If you reject the null hypothesis, how strongly are the two variables related?

6. Wesley Jennings, Bryanna Hahn Fox, and David Farrington (2014) investigated the relationship between tattoos and crime to determine whether the two were positively related. To test the notion that people with tattoos commit more crime, you take a random sample of 320 adults currently on probation. You determine whether they have tattoos and then get a count of the number of crimes they have committed as adults. Here are your data:

Tattoo Status	0–4 Adult Offenses	5–9 Adult Offenses	10–14 Adult Offenses	15 or More Adult Offenses	Total
No tattoos	78	56	34	15	183
Has tattoos	15	22	37	63	137
Total	93	78	71	78	320

a. What is the independent variable, and what is the dependent variable?

b. How many observations or cases are there?

c. What are the column marginals?

d. What are the row marginals?

e. What is the size of this contingency table?

f. How many offenders with tattoos have 10–14 adult offenses?

g. How many offenders without tattoos have 15 or more adult offenses?

h. How many degrees of freedom are there in this table?

i. Calculate the relative risk of having only 0–4 adult offenses for both tattoo statuses. What does this suggest?

j. Calculate the relative risk of having 15 or more adult offenses for both tattoo statuses.

k. Test the null hypothesis that the two variables are independent. Use an alpha level of .01 and state each step of your hypothesis test. If you reject the null hypothesis, how strongly are the two variables related?

STUDENT STUDY SITE

WANT A BETTER GRADE?

Get the tools you need to sharpen your study skills. Access practice quizzes, eFlashcards, data sets, and SPSS exercises at **study.sagepub.com/paternoster.**

CHAPTER 9

Hypothesis Tests Involving Two Population Means or Proportions

" *Basic research is what I am doing when I don't know what I'm doing.*

—Wernher von Braun

LEARNING OBJECTIVES

1. Identify the appropriate sampling distribution to use for a hypothesis test for large samples when you have a two-category independent variable and an interval- or ratio-level dependent variable.

2. Explain why you must use a slightly different hypothesis test when you cannot assume the variances for two groups are equal.

3. Describe the difference between independent groups and matched groups.

4. Conduct a hypothesis for the difference between means using the three variations of the *t* test and interpret the results.

5. Conduct a hypothesis for the difference between proportions and interpret the results.

Introduction

Imagine you are working for a state prison system and are in charge of testing a new batterer intervention program (BIP) designed to reduce recidivism for those convicted of intimate partner assaults. You have several individuals in the prison who were convicted of assaulting their intimate partners whom you randomly assign to either get the new BIP (called an experimental group) or be in a control group, whose group members do not receive the program. To measure individuals' approval of using violence to settle conflicts, you give all participants a survey both before the treatment (called a pretest) and after the treatment (called a posttest). To determine whether the BIP actually decreased the participants' approval of violence, you would have to conduct a hypothesis test between mean approval ratings for the pretest and posttest. In this case, the dependent variable would be the approval of violence scores and the independent variable would be a two-category variable indicating whether individuals were in the BIP or the control group. Luckily for you, you will be an expert on these types of tests after reading this chapter!

In this chapter, we will examine the statistical procedures that enable us to test hypotheses about the differences between two population means and two population proportions. We examine two different types of mean difference tests: one for independent samples and one for dependent or matched samples. The independent-samples test is designed to measure mean differences between *two* samples that are independent of each other or *two* subsets within the same sample (i.e., males and females). The key here is that we have two samples that are assumed to be independent. There are two different statistical tests for the difference between two independent samples; the appropriate one to use depends on what assumption we can make about the population variances. In contrast, the matched-groups or dependent-samples test is designed to measure the difference between means obtained for the same sample at two points in time or between two samples that are matched on certain characteristics so as to be as much alike as possible. This is the scenario we presented at the beginning of this section regarding the batterer intervention program. We also examine a test for the difference between two proportions in this chapter, which is a special case of a test for mean differences. In this chapter, we may use the terms "sample" and "group" interchangeably. Let's get started.

Explaining the Difference Between Two Sample Means

The hypothesis tests in this chapter are appropriate for the following variables: The independent variable is a two-level or binary categorical variable, and the dependent variable is continuous (interval/ratio). For example, one of the most persistent findings in criminology is the relationship between gender and the number of delinquent offenses committed. Consistently, males report having committed more delinquent acts than females. In a random sample of young males and females, then, the mean number of delinquent acts committed by the males is expected to be greater than the mean for females. In the language of causal analysis, gender is the independent variable that is predicted to "cause" high levels of delinquency, the dependent variable. In this example, gender is the dichotomous independent variable (male/female) and the number of committed delinquent acts is the dependent variable. Let's follow this example through to illustrate the kinds of problems we will encounter in this chapter.

If we were to take a random sample of 70 young males from some population, independently select an equal number of young females, and then ask each youth to self-report the number of times during the past year that he or she committed each of four delinquent offenses (theft, vandalism, fighting, and use of drugs), we would have two means: a mean for the sample of young men ($\bar{X}_{men}$) and a mean for the sample of young women ($\bar{X}_{women}$). We also would have two population means—one from the population of men (μ_{men}) and one from the population of women (μ_{women})—that we have not directly measured. Both the sample and the population also have standard deviations (remember, the sample standard

Student Study Site

Visit the open-access Student Study Site at **study.sagepub.com/paternoster** to access additional study tools including mobile-friendly eFlashcards, web quizzes, links to SAGE journal articles, additional data sets, SPSS exercises, and more!

deviation is *s* and the population standard deviation is σ). To keep these different components of samples and populations straight, we show them and their respective notations in Table 9.1.

Let's say that, consistent with previous research, the mean number of delinquent offenses committed for the sample of young males is greater than the mean for the sample of young females $(\overline{X}_m > \overline{X}_w)$. As we learned in Chapter 9, we can account for the difference between these two sample means in two very different ways.

One possible explanation for the difference between the male and female sample means is that there really is a difference between the rate at which young men and young women offend. What this explanation implies is that males and females come from different offending populations with different population means (Figure 9.1). This means that there are two distributions of the rate of delinquent offending: one for females (on the left) and one for males (on the right). The population mean for the number of delinquent acts committed is greater for men ($m_m = 20$) than it is for women ($m_w = 10$). Note that if this is true, then when we randomly select a sample of men and record their mean, and randomly select a sample of women and record their mean, more frequently than not the sample mean for men will be greater than the sample mean for women.

A second explanation for the observed difference in sample means between young men and young women is that the two population means are equal ($\mu = 17$), and it was just by chance that we happened to select a sample of males with a higher mean of delinquent offending than our female mean. This is illustrated in Figure 9.2, which shows two distributions of offending: one for the population of males and one for the population of females. Although they may differ in some respects (e.g., their respective standard deviations may be different), the two population means are the same, implying that the mean level of offending is the same for both genders. If this explanation is true, when we draw random samples from both populations, the two sample means will sometimes differ by chance alone, with the male mean sometimes being the larger of the two and the female mean other times being the larger of the two, and sometimes the two means will be equal. Over a large number of mean differences, the mean or average of those differences will be zero. The important point is that if the two population means are equal, the two sample means we obtained in this sample are different because of random sample variation and chance alone.

These two explanations have very different substantive implications. If the first explanation is true, then we will conclude that the mean number of delinquent offenses committed by males is significantly different from the mean number of offenses committed by females. Because the frequency of committing delinquent acts is significantly different between males and females, we will say that there is a "statistically significant" relationship between the independent variable of gender and the dependent variable of delinquency. What we are saying here is that the difference between the male and female sample means is so large that "chances are" the samples came from different populations. In a sense, this means that the sample difference is "real" (a real population

Table 9.1	Characteristics and Notations for Two-Sample Problems		
		Population 1	*Population 2*
Population mean		m_1	m_2
Population standard deviation		s_1	s_2
Sample mean		$\overline{X}_1$	$\overline{X}_2$
Sample standard deviation		s_1	s_2
Sample size		n_1	n_2

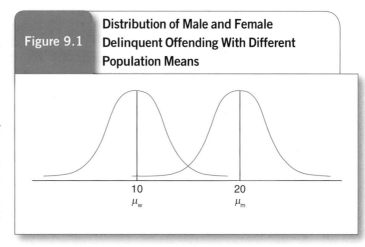

| Figure 9.1 | Distribution of Male and Female Delinquent Offending With Different Population Means |

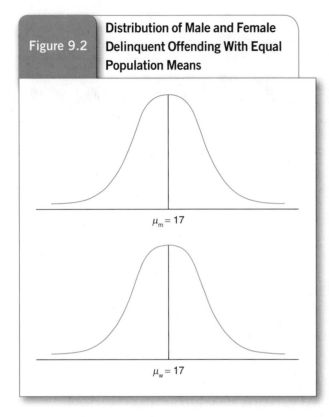

Figure 9.2 Distribution of Male and Female Delinquent Offending With Equal Population Means

$\mu_m = 17$

$\mu_w = 17$

difference). On the other hand, if the second explanation is true, then we will conclude that the observed difference between the male and female means is no greater than what we would expect to observe by chance alone despite the sample means being different. In this case, the sample difference does not reflect a real difference in the population—it's due to luck or chance or random sampling variation, whatever you want to call it.

In sum, because we have sample data, not population data, any difference we actually observe in our sample means may be due to "real differences" between males and females in how frequently they commit delinquent acts or just due to chance/sampling variability. Enter probability theory! With the help of probability theory, we can determine which explanation is *more likely* to be true. In deciding which of these two possible explanations is more likely, we will proceed exactly as we did in the last two chapters when we conducted formal hypothesis tests.

We will begin by assuming that there is no difference between the two population means. That is, we will begin with the null hypothesis that assumes the populations from which both of the samples were drawn have equal means $(\mu_m = \mu_w)$. With the use of probability theory and a new kind of sampling distribution, we will then ask, "Assuming that the population means are equal, how likely is it that we would have observed the difference between the two sample means that we actually observed?" If it is a likely event, where "likely" is defined by our alpha level, then we will conclude that our assumption of equal population means cannot be rejected. If, however, we find that the difference between our sample means is an unlikely or very rare event (say, an event with a probability of .05, .01, or .001), we will instead conclude that our assumption of equal population means is not likely true, and we will reject the null hypothesis.

In this chapter, we are interested in something called the *sampling distribution of sample mean differences*. We illustrate the process of hypothesis testing with two sample means in Figure 9.3.

Sampling Distribution of Mean Differences

To understand what a sampling distribution of mean differences is, imagine that we take a sample of males and an equal-sized sample of females from their respective populations, compute a mean for each sample, and then calculate the difference between the two sample means $(\bar{X}_1 - \bar{X}_2)$. Imagine that we do this for 10,000 samples, calculating the mean for each group and the difference between the two means so that we now have 10,000 of these mean difference scores $(10,000\ \bar{X}_1 - \bar{X}_2)$. We can then create a frequency distribution of these 10,000 mean difference scores. This theoretical distribution of the difference between 10,000 sample means is our **sampling distribution of sample mean differences**. We illustrate what this distribution might look like in Figure 9.4 and provide a summary of the characteristics of this sampling distribution here:

Sampling distribution of sample mean differences: Theoretical distribution of the difference between an infinite number of sample means.

1. The mean of the sampling distribution of the difference between two means, $m_1 - m_2$, is equal to the difference between the population means.

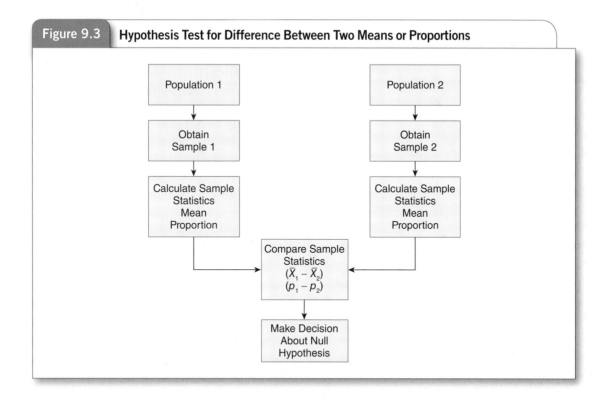

Figure 9.3 **Hypothesis Test for Difference Between Two Means or Proportions**

2. The standard deviation of the sampling distribution of the difference between two means $(\sigma_{\bar{X}_1-\bar{X}_2})$ is called the *standard error of the difference* between two means, and it reflects how much variation exists in the difference from sample to sample. In other words, it is the standard deviation of the large number of sample mean differences.

This sampling distribution of mean differences is analogous to the sampling distribution of the mean that we discussed in Chapter 8. What changes is that the sampling distribution in Figure 9.4 is composed of the *difference* between two sample means rather than the distribution of a single mean. In addition, the distribution of mean differences is centered about the difference between the two population means $(\mu_1 - \mu_2)$, not around a single population mean (μ).

The mean of this distribution of mean differences is determined by the difference between the two population means. If the two population means are equal $(\mu_m = \mu_w)$ as in Figure 9.2, the mean of the sampling distribution of mean differences will be 0 $(\mu_1 - \mu_2 = 0)$. As we stated earlier, even if the means in the population are equal, not every sample mean difference is expected to be equal to zero. Sometimes the male sample mean will be greater than the female sample mean, sometimes the female sample mean will be greater than the male sample mean, and sometimes they will be equal. What will be true, however, is that with a very large number of samples, the mean of the distribution of sample differences (the mean difference of the infinite number of sample differences) will be zero.

If the two population means are different, however, as they are in Figure 9.1 with the population mean for men being greater than that for women $(\mu_m > \mu_w)$, then most of the sample mean differences $(\bar{X}_1 - \bar{X}_2)$ will be positive. This will be true because in most of the sample comparisons the male mean will be greater than the female mean. In this case, the mean of the sampling distribution of differences will be greater than zero. More specifically, the mean of the sampling distribution will be equal to the difference between the two population means $(\mu_m - \mu_w)$.

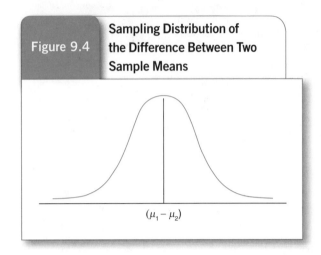

Figure 9.4 | Sampling Distribution of the Difference Between Two Sample Means

$(\mu_1 - \mu_2)$

Up to now, we have repeatedly stated that no matter what the value of the means for the two populations, when repeated random samples are taken, means are calculated, and differences between sample means are taken, not every mean difference will be exactly the same. There will, then, be dispersion about the mean of the sampling distribution of differences. You can see the spread about the mean of the sampling distribution of differences in Figure 9.4. This dispersion is measured by the standard deviation of sample mean differences, otherwise known as the standard error of the difference $(\sigma_{\bar{X}_1 - \bar{X}_2})$, which is defined as

$$\sigma_{\bar{X}_1 - \bar{X}_2} = \sqrt{\frac{\sigma_1^2}{n_1} + \frac{\sigma_2^2}{n_2}}$$ (Formula 9-1)

where

σ_1 = the standard deviation of the first population

σ_2 = the standard deviation of the second population

Not only do we know the mean and standard deviation of the sampling distribution of differences, we also are in a position to know its shape. An important statistical theorem states the following: If two independent random samples of size n_1 and n_2 are drawn from normal populations, then the sampling distribution of the difference between the two sample means $(\bar{X}_1 - \bar{X}_2)$ will be normally distributed.

We now can use the central limit theorem to generalize this to include any population whenever the sample sizes are large. That is, no matter what the shape of the two populations, if independent random samples of size n_1 and n_2 are drawn, the sampling distribution of the difference between the two sample means will approximate a normal distribution as n_1 and n_2 become large (both sample sizes > 30). With normal populations or with large enough samples from any population, then, the sampling distribution of differences between sample means will approximate normality.

This should sound very familiar to you because it is similar to what we did in Chapter 7. An appropriate statistical test for the difference between two sample means is either a z test or t test. Therefore, an appropriate sampling distribution would be either a z distribution or a t distribution. The z test for two means is appropriate whenever the two population variances (s_1 and s_2) are known. If these values are unknown, the t test for two means is the appropriate statistical test. Since we are seldom in a position to know the value of the population variances, the t test is more frequently applied. Keep in mind, however, that when the sample size gets large, the t and z distributions start to look the same. Now, let's go through some examples of different types of hypothesis tests involving two population means.

▣ Testing a Hypothesis About the Difference Between Two Means: Independent Samples

Independent random samples: Samples that are randomly and independently selected.

In this section, we will discuss the case of hypothesis tests for the difference between two *independent* sample means. In the case of **independent random samples**, we have two samples whose elements are randomly and independently selected. Random and independent selection occurs whenever there is a known probability of any element being selected into a sample, and the selection of an element into one sample has no effect on the selection of any element into the other sample. In other words, both samples are randomly selected and are independent of each other.

In our example, independence would occur if the selection of a male into one sample had no effect on the selection of a female into the other sample. The independence assumption is violated in the case of matched groups or dependent samples where an element is deliberately selected into a sample or when the same observations are found in both samples. We will review the special case of hypothesis testing presented by matched groups and dependent samples later in this chapter.

The statistical test we will conduct here is different from the t test we used in Chapter 7 in three ways: (1) Our sample statistic is not a single sample mean but rather the difference between two sample means ($\bar{X}_1 - \bar{X}_2$); (2) the mean of the sampling distribution is not the population mean (μ) but rather the difference between two population means ($m_1 - m_2$); and (3) the estimated standard deviation of the sampling distribution is the estimated standard deviation of the sampling distribution of the difference between sample means ($\hat{\sigma}_{\bar{X}_1-\bar{X}_2}$). The general formula for the t test involving the difference between two sample means can be expressed as

$$t_{\text{obt}} = \frac{\bar{X}_1 - \bar{X}_2}{\hat{\sigma}_{\bar{X}_1-\bar{X}_2}}$$

(Formula 9-2)

This t test requires that the two samples be independent random samples and that the dependent variable be measured at the interval or ratio level.

As you can see from equation 9-2, the t statistic is obtained by dividing the difference between the two sample means by the estimated standard deviation of the sampling distribution (the standard error of the difference). There are, however, two versions of the t test between two means. In one test, we can assume that the unknown population standard deviations are equal ($s_1 = s_2$); in the second case, we cannot make that assumption ($s_1 \neq s_2$). The importance of this is that our estimate of the standard error of the difference ($\hat{\sigma}_{\bar{X}_1-\bar{X}_2}$) is different for the two cases. We will examine the t test for both of these cases separately.

Model 1: Pooled Variance Estimate ($\sigma_1 = \sigma_2$)

If we can assume that the two unknown population standard deviations are equal ($\sigma_1 = \sigma_2$), we estimate the standard error of the difference using what is called a *pooled variance estimate*. Because the population standard deviations are not known, the decision of whether they are equal is based on the equality of the sample standard deviations (s_1 and s_2). Something called an F test is the appropriate test for the significance of the difference between the two sample standard deviations. Without going into too much detail here, the F test tests the null hypothesis that $\sigma_1^2 = \sigma_2^2$. If we fail to reject this null hypothesis, we can assume that the population standard deviations are equal and that the t test we will discuss in this section for the difference between two population means is the right test. If, however, we are led to reject this null hypothesis, we cannot make the assumption that the two population standard deviations are equal ($\sigma_1^2 \neq \sigma_2^2$), and we must estimate the standard error of the difference using what is called a *separate variance estimate,* which we will discuss later as Model 2: separate variance estimate. Since the F test has not yet been discussed, we will simply provide the information for you whether you can assume that the population standard deviations are equal (Model 1) or whether you cannot make that assumption (Model 2). We cover the F test in the next chapter.

In the pooled variance case, our estimate of the denominator of equation 9.2 above (the standard error of the difference) is

$$\hat{\sigma}_{\bar{X}_1-\bar{X}_2} = \sqrt{\frac{(n_1-1)s_1^2+(n_2-1)s_2^2}{n_1+n_2-2}}\sqrt{\frac{n_1+n_2}{n_1n_2}}$$

and the formula for the pooled variance *t* test is

$$t_{obt} = \frac{\bar{X}_1 - \bar{X}_2}{\sqrt{\dfrac{(n_1-1)s_1^2+(n_2-1)s_2^2}{n_1+n_2-2}}\sqrt{\dfrac{n_1+n_2}{n_1 n_2}}}$$

(Formula 9-3)

As we have done with other hypothesis tests, once we have our obtained value of *t* (t_{obt}), we will compare it with our critical value (t_{crit}) taken from our probability distribution (the *t* distribution) and make a decision about the null hypothesis. The critical value of *t* is based on our chosen alpha level, whether we have a one- or two-tailed test, and our degrees of freedom and is obtained from the *t* table (Table B.3 of Appendix B). You will remember from Chapter 7 that before using the *t* table, we need to determine the appropriate degrees of freedom in addition to our selected alpha level. When we are testing the difference between two sample means, the degrees of freedom are equal to ($n_1 + n_2 - 2$) in the independent-samples two-sample case for the *t* test. Once we have determined our degrees of freedom, we can go to the *t* table with our chosen alpha level and a one- or two-tailed test and find our critical value.

Let's go through an example of a formal hypothesis test using the *t* test. In this example, we will assume that we have conducted our *F* test and have failed to reject the null hypothesis about equal population standard deviations. Because we can assume that the population standard deviations are equal, then, we can use the pooled variance estimate of the standard error of the difference (Model 1).

Case Study

State Prison Expenditures by Region

Suppose that we are interested in regional differences in the cost of housing state prison inmates. Table 9.2 displays data from state prisons for two regions in the United States (West and Northeast). The dependent variable of interest is the cost per inmate per day, which is measured at the interval or ratio level. Let's say we believe that the average annual cost to house an inmate in state prisons will differ between the West and the Northeast, but we cannot say in which region it will be more costly. In this scenario, region would be the two-category independent variable (West vs. Northeast), and cost would be the dependent variable. We have reviewed the steps necessary to conduct a hypothesis test in Table 9.3. We will go through each of these steps using this example.

Step 1: Since we have no real idea about the nature of the relationship between region of the country and prison costs, a non-directional (two-tailed) hypothesis test is appropriate. The null hypothesis (H_0) will state that the mean annual cost to house prison inmates in the West is equal to the mean cost in the Northeast. The alternative hypothesis (H_1) will represent our belief that the regional means are not equal to each other. These hypotheses are formally stated as follows:

H_0: There is no relationship between region and prison costs OR $\mu_{West} = \mu_{Northeast}$

H_1: There is a relationship between region and prison costs OR $\mu_{West} \neq \mu_{Northeast}$

Step 2: To determine the validity of this null hypothesis, we will rely on the *t* statistic along with its corresponding probability sampling distribution. Because we can assume that the unknown population standard deviations are equal, we can estimate the standard error of the difference using a pooled variance estimate (Model 1).

Step 3: Let's adopt an alpha level equal to .05 ($\alpha = .05$). With this level of alpha, using a non-directional test and 14 ($8 + 8 - 2 = 14$) degrees of freedom, the critical value of *t* is equal to ± 2.145 ($t_{crit} = \pm 2.145$). Since we have a non-directional alternative hypothesis, the value of *t* we obtain from our statistical test must be equal to or greater than 2.145 or equal to or less than –2.145 in order to reject the null hypothesis of equal means. In other words, the obtained *t* value must be greater in absolute terms than 2.145 regardless of the sign. We show the two critical values and critical regions in Figure 9.5.

Step 4: Since we are assuming that the population standard deviations are equal, we can use a pooled variance estimate of the standard error of the difference. Please notice that in the preceding data, we have given you the sample standard deviation; to get the variance that the formula calls for, you will have to square the standard deviation. Sometimes we will provide the standard deviation, and sometimes we will provide the variances; you will have to be on your toes and alert as to which one you are given:

$$t_{obt} = \frac{\bar{X}_1 - \bar{X}_2}{\sqrt{\frac{(n_1-1)s_1^2 + (n_2-1)s_2^2}{n_1+n_2-2}} \sqrt{\frac{n_1+n_2}{n_1 n_2}}}$$

$$t_{obt} = \frac{85.37 - 132.42}{\sqrt{\frac{(8-1)(29.33)^2 + (8-1)(21.45)^2}{8+8-2}} \sqrt{\frac{8+8}{(8)(8)}}}$$

$$t_{obt} = \frac{-47.05}{\sqrt{\frac{(7)860.25 + (7)460.10}{14}} \sqrt{\frac{16}{64}}}$$

$$t_{obt} = \frac{-47.05}{\sqrt{\frac{6,021.75 + 3,220.7}{14}} \sqrt{.25}}$$

$$t_{obt} = \frac{-47.05}{\sqrt{660.18} \sqrt{.25}}$$

$$t_{obt} = \frac{-47.05}{25.69(.50)}$$

$$t_{obt} = \frac{-47.05}{12.85}$$

$$t_{obt} = -3.66$$

Step 5: The obtained value of *t* ($t_{obt} = -3.66$) falls into the critical region since $-3.66 < -2.145$ (or is

Table 9.2	Prison Expenditures per Inmate per Day by State and Region, 2011

State	*Daily Mean State Prison Operating Expenditures per Inmate (in Dollars)*
West	
Nevada	56.59
Idaho	53.55
Arizona	67.96
Montana	82.81
Colorado	83.22
California	129.92
Washington	128.48
Utah	80.41
Sample Statistics for the West	
$\bar{X}_1 = 85.37$ $s_1 = 29.33$ $n_1 = 8$	
Northeast	
New Hampshire	93.37
Pennsylvania	116.00
New York	164.59
New Jersey	150.32
Vermont	135.62
Connecticut	137.70
Maine	127.13
Rhode Island	134.61
Sample Statistics for the Northeast	
$\bar{X}_2 = 132.42$ $s_2 = 21.45$ $n_2 = 8$	

Source: Adapted from *The Cost of Prisons: What Incarceration Costs Taxpayers* © 2012 from the Vera Institute of Justice.

Table 9.3	Steps Taken When Conducting a Hypothesis Test

Step 1: Formally state your null (H_0) and research (H_1) hypotheses.

Step 2: Select an appropriate test statistic and the sampling distribution of that test statistic.

Step 3: Select a level of significance (alpha = α) and determine the critical value and rejection region of the test statistic based on the selected level of alpha and degrees of freedom.

Step 4: Conduct the test: Calculate the obtained value of the test statistic and compare it with the critical value.

Step 5: Make a decision about your null hypothesis and interpret this decision in a meaningful way based on the research question, sample, and population.

Figure 9.5	Critical *t* and Critical Region for Alpha = .05 (*df* = 14) and a Two-Tailed Test

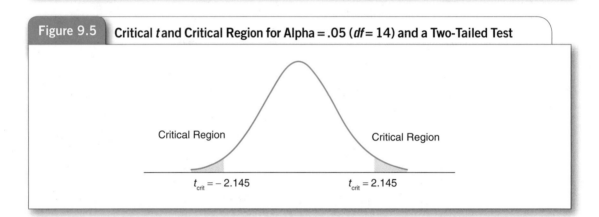

Critical Region   Critical Region

$t_{crit} = -2.145$ $t_{crit} = 2.145$

greater in absolute terms of the 2.145 needed). The data obtained from our sample, then, provide enough evidence for us to reject the null hypothesis that the population means are actually equal. We conclude that there is a significant relationship between region and annual cost to house prison inmates. The results of our test indicate that region—at least the West versus the Northeast—does affect the cost of incarcerating offenders housed in state prisons. In addition, the direction of this difference seems to be that it is significantly more expensive to house prison inmates in the Northeast than in the West. Let's go through another example.

Case Study

Social Disorganization and Crime

Ever since the days of the Chicago School in the 1920s, criminologists have postulated that states of social disorganization within a residential community increase the likelihood of various kinds of social problems, including unemployment, mental illness, and criminal victimization. One indicator that has been used to measure social disorganization within communities is the extent to which people move in and out of the community. Communities where very few families move in and move out are considered more stable and more organized than those where there is a great deal of population "turnover" in the neighborhoods. This is because in communities with relatively little turnover, residents live in the same place for a long time and get to know their neighbors, and as a result a sense of community becomes established. It is hypothesized that this sense of community and the network of social relationships between community members is responsible for the lower crime rates in these kinds of stable neighborhoods. In this hypothesis, the population turnover in a community is the independent variable and the rate of crime is the dependent variable.

Suppose we wanted to investigate the relationship between social disorganization and household crime. To do so, we collect a random sample of residents in a neighborhood and ask them how many times something has been stolen from or around their home (including their automobile) within the last 6 months (household theft). In addition, we ask them how long they have lived at their current address. From this survey, we divide our sample into two groups according to the length of time they have resided at their address: (1) those who have resided at their current address for less than 1 year, whom we will term "transient," and (2) those who have resided there for more than 1 year, whom we will term "stable." These two categories are our independent variable. We then calculate the mean number of times each group experienced a household theft, which is our dependent variable. For this hypothetical example, we obtain the following sample statistics:

Less Than 1 Year	More Than 1 Year
$\bar{X}_1 = 22.4$	$\bar{X}_2 = 16.2$
$s_1^2 = 4.3$	$s_2^2 = 4.1$
$n_1 = 49$	$n_2 = 53$

Step 1: Because we have some idea about the nature of the relationship between residential stability and risk of household victimization, we adopt a directional (one-tailed) hypothesis test. Since we believe that those who have lived in an area less than 1 year (the "transients") will be more vulnerable to becoming victims of household crime than those who have lived in the neighborhood longer (the "stables"), our alternative hypothesis states that the mean number of household victimizations experienced by residents who have lived at their current addresses for less than 1 year will be greater than the mean for those who have lived in their residences for more than 1 year. The null and alternative hypotheses are formally stated as follows:

$H_0: \mu_{\text{less than 1 year}} = \mu_{\text{more than 1 year}}$

$H_1: \mu_{\text{less than 1 year}} > \mu_{\text{more than 1 year}}$

Step 2: To determine the validity of the null hypothesis, we will rely on the t statistic along with its corresponding sampling distribution. Because we can assume that the unknown population standard deviations are equal, we can estimate the standard error of the difference using a pooled variance estimate.

Step 3: For this test, let's select an alpha level of .01. With $\alpha = .01$, using a directional test and degrees of freedom equal to 100 $[(n_1 + n_2 - 2) = (49 + 53 - 2 = 100)]$, the critical value of t that defines the rejection region can be found in Table B.3 of Appendix B. By using the degrees of freedom of 120 listed in the table (since that is the closest value we have to 100), we see that the critical value of t that defines the lower limit of the rejection region is 2.358. Therefore, to reject the null hypothesis, we must obtain a t value equal to or greater than 2.358. We use a positive value of t in this case because our alternative hypothesis states that the value of the first mean (for the "transients") will be greater than the value of the mean for the second group (the "stables"); the obtained value of t, therefore, is predicted to be positive. If we obtain a negative value of t, no matter how large it is, we must fail to reject the null hypothesis. We show the critical value of t and the critical region for this problem in Figure 9.6.

Step 4: The next step of our hypothesis test is to convert the difference between our sample means into a t value. Notice that you have been given the sample variances in this problem, so there is no need to square the terms again! We're just making sure you are paying attention!

$$t_{obt} = \frac{22.4 - 16.2}{\sqrt{\dfrac{(49-1)4.3 + (53-1)4.1}{49+53-2}}\sqrt{\dfrac{49+53}{(49)(53)}}}$$

$$t_{obt} = \frac{6.2}{\sqrt{\dfrac{(48)4.3 + (52)4.1}{100}}\sqrt{\dfrac{102}{2,597}}}$$

$$t_{obt} = \frac{6.2}{\sqrt{\dfrac{206.4 + 213.2}{100}}\sqrt{.039}}$$

$$t_{obt} = \frac{6.2}{\sqrt{\dfrac{419.6}{100}}\sqrt{.039}}$$

$$t_{obt} = \frac{6.2}{\sqrt{4.2}\sqrt{.039}}$$

$$t_{obt} = \frac{6.2}{(2.049)(.198)}$$

$$t_{obt} = \frac{6.2}{.406}$$

$$t_{obt} = 15.27$$

Step 5: The t value we obtained of 15.27 is substantially greater than the critical value of t (2.358) that was needed in order to reject the null hypothesis—it falls into the critical region. Since $t_{obt} > t_{crit}$, we will reject the null hypothesis that the population means are equal. This suggests that the observed sample mean difference is too large to be attributed to chance or sampling variation; therefore, we can assume that the mean rate of household victimization experienced by those who have recently moved to a neighborhood is greater than the mean rate experienced by those who have lived in their places of residence for more than 1 year. The results of our statistical test lend support to one of the premises of social disorganization theory; we have found that individuals who have just recently been in a state of transiency (e.g., have moved within the last year) are more likely to become victims of household crime than are those who have been more residentially stable (e.g., have not moved within the last year).

Figure 9.6   **Critical t and Critical Region for Alpha = .01 (df = 120) and a One-Tailed Test**

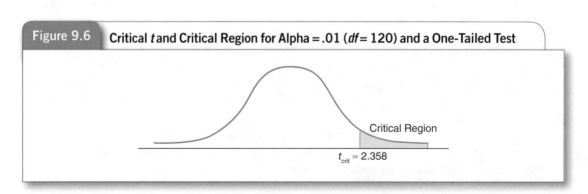

Critical Region

$t_{crit} = 2.358$

Case Study

Boot Camps and Recidivism

When crime rates in the United States were high in the mid-1980s to the early 1990s, a correctional program called correctional boot camps (sometimes called shock incarceration programs) became very popular in both state and federal prison systems. Although they were rapidly put in place, it was not always clear whether they reduced recidivism any better than regular correctional facilities. Despite their increased popularity, there have been only a few really rigorous attempts to evaluate their efficacy in reducing recidivism. Perhaps some of the most ambitious evaluations of boot camps have been conducted by Doris MacKenzie and her colleagues, who have compared graduates from boot camps with individuals sentenced for the same crimes but sent to prison instead (for a review, see MacKenzie, 2013).

Suppose we want to conduct our own experiment on the issue. We get the help of a local judge and randomly select, from a group of young adult offenders convicted of felony offenses, those who will go to a military-style boot camp and those who will be sent to the state prison for regular correctional programming. After their release, individuals are followed for 2 years. To collect information on offending behavior, we conduct interviews with the individuals and obtain official arrest data. Mean levels of offending behavior (for all crimes, including violent, property, and drug offenses) are calculated for both groups as follows:

Boot Camp Group	Prison Group
$\bar{X}_1 = 15.2$ offenses	$\bar{X}_2 = 15.9$ offenses
$s_1^2 = 4.7$	$s_2^2 = 5.1$
$n_1 = 32$	$n_2 = 29$

In this example, the type of custody (boot camp vs. prison) is our independent variable and the number of offenses committed is our dependent variable. To determine whether there is a significant difference in the mean rates of offending between the boot camp graduates and those released from prison, we must conduct a formal hypothesis test about the difference between two means. To help you learn the steps of formal hypothesis testing, we ask that you check off each step as we go through them.

Because there has been so little research on the efficacy of boot camps, and because the research that does exist is inconsistent, it would be hard to predict in advance which type of programming is more effective in reducing recidivism, so let's select a non-directional alternative hypothesis. The formal hypothesis statements are as follows:

$$H_0: \mu_{\text{boot camps}} = \mu_{\text{prison}}$$

$$H_1: \mu_{\text{boot camps}} \neq \mu_{\text{prison}}$$

The t test, along with its corresponding sampling distribution, is an appropriate statistical test for our data. Let's select an alpha level of .05. With a non-directional hypothesis test, $\alpha = .05$, and 59 degrees of freedom ($32 + 29 - 2 = 59$), we will use the critical value of t for 60 degrees of freedom because that is the closest value in Table B.3. We will reject the null hypothesis if our obtained t is either less than or equal to -2.00 or greater than or equal to $+2.00$. The critical values and corresponding critical regions are displayed in Figure 9.7. The obtained value of t is calculated as follows:

$$t_{\text{obt}} = \frac{15.2 - 15.9}{\sqrt{\dfrac{(32-1)4.7 + (29-1)5.1}{32+29-2}} \sqrt{\dfrac{32+29}{(32)(29)}}}$$

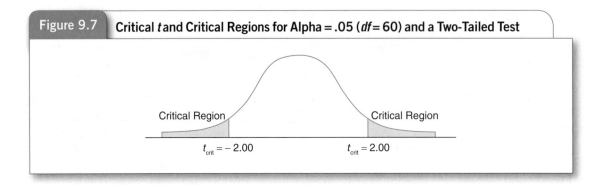

Figure 9.7 **Critical t and Critical Regions for Alpha = .05 (df = 60) and a Two-Tailed Test**

Critical Region

Critical Region

$t_{crit} = -2.00$

$t_{crit} = 2.00$

$$t_{obt} = \frac{-.7}{\sqrt{\frac{(31)4.7+(28)5.1}{59}}\sqrt{\frac{61}{928}}}$$

$$t_{obt} = \frac{-.7}{\sqrt{\frac{145.7+142.8}{59}}\sqrt{.066}}$$

$$t_{obt} = \frac{-.7}{\sqrt{\frac{288.5}{59}}\sqrt{.066}}$$

$$t_{obt} = \frac{-.7}{\sqrt{4.89}\sqrt{.066}}$$

$$t_{obt} = \frac{-.7}{(2.21)(.26)}$$

$$t_{obt} = \frac{-.7}{.57}$$

$$t_{obt} = -1.23$$

Our statistical test results in an obtained t value of –1.23. An obtained t of –1.23 does not lie within the critical region, so we must fail to reject the null hypothesis. Because we failed to reject the null hypothesis, we must conclude that the mean offending rates after release for boot camp and regular prison inmates are not significantly different from one another. This would be in line with much of the research to date on boot camps, which has shown that the core elements of boot camp programs—military-style discipline, hard labor, and physical training—do not reduce offender recidivism any better than regular prison (MacKenzie, 2013).

Model 2: Separate Variance Estimate ($\sigma_1 \neq \sigma_2$)

In the previous examples, we have assumed that the two population standard deviations were equal. Unfortunately, it will not always be possible for us to make this assumption about equal population standard deviations. In many instances, our F test will lead us to *reject* the null hypothesis that $s_1 = \sigma_2$ and we must conclude that the two population standard deviations are different. When this happens, we cannot use the pooled variance estimate of the standard error of the difference that we learned in the last section. Instead, we must estimate what is called a separate variance estimate of the standard error of the difference. The formula for this estimate is

$$\hat{\sigma}_{\bar{X}_1 - \bar{X}_2} = \sqrt{\frac{s_1^2}{n_1 - 1} + \frac{s_2^2}{n_2 - 1}}$$

With a separate variance estimate of the standard error of the difference, the formula for our t test now becomes

$$t_{obt} = \frac{\bar{X}_1 - \bar{X}_2}{\sqrt{\frac{s_1^2}{n_1 - 1} + \frac{s_2^2}{n_2 - 1}}}$$

(Formula 9-4)

The steps necessary to conduct a hypothesis test remain exactly the same as before except for determining the degrees of freedom. The correct degrees of freedom for the separate variance t test are not as easy as $n_1 + n_2 - 2$. In fact, the formula to calculate the degrees of freedom for a t test using the separate variance estimate is quite a bit more complicated. The following formula has been suggested to obtain the appropriate degrees of freedom for this test (Blalock, 1979; Hays, 1994):

$$df = \left[\frac{\left(\frac{s_1^2}{n_1 - 1} + \frac{s_2^2}{n_2 - 1} \right)}{\left(\frac{s_1^2}{n_1 - 1} \right)^2 \left(\frac{1}{n_1 + 1} \right) + \left(\frac{s_2^2}{n_2 - 1} \right)^2 \left(\frac{1}{n_2 + 1} \right)} \right] - 2$$

(Formula 9-5)

Wow! And you thought the degrees of freedom were relatively unimportant! The results of this formula should be rounded to the nearest integer to obtain the approximate degrees of freedom. Let's go through two examples using the separate variance estimate approach for the t test.

Case Study

Formal Sanctions and Intimate Partner Assault

In 1981, the first large-scale experiment to test the deterrent effects of arrest on domestic batterers, called the Minneapolis Domestic Violence Experiment, was conducted by Lawrence Sherman and Richard Berk (1984a, 1984b). The theoretical impetus for this experiment was guided by notions of specific deterrence. The primary research question driving the study was as follows: "Does arresting a man who has assaulted his partner decrease the probability that he will assault her in the future compared with less punitive interventions that are typically used such as separating the parties?" From their study, the researchers concluded that arrest provided the strongest deterrent to future violence and consequently was the preferred police response to domestic violence. This led to many jurisdictions implementing mandatory arrest policies for intimate partner assault.

To test the validity of experimental findings, an important canon of science is *replication*. Accordingly, the National Institute of Justice funded replication experiments of the Minneapolis experiment in six other cities. Unlike the original Minneapolis experiment, the published findings from these replications, which became known as the Spouse Assault Replication Program (SARP), did not uniformly find that arrest is an effective deterrent in spouse assault cases. The effect of arrest on intimate partner assault was revisited recently by Lawrence Sherman and Heather Harris (2015), who examined death rates among the original victims of domestic violence 23 years after the first study in Minneapolis. They found that victims whose abusers were arrested were more likely to die prematurely than those victims whose abusers were simply warned. Clearly, this latest study calls into further question the effectiveness of mandatory arrest policies.

Let's say we attempted to conduct our own study on a much smaller scale about the effects of an arrest policy on future domestic violence. By working with a police department, we would randomly assign arrested suspects who had assaulted their intimate partners to either short-term (no more than 3 hours) or long-term (4 or more hours) detention in jail after their arrest. We would then follow these offenders and victims for a 120-day period and record the number of new victimizations the partners reported to interviewers along with the number of calls to police during that period. The independent variable is the type of detention and the dependent variable is the number of intimate partner assaults perpetrated post-release. The hypothetical mean numbers of post-detention assaults, along with other sample statistics for both groups, are as follows:

Short-Term Detention	Long-Term Detention
$\bar{X}_1 = 6.4$	$\bar{X}_2 = 8.1$
$s_1 = 2.2$	$s_2 = 3.9$
$n_1 = 14$	$n_2 = 42$

We would like to test the null hypothesis that the population means for the two groups are equal. In saying this, we are suggesting that the length of detention after an arrest has no effect on the frequency with which intimate partner assault is committed in the immediate future. Suppose also that, based on an F test, we rejected the null hypothesis that the population standard deviations are equal; therefore, we must assume they are significantly different and use the separate variance t test as our statistical test.

Step 1: Because the literature on the efficacy in deterring intimate partner assault with stiff penalties is unclear, we will conduct a non-directional (two-tailed) alternative hypothesis that states the two population means are simply different. Our null hypothesis states that the two population means are equal or, stated in words, that there is no relationship between the type of detention experienced by arrested suspects and rates of intimate partner assault post-release. The hypotheses are formally stated as follows:

$H_0: \mu_{\text{short detention}} = \mu_{\text{long detention}}$

$H_1: \mu_{\text{short detention}} \neq \mu_{\text{long detention}}$

Step 2: As mentioned earlier, our statistical test will be the separate variance t test, and our sampling distribution will be the t distribution.

Step 3: We will select an alpha level of .01. To find our critical value of t and the critical region, we first need to determine the appropriate degrees of freedom. Based on formula 9-5, we can approximate our degrees of freedom as equal to

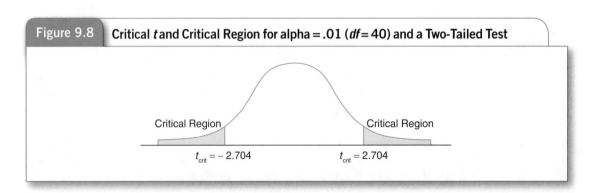

Figure 9.8 Critical t and Critical Region for alpha = .01 (df = 40) and a Two-Tailed Test

Critical Region

Critical Region

$t_{\text{crit}} = -2.704$

$t_{\text{crit}} = 2.704$

$$df = \left[\frac{\left(\dfrac{4.84}{14-1} + \dfrac{15.21}{42-1}\right)^2}{\left(\dfrac{4.84}{14-1}\right)^2\left(\dfrac{1}{14+1}\right) + \left(\dfrac{15.21}{42-1}\right)^2\left(\dfrac{1}{42+1}\right)}\right] - 2$$

$$df = \left[\frac{\left(\dfrac{4.84}{13} + \dfrac{15.21}{41}\right)^2}{\left(\dfrac{4.84}{13}\right)^2\left(\dfrac{1}{15}\right) + \left(\dfrac{15.21}{41}\right)^2\left(\dfrac{1}{43}\right)}\right] - 2$$

$$df = \frac{(.37+.37)^2}{(.37)^2(.07) + (.37)^2(.02)} - 2$$

$$df = \frac{(.74)^2}{.010+.003} - 2$$

$$df = \frac{.55}{.013} - 2$$

$$df = 42.3 - 2$$

$$df = 40.3$$

$$df = 40$$

With 40 degrees of freedom and an alpha of .01 for a two-tailed test, our critical values of t are ± 2.704 (per Table B.3 in Appendix B). Because we are doing a two-tailed or non-directional test, our critical region will consist of any t_{obt} less than or equal to -2.704 or greater than or equal to 2.704. We show the critical values and critical region in Figure 9.8.

We now calculate our obtained value of t as shown here (notice that we have given you the sample standard deviations rather than the variances):

$$t_{obt} = \frac{\bar{X}_1 - \bar{X}_2}{\sqrt{\dfrac{s_1^2}{n_1-1} + \dfrac{s_2^2}{n_2-1}}}$$

$$t_{obt} = \frac{6.4 - 8.1}{\sqrt{\dfrac{(2.2)^2}{14-1} + \dfrac{(3.9)^2}{42-1}}}$$

$$t_{obt} = \frac{6.4 - 8.1}{\sqrt{\dfrac{4.84}{14-1} + \dfrac{15.21}{42-1}}}$$

$$t_{obt} = \frac{-1.7}{\sqrt{\dfrac{4.84}{13} + \dfrac{15.21}{41}}}$$

$$t_{obt} = \frac{-1.7}{\sqrt{.37 + .37}}$$

$$t_{obt} = \frac{-1.7}{.86}$$

$$t_{obt} = -1.98$$

Our obtained t statistic is –1.98. Because this does not fall below the critical negative value of t (and, therefore, it does not fall into the critical region), we fail to reject the null hypothesis. Our conclusion, based on our sample results, is that there is no significant difference between the mean number of post-detention assaults for those who were given short-term detention and that for those who were given long-term detention in the population. Thus, it seems that there is no significant relationship between detention time and an arrested batterer's propensity to commit acts of violence in the future. Note that we also had to square the standard deviation that was provided to obtain the variance! Let's go through another quick example.

Case Study

Gender and Sentencing

An area that has received a great deal of research in criminology and criminal justice revolves around the idea of gender disparity in sentencing in both state and federal courts (Daly, 1987; Engen, Gainey, Crutchfield, & Weis, 2003; Starr, 2015; Steffensmeier, Kramer, & Streifel, 1993).

Controversy still exists over whether disparity in sentencing truly exists or whether observed gender differences in sentencing are due to legal characteristics of the offense or the offender. Some research has found that female defendants were sentenced for shorter prison terms than male defendants (Spohn & Spears, 1997; Starr, 2015), whereas other studies have found little or no evidence of gender disparity (Daly, 1994; Rapaport, 1991; Steffensmeier et al., 1993). Darrell Steffensmeier and his colleagues (1993), for example, went so far as to conclude, "When men and women appear in (contemporary) criminal court in similar circumstances and are charged with similar offenses, they receive similar treatment" (p. 411). You should have immediately recognized that gender in this scenario is the independent variable (a two-category, nominal-level variable) and the length of the sentence received is the continuous dependent variable.

Let's assume that we have a random sample of 50 male and 25 female defendants who were found guilty of burglary and sentenced to some time in prison. The mean sentence lengths received for male and female defendants, along with their respective standard deviations and sample sizes, are as follows:

Male Defendants	Female Defendants
$\overline{X}_1 = 12.02$	$\overline{X}_2 = 3.32$
$s_1 = 72.68$	$s_2 = 11.31$
$n_1 = 50$	$n_2 = 25$

Step 1: Let's say we believe that males will be sentenced more harshly than females. Accordingly, we state a directional (one-tailed) alternative hypothesis that the population mean sentence length is greater for male defendants than for female defendants. The null hypothesis is that the population means are equal:

$H_0: \mu_{males} = \mu_{females}$

$H_1: \mu_{males} > \mu_{females}$

Step 2: Our test statistic is the separate variance t test, and our sampling distribution is the t distribution.

Step 3: We will choose an alpha level of .05 ($\alpha = .05$). Based on formula 9-5, we determine that the approximate degrees of freedom is 56. (We will not show the work here, but it would be a good idea

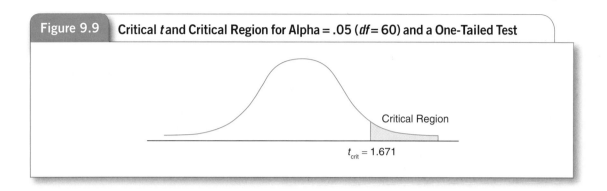

Figure 9.9 Critical *t* and Critical Region for Alpha = .05 (*df* = 60) and a One-Tailed Test

Critical Region

$t_{crit} = 1.671$

to compute this for yourself just for practice.) With 56 degrees of freedom, α = .05, and a one-tailed test, we can see from the *t* table that our critical *t* value is 1.671 (actually, this *t* score corresponds to 60 degrees of freedom, but it is the closest value we have to 56 degrees of freedom in the table). Since we have predicted that the population mean for males will be greater than the population mean for females, we will reject the null hypothesis if $t_{obt} \geq 1.671$ and we will fail to reject the null hypothesis if $t_{obt} < 1.671$. We show the critical value and the critical region in Figure 9.9.

Step 4: We will now calculate our obtained *t* value using the separate variance estimate, as shown:

$$t_{obt} = \frac{12.02 - 3.32}{\sqrt{\frac{(72.68)^2}{50-1} + \frac{(11.31)^2}{25-1}}}$$

$$t_{obt} = \frac{8.7}{\sqrt{107.80 + 5.33}}$$

$$t_{obt} = \frac{8.7}{\sqrt{113.13}}$$

$$t_{obt} = \frac{8.7}{10.64}$$

$$t_{obt} = .82$$

Note that we again had to square the standard deviation to obtain the variance! Our obtained *t* score of .82 is considerably less than the critical *t* of 1.671 and does not fall into the critical region. Our decision, then, will be to fail to reject the null hypothesis that there is no difference in the population means. We will conclude that, based on our sample data, there is not a significant relationship between sentence length received for burglary and gender of defendant in the population. Thus, the sentences handed down by judges for males convicted of robbery do not seem to be greater than the sentences received by females convicted of the same offense in the population. You may be thinking that the vast difference between the means should certainly have produced a significant result. However, remember that the test is also greatly influenced by the variation in each group—note the huge standard deviation around the mean sentence length for males!

So far, we have examined ways of comparing means across two independent samples or groups of cases. In the next section, we will examine a procedure called the matched-groups *t* test that is used to compare two means within the same or comparable group or sample. In this case, we cannot assume that we have two independent samples.

▣ Matched-Groups or Dependent-Samples *t* Test

In our application of the *t* test for the difference between two means in the previous section, we assumed that the two samples were independent of each other. That is, we assumed that the selection of the elements of one sample had no effect on the selection of the elements of the other sample. There are times when this assumption is deliberately violated. One instance of this lack of independence occurs when we have a "treatment" group and a "control" group. To make sure that the two groups are comparable with one another in as many ways as possible, each observation in one group is sometimes "matched" with an observation in the other group on relevant characteristics. Matching of samples can be done whenever it is not practical or ethical to randomly assign the "treatment." Matching subjects is done so that the only thing that differentiates the two groups is that one group received a certain type of treatment or was exposed to some phenomenon and the other group did not or was not.

For example, one way to determine the effect of counseling on future delinquency would be to collect data from two samples that are very similar to each other with the exception that one has received counseling (treatment group) and the other has not (control group). In such a study, an 18-year-old White male who lives in an urban area and has no criminal history might be placed in a sample that is to receive treatment (counseling), while another 18-year-old White male who lives in an urban area and has no criminal history might be "matched" to this treatment male but placed in a sample that is to receive no treatment (no counseling). In this case, the two subjects are matched with respect to five characteristics: age (they are both 18 years old), ethnicity (both White), gender (both males), residence (both urban dwellers), and criminal history (both have no criminal history). If the members of the two groups are effectively matched on important characteristics that are related to the dependent variable (such as age, minority status, gender, location of residence, and criminal history), then any observed differences between the two groups on the dependent variable after treatment (future delinquency) are unlikely to be due to these demographic characteristics. Rather, they are more likely to be due to the treatment, which in this example is counseling. The important point here is that by matching someone in one sample with a counterpart in a second sample, we have violated our assumption that the two samples are independent and so cannot use either of our two independent-samples *t* tests.

A second common use of **matched or dependent samples** occurs with "before-and-after" research designs, more generally referred to as pre–post designs. In this type of study, there is only one sample, but measures of the dependent variable are taken at two different points in time, "before" some intervention or treatment and again "after." For example, suppose we have access to only one group of arrested delinquents and all of them are going to receive counseling. In this case, we would have access to the individuals before and after they received counseling. Here, we might use self-report or official arrest data before and after counseling to determine whether counseling actually decreased rates of offending. However, this type of sample also violates our assumption of independence since the same persons appear in both groups. The subjects before the intervention cannot be independent of those after the intervention since they are the same people.

It should be clear to you that the two previously described *t* tests would not be appropriate because we would not have independent samples given that the elements of each sample were deliberately selected to be alike or, in fact, are the same people. In both the matched-groups and the pre–post designs, the independent observation is actually a *pair of cases,* not two independent groups. If we now consider *each pair* as an independent observation, we can conduct a statistical test based on the difference between the scores for each pair. In other words, we will make a pair-by-pair comparison by obtaining a difference score for each pair. Unlike the *t* test for independent samples that tests for the difference between two sample means ($\bar{X}_2 - \bar{X}_1$), the matched-groups or dependent-samples *t* test calculates the difference between the scores for each *pair* of subjects ($x_2 - x_1$) where a pair is either a pair of subjects who have been matched on some characteristics or the same person measured at two different points in time. In this example, one population consists of one of the matched groups or the group before the treatment, whereas the second population consists of the other matched group or the group after the treatment.

Matched or dependent samples: Samples in which individuals are either dependent or matched on several characteristics (age, race, gender, etc.) or "before-and-after" samples of the same people.

In the null hypothesis of the *t* test for matched groups or dependent samples, we will assume that the two populations are equal, which implies that the treatment or intervention has no effect. Under the null hypothesis, the difference between each pair of observations is expected to be zero, and the mean of the differences is also expected to be zero. The null hypothesis, then, presumes that the population mean of group differences will be zero. We will symbolize the mean of the population of group differences as μ_D, with the subscript D indicating that this is the difference between the two populations. The statistical test in a dependent-samples t test, then, is really a single-sample test of the hypothesis that $\mu_D = 0$ (the sample $\overline{X}_D$ statistic is the mean of the difference between each pair of scores in the sample).

Our procedure will be to determine the difference between each pair of scores ($X_D = x_2 - x_1$) in the sample, calculate the mean of these differences ($\overline{X}_D$), and then test whether this sample mean difference is equal to the expected population mean difference (μ_D) of zero. If the null hypothesis is true, then most of these X_D differences will be close to zero, as will the mean of the differences $\overline{X}_D$. If, however, the null hypothesis is not true, then the two scores will tend to be different from each other and the mean difference score will be greater than or less than zero. The greater the difference between each pair of scores, the greater the mean difference will be and the more likely we will be to reject the null hypothesis.

The formula for the t test with dependent samples is

$$t = \frac{\overline{X}_D - \mu_D}{s_D / \sqrt{n}}$$ (Formula 9-6)

Remember that we have drawn an analogy between the t test for matched samples and a hypothesis test involving a single population mean. In the t test in Chapter 7, where we dealt with one-population problems, we subtracted the population mean from the sample mean and divided by the standard deviation of the sampling distribution. This is exactly what we do in the independent-samples or matched-groups t test in formula 9-6. We subtract the population mean (μ_D) from the sample mean ($\overline{X}_D$), where the sample mean is the mean of the differences between each pair of scores in the sample, and we divide by the estimated standard deviation of the sampling distribution, which is the standard deviation of the observed difference scores. Note that the dependent-samples t test is based solely on the difference scores X_D (where $X_D = x_2 - x_1$) and the standard deviation of the difference scores (s_D).

Since the null hypothesis assumes that the population mean is zero ($\mu_D = 0$), we can drop that term from the numerator and the formula for the dependent-samples t test can be reduced to

$$t_{obt} = \frac{\overline{X}_D}{s_D/\sqrt{n}}$$ (Formula 9-7)

where

$$s_D = \sqrt{\frac{\Sigma(x_D - \overline{X}_D)^2}{n-1}}$$

or

$$s_D = \sqrt{\frac{\Sigma D^2 - \frac{(\Sigma D)^2}{n}}{n-1}}$$

The term s_D in equation 9-7 is just our old friend the standard deviation, and we gave you two ways to calculate it that you should recognize from Chapter 4 as the definitional and computational formulas for the standard deviation, respectively.

Once we have our obtained the t value, we do the same thing we have done with any t test discussed so far. We compare t_{obt} with t_{crit} and make a decision about our null hypothesis. We even go to the same t table as for independent-samples t tests (Table B.3 of Appendix B). The difference is that in the case of matched groups or dependent samples, since we have only n pairs of independent observations (rather than $n_1 + n_2$ observations as in the case of independent samples), we have $n - 1$ degrees of freedom where n is equal to the number of *pairs* of observations. If this sounds a bit confusing right now, no worries. A couple of examples will help to illustrate what is going on here. In each example, we will conduct a formal hypothesis test.

Case Study

Problem-Oriented Policing and Crime

Several recent studies have found that more than half of all crimes in a city are committed in only a few places. Some criminologists have called these places "hot spots" (Braga et al., 1999; Caplan, Kennedy, & Piza, 2013; Kennedy, Caplan, & Piza, 2013; Sherman, Gartin, & Buerger, 1989). Even within the most crime-ridden neighborhoods, it has been found that crime clusters at a few locations, while other areas remain relatively free of crime. The clustering of violent crime at particular locations suggests that there are important features of, or key dynamics at, these locations that give rise to frequent violence. Thus, focused crime prevention efforts have recently sought to modify these "criminogenic" conditions and reduce violence.

Problem-oriented policing strategies (similar to community policing) are increasingly used by urban jurisdictions to reduce crime in these high-activity or "hot spot" crime places. Problem-oriented policing challenges officers to identify and analyze the causes of problems behind a string of criminal incidents. Once the underlying conditions that give rise to crime problems are known, police officers can then develop and implement appropriate responses to reduce crime. For example, strategies include using community members as information sources to discuss the nature of the problems the community faces, the possible effectiveness of proposed responses, and the assessment of implemented responses. Other strategies target the social disorder problems inherent in these neighborhoods such as cleaning up the environment of the place and making physical improvements, securing vacant lots, and removing trash from the street.

Suppose we are interested in the efficacy of these policing strategies in reducing acts of violence in neighborhoods plagued by high rates of crime. We target 20 neighborhoods within a city and send out teams of community police officers to implement problem-oriented policing strategies in these neighborhoods. Before the program begins, we obtain the number of arrests for violent offenses that were made in each neighborhood within the 60 days prior to program implementation. After the program has been in place, we again obtain the number of arrests for violent offenses that were made in each neighborhood for a 60-day period. In this case, the program of having problem-oriented policing in the community is the independent variable and the number of violent offenses is the dependent variable. Notice that we have the same neighborhoods here; we have the number of crimes before and after the introduction of problem-oriented policing. We want to know whether the average number of arrests for violent offenses increased or decreased after the policing program was implemented. The hypothetical numbers of arrests for each time point are reported in the second and third columns of Table 9.4. We now are ready to conduct our hypothesis test.

Step 1: First, we state our null and research hypotheses. Our null hypothesis is that the mean difference score in the population is equal to zero. This implies that the problem-oriented policing had no effect on the number of arrests for violent offenses within neighborhoods. Since we are unsure what the exact effect of our problem-oriented policing strategy will be (maybe it will make things better, but maybe with more police it will make things worse or more crime will simply be seen), we will opt for a non-directional alternative hypothesis stating our belief that, on average, the number of arrests in neighborhoods after the new policing strategy was implemented will be different from the number of arrests before problem-oriented policing was implemented. The null and research hypotheses are formally stated as follows:

$H_0: \mu_D = 0$. This implies that the same number of crimes were committed before and after the policing program was put in place

$H_1: \mu_D \neq 0$. This implies that there is some effect of the policing program on crime, but we cannot state in advance if it decreases or increases crime

Step 2: The next step is to state our test statistic and the sampling distribution of that test statistic. Because we have dependent samples (the same community is used before and after the policing program was introduced), we use the dependent-samples t test as the statistical test and use the t distribution as our sampling distribution.

Step 3: The third step is to select our alpha level and determine the critical value and region. Let's select an alpha level of .01 ($\alpha = .01$) for this example. Because we have 20 pairs of observations ($n = 20$), we have 19 ($20 - 1 = 19$) degrees of freedom. We go to Table B.3 of Appendix B and find that for a two-tailed hypothesis test, $\alpha = .01$, and 19 degrees of freedom, the critical value of t is ± 2.861. Therefore, we will reject the null hypothesis if t_{obt} is less than or equal to -2.861 or if t_{obt} is greater than or equal to 2.861. We illustrate this for you in Figure 9.10.

Step 4: The fourth step of our hypothesis-testing procedure is to calculate the test statistic and compare it with our critical value.

For our first example of a matched-groups t test, we illustrate the calculations in detail. From equation 9-6, we see that we need to determine the mean of the difference scores and the estimated standard deviation of the difference scores. In Table 9.4, we report that the sum of the difference scores is equal to -48 (ΣX_D or $\Sigma (x_2 - x_1) = -48$). Note how these difference scores are created. For each neighborhood, we subtract the first score (before the policing program was implemented) from the second score (after the policing program was implemented). For example, the first pair of cases

Table 9.4	Number of Arrests for Violent Offenses in Neighborhoods Before (First Score) and After (Second Score) Implementation of Problem-Oriented Policing

Pair Number	First Score x_1	Second Score x_2	$x_2 - x_1$	$(x_2 - x_1)^2$
1	25	21	−4.00	16
2	29	25	−4.00	16
3	32	32	0.00	0
4	42	39	−3.00	9
5	21	25	4.00	16
6	29	25	−4.00	16
7	33	29	−4.00	16
8	35	36	1.00	1
9	32	29	−3.00	9
10	36	35	− 1.00	1
11	39	40	1.00	1
12	25	21	−4.00	16
13	27	25	−2.00	4
14	41	35	−6.00	36
15	36	35	− 1.00	1
16	21	23	2.00	4
17	38	31	−7.00	49
18	25	21	−4.00	16
19	29	25	−4.00	16
20	25	20	− 5.00	25
			$\Sigma = - 48$	$\Sigma = 268$
			$\overline{X}_D = -2.40$	

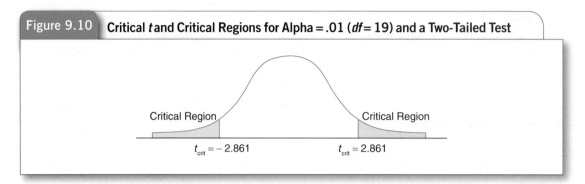

Figure 9.10 Critical *t* and Critical Regions for Alpha = .01 (*df* = 19) and a Two-Tailed Test

Critical Region

Critical Region

$t_{crit} = -2.861$

$t_{crit} = 2.861$

had 21 arrests after the problem-oriented policing strategy was implemented and 25 arrests before. The difference, then, is 21 − 25 = −4, or a reduction by 4 crimes. We do this for each neighborhood (each pair), sum across the pairs, and then divide by the number of pairs to obtain a mean difference score. All scores are added in calculating this mean difference score, including zeros and scores with negative signs. With 20 pairs of scores, the mean difference score for these data is −48 / 20, or −2.40 ($\overline{X}_D = -2.40$).

We now calculate the estimated standard deviation of the difference scores. This is just like calculating the standard deviation for any other group of scores except that the raw data are the difference scores and the mean is the mean of the difference scores. First, we will use the definitional formula for the standard deviation. We subtract the mean difference score from each difference score, square this difference, sum these squared differences, divide by the number of pairs minus 1, and then take the square root. This is equal to the standard deviation of the difference scores. To get the standard error or the standard deviation of the sampling distribution, divide this standard deviation by the square root of the sample size. The calculations necessary to find this are shown in Table 9.5.

We can place this into our definitional formula for the standard deviation (Chapter 4):

$$s_D = \sqrt{\frac{\Sigma(X_D - \overline{X}_D)^2}{n-1}}$$

The standard deviation of the difference scores is symbolized as s_D and, for this example, is calculated using the earlier standard deviation formula:

$$s_D = \sqrt{\frac{152.80}{19}}$$

$$s_D = \sqrt{8.042}$$

$$s_D = 2.836$$

Now that we have the standard deviation of the difference scores, we can calculate our test statistic:

$$t_{obt} = \frac{\overline{X}_D}{s_D/\sqrt{n}}$$

$$t_{obt} = \frac{-2.40}{2.836/\sqrt{20}}$$

$$t_{obt} = \frac{-2.40}{2.836 / 4.472}$$

$$t_{obt} = \frac{-2.40}{.634}$$

$$t_{obt} = -3.785$$

Table 9.5	Standard Deviations of the Sampling Distribution for the Number of Neighborhood Arrests for Violent Offenses Before (First Score) and After (Second Score) Problem-Oriented Policing Implementation

Pair	$x_D - \overline{X}_D$	$(x_D - \overline{X}_D)^2$
1	$-4 - (-2.4) = -1.60$	2.56
2	$-4 - (-2.4) = -1.60$	2.56
3	$0 - (-2.4) = 2.40$	5.76
4	$-3 - (-2.4) = -0.60$	0.36
5	$4 - (-2.4) = 6.40$	40.96
6	$-4 - (-2.4) = -1.60$	2.56
7	$-4 - (-2.4) = -1.60$	2.56
8	$1 - (-2.4) = 3.40$	11.56
9	$-3 - (-2.4) = -0.60$	0.36
10	$-1 - (-2.4) = 1.40$	1.96
11	$1 - (-2.4) = 3.40$	11.56
12	$-4 - (-2.4) = -1.60$	2.56
13	$-2 - (-2.4) = 0.40$	0.16
14	$-6 - (-2.4) = -3.60$	12.96
15	$-1 - (-2.4) = 1.40$	1.96
16	$2 - (-2.4) = 4.40$	19.36
17	$-7 - (-2.4) = -4.60$	21.16
18	$-4 - (-2.4) = -1.60$	2.56
19	$-4 - (-2.4) = -1.60$	2.56
20	$-5 - (-2.4) = -2.60$	6.76
$n = 20$		$\Sigma(X_D - \overline{X}_{D2}) = 152.80$

Step 5: Finally, we compare our obtained value of t (-3.785) with our critical value (± 2.861) and the critical region. Since t_{obt} falls within the critical region ($-3.785 < -2.861$), we can reject the null hypothesis that the mean of the differences is equal to zero. We will conclude that the number of post-arrests for violence is significantly different from the number of pre-arrests. The implementation of problem-oriented policing within our sample of neighborhoods seems to have had a significant impact in reducing the number of arrests for violent offenses made within neighborhoods in the population.

Case Study

Siblings and Delinquency

One of the most comprehensive studies ever undertaken on the causes of delinquent behavior was reported more than 60 years ago by Sheldon and Eleanor Glueck (1950). The Gluecks compared 500 institutionalized chronic delinquents with a matched group of 500 non-delinquents. Among their findings, the Gluecks reported that members of the delinquent group were more likely than the non-delinquents to come from broken homes and economically disadvantaged families, to have friends who were also delinquents, and to have parents who were cruel and erratic in their discipline.

Table 9.6 — Number of Delinquent Siblings for 15 Delinquent Youths and a Matched Group of 15 Non-Delinquent Youths and the Calculations Necessary for a Matched-Group t Test

Pair	Non-Delinquent Score X_1	Delinquent Score X_2	x_D $x_2 - x_1$	x_D^2 $(x_2 - x_1)^2$	$x_D - \bar{X}_D$	$(x_D - \bar{X}_D)^2$
1	1	3	2	4	2 − 1.40 = 0.60	0.36
2	0	2	2	4	2 − 1.40 = 0.60	0.36
3	0	1	1	1	1 − 1.40 = −0.40	0.16
4	1	4	3	9	3 − 1.40 = 1.60	2.56
5	2	1	−1	1	−1 − 1.40 = −2.40	5.76
6	0	3	3	9	3 − 1.40 = 1.60	2.56
7	2	2	0	0	0 − 1.40 = −1.40	1.96
8	1	4	3	9	3 − 1.40 = 1.60	2.56
9	0	1	1	1	1 − 1.40 = −0.40	0.16
10	0	2	2	4	2 − 1.40 = 0.60	0.36
11	0	0	0	0	0 − 1.40 = −1.40	1.96
12	1	2	1	1	1 − 1.40 = −0.40	0.16
13	0	2	2	4	2 − 1.40 = 0.60	0.36
14	1	3	2	4	2 − 1.40 = 0.60	0.36
15	0	0	0	0	0 − 1.40 = −1.40	1.96
$n = 15$			$\Sigma x_D = 21$ $\bar{X}_D = 21/15 = 1.40$ $\Sigma x_D^2 = 51$			$\Sigma(x_D - \bar{X}_D)^2 = 21.60$ $\Sigma_D = \sqrt{\dfrac{21.60}{15-1}} = 1.24$

Let's presume that, like the Gluecks, we have a group of 15 non-delinquents and a group of 15 delinquents who are matched with respect to social class, gender, age, race, and whether both parents are in the home. For each youth, we also have the number of siblings who he or she reports have been arrested for a crime. What we want to know is whether the delinquent youths have more delinquent siblings than the non-delinquent youths. In this scenario, whether a youth has been arrested for delinquency is the independent variable and the number of delinquent siblings is the dependent variable. The data from the two groups are reported in the second and third columns of Table 9.6.

Step 1: Our null hypothesis is that the number of delinquent siblings is not different between the two matched groups. In other words, we are assuming that the population mean for the difference between the pair of scores is zero. Based on our knowledge of the delinquency literature, we will make the directional (one-tailed) alternative hypothesis that the delinquent group will have more siblings who have violated the law than the non-delinquent group. Our prediction, therefore, is that if the number of law-violating siblings for the non-delinquent group is the first score and the number of law-violating siblings for the delinquent group is the second score, then the difference scores $(x_2 - x_1)$ will generally be positive and the population mean for the differences will be greater than zero. The hypotheses are formally stated as follows:

$H_0: \mu_D = 0$

$H_1: \mu_D > 0$

Step 2: Our test statistic will be the dependent-samples t test, and the sampling distribution will be the t distribution.

Step 3: For our hypothesis test, we will choose an alpha level of .05. Since our alternative hypothesis stated that the true population mean was greater than zero, our critical region will lie in the right tail of the sampling distribution. With $n - 1$ or 14 degrees of freedom, $\alpha = .05$, and a one-tailed test, we can find in the t table (Table B.3) that $t_{crit} = 1.761$. The critical region consists of all obtained t scores that are greater than or equal to 1.761. Therefore, we will fail to reject the null hypothesis if $t_{obt} < 1.761$. We show the critical t value and critical region in Figure 9.11.

Step 4: The second and third columns of Table 9.6 show the calculations necessary to determine both the mean and the standard deviation of the difference scores. We use the definitional formula for the standard deviation of the difference scores, but you would have obtained the same value with the computational formula! The value of t_{obt} is calculated as follows:

$$t_{obt} = \frac{\bar{X}_D}{\sqrt{\dfrac{\Sigma(D - \bar{X}_D)^2}{n-1}} / \sqrt{n}}$$

$$t_{obt} = \frac{1.40}{\sqrt{\dfrac{21.60}{14}} / \sqrt{15}}$$

$$t_{obt} = \frac{1.40}{\sqrt{1.54} / \sqrt{15}}$$

$$t_{obt} = \frac{1.40}{1.24 / 3.87}$$

$$t_{obt} = \frac{1.40}{.32}$$

$$t_{obt} = 4.375$$

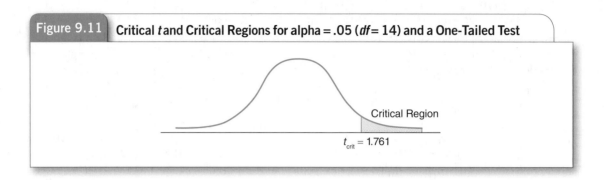

Figure 9.11 Critical *t* and Critical Regions for alpha = .05 (*df* = 14) and a One-Tailed Test

Critical Region

$t_{crit} = 1.761$

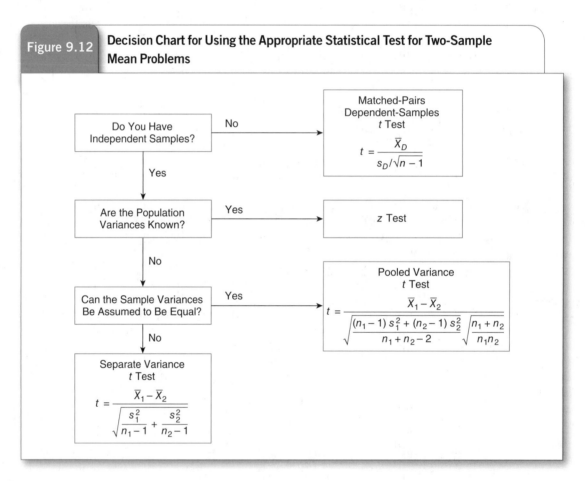

Figure 9.12 Decision Chart for Using the Appropriate Statistical Test for Two-Sample Mean Problems

Do You Have Independent Samples?

No → Matched-Pairs Dependent-Samples *t* Test

$$t = \frac{\overline{X}_D}{s_D/\sqrt{n-1}}$$

Yes ↓

Are the Population Variances Known?

Yes → *z* Test

No ↓

Can the Sample Variances Be Assumed to Be Equal?

Yes → Pooled Variance *t* Test

$$t = \frac{\overline{X}_1 - \overline{X}_2}{\sqrt{\frac{(n_1-1)\,s_1^2 + (n_2-1)\,s_2^2}{n_1+n_2-2}}\sqrt{\frac{n_1+n_2}{n_1 n_2}}}$$

No ↓

Separate Variance *t* Test

$$t = \frac{\overline{X}_1 - \overline{X}_2}{\sqrt{\frac{s_1^2}{n_1-1} + \frac{s_2^2}{n_2-1}}}$$

Step 5: The obtained value of our test statistic is 4.375. Because $t_{obt} > t_{crit}$, we can reject the null hypothesis that the mean population difference is zero. We conclude that there is a significant relationship in the population between delinquency and the number of delinquent siblings a youth has. In the population, we can assume delinquents have significantly more siblings who have violated the law than non-delinquents.

In this and the previous two sections of this chapter, we have examined several different types of statistical tests to test a hypothesis about two population means. This must present a somewhat bewildering picture, and we admit that it might seem a bit overwhelming right now. In selecting the appropriate test statistic for the two-sample mean problem, however, a good deal of confusion can be eliminated if you remember that you need to answer only a few fundamental questions before deciding which test is appropriate for your problem. Figure 9.12 summarizes these decisions. Think of this figure as a road map in deciding which statistical test you should use for two-sample mean problems. In the next section, we will examine hypothesis tests about the difference between two sample proportions.

Hypothesis Tests for the Difference Between Two Proportions: Large Samples

In this section, we will examine a statistical test for the significance of the difference between two population *proportions* (P_1 and P_2). Think of the difference of proportions test as a special case of the difference of means test. There are many cases in our discipline where this test is applicable.

Let's say we have a random sample of 100 persons and we asked each of them whether they favor the death penalty for those who commit first-degree murder. We arbitrarily assign a score of "0" for those who say no and a score of "1" for those who say yes. Let's assume that 89 of the 100 persons said they approved of the death penalty under that circumstance and 11 said they did not. Since there are only two values (0 = no and 1 = yes), we can treat this variable as being measured at the interval level. We can determine the mean of this variable by counting the number of "1" scores (or "0" scores) and dividing by n. Since we have 89 "1" scores, the mean would be 89 / 100, or .89. The mean for a binary variable (a variable with only two values coded as "0" and "1"), then, is the proportion of "1" scores—in this case, the proportion of our sample that was in favor of the death penalty. The mean, therefore, is actually the proportion of "1" scores. Even though the population is dichotomous (it is made up of 0s and 1s), we know from the central limit theorem that with a large enough sample, the distribution of sample means and the difference between two sample means will be approximately normal. Hence, we can use a z test and the z distribution to test hypotheses about the difference between two proportions.

In this section, we will consider only tests appropriate for data obtained from large independent samples. If $n\hat{p} \geq 5$ and $n\hat{q} \geq 5$ for each of the two samples (where $\hat{p}$ is the sample proportion and $\hat{q} = 1 - \hat{p}$), the sampling distribution of the difference between proportions will be approximately normal and we can use a z test as our test statistic.

In calculating the test statistic for the t test for two sample means, we subtracted one sample mean from the other and divided by the standard error of the difference between means. We will conduct the same procedure in our test for the difference between two proportions. In our z test for two proportions, we will subtract the two sample proportions ($\hat{p}_1 - \hat{p}_2$) and divide by our estimate of the standard deviation of the sampling distribution of the difference between proportions ($\hat{\sigma}_{P_1-P_2}$). This estimated standard deviation is also referred to as the standard error of the difference between proportions. The z test for the difference between proportions is

$$z_{obt} = \frac{\hat{p}_1 - \hat{p}_2}{\hat{\sigma}_{P_1-P_2}} = \frac{\hat{p}_1 - \hat{p}_2}{\sqrt{\hat{p}\hat{q}}\sqrt{\frac{n_1+n_2}{n_1 n_2}}}$$

(Formula 9-8)

where

$\hat{p}_1$ = the sample proportion for the first sample

$\hat{p}_2$ = the sample proportion for the second sample

$\hat{p} = \frac{n_1\hat{p}_1 + n_2\hat{p}_2}{n_1 + n_2}$

$\hat{q} = 1 - \hat{p}$

Again, notice that in formula 9-8 the p terms in the numerator have a subscript because they come from our two samples, whereas the p and q terms under the first radical in the denominator do not. Just as with all of the preceding hypothesis tests, once we have obtained the test statistic, we compare our z_{obt} with z_{crit} and make a decision about the null hypothesis. Let's go through an example.

Case Study

Education and Recidivism

One of the primary questions in the correctional literature is to determine what programs within the correctional setting decrease inmates' rates of recidivism once they are released. Recently, Ryang Kim and David Clark (2013) examined recidivism rates between inmates who participated in prison-based college programs and those who did not. Not surprisingly to some, they found that the recidivism rate for the inmates who had participated in the college program was lower than the recidivism rate for those who did not participate.

Let's say we have an independent random sample of 120 inmates from a correctional institution where 60 inmates in this group have received either their associate or baccalaureate degree while in prison and the remaining 60 inmates have received no educational curriculum whatsoever. Of the 60 who had received an education, 18% ($\hat{p}_1 = .18$) were rearrested within 1 year of their release from prison. Of the 60 who had not received any education, 38% ($\hat{p}_2 = .38$) were rearrested within the same time period. We wonder whether there is a significant difference between the percentage of released inmates who were rearrested (our measure of recidivism) for those who received an education in prison compared with those who did not. To answer this question, we need to conduct an explicit hypothesis test.

Step 1: Our null hypothesis is that the two samples came from populations with the same proportion of inmates who were rearrested after release. In other words, receiving an education while in prison had no effect on the likelihood of recidivating during the year after release. To be on the safe side, we test a non-directional (two-tailed) alternative hypothesis that the two proportions are simply different from each other. These hypotheses are stated as follows:

$H_0: P_1 = P_2$

$H_1: P_1 \neq P_2$

Step 2: To test these hypotheses, we select as our test statistic the z test for a difference of proportions. Since we have a large sample size, the z distribution will be our sampling distribution.

Step 3: We will select an alpha level of .01. For a two-tailed test, the critical level of z at $\alpha = .01$ is $z_{crit} = \pm 2.58$ (see Table B.2 in Appendix B or Table 7.1 in Chapter 7 for the critical values of z for common levels of alpha). Since this is a two-tailed test, the critical region lies in both tails of the z distribution and consists of all obtained z scores less than or equal to –2.58 or greater than or equal to 2.58. We will reject the null hypothesis if z_{obt} is less than or equal to –2.58 or greater than or equal to +2.58. Figure 9.13 shows the two critical regions and the critical z values.

Step 4: To make the calculations more manageable, we will find our obtained value of z in a series of steps.

Step 4a: We find the estimated value of the pooled population proportions:

$$\hat{p} = \frac{(60)(.18) + (60)(.38)}{60 + 60}$$

$$\hat{p} = \frac{10.8 + 22.8}{120}$$

$$\hat{p} = \frac{33.6}{120}$$

$$\hat{p} = .28$$

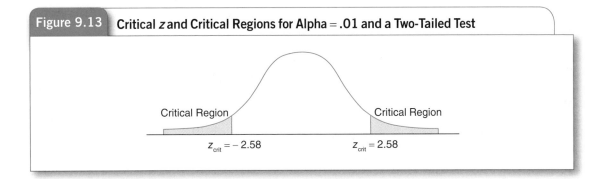

Figure 9.13 **Critical *z* and Critical Regions for Alpha = .01 and a Two-Tailed Test**

Critical Region

Critical Region

$z_{crit} = -2.58$ $z_{crit} = 2.58$

Step 4b: We find the standard error estimate of the difference between population proportions:

$$\hat{\sigma}_{p_1-p_2} = \sqrt{\hat{p}\,\hat{q}}\,\sqrt{\frac{n_1+n_2}{n_1 n_2}}$$

$$\hat{\sigma}_{p_1-p_2} = \sqrt{(.28).72}\,\sqrt{\frac{60+60}{60(60)}}$$

$$\hat{\sigma}_{p_1-p_2} = \sqrt{.20}\,\sqrt{\frac{120}{3,600}}$$

$$\hat{\sigma}_{p_1-p_2} = (.45)\sqrt{.033}$$

$$\hat{\sigma}_{p_1-p_2} = (.45)(.18)$$

$$\hat{\sigma}_{p_1-p_2} = .081$$

Step 4c: Finally, plugging our sample proportions into the numerator and this standard error estimate into the denominator of formula 9-8, we calculate the value of our obtained *z* test:

$$z_{obt} = \frac{\hat{p}_1 - \hat{p}_2}{\sqrt{\hat{p}\hat{q}}\,\sqrt{\frac{n_1+n_2}{n_1 n_2}}}$$

$$z_{obt} = \frac{.18-.38}{.081}$$

$$z_{obt} = \frac{-.2}{.081}$$

$$z_{obt} = -2.47$$

Step 5: Our obtained *z* statistic is –2.47. This value of z_{obt} just misses falling into our rejection region. Since it does not lie within the critical region, we must fail to reject the null hypothesis. We cannot conclude, based on our sample data, that in the population the proportion of inmates who recidivate is significantly different between those inmates who receive an education in prison and those who do not. To test yourself, conduct the same null hypothesis using an alpha of .05 (α = .05). What do you conclude?

🔲 Summary

In this chapter, we have examined techniques used to perform hypothesis tests to determine the difference between two means and two proportions. With unknown population variances, the statistical test for the difference between two means is conducted with a t test. If the test involves two independent random samples, we can choose from two different kinds of t tests. The first type is called a pooled variance t test. This test for two-sample means is appropriate when we can assume that the population standard deviations are equal. When we cannot maintain that assumption, the correct t test to use is the separate variance t test.

In addition to these tests for independent samples, we also examined a t test for matched groups or dependent samples. In this kind of t test, we are less interested in the difference between two means than in testing whether the difference between two sets of scores is equal to zero.

Finally, we learned how to test for the significance of the difference between two proportions and discovered that it was a special instance of the two-sample mean test.

Key Terms

➤ Review key terms with eFlashcards. Visit study.sagepub.com/paternoster.

independent random samples 226
matched or dependent samples 240

sampling distribution of sample mean
  differences 224

Key Formulas

Standard deviation of sample mean differences (formula 9-1):

$$\sigma_{\bar{X}_1-\bar{X}_2} = \sqrt{\frac{\sigma_1^2}{n_1} + \frac{\sigma_2^2}{n_2}}$$

General t test (formula 9-2):

$$t_{\text{obt}} = \frac{\bar{X}_1 - \bar{X}_2}{\hat{\sigma}_{\bar{X}_1-\bar{X}_2}}$$

Pooled variance t test (formula 9-3):

$$t_{\text{obt}} = \frac{\bar{X}_1 - \bar{X}_2}{\sqrt{\dfrac{(n_1-1)s_1^2 + (n_2-1)s_2^2}{n_1+n_2-2}} \sqrt{\dfrac{n_1+n_2}{n_1 n_2}}}$$

Separate variance t test (formula 9-4):

$$t_{\text{obt}} = \frac{\bar{X}_1 - \bar{X}_2}{\sqrt{\dfrac{s_1^2}{n_1-1} + \dfrac{s_2^2}{n_2-1}}}$$

Degrees of freedom for separate variance t test (formula 9-5):

$$df = \left[\frac{\left(\dfrac{s_1^2}{n_1-1} + \dfrac{s_2^2}{n_2-1} \right)^2}{\left(\dfrac{s_1^2}{n_1-1} \right)^2 \left(\dfrac{1}{n_1+1} \right) + \left(\dfrac{s_2^2}{n_2-1} \right)^2 \left(\dfrac{1}{n_2+1} \right)} \right] - 2$$

Dependent-samples t test (formula 9-7):

$$t_{\text{obt}} = \frac{\bar{X}_D}{s_D/\sqrt{n}}$$

Difference between proportions z test (formula 9-8):

$$z_{obt} = \frac{\hat{P}_1 - \hat{P}_2}{\sqrt{\hat{P}\hat{P}} \sqrt{\dfrac{n_1+n_2}{n_1 n_2}}}$$

Practice Problems

➤ Test your understanding of chapter content.
Take the practice quiz at study.sagepub.com/paternoster.

1. Explain the difference between independent and dependent variables. If you think that low self-control affects crime, which is the independent variable and which is the dependent variable?

2. When is it appropriate to use an independent-samples t test, and when is it appropriate to use a t test for dependent samples or matched groups?

3. John Worrall and colleagues found that the fear of losing the good opinion of one's family and peers kept people from driving home drunk (Worrall, Els, Piquero, & TenEyck, 2014). Let's say we have two independent random samples of people: those who think that their peers would disapprove of them for driving drunk and those who think that their peers either would not care or would approve of their driving drunk. We ask each person in each group to self-report the number of times that he or she has driven drunk during the past 12 months. Here are the results:

Would Not Approve of Driving Drunk	Would Approve of Driving Drunk
$n_1 = 40$	$n_2 = 25$
$x_1 = 2.1$	$x_2 = 8.2$
$s_1 = 1.8$	$s_2 = 1.9$

Test the null hypothesis that the two population means are equal against the alternative hypothesis that the group whose peers would not approve of driving drunk has a lower mean rate of driving drunk. In your hypothesis test, assume that the unknown population standard deviations are equal and use an alpha level of .01.

4. The use of monetary fines as a criminal sanction is being considered as one possible solution to the problem of prison overcrowding. Supporters of the use of fines contend that it would be both an effective deterrent to crime and a way to punish even moderately severe crimes without imprisonment. Critics argue that giving criminal offenders fines only increases their motivation to commit more crimes in order to pay their fines. You want to test the effect of fines versus incarceration on criminal behavior. You take a random sample of 150 convicted offenders who have been given a fine as punishment and follow them up for 3 years. You take a second independent random sample of 110 offenders recently released from prison and follow them up for 3 years. At the end of the 3-year follow-up period, you

find that 33% of those given a fine had been rearrested and 38% of those given a prison sentence had been rearrested. Test the null hypothesis that the proportions rearrested in the two groups are equal against the alternative hypothesis that they are different. Use an alpha level of .05.

5. Jason Ingram and William Terrill (2014) conducted some research on the perceptions that female and male police officers have of their roles, the public, and their departments. They concluded that female and male police officers do not view their jobs very differently. Let's say that we wanted to continue their work and were interested in how female and male police officers view one component of police work: the handling of domestic disputes. To do this research, we have created a scale that measures how important settling domestic disputes is and whether it is perceived as part of "police work." Those who score high on this scale think that the fair settling of domestic disturbances is of high priority and that it should be an important part of a police officer's duties. We have then taken two random samples. One is a sample of 50 male police officers, and the other is an independent random sample of 25 female police officers. We give each officer a questionnaire that includes our domestic dispute scale. The mean score for female officers is 21.3 with a standard deviation of 3.0. The mean score for male officers is 18.8 with a standard deviation of 4.5. Test the null hypothesis that the two population means are equal against the alternative hypothesis that the male mean is lower than the female mean. In your hypothesis test, *do not* presume that the population standard deviations are equal and use an alpha level of .05.

6. Capital punishment law is among the most complex bodies of law in our legal system. As a result, judges make frequent errors in capital cases in terms of their rulings regarding a change of venue, the decision to sequester jurors, questions of voir dire, suppression of evidence, and so on. When these errors are made, cases are often won on appeal and have to be retried or have a second penalty phase hearing. The Trial Judges Association thinks that only judges who have received special training should sit on capital cases because these judges would commit fewer errors and there would be fewer cases lost on appeal. You decide to test this hypothesis. You take a random sample of 15 judges who have received extensive training in capital punishment law. You match these judges with 15 other judges who have not received such training but are matched in terms of their number of years on the bench, experience as trial lawyers, gender, and age. You want the

two groups of judges to be alike in every way except the experience of capital punishment law training. The data on your matched groups of judges are as follows:

Number of Cases Lost on Appeal

Judge	Untrained	Trained
1	3	0
2	1	3
3	2	4
4	7	4
5	5	2
6	4	5
7	6	1
8	2	1
9	7	0
10	5	6
11	3	4
12	4	2
13	5	5
14	6	3
15	2	1

Test the null hypothesis that the mean difference in the number of cases lost on appeal for the two groups of judges is zero against the alternative hypothesis that the untrained judges lose more cases on appeal. Use an alpha level of .01.

7. Adrian Raine (1994) discussed some research in biological criminology suggesting that children with criminal parents are more likely to be criminals themselves than are children with noncriminal parents. Suppose you conduct a study on a random sample of 100 delinquent youths confined in a correctional institution and a random sample of 75 non-delinquent youths. You find that 43% of the delinquent youths have at least one criminal parent but that only 17% of the non-delinquent youths have a criminal parent. Test the null hypothesis that the two population proportions are equal against the alternative hypothesis that the delinquent group has a greater proportion of criminal parents. Use an alpha level of .01.

8. It is common wisdom to believe that dropping out of high school leads to delinquency. For example, Travis Hirschi's (1969) control theory might predict that those with little or no commitment to education are delinquent more often than those with strong educational commitments. In his general strain theory, however, Robert Agnew (1992) might predict that dropping out of school would lower one's involvement in delinquency because it would get youths out of an aversive and painful environment. You want to examine the relationship between dropping out of high school and delinquency. You have a random sample of 11 students. You have the number of delinquent offenses that each student reported committing during the year before dropping out of school and the number of offenses that each reported committing during the year after dropping out of school. Here are those data:

Number of Delinquent Acts

Person	Before	After
1	5	7
2	9	5
3	2	3
4	7	7
5	8	11
6	11	13
7	8	4
8	8	10
9	5	7
10	2	1
11	9	3

Test the null hypothesis that the mean difference between the two sets of scores is zero against the alternative hypothesis that it is different from zero. Use an alpha level of .05.

STUDENT STUDY SITE

WANT A BETTER GRADE?

Get the tools you need to sharpen your study skills. Access practice quizzes, eFlashcards, data sets, and SPSS exercises at **study.sagepub.com/paternoster.**

CHAPTER 10

Hypothesis Tests Involving Three or More Population Means

Analysis of Variance

"The analysis of variance is not a mathematical theorem, but rather a convenient method of arranging the arithmetic.

To call in the statistician after the experiment is done may be no more than asking him to perform a post-mortem examination: he may be able to say what the experiment died of."

—Sir Ronald Fisher

LEARNING OBJECTIVES

1. Explain why multiple *t* tests are not appropriate when an independent variable has more than two categories.

2. Describe the importance of the variance in testing the difference between means.

3. Identify and interpret the total, between-groups, and within-group sums of squares and their relationship to testing the difference between means.

4. Conduct a hypothesis for the difference among three or more group means and interpret the results.

5. Describe the purpose of John Tukey's honest significant difference (HSD) test.

6. State the difference between measures of association and the analysis of variance (ANOVA) hypothesis test.

▣ Introduction

In Chapter 9, we were interested in the relationship between an independent variable that has only two values or levels and a continuous dependent variable. There will be many times, however, when our independent variable is a categorical variable that has more than two values. For example, suppose we were interested in finding out whether the sentence given to armed robbers (measured in months) varied by the race of the defendant. Suppose also that our independent variable (race of defendant) consisted of the following categories: White, Black, Hispanic, and Asian. Here we have a continuous dependent variable, and our independent variable has four values. In this chapter, we will examine cases like this where we have an independent variable with three or more levels or categories and a continuous (interval/ratio) dependent variable. Just as in the last chapter, we are also interested in the difference between the means of different groups. In this chapter, however, we have three or more groups, and for reasons we will explain, applying the t test to more than two groups is not appropriate. In this chapter you will learn about a technique called analysis of variance, which relies on the F probability distribution. In addition, because we have more than two means, the results of a null hypothesis that three or more population means are equal can tell us that at least one pair of the means may be different from each other, but it does not tell us which pair or pairs. You will also learn how to conduct a test called John Tukey's honest significant difference (HSD) test to determine which of your group means are significantly different from each other. What neither the F test nor Tukey's HSD test can do, however, is tell us about the *strength* of the relationship between our independent and dependent variables. Therefore, we will conclude our discussion by learning how to calculate something called eta squared (η^2), which measures the strength of the relationship between an independent variable and a dependent variable in an analysis of variance.

▣ The Logic of Analysis of Variance

The Problem With Using a *t* Test With Three or More Means

To illustrate the problem with using the t test we learned in the last chapter when we have more than two means, let's go back to our scenario of examining the difference between the sentence received for armed robbery for a sample of White, Black, Hispanic, and Asian defendants. With the tools we now have in our toolbox, we might be tempted just to do a series of pairwise t tests. That is, we could use our t test for independent samples and conduct the hypothesis test at some level of significance (say, $\alpha = .05$) that each pair of population means is equal against the alternative hypothesis that each pair is not equal. Note that if we did this, we would have a lot of pairwise t tests to perform. With four groups, we would have to do six different t tests:

$$\mu_{\text{White}} - \mu_{\text{Black}} \; ; \; \mu_{\text{White}} - \mu_{\text{Hispanic}} \; ; \; \mu_{\text{White}} - \mu_{\text{Asian}} \; ; \; \mu_{\text{Black}} - \mu_{\text{Hispanic}} \; ; \; \mu_{\text{Black}} - \mu_{\text{Asian}} \; ; \; \mu_{\text{Hispanic}} - \mu_{\text{Asian}}$$

Student Study Site

Visit the open-access Student Study Site at study.sagepub.com/paternoster to access additional study tools including mobile-friendly eFlashcards, web quizzes, links to SAGE journal articles, additional data sets, SPSS exercises, and more!

We would, therefore, have a lot of work to do. That's not the real problem with this strategy, however. The main problem in doing a series of t tests with the same data is that the significance level of our hypothesis test assumes that the sample means are independent. When we use the same sample means for multiple significance tests (note that the White group mean in the preceding example is used in three separate hypothesis tests), this assumption of independence is violated. The problem with doing these multiple t tests with our one set of data, therefore, is that our alpha level increases with each hypothesis test. That is, although our first t test hypothesis test is done with an alpha level of .05, the next hypothesis test using one of same samples has an alpha higher than .05 because the assumption of independence is violated. What this means is that for our six separate hypothesis tests, the probability of making a Type I error in rejecting a true null hypothesis is not .05 but greater than that, sometimes much greater. In conducting multiple means tests with the same data, therefore, we do not have a consistently true alpha level.

Because of this, we need a tool where we can compare multiple population means and maintain a consistently true alpha level. This tool, which we will learn in this chapter, is called the **analysis of variance,** or ANOVA for short. The analysis of variance test is to be used when we are interested in conducting a hypothesis test where we have a continuous (interval/ratio) dependent variable and an independent variable that is categorical (nominal or ordinal) with three or more values.

Let's assume we have three population means whose equality we are testing ($\mu_1 = \mu_2 = \mu_3$). Our hypothesis test is called the analysis of variance because in testing this hypothesis, we are not going to examine the means directly; rather, we are going to examine the variances. That is why the test is called an analysis of *variance*. Now, it may seem very odd to do a hypothesis test about population means by examining variances, so allow us to explain with an example.

Case Study

Police Responses to Intimate Partner Assault

The example we are going to use to illustrate ANOVA examines the differential effects of three different kinds of police response to an intimate partner assault call: (1) simply separate the couple and do nothing else, (2) separate the couple and require counseling for the offender, and (3) arrest the offender. The outcome we are interested in is the number of times during the following year that the police are called back to the address on another domestic violence call involving the same offender. Our nominal-level independent variable is the police response to domestic violence, and there are three values or categories: separate, counsel, and arrest. Our interval- and ratio-level dependent variable is the number of return calls to the address against the same offender. Let's assume that we have a sample of 100 persons in each group, for a total sample size of 300, and that after a year we calculate the mean number of return visits to the house for each group.

Figure 10.1(a) shows a hypothetical distribution of the number of times the police have to return to the house for each of the three groups. Note that the three group means are very different. The mean number of return visits is highest for the separate-only group, next highest for the counsel group, and lowest for the arrest group. Note also that although the three group means are very different from each other, the scores within each group are not that different from their own unique group mean. In other words, each score within each group clusters fairly tightly around its group mean. In sum, scores do not vary that much within groups, but the mean scores vary a great deal across the three groups. Based on this figure and our "eyeball test," we would be tempted to conclude that how the police respond to a domestic violence call does indeed make a difference in terms of the effect on the suspect, that is, that there is a "treatment effect." Suspects who have been arrested seem least likely to repeat their offense during the subsequent year compared with those counseled and those separated, and the counseled group of suspects seems to do better than those who are simply told to leave the scene. In fact, the latter group has the highest number of new offenses. In other words, it looks as if $\bar{X}_{arrest} \neq \bar{X}_{counsel} \neq \bar{X}_{separate}$. If we think in terms of population means rather than sample means, it looks as if $\mu_{arrest} \neq \mu_{counsel} \neq \mu_{separate}$.

Figure 10.1(b) shows a different set of hypothetical distributions for the same data. In this hypothetical case, even though the three group means are the same as in Figure 10.1(a), there is much greater variability within each group. The scores within each group no longer cluster tightly about the group mean but rather are highly variable, overlapping sometimes with the scores from another group. It looks like there is more variability within a group than there is

Analysis of variance (ANOVA): Statistical model used to test the differences among three or more group means.

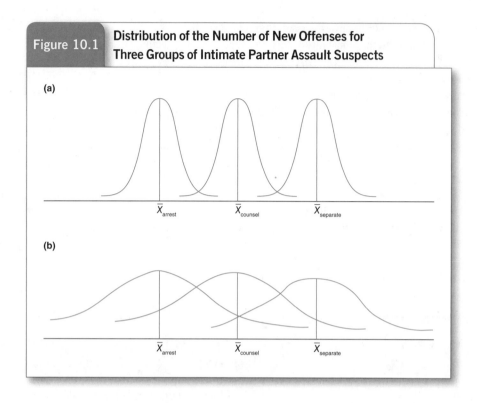

Figure 10.1 Distribution of the Number of New Offenses for Three Groups of Intimate Partner Assault Suspects

between groups. In this set of distributions, we are less tempted to conclude that there is a clear "treatment effect" due to the different police responses to domestic violence. Now it looks like $\bar{X}_{\text{arrest}} = \bar{X}_{\text{counsel}} = \bar{X}_{\text{separate}}$ or, again with respect to the population that we want to generalize to, $\mu_{\text{arrest}} = \mu_{\text{counsel}} = \mu_{\text{separate}}$. We came to this tentative conclusion by comparing the variability within each group with that across the three groups. This comparison of within-group variability with between-group or across-group variability is at the heart of the analysis of variance. All we have to do is change the word "variability" to "variance" and we can see that an analysis of variance is based on comparing the variance within groups with the variance between groups to draw a conclusion about the equality of group means.

Types of Variance: Total, Between-Groups, and Within-Group Variance

In the analysis of variance test, we calculate three different types of variance: the total variance, the between-groups variance, and the within-group variance. To refresh your memory, here is the formula we have used for the sample variance:

$$s^2 = \frac{\Sigma(x - \bar{X})^2}{n-1}$$

(Formula 10-1)

To calculate a variance, therefore, we simply take the difference between a score and the mean of those scores, square that difference, sum over all scores, and divide by the degrees of freedom ($n - 1$). As you can see, we can calculate a variance for any group of scores; all we need to calculate a variance is a mean. Technically, the statistical test in an analysis of variance is called the F test, which is actually a ratio of the variance between groups to the variance within groups. It is the F test that we use to test the null hypothesis about the equality of three or more population means. Let's first examine the different sorts of variability or sources of variance we have in this "three or more population mean" problem, and then we'll get to the *F* test.

Continuing with our example from the previous section, let's assume we want to test the null hypothesis about the equality of the mean number of new offenses for our three groups of domestic violence offenders we discussed previously. In that example, we had a group of suspects who were arrested by the police in response to a "911" call for domestic violence, a group of suspects who were given mandatory counseling, and a group of suspects who were only physically separated from their victims. Our dependent variable was the number of new domestic violence offenses committed by the same offender during the following year. For simplicity's sake, let's say we have a sample of five offenders in each of our three groups. The number of new offenses for each offender and the mean for each group are shown in Table 10.1.

Table 10.1 Number of New Offenses for Suspects Arrested, Counseled, or Separated by Police in Response to a 911 Call for Intimate Partner Assault

Arrested	Counseled	Separated
0	6	8
2	4	10
1	4	9
1	6	10
1	5	8
$\bar{X}_{arrest} = 1.0$	$\bar{X}_{counsel} = 5.0$	$\bar{X}_{separate} = 9.0$

You can see that the mean number of new offenses differs across the three groups. Those arrested have on average 1 new subsequent offense, those counseled committed on average 5 new offenses, and those merely separated had an average of 9 new offenses during the year that followed. We cannot, of course, conclude on the basis of these sample data that the way the police respond affects the number of new offenses in the population. That is, we cannot automatically conclude from these different sample means that $\mu_{arrest} \neq \mu_{counseled} \neq \mu_{separated}$ because our observed sample means may differ from each other by chance alone. That is, sampling variation, instead of a real difference between the population means, may be accounting for the observed differences in our sample means. Our decision to rule out the possibility of sampling variation is going to be based on a formal hypothesis test using the analysis of variance.

For the data in Table 10.1, we can calculate a couple of different means. The first mean we will calculate is the mean number of new offenses for each group separately—that is, a mean number of new offenses for each of the arrested, counseled, and separated treatment groups. We have already done this in Table 10.1, and the three means are reported at the bottom of each group. Let's call these three means the within-group means. Now let's calculate another mean by ignoring the fact that someone belongs in a particular group. We will add together all 15 scores, ignoring group membership, and divide by 15. Let's call this mean the "grand mean" because it is the overall mean for all the scores. The grand mean is calculated as

$$\bar{X}_{grand} = \frac{0+2+1+1+1+6+...+9+10+18}{15}$$
$$\bar{X}_{grand} = 5$$

Ignoring the group that someone falls into, then, the average number of new domestic offenses for these 15 offenders is 5. Let's calculate a third mean, this time by summing the three group means and then dividing by 3, and we'll call this the between-groups mean:

$$\bar{X}_{between} = \frac{1+5+9}{3}$$
$$\bar{X}_{between} = 5$$

The between-groups mean is the same as the grand mean whenever there are the same number of observations in each group, as is the case here.

So now we have three different means: (1) a unique mean for each of our three groups; (2) a mean for the entire set of scores, ignoring the group that the score came from; and (3) a mean for the three groups. With these means, we are now going to calculate a couple of different measures of *variability* where variability is defined as the difference between a given score and the mean of those scores. First, we are going to calculate a measure of *total variability,* which is the difference between an individual score (x_i) and the grand mean or the mean of all the scores $(x_i - \bar{X}_{grand})$. This total variability can be divided into two separate components. One component of the total variability is the difference between an individual score and the mean of the group to which an individual belongs $(x_i - \bar{X}_k)$ where $\bar{X}_k$ is the mean for the kth group (in our example here, $k = 3$). This is a measure of *within-group variability.* There is variation within a group not because the people within it received a different treatment by the police (because all persons within a group received the same treatment), but for other reasons—reasons we have not measured. In other words, within-group variability measures how different the scores are from the mean of the group.

The second component of the total variability is the difference between the group mean and the grand mean $(\bar{X}_k - \bar{X}_{grand})$. This is a measure of between-groups variability. There is variation between groups because offenders in different groups received a different "treatment" (police response), and the effect of the treatment may be to give them different "x" scores. In other words, there is a group "treatment effect." For example, there are on average a different number of offenses committed between the groups because offenders in a case of domestic violence respond to being arrested differently than they do to being counseled or separated. Between-groups variability measures how different the group means are from the overall mean. By separating the two types of variability, we can determine which type contributes more to the total variability.

Let's illustrate this with our data. The total variability for the first case in the arrested group is equal to $(0-5)=-5$. This person has 5 fewer offenses than the overall average number of offenses (the grand mean, $\bar{X}_{grand}$). We will now break this variability down into two components. First is the within-group variability, which is the difference between the individual score and the group mean. Since the mean of the first group (the arrested group) is 1, this component is equal to -1 $(0-1=-1)$. Part of the total variability for the first person, then, is because the number of new offenses for this person is 1 less than the average for the group that person is in (the arrested group). The between-groups variability is the difference between the mean of the group to which the person belongs and the grand mean, or -4 $(1-5=-4)$. Most of the total variability for this person is due to the fact that those in the arrested group have fewer new offenses than the overall average. Let's illustrate:

Total Variability		Within-Group Variability		Between-Groups Variability
$(x_i - \bar{X}_{grand})$	=	$(x_i - \bar{X}_k)$	+	$(\bar{X}_k - \bar{X}_{grand})$
$(0-5)$	=	$(0-1)$	+	$(1-5)$
-5	=	-1	+	-4
-5	=	-5		

Another way to describe this is (Individual score − Grand mean) = (Individual score − Group mean) + (Group mean − Grand mean).

Let's now do the same thing for the first case in the counseled group. We will divide the total amount of variability (the difference between the individual's score and the grand mean) into both within-group variability (the difference between the individual's score and the mean of the group he or she is in) and between-groups variability (the difference between the mean of the group the person is in and the grand mean) sources:

Total Variability		Within-Group Variability		Between-Groups Variability
$(x_i - \bar{X}_{grand})$	=	$(x_i - \bar{X}_k)$	+	$(\bar{X}_k - \bar{X}_{grand})$
$(6-5)$	=	$(6-5)$	+	$(5-5)$
1	=	1	+	0
1	=	1		

In this case, all of the variability is due to within-group variability. Finally, let's take the first person in the separated group and decompose that person's total variability into its two components:

Total Variability		Within-Group Variability		Between-Groups Variability
$(x_i - \bar{X}_{grand})$	=	$(x_i - \bar{X}_k)$	+	$(\bar{X}_k - \bar{X}_{grand})$
$(8 - 5)$	=	$(8 - 9)$	+	$(9 - 5)$
3	=	−1	+	4
3	=	3		

The total variability for this person is a +3, and most of this is because this person's group (suspects separated by police) has a higher mean number of new offenses than the other two groups (i.e., it's due to variability between groups).

What the analysis of variance does, therefore, is calculate the overall or total variability for each observation and then partition it into the "within" and "between" components. You should be able to see that if the lion's share of this total variability for these domestic violence data is due to variability within groups and the variability between groups is relatively small [see Figure 10.1(b)], we are not so likely to conclude that the group means are different and, thus, not so likely to conclude that the population means are different from each other (i.e., that the "treatment" does not work). If, however, most of the total variability is due to that between groups and the variability within groups is relatively small [see Figure 10.1(a)], we suspect that there really is a group "treatment effect" and that the population means really are different from each other. Although we have been talking about variability, the analysis of variance F test is really based on two types of *variance* that we will demonstrate next.

First, we are going to take each of our three sources of variability—total, within-group, and between-groups variability—and square them. These different components are called the *sums of squares*. For example, let's take the simple formula we used for total variability $(x_i - \bar{X}_{grand})$ and do two things to it: (1) square the difference and (2) require that we take this squared difference for every score or observation. If we do this, the squared difference between each score and the grand mean is given a special term; it is called the **total sum of squares**, or SS_{total}. This formula is

$$SS_{total} = \sum_i \sum_k (x_{ik} - \bar{X}_{grand})^2 \qquad \text{(Formula 10-2)}$$

where i refers to the individual x score and k refers to the group. This formula says that the total sum of squares is obtained by subtracting the grand mean from each score ignoring group membership, squaring that difference, and then summing over all scores (the summation signs $\sum_i \sum_k$ instruct us to start with the first i score in the first of k groups and to continue until we have done the last i score in the last of k groups). Note that this total sum of squares looks a lot like the numerator of an estimate of the variance that we see in equation 10-1; it's a squared difference of some score from the mean.

We are now going to take our within-group variability and with it derive an estimate of the squared difference of each score in a group from the mean of that group. This squared difference of each score from the mean of the group is called the **within-group sum of squares**, or (SS_{within}):

$$SS_{within} = \sum_i \sum_k (x_{ik} - \bar{X}_k)^2 \qquad \text{(Formula 10-3)}$$

In words, this formula tells us to start with the first group ($k = 1$) and take the first person in this group ($i = 1$), subtract the group mean from this xi score, square this difference, repeat this for each person in the first group, and then sum the squared differences.

Total sum of squares: Measures the total variability in the sample for an ANOVA.

Within-group sum of squares: Measures the variability within a group for an ANOVA.

Then, go to the first person in the second group ($k = 2$) and do the same thing for each person in this group. Continue until you have squared the difference between the score for the last person in the last group and that group mean. Note that this within-group sum of squares also looks a lot like the numerator of an estimate of the variance in equation 10-1. Like the total sum of squares, it too is a squared difference of the mean from some score.

Finally, we are going to take our measure of the variability between groups and derive an estimate of the squared difference of each group mean from the grand mean. This squared difference of each group mean from the grand mean is called the **between-groups sum of squares**, or (SS_{between}):

$$SS_{\text{between}} = \sum_i \sum_k (\bar{x}_k - \bar{X}_{\text{grand}})^2 \qquad \text{(Formula 10-4)}$$

In words, this formula tells us to take the first group mean and subtract the grand mean from that and square the difference, then do the same for each of the i persons in that group and sum over the number of cases in that group. After that, do the same thing for each of the other k groups and sum over groups. Note that this between-groups sum of squares also looks a lot like the numerator of an estimate of the variance in equation 10-1. Like the total and within-group sums of squares, the sum of squares between groups also is a squared difference of the mean from some score. The three sums of squares have this property:

$$SS_{\text{total}} = SS_{\text{within}} + SS_{\text{between}}$$

Accordingly, we only need to calculate two sources of the sum of squares, and the third can be found by subtraction (i.e., $SS_{\text{total}} - SS_{\text{within}} = SS_{\text{between}}$) or addition ($SS_{\text{within}} + SS_{\text{between}} = SS_{\text{total}}$).

We now have three sum of squares measures: total, within-group, and between-groups sums of squares. Each of these sum of squares measures is the numerator of an estimate of a source of variance, total variance, within-group variance, and between-group variance. Looking at equation 10-1, to complete our formulas for each of these three variances, we need to divide each sum of squares by its respective degrees of freedom. Just as there are three different sums of squares, there are three corresponding degrees of freedom:

$$\textbf{Total degrees of freedom} = df_{\text{total}} = n - 1$$

$$\textbf{Within-group degrees of freedom} = df_{\text{within}} = n - k$$

$$\textbf{Between-groups degrees of freedom} = df_{\text{between}} = k - 1$$

where
$n =$ total number of observations
$k =$ number of groups

As with the sum of squares,

$$df_{\text{total}} = df_{\text{within}} + df_{\text{between}}$$

So we have to calculate only two sources of degrees of freedom and then can obtain the third by subtraction or addition.

We now have three different variance estimates:

Between-groups sum of squares:
Measures the variability between groups for an ANOVA.

$$\textbf{Total variance} = \frac{SS_{\text{total}}}{df_{\text{total}}} = \frac{\sum_i \sum_k (x_{ik} - \bar{X}_{\text{grand}})^2}{n - 1} \qquad \text{(Formula 10-5)}$$

$$\text{Within-group variance} = \frac{SS_{\text{within}}}{df_{\text{within}}} = \frac{\sum_i \sum_k (x_{ik} - \overline{X}_k)^2}{n-k}$$

(Formula 10-6)

$$\text{Between-groups variance} = \frac{SS_{\text{between}}}{df_{\text{between}}} = \frac{\sum_i \sum_k (x_k - \overline{X}_{\text{grand}})^2}{k-1}$$

(Formula 10-7)

The F test that is the test statistic for the analysis of variance is simply the ratio of the between-groups variance to the within-group variance:

$$F = \frac{SS_{\text{between}}/df_{\text{between}}}{SS_{\text{within}}/df_{\text{within}}} = \frac{\text{Variance between groups}}{\text{Variance within groups}}$$

(Formula 10-8)

Note that this F *statistic* will become larger as the variance between groups becomes larger relative to the variance within groups. This corresponds to Figure 10.1(a). Large values of the F statistic, then, lead us to reject the null hypothesis of equal population means. What we do not yet know, however, is how large our obtained F must be in order for us to reject the null hypothesis of equal population means. We do know that even if the three population means are the same, our sample means will be different due simply to sample variation or chance. By now, it should be no surprise that we need to conduct a formal hypothesis test to rule out chance.

Like any test statistic we have discussed (e.g., the t, z, or chi-square test), to conduct our hypothesis test, we need to select a level of significance, or alpha level, and then find a critical value of our test statistic from the appropriate probability distribution. In this case, involving a hypothesis test of three or more population means, we know that our test statistic is the analysis of variance F test. The F statistic follows an F *distribution*. Critical values of F can be obtained from Table B.5 in Appendix B. There are two F tables here: one table in which the alpha level is .05 and another for a .01 level of significance. To find the critical value of F at some alpha level, we also need to know two types of degrees of freedom. The between-groups degrees of freedom are found at the top of each of the two tables, forming columns, and the within-group degrees of freedom are found down the left side of the tables, forming rows. To find the correct critical value of F, then, you need to know your alpha level, identify the column corresponding to your between-groups degrees of freedom, and finally identify the correct row corresponding to your within-group degrees of freedom. The value of F found at the convergence of that column and that row is your critical F for a given alpha level. Since the obtained F statistic is based on a *sum of squares* (deviations from some mean, squared), we will have only positive values of F. The F statistic can never be negative. Our decision, then, will always be to reject the null hypothesis when our obtained F is greater than or equal to our critical F.

Since we have all the necessary tools to do an analysis of variance, we should now move on and actually test a hypothesis about equal population means. Let's use data in Table 10.1, which reported the number of new offenses for three groups of offenders who were given different treatments by the police responding to a 911 call for intimate partner assault.

Conducting a Hypothesis Test With ANOVA

In an analysis of variance, the hypothesis test involves the equality of three or more population means. In our example, we want to know whether the mean number of new offenses for the arrested, counseled, and separated populations is equal. The null hypothesis is expressed as $\mu_{\text{arrest}} = \mu_{\text{counsel}} = \mu_{\text{separate}}$. When we fail to reject the null hypothesis, therefore, we are assuming that the population means are equal. This conclusion implies that the different "treatments," or police responses to intimate partner assault, make no difference in terms of the number of new offenses committed—that arrest is no better than counseling or separating offenders in reducing the number of new offenses. The alternative hypothesis in an analysis of variance always states that the population means are simply different from each other (i.e., that they are not equal): $\mu_{\text{arrest}} \neq \mu_{\text{counsel}} \neq \mu_{\text{separate}}$. When we reject the null hypothesis, therefore, we are concluding that at least two of the population means are different. There is no directional alternative hypothesis test in an analysis of variance; the alternative hypothesis is always that the population means are not equal. When we reject the null hypothesis, the only thing we know for sure is that at least one population mean is significantly different from at least one other population mean. We do not know from the analysis of variance test which specific population means are different from each other. This will require an additional step, which we will get to later in the chapter. Let's now do our hypothesis test with the data on police response to domestic violence. As always, we do it in a series of five steps.

Step 1:

$H_0: \mu_{arrest} = \mu_{counsel} = \mu_{separate}$. In other words, the different police responses to intimate partner assault have no effect on the number of new offenses.

$H_1: \mu_{arrest} \neq \mu_{counsel} \neq \mu_{separate}$. The alternative or research hypothesis states that the type of response the police make to a call for an intimate partner assault does make a difference in the number of new offenses.

Step 2: Since we are testing a hypothesis about the equality of more than two population means, we recognize this as an analysis of variance test. Our test statistic is the F test, and we use the F probability distribution.

Step 3: For this problem, we are going to select an alpha level of .05. To find our critical value of F, we need to determine our two degrees of freedom: within group and between groups.

The within-group degrees of freedom is equal to $n - k$ where n is the total number of observations and k is the number of groups. In our problem, $n = 15$ and $k = 3$, so the within-group degrees of freedom is equal to $15 - 3 = 12$. The between-groups degrees of freedom is equal to $k - 1$. With three groups, the between-groups degrees of freedom for this problem is equal to $3 - 1 = 2$. We can now go to the appropriate F table with an alpha of .05, 12 within-group degrees of freedom, and 2 between-groups degrees of freedom. We use the 2 between-groups degrees of freedom in Table B.5 to find the correct column, and we use the 12 within-group degrees of freedom to find the correct row. We can see that with an alpha of .05, and 2 and 12 degrees of freedom, the critical value of F is 3.88. The critical region consists of all values of F equal to or greater than 3.88, and our decision rule is to reject the null hypothesis when $F_{obt} \geq 3.88$.

Step 4: We now need to calculate our obtained value of F. To do this, we need to calculate our three sources of variance. We will do this in a series of steps as well. Our first step will be to find the three sums of squares. We show all the calculations in Table 10.2. We provide the calculations to obtain all three sums of squares, but recall that we could have calculated only two and obtained the third by subtraction or addition.

For example, we could have calculated the total and within-group sums of squares and then subtracted these two to get the between-groups sum of squares:

$$SS_{total} - SS_{Within} = SS_{between}$$
$$170 - 10 = 160$$

Or we could have calculated the between-groups and within-group sums of squares and obtained the total sum of squares by addition:

$$SS_{between} + SS_{Within} = SS_{total}$$
$$10 + 160 = 170$$

We recommend that you calculate all three sources of sum of squares until you are completely comfortable with doing an analysis of variance.

Now that we have our sum of squares from Table 10.2, we need to determine the degrees of freedom:

$df_{within} = n - k = 15 - 3 = 12$ within-group degrees of freedom

$df_{between} = k - 1 = 3 - 1 = 2$ between-groups degrees of freedom

$df_{total} = n - 1 = 15 - 1 = 14$ total degrees of freedom

Table 10.2 **Calculations of Sums of Squares for Analysis of Variance Test**

Total Sum of Squares			
$(X_i - \bar{X}_{grand})$	$(X_i - \bar{X}_{grand})^2$	$(4 - 5) = -1$	1
		$(6 - 5) = 1$	1
$(0 - 5) = -5$	25	$(5 - 5) = 0$	0
$(2 - 5) = -3$	9	$(8 - 9) = -1$	1
$(1 - 5) = -4$	16	$(10 - 9) = 1$	1
$(1 - 5) = -4$	16	$(9 - 9) = 0$	0
$(1 - 5) = -4$	16	$(10 - 9) = 1$	1
$(6 - 5) = 1$	1	$(8 - 9) = -1$	1
$(4 - 5) = -1$	1		$\Sigma = 10$

Between-Groups Sum of Squares	
$(\bar{X}_k - \bar{X}_{grand})$	$(\bar{X}_k - \bar{X}_{grand})^2$

Total Sum of Squares continued:

$(X_i - \bar{X}_{grand})$	$(X_i - \bar{X}_{grand})^2$
$(4 - 5) = -1$	1
$(6 - 5) = 1$	1
$(5 - 5) = 0$	0
$(8 - 5) = 3$	9
$(10 - 5) = 5$	25
$(9 - 5) = 4$	16
$(10 - 5) = 5$	25
$(8 - 5) = 3$	9
	$\Sigma = 170$

Within-Group Sum of Squares	
$(X_i - \bar{X}_k)$	$(X_i - \bar{X}_k)^2$
$(0 - 1) = -1$	1
$(2 - 1) = -1$	1
$(1 - 1) = 0$	0
$(1 - 1) = 0$	0
$(1 - 1) = 0$	0
$(6 - 5) = 1$	1
$(4 - 5) = -1$	1

Between-Groups Sum of Squares	
$(\bar{X}_k - \bar{X}_{grand})$	$(\bar{X}_k - \bar{X}_{grand})^2$
$(1 - 5) = -4$	16
$(1 - 5) = -4$	16
$(1 - 5) = -4$	16
$(1 - 5) = -4$	16
$(1 - 5) = -4$	16
$(5 - 5) = 0$	0
$(5 - 5) = 0$	0
$(5 - 5) = 0$	0
$(5 - 5) = 0$	0
$(5 - 5) = 0$	0
$(9 - 5) = 4$	16
$(9 - 5) = 4$	16
$(9 - 5) = 4$	16
$(9 - 5) = 4$	16
$(9 - 5) = 4$	16
	$\Sigma = 160$

We can verify that these are correct because the sum of the within-group and between-groups degrees of freedom should equal the total degrees of freedom, and the total degrees of freedom is equal to 1 less than the total number of observations.

Now we are ready to calculate the estimates of our within-group variance and between-groups variance that go into the F statistic. Recall that the estimate of each source of variance is obtained by dividing the sum of squares by its respective degrees of freedom. We will put this information into what is frequently called an F test summary table. This summary table shows the sum of squares, the degrees of freedom, the estimated variance, and the obtained F statistic. For our example, we provide this F table in Table 10.3. The value of the F statistic reported in Table 10.3 is obtained by taking the ratio of the between-groups variance to the within-group variance ($80 / .83 = 96.39$).

Table 10.3 — Summary F Table for Police Response to Domestic Violence Data

Source	Sum of Squares	df	Variance	F
Between groups	160	2	80.00	96.39
Within group	10	12	0.83	
Total	170	14		

Step 5: Since $F_{obt} > F_{crit}$ (96.39 > 3.88), our obtained F statistic falls into the critical region, so our decision is to reject the null hypothesis in favor of the alternative. We would conclude, then, that $\mu_{arrest} \neq \mu_{counsel} \neq \mu_{separate}$. We are saying two things in making this conclusion. First, we are saying that the independent variable, type of police response to intimate partner assault, is related to the number of new domestic violence acts an offender subsequently commits. However, the only thing we can conclude is that at least one population mean is significantly different from one other population mean. In other words, we know that the three populations of arrested, counseled, and separated suspects have different means, but we do not know which specific population means are different from which others. We could be rejecting the null hypothesis because $\mu_{arrest} \neq \mu_{counsel} \neq \mu_{separate}$, because $\mu_{arrest} \neq \mu_{counsel}$, because $\mu_{arrest} \neq \mu_{separate}$, or because $\mu_{counsel} \neq \mu_{separate}$. We simply don't know, on the basis of our F test, which of these is true or if all are true. Since we rejected the null hypothesis, however, we know that at least one of these inequalities is true. To decide which particular population means are different, we have to do some more calculations.

After the F Test: Testing the Difference Between Pairs of Means

Tukey's Honest Significant Difference Test

Once we have rejected the null hypothesis in an analysis of variance, our attention next turns to the question: "Which means are significantly different from which other means?" We will answer this question by conducting a statistical test about the difference between two population means. There are several different statistical tests in the literature that can do this, each one appropriate under different situations. For our purposes here, we will learn one of the most frequently used tests, **Tukey's honest significant difference (HSD) test**. Tukey's HSD test requires that we calculate something called the **critical difference (CD) score**:

$$CD = q\sqrt{\frac{\text{Within-group variance}}{n_k}}$$

(Formula 10-9)

where
n_k = the number of cases in each of the k groups
q = the studentized range statistic

Notice that the numerator requires equal sample sizes for the HSD test. When sample sizes are not equal, there are other tests to use. Values of the studentized range statistic can be found in Table B.6 in Appendix B. You need three pieces of information to find the correct value of q to use in equation 10-9: your selected alpha level (α), your degrees of freedom within groups (df_{within}), and the number of groups you have (k). What the critical difference gives us is the minimum absolute value of the difference between two sample means that would lead us to reject the null hypothesis of their equality. Now this last sentence, although accurate, is entirely too confusing to be helpful. We can best explain things by going through an example using the HSD test.

Tukey's honest significant difference (HSD) test: Tests the difference between a series of group mean combinations after the null hypothesis from an ANOVA has been rejected.

Critical difference (CD) score: Calculated by Tukey's honest significant difference test to determine the significant difference between a series of group mean combinations after the null hypothesis from an ANOVA has been rejected.

In our analysis of variance in the last section, we rejected the null hypothesis that $\mu_{arrest} = \mu_{counsel} = \mu_{separate}$ in favor of the alternative hypothesis that $\mu_{arrest} \neq \mu_{counsel} \neq \mu_{separate}$. We now want to know which of these three population means is significantly different from which others. To find out, we will use our sample means and conduct a Tukey's HSD test of *each pair* of sample means. That is, we will examine the difference between our sample means to make an inference about the equality of the unknown population means. Unlike a series of independent-samples *t* tests, however, Tukey's HSD will give us an honest level of significance or alpha for each of our sample mean comparisons (that's why it's called Tukey's *honest* significant difference test).

First, we will list our null and alternative hypotheses for each population mean comparison (notice that these three hypotheses constitute all possible two-mean comparisons):

$H_0: \mu_{arrest} = \mu_{counsel}$

$H_1: \mu_{arrest} \neq \mu_{counsel}$

$H_0: \mu_{arrest} = \mu_{separate}$

$H_1: \mu_{arrest} \neq \mu_{separate}$

$H_0: \mu_{counsel} = \mu_{separate}$

$H_1: \mu_{counsel} \neq \mu_{separate}$

Second, we will calculate the value of the critical difference using equation 10-9. In Tukey's HSD test, we use the same level of significance we employed in the analysis of variance *F* test ($a = .05$ in the preceding example). To calculate CD, we need to get the value of q, or the studentized range statistic, and to obtain this, we need to go to Table B.6 in Appendix B with our alpha level (.05), the within-group degrees of freedom ($df_{within} = 12$), and the number of groups ($k = 3$). With this information, we can see that the value of q is equal to 3.77. We can now put this value into equation 10-9 for the CD with the other values (the within-group variance and the number of people in each group):

$$CD = 3.77 \sqrt{\frac{.83}{5}}$$
$$CD = 1.54$$

We have a critical difference score of 1.54. This means that the absolute value of the difference between any two sample means that we test must be greater than or equal to 1.54 for us to reject the null hypothesis of equal population means. Keep in mind that we need to compare the CD score with the *absolute value* of the difference between two sample means.

With our critical difference score of 1.54, let's calculate the absolute value of the difference between each of the three pairs of sample means. First, let's calculate the difference in the mean number of new offenses between the arrested group and the counseled group:

$$
\begin{array}{r}
1 \\
-5 \\
\hline
|4|
\end{array}
$$

Since the absolute value of the difference between these two sample means is greater than the critical difference score of 1.54, we can conclude that the two population means are significantly different from each other. We will decide, therefore, that $\mu_{arrest} \neq \mu_{counsel}$ and that the population of offenders who are arrested for domestic violence have significantly fewer new offenses on average than those who are counseled. Second, let's calculate the absolute value of the difference in the mean number of new offenses between the arrested group and the separated group:

$$
\begin{array}{r}
1 \\
-9 \\
\hline
|8|
\end{array}
$$

Since the absolute value of the difference between these two sample means is greater than our critical difference score of 1.54, we will conclude that these two population means are also significantly different from each other. We will decide that $\mu_{arrest} \neq \mu_{separate}$ and that domestic violence offenders who are arrested have significantly fewer new offenses on average than those who are separated from their partners. Finally, let's calculate the absolute value of the difference between the mean number of new offenses for the counseled group and the separated group:

$$
\begin{array}{r}
5 \\
-9 \\
\hline
|4|
\end{array}
$$

Since the absolute value of the difference between these two sample means is greater than the critical difference score of 1.54, we will conclude that the population mean number of new offenses is significantly different for those offenders who are counseled and those who are separated from their partners. It seems that counseling offenders of domestic violence is more effective in reducing the number of new offenses than merely separating the couple.

In sum, the analysis of variance test and the series of Tukey's honest significant difference tests tell us that how the police respond to an incident of domestic violence does make a difference. At least in terms of reducing the number of new offenses committed by the same offender is concerned, arrest leads to the fewest new offenses on average, counseling leads to significantly more new offenses than arrest but to significantly fewer offenses than just separating the couple, and a police response of separating the pair is the least effective in curbing future acts of intimate partner assault. In this particular example, all three sample means were significantly different from each other, but remember that this will not always be the case and you will have to interpret your results accordingly.

▣ A Measure of Association Test With ANOVA

In the previous sections, we conducted the F test of an analysis of variance and Tukey's HSD test to assess the relationship between the type of police response to domestic violence and the number of new offenses committed by an offender. When we rejected the null hypothesis in the analysis of variance, we concluded that there was a relationship between the type of response the police make to domestic violence and the number of new offenses subsequently committed. What neither the F test nor the Tukey's HSD test told us, however, was the *strength* of the relationship between our independent and dependent variables. As we have learned in previous chapters, concluding that there is a relationship between two variables in the population, which is what a hypothesis test does, gives no clue as to the magnitude or strength of the relationship between them. To assess the strength of a relationship between two variables, we must use an appropriate measure of association.

Recall that in the analysis of variance, we calculated three different sums of squares: total, between-groups, and within-group sum of squares. The total sum of squares measures the total amount of variability that exists among the scores. The between-groups variability measures the amount of variability due to group membership. This variability reflects the extent to which the groups differ from each other on the dependent variable, and it captures a "treatment effect." If there is a substantial amount of this variability, then it would seem that the group membership matters, at least as far as the dependent variable is concerned. Finally, the within-group variability measures the amount of variability that is unaccounted for by group membership. Since everyone within a group shares the same group membership, these persons cannot differ because of different group effects. In fact, since they have the same level of the independent variable, we do not know exactly why the scores within a group are different, so this variability is unexplained or unaccounted for (it's just "noise" or error). With this in mind, think of the total sum of squares as consisting of total variability, the between-groups sum of squares as consisting of explained variability (variability explained by membership in the group), and the within-group sum of squares as consisting of unexplained variability.

Recall also that the sum of the between-groups and within-group sums of squares is equal to the total sum of squares. The total variability in the scores, or the total sum of squares, then, is equal to two components: an explained component (the between-groups sum of squares) and an unexplained component (the within-group sum of squares). If we take the ratio of the between-groups sum of squares to the total sum of squares, then, we have a ratio of explained variability to total variability, and from this we get an estimate of the proportion of the total variability that is explained. The greater the amount of the total variability that is explained or due to variation in the independent variable, the stronger the relationship there is between it and the dependent variable. Fortunately, we have a way to quantify this that we explain next.

Eta Squared (Correlation Ratio)

This discussion of explained, unexplained, and total variability is the conceptual basis behind one measure of association with ANOVA called **eta-squared** or the **correlation ratio**:

$$\eta^2 = \frac{SS_{between}}{SS_{total}}$$

(Formula 10-10)

Eta squared measures the strength of the relationship between an independent variable and a dependent variable in an analysis of variance. More specifically, it measures the amount of variance in the dependent variable that is explained by the independent variable. Eta squared can range from 0, indicating no relationship between the independent and dependent variables, to 1.0, indicating a perfect relationship between the two variables. A perfect relationship means that all of the variability (you are explaining all of variance in the dependent variable with the independent variable) among the scores of the dependent variable is due to differences in group membership on the independent variable, and there is no within-group variability. What we are saying here is that all our variability is due to treatment, and nothing is due to noise or error. A zero relationship means that none of the variability (you are explaining none of variance in the dependent variable with the independent variable) among the scores is due to differences in group membership, and everything is due to within-group variability (noise or error). In between these values, we can follow our old rule of thumb about measures of association and state that values of eta squared between 0 and .29 can be interpreted as a "weak" relationship, values between .30 and .59 indicate a "moderate" relationship, and values greater than .60 reflect a "strong" relationship. More specifically, we can multiply the obtained value of eta squared we get by 100 to estimate the percentage of the variance in the dependent variable that is explained by the independent variable.

Let's use our data on police response to intimate partner assault as an example and calculate the value of eta squared:

$$\eta^2 = \frac{160}{170}$$
$$\eta^2 = .94$$

We have a very strong relationship between type of police response and the number of subsequent offenses. Multiplying eta squared by 100 tells us that 94% of the variability in the number of offenses committed is due to differences in police response.

Eta squared: Describes the ratio of variance explained in the dependent variable by an independent variable.

🔲 A Second ANOVA Example: Caseload Size and Success on Probation

In our second example, we are interested in the relationship between the number of cases that a probation officer has to supervise and how successful probation is in terms of the number of probation infractions or new offenses committed by a probationer. There has been some controversy in the criminal justice literature about this issue. Some studies have found that smaller caseload sizes for probation officers are more effective in reducing new offenses or probation violations, whereas other studies have indicated that the number of cases a probation officer has to supervise has no effect on success. This is an important issue because we would like to reduce the number of probation violations, but reducing probation supervision size costs money. To examine the relationship between the caseload size a probation officer has and success on probation, we take a sample of women who were convicted by a court and sentenced to 4 years of probation each. Of these women, 10 were randomly assigned to probation officers who had "low" caseloads (fewer than 25 cases to supervise), 10 were randomly assigned to probation officers who had "moderate" caseloads (between 25 and 50 cases), and 10 were randomly assigned to probation officers who had "heavy" caseloads (more than 50 cases). For each of these women, we identify the number of probation infractions or new crimes they committed while they were on probation over the 4-year period. The data are shown in Table 10.4.

We want to test the null hypothesis that $\mu_{low} = \mu_{moderate} = \mu_{heavy}$ against the alternative hypothesis that $\mu_{low} \neq \mu_{moderate} \neq \mu_{heavy}$. We will use an alpha of .01 for this hypothesis test, and all of the steps are shown as follows.

Table 10.4 Size of Probation Officer Caseload and Number of Crimes and Violations Committed on Release

Caseload Supervision Size		
Low	Moderate	Heavy
7	10	11
12	14	8
13	8	7
5	7	10
8	9	9
11	11	9
10	13	7
14	12	8
9	8	3
6	8	3
$\bar{X}_{low} = 9.5$	$\bar{X}_{moderate} = 10.0$	$\bar{X}_{heavy} = 7.5$

Step 1:

$H_0: \mu_{low} = \mu_{moderate} = \mu_{heavy}$

$H_1: \mu_{low} \neq \mu_{moderate} \neq \mu_{heavy}$

Step 2: This is a problem involving the equality of three population means, so the correct statistical test is the F test of an analysis of variance. The F test has an F probability distribution.

Step 3: We will use an alpha of .01. Our within-group degrees of freedom $(n - k)$ is equal to 27 (30 total subjects and 3 groups), and our between-groups degrees of freedom $(k - 1)$ is equal to 2. With 2 and 27 degrees of freedom, our critical value of F with $\alpha = .01$ is 5.49, and the critical region comprises all F values greater than or equal to 5.49. Our decision rule is to reject the null hypothesis if $F_{obt} \geq 5.49$.

Step 4: The calculations for the total, between-groups, and within-group sums of squares are shown in Table 10.5. With the sum of squares and degrees of freedom, we can then calculate the between-groups and within-group variance and the F statistic. The analysis of variance summary table is shown in Table 10.6.

Table 10.5 Calculations for Caseload Size and Probation Success

Total Sum of Squares		Within-Group Sum of Squares		Between-Groups Sum of Squares	
$(X_i - \bar{X}_{grand})$	$(X_i - \bar{X}_{grand})^2$	$(X_i - \bar{X}_k)$	$(X_i - \bar{X}_k)^2$	$(\bar{X}_k - \bar{X}_{grand})$	$(\bar{X}_k - \bar{X}_{grand})^2$
7 − 9 = −2	4	7 − 9.5 = −2.5	6.25	9.5 − 9 = 0.5	0.25
12 − 9 = 3	9	12 − 9.5 = 2.5	6.25	9.5 − 9 = 0.5	0.25
13 − 9 = 4	16	13 − 9.5 = 3.5	12.25	9.5 − 9 = 0.5	0.25
5 − 9 = −4	16	5 − 9.5 = −4.5	20.25	9.5 − 9 = 0.5	0.25
8 − 9 = −1	1	8 − 9.5 = −1.5	2.25	9.5 − 9 = 0.5	0.25
11 − 9 = 2	4	11 − 9.5 = 1.5	2.25	9.5 − 9 = 0.5	0.25
10 − 9 = 1	1	10 − 9.5 = 0.5	0.25	9.5 − 9 = 0.5	0.25
14 − 9 = 5	25	14 − 9.5 = 4.5	20.25	9.5 − 9 = 0.5	0.25
9 − 9 = 0	0	9 − 9.5 = −0.5	0.25	9.5 − 9 = 0.5	0.25
6 − 9 = −3	9	6 − 9.5 = −3.5	12.25	9.5 − 9 = 0.5	0.25
10 − 9 = 1	1	10 − 10 = 0	0.00	10 − 9 = 1	1.00
14 − 9 = 5	25	14 − 10 = 4	16.00	10 − 9 = 1	1.00
8 − 9 = −1	1	8 − 10 = −2	4.00	10 − 9 = 1	1.00
7 − 9 = −2	4	7 − 10 = −3	9.00	10 − 9 = 1	1.00
9 − 9 = 0	0	9 − 10 = −1	1.00	10 − 9 = 1	1.00
11 − 9 = 2	4	11 − 10 = 1	1.00	10 − 9 = 1	1.00
13 − 9 = 4	16	13 − 10 = 3	9.00	10 − 9 = 1	1.00
12 − 9 = 3	9	12 − 10 = 2	4.00	10 − 9 = 1	1.00
8 − 9 = −1	1	8 − 10 = −2	4.00	10 − 9 = 1	1.00
8 − 9 = −1	1	8 − 10 = −2	4.00	10 − 9 = 1	1.00
11 − 9 = 2	4	11 − 7.5 = 3.5	12.25	7.5 − 9 = −1.5	2.25
8 − 9 = −1	1	8 − 7.5 = 0.5	0.25	7.5 − 9 = −1.5	2.25
7 − 9 = −2	4	7 − 7.5 = −0.5	0.25	7.5 − 9 = −1.5	2.25
10 − 9 = 1	1	10 − 7.5 = 2.5	6.25	7.5 − 9 = −1.5	2.25
9 − 9 = 0	0	9 − 7.5 = 1.5	2.25	7.5 − 9 = −1.5	2.25
9 − 9 = 0	0	9 − 7.5 = 1.5	2.25	7.5 − 9 = −1.5	2.25
7 − 9 = −2	4	7 − 7.5 = −0.5	0.25	7.5 − 9 = −1.5	2.25
8 − 9 = −1	1	8 − 7.5 = 0.5	0.25	7.5 − 9 = −1.5	2.25
3 − 9 = −6	36	3 − 7.5 = −4.5	20.25	7.5 − 9 = −1.5	2.25
3 − 9 = −6	36	3 − 7.5 = −4.5	20.25	7.5 − 9 = −1.5	2.25
	Σ = 234		Σ = 199		Σ = 35

Table 10.6	Summary *F* Table for the Relationship Between Caseload Size and Success on Probation			
Source	Sum of Squares	df	Variance	F
Between groups	35	2	17.50	2.374
Within group	199	27	7.37	
Total	234	29		

Step 5: We have an obtained *F* value of 2.374. Since this is less than our critical *F* value of 5.49, our decision is to fail to reject the null hypothesis. We will conclude that $\mu_{low} = \mu_{moderate} = \mu_{heavy}$ and that the intensity of the probation officer's caseload has no effect on the success of her or his clients. Since we failed to reject the null hypothesis, we do not need to examine our individual pairs of sample means with Tukey's HSD. The HSD test is appropriate only after we reject the null hypothesis in an analysis of variance. We can, however, calculate eta squared:

$$\eta^2 = \frac{35}{234}$$

$$\eta^2 = .15$$

A magnitude of .15 is small; caseload size is able to explain only 15% of the variance in success on probation, strengthening our conclusion that caseload size is not related to success on probation.

🔲 Summary

In this chapter, we studied the analysis of variance. Although this statistical technique is called an analysis of *variance*, it is used to test a hypothesis about the equality of three or more population *means*. In an analysis of variance, we have an independent variable that is measured at the nominal or ordinal level and has three or more values, or levels, and a continuous (interval/ratio) dependent variable. The test statistic is the *F* statistic and is the ratio of the variability that exists between groups to the variability that exists within groups. The variability between groups reflects differences due to "treatment" or the independent variable, whereas variability within groups reflects noise or error. A high *F* statistic means that there is more between-groups variance than within-group variance, a finding that would lead us to reject the null hypothesis of equal population means.

When we reject the null hypothesis in an analysis of variance, we conclude that some of the population means are not equal, although we do not know which specific ones are different on the basis of the *F* test alone. To identify which population means are significantly different, we use Tukey's HSD test. Finally, we learned about a measure of association in an analysis of variance, eta squared. Eta squared measures the amount of variability in the dependent variable that is explained by the independent variable. The larger the magnitude of eta squared, the stronger the relationship between the independent and dependent variables.

Key Terms

▶ Review key terms with eFlashcards. Visit study.sagepub.com/paternoster.

analysis of variance (ANOVA)   257
between-groups sum of squares   262
critical difference (CD) score   266
eta squared   269

total sum of squares   261
Tukey's honest significant difference (HSD) test   266
within-group sum of squares   261

Key Formulas

Variance of a sample (formula 10-1):

$$s^2 = \frac{\Sigma(x - \bar{X})^2}{n-1}$$

Total sum of squares (SS_{total}) (formula 10-2):

$$SS_{total} = \sum_i \sum_k (x_{ik} - \bar{X}_{grand})^2$$

Within-group sum of squares (SS_{within}) (formula 10-3):

$$SS_{within} = \sum_i \sum_k (x_{ik} - \bar{X}_k)^2$$

Between-groups sum of squares ($SS_{between}$) (formula 10-4):

$$SS_{between} = \sum_i \sum_k (\bar{X}_k - \bar{X}_{grand})^2$$

Formulas to estimate the three types of variance (formulas 10-5 through 10-7):

$$\text{Total variance:} \frac{SS_{total}}{df_{total}} = \frac{\sum_i \sum_k (x_{ik} - \bar{X}_{grand})^2}{n-1}$$

$$\text{Within-group variance:} \frac{SS_{within}}{df_{within}} = \frac{\sum_i \sum_k (x_{ik} - \bar{X}_k)^2}{n-k}$$

Between-groups variance : $\dfrac{SS_{between}}{df_{between}} = \dfrac{\sum_i \sum_k (\bar{X}_k - \bar{X}_{grand})^2}{k-1}$

Formula for calculating F (formula 10-8):

$$F : \frac{SS_{between}/df_{between}}{SS_{within}/df_{within}} = \frac{\text{Variance between groups}}{\text{Variance within group}}$$

Turkey's honest significant difference (HSD) test: Critical difference score (formula 10-9):

$$CD = q\sqrt{\frac{\text{Within-group variance}}{n_k}}$$

Eta squared or the correlation ratio (formula 10-10):

$$\eta^2 = \frac{SS_{between}}{SS_{total}}$$

Practice Problems

> Test your understanding of chapter content.
> Take the practice quiz at study.sagepub.com/paternoster.

1. When is it appropriate to perform an analysis of variance with our data? What type of variables do we need?

2. What statistical technique should we use if we have a continuous dependent variable and a categorical independent variable with only two categories?

3. Why do we call this statistical technique an analysis of *variance* when we are really interested in the difference among population *means*?

4. What two types of variance do we use to calculate the F ratio?

5. How do we determine the df_{total}, $df_{between}$, and df_{within}?

6. Meagan Tucker and Christina Rodriguez (2014) published an article in which they argued that stress contributes directly to increased risks of physical child maltreatment. Let's say you want to test this hypothesis. You have a random sample of 30 women with young children living at home. Based on questions about their home life and possible sources of stress, you are able to place them into one of three groups: "high stress," "medium stress," or "low stress." You then ask the women individually how many times they have physically punished their children during the past month. You think that stress might be related to the use of physical punishment. The following are the data from your sample:

Number of Times Physical Punishment Used Last Month

Level of Stress		
High	Medium	Low
x	x	x
4	2	3
6	4	1
12	5	2
10	3	0
5	0	2
9	3	2
8	2	4
11	5	1
10	5	0
8	4	1

With these data, do the following:

a. Identify the independent and dependent variables.

b. Calculate the total, between-groups, and within-group sums of squares.

c. Determine the correct number of degrees of freedom, calculate the ratio of sum of squares to degrees of freedom, and determine the F ratio.

d. With an alpha of .05, test the null hypothesis that the three population means are equal against the alternative hypothesis that some of them are different.

e. If appropriate, conduct a mean comparison for each pair of means using Tukey's HSD test.

f. Calculate the value of eta squared and make a conclusion about the strength of the relationship between a mother's stress level and the frequency with which she punishes her child.

7. One of the most pressing social problems is the problem of drunk driving. Drunk driving causes untold human suffering and has profound economic effects. States have tried various things to inhibit drunk driving. Some states have tried to cut down on drunk driving within their borders by "getting tough" with drunk drivers. One way to do this is to suspend their driver's licenses and impose heavy fines, as well as jail and prison sentences, on those convicted of drunk driving. Other states have tried a "moral appeal" by mounting public relations campaigns

that proclaim the harm and injury produced by drunk driving. You want to determine the effectiveness of these strategies. You calculate the rate of drunk driving per 100,000 residents for each of the 50 states, and you classify each state into one of three categories: a "get tough" state, a "moral appeal" state, or a "control" state. The latter states do nothing special to those who get caught drinking and driving. Your summary data look like the following:

Get Tough States	Moral Appeal States	Control States
$n_1 = 15$	$n_2 = 15$	$n_3 = 15$
$\bar{X}_1 = 125.2$	$\bar{X}_2 = 119.7$	$\bar{X}_3 = 145.3$

Part of the summary F table looks like this:

	Sum of Squares	df	SS/df	F
Between groups	475.3			
Within group	204.5			
Total	679.8			

With these summary data, do the following:

a. Identify the independent and dependent variables.

b. Determine the correct number of degrees of freedom, calculate the ratio of sum of squares to degrees of freedom, and determine the F ratio.

c. With an alpha of .01, test the null hypothesis that the three population means are equal against the alternative hypothesis that some of them are different.

d. If appropriate, conduct a mean comparison for each pair of means using Tukey's HSD test.

e. Calculate the value of eta squared and make a conclusion about the strength of the relationship between sanction policy and the rate of drunk driving.

8. In a 2014 article, Nancy Steinmetz and Mark Austin suggested that there are areas of a college campus that might be characterized as evoking a greater fear of crime. These "fear spots" are defined geographical areas where people feel vulnerable to criminal victimization. As a research project, you want to find out why particular areas are feared more than others. You think it is because people's perceptions of their risk of criminal victimization are strongly related to their actual risks of being the victim of a crime. Let's say that you identified five geographical areas in your city that vary in terms of how much fear people felt when going into those areas ("high fear" spot

to "very low fear" spot). You then went into each of those areas and asked a random sample of 50 people how many times they had been the victim of a crime during the last 5 years. You found the following mean numbers of victimizations for these areas:

	Very High Fear Spot	High Fear Spot	Medium Fear Spot	Low Fear Spot	Very Low Fear Spot
Mean	14.5	14.3	14.7	13.4	13.9
n	50	50	50	50	50

Part of your summary F table looks like this:

	Sum of Squares	df	SS/df	F
Between groups	12.5			
Within group	616.2			
Total	628.7			

With these summary data, do the following:

a. Identify the independent and dependent variables.

b. Determine the correct number of degrees of freedom, calculate the ratio of sum of squares to degrees of freedom, and determine the F ratio.

c. With an alpha of .05, test the null hypothesis that the four population means are equal against the alternative hypothesis that some of them are different.

d. If appropriate, conduct a mean comparison for all pairs of means using Tukey's HSD test.

e. Calculate the value of eta squared and make a conclusion about the strength of the relationship between fear spot and number of actual criminal victimizations.

9. In their study of the influence of delinquent peers, Constance Chapple, Jamie Vaske, and Meredith Worthen (2014) suggested that females who have more friends are at greater risk for receiving delinquent peer pressure. To test their notion, you take a random sample of girls and classify them into one of three groups: those who "have a lot of friends," those who "have some friends," and those who "have a few friends." You then ask each girl to self-report the number of delinquent offenses her friends had encouraged her to do. The following table shows the number of delinquent acts encouraged by friends for each female:

Number of Delinquent Acts Committed

How Many Friends Each Female Has		
A Lot	Some	A Few
5	7	2
8	5	3
9	4	0
4	9	3
7	6	1
10	4	3
6	7	2

With these data, do the following:

a. Identify the independent and dependent variables.

b. Calculate the total, between-groups, and within-group sums of squares.

c. Determine the correct number of degrees of freedom, calculate the ratio of sum of squares to degrees of freedom, and determine the F ratio.

d. With an alpha of .05, test the null hypothesis that the three population means are equal against the alternative hypothesis that some of them are different.

e. If appropriate, conduct a mean comparison for each pair of means using Tukey's HSD test.

f. Calculate the value of eta squared and make a conclusion about the strength of the relationship between the number of friends a girl has and the number of crimes she is encouraged to do by her peers.

STUDENT STUDY SITE

WANT A BETTER GRADE?

Get the tools you need to sharpen your study skills. Access practice quizzes, eFlashcards, data sets, and SPSS exercises at **study.sagepub.com/paternoster.**

CHAPTER 11

Bivariate Correlation and Ordinary Least-Squares Regression

> *One of the first things taught in introductory statistics textbooks is that correlation is not causation. It is also one of the first things forgotten.*
>
> —Thomas Sowell

LEARNING OBJECTIVES

1. Describe the difference between a positive relationship and a negative relationship between two continuous (interval/ratio) level variables.

2. Conduct and interpret a scatterplot between two continuous (interval/ratio) level variables.

3. Calculate and interpret the correlation coefficient and the coefficient of determination.

4. Describe how the ordinary least-squares (OLS) regression equation is different from the correlation coefficient and why they are both useful.

5. Calculate and interpret the OLS regression equation and interpret the intercept and slope coefficient.

6. Explain how to use the OLS regression equation for prediction.

7. Conduct and interpret null hypothesis tests for both the correlation and slope coefficients.

🔲 Introduction

You have probably heard the adage that "correlation is not causation," but you have probably never known the true meaning of correlation. Although we have discussed several different statistics to test the significance of bivariate relationships already, in this chapter we will introduce you to the correlation coefficient along with its counterpart, the ordinary least-squares (OLS) regression coefficient. When both an independent variable and a dependent variable are measured at the interval/ratio level, the strength of the association or relationship between them is usually referred to as the correlation between two variables. And when we have only one independent variable, the relationship is referred to as a **bivariate correlation**. In this chapter, you first will learn how to construct a scatterplot graphically depicting the relationship between a quantitative independent variable and a quantitative dependent variable. You will then learn about the statistics that quantify this relationship, including the correlation coefficient, the coefficient of determination, and the slope coefficient from an ordinary least-squares regression equation. The measures all assume that the relationship between the independent variable and the dependent variable is linear. Our attention in this chapter will be limited to the bivariate case where we have one independent variable (x) and one dependent variable (y). In Chapter 12, we will examine the multivariate case where we have more than one independent variable.

🔲 Graphing the Bivariate Distribution Between Two Quantitative Variables: Scatterplots

Throughout this book, we have tried to stress the importance and usefulness of displaying data graphically. Let's again remind you that it is no less true in statistics than in real life that "a picture is worth a thousand words." When you are first examining two interval- and ratio-level variables, one of the most instructive things you can do is to draw a picture or graph of what the two variables look like when examined together. In the bivariate case, the graphical display of two interval- and ratio-level variables is called a **scatterplot** or a scattergram. It is called this because the picture looks like points scattered across your graph. The pattern, or scatter, of data points provides valuable information about the relationship (or lack of a relationship) between the variables. Let's begin this discussion with a simple illustration. In the list that follows, we have data on two variables for 10 observations:

Bivariate correlation: Measures the linear relationship between two variables.

Scatterplot: Graphical display of the linear relationship between two interval/ratio-level variables. Also called a scattergram.

Observation	x Score	y Score
1	3	3
2	5	5
3	2	2
4	4	4
5	8	8
6	10	10
7	1	1
8	7	7
9	6	6
10	9	9

Student Study Site

Visit the open-access Student Study Site at **study.sagepub.com/paternoster** to access additional study tools including mobile-friendly eFlashcards, web quizzes, links to SAGE journal articles, additional data sets, SPSS exercises, and more!

We can construct a scatterplot for these data by first drawing a graph with two axes. The first axis of this graph is the horizontal axis (x), or abscissa. The second axis of the graph is formed at a right angle to the first axis and is the vertical axis (y), or ordinate. We will label the horizontal axis the x axis and will display the x variable on that axis. To do this, simply place the original measurement scale for the x variable at equal intervals along the axis. We will label the vertical axis the y axis and will display the y variable along that axis. Again, place the measurement scale for the y variable along the vertical axis.

Once you have done this, you can begin to graph your data points. For each observation, find the position of its x score along the horizontal axis. Then follow in a straight line up from that point until you find the corresponding position of its y score along the vertical axis. Place a dot or point here. For example, for the first observation, go along the x axis until you find "3." Then go straight up from that point until you reach "3" on the y axis. Place a point here. This point represents the position on the graph for the xy score of the first observation, which had a score of 3 on both the x and y variables. Continue to do this for each of the 10 observations, placing a point when you have found the intersection of each x and y score. You can see the collection of data points, called the scatterplot, in Figure 11.1.

What does this scatterplot tell us about the x and y scores? Note that all the scores fall on a straight line that ascends from the bottom left of the scatterplot to the top right. This is because in this case there is a unique relationship between the x and y scores. The y score is always the same as its corresponding x score. That is, if the y score is 4, the corresponding x score is 4, and if the y score is 6, the x score is 6. Therefore, those observations that have high x scores also have high y scores, and those with low x scores also have low y scores. Note also that when the x score increases by 1 unit, the y score also increases by exactly 1 unit. For example, when the x score changes from 4 to 5, the corresponding score for the y variable changes from 4 to 5—an increase of 1 unit. Whenever two variables are related in this manner—when high scores on one variable (x) also have high scores on a second variable (y) and an increase in one score is associated with an increase in the other score—we have a **positive correlation**, or positive relationship, between x and y. As you can clearly see, there is a clear pattern to these data, with increasing x scores corresponding to increasing y scores.

In the list that follows and in Figure 11.2, we have a different set of x and y scores for 10 observations:

Observation	x Score	y Score
1	2	9
2	4	7
3	9	2
4	7	4
5	8	3
6	1	10
7	5	6
8	6	5
9	10	1
10	3	8

Positive correlation: As the independent variable increases, the dependent variable also increases.

Negative correlation: As the independent variable increases, the dependent variable decreases.

In this case, the data points are still on a straight line, but the pattern is different from that in Figure 11.1. In Figure 11.2, the pattern of the points is one that descends from the top left corner to the bottom right. This is because those observations that have high scores on the x variable have *low* scores on the y variable, and those observations with low scores on the x variable have *high* scores on the y variable. Whenever high scores on one variable (x) correspond to low scores on a second variable (y), we have a **negative correlation**, or negative relationship, between x and y. There is, then, a clear pattern to the scatterplot of scores whenever the two variables are negatively correlated—a band or line of descending scores runs from the top left corner of the graph to the bottom right.

Figures 11.1 and 11.2 illustrate that when two variables (x and y) are correlated, their scores vary together or covary; this is termed *covariation* in statistics. As the scores on the x variable change or vary, the scores on the y variable change or vary. How, or the direction in which, they change is a function of the direction of the correlation.

Figure 11.1 Positive Relationship Between x and y

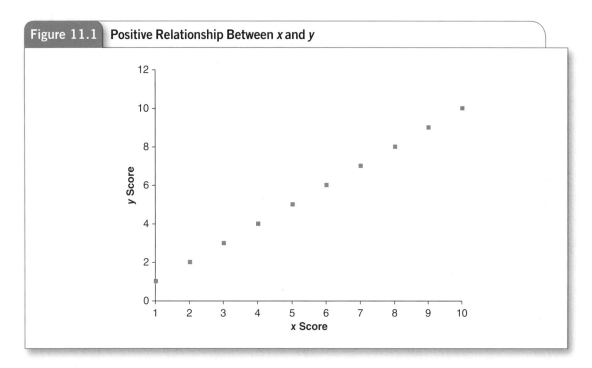

Figure 11.2 Negative Relationship Between x and y

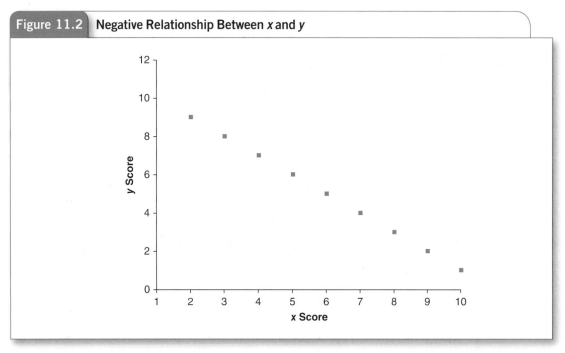

With the positive correlation in Figure 11.1, as the x scores increase, the y scores increase (similarly, as x decreases, y decreases). With the negative correlation in Figure 11.2, as the x scores increase, the y scores decrease (similarly, as x decreases, y increases). In a positive correlation, then, the two variables covary in the same direction (x increases and y increases; x decreases and y decreases). In a negative correlation, the two variables covary in the opposite direction (x increases and y decreases; x decreases and y increases).

In the list that follows, we have a third set of x and y scores for 10 observations:

Observation	x Score	y Score
1	6	4
2	9	4
3	2	4
4	7	4
5	3	4
6	4	4
7	1	4
8	8	4
9	5	4
10	10	4

Figure 11.3 presents the scatterplot of these scores. Note that, unlike the previous two figures, there is no ascending or descending pattern to the scores in this scatterplot. In fact, the scores are perfectly horizontal because for different values of x, the y score is always the same ($y = 4$). In other words, the x variable and the y variable do not covary. As x increases or decreases, the value of y stays the same; there is no relationship between x and y. To state this one more way, variations in x (increases and decreases) do not result in systematic variations in y.

One thing that we can easily learn from a scatterplot, then, is the *direction* of a relationship between two quantitative variables. By the direction of a relationship, we mean whether it is positive or negative. When the scatterplot looks like Figure 11.1, where the pattern of scores resembles an upward slope, we can conclude that the two variables are positively related. In this case, there is positive covariation. When the scatterplot looks like Figure 11.2, where the pattern of scores has a downward slope, we can conclude that the two variables are negatively related. There is negative covariation. And finally, when the scatterplot resembles Figure 11.3, where there is no clear upward or downward slope but rather a flat line, we can presume that the two variables are not correlated with one another.

In addition to the direction of a relationship, what else can we determine by examining the scatterplot of x and y scores? Let's return to the data illustrated in Figure 11.1. Without being too precise, let's draw a straight line that goes through each data point. We show this in Figure 11.4. This figure illustrates that if we were to connect the data points, the straight line would go through each data point in its upward slope. In other words, each point would fall exactly on that straight upward-moving line. Later in this chapter, we will have more to say about how to fit this straight line to our data points. For now, we will simply note that this line is called the linear **regression line**. In the example presented in Figures 11.1 and 11.4, where all the data points fall exactly on a straight upward-sloping line, we say that the two variables have a *perfect positive correlation*—positive because the regression line slopes upward and perfect because all the points fall exactly on the line. Note that we can also draw a straight line through the data points in Figure 11.2, as shown in Figure 11.5. Here again, all the data points lie precisely on the line, but in this case the line slopes downward. This figure illustrates a *perfect negative correlation* between two variables.

A line through the data points in Figure 11.3 is shown in Figure 11.6. Note that this straight line has neither an upward slope nor a downward slope but is instead a flat line

Regression line: Line depicting the relationship between independent and dependent variables determined by an ordinary least-squares regression equation.

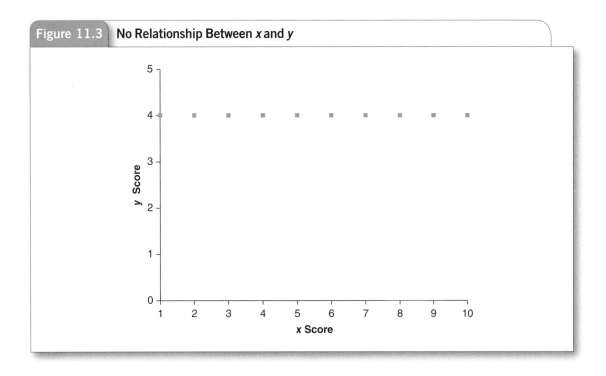

Figure 11.3   No Relationship Between *x* and *y*

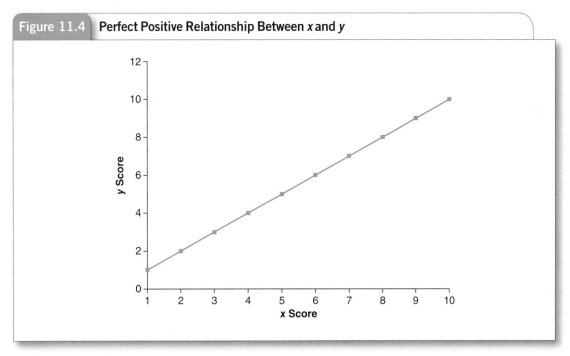

Figure 11.4   Perfect Positive Relationship Between *x* and *y*

that is horizontal to the *x* axis. This line has no slope. As we suggested earlier, in this example we have no correlation between *x* and *y*. It might be said that Figure 11.6 presents an example of two variables with absolutely no correlation.

In addition to direction, the second valuable thing we can learn from a scatterplot, then, is an indication of the *strength* or *magnitude* of the relationship. The strength of a relationship can be judged by examining the spread of the data points around a straight line, called the regression line, which passes through them. The closer the data points are

There is one other very important thing we can learn from a scatterplot, and that is how to predict the score on one variable (the *y* variable) from the score on another variable (the *x* variable). Figures 11.7 and 11.8 show the previous examples of a perfect positive correlation between *x* and *y* and no correlation, respectively. In these figures, the two axes and the straight regression line have been extended to include additional scores. Let's first look at Figure 11.7. In

Figure 11.7 Predicting *y* Scores ($\hat{y}$) from *x* Scores With Perfect Positive Correlation

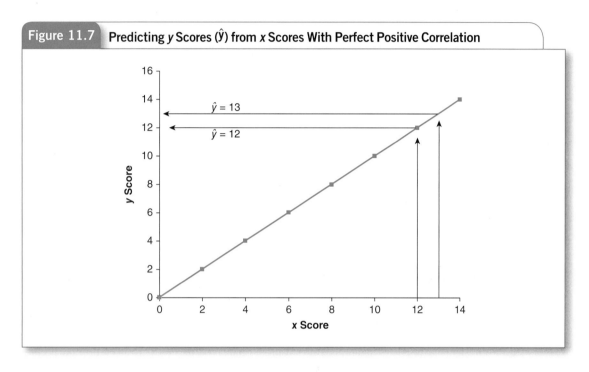

Figure 11.8 Predicting *y* Scores ($\hat{y}$) from *x* Scores With No Correlation

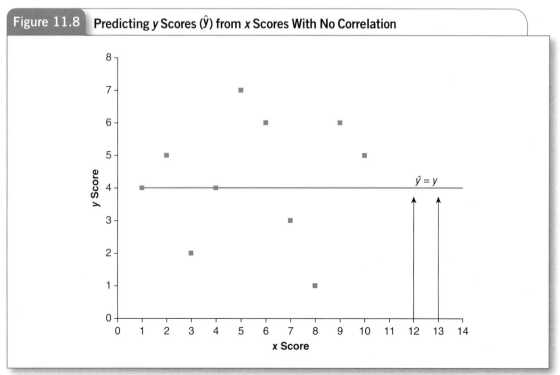

this figure, we want to predict what someone's y score would be if she or he had an x score of 12. To find the *predicted value* of y (denoted by the symbol $\hat{y}$ to distinguish it from its *actual value y*), we first find the value of x on the x axis ($x = 12$). Next we draw a straight line up to the regression line, and from that point we draw another straight line parallel to the x axis across to the y axis. The predicted value of y ($\hat{y}$) is the value of y where this line touches the y axis. In this case, our predicted value of y with $x = 12$ would be 12 ($\hat{y} = 12$). We could follow the same procedure and determine that for $x = 13$, our predicted y score would also be 13.

In Figure 11.8, which shows no strong correlation between x and y, we could also make predictions about y based on information about x, but in this case the predictions would all be the same. That is, no matter what the observed x score, if we were to draw a straight line up from the x axis to the regression line and then another line over to the y axis, we would have the same predicted y score ($\hat{y} = 4$). With an observed x score of 12, our predicted y would be 4, and with an observed x score of 13, our predicted value of y would also be 4. In the case of no correlation between two variables, there is no unique predicted score for y at different values of x. Instead, no matter what the x score, the predicted y score will always be the same. In other words, knowledge of x does not help us to predict the value of y.

Relationships or correlations between variables in the real world rarely have such obvious or perfect patterns. When real crime data are used, patterns become a little less clear.

Case Study

Causes of State-Level Crime

Now that you understand what can be learned from a scatterplot, let's examine some real data. Let's say we are interested in the factors related to violent crime. From our review of the literature, we determine that poverty and economic deprivation are often found to be related to murder. One way to look at this relationship between poverty and murder would be to examine the correlation between a state's poverty rate (we will designate this as our x or independent variable) and its rate of homicide (our y or dependent variable). More specifically, we use the percentage of the state's population that lives below the poverty level as our independent variable (x) and the homicide rate for each state, obtained from the Federal Bureau of Investigation's (FBI) Uniform Crime Reports, as our dependent variable (y). The state, then, is our level of analysis.

To examine this issue, we take a random sample of 20 states ($n = 20$) and record the murder rate in each state (y), along with the state's rate of poverty for the year 2013 (x). These data are shown in Table 11.1. Based on these data, we create the scatterplot displayed in Figure 11.9. This was created the same way as the other scatterplots were created, by first drawing the x and y axes to accommodate both variables and then simply finding the data point for each case. For example, for the first state, Alaska, we go over to 9.0 on the horizontal or x axis and then up to 3.2 on the vertical or y axis. This point then becomes the point that represents Alaska on our scatterplot.

What kind of relationship do you see in Figure 11.9? By "eyeballing" the data, we can draw a straight line that we think runs though the data points; however, unlike our hypothetical data, these data points do not all fall perfectly on any one line. Instead, we will have to draw our line in such a way that it comes as close to all the data points as possible. A line that appears to fit the data is drawn through the scatterplot and displayed in Figure 11.10. As before, we will use this line to summarize the pattern and strength of the relationship between our two variables, keeping in mind that we know the farther the points are away from the line, the weaker the linear relationship—positive or negative.

Based on what we have learned so far in this chapter, we can conclude two things from this scatterplot. First, there does seem to be a positive correlation between poverty and murder rates. The general pattern of the data points, and the line that runs through them, is an upward slope, indicating that as the rate of poverty increases (as x increases), the murder rate also increases (y increases). States that have high poverty rates, then, also tend to have higher rates of murder. Second, the correlation between the two variables is far from perfect. None of the data points falls exactly on the straight line.

In fact, many of these points lie fairly far below or above the line. What we can tell from this scatterplot, then, is that we have a nonperfect positive correlation between a state's murder rate and its poverty rate. These types of relationships are more typical of real crime data than the hypothetical data we examined earlier.

In Table 11.2, we have the same random sample of states but two different variables. In this table, the x variable is the percentage of the population in the state that lives in a nonmetropolitan (rural) area, and the y variable is the rate of robbery. We examine this relationship because we suspect that there is a correlation between how rural or nonmetropolitan a state is and its robbery rate. We think that rural states have lower rates of robbery than urban states because they are likely to be more cohesive, more homogeneous, and less socially disorganized. This is a prediction based on the early "Chicago School" of crime and social disorganization.

Figure 11.11 depicts the scatterplot of the data in Table 11.2. Here we see a downward-sloping pattern of data points. This indicates the existence of a negative correlation between rural population and violent crime. States that are more rural, such as Alaska and Maine, have lower rates of robbery than less rural states, such as California. As in the last example, however, the negative correlation between rural population and robbery rates is less than perfect. Not all of the points lie exactly on the regression line.

Table 11.1	Murder Rate per 100,000 and Percentage of Individuals in State Living Below the Poverty Level for 20 States, 2013

State	Murder Rate (y)	Poverty Rate (x)
Alaska	3.2	9.0
Arizona	5.5	16.5
California	5.4	14.2
Delaware	4.6	10.8
Florida	5.5	14.9
Indiana	5.3	14.4
Louisiana	12.3	17.3
Maine	2.0	12.3
Maryland	7.7	9.1
Massachusetts	2.7	10.3
Michigan	6.3	16.2
Missouri	6.6	14.6
Nebraska	2.5	12.3
New Jersey	3.7	9.4
New Mexico	10.0	18.0
New York	4.0	14.2
Pennsylvania	5.4	12.5
South Carolina	6.7	17.1
Texas	5.4	17.2
Wyoming	2.0	9.8

Source: Adapted from the Uniform Crime Reports and *Population by Age and Sex* from the FBI (2014) and the U.S. Bureau of the Census (2014), respectively.

Figure 11.9	**Scatterplot of Poverty Rate (x) and Murder Rate (y) for 20 States**

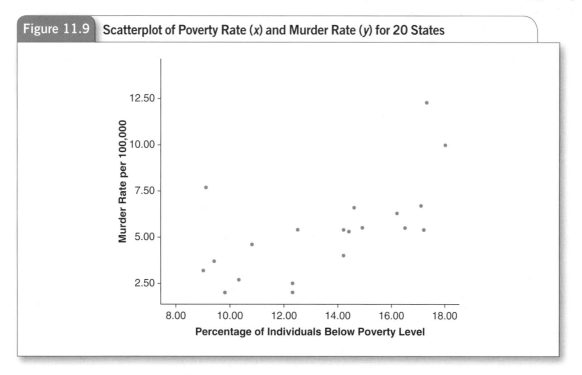

| Figure 11.10 | Scatterplot of Poverty Rate (x) and Murder Rate (y) for 20 States With Regression Line |

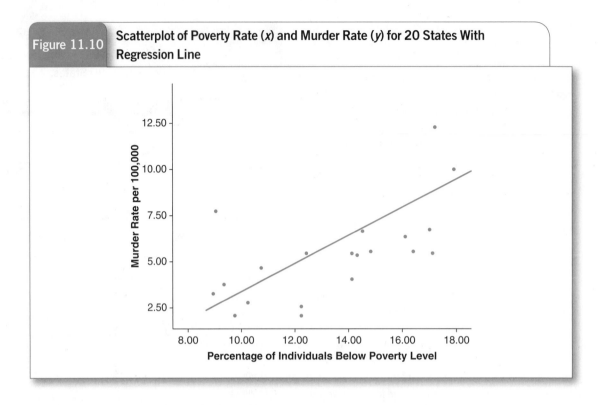

| Table 11.2 | Robbery Rate per 100,000 and Percentage of Individuals in State Living in Rural Areas for 20 States, 2013 |

State	Robbery Rate (y)	% Rural (x)	State	Robbery Rate (y)	% Rural (x)
Alaska	94.0	30.4	Michigan	126.5	25.5
Arizona	123.9	9.5	Missouri	127.1	28.6
California	173.7	5.1	Nebraska	74.7	28.4
Delaware	189.7	17.4	New Jersey	133.7	5.4
Florida	166.8	9.1	New Mexico	98.7	22.1
Indiana	129.4	27.4	New York	144.5	12.3
Louisiana	142.3	27.0	Pennsylvania	142.4	22.2
Maine	30.3	57.4	South Carolina	126.0	34.3
Maryland	210.7	12.8	Texas	153.6	14.5
Massachusetts	114.1	8.4	Wyoming	14.3	30.5

Source: Adapted from the Uniform Crime Reports and *Population by Age and Sex* from the FBI (2014) and the U.S. Bureau of the Census (2014), respectively.

Figure 11.11	Scatterplot of Percentage Rural (x) and Robbery Rate (y) for 20 States With Regression Line

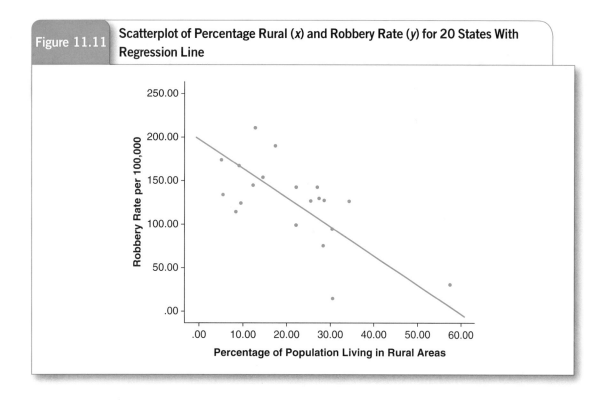

Table 11.3	Burglary Rate per 100,000 and Divorce Rate per 1,000 in State Living in Rural Areas for 20 States, 2013

State	Burglary Rate (y)	Divorce Rate (x)	State	Burglary Rate (y)	Divorce Rate (x)
Alaska	514.2	7.8	Michigan	768.1	5.4
Arizona	817.3	5.4	Missouri	733.5	6.5
California	622.1	5.8	Nebraska	499.4	6.7
Delaware	784.0	5.4	New Jersey	424.2	5.1
Florida	981.2	7.5	New Mexico	1117.3	5.1
Indiana	815.9	7.9	New York	321.6	6.4
Louisiana	1036.4	7.1	Pennsylvania	439.2	5.3
Maine	510.4	7.2	South Carolina	991.7	7.4
Maryland	647.5	5.8	Texas	967.4	7.1
Massachusetts	524.1	5.5	Wyoming	399.8	8.2

Source: Adapted from the Uniform Crime Reports and *Population by Age and Sex* from the FBI (2014) and the U.S. Bureau of the Census (2014), respectively.

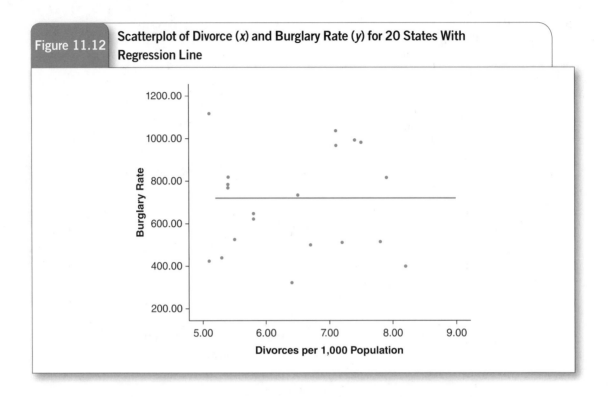

Figure 11.12 Scatterplot of Divorce (*x*) and Burglary Rate (*y*) for 20 States With Regression Line

Let's say we make a third conjecture about our random sample of 20 states. Let's hypothesize that states with high divorce rates also have high rates of burglary. In Table 11.3, we record the number of divorces per 1,000 residents of each state on the *x* axis and record the burglary rate on the *y* axis. We create a scatterplot for these data in Figure 11.12. Unlike the other two scatterplots using the state-level crime data, however, this one has no clear or discernible pattern. That is, it slopes neither upward nor downward. Also, unlike our hypothetical data, these data points do not lie on a perfectly horizontal line. The line that probably best describes this pattern of data would generally be flat, running through the middle of the data. Moreover, most data points in this scatterplot would be far from the straight line we drew. From this, we would conclude that there probably is very little correlation between these two variables.

In sum, by graphically representing the relationship between two interval- and ratio-level variables in a scatterplot, we can learn about the direction of the relationship or correlation between *x* and *y*—and a little bit about its strength. If the pattern of the data points and a line drawn through them is an ascending one, we can conclude that the correlation between *x* and *y* is positive and linear. If the pattern is a descending one, we can conclude that the correlation is negative and linear. If there is no pattern to the data and the line we draw through the data points is almost horizontal, we can conclude that there is very little correlation between the two variables. We can estimate the strength of the relationship by examining the distance between the actual data points and the straight line. The closer the data points cluster around this line, the stronger the correlation between *x* and *y*. Correlations that are not strong generally have data points that fall far above and/or below the line. It would be nice if there were a numerical indicator that told us the extent of correlation between two variables, wouldn't it? Fortunately, there is, and we discuss it next.

▣ The Pearson Correlation Coefficient

The statistic used to measure the linear correlation between two interval- and ratio-level variables is called the **Pearson correlation coefficient** or *Pearson product–moment correlation coefficient*. We will refer to this statistic simply as Pearson's r, named after its originator, the statistician Karl Pearson. Pearson's r measures the strength of the *linear* correlation between two continuous (interval- and ratio-level) variables. The statistic r is our sample estimate of the correlation between the two variables in the population. The population correlation coefficient is designated by ρ, the Greek letter rho.

Pearson's correlation coefficient is standardized. By this, we mean that the magnitude of r does not depend on the natural units of measurement of the x and y variables (e.g., dollars, crimes, IQ points). No matter what the unit of measurement, Pearson's r assumes a value of 0 whenever there is no linear correlation between two variables, and it attains a maximum value of ± 1.0 when there is a perfect linear correlation between two variables. Figure 11.13 displays a guide to aid you in the interpretation of Pearson's r. A correlation of ± 1.0 occurs when all points fall exactly on a straight regression line. A Pearson correlation coefficient of +1.00 means that there is a perfect positive correlation between two variables (as in Figure 11.1), an r of –1.00 means that there is a perfect negative correlation (as in Figure 11.2), and an r of 0.00 means that there is absolutely no linear relationship. The closer the data points cluster around the regression line, the stronger the correlation between the two variables and the higher the value of r will be. If there is no linear pattern in data points, the value of r will be closer to zero, indicating very little linear relationship between the two variables.

The calculation of Pearson's r is relatively straightforward and involves arithmetic operations you are already very familiar with. Because a definitional formula helps us to describe what the coefficient is actually doing, we are first going to show you that. The definitional formula for Pearson's r is

$$r = \frac{\Sigma(x - \bar{X})(y - \bar{Y})}{\sqrt{\left[\Sigma(x - \bar{X})^2\right]\left[\Sigma(y - \bar{Y})^2\right]}}$$

(Formula 11-1)

The first term in the numerator of this equation is simply the difference between an x score and its mean, whereas the second term is the difference between a y score and its mean. In the definitional formula for the correlation coefficient, we multiply these difference scores by each other, we do this for each pair of difference scores, and then we sum over all scores. In other words, we take the difference between the first person's x score and the mean of x, take the difference between the first person's y score and the mean of y, and then

> **Pearson correlation coefficient:**
> Statistic that quantifies the direction and strength of the relationship between two interval/ratio-level variables.

Figure 11.13	Interpretation of Pearson's *r* Values

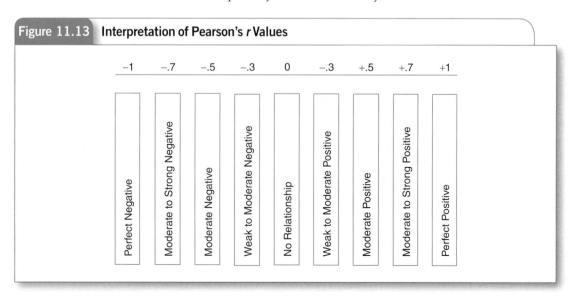

multiply those two differences. We do this for each observation and sum over observations. Since the mean is defined in statistical terms as the *first moment*, the terms $(x - \bar{X})$ and $(y - \bar{Y})$ are referred to as the first moments about the mean. The correlation coefficient, then, is based on the product of the first moments about the mean of x and y; hence, it is often referred to as the *product–moment* correlation coefficient.

The product of $(x - \bar{X})$ and $(y - \bar{Y})$ captures the *covariation* between x and y. That is, it measures the extent to which the x and y scores vary together, or covary. The stronger the relationship between the two variables, the greater the covariance. A covariation of zero implies that the two variables are not correlated, a positive covariation implies positive correlation, and a negative covariation implies negative correlation. We cannot simply use the size of the covariation as our measure of correlation, however. First of all, the magnitude of the covariation is a function of the measurement units of the variables. For example, other things being equal, we would obtain a much greater covariation if one of our variables were measured in pennies rather than dollars or measured in days rather than months or years. Second, the covariance can often be greater than 1.0, so we have no clear interpretation for it. We can, however, standardize the covariation—that is, make its value independent of the units of measurement. We do this by dividing the covariation in x and y by a term that includes both the variation in x and the variation in y. These terms form the denominator of the correlation coefficient in equation 11-1, and it should look very familiar to you. It is simply the product of two terms: the amount of variation in the x variable and the amount of variation in the y variable. The correlation coefficient, then, expresses the ratio of the covariation in x and y to the product of the variation in x and the variation in y. It has a lower limit of -1.0 and an upper limit of $+1.0$ and is equal to 0 if there is no linear relationship between two variables.

As you can imagine from going over formula 11-1 in your head, the necessary calculations to estimate r are enough to make you faint. Fortunately, there is a computational formula that involves fewer operations and, therefore, fewer chances of making computational errors. The computing formula for the Pearson correlation coefficient is

$$r = \frac{n\Sigma xy - (\Sigma x)(\Sigma y)}{\sqrt{\left[n\Sigma x^2 - (\Sigma x)^2 \right]\left[n\Sigma y^2 - (\Sigma y)^2 \right]}} \qquad \text{(Formula 11-2)}$$

Even this formula may appear forbidding to you, but fear not, we can break it down into five simple components that we can then plug into the formula and solve. The computational formula requires the following five sums:

1. Σxy = the sum of each x score times its corresponding y score

2. Σx = the sum of the x scores

3. Σy = the sum of the y scores

4. Σx^2 = the sum of the squared x scores $(x_1^2 + x_2^2 + \cdots + x_n^2)$

5. Σy^2 = the sum of the squared y scores $(y_1^2 + y_2^2 + \cdots + y_n^2)$

We will use this computational formula to calculate the value of r for the state data in Tables 11.1, 11.2, and 11.3. In calculating the value of r, it will be helpful if you first calculate each of the five sums and then insert them into the formula. A listing of the sums in separate columns will make keeping track of the different components of the formula easier. We have provided these calculations in Tables 11.4, 11.5, and 11.6, although you should first try to calculate them yourself.

For the state-level data in Table 11.4, which reports the murder rates and poverty rates for 20 randomly selected states, we calculate the value of r as follows:

$$r = \frac{n\Sigma xy - (\Sigma x)(\Sigma y)}{\sqrt{\left[n\Sigma x^2 - (\Sigma x)^2 \right]\left[n\Sigma y^2 - (\Sigma y)^2 \right]}}$$

$$r = \frac{(20)(1,535.1) - (270.1)(106.8)}{\sqrt{\left[(20)(3,821.8) - (270.1)^2 \right]\left[(20)(697.8) - (106.8)^2 \right]}}$$

$$r = \frac{30,702 - 28,846.7}{\sqrt{[76,436 - 72,954][13,956 - 11,406.2]}}$$

$$r = \frac{1,855.3}{\sqrt{(3,482)(2,549.8)}}$$

$$r = \frac{1,855.3}{\sqrt{8,878,403.6}}$$

$$r = \frac{1,855.3}{2,979.7}$$

$$r = .62$$

| Table 11.4 | Calculation of Pearson Correlation Coefficient, *r*, for Correlation Between State Murder Rate and Poverty Rate (Table 11.1) |

State	Poverty Rate (x)	Murder Rate (y)	x^2	y^2	xy
Alaska	9.0	3.2	81.0	10.2	28.8
Arizona	16.5	5.5	272.3	30.3	90.8
California	14.2	5.4	201.6	29.2	76.7
Delaware	10.8	4.6	116.6	21.2	49.7
Florida	14.9	5.5	222.0	30.3	82.0
Indiana	14.4	5.3	207.4	28.1	76.3
Louisiana	17.3	12.3	299.3	151.3	212.8
Maine	12.3	2.0	151.3	4.0	24.6
Maryland	9.1	7.7	82.8	59.3	70.1
Massachusetts	10.3	2.7	106.1	7.3	27.8
Michigan	16.2	6.3	262.4	39.7	102.1
Missouri	14.6	6.6	213.2	43.6	96.4
Nebraska	12.3	2.5	151.3	6.3	30.8
New Jersey	9.4	3.7	88.4	13.7	34.8
New Mexico	18.0	10.0	324.0	100.0	180.0
New York	14.2	4.0	201.6	16.0	56.8
Pennsylvania	12.5	5.4	156.3	29.2	67.5
South Carolina	17.1	6.7	292.4	44.9	114.6
Texas	17.2	5.4	295.8	29.2	92.9
Wyoming	9.8	2.0	96.0	4.0	19.6
$n = 20$	$\Sigma x = 270.1$	$\Sigma y = 106.8$	$\Sigma x^2 = 3,821.8$	$\Sigma y^2 = 697.8$	$\Sigma xy = 1,535.1$

What does this correlation between a state's murder rate and level of poverty of $r = .62$ tell us? Well, the sign of the correlation coefficient informs us that there is a positive linear correlation between a state's murder rate and the percentage of the population that lives below the poverty level. Those states with high murder rates also tend to have high rates of poverty. How do we interpret the magnitude of this correlation? Recall that the value of a Pearson correlation coefficient varies between –1.0 (a perfect negative correlation) and +1.0 (a perfect positive correlation), with 0 indicating no correlation. One thing we can say about our correlation of .62 is that it is close to .50 and, therefore, indicates a moderately strong relationship. Unfortunately, there are no clear and agreed-on rules that tell us what constitutes a "weak," "moderate," or "strong" correlation. It is entirely subjective. We will provide a more exact interpretation of the magnitude of r in the next section, but for now we will use less precise terms such as "moderately strong" and "weak." We can conclude from this, then, that there is a moderately strong positive correlation between a state's poverty rate and its murder rate.

Table 11.5 Calculation of Pearson Correlation Coefficient, r, for Correlation Between Percentage of Population Living in Rural Areas in a State and Rate of Robbery for 20 States (Table 11.2)

State	Rural Area (%) (x)	Robbery Rate (y)	x^2	y^2	xy
Alaska	30.4	94.0	924.2	8836.0	2857.6
Arizona	9.5	123.9	90.3	15351.2	1177.1
California	5.1	173.7	26.0	30171.7	885.9
Delaware	17.4	189.7	302.8	35986.1	3300.8
Florida	9.1	166.8	82.8	27822.2	1517.9
Indiana	27.4	129.4	750.8	16744.4	3545.6
Louisiana	27.0	142.3	729.0	20249.3	3842.1
Maine	57.4	30.3	3294.8	918.1	1739.2
Maryland	12.8	210.7	163.8	44394.5	2697.0
Massachusetts	8.4	114.1	70.6	13018.8	958.4
Michigan	25.5	126.5	650.3	16002.3	3225.8
Missouri	28.6	127.1	818.0	16154.4	3635.1
Nebraska	28.4	74.7	806.6	5580.1	2121.5
New Jersey	5.4	133.7	29.2	17875.7	722.0
New Mexico	22.1	98.7	488.4	9741.7	2181.3
New York	12.3	144.5	151.3	20880.3	1777.4
Pennsylvania	22.2	142.4	492.8	20277.8	3161.3
South Carolina	34.3	126.0	1176.5	15876.0	4321.8
Texas	14.5	153.6	210.3	23593.0	2227.2
Wyoming	30.5	14.3	930.3	204.5	436.2
$n = 20$	$\Sigma x = 428.3$	$\Sigma y = 2,516.4$	$\Sigma x^2 = 12,188.8$	$\Sigma y^2 = 359,678.1$	$\Sigma xy = 46,331.2$

Table 11.5 reports the calculations necessary to estimate the correlation between the percentage of a state's population that lives in a nonmetropolitan area and its rate of robbery. The correlation between these two variables is calculated as follows, but we will refresh your memory of the formula:

$$r = \frac{n\Sigma xy - (\Sigma x)(\Sigma y)}{\sqrt{\left[n\Sigma x^2 - (\Sigma x)^2\right]\left[n\Sigma y^2 - (\Sigma y)^2\right]}}$$

$$r = \frac{(20)(46,331.2) - (428.3)(2,516.4)}{\sqrt{\left[(20)(12,188.8) - (428.3)^2\right]\left[(20)(359,678.1) - (2,516.4)^2\right]}}$$

$$r = \frac{926,624 - 1,077,774.}{\sqrt{[243,776 - 183,440.9][7,193,562 - 6,332,269]}}$$

$$r = \frac{-151,150.1}{\sqrt{(60,335.1)(861,293)}}$$

$$r = \frac{-151,150.1}{\sqrt{51,966,199,284}}$$

$$r = \frac{-151,150.1}{227,961}$$

$$r = -.66$$

This coefficient ($r = -.66$) indicates that there is a moderately negative linear correlation between percentage of rural population and a state's robbery rate. As we predicted, states with a higher percentage of its population living in a rural area have lower rates of robbery than more urban states.

And finally, Table 11.6 reports the calculations to estimate the correlation between a state's divorce rate and its rate of burglary. The correlation is

$$r = \frac{(20)(89,736.6) - (128.6)(13,915.3)}{\sqrt{\left[(20)(847.5) - (128.6)^2\right]\left[(20)(10,722,261.6) - (13,915.3)^2\right]}}$$

$$r = \frac{1,794,732 - 1,789,507.6}{\sqrt{[16,950 - 16,538][214,445,232 - 193,635,574.1]}}$$

$$r = \frac{5,222.4}{\sqrt{(412)(20,809,657.9)}}$$

$$r = \frac{5,222.4}{\sqrt{8,573,579,055}}$$

$$r = \frac{5,222.4}{92,593.6}$$

$$r = .056$$

How would you interpret this correlation of .056? It is closer to zero than the other correlation coefficients. In fact, it is almost zero! This indicates that there is a very weak positive linear correlation between a state's divorce rate and its rate of burglary. Consistent with the appearance of our scatterplot, then, there is not a very strong linear relationship between these two variables. The divorce rate does not appear to influence rates of burglary.

In our examination of the three relationships, we have found a moderately strong positive correlation between a state's murder rate and its poverty rate, a moderately strong negative correlation between a state's percentage of rural population and its rate of robbery, and not much of a linear correlation between a state's divorce rate and its burglary rate.

Table 11.6	Calculation of Pearson Correlation Coefficient, r, for Correlation Between Divorce Rate in a State and Rate of Burglary for 20 States (Table 11.3)

State	Divorce Rate (x)	Burglary Rate (y)	x^2	y^2	xy
Alaska	7.8	514.2	60.8	264401.6	4010.8
Arizona	5.4	817.3	29.2	667979.3	4413.4
California	5.8	622.1	33.6	387008.4	3608.2
Delaware	5.4	784.0	29.2	614656.0	4233.6
Florida	7.5	981.2	56.3	962753.4	7359.0
Indiana	7.9	815.9	62.4	665692.8	6445.6
Louisiana	7.1	1036.4	50.4	1074125	7358.4
Maine	7.2	510.4	51.8	260508.2	3674.9
Maryland	5.8	647.5	33.6	419256.3	3755.5
Massachusetts	5.5	524.1	30.3	274680.8	2882.6
Michigan	5.4	768.1	29.2	589977.6	4147.7
Missouri	6.5	733.5	42.3	538022.3	4767.8
Nebraska	6.7	499.4	44.9	249400.4	3346.0
New Jersey	5.1	424.2	26.0	179945.6	2163.4
New Mexico	5.1	1117.3	26.0	1248359	5698.2
New York	6.4	321.6	41.0	103426.6	2058.2
Pennsylvania	5.3	439.2	28.1	192896.6	2327.8
South Carolina	7.4	991.7	54.8	983468.9	7338.6
Texas	7.1	967.4	50.4	935862.8	6868.5
Wyoming	8.2	399.8	67.2	159840.0	3278.4
$n = 20$	$\Sigma x = 128.6$	$\Sigma y = 13,915.3$	$\Sigma x^2 = 847.5$	$\Sigma y^2 = 10,772,261.6$	$\Sigma xy = 89,736.6$

Although we can interpret a perfect positive correlation as +1.0, a perfect negative correlation as –1.0, and no linear correlation at all as 0.0, what do correlations that fall in between these extremes mean? Although Figure 11.13 provides accepted adjectives to describe correlations that fall between 0 and ±1, there is another statistic that enables us to interpret more precisely the strength of the relationship between two variables. This statistic is called the coefficient of determination, and we turn to it next.

A More Precise Way to Interpret a Correlation: The Coefficient of Determination

The **coefficient of determination**, r^2, enables us to interpret more definitively the strength of the association between two interval- and ratio-level variables. It is very easy to obtain once we have already calculated the correlation coefficient. As the symbol r^2 suggests, the coefficient of determination is simply the square of the Pearson correlation coefficient. It is interpreted as *the proportion of the variation in the y variable that is explained by the x variable.* Remember, what we are trying to do is to explain variation in the dependent or *y* variable. We want to know why everyone is not the same on *y,* that there is variation in *y,* and that what explains variation in *y* is variation in the independent variable, *x.* So, a good question to ask of our *x* variable is, "How much of the variation in *y* are you explaining?" When the value of r^2 is multiplied by 100 to get a percentage, it is interpreted as the *percentage of the variation* in the *y* variable that is explained by the *x* variable.

> **Coefficient of determination (r^2):**
> Percentage of the variation in the dependent variable (*y*) that is explained by the independent variable (*x*).

For example, our correlation between the poverty rate and the murder rate for our 20 states was .62. The coefficient of determination is $(.62)^2$, or .38, and can be understood as the amount of variance in murder rates that is explained by the rate of poverty. In this example, 38% of the variation in states' murder rates is explained by state-level rates of poverty. The correlation between percentage rural population and the robbery rate was –.66. The coefficient of determination is $(-.66)^2$, or .44, which indicates that 44% of the variation in robbery crime rates for these 20 states is explained by the percentage of the state's population that is living in a rural area. Finally, the correlation between the divorce rate and a state's burglary rate is $(.056)^2$, or .003. This indicates that less than 1% of the variation in burglary rates is explained by the divorce rate in states.

The amount of variation explained varies from 0% to 100%. The more variation that is explained, the stronger the association or relationship between the two variables. If two variables are perfectly related, the amount of explained variation will be 100% ($+1.0^2 = -1.0^2 = 1.0 \times 100\%$). If two variables are perfectly unrelated (independent), the amount of variation one variable explains in the other will be 0%. Obviously, the more variation one variable explains in another, the more accurate the predictions of a *y* variable from an *x* variable will be. The magnitude of r^2, the coefficient of determination, then, is the proportion of variation in *y* that is explained by *x.* As the amount of explained variation increases, r^2 increases. The greater the proportion of the total variation that is explained by the independent variable, the stronger the linear relationship between *x* and *y.* As you can see, the coefficient of determination (r^2) is a very useful measure of association between two continuous variables. Unlike the correlation coefficient (*r*), values of the coefficient of determination between 0 and 1.0 are readily interpretable. Another way to think of this is that values of r^2 reflect the amount of improvement in our predictive accuracy. There is an additional way to describe a linear relationship between *x* and *y,* which we turn to next.

▣ The Least-Squares Regression Line and the Slope Coefficient

The correlation coefficient (*r*) and the coefficient of determination (r^2) are two very helpful statistics in understanding the linear relationship between two interval/ratio variables. One advantage of them both is that you can compare the relative strength of a relationship across different variables and everyone will be able to judge the strength. For example, we know that a relationship that has a correlation of .70 is a stronger relationship than one that has a correlation of .45. Unfortunately, because the values of these statistics are standardized, they don't tell us exactly how a particular independent variable will affect a given dependent variable. The **least-squares regression line** not only provides information about the strength and direction of the relationship between *x* and *y* but also enables us to predict values of *y* from values of *x* more precisely. In fact, it tells us exactly what happens to *y* for every 1-unit increase in *x.*

──────── **Case Study** ────────

Age and Delinquency

To understand the idea behind the least-squares regression line, we first need to examine how the line is constructed and why it is called the "least-squares" regression line. Let's begin our discussion of the least-squares regression line by looking at the

> **Least-squares regression line:**
> Regression line based on the least-squares function to calculate an equation that characterizes the best-fitting line between two interval/ratio variables.

Table 11.7	Hypothetical Data for 20 Students	
Student	Age (x)	Self-Reported Delinquency (y)
1	12	0
2	12	2
3	12	1
4	12	3
5	13	4
6	13	2
7	13	1
8	14	2
9	14	5
10	14	4
11	15	3
12	15	4
13	15	6
14	15	8
15	16	9
16	16	7
17	16	6
18	17	8
19	17	10
20	17	7

hypothetical data in Table 11.7. This table shows the age of a random sample of 20 youths and the number of self-reported acts of delinquency committed by each youth during the previous year. Age is our designated independent (x) variable, and the number of self-reported delinquent acts is our dependent (y) variable. Note that both of these variables are measured at the interval/ratio level.

The first thing to note in Table 11.7 is that for any given x value, there are different values for y. This means that there are several youths who are the same age but have not committed the same number of delinquent acts. For example, of the four 12-year-old youths in the sample, one committed 0 delinquent acts, one committed 1 delinquent act, one committed 2 delinquent acts, and one committed 3 delinquent acts. The three 13-year-old youths committed different numbers of delinquent acts as well. For each value of x, then, there are a number of different y values. Think of these different y values at each value of x as constituting a distribution of y scores. Since there are seven different x scores, there are seven different distributions of y scores. Another way to express this is to say that for every fixed value of x, there is a corresponding distribution of y scores. In statistics, these distributions of y scores are often called conditional distributions since the distribution of y scores depends, or is conditional, on the value of x.

Figure 11.14 is the scatterplot illustrating these data. We can tell from "eyeballing" this scatterplot that age and self-reported delinquency are positively related to one another and that this relationship looks reasonably strong and linear. The goal of least-squares regression is to fit a straight line to these data in such a way that the line comes as close to the original data points as possible.

Recall from Chapter 3 that we can determine a central score within a distribution of scores that arithmetically varies the least from all other scores in the distribution. This point of minimum variation, you will remember, is the mean. The mean is that one score around which the variation of the other scores is the smallest or is minimized. In mathematical terms, the mean satisfies the expression

$$\Sigma(x - \bar{X})^2 = \text{Minimum variance}$$

This expression simply means that the sum of the squared differences (deviations) around any mean is the minimum value that can be defined. Arithmetically, we know that if any value other than the mean were used in the expression, the obtained value would be greater than if the mean is used. In other words, in any distribution of scores, the mean will be that score that is closest to all the other scores.

This property of the mean holds true even for a conditional distribution of scores such as that shown in Table 11.7. If we calculate a mean of y at each value of x (called the conditional mean of y), this mean will be the score that is closest to all other y scores at

Conditional means of *y*: Means of y calculated for every value of x.

that given value of x. We have calculated each of these conditional y means for you and report the results in Table 11.8. These conditional means were calculated like any other mean by summing all values of y and then dividing by the total number of these y scores. For example, there were four y scores (number of self-reported delinquent acts) for those at 12 years of age: 0, 2, 1, and 3. The mean number of self-reported delinquent acts for these four 12-year-old youths, therefore, is $(0+2+1+3)/4=1.5$. This mean indicates that the 12-year-olds from this sample reported committing an average of 1.5 delinquent acts. We can similarly calculate conditional means of y for each age, as we show in Table 11.8. In Figure 11.15, we show the scatterplot that includes points for both the original scores and each of the conditional means (shown by $\bar{Y}$).

Since the conditional means $(\bar{Y})$ minimize the variance of the y scores at each value of x, the straight line that comes the closest to going through each value of $\bar{Y}$ will be our best-fitting line. By "best fitting," we mean that it is the line that will minimize the variation of the conditional y scores about that line. Because the variance is measured by the squared deviations from the mean $(y-\bar{Y})^2$, this regression line is the *least-squares* regression line, and the estimation procedure is referred to as ordinary least-squares (OLS) regression. The least-squares regression line, therefore, is the line where the squared deviations of the conditional means for the y scores $(\bar{Y})$ are the least. Figure 11.16 is the scatterplot of the conditional values from Figure 11.15. We have also included the regression line and the distance (drawn with a vertical line) between each conditional mean and the regression line. This regression line is the best-fitting line in the sense that it is calculated in such a way that this vertical distance is at a minimum. This is simply a beautiful equation!

Mathematically, the equation that defines this least-squares regression line takes the general linear form in the sample as

$$y = a + bx \qquad \text{(Formula 11-3)}$$

where
  y = the score on the y variable
  a = the y intercept or constant
  b = the slope of the regression line
  x = the score on the x variable

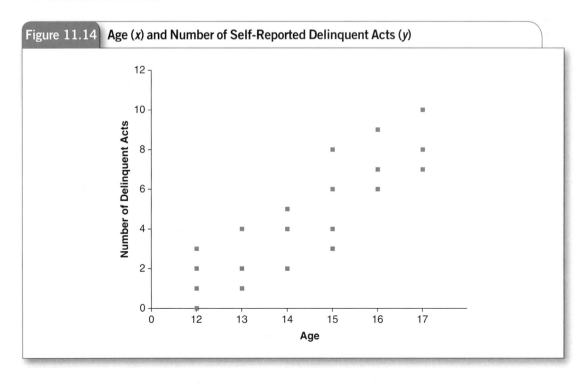

Figure 11.14 **Age (x) and Number of Self-Reported Delinquent Acts (y)**

Table 11.8	Conditional Means (means of *y* for fixed values of *x*) for the Data on Age and Self-Reported Delinquency	

Age	*y* Scores	Conditional $\bar{Y}$
12	0, 1, 2, 3	1.5
13	4, 2, 1	2.3
14	2, 5, 4	3.7
15	3, 4, 6, 8	5.2
16	9, 7, 6	7.3
17	8, 10, 7	8.3

There are two new terms in this equation, the intercept and the slope, that must be defined and explained. The **y intercept** (*a*), or constant, is the point where the regression line crosses the *y* axis. As you can determine from the equation, it is equal to the value of *y* whenever *x* = 0. The **slope** of the regression line, *b*, often called the regression coefficient, measures the amount of change produced in the *y* variable by a 1-unit increase in the *x* variable, and the sign indicates the direction of that change. For example, a slope of 2 indicates that a 1-unit increase in *x* produces a 2-unit increase in *y*. A slope of –2 indicates that a 1-unit increase in *x* produces a 2-unit decrease in *y*. If the slope in our age and delinquency example were 2, this would indicate that a 1-year increase in age (a 1-unit change in *x*) would increase the number of self-reported delinquent acts by 2 (a 2-unit change in *y*).

From our sample data, we can estimate our regression equation when we know the values of the intercept and slope. Both values are derived from the original data. We determine the intercept (*a*) by first computing the value of the slope (*b*). The definitional formula for estimating the slope of a regression line is

$$b = \frac{\Sigma(x - \bar{X})(y - \bar{Y})}{\Sigma(x - \bar{X})^2}$$

(Formula 11-4)

y intercept: Value of *y* in an ordinary least-squares regression equation when *x* is equal to 0.

Slope: Term in an ordinary least-squares regression equation that indicates the change in *y* associated with a 1-unit change in *x*.

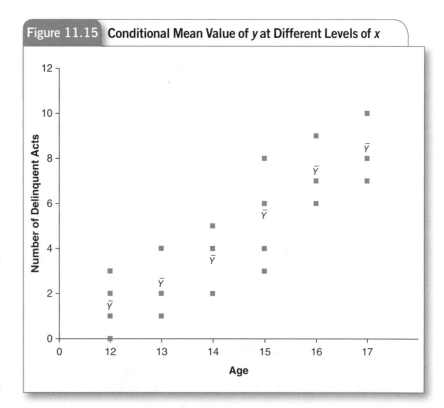

Figure 11.15	Conditional Mean Value of *y* at Different Levels of *x*

This should look very familiar to you by now. The numerator of the equation is simply the product of each x score minus its mean and each y score minus its mean summed over all observations. Remember that the product of these two differences is referred to as the *covariation* between x and y. It measures the extent to which x and y vary together, or *covary*. If we divide this sum by n, what we get is called the *covariance* between x and y. The denominator of equation 11-4 is the squared deviation of each x score about its mean (the sum of squares for x). When divided by n, this is the variance. The slope coefficient, then, can be understood as the ratio of the covariance between x and y to the variance in x.

Note that the covariation between x and y, the numerator in the formula for b, can be either positive or negative. Calculating the slope (b) from this definitional formula would be a tiresome (and error-prone) task. Fortunately, as with the Pearson correlation coefficient, there is a much easier computational formula for b:

$$b = \frac{n\Sigma xy - (\Sigma x)(\Sigma y)}{n\Sigma x^2 - (\Sigma x)^2}$$

(Formula 11-5)

At first glance, this formula looks no easier to use than the definitional formula. But it, too, should be familiar to you by now. We can break this monster up into five component parts that are really quite simple to compute.

1. $\Sigma xy =$ the sum of the product formed by multiplying each x score by each y score and then summing over all scores

2. $\Sigma x =$ the sum of the x scores

3. $\Sigma y =$ the sum of the y scores

4. $\Sigma x^2 =$ the sum of the squared x scores $(x_1^2 + \cdots + x_2^2 + \cdots + x_n^2)$

5. $(\Sigma x)^2 =$ the sum of the x scores squared $(x_1 + \cdots + x_2 + \cdots + x_n)^2$

6. $n =$ The number of observations, or sample size

We will first illustrate the calculation of b with the hypothetical age and self-reported delinquency data in Table 11.7. We will then return to the example involving our real state-level data.

The calculations necessary to find b for the data in Table 11.7 are shown in Table 11.9. In this table, the component elements of the formula are represented by separate columns. With this information, we can calculate the slope using formula 11.6:

$$b = \frac{n\Sigma xy - (\Sigma x)(\Sigma y)}{n\Sigma x^2 - (\Sigma x)^2}$$

$$b = \frac{(20)(1,409) - (288)(92)}{(20)(4,206) - (288)^2}$$

$$b = \frac{28,180 - 26,496}{84,120 - 82,944}$$

$$b = \frac{1,684}{1,176}$$

$$b = 1.43$$

The slope coefficient, b, in this example is 1.43. It is positive, indicating that there is a positive linear relationship between age and the number of self-reported delinquent acts. The value of 1.43 indicates that as age increases by 1 unit (in this case, we know 1 unit is 1 year), the number of self-reported delinquent acts increases by 1.43 acts.

Once we have obtained our estimated slope coefficient, it is easy enough to find the intercept (a) in our regression equation. The first step is to find the mean values of both the x and y distributions. We do this by dividing Σx by n

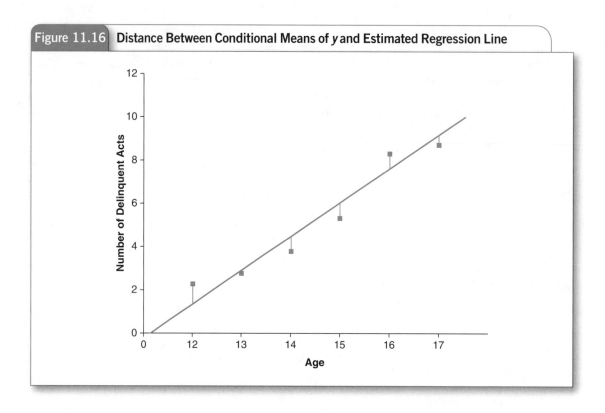

Figure 11.16 **Distance Between Conditional Means of *y* and Estimated Regression Line**

and then doing the same for the *y* scores. For the data on self-reported delinquent acts, $\bar{X} = 14.4$ (288 / 20) and $\bar{Y} = 4.6$ (92/20). Because the regression line will always pass through the mean values of both *x* and *y*, represented by $\bar{X}$ and $\bar{Y}$, we simply have to substitute these terms into the equation

$$\bar{Y} = a + b\bar{X}$$

Then, by substitution, we obtain

$$a = \bar{Y} - b\bar{X}$$

For our example, the solution would be

$$a = 4.6 - (1.43)(14.4)$$
$$a = 4.6 - 20.59$$
$$a = -15.99$$

Thus, the regression line will cross the *y* axis at the point where *y* = –15.99 when the value of *x* equals 0. We can now specify our complete regression equation:

$$y = a + bx$$
$$y = -15.99 + (1.43)x$$

| Table 11.9 | Calculations for Determining the Slope (b) for the Data on Age and Self-Reported Delinquency | | | |

ID Number	Age (x)	Self-Reported Delinquency (y)	x^2	xy
1	12	0	144	0
2	12	2	144	24
3	12	1	144	12
4	12	3	144	36
5	13	4	169	52
6	13	2	169	26
7	13	1	169	13
8	14	2	196	28
9	14	5	196	70
10	14	4	196	56
11	15	3	225	45
12	15	4	225	60
13	15	6	225	90
14	15	8	225	120
15	16	9	256	144
16	16	7	256	112
17	16	6	256	96
18	17	8	289	136
19	17	10	289	170
20	17	7	289	119
$n = 20$	$\Sigma x = 288$	$\Sigma y = 92$	$\Sigma x^2 = 4,206$	$\Sigma xy = 1,409$

A brief word about the intercept is in order. The intercept is where the regression line crosses the y axis, and it is the expected value of the dependent variable y when the independent variable is equal to zero. We have an intercept of −15.99, which would mean that the expected number of delinquent acts when age is equal to zero is a negative 16. That doesn't make much sense, does it? This is because the intercept is substantively meaningful only when an x value of zero has some meaning. It may make sense to speak of 0 dollars, but it makes no real sense to speak of an age equal to 0. In this case, then, when a zero value of the independent variable has no real meaning, neither does the intercept. In other words, sometimes the intercept has a substantive meaning and sometimes it does not have one. In most cases, we don't spend a great deal of time interpreting the intercept because what we really want to know is the relationship between x and y. As such, we focus on interpreting the slope.

🔲 Using the Regression Line for Prediction

After we have computed the regression equation, we can use it to estimate the **predicted value of y ($\hat{y}$)** for any given value of x. To find predicted values of y, we simply use our regression equation and substitute values for x. For example, using the regression equation for age and self-reported delinquent acts, the expected number of delinquent acts for a 17-year-old youth would be

$$\hat{y} = -15.99 + (1.43)(17)$$
$$\hat{y} = 8.32$$

This predicted value indicates that we would expect approximately 8 self-reported delinquent acts to be reported by a 17-year-old youth. In reality, this predicted y value is simply our "best guess" based on the estimated regression line. It does not mean that every 17-year-old will report 8 delinquent acts. Since age and delinquency are linearly related, however, it does mean that our best guess when using the regression equation is better than guessing the number of delinquent acts without it or just using the overall mean number of delinquent acts as our best guess. The stronger the linear relationship between age and self-reported delinquency, the better or more accurate our estimate will be.

We now know two data points that lie exactly on our estimated regression line: the one corresponding to the means of the x and y values ($\bar{X} = 14.4$, $\bar{Y} = 4.6$) and the one corresponding to the predicted value of y when x = 17 ($\bar{Y} = 8.32$) from our prediction equation earlier. Knowing two data points that lie on our regression line enables us to draw the regression line with precision rather than simply "eyeballing" the line. We simply draw a straight line that runs through these two data points, as shown in Figure 11.17. This line represents the "best-fitting" regression line that we could obtain to describe the relationship between age and self-reported delinquency.

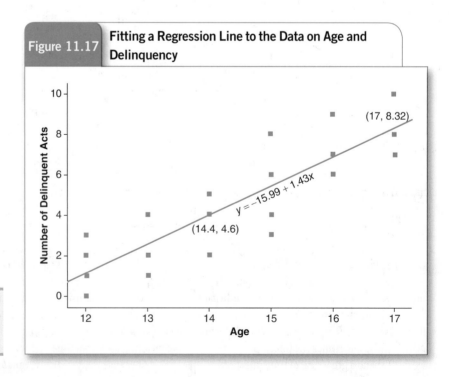

Figure 11.17 Fitting a Regression Line to the Data on Age and Delinquency

Predicted value of of y($\hat{y}$): Value of the dependent variable predicted by a regression equation.

Case Study

Predicting State Crime Rates

Let's return now to our state-level data and estimate the value of the slope coefficient for each of the three relationships we examined earlier with the correlation coefficient. In Table 11.1, we reported the rate of poverty (x) and murder rate (y) for each of the randomly selected 20 states. When we plotted these data in a scatterplot (Figure 11.9), we observed a positive relationship between these two variables. This was confirmed by calculation of the correlation coefficient, $r = .62$, which told us there was a moderate to strong positive relationship between poverty and murder in states. We also know that poverty rates explain 38% of the variation in rates of murder ($r^2 = .38$, or 38%).

Now we will fit a regression line to these data by determining first the slope (b) and then the intercept (a). Because we needed the same information to calculate the correlation coefficient, the calculations necessary to find the slope are already provided for you in Table 11.4. With these calculations and formula 11-5, we can estimate the slope coefficient as

$$b = \frac{20(1,535.1) - (270.1)(106.8)}{20(3,821.8) - (270.1)^2}$$

$$b = \frac{30,702 - 28,846.7}{76,434 - 72,954}$$

$$b = \frac{1,855.3}{3,482}$$

$$b = .53$$

As with the correlation coefficient, the slope coefficient is positive, indicating that there is a positive linear relationship between a state's murder rate and its poverty rate. The magnitude of the slope is .53, which tells us that a 1-unit change in the rate of poverty (a 1% increase in poverty since the poverty variable is measured as the percentage of the population living below the poverty level) increases the murder rate by .53 unit. There is, then, a positive linear relationship between a state's poverty rate and its murder rate. This slope appears small, but when you examine the murder rates you can see that the range for this variable is not very large, hence the relatively small size of b. As we will soon see, it does not indicate that there is a weak relationship between poverty and rates of murder. To increase our understanding, we can add units to x to determine the change in y. For example, if a 1-unit increase in poverty increases the murder rate by .53 unit, we know that a 5-unit increase in poverty will increase the rate of murder by 2.65 units ($5 \times .53 = 2.65$). This, then, enables us to demonstrate more meaningfully the effect of x on y; increasing the poverty rate by 5%, in this case, will serve to increase the rate of murder by 2.65 murders per 100,000 population.

Let's move on to solve for the entire regression equation. Knowing the value of b and the mean values of x (poverty rate) and y (murder rate), we can now solve for the intercept (a). The mean homicide rate for these 20 states is 5.3 (106.8 / 20), and the mean rate of poverty is 13.5 (270.1 / 20). The intercept then, is equal to

$$a = \bar{Y} - b\bar{X}$$

$$a = 5.3 - (.53)(13.5)$$

$$a = 5.3 - 7.16$$

$$a = -1.86$$

The point where the regression line crosses the y axis when x is equal to 0 is where $y = -1.86$. We can now write our full regression equation for these data as

$$y = a + bx$$
$$y = -1.86 + .53(x)$$

With this regression equation, we can now estimate the predicted value of y ($\hat{y}$) at any given value of x. For example, the predicted murder rate for a state with a poverty rate of 17 would be

$$y = a + bx$$
$$y = -1.86 + .53(17)$$
$$y = -1.86 + 9.01$$
$$y = 7.15$$

Exactly what does this predicted value mean? It means that we would predict a state with 17% of its population living below the poverty level would have a murder rate of 7.15 per 100,000. Keep in mind that this is our predicted value of y based on our regression equation estimated from the sample data. It represents our "best guess" of what y will be at a given value of x. It does not mean that the y score will be that exact value. Unless all of the sample data points lie exactly on the regression line (which would mean that our two variables were perfectly correlated), our predicted y values ($\hat{y}$) will usually be different from our observed y value. In regression analysis, this error in predicting the dependent variable is often called the **residual**. In the case of perfect correlation, we can predict one score from another without error and our residuals will be zero. The closer the data points are to the estimated regression line, therefore, the more accurate our predicted y scores and the smaller the residuals. The farther the data points are from the line, the less accurate our predicted y scores and the greater the residuals will be. Because we always have error in prediction, we must rewrite the regression equation as

$$y = a + bx + e$$

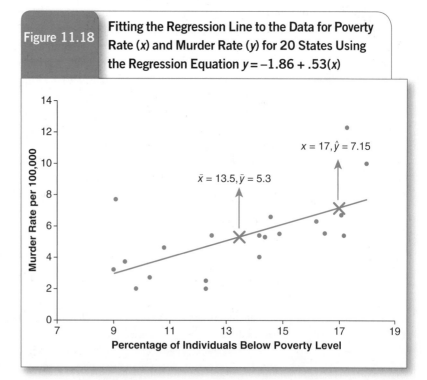

Figure 11.18 Fitting the Regression Line to the Data for Poverty Rate (x) and Murder Rate (y) for 20 States Using the Regression Equation $y = -1.86 + .53(x)$

Residual: Difference between the predicted value of y from the regression equation and the observed value at a given x score.

where e is the symbol for the error term. The error term reflects the fact that other factors are related to the dependent variable than the one independent variable we have included in our model. This refers to the fact that several factors, not just the one we are looking at, usually help to explain a given y variable. If we are examining only one of them, we will not be able to predict y with perfect precision. In other words, when we look only at x and ignore other factors that influence y, our predictions will contain some amount of error. The more y is determined solely by x, the less error we will have. We will have more to say about this in the next chapter, which is about multiple regression. For now, let's return to our problem.

With our predicted value of $\hat{y} = 7.15$ with an x score of 17, we now have two data points that fall exactly on our regression line, including the value for the means of x and y ($X = 13.5$, $\bar{Y} = 5.3$). Connecting these two points with a straight line will give us our best-fitting regression line that describes the relationship between the murder rate and the poverty rate. This is shown in Figure 11.18.

Let's go through another example. In Table 11.2, we reported data for 20 states regarding the percentage of each state's population living in a nonmetropolitan area (x) and its robbery rate (y). In the scatterplot we constructed from these data (Figure 11.11), we observed a negative relationship between these two variables. This was confirmed by the sign of the correlation coefficient ($r = -.66$). The magnitude of the correlation coefficient indicated that the percentage of the population that was rural in a state could explain 44% of the variation in robbery ($r^2 = .44$). Now, we will fit a regression line to these data by determining first the slope (b) and then the intercept (a). The calculations necessary to calculate the slope were provided in Table 11.5. With these calculations and formula 11-5, we can estimate the slope coefficient to be

$$b = \frac{n\Sigma xy - (\Sigma x)(\Sigma y)}{n\Sigma x^2 - (\Sigma x)^2}$$

$$b = \frac{(20)(46,331.2) - (428.3)(2,516.4)}{(20)(12,188.8) - (428.3)^2}$$

$$b = \frac{926,624 - 1,077,774.1}{243,776 - 183,440.9}$$

$$b = \frac{-151,150.1}{60,335.1}$$

$$b = -2.51$$

The sign of the slope is negative, indicating a negative linear relationship between percentage rural and a state's robbery rate. This means that for every 1-unit increase in x, there is a b-unit *decrease* in y. Thus, the magnitude of the slope tells us that for each 1% increase in the state's population that is rural, the robbery rate declines by 2.51 units per 100,000. In other words, the greater the percentage of a state's population that lives in a rural area, the lower the rate of robbery. States with larger percentages of urban residents, therefore, have higher rates of robbery.

We can next calculate the mean for the x variable (percentage nonmetropolitan) as 428.3 / 20 = 21.4 and the mean of y (robbery rate) as 2,516.4 / 20 = 125.8. With this information, we can determine the intercept:

$$a = 125.8 - (-2.51)(21.4)$$

$$a = 125.8 - (-53.7)$$

$$a = 179.5$$

The point where the regression line crosses the y axis when the value of x is equal to 0 is $y = 179.5$. We can now write our full regression equation as

$$y = a + bx$$

$$y = 179.5 + -2.51(x)$$

With this regression equation, we can estimate a predicted value of the robbery rate ($\hat{y}$) for a given value of percentage rural population. If the percentage of the state that lives in a nonmetropolitan area is 10%, our predicted rate of robbery will be

$$\hat{y} = 179.5 + -2.51(10)$$

$$\hat{y} = 179.5 + -25.1$$

$$\hat{y} = 154.4$$

Given a state with 10% rural population, then, we would predict a robbery rate of 154.4 robberies per 100,000. We now have two data points that lie exactly on the estimated regression line. One of these points is the mean of the x and y variables ($\bar{X}, \bar{Y}$), which is (21.4, 125.8), and the other is our x value of 10 and the predicted value of $y(\hat{y})$, equal to 154.4. With these two points, we can draw a straight line that runs through both of them to establish our regression line; this line represents the best-fitting regression line that describes the linear relationship between these data. We have drawn this line for you on the scatterplot presented in Figure 11.19.

Our final example using the state-level data involved the relationship between the divorce rate in a state and its burglary rate. Recall that the original data for these variables, along with the calculations necessary for determining b, were presented in Table 11.6. In our scatterplot from these data (Figure 11.12), we could not discern any clear upward or downward linear pattern in the data points. This suggested to us that the two variables were not very strongly linearly related to one another. The correlation coefficient we obtained of $r = .056$ confirmed this suspicion, indicating that the divorce rate explained less than 1% of the variation in burglary in states. Now, we will more precisely fit a least-squares regression line to the data.

As in our other examples, we will begin by estimating the slope of the regression line (b) using the calculations provided for us in Table 11.6.

With these calculations, we can derive an estimate of b as

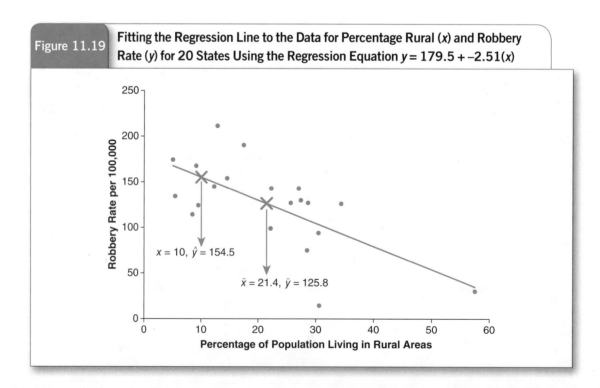

Figure 11.19 Fitting the Regression Line to the Data for Percentage Rural (x) and Robbery Rate (y) for 20 States Using the Regression Equation $y = 179.5 + -2.51(x)$

$$b = \frac{n\Sigma xy - (\Sigma x)(\Sigma y)}{n\Sigma x^2 - (\Sigma x)^2}$$

$$b = \frac{(20)(89,736.6) - (128.6)(13,915.3)}{(20)(847.5) - (128.6)^2}$$

$$b = \frac{1,794,732 - 1,789,507.6}{16,950 - 16,538}$$

$$b = \frac{5222.4}{412}$$

$$b = 12.68$$

The sign and magnitude of the slope coefficient indicate that as the divorce rate in a state increases by 1 unit, the rate of burglary increases by 12.68 units per 100,000. There is, then, a positive linear relationship between a state's divorce rate and its corresponding rate of burglary. The mean value of the divorce rate is 6.43 (128.6 / 20), and the mean burglary rate is 695.77 (13,915.3 / 20) per 100,000. With these values, the estimated value of the intercept can be determined as

$$a = \bar{Y} - b\bar{X}$$

$$a = 695.77 - 12.68(6.43)$$

$$a = 695.77 - 81.53$$

$$a = 614.24$$

The point where the regression line crosses the y axis (the y intercept) is where $y = 614.24$. Our complete regression equation for these data can now be defined as

$$y = a + bx$$

$$y = 614.24 + 12.68(x)$$

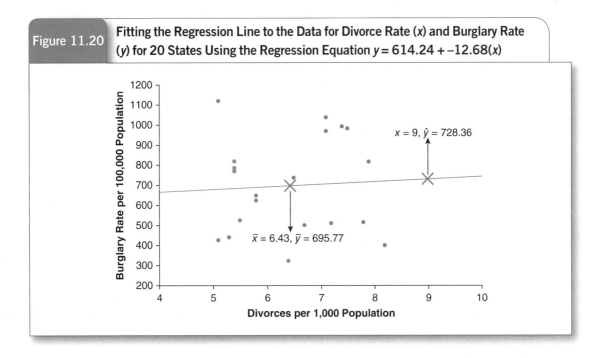

Figure 11.20 **Fitting the Regression Line to the Data for Divorce Rate (x) and Burglary Rate (y) for 20 States Using the Regression Equation $y = 614.24 + -12.68(x)$**

For any value of x, we can now estimate a predicted value of $y(\hat{y})$. For example, the predicted burglary rate for a state with a divorce rate equal to 9 per 1,000 would be

$$\hat{y} = 614.24 + 12.68(9)$$

$$\hat{y} = 614.24 + 114.12$$

$$\hat{y} = 728.36$$

Thus, if a state's divorce rate were 9 divorces per 1,000 residents, then based on our estimated regression equation, we would predict that there would be approximately 728 burglaries per 100,000 residents. By knowing this data point along with the mean values of both variables ($\overline{X} = 6.43$, $\overline{Y} = 695.77$), we can now draw our regression line by drawing a straight line that goes through these two points. This is shown in Figure 11.20. Note that this regression line is much more horizontal (flat) than the other two regression lines we have drawn using the state-level data, indicating that the divorce rates do not seem to affect burglary rates in states.

Comparison of b and r

In understanding the linear relationship between two continuous variables, we have discussed the slope coefficient (b) and the correlation coefficient (r). You may be wondering at this point why two statistics are necessary. Couldn't we estimate just one with our sample data and be done with it? The quick answer to your question (and you should know by now that there is *never* really a quick answer) is that although the two measures have some similar properties, they tell us somewhat different things about our continuous variables.

Note that the slope coefficient is interpreted in terms of the original units of measurement of the variables. That is, an increase of 1 in the x variable's unit of measurement (percentage below the poverty level, percentage rural population) changes (increases/decreases) the y variable by b units (murder rate per 100,000 and robbery rate per 100,000). Beyond this interpretation, however, there is no information that conveys the magnitude of the relationship. If, for example, we were to change units of measurement, say from dollars to pennies or from rates per 10,000 to rates per 100,000, the magnitude (but not the direction) of our slope coefficient would correspondingly change. That is why we cannot simply assume that a small slope coefficient indicates that the strength of the linear relationship is also small. A small slope coefficient may pack quite a wallop in terms of how strongly related it is to the dependent variable!

Notice, for example, that the slope coefficient in the regression equation for the divorce rate and the rate of burglary was equal to 12.68 ($b = 12.68$), but the slope coefficient in the regression equation for the poverty rate and the rate of murder was equal to .53 ($b = .53$). We cannot compare the magnitude of these two coefficients and conclude that the relationship between divorce and burglary is stronger than the relationship between poverty and murder. The reason why the slope coefficient for the poverty rate is so much smaller than that for the divorce rate is that there is so little variation in our rates of murder and that the rates themselves are much smaller than the rates of burglary. For example, the range of murder rates for our 20 states is from 2 to 12.3 per 100,000 population, whereas the range of burglary rates is from 321.6 to 1,117.3 per 100,000. This range and variation for the burglary rate is much larger than that for the murder rate, and this magnitude of difference in the units of measurement is reflected in the magnitude of the slope (b). The correlation coefficient, however, is like a standardized linear measure of association. Its magnitude does not depend on what metric of measurement the variables are measured in. That is why we need the values of both the regression coefficient (b) and Pearson's correlation coefficient (r). The regression coefficient (b) gives us the more precise indicator of the linear change in y associated with a change in x, whereas the correlation coefficient (r) standardizes the magnitude of this relationship so that we can compare the relative strength of relationships across different cases and across different variables. When we examine the correlation coefficients for both cases, we see that the correlation is much stronger for the relationship between murder and poverty ($r = .62$) than for the relationship between divorce and burglary ($r = .056$).

In sum, the slope coefficient measures the *form* of the linear relationship between x and y but is expressed in terms of the units of measurement of the variables. The correlation coefficient can tell us about the *strength* of the linear relationship between two continuous variables, but it tells us nothing about the precise nature of that relationship. We cannot use the value of r to predict y values because we do not know how much of an impact x has on y, nor do we know the original measurement units of the variables. Again, this is because the correlation coefficient is standardized. For this reason, it is important to calculate and report both the slope coefficient (b) and the correlation coefficient (r). Knowing the values of both b and r, however, still does not tell us whether there is a significant relationship between x and y. For this, we need to perform a hypothesis test.

Testing for the Significance of *b* and *r*

Because the slope (b) and correlation coefficient (r) are only sample estimates of their respective population parameters (β and ρ), we must test for the statistical significance of b and r. In returning to our state-level data, the question we want to address concerns the relationship between x and y for the 50 states, not just for our sample of 20 states. We also include jurisdictions that did not report data to the FBI for the Uniform Crime Reports as our target population. The null hypothesis used for the slope and the correlation coefficient in the population assumes that there is no linear relationship between the x and y variables in the population. Remember that when there is no linear relationship between two variables, both the slope and the correlation coefficient will be equal to zero. Since the numerators for the slope and the correlation coefficient are identical, a hypothesis test about the slope is also a hypothesis test about the correlation coefficient in the bivariate case. The alternative hypothesis assumes that there is a linear relationship between the x and y variables in the population and, thus, that the slope and correlation coefficient are significantly different from zero. As with many other hypothesis tests, the alternative hypothesis can be stated as a one-tailed or two-tailed test. Formally stated, the null and alternative hypotheses for the slope and regression coefficient in the population would be

H_0: β and $\rho = 0$, or there is no relationship between x and y

H_1: β and $\rho \neq 0$, or there is a relationship between x and y

H_1: β and $\rho > 0$, or there is a positive relationship between x and y

H_1: β and $\rho < 0$, or there is a negative relationship between x and y

Remember, we refer to the population parameters in the hypotheses because that is what we are really testing—the relationship between the variables in the population. Before we conduct our hypothesis test, however, we must be sure that our data meet certain assumptions. A few of these assumptions are familiar to you. For example, we must assume that the data were randomly selected. Second, we must assume that both variables are normally distributed. Third, we must assume that the data are continuous—that they are measured at the interval/ratio level. Fourth, we must assume that the nature of the relationship between the two variables is linear. The fifth assumption is really a set of assumptions about the error term. It is assumed that the error component of a regression equation is independent of, and therefore uncorrelated with, the independent or x variable, that it is normally distributed, that it has an expected value of zero, and that it has constant variance across all levels of x. The last assumption is called the assumption of **homoscedasticity**. The assumption of homoscedasticity is simply that the variance of the conditional y scores is the same at each value of x.

> **Homoscedasticity:** Assumption in ordinary least-squares regression that the error terms are constant across all values of x.

Assumptions for Testing Hypotheses about β and ρ

1. The observations were randomly selected.

2. Both variables have normal distributions.

3. The two variables are measured at the interval/ratio level.

4. The variables are related in a linear form.

5. The error component is independent of, and therefore uncorrelated with, the independent or x variable, is normally distributed, has an expected value of zero, and has a constant variance across all levels of x (assumption of homoscedasticity).

The assumption of homoscedasticity, as well as the assumption of linearity, may be assessed by examining the scatterplots. In Figure 11.21, the relationship between x and y is linear, and the assumption of homoscedasticity is met. At each value of x, the variance of y is the same. In other words, the conditional distribution of the y scores at fixed values of x shows the same dispersion. No value of x has a variance in the y scores that is significantly higher or lower compared with the other values of x. In Figure 11.22, however, the assumption of homoscedasticity is violated. Although the relationship is linear, the variance of the y scores is much greater at higher values of x than at lower values. This can be seen from the fact that there is a "wedge" pattern in the y scores as x increases. The spread, or dispersion, of y scores is greater when x is greater than 15. When the assumption of linearity is violated, linear-based statistics such as the Pearson correlation coefficient and the least-squares regression coefficient are not appropriate. When the assumption of homoscedasticity is not supported, you may have to make what are called transformations of your data. That topic, you will be relieved to learn, is beyond the scope of this book. You should be aware, however, that a careful inspection of your scatterplot is always the first order of business because it can warn you of potential problems with your data.

If all assumptions have been met, the significance test for r and b is relatively straightforward. With the null hypothesis of no linear relationship, the distribution of the sample r values (and b values) is approximated with the t distribution, with the degrees of freedom equal to $n - 2$. The t statistic for this test has the following formula:

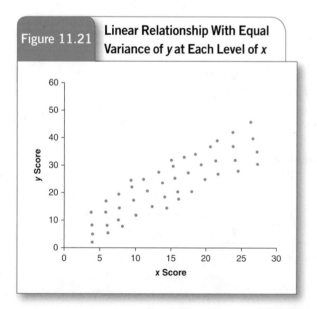

Figure 11.21 Linear Relationship With Equal Variance of y at Each Level of x

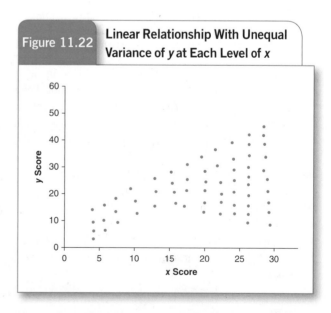

Figure 11.22 Linear Relationship With Unequal Variance of y at Each Level of x

$$t = r\sqrt{\frac{n-2}{1-r^2}}$$
(Formula 11-6)

where

r = the estimated sample r

n = the sample size

For our sample of state data, let's test for the significance of a linear relationship among the three sets of variables. Because we have some idea about the relationship between each independent and dependent variable, we will use one-tailed tests with an alpha level of .05 (one-tailed) and 18 degrees of freedom (20 − 2 = 18). We lose 2 degrees of freedom because we are estimating two parameters in our regression model: the intercept and the slope. From the t table in Table B.3 of Appendix B, we can see that for a one-tailed test with an alpha of .05 and 18 degrees of freedom, the critical t value is 1.734. Let's get going.

Case Study

Murder and Poverty

Step 1: For the relationship between the poverty rate and the murder rate, we found that $r = .62$ and $b = .53$. Our null hypothesis is that the slope and correlation coefficient are zero—that is, there is no linear relationship between murder and poverty. Because we believe that there is a positive relationship between the poverty rate and the murder rate, our research or alternative hypothesis is that both coefficients will be significantly greater than zero, or that as state poverty rates increase, so do murder rates:

H_0: β and ρ for murder and poverty rates = 0, or there is no relationship between murder and poverty rates in the population.

H_1: β and ρ for murder and poverty rates > 0, or there is a relationship between murder and poverty rates in the population.

Step 2: To test this null hypothesis, we will use the t statistic and its respective sampling distribution. The question we are really asking is, "If there was no linear relationship between the poverty rate and murder rate in the population, how likely is it that we would obtain a sample r of .62 or greater or a sample b of .53 or greater?"

Step 3: We have already decided to use a one-tailed test with an alpha level of .05 ($\alpha = .05$). The critical value of t from the t table in Appendix B.3 tells us that our obtained value of t for this test must be greater than 1.734 to reject the null hypothesis. So, our decision will be to reject the null hypothesis if $t_{obt} \geq 1.734$.

Step 4: Calculate the obtained value of t:

$$t = .62\sqrt{\frac{20-2}{1-(.62)^2}}$$

$$t = .62\sqrt{\frac{18}{1-.38}}$$

$$t = .62\sqrt{\dfrac{18}{.62}}$$

$$t = .62\sqrt{29.03}$$

$$t = .62(5.39)$$

$$t = 3.34$$

Step 5: Since our obtained t of 3.34 is greater than the critical t value of 1.734, we can reject the null hypothesis and conclude that there is a statistically significant relationship between poverty rate and murder rate for the 50 U.S. states. States with higher rates of poverty also have higher rates of murder in the population.

Case Study

Robbery Rates and Rural Population

Let's move on to our data examining the relationship between percentage rural population and robbery. With our sample of 20 states, we found a correlation of $r = -.66$ and a slope of $b = -2.50$. Because we believe that states that have higher rates of rural population will tend to have lower rates of robbery, we will assume that the values of b and r also will be negative. This is reflected in our research hypothesis that follows, which states that the values of b and r in the population will be less than 0. The first step is to formalize our null and research hypotheses:

H_0: β and ρ for violent crime and rural $= 0$, or there is no relationship between violent crime and percentage rural in the population.

H_1: β and ρ for violent crime and rural < 0, or there is a relationship between violent crime and percentage rural in the population.

By using an alpha $= .05$ with 18 degrees of freedom for a one-tailed test, we have a critical value of t equal to -1.734. We will reject the null hypothesis if t_{obt} is less than or equal to -1.734, and we will fail to reject the null hypothesis if it is greater than -1.734. We can next calculate the obtained value of t from the sample data:

$$t = -.66\sqrt{\dfrac{20-2}{1-(-.66)^2}}$$

$$t = -.66\sqrt{\dfrac{18}{1-.44}}$$

$$t = -.66\sqrt{\dfrac{18}{.56}}$$

$$t = -.66\sqrt{32.14}$$

$$t = -.66(5.67)$$

$$t = -3.74$$

Since the obtained t value of -3.74 is less than the critical t value of -1.734, we can reject the null hypothesis of no linear relationship. We can conclude that there is a significant negative linear relationship between percentage rural and rate of robbery for the 50 states. States with higher percentages of their population in rural areas tend to have significantly lower robbery rates.

Case Study

Burglary Rates and Divorce

Finally, let's test the null hypothesis that there is no significant linear relationship between the divorce rate and the burglary rate. The sample correlation for our data was $r = .056$, and the estimated sample slope coefficient was $b = 12.68$. Our research hypothesis will assume that there is a positive relationship between the divorce rate and the burglary rate, and along with the null hypothesis, it is formally stated as follows:

H_0: β and ρ for burglary and divorce $= 0$, or there is no relationship between the divorce rate and the burglary rate in the population.

H_1: β and ρ for burglary and divorce > 0, or there is a relationship between the divorce rate and the burglary rate in the population.

We are again using a one-tailed hypothesis. With 18 degrees of freedom and $\alpha = .05$, the critical value of t is 1.734. We will reject the null hypothesis if $t_{obt} \geq 1.734$, and we will fail to reject it if $t_{obt} < 1.734$. The t statistic we would obtain for this relationship is

$$t = .056\sqrt{\frac{18}{1-(.056)^2}}$$

$$t = .056\sqrt{\frac{18}{1-.0031}}$$

$$t = .056\sqrt{\frac{18}{.9969}}$$

$$t = .056\sqrt{18.06}$$

$$t = .056(4.25)$$

$$t = .24$$

In this case, the obtained t statistic is almost equal to zero. The value of .24 is much less than the critical t value of 1.732. Therefore, we must fail to reject the null hypothesis. We must conclude that there is not a significant linear relationship between the divorce rate and the burglary rate at the state level. The divorce rate within states does not seem to affect the burglary rate.

🔲 Summary

In this chapter, we have been concerned with the relationship between two continuous (interval/ratio) level variables. This relationship is often expressed in terms of the correlation between them. In examining the correlation between two continuous variables (x and y), a very important first step is to create a scatterplot or scattergram. The scatterplot is a graphical display of your joint xy data points. From the pattern of these data points, you can discern whether the relationship between your variables is linear (a pattern resembling a straight line), whether the relationship is nonlinear (a pattern resembling a curved line), or whether there is no relationship between them (no pattern but a random scatter of points). If the relationship is linear, you can tell from the scatterplot whether it is positive (the line is ascending) or negative (the line is descending). You can also make a preliminary judgment from your scatterplot about the strength of the linear relationship by roughly sketching a straight line that passes as close to as many data points as possible and examining how close the points fall to the line. The closer the data points cluster to the line, the stronger the linear relationship between the variables.

A more precise way to draw your regression line and calculate predicted values of $y(\hat{y})$, however, would be to use the mathematical equation for a straight line ($y = a + bx$). If your data are linearly related, this regression line is estimated in such a way that it provides the "best linear fit" to your data. Rather than "eyeballing" the data and drawing a line that seems to come closest to the data points, this equation for the straight line will give us the best fit in terms of minimizing the squared difference between each data point and the mean of y at fixed values of x. This is the idea of the "least-squares" regression line. One term in the regression equation is the slope (b), which measures the steepness of the line. The magnitude of the slope measures the effect of the x variable on the y variable with a 1-unit change in x, and its sign tells us the direction of the relationship. Unfortunately, since the magnitude of the slope coefficient is expressed in terms of the natural units of measurement of the x and y variables, it is not a very convenient measure of association.

A standardized measure of association for continuous variables is the Pearson correlation coefficient (r). The sign of the correlation coefficient is the same as that of its corresponding slope. The value of the correlation coefficient is that it is bounded by ±1.0, so as the relationship between x and y gets stronger, the magnitude of r gets closer to ±1.0. The drawback to the correlation coefficient as a measure of association is that although an r of 0 is indicative of no correlation and an r of ±1.0 indicates a perfect correlation, the magnitudes between these values are not so easy to interpret beyond subjective assessments such as "weak" and "moderately strong" correlations.

The squared value of r (r^2), the coefficient of determination, is, however, readily interpretable at all magnitudes. The value of r^2 reflects the amount of variation in the y variable that is explained by the x variable. Another way to understand this is to view the value of r^2 as an indication of how much we improve our prediction of y by knowing the value of x.

Finally, we examined how to test for the existence of a significant relationship between an independent variable and a dependent variable in the population by using a t test.

Key Terms

➤ Review key terms with eFlashcards. Visit study.sagepub.com/paternoster.

bivariate correlation 277
coefficient of determination (r^2) 294
conditional means of y 296
homoscedasticity 309
least-squares regression line 295

negative correlation 278
Pearson correlation coefficient 289
positive correlation 278
predicted value of y ($\hat{y}$) 302
regression line 280

residual 304
scatterplot 277
slope 298
y intercept 298

Key Formulas

Definitional formula for Pearson's r (formula 11-1):

$$r = \frac{\Sigma(x - \bar{X})(y - \bar{Y})}{\sqrt{\left[\Sigma(x - \bar{X})^2\right]\left[\Sigma(y - \bar{Y})^2\right]}}$$

Computational formula for Pearson's correlation coefficient (formula 11-2):

$$r = \frac{n\Sigma xy - (\Sigma x)(\Sigma y)}{\sqrt{\left[n\Sigma x^2 - (\Sigma x)^2\right]\left[n\Sigma y^2 - (\Sigma y)^2\right]}}$$

Sample regression line (formula 11-3):

$$y = a + bx$$

Definitional formula for the slope coefficient
(formula 11-4):

$$b = \frac{\Sigma(x - \bar{X})(y - \bar{Y})}{\Sigma(x - \bar{X})^2}$$

Computational formula for the slope coefficient
(formula 11-5):

$$b = \frac{n\Sigma xy - (\Sigma x)(\Sigma y)}{n\Sigma x^2 - (\Sigma x)^2}$$

t statistic for testing null hypothesis about b and r
(formula 11-6):

$$t = r\sqrt{\frac{n-2}{1-r^2}}$$

Practice Problems

➤ Test your understanding of chapter content.
Take the practice quiz.

1. Interpret the following Pearson correlation coefficients:

   a. An r of –.55 between the crime rate in a neighborhood and the median income level per household.

   b. An r of .17 between the number of hours spent working after school and self-reported delinquency.

   c. An r of .74 between the number of prior arrests and the length of sentence received for most recent conviction.

   d. An r of –.12 between the number of jobs held when 15 to 17 years old and the number of arrests as an adult.

   e. An r of –.03 between a state's divorce rate and its rate of violent crime.

2. Square each correlation coefficient in problem 1 and interpret the coefficient of determination.

3. Interpret the following regression slope coefficients:

   a. A b of –.017 between the dollar fines given by a federal court for white-collar crimes and the number of citations for price fixing.

   b. A b of .715 between the percentage unemployed and property crime rates.

   c. A b of 1,444.53 between a police officer's years of education and his or her salary.

4. In 2014 research, Callie Burt, Gary Sweeten, and Ronald Simons found a moderately strong relationship between scores on a low self-control scale and self-reported acts of crime. Persons with low self-control admitted committing more criminal acts. Let's say you wanted to replicate this study. With the following data for self-control (x) (assume that high scores on this scale mean low self-control) and self-reported delinquency (y), do or answer the following:

   a. Draw a scatterplot of your data points.

   b. Calculate what the slope of the regression line would be.

   c. Determine what the y intercept is.

   d. What is the predicted number of self-reported offenses (y) when the score on the self-control scale is equal to 70?

   e. Calculate the value of r and test for its significance with an alpha level of .01.

   f. How much of the variation in self-reported delinquency is explained by self-control?

   g. What would you conclude about the relationship between self-control and delinquency? Are your findings consistent with those reported by Burt and her colleagues?

Self-Control (x)	Self-Reported Delinquency (y)
45	5
63	10
38	2
77	23
82	19
59	7
61	17
88	24
52	14
67	20

5. Kyung-Shick Choi, Mitch Librett, and Taylor Collins (2014) found that a gunshot detection system, Shotspotter™, significantly reduced the time it took police to respond to a gun-related crime. You are interested in determining whether this faster police response time (x) will lower the crime rate (y) in a given community and, conversely, whether a longer response time is associated with a higher crime rate. You have the following data on the average time it takes the police to respond to a call by a citizen for help in a community as well as that community's rate of crime. With these data, do or answer the following:

   a. Draw a scatterplot of your data points.

   b. Calculate what the slope of the regression line would be.

   c. Determine what the y intercept is.

   d. What is the predicted rate of crime (ŷ) when the police response time is 11 minutes?

   e. Calculate the value of r and determine whether it is significantly different from zero with an alpha level of .05.

   f. How much of the variation in the rate of crime is explained by police response time?

   g. What would you conclude about the relationship between police response time and crime?

Police Response Time in Minutes (x)	Community Rate of Crime per 1,000 (y)
14	82.9
3	23.6
5	42.5
6	39.7
5	63.2
8	51.3
7	58.7
4	44.5
10	61.2
12	73.5

6. A group of citizens has filed a complaint with the police commissioner of a large city. In this complaint, they allege that poor neighborhoods receive significantly less protection than more affluent neighborhoods. The commissioner asks you to examine this issue, and you have the following data on the percentage of the population in the neighborhood that is on welfare (x) and the number of hours of daily police patrols (y) in a sample of 12 communities in the city. With these data in mind, do or answer the following:

   a. Draw a scatterplot of the data points.

   b. Calculate what the slope of the regression line would be.

   c. Determine what the y intercept is.

   d. What is the predicted number of hours of foot patrol (ŷ) when the percentage unemployed is 30%?

   e. Calculate the value of r and test its significance with an alpha of .01.

   f. How much of the variation in the number of hours of police patrol is explained by the percentage of the population on welfare?

   g. What would you conclude about the relationship between percentage on welfare and number of police patrols?

   h. Calculate the value of b and r again, but this time leave out community numbers 11 and 12. What do you conclude now? What do you think causes these very different findings? Draw a scatterplot of these data and compare it with the one in part 6a.

Community Number	Percentage on Welfare (x)	Hours of Daily Police Patrol (y)
1	40	20
2	37	15
3	32	20
4	29	20
5	25	15
6	24	20
7	17	15
8	15	20
9	12	10
10	8	20
11	4	40
12	2	50

Controlling for a Third Variable

Multiple Ordinary Least Squares Regression

❝ *Conquest is easy. Control is not.*

—Captain James T. Kirk, stardate unknown ❞

LEARNING OBJECTIVES

1. Explain the importance of controlling for multiple independent variables when predicting a dependent variable.

2. Describe the difference between a bivariate correlation and a partial correlation coefficient.

3. Interpret a multiple coefficient of determination and be able to calculate the change in the multiple R^2.

4. Interpret the hypothesis test for a multiple regression model and understand how it is different from the hypotheses tests for partial slope coefficients.

5. Calculate the multiple regression equation and be able to identify it from SPSS output.

6. Interpret the partial slope coefficient and its corresponding null hypothesis test.

7. Describe how the beta weights are different from unstandardized slope coefficients.

Introduction

This chapter represents a very exciting transition in our statistical analysis adventures! Most of our work with inferential statistics has involved bivariate relationships—examining the effects of one independent variable on a dependent variable. However, in our discipline, and in all social sciences more generally, it is virtually never the case that one independent variable alone sufficiently explains the dependent variable. In reality, there are usually several factors that jointly influence the dependent variable. For example, delinquency is affected not only by school grades but also by the delinquency of our friends, our relationships with parents, whether we have jobs during the school year, and a host of other factors. Recidivism is influenced not just by the type of crime someone committed but by many factors, including whether the person received educational training while in prison, or mental health and substance abuse treatment, and the support he or she received after release. We need, therefore, to build on our knowledge of the bivariate regression model by adding more independent variables to that model. When we examine the effect of more than one independent variable on a dependent variable, we employ what is called a multivariate regression model. As the name implies, in the *multivariate* model, we have more than one independent variable whose relationships with the dependent variable we wish to estimate. An implicit assumption of the multivariate regression model, therefore, is that there is more than one independent variable that explains the dependent variable and the purpose of the model is to estimate the effect of each of these independent variables simultaneously. In the multivariate model, therefore, we have a correlation coefficient and a regression coefficient for each of the independent variables in the model. The corresponding correlation coefficient is called the *partial correlation coefficient,* and the regression coefficient is called the *partial regression coefficient.* In this chapter, we will introduce some of the most important features of the multivariate regression model and partial correlation coefficient.

What Do We Mean by Controlling for Other Important Variables?

Identifying the causes of phenomena—figuring out why things happen—is the goal of much research. Unfortunately, valid explanations for the causes of things, including crime and the workings of the criminal justice system, are rarely very simple. When we assume that a change in one variable leads to or produces a change in another variable, we are assuming that these two variables are causally related. Establishing the existence of a causal effect between an independent variable and a dependent variable is often termed "making a causal inference." The language we use in criminology and criminal justice often implies causality. For example, if a research study finds that arrested men who assault their intimate partners are less likely to assault their partners in the future compared with assaulters who were not arrested, the researcher may conclude that arrest was causally related to this decrease in the likelihood of future violence. When it is found that inmates who participated in a therapeutic community within prison are less likely to recidivate than those who did not participate, we often say that the reduced crime on release was produced or caused by their involvement in a rehabilitation program. But establishing a causal relationship through research is actually very difficult. Specifically, three things need to exist before we can conclude that a causal connection exists between two variables:

1. There must be an empirical association between them.
2. The independent variable must precede the dependent variable in time.
3. Other possible causes of the dependent variable must be explicitly considered. That is, the relationship between two variables must be nonspurious, which means it is not caused by a third variable.

Multivariate regression model:
A regression model predicting one dependent variable with two or more independent variables.

Student Study Site

Visit the open-access Student Study Site at
study.sagepub.com/paternoster to access
additional study tools including mobile-friendly
eFlashcards, web quizzes, links to SAGE journal
articles, additional data sets, SPSS exercises,
and more!

The first criterion, demonstrating that there is a statistical association or correlation between the independent and dependent variables, is generally the easiest to satisfy. In fact, we know you have become relatively good at this by now! Establishing the second criterion—that the independent variable occurred prior to the dependent variable—is sometimes very easy and sometimes very difficult. The easy form of the correct temporal order occurs when it is logically impossible for the dependent variable to come first. For example, if we find that males are more likely to drop out of high school than females, the correct temporal order can only be that something about gender causes males to have a higher risk of dropping out since dropping out cannot logically cause gender. The more difficult form of the correct temporal order of our causal variables can frequently be accomplished by a careful research design. The third criterion, nonspuriousness, is related to the subject matter of this chapter. **Nonspuriousness** between two variables means that the relationship between them is not caused by a third factor or factors that may be related to them both. When a third variable (z), sometimes called an extraneous variable, causes both the independent variable (x) and the dependent variable (y), there will be a correlation between x and y, but this correlation is present because they are both outcomes of the third variable, z. Thus, x and y are not *causally* related to each other but rather are spuriously related; they (x and y) are simply two outcomes of a common cause (z). They are said to be spuriously related because they both depend on z and not on each other.

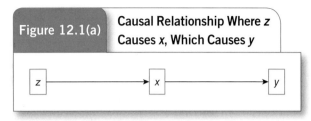

Figure 12.1(a) Causal Relationship Where z Causes x, Which Causes y

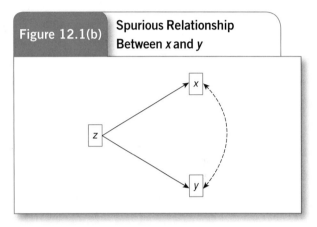

Figure 12.1(b) Spurious Relationship Between x and y

Figure 12.1(a) shows a causal relationship among three variables, x, y, and z. The variable z causes x, and x in turn causes y. In this figure, the relationship between x and y is causal. In Figure 12.1(b), we have the situation where z is the common cause of both x and y. Here, the dashed line indicates that x and y are correlated not because one causes the other but simply because they both depend on z. One of the most vexing problems in making inferences about causality, then, is the possibility that one has not really measured the causal effect of one variable on another because there is some third factor causing them both. To help us make more valid causal inferences, then, we need to measure and consider other variables and control for their effects. One powerful way to control for the effects of other variables is to collect data from a randomized experiment. In a randomized experiment, subjects are randomly placed into "treatment" or "control" groups. Because the assignment into these groups is random, the groups can be considered equivalent. Suppose we wanted to determine whether a prison job training program reduced recidivism after release. If we randomly assigned inmates to either receive the program or not, the only difference between the two groups after release would be whether they received treatment. As such, if the people who received the job training had lower rates of recidivism compared with those who did not, we can be relatively certain that the program had something to do with this difference.

It is not always possible to conduct true experiments, however. If we are interested in the effect of a good marriage on offenders quitting crime, how can we randomly assign people to get married or not get married or assign some to a good marriage and some to a bad marriage or no marriage? As you can see, there are many instances where a randomized experimental design cannot or cannot easily be used; in social science, we more frequently than not have observational data rather than experimental data. In collecting observational data, we observe but do not manipulate who gets the "treatment" and who does not. For example, we simply observe those who are married or have good marriages and those who are not married or have bad marriages. Since we do not have control with the randomization of subjects, in observational data we must control for spuriousness statistically. One common technique used statistically to control for the effects of other variables is multiple regression analysis. But before we discuss this more advanced technique, we want to illustrate the concept of statistical control with an easier to understand partial cross-tabulation table.

Nonspuriousness: When a relationship between two variables is not explained by a third variable.

Illustrating Statistical Control With Partial Tables

Case Study

Boot Camps and Recidivism

The top panel of Figure 12.2 depicts data from a hypothetical study examining the relationship between attending a boot camp prison (a highly regimented, discipline-focused correctional program) and whether people committed a crime after prison (recidivism). As you can see, the 2 × 2 table reveals that prisoners who attended boot camp were slightly less likely to recidivate (47%) than those who did not attend the boot camp (55%). The bottom panel of Figure 12.2, however, depicts this same relationship between attending boot camp and recidivism while holding constant the offenders' gender. In this case, "holding constant" means looking at the relationship between two variables (boot camp attendance and recidivism) within separate levels of a third variable (gender). In this example, notice that in looking at the relationship between attending a boot camp prison and recidivism, we have turned gender into a constant. In the males-only table, the relationship between boot camp participation and recidivism cannot be due to gender, and the same holds for the females-only table.

This bottom table is referred to as a partial cross-tabulation table; it examines the relationship between boot camp attendance and recidivism separately for males and females. When gender is held constant, a much different picture emerges. Within categories of gender, there is no relationship between going to a boot camp and the risk of recidivism. The original relationship between recidivism and boot camp attendance is spurious. It was present primarily because gender is correlated with both going to boot camp and the risk of recidivism. Attending boot camp just appears to reduce recidivism because males were both less likely to attend boot camp and more likely to commit crimes after prison regardless of whether they attended boot camp or a regular correctional facility.

Figure 12.2 Data From a Hypothetical Study Examining the Relationship Between Attending a Boot Camp Prison and the Likelihood of Committing Crimes After Prison (Recidivating)

All Prisoners, n = 350

	Attended Boot Camp	Did Not Attend Boot Camp
Recidivated	75 / 47%	105 / 55%
Did Not Recidivate	85 / 53%	85 / 45%
	160	190

Female Prisoners, n = 150 / Male Prisoners, n = 200

	Attended Boot Camp	Did Not Attend	Attended Boot Camp	Did Not Attend
Recidivated	40 / 40%	20 / 40%	30 / 60%	90 / 60%
Did Not Recidivate	60 / 60%	30 / 60%	20 / 40%	60 / 40%
	100	50	50	150

This example illustrates the utility of statistical control. If the original bivariate relationship between an independent variable and a dependent variable still holds even after we have controlled for other variables, we can have more confidence that these variables may actually be causally related. If the original relationship between the two variables disappears, however, those two original variables may be only spuriously related. As we shall see, the multivariate regression equation gives us the same kind of statistical control that exists in the partial cross-tabulation tables.

The Multiple Regression Equation

As we suggested earlier, the **multiple regression equation** (or model) is simply a straightforward extension of the bivariate regression model. The difference between the bivariate and multiple regression models is that the latter has more than one independent variable. In the case of the multiple regression model, we aim to estimate the effect of several independent variables on a dependent variable. Given that there are several independent variables, there will be more than one slope coefficient to estimate. In fact, there will be one slope coefficient for each independent variable that is in the model. Formally, the multiple regression model for the population specifies the dependent variable (y) as being a linear function of two or more independent variables (x_1, x_2, etc.) plus an error term that encompasses various omitted factors that are also related to y but we have not included in our model. The multivariate regression model estimated from sample data is represented as

$$y = a + b_1 x_1 + b_2 x_2 + \cdots b_k x_k + \varepsilon \qquad \text{(Formula 12-1)}$$

The intercept (a) in this multivariate equation is the predicted value of y when *all* independent variables are equal to 0. The interpretation of the slope coefficient (b), which is identified by subscripts, is somewhat different from the bivariate case. Technically, slope coefficients estimated with multiple regression equations are referred to as **partial slope coefficients** or **partial regression coefficients**. The first slope coefficient in equation 12-1, b_1, is the partial slope of the linear relationship between the first independent variable and the dependent variable, y, holding all other variables in the model constant. By "holding all other variables constant," we mean after taking their effect on the dependent variable into account. The second slope coefficient, b_2, is the partial slope of the linear relationship between the second independent variable and y, holding all other variables in the model constant. If you were using five independent variables to predict a dependent variable, there would be five partial slope coefficients, each denoted by its subscript (b_1, b_2, b_3, b_4, and b_5).

Each slope coefficient indicates the expected change in the y variable associated with a 1-unit change in a given independent variable when all other independent variables in the model are held constant. This last component of the interpretation, "when all other independent variables are held constant," is important. It is this statistical control that enables us to separate the effect of one independent variable from the effects of other independent variables in the regression model. In other words, the partial slope coefficient measures the effect of one independent variable on the dependent variable when the effects of all the other independent variables in the model on the dependent variable have been considered (e.g., statistically controlled for).

The final term in the multiple regression equation is the error term, ε. As in the bivariate model, the error component in the multiple regression model reflects those explanatory variables that are not included in the model. The practice of good regression analysis consists of including in the model those explanatory variables that are most strongly related to the dependent variable—and unrelated to the other independent variables included in the model. Although the multiple regression equation can be estimated using a large number of independent variables, for ease of presentation, we will concentrate on equations using only two independent variables.

Multiple regression equation: Equation estimated with two or more independent variables predicting one dependent variable.

Partial slope coefficient: Effect of an independent variable on the dependent variable after controlling for one or more other independent variables.

Assumptions of the Multivariate Regression Model

1. The observations are independent.

2. All values of y are normally distributed at each value of x.

3. The dependent variable is measured at the interval/ratio level.

4. The relationship between the dependent variable and each of the independent variables is linear.

5. The error term (ε) is independent of, and therefore uncorrelated with, each of the independent variables; is normally distributed; has an expected value of 0; and has constant variance across all levels of x.

6. The independent variables are not highly correlated among themselves. That is, there is no multicollinearity.

The assumptions of the multiple regression model are identical to those for the case of one independent variable except for the addition of one new assumption (see the accompanying boxed list). The new assumption in the multivariate regression model is that the independent variables are independent of, or uncorrelated with, one another. Having independent variables that are highly correlated is referred to as the problem of multicollinearity. That was the point we were making when we said that the ideal regression analysis is to select independent variables that are strongly related to the dependent variable *and only weakly related or unrelated to each other*. This problem did not arise in the case of one independent variable, but it will be a constant concern as we add to the list of independent variables in our model.

Why is it so important that the independent variables be uncorrelated with one another? To answer this question, think carefully about what we want to do in multiple regression analysis. We have a dependent variable that we are trying to explain. We have at least two independent variables that may explain this dependent variable. We would like to learn two important things from our multiple regression analysis: (1) How much of the variation in the dependent variable are we explaining by our two independent variables together? (2) How much of this combined explained variation can we say is *uniquely* due to each of the independent variables? The first question asks how much we can explain in the dependent variable. The second asks how much of what we explain is due to the unique contribution of *each* of our independent variables. It is this second question that is difficult to answer when the independent variables are correlated.

Think of two independent variables as lying on a continuum from being completely unique variables with absolutely nothing in common (their correlation is zero) to being identical to one another and having everything in common (their correlation is ±1.0). At one end of this continuum are two variables that are completely unique. These variables are not related to each other, so the correlation between them is near zero or zero. When two variables are correlated, however, it means that they share something in common; they are both measuring some of the same things. The lower the correlation, the more they are unique and the less they have in common; the higher the correlation, the less unique they are and the more they have in common. When two independent variables are completely uncorrelated, we are able to separate the combined explained variance of the dependent variable into unique components. For example, we can specify that of the 60% of explained variance in the dependent variable (y), two thirds of that is due to x_1 and the other one third is due to x_2. As two independent variables become correlated, however, some of the explained variance in the dependent variable cannot be uniquely attributed to one or the other variable. That is, some of the explained variance cannot be said to be due to x_1 or x_2 but can only be said to be due to their shared influence. The stronger the correlation between the two independent variables, the less of the explained variance we can attribute to the unique effect of each variable and the more we must attribute to the explained variance that they share. When the two variables are very highly correlated, we can attribute no unique explained variance to either of them and all of the explained variance in the dependent variable is shared between the two.

Multicollinearity: Occurs whenever the independent variables in your regression equation are too highly correlated with one another.

When the independent variables in a regression equation are highly correlated with one another, they are said to be *collinear*. This means that there is a relationship between or among the independent variables. The final assumption simply notes that you want to avoid multicollinearity in multiple regression analysis. As we stated earlier, you want your independent variables to be strongly correlated with the dependent variable but not highly correlated with each other. Now let's return to the multiple regression model described in equation 12-1 and consider some data to illustrate and give meaning to the concepts we have discussed so far.

Case Study

Predicting Delinquency

Table 12.1 presents hypothetical data from a random survey of 23 high school students who were queried about a number of things, including the number of self-reported delinquent acts during the past year (y), their age (x_1), and how emotionally close they felt to their families (x_2), with a higher score on the close family scale corresponding to a closer connection between the student and family. Two indexes or scales were created that measured students' self-reported delinquency and family closeness. From these data, we are going to estimate the effect that both age and family closeness have on rates of delinquency.

For the sake of this example, let's say that we believe that age will be positively related to delinquency and that family closeness will be negatively related to delinquency. Thus, older students will tend to have higher delinquency scores, and those who are closer to their families will tend to have lower rates of delinquency. In this example, delinquency is our dependent variable (y), whereas age (x_1) and family closeness (x_2) are our two independent variables. Our two-variable regression model, then, looks like this:

$$\text{Delinquency}(y) = a + b_1(\text{age}) + b_2(\text{family closeness}) + \varepsilon$$

The means, standard deviations, and correlation coefficients are presented at the bottom of Table 12.1.

The first step we need to take in computing our multiple regression equation is to calculate each partial slope. The formulas used for calculating partial slope coefficients are

$$b_1 = \left(\frac{s_y}{s_{x1}}\right)\left(\frac{r_{yx_1} - \left(r_{yx_2}\right)\left(r_{x_1x_2}\right)}{1 - r_{x_1x_2}^2}\right) \qquad \text{(Formula 12-2)}$$

$$b_2 = \left(\frac{s_y}{s_{x2}}\right)\left(\frac{r_{yx_2} - \left(r_{yx_1}\right)\left(r_{x_1x_2}\right)}{1 - r_{x_1x_2}^2}\right) \qquad \text{(Formula 12-3)}$$

where

$\quad b_1 =$ the partial slope of x_1 on y
$\quad b_2 =$ the partial slope of x_2 on y
$\quad s_y =$ the standard deviation of y
$\quad s_{x_1} =$ the standard deviation of the first independent variable (x_1)
$\quad s_{x_2} =$ the standard deviation of the second independent variable (x_2)
$\quad r_{yx_1} =$ the bivariate correlation between y and x_1
$\quad r_{yx_2} =$ the bivariate correlation between y and x_2
$\quad r_{x_1x_2} =$ the bivariate correlation between x_1 and x_2

Note that you need not only the bivariate correlation coefficient between each of the two independent variables and the dependent variable (r_{yx_1} and r_{yx_2}) but also the bivariate correlation between the two independent variables ($r_{x_1x_2}$).

| Table 12.1 | | Calculations Necessary to Compute the Partial Slope Coefficient Between Delinquency and Both Age and Family Closeness ($n = 23$) | | | | | |

Delinquency y	Age x_1	Family Closeness x_2	y^2	x_1^2	x_2^2	$x_1 y$	$x_2 y$
80	17	10	6,400	289	100	1,360	800
60	15	20	3,600	225	400	900	1,200
50	14	25	2,500	196	625	700	1,250
70	17	15	4,900	289	225	1,190	1,050
10	13	35	100	169	1,225	130	350
15	13	30	225	169	900	195	450
20	14	28	400	196	784	280	560
5	13	40	25	169	1,600	65	200
70	13	15	4,900	169	225	910	1,050
55	14	20	3,025	196	400	770	1,100
40	15	25	1,600	225	625	600	1,000
35	16	20	1,225	256	400	560	700
10	17	30	100	289	900	170	300
15	16	25	225	256	625	240	375
10	14	20	100	196	400	140	200
15	16	25	225	256	625	240	375
0	14	25	0	196	625	0	0
0	13	35	0	169	1,225	0	0
20	14	20	400	196	400	280	400
0	13	20	0	169	400	0	0
20	14	30	400	196	900	280	600
45	16	30	2,025	256	900	720	1,350
50	17	25	2,500	289	625	850	1,250
$\Sigma = 695$	$\Sigma = 338$	$\Sigma = 568$	$\Sigma = 34,875$	$\Sigma = 5,016$	$\Sigma = 15,134$	$\Sigma = 10,580$	$\Sigma = 14,560$

$\bar{Y} = 30.22$ $\bar{X}_{x_1} = 14.70$ $\bar{X}_{x_2} = 24.70$
$s_y = 25.11$ $s_{x_1} = 1.49$ $s_{x_2} = 7.09$
$r_{yx_1} = .445$
$r_{yx_2} = -.664$
$r_{x_1x_2} = -.366$

In our examples of the multiple regression model, we will go through the calculations of each component of the partial slope coefficient, but we will provide you with each bivariate correlation coefficient.

As shown in the tables, the bivariate correlation coefficients indicate that the relationship between age and delinquency is positive ($r = .445$) and the relationship between family closeness and delinquency is negative ($r = -.664$). These correlation coefficients suggest that older students tend to have higher levels of delinquency but that students with stronger family closeness tend to have lower levels of delinquency. In addition, age and family closeness are negatively related to each other ($r_{x_1 x_2} = -.366$); older youths are less close to their families than younger youths. The correlation between our two independent variables ($r = -.366$) is not very high, so we do not have to worry about the problem of multicollinearity.

With these correlation coefficients, together with the standard deviation of each of the variables and formulas 12-2 and 12-3, we can calculate the partial slope coefficient for each independent variable. From these partial slope coefficients, we will be able to ascertain the effect of each independent variable on the dependent variable while holding the other independent variable constant. These calculations are shown for you as follows.

Partial slope coefficient for the effect of age on delinquency:

$$b_1 = \left(\frac{25.11}{1.49} \right)\left(\frac{.445 - (-.664)(-.366)}{1 - (-.366)^2} \right)$$

$$b_1 = (16.85)\left(\frac{.445 - .243}{1 - .134} \right)$$

$$b_1 = (16.85)\left(\frac{.202}{.866} \right)$$

$$b_1 = (16.85)(.233)$$

$$b_1 = 3.93$$

Partial slope coefficient for the effect of family closeness on delinquency:

$$b_2 = \left(\frac{25.11}{7.09} \right)\left(\frac{-.664 - (.445)(-.366)}{1 - (-.366)^2} \right)$$

$$b_2 = (3.54)\left(\frac{-.664 - (-.163)}{1 - .134} \right)$$

$$b_2 = (3.54)\left(\frac{-.501}{.866} \right)$$

$$b_2 = (3.54)(-.58)$$

$$b_2 = -2.05$$

The partial slope coefficient for the effect of age on delinquency is $b_1 = 3.93$. This indicates that, on average, with every 1-year increase in age (since age is measured in years), the delinquency score increases by 3.93 offenses while holding an individual's closeness to family constant. Similarly, the partial slope coefficient for the effect of family closeness on the delinquency score is $b_2 = -2.05$. This indicates that, on average, for every 1-unit increase in an individual's family closeness, there is a 2.05-unit decrease in delinquency while holding an individual's age constant.

Now that we have obtained the partial slope coefficients for the independent variables of age (b_1) and family closeness (b_2), we can compute the final unknown element in the least-squares regression equation, the intercept (a). This is done in the same way we obtained the intercept in the bivariate regression equation—by substituting the mean of the dependent variable ($\bar{Y}$) and the means of the two independent variables ($\bar{X}_{x_1}$ and $\bar{X}_{x_2}$) into the equation below and solving for a:

$$a = \bar{Y} - b_1 \bar{X}_1 - b_2 \bar{X}_2$$
$$a = 30.22 - 3.93(14.70) - (-2.05)(24.70)$$
$$a = 30.22 - (57.77) - (-50.64)$$
$$a = 23.09$$

The intercept value in these equations indicates that when both independent variables are equal to zero, the average value of y will be equal to 23.09. Now that we have solved for the intercept (a) and both partial regression slopes, our multiple regression equation for delinquency can be expressed as

$$\hat{y} = a + b_1 x_1 + b_2 x_2$$
$$\hat{y} = 23.09 + (3.93)(x_1) + (-2.05)(x_2)$$
$$\hat{y} = 23.09 + (3.93)(\text{age}) + (-2.05)(\text{family closeness})$$

Just like the bivariate regression equation we examined in the last chapter, this least-squares multiple regression equation provides us with the best-fitting line to our data. However, we can no longer represent the equation graphically with a simple straight line fitted to a two-dimensional (x and y) scattergram. With two independent variables in our regression, we have to use our imagination to visualize the fitting of a regression plane to a three-dimensional scatter of points that is defined by each of the coefficients (a, b_1, and b_2). As you can imagine, this exercise in imagery becomes even more complex as more independent variables are brought into the equation. With k independent variables, the regression equation is represented by a plane in k-dimensional space. However, we can still use this multivariate equation to predict scores on our dependent variable, number of delinquent acts committed, from scores on the independent variables of age and family closeness. For example, our best prediction of a delinquency score ($\hat{y}$) for an 18-year-old and a score of 15 on the family closeness index would be obtained by substituting these two x values into the least-squares regression formula as shown:

$$\hat{y} = a + b_1 x_1 + b_2 x_2$$
$$\hat{y} = 23.09 + 3.93(18) + (-2.05)15$$
$$\hat{y} = 23.09 + 70.74 + (-30.75)$$
$$\hat{y} = 63.08$$

Our multiple regression equation predicts that an 18-year-old with a score of 15 on the family closeness index (relatively low, meaning poor family closeness) would have a predicted delinquency score of 63.08. It is always informative to compare predicted values of y for two different scores on the same independent variable while holding the other independent variables constant. So let's predict what the delinquency score would be for that same 18-year-old (18), but this time with a relatively strong closeness to family (30 rather than 15). By using our regression equation, the predicted delinquency score would be

$$\hat{y} = 23.09 + 3.93(18) + (-2.05)30$$

$$\hat{y} = 23.09 + 70.74 + (-61.50)$$

$$\hat{y} = 32.33$$

As you can see here, by doubling the family closeness score for an 18-year-old, the predicted delinquency score is reduced by almost half from 63.08 to 32.33.

We want to emphasize a note of caution in comparing partial slope coefficients. Remember that you cannot compare the relative strength of a relationship between x and y based on the magnitude of b, the partial slope coefficient. Specifically, just because the partial slope for age on delinquency scores was 3.93 while holding family closeness constant, and that slope coefficient for family closeness on delinquency scores was –2.05 while holding age constant, we cannot conclude that the effect of age on delinquency is stronger than the effect of family closeness. Similar to the bivariate model in the last chapter, *in a multiple regression analysis, you cannot determine which independent variable has the strongest effect on the dependent variable by comparing unstandardized partial slope coefficients*. Remember from our discussion in the last chapter that the slope coefficient is measured in terms of the unit of measurement of the x variable—that is, a 1-unit change in x produces a b-unit change in the y variable. The size of the partial slope coefficient, then, reflects the underlying units of measurement. In the bivariate model, we solved this problem by calculating a standardized coefficient that was not dependent on the independent variable's unit of measurement: the correlation coefficient. A similar standardized coefficient in multiple regression is called the *standardized partial slope* or *beta weight*. (This is not to be confused with beta, the population parameter for the slope coefficient.) We will examine beta weights next.

▣ Comparing the Strength of a Relationship Using Beta Weights

To compare the effects of two independent variables on a dependent variable, it is necessary to remove differences in the units of measurement (e.g., dollars compared with cents, years compared with months). One way of doing this is to convert all of the variables in the regression equation to a common measurement scale. This can be achieved by computing a *standardized partial slope coefficient,* called a beta weight, from the obtained partial slope coefficient. If we do this, we will have two partial slope coefficients for each independent variable, one standardized (the beta weight) and one in the original measurement scale.

The formulas used to obtain standardized partial slopes or **beta weights**, symbolized as b^*, from a multiple regression equation with two independent variables are

$$b^*_{x_1} = b_{x_1}\left(\frac{s_{x_1}}{s_y}\right)$$ (Formula 12-4)

$$b^*_{x_2} = b_{x_2}\left(\frac{s_{x_2}}{s_y}\right)$$ (Formula 12-5)

> **Beta weight:** Standardized slope coefficient in an ordinary least-squares regression model.

As the formulas indicate, computation of the beta weight involves multiplying the partial slope coefficient (b_1) obtained for an independent variable by the ratio of the standard deviation of that variable (s_{x_1}) to the standard deviation of the dependent variable (s_y). The interpretation of a beta weight is relatively straightforward. Like a partial slope coefficient, beta coefficients can be either positive or negative. A positive beta coefficient indicates a positive linear relationship between the independent and dependent variables, whereas a negative beta weight indicates a negative linear relationship. The standardized partial slope will always have the same sign as the unstandardized partial slope. Similar to the interpretation of a correlation coefficient, the larger the beta weight, the stronger the relationship between the independent and dependent variables. More specifically, the beta weights show the expected change in a standardized score on the dependent variable for a 1-unit change in a standardized score of the independent variable while holding the other independent variable constant. If we want to know the *relative importance* of two variables, then, we can compare the absolute value of the magnitudes of their respective beta weights. The variable with the larger beta weight has the stronger effect on the dependent variable.

Let's go through an example using the delinquency data. Recall that the partial slope coefficient for age (b_1) was equal to 3.93 and the partial slope coefficient for family closeness (b_2) was equal to –2.05. The standard deviations for age and family closeness are 1.49 and 7.09, respectively (Table 12.1). To determine the beta weight for each independent variable, we simply plug these values into equations 12-4 and 12-5:

$$b^*_{x_1} = (3.93)\left(\frac{1.49}{25.11}\right)$$
$$b^*_{x_1} = .233$$
$$b^*_{x_2} = (-2.05)\left(\frac{7.09}{25.11}\right)$$
$$b^*_{x_2} = .579$$

By using the absolute value of these beta weights, we can compare the effect of one independent variable on the dependent variable with the effect of the other without our comparison being distorted by a variable's unit of measurement. From the beta weights displayed earlier, we can immediately ascertain that family closeness has a much stronger relationship with delinquency $\left(b^*_{x_2} = |-.579|\right)$ than does age $\left(b^*_{x_1} = |.233|\right)$.

There are two other ways of assessing the relative importance of independent variables in a multiple regression analysis. One method you are already familiar with from our treatment of bivariate regression is to calculate correlation coefficients and coefficients of determination. The second way is to compare the absolute value of the magnitude of the obtained t value for each independent variable from a hypothesis test that the slope coefficient is equal to zero. We will explore the multivariate equivalent of correlation coefficients and coefficients of determination in the next section, and then we will examine hypothesis tests for the significance of partial slope coefficients in the section after that.

▣ Partial Correlation Coefficients

Partial correlation coefficient: Correlation between two variables after controlling for a third variable.

Multiple coefficient of determination (R^2): Value of R^2 when there are two or more independent variables predicting a dependent variable.

Another way of addressing the relative effects of our independent variables is to compute something called the **partial correlation coefficient**. We can also compute the **multiple coefficient of determination (R^2)**. Both of these coefficients enable us to investigate the question of the relative importance of independent variables, although they do so in somewhat different ways. Interpreting the partial correlation coefficient and multiple coefficient of determination, however, is analogous to interpreting their bivariate equivalents, so you should have no problem with this section. We will begin our discussion with the partial correlation coefficient.

The magnitude of a partial correlation coefficient indicates the correlation or strength of the linear relationship between a given independent variable and a dependent variable when the effect of another independent variable is held constant or removed. The partial correlation coefficient is, therefore, like the Pearson correlation coefficient you learned about in the last chapter, only now we are controlling for another variable. In the example we are currently using, the partial correlation between age and delinquency would measure the relationship between these two variables when the effect of closeness to the family has been removed or controlled. Similarly, the partial correlation between family closeness and delinquency would measure the relationship between these variables when the effect of the person's age has been controlled.

In referring to the partial correlation coefficient, we will continue with the same subscripts we have used throughout this chapter with one additional twist. We will use the partial correlation symbol $r_{yx_1 . x_2}$ to show the correlation between the dependent variable (y) and the first independent variable (x_1) while controlling for the second independent variable (x_2). Similarly, we will use the partial correlation symbol $r_{yx_2 . x_1}$ to show the correlation between the dependent variable (y) and the second independent variable (x_2) while controlling for the first independent variable (x_1). The subscript to the right of the dot indicates the variable whose effect is being controlled. The formulas used to obtain partial correlation coefficients for two independent variables with a dependent variable are

$$r_{yx_1 . x_2} = \frac{r_{yx_1} - \left(r_{yx_2}\right)\left(r_{x_1 x_2}\right)}{\sqrt{1 - r_{yx_2}^2}\sqrt{1 - r_{x_1 x_2}^2}} \qquad \text{(Formula 12-6)}$$

$$r_{yx_2 . x_1} = \frac{r_{yx_1} - \left(r_{yx_1}\right)\left(r_{x_1 x_2}\right)}{\sqrt{1 - r_{yx_1}^2}\sqrt{1 - r_{x_1 x_2}^2}} \qquad \text{(Formula 12-7)}$$

In Table 12.1, we have all the values we need to calculate these coefficients for our delinquency data. Recall that the bivariate correlation between age and delinquency was $r_{yx_1} = .445$, the correlation between family closeness and delinquency was $r_{yx_2} = -.664$, and the correlation between age and family closeness was $r_{x_1 x_2} = -.366$. With this information, we can now compute the partial correlation coefficients for both independent variables as shown in the following equations.

Partial correlation coefficient for age and delinquency while controlling for family closeness:

$$r_{yx_1 . x_2} = \frac{.445 - (-.664)(-.366)}{\sqrt{1 - (-.664)^2}\sqrt{1 - (-.366)^2}}$$

$$r_{yx_1 . x_2} = .29$$

Partial correlation coefficient for family closeness and delinquency while controlling for age:

$$r_{yx_1 . x_2} = \frac{-.664 - (.445)(-3.66)}{\sqrt{1 - (.445)^2}\sqrt{1 - (-.366)^2}}$$

$$r_{yx_1 . x_2} = -.60$$

The partial correlation between age and delinquency is .29 while controlling for family closeness. The partial correlation between family closeness and delinquency is –.60 while controlling for age. Since the partial correlation for family closeness (–.60) is greater than the partial correlation for age (.29) in absolute value, family closeness has the stronger effect on a student's involvement in delinquent behavior. This is consistent with our conclusion when we used beta weights (standardized partial slopes). In general, the relative explanatory power of two independent variables can be determined by comparing their partial correlation coefficients. The variable with the largest partial correlation coefficient (absolute value) has the strongest relationship with the dependent variable.

We should note here that the reason why the partial correlation coefficients for both independent variables is less than their respective bivariate correlation coefficients is that since the two independent variables are themselves correlated ($r_{x_1 x_2} = -.366$), they share a certain amount of the total explanatory power or explained variance. In other words, in this particular regression model, there are four sources that explain delinquency:

1. That which is due uniquely to the effect of age
2. That which is due uniquely to the effect of family closeness
3. That which is due to the *joint effect* of age and family closeness
4. That which is due to all other factors not explicitly included in the model but whose effect is manifested through the error term (ε)

What the partial correlation (and partial slope) coefficients reflect is the unique effect of each independent variable on the dependent variable. That is, they reveal the effect of each independent variable that is not shared with the other independent variable. The greater the correlation between the two independent variables ($r_{x_1 x_2}$), the weaker the first two sources and the stronger the joint effect.

We illustrate this point in Figure 12.3, which shows a Venn diagram. Think of the entire area of the Venn diagram as the variance explained in the dependent variable. Some of this variance is explained uniquely by x_1, the first independent variable, and some of this variance is uniquely explained by x_2, the second independent variable. The intersection of the two circles is the variation in the dependent variable that is jointly explained by x_1 and x_2. The intersection shows that the two independent variables are correlated with each other. The stronger the correlation between the two independent variables, the larger the size of the intersection and the more difficult it is to untangle their unique effects from their joint effects. In one extreme case, where the two variables are not correlated at all, there is no intersection and all the variance in the dependent variable is uniquely explained by the two independent variables. In the other extreme case, where the correlation between x_1 and x_2 is 1.0, all of the area is covered by the intersection and all variance in the dependent variable is jointly explained. In this instance, you could use one of the independent variables to explain variation in the dependent variable, but you can't use both because it would violate the multicollinearity assumption. More practically, however, why would you need to include both given that they would be identical and provide perfectly redundant information?

Multiple Coefficient of Determination, R^2

Another way to disentangle the separate effects of the independent variables on the dependent variable is to compute the increase in the amount of explained variance when each independent variable is separately added to the regression model. With two independent variables, this requires taking the amount of variation in the dependent variable explained by both independent variables (called the multiple coefficient of determination, or R^2, for the full model) and subtracting the amount of variance explained by each independent variable when it is alone in the model (called the R^2 for the reduced model). This gives you the amount of variance that is explained uniquely by each independent variable ($R^2_{\text{full}} - R^2_{\text{reduced}}$).

To do this, of course, requires knowing how much of the variance in the dependent variable is explained by both independent variables together. We obtain this value by computing what is termed the multiple coefficient of determination, which is symbolized by a capital R^2 to differentiate it from the bivariate coefficient of determination r^2. The multiple coefficient of determination indicates the proportion of variance in the dependent variable that is explained by all the independent variables combined. You might think of the multiple coefficient of determination as an indicator of how well your model fits the data in terms of the combined ability of the independent variables to explain the dependent variable. The range of R^2 is from 0%, which indicates that the independent variables explain no variance in the dependent variable, to a maximum of 100%, which indicates that the independent variables explain all of the variance. As the independent variables explain a larger amount of the variance (i.e., as R^2 approaches 100%), the estimated regression model provides a better fit to the data.

Calculating the R^2 in a multivariate model should be easy, right? If the r^2 for the effect of age on delinquency is .20 [$(.445)^2$] and the r^2 for the effect of family closeness on delinquency is .44 [$(-.664)^2$], we can simply add these two together and conclude that when both variables are in the model, our R^2 should be .64. Unfortunately, to obtain the multiple coefficient of determination, we cannot simply add together the separate bivariate coefficients of determination. Why not? Remember that the independent variables are also virtually always correlated with each other (see Figure 12.3). If the independent variables in a multiple regression equation are correlated, the estimated value of R^2 reflects both the amount of variance that each variable uniquely explains and the amount that they share through their joint correlation. As a result, there will be a joint effect on the dependent variable that cannot be attributed to one variable alone. Again, the amount of this joint effect is a function of the extent to which the two independent variables are correlated themselves. The more highly correlated our inde-

Figure 12.3 Variance in Dependent Variable Explained Uniquely by Independent Variables x_1 and x_2 and Variance Jointly Explained

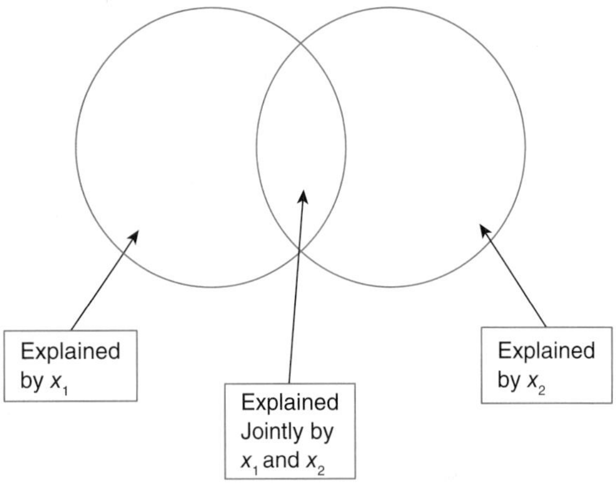

pendent variables are, and the more explained variance they share, the less likely the separate r^2 values will sum to the R^2. What we need, therefore, is a way to calculate the real R^2 value.

For a regression equation with two independent variables, the multiple coefficient of determination is found with the following formula:

$$R^2 = r_{yx_1}^2 + (r_{yx_2.x_1}^2)(1 - r_{yx_1}^2)$$

(Formula 12-8)

where

R^2 = the multiple coefficient of determination
$r_{yx_1}^2$ = the bivariate correlation between x_1 and y, squared
$r_{yx_2.x_1}$ = the partial correlation of x_2 and y while controlling for x_1, squared
$r_{yx_1}^2$ = the bivariate correlation between x_1 and y, squared

Before we explain the different components of this formula, let's compute the multiple coefficient of determination with our delinquency data. We have already calculated all of the values we need, so we can simply plug them into formula 12-8:

$$R^2 = (.445)^2 + (-.602)^2 \left[1 - (.445)^2\right]$$
$$R^2 = (.198) + (.362)(.802)$$
$$R^2 = (.198) + .290$$
$$R^2 = .488$$

This R^2 indicates the proportion of variance explained in the dependent variable by both independent variables in the regression equation. The obtained R^2 of .488 indicates that combined age and family closeness scores together explain almost one half (49%) of the variation in delinquency scores. Notice right away that this value of R^2 is not the same as the sum of the individual r^2 values, and now you know why—shared variance between x_1 and x_2.

Calculating Change in R^2

How can we disentangle the contribution of each independent variable to this total explained variance? What does the formula for the multiple coefficient of determination (formula 12-8) do? It first lets one independent variable do all the explaining in the dependent variable that it can. That is the first expression after the equals sign ($r_{yx_1}^2$). The value of this term is simply the square of the bivariate correlation coefficient between the first independent variable and the dependent variable. After the first independent variable has done all of the explaining it can, the second variable is then given the chance to explain what *it* can of the remaining unexplained variation. That is the second term in the expression. This term is the squared partial correlation coefficient between the second independent variable and the dependent variable (controlling for the first independent variable) multiplied by the proportion of variance that the first variable cannot explain:

$$R^2 \quad = \quad r_{yx_1}^2 \quad + \quad \left[(r_{yx_2.x_1}^2)(1 - r_{yx_1}^2) \right]$$

$$\begin{pmatrix} \text{Proportion} \\ \text{explained by both} \\ \text{independent} \\ \text{variables} \end{pmatrix} = \begin{pmatrix} \text{Proportion} \\ \text{explained by the} \\ \text{first independent} \\ \text{variable} \end{pmatrix} + \left(\begin{pmatrix} \text{Proportion explained by} \\ \text{the second independent} \\ \text{variable after controlling for} \\ \text{first independent variable} \end{pmatrix} \times \begin{pmatrix} \text{Proportion unexplained} \\ \text{by the first independent} \\ \text{variable} \end{pmatrix} \right)$$

The magnitude of R^2 will be the same no matter which of the two independent variables appears first. The following two formulas, then, will produce identical results:

$$R^2 = r_{yx_1}^2 + (r_{yx_2.x_1}^2)(1 - r_{yx_1}^2)$$

and

$$R^2 = r_{yx_2}^2 + (r_{yx_1.x_2}^2)(1 - r_{yx_2}^2)$$

In the first formula, we let x_1 explain all the variance it can in the dependent variable, and then we let x_2 explain what it can of the remaining variance. In the second formula, we let x_2 first do all the explaining *it* can in the dependent variable, and then we let x_1 explain what remains. The combined explanatory power of the two variables will always be the same. However, although the value of R^2 will be the same no matter which variable is considered first, the amount of explained variance that is attributed to a given variable will differ depending on the order that it appears in the formula. The first variable considered will explain more variance unless the two independent variables are not correlated at all. If there is a substantial correlation between the two independent variables, the first variable considered will be "given credit" for the explained variance that they share. In this circumstance, the variance explained by the second variable that is not already explained by the first will be small. It is, therefore, a good idea to estimate R^2 with each variable appearing first to see how much additional variance the second-considered variable can explain above that explained by the first-considered variable.

As you can now perhaps see, the expression for the multiple coefficient of determination can give us some idea of the contribution to the total explained variance made by each variable. To see this more clearly, we can rewrite our two expressions for the multiple coefficient of determination as follows:

$$R_{yx_1 x_2}^2 - r_{yx_1}^2 = \left(r_{yx_2.x_1}^2 \right)\left(1 - r_{yx_1} \right)^2$$

$$R_{yx_1 x_2}^2 - r_{yx_2}^2 = \left(r_{yx_1.x_2}^2 \right)\left(1 - r_{yx_2} \right)^2$$

In the first formula, the expression on the left-hand side of the equals sign is the difference between the total amount of explained variance in the two-variable regression model and the amount that would be explained by the first variable if it alone appeared in the regression equation. You can see that the latter is just the squared bivariate correlation between the first independent variable and the dependent variable. The expression to the right of the equals sign reflects the amount of variance explained by the second variable that is left unexplained by the first. This latter component of the total explained variance is often referred to as the **R^2 change** because it reflects the change in the amount of variance explained when the second variable is entered into the regression model. If the change in variance explained is substantial, it tells us that the second variable can give us information about the dependent variable that we do not get from the first independent variable.

The second formula is a corollary formula for R^2 change. The expression on the left-hand side of the equals sign is the difference between the total amount of explained variance in the two-variable regression model and the amount that would be explained by the second variable if it alone appeared in the regression equation. The $r^2_{yx_2}$ term is just the squared bivariate correlation between the second independent variable and the dependent variable in the one-variable regression model. The expression to the right of the equals sign reflects the amount of variance explained by the first independent variable that is left unexplained by the second. This formula measures the change in explained variance that we can uniquely attribute to the first independent variable because it reflects the amount of variance it explains over and above that explained by the second independent variable. We will illustrate the R^2 change term with our delinquency data.

First, let's let age explain all the variance in the dependent variable that it can:

$$R^2 = (.445)^2 + (-.602)^2 \left[1 - (.445)^2 \right]$$
$$R^2 = .198 + (.362)(.802)$$
$$R^2 = .198 + .290$$
$$R^2 = .488$$

In this calculation of the multiple coefficient of determination for delinquency scores, age is the independent variable considered first. It explains 19.8% of the total 48.8% of the explained variance in delinquency scores. After age explains all it can, family closeness is considered and it explains the remaining 29%. The change in the value of R^2 when family closeness is added to the regression model, then, is 29%.

In the calculations that follow, family closeness scores appear first. Family closeness is given the opportunity to explain all the variance in delinquency that it can, and then age is entered to explain the remaining variance left unexplained:

$$R^2 = (-.664)^2 + (.290)^2 \left[1 - (-.664)^2 \right]$$
$$R^2 = .441 + (.084)(.559)$$
$$R^2 = .441 + .047$$
$$R^2 = .488$$

The combined variance explained is still 48.8%, so no matter which variable is considered first, the total amount of explained variance remains the same. We find here that family closeness explains 44.1% of the variance when considered first, and age explains an additional 4.7% of the variance above and beyond that explained by the family closeness variable. Thus, the change in the value of R^2 when age is added to the regression model is only 4.7%. Since the change in R^2 when family closeness is added to the model is 29% and the change in R^2 when age is added to the model is not quite 5%, we would conclude that family closeness is a more important variable in explaining delinquency than age.

You should also note here that about one half of the variance in delinquency remains unexplained by age and family closeness ($1 - R^2 = .512$, or 51%). This gives us a clue that there are factors other than age and family closeness that help to explain why some kids are more likely than others to engage in delinquent activity. This would lead us on a search for other suitable independent variables to add to our regression model. We would then add a third or fourth independent variable or more independent variables to our model. To make a good explanatory model, then, we should also include other factors theorized or empirically found to be associated with the dependent variable but not strongly correlated with the other independent variables.

> **R^2 change:** Reflects the change in the amount of variance explained when a second variable is entered into a regression model.

We should seek advice from the empirical literature predicting delinquency or delinquency theory to determine what other factors should be included in our model!

The next questions we need to address are as follows: (1) Is there a statistically significant relationship between the independent variables in our multiple regression equation and the dependent variable? (2) Is there a significant relationship between each of the independent variables singly and the dependent variable? We will discuss issues of hypothesis testing with multiple regression models in the next section.

Hypothesis Testing in Multiple Regression

So far in this chapter, we have focused on calculating and interpreting the various coefficients associated with multiple regression analysis. However, since we are really interested in knowing whether the total amount of variance explained is significantly different from zero, and in estimating the value of the *population* partial slope coefficients (β_1 and β_2) from the sample coefficients (b_1 and b_2), we must now examine issues of hypothesis testing. In multiple regression analysis, we are interested in testing hypotheses about the multiple coefficient of determination and the partial slope coefficients. Calculating the standard error of these coefficients for these hypothesis tests, however, gets a bit labor-intensive and tricky. For this reason, we are going to rely on statistical output from the computer software package SPSS (Statistical Package for the Social Sciences) to conduct the hypotheses tests. In the remainder of this chapter, therefore, we will simply report the results of the calculations and work through the interpretation with you. With the data we use, you can use any other statistical software package and you will get the identical information we provide.

Figure 12.4 presents the SPSS computer output for the multiple regression equation predicting delinquency that we have been examining. As a reminder, SPSS displays only three decimal places; however, if you are in SPSS and you click on the coefficient, you will see that there are actually six decimal places being used for the calculations. That is why the numbers we calculate by hand with only three decimal places may not be exactly like those calculated by SPSS. Despite this difference in accuracy, if you use the output displayed in the last coefficient box, you can see that the regression equation is virtually identical to the one we calculated by hand:

$$y = 23.10 + 3.92(\text{age}) + -2.05(\text{family attachments})$$

The first null hypothesis of interest states that all slope coefficients in the regression equation are equal to zero. This is the same as saying that the multiple coefficient of determination R^2 is equal to zero in the population. The alternative hypothesis states that the slopes for all independent variables when used together are not equal to zero. This can be expressed as shown:

$$H_0: \beta_1, \beta_2, \beta_3, \ldots, \beta_k = 0 \quad \text{or} \quad R^2 = 0$$
$$H_1: \beta_1, \beta_2, \beta_3, \ldots, \beta_k \neq 0 \quad \text{or} \quad R^2 \neq 0$$

For us to reject the null hypothesis, only one of the partial slope coefficients needs to be significantly different from zero. To determine the results of this hypothesis test, we need to examine the boxes labeled "Model Summary" and "ANOVA." The former displays the results of the sample R^2, which we have already calculated by hand to be .488.

An F test is used to test the null hypothesis that the population R^2 is equal to zero. This F test is comparable to the F test we conducted with the analysis of variance. It is based on two sources of variability in our data: explained and unexplained variability. These correspond to two estimates of the population variance: explained/regression variance and unexplained/residual variance. You should be familiar with these terms from the previous chapter on bivariate regression models. The regression variance is the variance in the data we can explain from our regression equation. Hence, it is often referred to as explained variance. It is estimated as the ratio of the regression sum of squares to its degrees of freedom. The regression sum of squares is the sum of the squared differences between the predicted value of y ($\hat{y}$), based on the regression equation, and the mean of y ($\bar{Y}$). The number of degrees of freedom for the regression sum of squares is equal to p where p is the number of predictors or independent variables in the regression model. This ratio of regression sum of squares to degrees of freedom is one estimate of the population variance. In Figure 12.4, this estimate of the variance is labeled the regression "Mean Square." The residual variance is the variance in our data unexplained by the regression equation. It is estimated as the ratio of the residual sum of squares to its degrees of freedom. The residual sum of squares is the sum of the squared differences between the observed value of y and its predicted value ($\hat{y}$). The number of degrees of freedom for the residual sum of squares is equal to $n - (p + 1)$ (the extra 1 is for the

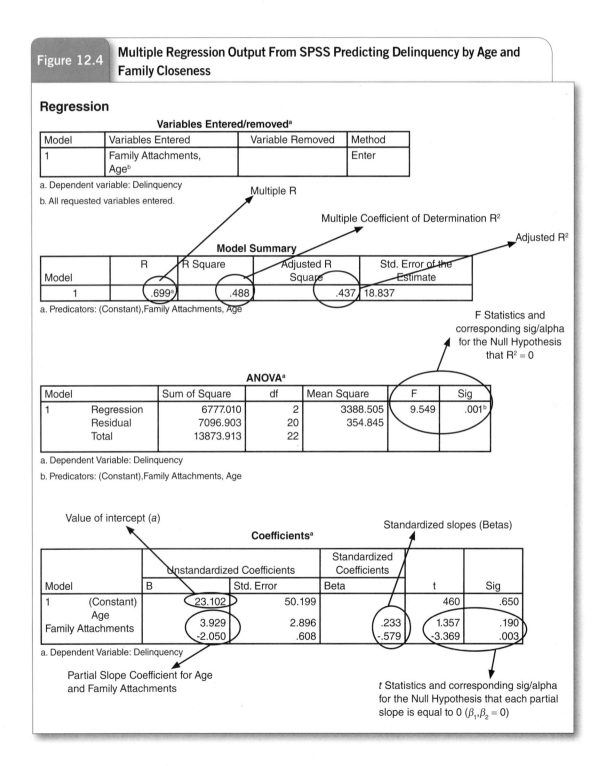

Figure 12.4 Multiple Regression Output From SPSS Predicting Delinquency by Age and Family Closeness

Regression

Variables Entered/removed[a]

Model	Variables Entered	Variable Removed	Method
1	Family Attachments, Age[b]		Enter

a. Dependent variable: Delinquency

b. All requested variables entered.

Multiple R

Multiple Coefficient of Determination R²

Adjusted R²

Model Summary

Model	R	R Square	Adjusted R Square	Std. Error of the Estimate
1	.699[a]	.488	.437	18.837

a. Predictors: (Constant), Family Attachments, Age

F Statistics and corresponding sig/alpha for the Null Hypothesis that R² = 0

ANOVA[a]

Model		Sum of Square	df	Mean Square	F	Sig
1	Regression	6777.010	2	3388.505	9.549	.001[b]
	Residual	7096.903	20	354.845		
	Total	13873.913	22			

a. Dependent Variable: Delinquency

b. Predictors: (Constant), Family Attachments, Age

Value of intercept (a)

Standardized slopes (Betas)

Coefficients[a]

Model		Unstandardized Coefficients		Standardized Coefficients	t	Sig
		B	Std. Error	Beta		
1	(Constant)	23.102	50.199		460	.650
	Age	3.929	2.896	.233	1.357	.190
	Family Attachments	-2.050	.608	-.579	-3.369	.003

a. Dependent Variable: Delinquency

Partial Slope Coefficient for Age and Family Attachments

t Statistics and corresponding sig/alpha for the Null Hypothesis that each partial slope is equal to 0 ($\beta_1, \beta_2 = 0$)

intercept). This ratio of residual sum of squares to degrees of freedom is the second estimate of the population variance, and in Figure 12.4 it is labeled the residual "Mean Square."

The F test for the significance of R^2 is based on the ratio of these two estimates of variance or mean squares:

$$F = \frac{\text{Regression variance}}{\text{Residual variance}}$$

This is the same as

$$F = \frac{\text{Mean square for the regression}}{\text{Mean square for the residual}}$$

The obtained value of F can be directly compared with a critical F at a chosen alpha level with p and $n - (p + 1)$ degrees of freedom. If $F_{obt} > F_{crit}$, your decision is to reject the null hypothesis. Luckily for you, most software programs, including SPSS, give you the exact probability of getting this sample statistic, F, if the null hypothesis is true. In this case, we can see under the "Sig" (abbreviation for significance) column after the F value that the exact significance or alpha in this case is equal to .001. This tells us that we would be wrong in rejecting the null hypothesis less than one time in a thousand! If this exact significance is lower than our chosen alpha, we can reject the null hypothesis. If the reported significance is greater than your alpha level, you fail to reject the null hypothesis. For example, if we chose an alpha of .05 and the significance we obtained was .07, that would be telling us that we would be wrong 7% of the time, which is more than the 5% we are willing to be wrong. In that case, we must fail to reject the null hypothesis.

Let's continue with our example more formally. Our formal null and alternative hypotheses for this test state are as follows:

$$H_0: \beta_{\text{age}} \text{ and } \beta_{\text{attachment}} = 0 \quad \text{or} \quad R^2_{\text{age, attachment}} = 0$$

$$H_1: \beta_{\text{age}} \text{ and } \beta_{\text{attachment}} \neq 0 \quad \text{or} \quad R^2_{\text{age, attachment}} \neq 0$$

Let's use an alpha of .05 for our hypothesis test, so our decision rule will be to reject the null hypothesis if the estimated probability of our obtained F statistic is .05 or less. Figure 12.4 tells us that the probability of obtaining an F value of 9.549 if the null hypothesis is true is equal to .001. This significance is less than alpha = .05, so we can safely reject the null hypothesis that both of the slope coefficients, when used together to predict the dependent variable, are equal to zero. We can instead conclude that there is a significant linear relationship between at least one of the independent variables (age or family closeness) and delinquency scores for high school students.

If we want to know which specific partial slopes are significantly different from zero, we must perform hypothesis tests on our individual slope coefficients. The hypothesis tests associated with partial slopes are very similar to the tests we conducted in the last chapter for bivariate slope coefficients. Specifically, we want to determine whether each partial slope coefficient is significantly different from zero. The null hypothesis in this case would state that the true population parameter for each independent variable β is equal to zero. Just as we did with the bivariate slope hypothesis tests in the last chapter, we use the t statistic and sampling distribution to test this hypothesis. The calculations for the t statistic in the multiple regression case are, however, much more complicated. The t statistic we use for our partial slope coefficient hypothesis test is simply the ratio of the partial slope to the standard error of the slope:

$$t = \frac{b_i}{s_{bi}}$$

The sampling distribution used for this t statistic is the Student's t with $(n - p - 1)$ degrees of freedom where p is the number of independent variables in the regression equation.

This formula may look simple, but the complicated part is in estimating the denominator—the standard error of the partial slope. For a two-variable multiple regression problem (x_1 and x_2), the estimate for the standard error of the slope can be derived from the following formulas:

$$S_{byx_1.x_2} = \sqrt{\frac{\text{Residual mean square}}{\Sigma x_1^2 (1 - r_{x_1 x_2}^2)}}$$

$$S_{byx_2.x_1} = \sqrt{\frac{\text{Residual mean square}}{\Sigma x_2^2 (1 - r_{x_1 x_2}^2)}}$$

where

$\Sigma x_1^2 =$ the sum of the squared x_1 scores

$\Sigma x_2^2 =$ the sum of squared x_2 scores

$r_{x_1 x_2}^2 =$ the squared correlation coefficient between x_1 and x_2

If we are going to make a decision by calculating this t value by hand, the next step in our hypothesis test is to select an alpha level with the appropriate degrees of freedom and determine what the critical value of t is. You can now select an alpha level (let's use an alpha of .05) and go to the t table (Table B.3 in Appendix B) with $n - p - 1$ degrees of freedom and find the critical value of t. For this example, with $n = 23$ and $p = 2$ (we have two independent variables), we have $23 - 2 - 1$, or 20, degrees of freedom. The critical value of t with $\alpha = .05$ for a two-tailed hypothesis test and 20 degrees of freedom is ± 2.086. If our obtained t is greater than or equal to 2.086 or less than or equal to -2.086, we will reject the null hypothesis.

Again, however, we will rely on the computer output to do our calculations for us. The necessary information to conduct a hypothesis test is shown in Figure 12.4, displayed in the box labeled "Coefficients" where we found the regression equation coefficients. In this box, you will find the partial slopes (β), the standard error of each slope, the beta coefficients (beta weights or standardized partial slopes), the resulting t value obtained for each slope, and the *exact* significance level (two-tailed) that corresponds to each t value. We are interested in testing the null hypothesis associated with each partial slope coefficient, which states that there is no relationship in the population between age and delinquency when holding family closeness constant and that there is no linear relationship in the population between family closeness and delinquency when holding age constant. That is, we are testing the null hypothesis that the population parameters, β_{x_1} and β_{x_2}, are each equal to zero. The alternative hypotheses state that the slope coefficients in the population are not equal to zero, which means this will be a two-tailed hypothesis test. These null and alternative hypotheses for each partial slope can be expressed as follows:

$$H_0 : \beta_{\text{age}} = 0$$

$$H_1 : \beta_{\text{age}} \neq 0$$

$$H_0 : \beta_{\text{family attachment}} = 0$$

$$H_1 : \beta_{\text{family attachment}} \neq 0$$

Like the F test, the output provided by most computer software packages gives the *exact probability* of each t statistic (two-tailed) under the assumption that the null hypothesis is true. This exact probability is displayed in Figure 12.4 under the column labeled "Sig" (for the significance of t) for each slope. Note that we do not care about the significance of the intercept. Your decision to reject the null hypothesis about the partial slope coefficients is the same as before. If this reported significance is less than or equal to your chosen alpha level, your decision is to reject the null hypothesis. If the reported probability is greater than your selected alpha level, your decision is to fail to reject the null hypothesis. Remember that if you are conducting a one-tailed hypothesis test, you need to cut this reported exact probability in half. To conduct our hypothesis test, all we need now is the obtained t statistic for each partial slope coefficient and its corresponding level of significance. You can find the obtained t values under the heading "t" in Figure 12.4 and their significance in the final column.

We can see from Figure 12.4 that the partial slope coefficient for the effect of age on delinquency is 3.929 and the obtained t value for that partial slope coefficient is 1.357. The exact probability or significance (alpha) of a sample slope coefficient this large if the population coefficient were actually zero is .190 (significance = .190). This means that if we reject the null hypothesis, we will be wrong about 19% of the time. We are willing to be wrong only 5% of the time (α = .05). Thus, we must fail to reject the null hypothesis. We would conclude, therefore, that there is no significant relationship between age and delinquency in the population once students' closeness to their families is controlled.

The partial slope coefficient for family closeness is –2.05, and the obtained t value is –3.369. If we look at the exact probability, we can see that the probability of getting a t that large if the null hypothesis is true is only .003. Since the exact probability is less than .05 (.003 < .05), we will reject this null hypothesis. Let's put this another way: If the partial slope coefficient in the population were actually zero, we would obtain a sample value of –2.05 by chance alone less than 3 times out of 1,000—less than 1% of the time. This is much less than our alpha of .05. As such, we will reject the null hypothesis that the slope coefficient in the population is equal to zero and conclude that there is a significant negative linear effect of family closeness on delinquency even after controlling for age. In the population, then, we can conclude that youths with stronger closeness to their families will have lower levels of delinquency.

We suggested to you earlier that in addition to its use in conducting hypothesis tests, the obtained t statistic can also be used to compare the relative effects of two independent variables on the dependent variable. If you want to know which independent variable has the stronger effect, simply compare the absolute value of each variable's obtained t statistic. For a given regression equation, the greater the t_{obt}, the stronger the effect the variable has on the dependent variable. In our example, the obtained t for the partial slope for age was 1.357, and the t_{obt} for family closeness was –3.369. Since the absolute value of 3.369 is greater than 1.357, we would conclude that family closeness has a stronger effect on delinquency than on age. This conclusion is consistent with our earlier findings using the standardized slope coefficients.

Before we move onto another example, let's discuss one more piece of information that most regression statistical software packages provide—the adjusted R^2 statistic. You can see from the information provided in Figure 12.4 that although the value of R^2 is .488, the adjusted R^2 is less than that at .437. What the adjusted R^2 does is take into account how many independent variables you have in the model and how well they are explaining the dependent variable. If you want to have a larger value of R^2 for your model, you might just keep including independent variables—if you do, the R^2 will not decrease but will increase (unless the model "blows up" and you get a negative R^2, a sure sign you did something wrong). Of course, you might just be adding variables that increase your R^2 by a tiny amount but do not do much explaining. The "adjustment" that the adjusted R^2 does is actually a penalty for including independent variables in your model that are not doing any explaining—it penalizes you for adding independent variables that do not explain much of the dependent variable. The value of the adjusted R^2 tells you the percentage of variance explained by the independent variables that are actually affecting the dependent variable. If you add an independent variable to your model that is actually doing its job and explaining the dependent variable, your adjusted R^2 will be greater than your unadjusted R^2. If, however, you are adding variables that are not very good at explaining y, your adjusted R^2 will be lower than your unadjusted R^2. In our earlier case, this is what we see, so we suspect that one of our independent variables is not really pulling its explanatory weight, and given the t values, it is probably age. The formula for the adjusted R^2 statistic is

$$R^2_{adjusted} = R^2 - \frac{k(1-R^2)}{n-k-1}$$

(Formula 12-9)

Let's move on to another example from the criminal justice literature. For the remainder of the chapter, we will emphasize the interpretation of multiple regression analysis rather than the calculation of these coefficients.

⊡ Another Example: Prison Density, Mean Age, and Rate of Inmate Violence

Research that has examined the factors related to inmate misconduct in prison settings, which includes both minor offenses and serious violence, has found many relevant explanatory variables, including those at the institutional level (i.e., security level of prison and cleanliness of housing) and those measuring individual attributes of prisoners (i.e., mean age and the criminal history of inmates). One institutional aspect that has received a great deal of attention is prison overcrowding. Results of this research have remained inconsistent. A recent study by David Bierie (2012) took a novel approach to study this issue by surveying staff in 114 federal prisons across the United States. By using U.S. Bureau of Prison data to measure the dependent variable of inmate violence within each prison, Bierie included a measure of prison overcrowding as one of the independent variables along with a measure of prison conditions obtained from survey questions asking staff members about the presence of things like insects and rodents, inadequate sanitation, and noise in the prison.

Let's set up a hypothetical study investigating the extent to which prison overcrowding is related to the rate of inmate-to-inmate assault. To do this, we select a sample of prisons and collect data for three variables: inmate-to-inmate assault rates (dependent variable), prison population density (which we will use as our measure of overcrowding), and the mean age of inmates in the facility, with density and mean age as our independent variables. The unit of analysis here is the prison, not individual inmates. We operationalize the "prison density index" by dividing a prison's inmate population by the prison's official rated inmate capacity. For example, if a prison had a population of 500 and a rated capacity of 400, it would yield a density index of 1.25, indicating that the facility was 25% overcapacity or overcrowded by 25%. We suspect that the rate of inmate assault is positively related to the extent to which the prison is overcrowded. We collect information on age because previous research has found that, compared with facilities with older populations, prisons with younger inmates tend to have higher rates of inmate-to-inmate assault.

The hypothetical data we obtain from a random sample of 30 correctional facilities is presented in Table 12.2. Also reported in this table are all of the component values necessary to calculate the bivariate correlation coefficients between each of the variables in addition to the correlation coefficients themselves. We will not go through the labor of computing these correlation coefficients by hand here, but it would be a good exercise for you to do so on your own before moving on.

The bivariate correlation coefficients shown in Table 12.2 indicate that both independent variables have moderately strong relationships with the dependent variable. The relationship between overcrowding (prison density) and inmate-to-inmate assault rates is moderate and positive ($r = .61$), indicating that overcrowding within prisons tends to increase the number of assaults between inmates. The correlation between the age of inmates and inmate-to-inmate assault rates is negative and moderately strong ($r = -.76$), indicating that prisons with younger inmate populations tend to have higher assault rates than prisons with older inmate populations. The correlation between our two independent variables is $-.55$. Although not small, the R^2 value is only .30, indicating that 30% of the variance in one independent variable is explained by the other. The correlation is not large enough to create a problem of multicollinearity.

With these bivariate correlation coefficients and the respective standard deviations of each variable, we can calculate the partial slope coefficients from equations 12-3 and 12-4. The partial slope coefficient for prison overcrowding regressed on inmate assault rates is

$$b_1 = \left(\frac{3.78}{.27} \right) \left(\frac{.61 - (-.76)(-.55)}{1 - (-.55)^2} \right)$$

$$b_1 = (14) \left(\frac{.61 - .42}{1 - .30} \right)$$

$$b_1 = (14) \left(\frac{.19}{.79} \right)$$

$$b_1 = 3.8$$

The partial slope coefficient for mean age of prison inmate population regressed on inmate assault rates is

$$b_2 = \left(\frac{3.78}{4.19} \right) \left(\frac{-.76 - (.61)(-.55)}{1 - (-.55)^2} \right)$$

$$b_2 = (.9) \left(\frac{-.76 - (-.34)}{1 - .30} \right)$$

$$b_2 = (.9) \left(\frac{-.42}{.70} \right)$$

$$b_2 = -.54$$

| Table 12.2 | Hypothetical Inmate-to-Inmate Assault Rates per 100 Inmate Population, Prison Density Index (overcrowding), and Mean Age of Inmates for a Random Sample of 30 Prisons | | | |

Case	Prison	Assault Rate y	Density Index x_1	Mean Age x_2
1	Prison A	10.2	1.5	25.8
2	Prison B	8.2	1.0	32.1
3	Prison C	11.3	1.6	26.2
4	Prison D	9.2	1.2	29.6
5	Prison E	5.3	1.0	34.5
6	Prison F	8.5	1.1	27.5
7	Prison G	8.6	1.3	30.2
8	Prison H	7.5	0.9	33.2
9	Prison I	15.3	1.9	27.2
10	Prison J	10.5	1.5	26.3
11	Prison K	12.5	1.5	28.3
12	Prison L	5.4	1.1	32.3
13	Prison M	10.5	1.4	23.5
14	Prison N	15.4	1.4	24.5
15	Prison O	12.8	1.2	24.5
16	Prison P	13.5	1.3	27.5
17	Prison Q	17.5	1.8	25.8
18	Prison R	11.5	1.6	32.6
19	Prison S	19.0	1.4	21.2
20	Prison T	14.2	1.2	26.5
21	Prison U	11.4	1.6	32.0
22	Prison V	9.8	1.1	29.9
23	Prison W	6.6	0.9	36.2
24	Prison X	8.9	1.0	35.0
25	Prison Y	10.6	1.1	29.8
26	Prison Z	12.5	1.2	25.6
27	Prison AA	7.4	1.1	33.5
28	Prison BB	3.3	1.2	38.2
29	Prison CC	17.5	1.7	25.2
30	Prison DD	13.2	0.9	33.1
		$\Sigma_y = 328.10$	$\Sigma x_1 = 38.7$	$\Sigma x_2 = 877.80$
		$\bar{Y} = 10.94$	$\bar{X}_{x_1} = 1.29$	$\bar{X}_{x_2} = 29.26$
		$s_y = 3.78$	$s_{x_1} = .27$	$s_{x_2} = 4.19$
		$\Sigma y^2 = 4002.07$	$\Sigma x_1^2 = 52.11$	$\Sigma x_2^2 = 26{,}193.2$
	$\Sigma yx_1 = 441.7$	$\Sigma yx_2 = 9{,}251.0$	$\Sigma x_1 x_2 = 1{,}114.2$	
	$r_{yx_1} = .61$	$r_{yx_2} = -.76$	$r_{x_1 x_2} = -.55$	

The partial slope coefficient for overcrowding, b_1, indicates that, on average, inmate-to-inmate assault rates increase by a value of 3.8 with every 1% increase in prison overcrowding while holding constant the mean age of the inmate population. The partial slope coefficient for mean inmate age, b_2, indicates that, on average, assault rates between inmates decrease by $-.54$ with every 1-year increase in mean age while holding constant prison density.

These partial slopes help us to determine the form of the linear effect for a given independent variable. However, since their magnitude is affected by the underlying units of measurement, they are not very useful in comparing relative effects across independent variables. This is why it is necessary to calculate other statistics such as the standardized partial slope coefficient or beta weight (b^*). Before we do this, however, we will solve the multiple regression equation for this model:

$$y = a + b_1 x_1 + b_2 x_2$$
$$y = a + (3.8)x_1 + (-.54)x_2$$

Now that we have obtained the partial slopes for overcrowding (b_1) and age (b_2), we can compute the intercept value by substituting the mean of the dependent variable and the means of the two independent variables (Table 12.2) into the equation:

$$a = \bar{y} - b_1 \bar{x}_1 - b_2 \bar{x}_2$$
$$a = 10.94 - (3.8)(1.29) - (-.54)(29.26)$$
$$a = 10.94 - 4.90 - (-15.8)$$
$$a = 21.84$$

The intercept value we obtained from these equations indicates that when both independent variables are equal to zero, the average value of y, our inmate assault rate, will be equal to 21.84. This gives us the full multiple regression equation as follows:

$$y = 21.84 + 3.8(\text{overcrowding}) - .54(\text{mean age})$$

Now that we have solved for the intercept and both partial slope coefficients, we can obtain predicted values of y based on given values of our two independent variables. For example, the predicted rate of inmate assaults in a prison with a density index of 1.6 and a mean inmate age of 24 would be

$$\hat{y} = 21.84 + (3.8)(1.6) + (-.54)(24)$$
$$\hat{y} = 21.84 + 6.08 + (-12.96)$$
$$\hat{y} = 14.96$$

Our least-squares multiple regression equation predicts that a prison with an overcrowding index of 1.6 and a mean inmate age of 24 would have an inmate-to-inmate assault rate of about 15. Remember that the predictions we make using this regression equation will not be perfect, and we will continue to have error in our regression equation and our predictions from that equation.

Now let's return to the issue of comparing the relative magnitude of the effects for our two independent variables. Recall that standardized partial slope coefficients, called beta weights (b^*), are one way to achieve this end.

By using formulas 12-4 and 12-5, let's compute the beta weights for overcrowding and mean age:

$$b^*_{density} = (3.8)\left(\frac{.27}{3.78}\right)$$

$$b^*_{density} = (3.8)(.071)$$

$$b^*_{density} = .270$$

$$b^*_{age} = (-.54)\left(\frac{4.19}{3.78}\right)$$

$$b^*_{age} = (-.54)(1.108)$$

$$b^*_{age} = -.598$$

The absolute value of the beta weight obtained for age is more than double that of the beta weight obtained for prison overcrowding (−.598 vs. .270). This indicates that mean inmate age in prison settings has a much stronger effect on inmate-to-inmate assaults than the extent to which the prison is overcrowded.

Another way of assessing the relative importance of the independent variables in predicting the dependent variable is through the partial correlation coefficients and a partitioning of the multiple coefficient of determination. By using formulas 12-6 and 12-7, respectively, let's first compute the partial correlation coefficients $r_{yx_1.x_2}$ and $r_{yx_1.x_2}$.

The partial correlation coefficient for overcrowding and assault when controlling for age is

$$r_{yx_1.x_2} = \frac{.61-(-.76)(-.55)}{\sqrt{1-(-.76)^2}\sqrt{1-(-.55)^2}}$$

$$r_{yx_1.x_2} = \frac{.61-.42}{\sqrt{1-.58}\sqrt{1-.30}}$$

$$r_{yx_1.x_2} = \frac{.19}{(.648)(.837)}$$

$$r_{yx_1.x_2} = \frac{.19}{.542}$$

$$r_{yx_1.x_2} = .351$$

The partial correlation coefficient for age and assaults when controlling for overcrowding is

$$r_{yx_2.x_1} = \frac{-.76-(.61)(-.55)}{\sqrt{1-(.61)^2}\sqrt{1-(-.55)^2}}$$

$$r_{yx_2.x_1} = \frac{-.76-(-.34)}{\sqrt{1-.37}\sqrt{1-.30}}$$

$$r_{yx_2.x_1} = \frac{-.42}{(.794)(.837)}$$

$$r_{yx_2.x_1} = \frac{-.42}{.66}$$

$$r_{yx_2.x_1} = -.636$$

The partial correlation coefficient between age and assault when controlling for prison overcrowding is equal to −.636. Its absolute value is greater than the partial correlation between overcrowding and assault when controlling for inmate age (.351). This would lead us to conclude that age is more important than overcrowding in explaining inmate assault rates.

With these partial correlation coefficients, we can calculate the multiple coefficient of determination. By using formula 12-8, we obtain the multiple coefficient of determination for overcrowding and age on assault as follows:

$$R^2_{yx_2x_1} = (.61)^2 + (-.636)^2 \left[1 - (.61)^2 \right]$$

$$R^2_{yx_2x_1} = (.37) + (.41)(1 - .37)$$

$$R^2_{yx_2x_1} = .63$$

The obtained $R^2_{yx_1x_2} = .63$ indicates that both overcrowding and mean age, when used together, explain 63% of the variance in inmate-to-inmate assault rates within prisons.

With the multiple coefficient of determination calculated, we can now determine the relative contribution in explained variance made by each independent variable. Recall that we do this by subtracting the bivariate coefficient of determination for each variable from the multiple coefficient of determination. For example, to determine the relative contribution of age in explaining assault rates, we simply subtract the bivariate coefficient of determination for overcrowding on inmate assaults $(r_{yx_1})^2$ from the multiple coefficient of determination. This will give us the proportion of explained variance added to the total when mean age is added to the model explaining inmate assault rates.

In the calculated multiple coefficient of determination, we found that prison density by itself explains 37% of the variance in inmate assault rates. When age is considered, it contributes an additional 26% to the total explained variance over and above that explained by prison density. The R^2 change value for age, then, is 26% (63% – 37%). This indicates that age contributes unique information about the dependent variable of assault rates that is not available through knowledge of overcrowding.

When age is the first variable considered, we find that

$$R^2_{yx_1x_2} = (-.76)^2 + (.351)^2 \left[1 - (-.76)^2 \right]$$

$$R^2_{yx_1x_2} = (.58) + (.12)(.42)$$

$$R^2_{yx_1x_2} = .58 + .05$$

$$R^2_{yx_1x_2} = .63$$

By itself, age explains 58% of the total variance, whereas prison overcrowding explains only 5% additional variance beyond that explained by age. It would seem, then, that although both variables contribute to the total explained variance, the age of the inmates gives us more information about assault rates than does the extent of overcrowding.

Even though the adjusted value of R^2 is already displayed for you in Figure 12.5, you can see that if we plugged the appropriate values into the equation, we would obtain the same result:

$$R^2_{adjusted} = .63 - \frac{(2)(1 - .63)}{30 - 2 - 1}$$

$$R^2_{adjusted} = .63 - \frac{(2)(.37)}{27}$$

$$R^2_{adjusted} = .60$$

In this example, the unadjusted R^2 value is .63 and its adjusted value is .60, so the shrinkage in the amount of explained variance in this particular regression model is slight, but when using multiple regression, we recommend that you examine both the unadjusted and adjusted R^2 values.

Let's move on to testing the significance of our partial slope coefficients and the significance of the entire multiple regression equation. We first want to address the extent to which there is a significant linear relationship among the dependent variable, the number of inmate assaults, and our two independent variables, prison overcrowding and inmate age, considered in combination. The null and research hypotheses for this test can be expressed as follows:

$$H_0 = \beta_{\text{overcrowding}}, \ \beta_{\text{age}} = 0, \text{ or } R^2_{\text{overcrowding,age}} = 0$$

$$H_1 = \beta_{\text{overcrowding}}, \ \beta_{\text{age}} \neq 0, \text{ or } R^2_{\text{overcrowding,age}} \neq 0$$

As we stated earlier, this hypothesis test really determines whether the R^2 value is significantly different from zero. If we reject this null hypothesis, we can conclude that at least one of the partial slope coefficients is significantly different from zero. Our next set of hypothesis tests will then determine which specific slopes are significantly different from zero.

We will use the F statistic and sampling distribution to test the null hypothesis about R^2. For this example, we are going to rely on both the SPSS output and finding the critical value of F to make our decision. We will adopt an alpha level of .01 for this test and will find F_{crit} with the appropriate degrees of freedom. With a sample size of 30 and two independent variables, our F test has 2 and 27 degrees of freedom. For an alpha level of .01 with 2 and 27 degrees of freedom, our critical value of F is 5.49. Our decision rule, then, is to reject the null hypothesis if $F_{\text{obt}} \geq 5.49$ and to fail to reject if $F_{\text{obt}} < 5.49$.

All of the information necessary to make a decision about the null hypothesis is provided in the top portion of Figure 12.5. The obtained value of F for the entire equation is equal to 23.201. Since an F_{obt} of 23.201 is greater than the critical F of 5.49, our decision is to reject the null hypothesis. We can see that the exact significance level is really much less than .01—it is .000. You may be thinking, "Does this mean that we risk 0% error?" Remember that there are actually six decimal places for this number, but you can't see them all because SPSS displays only three decimals. As such, rest assured that there is a one somewhere in this significance level because when working with probability theory, you can never be 100% certain or risk 0% error! Still, we can safely reject the null hypothesis (at least at the .001 level) in this case and conclude that there is a significant linear relationship between prison overcrowding and the mean age of the inmate population when they are used together to predict rates of inmate-to-inmate assault.

We will next determine exactly which independent variable(s) is (are) significant in predicting the dependent variable. The null hypotheses we are testing are that the population parameters, β_1 and β_2, are each equal to zero. The alternative hypotheses state that the slope coefficients for the effect of inmate age and prison overcrowding on inmate assaults in the population are not equal to zero. These hypothesis tests can be formally expressed as follows:

$$H_0: \beta_{\text{overcrowding}} = 0$$

$$H_1: \beta_{\text{overcrowding}} \neq 0$$

$$H_0: \beta_{\text{age}} = 0$$

$$H_1: \beta_{\text{age}} \neq 0$$

The next step in our hypothesis test is to select an alpha level, determine our degrees of freedom, and identify the critical value of our test statistic. Let's continue with the alpha of .01. The statistic we will use to test our null hypothesis is Student's t, and the sampling distribution we will use is the t distribution with $n - p$ degrees of freedom (where p is equal to the number of independent variables in our regression model). We will conduct this hypothesis test with the exact probability of t_{obt}.

From Figure 12.5, you can see that the partial slope coefficient for the effect of age on inmate assaults is $-.547$ (because of rounding errors, our hand calculation of this b was $-.54$), and the t statistic is -4.317, with an exact two-tailed probability of this t_{obt} being equal to .000. Since this probability is less than our critical alpha of .01, we are led to reject the null hypothesis. Our conclusion will be that the age of the inmate population is significantly related to the rate of inmate-to-inmate assault even after controlling for the overcrowding index. As the mean age of the inmate population increases, rates of assault between inmates decrease. In other words, our sample data indicate that prisons with younger inmate populations tend to have significantly higher rates of assault between inmates than prisons with older inmate populations even after controlling for the effects of overcrowding.

Regression

Variables Entered/Removed[a]

Model	Variables Entered	Variables Removed	Method
1	Mean Age of inmates, Overcrowding index[b]		Enter

a. Dependent Variable: Inmate to Inmate Assault Rate

b. All requested variables entered.

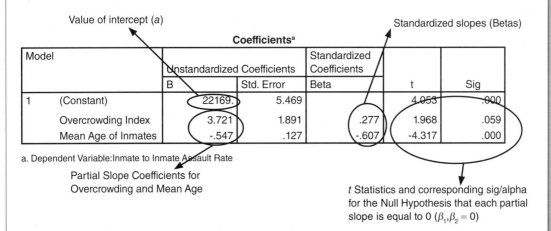

Multiple R

Multiple Coefficient of Determination R²

Model Summary

Model	R	R Square	Adjusted R Square	Std. Error of the Estimate
1	.795[a]	.632	.605	2.3742

a. Predictors, (Constant),Mean Age of Inmates Overcrowding Index

F Statistic and corresponding sig/alpha for the Null Hypothesis that R² = 0

ANOVA[a]

Model		Sum of Squares	df	Mean Square	F	Sig.
1	Regression	261.556	2	130.778	23.201	.000[b]
	Residual	152.193	27	5.637		
	Total	413.750	29			

a. Dependent Variable: Inmate to Inmate Assault Rate

b. Predictors: (Constant), Mean Age of Inmates, Overcrowding Index

Value of intercept (a)

Standardized slopes (Betas)

Coefficients[a]

Model		Unstandardized Coefficients		Standardized Coefficients		
		B	Std. Error	Beta	t	Sig
1	(Constant)	22169.	5.469		4.053	.000
	Overcrowding Index	3.721	1.891	.277	1.968	.059
	Mean Age of Inmates	-.547	.127	-.607	-4.317	.000

a. Dependent Variable:Inmate to Inmate Assault Rate

Partial Slope Coefficients for Overcrowding and Mean Age

t Statistics and corresponding sig/alpha for the Null Hypothesis that each partial slope is equal to 0 ($\beta_1, \beta_2 = 0$)

The slope coefficient for the effect of prison density on inmate assaults is 3.721 with a *t* value of 1.968. This corresponds to an exact two-tailed probability level of .059. Since this is greater than our alpha level of .01, we must fail to reject the null hypothesis that the slope coefficient in the population for prison overcrowding is equal to zero. We conclude that there is no significant linear relationship between overcrowding and rate of inmate-to-inmate assault within prisons. Finally, note that the absolute value of t_{obt} for age (4.317) is greater than that for prison density (1.968). This would also lead us to believe that inmate age has more of an effect than prison density on the rate of inmate assault. As such, despite the fact that both independent variables were related to inmate-to-inmate assault at the bivariate level, when they were used to predict the assault rate after controlling for each other, only the mean age retained its significance.

Before we conclude, we want to provide one more multiple regression example that includes a dichotomous independent variable. No worries, however, as we are going to rely exclusively on SPSS output for this example with our focus on interpretation!

Case Study

Using a Dichotomous Independent Variable: Predicting Murder Rates in States

The data for this case study come from the state-level data we introduced in the last chapter. The dependent variable we are going to examine is state rates of murder, and the independent variables will be the percentage of individuals in states who live below the poverty line and a dichotomous variable indicating whether the state resides in the southern region of the United States (coded 1) or not (coded 0). We are examining this southern indicator to test the southern culture of honor thesis documented by a classic experiment by Richard Nisbett and Dov Cohen (1996). After their experiment, they contended that southerners were more likely to approve of violence as a form of social control in response to perceived insults and in defense of self or their homes (Nisbett & Cohen, 2014). It is this tolerance of violence in the defense of honor, some contend, that is responsible for higher rates of murder in the South. Recent research, however, has failed to find a relationship between an individual's defensive gun use and whether he or she lived or was born in the South (Copes, Kovandzic, Miller, & Williamson, 2014). Viviana Andreescu, John Shutt, and Gennaro Vito (2011) found that homicide rates did not significantly differ in Appalachian counties in the South versus the non-South after controlling for other cultural and structural variables like family stability. In our case study here, we will use this regional indicator to illustrate how to interpret the slope of a dichotomous variable. We want to state at the outset that dichotomies must be coded "0" and "1" to be easily interpreted in ordinary least-squares (OLS) regression analyses. Although we are relying on SPSS, we have provided the data and all coefficients necessary for hand calculations in Table 12.3 if you want to have some extra practice!

Figure 12.6 provides the SPSS output for our regression model predicting the murder rates with state poverty and regional location. We have not placed circles around the coefficients in this example so as to help you learn how to read output. We will start with the model summary statistics of the multiple R and R^2. The multiple R indicates a moderate to strong relationship between the murder rate in states and independent variables of poverty and regional location. Together, these independent variables explain 49% (.49) of the variance in murder rates according to the R^2 statistic. The null and research hypotheses for this are

$$H_0 = \beta_{poverty},\ \beta_{region} = 0,\ \text{or}\ R^2_{poverty,\ region} = 0$$
$$H_1 = \beta_{poverty},\ \beta_{region} \neq 0,\ \text{or}\ R^2_{poverty,\ region} \neq 0$$

Let's adopt an alpha/significance level for this test of .05. We can see in the analysis of variance (ANOVA) summary statistics that the value of F for this test is equal to 8.17, which corresponds to a significance level of .003. This tells us that we will be wrong in rejecting the null hypothesis less than 1% of the time. Since we are willing to be wrong 5% of the time in this case ($\alpha = .05$), we can reject the null hypothesis and conclude that at least one of the independent variables has a significant linear relationship with murder rates in states.

Moving on to the regression model in the "Coefficients" box in Figure 12.6, we see the value of the intercept (*a*), which is provided in the row labeled "constant," is equal to –1.617. Along with the unstandardized slope coefficients for the independent variables, this tells us that the linear regression equation is

$$y = -1.617 + .475_{\text{poverty}} + 1.812_{\text{region}}$$

The slope for poverty indicates that for a 1-unit increase in poverty in states, the murder rate increases by .475 unit even while holding constant regional location. The null hypothesis test for this slope is

$$H_0 = \beta_{\text{poverty}} = 0$$
$$H_1 = \beta_{\text{poverty}} \neq 0$$

Figure 12.6 indicates that the *t* statistic for this test is equal to 3.145 and corresponds to a significance level of 006. This tells us that we will be wrong in rejecting the null hypothesis less than 1% of the time, which is lower than our alpha of .05. As such, we can safely reject this null hypothesis and conclude that there is a significant linear relationship between poverty and murder at the state level net of regional location. States that have higher rates of poverty also have higher rates of murder.

Now let's move on to the slope coefficient for regional location in the South. This is not a continuous independent variable, but it has only two values: 0 for those states not in the South and 1 for those states in the South. So how do we interpret this? The 1-unit increase in *x* is actually what happens to *y* when *x* changes from 0 to 1, which in this case is the non-South to the South. The unstandardized slope here tells us that when states reside in the South, the murder rate increases by 1.812 units after controlling for poverty. You can perhaps more easily see this if we predict the value of murder for states in the South versus the non-South while holding constant poverty at its mean ($\bar{X}_{\text{poverty}} = 13.5$). Let's first predict the murder rate for a state with an average poverty rate (13.5) that resides in the non-South (coded 0):

$$\hat{y} = -1.617 + .475(13.5) + 1.812(0)$$
$$\hat{y} = -1.617 + 6.413 + 0$$
$$\hat{y} = 4.796$$

Now let's predict the murder rate with the same average poverty rate but this time residing in the South (coded 1):

$$\hat{y} = -1.617 + .475(13.5) + 1.812(1)$$
$$\hat{y} = -1.617 + 6.413 + 1.812$$
$$\hat{y} = 6.608$$

As you can see, the difference between these predicted values of murder is about 1.812, which is the value of the partial slope coefficient for the variable "State in South" in the model. Now let's test the null hypothesis that there is no relationship between regional location and rates of murder:

$$H_0 = \beta_{\text{region}} = 0$$
$$H_1 = \beta_{\text{region}} \neq 0$$

As shown in Figure 12.6, the *t* value for southern location is equal to 1.864 and corresponds to a significance level of .080. That tells us that instead of the 5% error we are willing to make, we would be wrong in this case 8% of the time. As

Table 12.3	Data and Calculations Necessary to Compute the Partial Slope Coefficient Among Murder Rates, Poverty Rate, and South Region (0 = Non-South, 1 = South) for $n = 20$ States

Case	State	Murder Rate y	Percentage Poor x_1	Southern Region x_2
1	Alaska	3.2	9.0	0
2	Arizona	5.5	16.5	0
3	California	5.4	14.2	0
4	Delaware	4.6	10.8	1
5	Florida	5.5	14.9	1
6	Indiana	5.3	14.4	0
7	Louisiana	12.3	17.3	1
8	Maine	2.0	12.3	0
9	Maryland	7.7	9.1	1
10	Massachusetts	2.7	10.3	0
11	Michigan	6.3	16.2	0
12	Missouri	6.6	14.6	0
13	Nebraska	2.5	12.3	0
14	New Jersey	3.7	9.4	0
15	New Mexico	10.0	18.0	0
16	New York	4.0	14.2	0
17	Pennsylvania	5.4	12.5	0
18	South Carolina	6.7	17.1	1
19	Texas	5.4	17.2	1
20	Wyoming	2.0	9.8	0
		$\Sigma_y = 106.8$	$\Sigma x_1 = 270.1$	$\Sigma x_2 = 6$
		$\bar{Y} = 5.34$	$\bar{X}_{x_1} = 13.5$	$\bar{X}_{x_2} = .30$
		$s_y = 2.59$	$s_{x_1} = 3.03$	$s_{x_2} = .47$
		$\Sigma y^2 = 697.4$	$\Sigma x_1^2 = 3821.8$	$\Sigma x_2^2 = 6$
	$\Sigma yx_1 = 1534.8$	$\Sigma yx_2 = 42.2$	$\Sigma x_1 x_2 = 86.4$	
	$r_{yx_1} = .62$	$r_{yx_2} = .44$	$r_{y_1 x_2} = .56$	
			$r_{x_1 x_2} = .20$	

such, we must fail to reject the null hypothesis in this case and generalize that there is no relationship between murder rates in the South and the non-South after controlling for poverty. We could have gotten a hint from this also by comparing the unadjusted value of R^2 (.49) with the adjusted value (.43). The value diminishes when we add a second independent

Figure 12.6 Multiple Regression Output From SPSS Predicting Murder Rates With Percentage Poor and Southern Region (0 = Non-South and 1 = South) for *n* = 20 States

Variables Entered/Removed[a]

Model	Variables Entered	Variables Removed	Method
1	State in South, Percent Individuals below poverty[b]		Enter

a. Dependent Variable: Murder Rate per 100K
b. All requested variables entered.

Model Summary

Model	R	Square	Adjusted R Square	Std. Error of the Estimate
1	.700[a]	.490	.430	1.9525

a. Predictors: (Constant), State in South, Percent Individuals below poverty

ANOVA[a]

Model		Sum of Squares	df	Mean Square	F	Sig.
1	Regression	62.298	2	31.149	8.170	.003[b]
	Residual	64.810	17	3.812		
	Total	127.108	19			

a. Dependent Variable: Murder Rate per 100K
b. Predictors: (Constant), State in South, Percent Individuals below poverty

Coefficients[a]

Model		Unstandardized Coefficients B	Std.Error	Standardized Coefficients Beta	t	Sig.
1	(Constant)	−1.617	2.049		−.789	.441
	Percent Individuals below poverty	.475	.151	.556	3.145	.006
	State in South	1.812	.972	.329	1.864	.080

a. Dependent Variable: Murder Rate per 100K

variable that is not explaining very much of the dependent variable—in this case, the variable "State in the South." The penalty we incur for including variables that are not explaining the dependent variable, then, is a drop in the R^2 value.

Summary

In this chapter, we have examined techniques of multiple regression analysis. The multiple regression model is really a straightforward extension of the bivariate model, or model with one independent variable. The slope coefficient in the multiple regression model, the partial slope coefficient, reflects the change in the dependent variable for a 1-unit change in one independent variable while all other independent variables are held constant. The relative explanatory power of independent variables can be assessed by partial correlation coefficients, beta weights, standardized regression coefficients, the value of the R^2 change, and the absolute value of the *t* ratios. In deciding which explanatory variables to include in a multiple regression model, the optimal strategy is to include those variables that are strongly correlated with the dependent variable but uncorrelated with other independent variables. We have also illustrated how to examine the relationship between a dichotomous independent variable coded 0 and 1 within an OLS regression model.

Key Terms

> Review key terms with eFlashcards. Visit study.sagepub.com/paternoster.

beta weight   327
multicollinearity   322
multiple coefficient of determination
   (R^2) 328

multiple regression equation   321
multivariate regression model   318
nonspuriousness   319
partial correlation coefficient   328

partial slope coefficient   321
R^2 change   333

Key Formulas

Multivariate regression equation (formula 12-1):

$$y = a + b_1 x_1 + b_2 x_2 + \cdots b_k x_k + \varepsilon$$

Partial slope coefficients (formulas 12-2 and 12-3):

$$b_1 = \left(\frac{s_y}{s_{x_1}}\right)\left(\frac{r_{yx_1} - (r_{yx_2})(r_{x_1 x_2})}{1 - r_{x_1 x_2}^2}\right)$$

$$b_2 = \left(\frac{s_y}{s_{x_2}}\right)\left(\frac{r_{yx_2} - (r_{yx_1})(r_{x_1 x_2})}{1 - r_{x_1 x_2}^2}\right)$$

Beta weights (formulas 12-4 and 12-5):

$$b^*_{x_1} = b_{x_1}\left(\frac{s_{x1}}{s_y}\right)$$

$$b^*_{x_2} = b_{x_2}\left(\frac{s_{x2}}{s_y}\right)$$

Partial correlation coefficients (formulas 12-6 and 12-7):

$$r_{yx_1 . x_2} = \frac{r_{yx_1} - (r_{yx_2})(r_{x_1 x_2})}{\sqrt{1 - r_{yx_2}^2}\ \sqrt{1 - r_{x_1 x_2}^2}}$$

$$r_{yx_2 . x_1} = \frac{r_{yx_1} - (r_{yx_1})(r_{x_1 x_2})}{\sqrt{1 - r_{yx_1}^2}\ \sqrt{1 - r_{x_1 x_2}^2}}$$

Multiple coefficient of determination (R^2) (formula 12-8):

$$R^2 = r_{yx_1}^2 + (r_{yx_2 . x_1}^2)(1 - r_{yx_1}^2)$$

Adjusted R^2 (formula 12-9):

$$R^2_{\text{adjusted}} = R^2 - \frac{k(1 - R^2)}{n - k - 1}$$

Practice Problems

> Test your understanding of chapter content.
> Take the practice quiz.

1. Suppose we were interested in the extent to which rates of divorce and mean age of the population within states affected state-level rates of violent crime. To examine these relationships, we took a random sample of 35 states and obtained the divorce rate per 100,000 population for each, the mean age in each state, and rates of violent crime per 100,000.

   Assume that we obtained the multiple regression output shown in the table below. With this output, answer the following questions:

   a. Specify the exact least-squares multiple regression equation.

   b. Interpret both partial slope coefficients and the intercept value.

   c. By using this output, how would you examine the relative importance of each independent variable?

   d. What is the total variance explained?

   e. Conduct a hypothesis test using the obtained output for both the entire regression model and the

Figure 12.7	Multiple Regression Output for Problem 1: Predicting the Violent Crime Rate for States

Variables Entered/Removed[a]

Model	Variables Entered	Variables Removed	Method
1	Divorce Mean Age		Enter

Model Summary

Model	R	R Square	Adjusted R Square	Std. Error of the Estimate
1	.795[a]	.632	.609	1.9525

a. Predictors: (Constant), Divorce, Mean Age

ANOVA[a]

Model		Sum of Squares	df	Mean Square	F	Sig.
1	Regression	324.538	2	162.26	27.531	.000[b]
	Residual	188.604	20	5.893		

a. Dependent Variable: Violent Crime Rate per 100,000
b. Predictors: (Constant), Divorce, Mean Age

Coefficients[a]

Model		Unstandardized Coefficients B	Std. Error	Standardized Coefficients Beta	t	Sig.
1	(Constant)	19.642	2.736		.600	.552
	Divorce	.871	.119	.594	4.268	.000
	Mean Age	-.146	.158	-.133	-3.110	.001

independent slope coefficients. Use a two-tailed alpha level of .01 for both tests. What are your formal hypothesis statements? What do you conclude based on the F test and the two t tests?

2. Suppose we are interested in the reasons why escapes occur in local jails. To investigate this issue, we take a random sample of 30 jails. We ask the jail managers how many escapes they had from their facilities during the past year. This is our dependent variable. Based on our knowledge of the literature, we also know that work-related morale and the extent to which facilities are understaffed affect things like supervision and motivation to identify and solve problems. To measure the level of morale, we ask jail employees to respond to a number of items regarding their morale (e.g., "I think my supervisors appreciate my work," "I feel secure in my job," "I like the people I work with"). With their responses, we compute a morale index, with high scores indicating high morale and low scores indicating low morale. To determine the extent to which an institution is understaffed, we construct a jail staff-to-inmate ratio. Again, high scores indicate a large number of staff members relative to inmates and low scores indicate a small number of staff members relative to inmates. The data we obtain are listed in the table that begins to the right:

a. What would the values of b_1 and b_2 be from these sample statistics? Interpret these coefficients.

b. From your calculated partial slope coefficients and sample means, solve for the value of the intercept (a). What is the complete multiple regression equation?

c. By using the earlier multiple regression equation, predict the value of y (number of escapes) from a morale score of 8 and a staff ratio score of .3.

d. Calculate the beta weights for each of the partial slope coefficients. What do they tell you about the relative importance of each independent variable?

e. Calculate the multiple coefficient of determination from these sample statistics. What does this coefficient indicate?

Jail	# of Escapes	Morale Score	Staff-to-Inmate Ratio
1	12.00	3.00	.22
2	10.00	7.00	.41
3	3.00	14.00	.66
4	7.00	8.00	.45
5	9.00	9.00	.32

(Continued)

(Continued)

6	13.00	5.00	.33
7	17.00	2.00	.10
8	12.00	5.00	.30
9	15.00	4.00	.20
10	9.00	5.00	.50
11	3.00	7.00	.60
12	5.00	3.00	.40
13	11.00	2.00	.20
14	14.00	5.00	.50
15	7.00	8.00	.40
16	10.00	5.00	.20
17	14.00	3.00	.30
18	15.00	2.00	.40
19	17.00	2.00	.10
20	6.00	8.00	.20
21	9.00	4.00	.20
22	3.00	10.00	.50
23	2.00	11.00	.60
24	4.00	7.00	.30

25	13.00	2.00	.30
26	11.00	8.00	.50
27	14.00	4.00	.30
28	9.00	4.00	.30
29	5.00	11.00	.40
30	4.00	14.00	.50

The statistics necessary to calculate the slope coefficients are as follows:

$\Sigma_y = 283$	$\Sigma_{x_1} = 182$	$\Sigma_{x_2} = 10.7$
$s_y = 4.49$	$s_{x_1} = 3.47$	$s_{x_2} = .15$
$\bar{y} = 9.43$	$\bar{x}_1 = 6.07$	$\bar{x}_2 = .36$
$\Sigma y^2 = 3255$	$\Sigma x_{x_1}^2 = 1454$	$\Sigma x_{x_1}^2 = 4.44$
	$r_{yx_1} = -.77$	
	$r_{yx_2} = -.63$	
	$r_{x_1x_2} = .67$	
$r_{yx_1.x_2} = -.59$	$r_{yx_2.x_1} = -.245$	

Figure 12.8 Multiple Regression Output for Problem 3: Jurors' Religious Characteristics and Their Verdicts and Sentencing Decisions

Variables Entered/Removed[a]

Model	Variables Entered	Variables Removed	Method
1	ENV, REL		Enter

Model Summary

Model	R	R Square	Adjusted R Square
1	.811[a]	.659	.602

a. Predictors: (Constant), ENV, REL

ANOVA[a]

Model		Sum of Squares	df	Mean Square	F	Sig.
1	Regression	481.341	2	240.670	11.565	.001[b]
	Residual	249.058	12	20.754		

Coefficients[a]

Model		Unstandardized Coefficients B	Std. Error	Standardized Coefficients Beta	t	Sig.
1	(Constant)	16.245	5.514		2.946	.012
	ENV	-1.467	.443	-.608	-3.312	.006
	REL	1.075	.570	.346	1.184	.084

3. In a 2014 article, Monica Miller, Jonathan Maskaly, Clayton Peoples, and Alexandra Sigillo conducted a study on jurors' religious characteristics and their verdicts and sentencing decisions. They found that those people who were high on religious fundamentalism saw the character of the offender rather than environmental factors as a cause of crime and, therefore, were more punitive in their response to crime. You wanted to conduct a similar study. You first developed three attitude scales: one that measured punitiveness toward the criminal (PUN), one that measured religious fundamentalism (REL), and one that measured a person's belief that environmental factors are responsible for crime (ENV). Those who score high on the punitiveness scale want to punish convicted criminals severely, those who score high on the religious fundamentalism scale take a strict interpretation of the Bible, and those who score high on the environmental factors scale think that social factors are to blame for crime rather than the evil character of offenders. Based on the Miller and colleagues' study, you expect that religious fundamentalism will be positively related to punitiveness and that a belief in environmental causes of crime will be negatively related to punitiveness. You take a random sample of 15 persons who respond to a questionnaire that contains your attitude scales. You conduct a multiple regression analysis on your data and present the results in Figure 12.8. With this output, answer the following questions.

a. Specify the exact least-squares multiple regression equation.

b. Interpret both partial slope coefficients and the intercept value.

c. By using this output, how would you examine the relative importance of each independent variable?

d. What is the total variance explained?

e. Conduct a hypothesis test using the obtained output for both the entire regression model and the independent slope coefficients. Use an alpha level of .01 for both tests. What are your formal hypothesis statements? What do you conclude based on the F test and the two t tests?

f. By using the multiple regression equation, predict the punitiveness score for a person who has a religious fundamentalism score of 8 and an environmental factor score of 2.

STUDENT STUDY SITE

WANT A BETTER GRADE?

Get the tools you need to sharpen your study skills. Access practice quizzes, eFlashcards, data sets, and SPSS exercises at **study.sagepub.com/paternoster.**

Appendix A

Review of Basic Mathematical Operations

> *I never did very well in math—I could never seem to persuade the teacher that I hadn't meant my answers literally.*
>
> —Calvin Trillin

Introduction

Many of you undoubtedly have avoided taking a statistics class because you believed that the mathematics involved would be too difficult for your meager skills. After many years of teaching undergraduate statistics courses, we have probably heard all the stories.

Some students protest, "I'm not very good at math, so how can I ever hope to pass a statistics course? Statistics is nothing but math!" Others are more pessimistic: "I've *never* been good at math. I did lousy in junior high, high school, and college. I just have a mental block against doing math!" Others are only slightly more optimistic, claiming that they are simply rusty: "I haven't had a math course since high school. I've forgotten everything since then!"

This anxiety you brought with you to the course was probably only made worse when you thumbed through the chapters of this book, seeing all the equations, formulas, and strange symbols. Even letters in a different alphabet! "Boy," you thought, "I am sunk. Maybe I should change my major or start planning for summer school!" Put your mind at rest; you need do none of those things. The study of statistics does require some mathematical skills, but they are no more than the ability to add, subtract, multiply, and divide. Let us assure you that if you can do these simple mathematical operations, you can do statistics.

In this statistics text, we have emphasized the conceptual and logical dimension of statistical analyses of crime data. Most complex statistical analyses are now performed by computer programs. You will undoubtedly learn one of these programs in this or some other course. The study site for this text introduces you to one such statistical software program called SPSS. This stands for the Statistical Package for the Social Sciences. This is only one such statistical package that will do the calculations for you for the statistics described in this book. There are many others available, and all of them perform high-speed and accurate calculations of simple and complex statistics.

Although computer software programs can perform the calculations for us much quicker than we could by hand and with far greater accuracy, we need to know some basics about statistics so that we know which statistical analyses to perform in which situations. We also need to know how to interpret and diagnose the mass of statistical information most computer programs spit out for us. In other words, no matter how fast, accurate, or sophisticated the statistical computer package you use, *you still need to know what you are doing.* Therefore, in this statistics course, you need to learn how to hand calculate the various statistical procedures.

The hand calculation of statistics is not that daunting a task. Again, all you need to know how to do mathematically is add, subtract, multiply, and divide. The task will be made simpler by two things we have provided in each chapter of the text:

1. Clear and simplified examples.

2. A step-by-step approach in which even the most difficult statistical procedures are broken down into simple steps.

In addition, you will probably find it necessary to use a hand calculator to do the numerical operations for you. There are a great many kinds of calculators on the market now. Some of these calculators seem as complex as personal computers with graphic screens and everything! Others, in addition to basic mathematical operations, actually calculate some of the statistics in this book for you such as standard deviations and correlation coefficients.

We would recommend that you use a calculator for your calculations. You do not, however, need a very fancy or expensive one. All you really need is a calculator that, in addition to mathematical operations such as adding and subtracting, has a square root key ($\sqrt{}$) and a square key (x^2). The square key will enable you to square (multiply by itself) any number. A simple calculator that does these things is all you really need to work the problems described in this text.

Before we describe some simple mathematical operations, we would like to show you some common symbols used in statistics. Mathematical operations involve many symbols in their own right; as if this were not difficult enough, many statistics are symbolized by Greek letters. To help you through the symbolism, the following are some common math symbols and Greek letters you will find in this text:

Common Greek Letters Used In Statistics

Uppercase	Lowercase	
A	α	Alpha
B	β	Beta
Γ	γ	Gamma
Δ	δ	Delta
E	ε	Epsilon
Λ	λ	Lambda
M	μ	Mu
P	ρ	Rho
Σ	σ	Sigma
T	τ	Tau
Φ	ϕ	Phi
X	χ	Chi

Common Mathematical Symbols

+	Addition	>	Is greater than
−	Subtraction	≥	Is greater than or equal to
×	Multiplication	≈	Is approximately equal to
/ or ÷	Division	x^2	The number x squared
=	Equals	$\sqrt{x}$	The square root of the number x
≠	Is not equal to	ln x	The natural log of the number x
±	Plus or minus	log x	The common log of the number x
<	Is less than	$|x|$	The absolute value of the number x
≤	Is less than or equal to		

Mathematical Operations

Most of you are familiar with the four basic mathematical operations: addition, subtraction, multiplication, and division. In this text, the operations of addition and subtraction are shown with their common symbols, + and −. In the text, the operations of multiplication and division are shown with several different symbols. For example, the operation of multiplying x by y may be shown as xy, $x \times y$, or $(x)(y)$. The operation of dividing x by y may be shown as $x \div y$ or x / y.

In addition to the standard operations of addition, subtraction, multiplication, and division, there are three other very frequent mathematical operations in statistics. One of these is the squaring of a number. A number squared is symbolized by the number being squared shown with a superscript of 2. For example, 4 squared is shown as 4^2, and 7 squared is shown as 7^2. When you square a number, you multiply that number by itself, so 4 squared is equal to $4 \times 4 = 16$, and 7 squared is equal to $7 \times 7 = 49$. These expressions tell us that 4 squared is equal to 16 and that 7 squared is equal to 49. One squared is equal to 1 because $1^2 = 1 \times 1 = 1$. When calculating the square of fractions, it is probably easier first to convert the fraction to a decimal and then square. For example, the square of one half $(^1/_2)^2$ would be equal to $.50^2$ or $(.50)(.50) = .25$. The square of one third $(^1/_3)^2$ would be equal to $.33^2$ or $(.33)(.33) = .1089$.

A second frequent mathematical operation in statistics is taking the square root of a number. This is symbolized by placing the number we want the square root of within something called a radical sign ($\sqrt{}$). For example, the square root of 2 is shown as $\sqrt{2}$, and the square root of 9 is shown as $\sqrt{9}$. The square root of a number is the value that, when squared, results in the original number. For example, the square root of 9 is 3 ($\sqrt{9} = 3$) because when 3 is squared, we obtain 9 ($3^2 = 3 \times 3 = 9$). The square root of 25 is 5 ($\sqrt{25} = 5$) because when 5 is squared, we obtain 25 ($5^2 = (5)(5) = 25$). As with the squaring of fractions, it will probably be easier to convert a fraction into a decimal before taking the square root. For example, the square root of one half ($\sqrt{1/2}$) is equal to $\sqrt{.5}$, which is equal to .707 because $.707^2 = .5$. The square root of a negative number, $\sqrt{-x}$, is not defined because there is no number x that, when squared (multiplied by itself), results in a negative number. This is because the multiplication of two negative numbers always results in a positive product.

The third other operation that you will frequently see in this text is the summation operation. This is actually an addition operation, but because it appears with its own symbol, we need to call special attention to it. The operation of summation is symbolized by the uppercase Greek letter sigma (Σ). The summation sign stands for "the sum of," and the operation requires you to add a series of scores for a given variable. For example, presuming that there are five scores for the variable "Age" (itself symbolized as x), the ages of five persons might be as follows:

$$x_1 = 13 \qquad x_4 = 20$$

$$x_2 = 18 \qquad x_5 = 17$$

$$x_3 = 25$$

The operation Σx instructs you to sum or add each of these x scores or ages. That is, instead of stating that you should take the first person's age and add it to the second person's age, and then add this sum to the third person's age, and so on, a formula will simply state the sum of all the x scores or Σx. In this example, then, $\Sigma x = 13 + 18 + 25 + 20 + 17 = 93$. Think of the symbol Σ, then, as a mathematical operation that says "add up all of the x scores and determine the sum."

Order of Operations

Many statistical formulas require you to perform several mathematical operations at once. At times, these formulas may seem very complex, requiring addition, division, squaring, square roots, and summation. Your task of comprehending statistical formulas would not be so difficult if it did not matter how all the calculations were performed as long as they were all completed. Unfortunately, however, statistical formulas require not only that all mathematical operations be conducted but also that they be conducted in the right order because you will get different results depending on the order in which the operations are performed!

For example, take the following very simple equation that requires you to add and divide a few numbers:

$$15 + 10 \div 5$$

Note that you will get completely different results depending on whether you complete the addition before dividing or do the dividing first:

$$(15 + 10) \div 5 \qquad 15 + (10 \div 5)$$

$$25 \div 5 = 5 \qquad 15 + 2 = 17$$

As you can see, the order in which you perform your mathematical operations does make a substantial difference and must, therefore, be correctly followed. Fortunately, there are some standard rules that tell you the order in which operations should be performed. Furthermore, we would like to emphasize that even the most complex formula or mathematical expression can be simplified by solving it in sequential steps. We now illustrate these rules of operation and our recommended step-by-step approach for solving mathematical expressions.

The first rule is that any operation that is included in parentheses should be performed before operations not included in parentheses. For example, for the expression

$$15 + (10 \div 5) \times (7 \times 2)$$

the order of operations would be first to divide 10 by 5 and multiply 7 by 2. We now have simplified the expression to

$$15 + 2 \times 14$$

How do we solve the remainder of this? Do we first add 15 + 2 and then multiply by 14 to get 238? Or do we first multiply 2 by 14 and then add 15 to get 43?

The second rule of the order of operations is that you should first obtain all squares and square roots, then perform multiplication and division, and last complete any addition and subtraction. Because in the expression just listed we have no squares or square roots to calculate, we know that we should first multiply the 2 and 14 to get 28:

$$15 + 28$$

After this, we should add 28 to 15 to get the final sum of 43.

To summarize, the rules of operation for solving mathematical expressions are, in order:

- Solve all expressions in parentheses.
- Determine the value of all squares and square roots.
- Perform all division and multiplication operations.
- Perform all addition and subtraction operations.

We will practice these rules with some exercises momentarily, but first we need to illustrate the parentheses rule in combination with the rule of squares.

The rules are to perform all operations within parentheses first, then squares and square roots, next multiplication and division, and then addition and subtraction. As an example, assume that we have the following six scores: 46, 29, 61, 14, 33, and 25. With these scores, examine the two expressions, Σx^2 and $(\Sigma x)^2$. These two expressions look virtually identical because they both require a summation of scores and that a number be squared. Note, however, that in the first expression there are no parentheses. We know that the summation sign tells us that we have to add the six scores. Before we do this, however, following the correct order of operations, we must first square each x score and then sum all of them:

$$\begin{aligned} \Sigma x^2 &= 46^2 + 29^2 + 61^2 + 14^2 + 33^2 + 25^2 \\ &= 2{,}116 + 841 + 3{,}721 + 196 + 1{,}089 + 625 \\ &= 8{,}588 \end{aligned}$$

In this first expression, then, we have followed the order of operations by first squaring each x score and then taking the sum (squaring before addition).

Note that in the second expression, we have parentheses $(\Sigma x)^2$. As the order of operations is to conduct all calculations within parentheses first, this expression tells us first to sum the six scores and then square the sum:

$$\begin{aligned} (\Sigma x^2) &= (46 + 29 + 61 + 14 + 33 + 25)^2 \\ &= 208^2 \\ &= 43{,}264 \end{aligned}$$

To reiterate the point made earlier, Σx^2, called the sum of the x squares, is obtained by first squaring each x score and then adding all squared numbers. This is different from the expression, $(\Sigma x)^2$, called the sum of the xs, squared, which is obtained by first adding up all the x scores and then squaring the sum.

Operations With Negative Numbers and Fractions in Denominators

In many statistical calculations, you have both positive and negative scores. Positive scores are shown with no sign at all, so that a positive 10 appears as 10. Negative numbers are shown with a minus sign in front of them, so that a negative 10 appears as –10. Negative numbers are less than zero, and positive numbers are greater than zero. It is important to keep track of the signs of numbers because it makes a substantial difference for the final result of a mathematical operation.

For example, when a positive number is added to a positive number, nothing special happens, and the sum of the two numbers can be obtained directly: $10 + 14 = 24$. When a negative number is added to a positive number, however, it has the same effect as subtraction. For example, adding a negative 14 to 10 is the same thing as subtracting 14 from 10: $10 + (-14) = 10 - 14 = (-4)$. When a positive number is subtracted from another positive number, nothing special happens, and the difference between the two numbers can be obtained directly: $25 - 10 = 15$. When a negative number is subtracted from either a positive or negative number, its sign changes to that of a positive number, so that $25 - (-10) = 25 + 10 = 35$; $(-10) - (-7) = (-10) + 7 = (-3)$. Remember, then, that the subtraction of a negative number changes the sign of the number from negative to positive.

When two positive numbers are multiplied, nothing special happens, and the product of the two numbers can be obtained directly: $6 \times 3 = 18$. When two numbers are multiplied and one is positive and the other negative, the resulting product is negative. For example: $25 \times (-3) = -75$; $(-14) \times 5 = -70$. When two negative numbers are multiplied, the resulting product is always positive: $(-23) \times (-14) = 322$. So the rule is that the multiplication of either two positive or two negative numbers results in a positive product, whereas the multiplication of one positive and one negative number results in a negative product.

The same pattern occurs when the operation is division rather than multiplication. When two positive numbers are divided, nothing special happens, and the result (the *quotient*) is positive: $125 \div 5 = 25$; $10 \div 20 = .5$. When two numbers are divided and one is positive and the other negative, the quotient is negative: $250 \div (-25) = (-10)$; $(-33) \div 11 = -3$. When two negative numbers are divided, the quotient is always positive: $(-16) \div (-4) = 4$. So the rule is that the division of either two positive or two negative numbers results in a positive quotient, whereas the division of one positive and one negative number results in a negative quotient.

Rounding Numbers Off

Whenever you are working with statistical formulas, you need to decide how precise you want your answer to be. For example, should your answer be correct to the tenth decimal place? The fifth? The third? It is also important to decide when to round up and when to round down. For example, having decided that we want to be accurate only to the second decimal place, should the number 28.355 be rounded up to 28.36 or rounded down to 28.35? It is important to make these decisions explicit because two people may get different answers to the same statistical problem simply because they employed different rounding rules.

Unfortunately, no rule about when to round off can always be hard and fast. When we are dealing with large numbers, we can frequently do our calculations with whole numbers (integers). In this case, we would not gain much precision by carrying out our calculations to one or two decimal places. When we are dealing with much smaller numbers, however, it may be necessary, to be as precise as possible, to take a number out to three or four decimal places in our calculations. With smaller numbers, there is a substantial gain in precision by including more decimal places in our calculations. Whenever possible, however, we have tried to limit our precision to two decimal places. This means that most of the time, numbers will include only two decimal places. We warn you, however, that this will not always be the case.

The question about how to round can be answered a little more definitively. When rounding, the following convention should be applied. When deciding how to round, look at the digit to the right of the last digit you want to keep. If you are rounding to the second decimal place, then, look at the third digit to the right of the decimal point. If this digit is larger than 5, you should round up. For example, 123.148 becomes 123.15 and 34.737 becomes 34.74. If this digit is less than 5, you should round down. For example, 8.923 becomes 8.92 and 53.904 becomes 53.90.

What do you do in the case where the third digit is a 5, as in 34.675, for example? Do you round up or round down? You cannot simply say that you should always round up or always round down because there will be systematic bias to your rounding decision. Your decision rule will be consistent to be sure, but it will be biased because numbers are always being overestimated (if rounded up) or underestimated (if rounded down). You would like your decision rule to be consistent but consistently fair—that is, never in the same direction. This way, sometimes the 5 will be rounded up and sometimes it will be rounded down, and the number of times it is rounded up and down will be approximately the same. One way to ensure this is to adopt the following rounding rule: If the third digit is a 5, then look at the digit immediately before the 5; if that digit (the second decimal place) is an even number, then round up; if it is an odd number, then round down. For example, the number 34.675 should be rounded down to 34.67 because the number immediately *before* the 5 is an odd number. The number 164.965 should be rounded up to 164.97 because the number before the 5 is an even number. Note that the number of occasions you will decide to round up (if the immediately preceding digit is an even number 0, 2, 4, 6, or 8) is the same as the number of occasions when you will decide to round down (if the immediately preceding digit is an odd number 1, 3, 5, 7, 9). Because even numbers should appear in our calculations as frequently as odd numbers, there is no bias to our rounding decision rule.

Examples

Let's go through a few examples step by step to make sure that we understand all the rules and procedures. We will begin by solving the following problem:

$$25 + 192 - (3 + 5)^2$$

Following the rules of operation, we first solve within the parentheses:

$$25 + 192 - (8)^2$$

Then we square the 8:

$$25 + 192 - 64$$

Now we can solve for the final answer either by adding 25 to 192 and then subtracting 64 or by subtracting 64 from 192 and then adding 25. Either way, we get the same result:

$$217 - 64 = 153$$

$$25 + 128 = 153$$

Now let's solve a more complicated-looking problem. Please note that this problem is only more *complicated-looking*. When we solve it step by step, you will see that it is very manageable and that all you really need to know is addition, subtraction, multiplication, and division:

$$[32 + 17)^2 / 10] + [\sqrt{16}/(10 - 6)^2]$$

First, we solve within parentheses:

$$[(49)^2 / 10] + [\sqrt{16}/(4)^2]$$

Then we calculate all squares and square roots:

$$(2{,}401/10) + (4/16)$$

Next we do the division:

$$240.1 + .25$$

Finally, we do the addition:

$$240.35$$

Here is one more problem, and it's probably as difficult as any you will encounter in this book:

$$\sqrt{\frac{(116 - 27)^2 + 21}{\sqrt{15 + 1}}} - \frac{(212 - 188)}{2}$$

Following the rules of operations, we first want to solve within all the parentheses:

$$\sqrt{\frac{(89)^2 + 21}{\sqrt{15 + 1}}} - \frac{24}{2}$$

Then we calculate all squares and square roots. Note, however, that in the denominator of the first term, we first have to use addition (15 + 1) before taking the square root of the sum. Note also that we cannot take the square root of the

entire first term until we solve for all that is under the square root sign:

$$\sqrt{\frac{7{,}921 + 21}{4}} - 12$$

Now we continue to solve that part of the problem within the square root by first completing the numerator (by addition) and then dividing:

$$\sqrt{\frac{7{,}942}{4}} - 12$$

$$\sqrt{1{,}985.5} - 12$$

Finally, now that we have completed all the operations within the square root sign, we can complete that:

$$44.56 - 12$$

Note that the result for the first expression was 44.558. Because the third decimal place is greater than 5, we round the second digit up, so that 44.558 becomes 44.56. Then we complete the problem by subtracting 12:

$$32.56$$

We hope that you now feel greater confidence in solving math equations. As long as things are performed in a step-by-step manner, in accordance with the rules of operations, everything in any equation can be solved relatively easily. To make sure that you comprehend these rules, as well as to brush up on your math skills, complete the following exercises.

We have provided answers for you at the end of the section. If you can do these problems, you are ready to tackle any of the statistics problems in this text. If some of the problems in the exercises give you difficulty, simply review that section of this appendix or consult a mathematics book for some help.

Practice Problems

1. Calculate each of the following:
   a. $5^2 + 3$
   b. $(35/7) - 4$
   c. $\sqrt{16} + 7 - (4/2)$
   d. $[(35)(.3)] / 10 + 15$

2. Calculate each of the following:

   a. $45 + \sqrt{\dfrac{125}{15 - (3)^2}}$

   b. $18 + (12 \times 10)\sqrt{150} - 50$

   c. $(18 + 12) \times 10\sqrt{150} - 50$

   d. $[(23 + 17) - (5 \times 4)] / (8 + 2)^2$

   e. $(-5) \times 13$

   f. $(-5) \times (-13)$

   g. $[18 + (-7)] \times [(-4) - (-10)]$

   h. $125 / -5$

   i. $450 - [(-125 / -10) / 2]$

3. With the 10 scores 7, 18, 42, 11, 34, 65, 30, 27, 6, and 29, perform the following operations:

   a. Σx

   b. $(\Sigma x)^2$

   c. Σx^2

4. Round the following numbers off to two places to the right of the decimal point:

   a. 118.954

   b. 65.186

   c. 156.145

   d. 87.915

   e. 3.212

   f. 48.565

   g. 48.535

Solutions to Problems

1. a. 28

   b. 1 (Remember to do the division before the subtraction.)

   c. 13

   d. 16.05

2. a. 49.56

   b. 128

   c. 290

   d. .20 (Remember to do all operations within parentheses first, starting with the innermost parentheses.)

   e. −65

   f. 65

   g. 66

   h. −25

   i. 443.75 (Following the rules of operation, you should have divided the two negative numbers (−125 and −10) first, then divided by 2, and finally subtracted that quotient from 450.)

3. a. This expression says to sum all x scores: $7 + 18 + 42 + 11 + 34 + 65 + 30 + 27 + 6 + 29 = 269$.

   b. Note the parentheses in this expression. It tells you to first sum all the x scores and then square the sum: $(7 + 18 + 42 + 11 + 34 + 65 + 30 + 27 + 6 + 29)^2 = (269)^2 = 72{,}361$.

   c. Following the order of operations, first square each x score and then sum these squared scores: $7^2 + 18^2 + 42^2 + 11^2 + 34^2 + 65^2 + 30^2 + 27^2 + 6^2 + 29^2 = 49 + 324 + 1{,}764 + 121 + 1{,}156 + 4{,}225 + 900 + 729 + 36 + 841 = 10{,}145$.

4. a. 118.95

   b. 65.19

   c. 156.15 (Round up because the number to the left of the 5 is an even number.)

   d. 87.91 (Round down because the number to the left of the 5 is an odd number.)

   e. 3.21

   f. 48.57

   g. 48.53

Appendix B

Statistical Tables

Table B.1 Table of Random Numbers

16408	81899	04153	53381	79401	21438	83035	92350	36693	31238	59649	91754	72772
18629	81953	05520	91962	04739	13092	97662	24822	94730	06496	35090	04822	86774
73115	35101	47498	87637	99016	71060	88824	71013	18735	20286	23153	72924	35165
57491	16703	23167	49323	45021	33132	12544	41035	80780	45393	44812	12515	98931
30405	83946	23792	14422	15059	45799	22716	19792	09983	74353	68668	30429	70735
16631	35006	85900	98275	32388	52390	16815	69298	82732	38480	73817	32523	41961
96773	20206	42559	78985	05300	22164	24369	54224	35083	19687	11052	91491	60383
38935	64202	14349	82674	66523	44133	00697	35552	35970	19124	63318	29686	03387
31624	76384	17403	53363	44167	64486	64758	75366	76554	31601	12614	33072	60332
78919	19474	23632	27889	47914	02584	37680	20801	72152	39339	34806	08930	85001
03931	33309	57047	74211	63445	17361	62825	39908	05607	91284	68833	25570	38818
74426	33278	43972	10119	89917	15665	52872	73823	73144	88662	88970	74492	51805
09066	00903	20795	95452	92648	45454	09552	88815	16553	51125	79375	97596	16296
42238	12426	87025	14267	20979	04508	64535	31355	86064	29472	47689	05974	52468
16153	08002	26504	41744	81959	65642	74240	56302	00033	67107	77510	70625	28725
21457	40742	29820	96783	29400	21840	15035	34537	33310	06116	95240	15957	16572
21581	57802	02050	89728	17937	37621	47075	42080	97403	48626	68995	43805	33386
55612	78095	83197	33732	05810	24813	86902	60397	16489	03264	88525	42786	05269
44657	66999	99324	51281	84463	60563	79312	93454	68876	25471	93911	25650	12682
91340	84979	46949	81973	37949	61023	43997	15263	80644	43942	89203	71795	99533
91227	21199	31935	27022	84067	05462	35216	14486	29891	68607	41867	14951	91696
50001	38140	66321	19924	72163	09538	12151	06878	91903	18749	34405	56087	82790
65390	05224	72958	28609	81406	39147	25549	48542	42627	45233	57202	94617	23772
27504	96131	83944	41575	10573	08619	64482	73923	36152	05184	94142	25299	84387
37169	94851	39117	89632	00959	16487	65536	19071	39782	17095	02330	74301	00275
11508	70225	51111	38351	19444	66499	71945	05422	13442	78675	84081	66938	93654
37449	30362	06694	54690	04052	53115	62757	95348	78662	11163	81651	50245	34971
46515	70331	85922	38329	57015	15765	97161	17869	45349	61796	66345	81073	49106
30986	81223	42416	58353	21532	30502	32305	86482	06174	07901	54339	58861	74818
63798	64995	46583	09785	44160	78128	83991	42865	92520	83531	80377	35909	81250

82486	84846	99254	67632	43218	50076	21361	64816	51202	88124	41870	52689	51275
21885	32906	92431	09060	64297	51674	64126	62570	26123	05155	59194	52799	28225
60336	98782	07408	53458	13564	59089	26445	29789	85205	41001	12535	12133	14645
43937	46891	24010	25560	86355	33941	25786	54990	71899	15475	95434	98227	21824
97656	63175	89303	16275	07100	92063	21942	18611	47348	20203	18534	03862	78095
03299	01221	05418	38982	55758	92237	26759	86367	21216	98442	08303	56613	91511
79626	06486	03574	17668	07785	76020	79924	25651	83325	88428	85076	72811	22717
85636	68335	47539	03129	65651	11977	02510	26113	99447	68645	34327	15152	55230
18039	14367	61337	06177	12143	46609	32989	74014	64708	00533	35398	58408	13261
08362	15656	60627	36478	65648	16764	53412	09013	07832	41574	17639	82163	60859
79556	29068	04142	16268	15387	12856	66227	38358	22478	73373	88732	09443	82558
92608	82674	27072	32534	17075	27698	98204	63863	11951	34648	88022	56148	34925
23982	25835	40055	67006	12293	02753	14827	23235	35071	99704	37543	11601	35503
09915	96306	05908	97901	28395	14186	00821	80703	70426	75647	76310	88717	37890
59037	33300	26695	62247	69927	76123	50842	43834	86654	70959	79725	93872	28117
42488	78077	69882	61657	34136	79180	97526	43092	04098	73571	80799	76536	71255
46764	86273	63003	93017	31204	36692	40202	35275	57306	55543	53203	18098	47625
03237	45430	55417	63282	90816	17349	88298	90183	36600	78406	06216	95787	42579
86591	81482	52667	61582	14972	90053	89534	76036	49199	43716	97548	04379	46370
38534	01715	94964	87288	65680	43772	39560	12918	86537	62738	19636	51132	25739

Source: Adapted with permission from Beyer, W. H. (Ed.). 1991. CRC Standard Probability and Statistics: Tables and Formulae, XII.3. Boca Raton, FL: CRC Press.

Table B.2 — Area Under the Standard Normal Curve (z Distribution)*

z	.00	.01	.02	.03	.04	.05	.06	.07	.08	.09
0.0	.0000	.0040	.0080	.0120	.0160	.0199	.0239	.0279	.0319	.0359
0.1	.0398	.0438	.0478	.0517	.0557	.0596	.0636	.0675	.0714	.0753
0.2	.0793	.0832	.0871	.0910	.0948	.0987	.1026	.1064	.1103	.1141
0.3	.1179	.1217	.1255	.1293	.1331	.1368	.1406	.1443	.1480	.1517
0.4	.1554	.1591	.1628	.1664	.1700	.1736	.1772	.1808	.1844	.1879
0.5	.1915	.1950	.1985	.2019	.2054	.2088	.2123	.2157	.2190	.2224
0.6	.2257	.2291	.2324	.2357	.2389	.2422	.2454	.2486	.2517	.2549
0.7	.2580	.2611	.2642	.2673	.2704	.2734	.2764	.2794	.2823	.2852
0.8	.2881	.2910	.2939	.2967	.2995	.3023	.3051	.3078	.3106	.3133
0.9	.3159	.3186	.3212	.3238	.3264	.3289	.3315	.3340	.3365	.3389
1.0	.3413	.3438	.3461	.3485	.3508	.3531	.3554	.3577	.3599	.3621
1.1	.3643	.3665	.3686	.3708	.3729	.3749	.3770	.3790	.3810	.3830
1.2	.3849	.3869	.3888	.3907	.3925	.3944	.3962	.3980	.3997	.4015
1.3	.4032	.4049	.4066	.4082	.4099	.4115	.4131	.4147	.4162	.4177
1.4	.4192	.4207	.4222	.4236	.4251	.4265	.4279	.4292	.4306	.4319
1.5	.4332	.4345	.4357	.4370	.4382	.4394	.4406	.4418	.4429	.4441
1.6	.4452	.4463	.4474	.4484	.4495	.4505	.4515	.4525	.4535	.4545
1.7	.4554	.4564	.4573	.4582	.4591	.4599	.4608	.4616	.4625	.4633
1.8	.4641	.4649	.4656	.4664	.4671	.4678	.4686	.4693	.4699	.4706
1.9	.4713	.4719	.4726	.4732	.4738	.4744	.4750	.4756	.4761	.4767
2.0	.4772	.4778	.4783	.4788	.4793	.4798	.4803	.4808	.4812	.4817
2.1	.4821	.4826	.4830	.4834	.4838	.4842	.4846	.4850	.4854	.4857
2.2	.4861	.4864	.4868	.4871	.4875	.4878	.4881	.4884	.4887	.4890
2.3	.4893	.4896	.4898	.4901	.4904	.4906	.4909	.4911	.4913	.4916
2.4	.4918	.4920	.4922	.4925	.4927	.4929	.4931	.4932	.4934	.4936
2.5	.4938	.4940	.4941	.4943	.4945	.4946	.4948	.4949	.4951	.4952
2.6	.4953	.4955	.4956	.4957	.4959	.4960	.4961	.4962	.4963	.4964
2.7	.4965	.4966	.4967	.4968	.4969	.4970	.4971	.4972	.4973	.4974
2.8	.4974	.4975	.4976	.4977	.4977	.4978	.4979	.4979	.4980	.4981
2.9	.4981	.4982	.4982	.4983	.4984	.4984	.4985	.4985	.4986	.4986
3.0	.4987	.4987	.4987	.4988	.4988	.4989	.4989	.4989	.4990	.4990

Source: Adapted with permission from Frederick Mosteller and Robert E. K. Rourke, 1973. *Sturdy Statistics.* Table A-1. Reading, MA: Addison–Wesley.

*Proportion of the area under the normal curve corresponding to the distance between the mean (0) and a point that is z standard deviation units away from the mean.

Table B.3 The *t* Distribution

	Level of Significance for a One-Tailed Test					
	.10	.05	.025	.01	.005	.0005
	Level of Significance for a Two-Tailed Test					
	.20	.10	.05	.02	.01	.001
1	3.078	6.314	12.706	31.821	63.657	636.619
2	1.886	2.920	4.303	6.965	9.925	31.598
3	1.638	2.353	3.182	4.541	5.841	12.941
4	1.533	2.132	2.776	3.747	4.604	8.610
5	1.476	2.015	2.571	3.365	4.032	6.859
6	1.440	1.943	2.447	3.143	3.707	5.959
7	1.415	1.895	2.365	2.998	3.499	5.405
8	1.397	1.860	2.306	2.896	3.355	5.041
9	1.383	1.833	2.262	2.821	3.250	4.781
10	1.372	1.812	2.228	2.764	3.169	4.587
11	1.363	1.796	2.201	2.718	3.106	4.437
12	1.356	1.782	2.179	2.681	3.055	4.318
13	1.350	1.771	2.160	2.650	3.012	4.221
14	1.345	1.761	2.145	2.624	2.977	4.140
15	1.341	1.753	2.131	2.602	2.947	4.073
16	1.337	1.746	2.120	2.583	2.921	4.015
17	1.333	1.740	2.110	2.567	2.898	3.965
18	1.330	1.734	2.101	2.552	2.878	3.922
19	1.328	1.729	2.093	2.539	2.861	3.883
20	1.325	1.725	2.086	2.528	2.845	3.850
21	1.323	1.721	2.080	2.518	2.831	3.819
22	1.321	1.717	2.074	2.508	2.819	3.792
23	1.319	1.714	2.069	2.500	2.807	3.767
24	1.318	1.711	2.064	2.492	2.797	3.745
25	1.316	1.708	2.060	2.485	2.787	3.725
26	1.315	1.706	2.056	2.479	2.779	3.707
27	1.314	1.703	2.052	2.473	2.771	3.690
28	1.313	1.701	2.048	2.467	2.763	3.674
29	1.311	1.699	2.045	2.462	2.756	3.659
30	1.310	1.697	2.042	2.457	2.750	3.646
40	1.303	1.684	2.021	2.423	2.704	3.551
60	1.206	1.671	2.000	2.390	2.660	3.460
120	1.289	1.658	1.980	2.358	2.617	3.373
∞	1.282	1.645	1.960	2.326	2.576	3.291

Source: Table B.3 is adapted with permission from Table III of R. A. Fisher and F. Yates, *Statistical Tables for Biological, Agricultural and Medical Research* (6th ed.). Published by Longman Group UK Ltd., 1974.

Table B.4 **Critical Values of the Chi-Square Statistic at the .05 and .01 Significance Levels**

Area to the Right of the Critical Value			Area to the Right of the Critical Value		
	Level of Significance			Level of Significance	
df	.05	.01	df	.05	.01
1	3.841	6.635	21	32.671	38.932
2	5.991	9.210	22	33.924	40.289
3	7.815	11.345	23	33.924	40.289
4	9.488	13.277	24	36.415	42.980
5	11.070	15.086	25	37.652	44.314
6	12.592	16.812	26	38.885	45.642
7	14.067	18.475	27	40.113	46.963
8	15.507	20.090	28	41.337	48.278
9	16.919	21.666	29	42.557	49.588
10	18.307	23.209	30	43.773	50.892
11	19.675	24.725	40	55.758	63.691
12	21.026	26.217	50	67.505	76.154
13	22.362	27.688	60	79.082	88.379
14	23.685	29.141	70	90.531	100.425
15	24.996	30.578	80	101.879	112.329
16	26.296	32.000	90	113.145	124.116
17	27.587	33.409	100	124.342	135.807
18	28.869	34.805			
19	30.144	36.191			
20	31.410	37.566			

Source: Adapted from Donald Owen, Handbook of Statistical Tables, © 1962 by Addison–Wesley Publishing Company, Inc. Reprinted by permission of Addison–Wesley Publishing Company, Inc.

Table B.5a   The *F* Distribution ($\alpha = .01$ in the right tail)

df (within) ↓ \ df (between) →	Numerator Degrees of Freedom								
	1	2	3	4	5	6	7	8	9
1	4052.2	4999.5	5403.4	5624.6	5763.6	5859.0	5928.4	5981.1	6022.5
2	98.503	99.000	99.166	99.249	99.299	99.333	99.356	99.374	99.388
3	34.116	30.817	29.457	28.710	28.237	27.911	27.672	27.489	27.345
4	21.198	18.000	16.694	15.977	15.522	15.207	14.976	14.799	14.659
5	16.258	13.274	12.060	11.392	10.967	10.672	10.456	10.289	10.158
6	13.745	10.925	9.7795	9.1483	8.7459	8.4661	8.2600	8.1017	7.9761
7	12.246	9.5466	8.4513	7.8466	7.4604	7.1914	6.9928	6.8400	6.7188
8	11.259	8.6491	7.5910	7.0061	6.6318	6.3707	6.1776	6.0289	5.9106
9	10.561	8.0215	6.9919	6.4221	6.0569	5.8018	5.6129	5.4671	5.3511
10	10.044	7.5594	6.5523	5.9943	5.6363	5.3858	5.2001	5.0567	4.9424
11	9.6460	7.2057	6.2167	5.6683	5.3160	5.0692	4.8861	4.7445	4.6315
12	9.3302	6.9266	5.9525	5.4120	5.0643	4.8206	4.6395	4.4994	4.3875
13	9.0738	6.7010	5.7394	5.2053	4.8616	4.6204	4.4410	4.3021	4.1911
14	8.8616	6.5149	5.5639	5.0354	4.6950	4.4558	4.2779	4.1399	4.0297
15	8.6831	6.3589	5.4170	4.8932	4.5556	4.3183	4.1415	4.0045	3.8948
16	8.5310	6.2262	5.2922	4.7726	4.4374	4.2016	4.0259	3.8896	3.7804
17	8.3997	6.1121	5.1850	4.6690	4.3359	4.1015	3.9267	3.7910	3.6822
18	8.2854	6.0129	5.0919	4.5790	4.2479	4.0146	3.8406	3.7054	3.5971
19	8.1849	5.9259	5.0103	4.5003	4.1708	3.9386	3.7653	3.6305	3.5225
20	8.0960	5.8489	4.9382	4.4307	4.1027	3.8714	3.6987	3.5644	3.4567
21	8.0166	5.7804	4.8740	4.3688	4.0421	3.8117	3.6396	3.5056	3.3981
22	7.9454	5.7190	4.8166	4.3134	3.9880	3.7583	3.5867	3.4530	3.3458
23	7.8811	5.6637	4.7649	4.2636	3.9392	3.7102	3.5390	3.4057	3.2986
24	7.8229	5.6136	4.7181	4.2184	3.8951	3.6667	3.4959	3.3629	3.2560
25	7.7698	5.5680	4.6755	4.1774	3.8550	3.6272	3.4568	3.3239	3.2172
26	7.7213	5.5263	4.6366	4.1400	3.8183	3.5911	3.4210	3.2884	3.1818
27	7.6767	5.4881	4.6009	4.1056	3.7848	3.5580	3.3882	3.2558	3.1494
28	7.6356	5.4529	4.5681	4.0740	3.7539	3.5276	3.3581	3.2259	3.1195
29	7.5977	5.4204	4.5378	4.0449	3.7254	3.4995	3.3303	3.1982	3.0920
30	7.5625	5.3903	4.5097	4.0179	3.6990	3.4735	3.3045	3.1726	3.0665
40	7.3141	5.1785	4.3126	3.8283	3.5138	3.2910	3.1238	2.9930	2.8876
60	7.0771	4.9774	4.1259	3.6490	3.3389	3.1187	2.9530	2.8233	2.7185
120	6.8509	4.7865	3.9491	3.4795	3.1735	2.9559	2.7918	2.6629	2.5586
∞	6.6349	4.6052	3.7816	3.3192	30173	2.8020	2.6393	2.5113	2.4073

Table B.5b — The F Distribution ($\alpha = .01$ in the right tail)

df (within)	10	12	15	20	24	30	40	60	120	∞
1	241.88	243.91	245.95	248.01	249.05	250.10	251.14	252.20	253.25	254.31
2	19.396	19.413	19.429	19.446	19.454	19.462	19.471	19.479	19.487	19.496
3	8.7855	8.7446	8.7029	8.6602	8.6385	8.6166	8.5944	8.5720	8.5494	8.5264
4	5.9644	5.9117	5.8578	5.8025	5.7744	5.7459	5.7170	5.6877	5.6581	5.6281
5	4.7351	4.6777	4.6188	4.5581	4.5272	4.4957	4.4638	4.4314	4.3985	4.3650
6	4.0600	3.9999	3.9381	3.8742	3.8415	3.8082	3.7743	3.7398	3.7047	3.6689
7	3.6365	3.5747	3.5107	3.4445	3.4105	3.1758	3.3404	3.3043	3.2674	3.2298
8	3.3472	3.2839	3.2184	3.1503	3.1152	3.0794	3.0428	3.0053	2.9669	2.9276
9	3.1373	3.0729	3.0061	2.9365	2.9005	2.8617	2.8259	2.7872	2.7475	2.7067
10	2.9782	2.9110	2.8450	2.7740	2.7372	2.6996	2.6609	2.6211	2.5801	2.5379
11	2.8536	2.7876	2.7186	2.6464	2.6090	2.5705	2.5309	2.4901	2.4480	2.4045
12	2.7534	2.6866	2.6169	2.5436	2.5055	2.4663	2.4259	2.3842	2.3410	2.2962
13	2.6710	2.6037	2.5331	2.4589	2.4202	2.1801	2.3392	2.2966	2.2524	2.2064
14	2.6022	2.5342	2.4630	2.3879	2.3487	2.1082	2.2664	2.2229	2.1778	2.1307
15	2.5437	2.4753	2.4034	2.3275	2.2878	2.2468	2.2043	2.1601	2.1141	2.0658
16	2.4935	2.4247	2.3522	2.2756	2.2354	2.1938	2.1507	2.1058	2.0589	2.0096
17	2.4499	2.3807	2.3077	2.2304	2.1898	2.1477	2.1040	2.0584	2.0107	1.9604
18	2.4117	2.3421	2.2686	2.1906	2.1497	2.1071	2.0629	2.0166	1.9681	1.9168
19	2.3779	2.3080	2.2341	2.1555	2.1141	2.0712	2.0264	1.9795	1.9302	1.8780
20	2.3479	2.2776	2.2033	2.1242	2.0825	2.0391	1.9938	1.9464	1.8963	1.8432
21	2.3210	2.2504	2.1757	2.0960	2.0540	2.0102	1.9645	1.9165	1.8657	1.8117
22	2.2967	2.2258	2.1508	2.0707	2.0283	1.9842	1.9380	1.8894	1.8380	1.7831
23	2.2747	2.2036	2.1282	2.0476	2.0050	1.9605	1.9139	1.8648	1.8128	1.7570
24	2.2547	2.1834	2.1077	2.0267	1.9838	1.9390	1.8920	1.8424	1.7896	1.7330
25	2.2365	2.1649	2.0889	2.0075	1.9643	1.9192	1.8718	1.8217	1.7684	1.7110
26	2.2197	2.1479	2.0716	1.9898	1.9464	1.9010	1.8533	1.8027	1.7488	1.6906
27	2.2043	2.1323	20558	1.9736	1.9299	1.8842	1.8361	1.7851	1.7306	1.6717
28	2.1900	2.1179	2.0411	1.9586	1.9147	1.8687	1.8203	1.7689	1.7138	1.6541
29	2.1768	2.1045	2.0275	1.9446	1.9005	1.8543	1.8055	1.7537	1.6981	1.6376
30	2.1646	2.0921	2.0148	1.9317	1.8874	1.8409	1.7918	1.7396	1.6835	1.6223
40	2.0772	2.0035	1.9245	1.8389	1.7929	1.7444	1.6928	1.6373	1.5766	1.5089
60	1.9926	1.9174	1.8364	1.7480	1.7001	1.6491	1.5943	1.5343	1.4673	1.3893
120	1.9105	1.8337	1.7505	1.6587	1.6084	1.5543	1.4952	1.4290	1.3519	1.2539
∞	1.8307	1.7522	1.6664	1.5705	1.5173	1.4591	1.3940	1.3180	1.2214	1.0000

Numerator Degrees of Freedom

Table B.6 The Studentized Range Statistic, q

q Value When Alpha = .05

df (within)	k=2	3	4	5	6	7	8	9	10	11	12	13	14	15	16	17	18	19	20
1	18.0	27.0	32.8	37.1	40.4	43.1	45.4	47.4	49.1	50.6	52.0	53.2	54.3	55.4	56.3	57.2	58.0	58.8	59.6
2	6.09	8.3	9.8	10.9	11.7	12.4	13.0	13.5	14.0	14.4	14.7	15.1	15.4	15.7	15.9	16.1	16.4	16.6	16.8
3	4.50	5.91	6.82	7.50	8.04	8.48	8.85	9.18	9.46	9.72	9.95	10.15	10.35	10.52	10.69	10.84	10.98	11.11	11.24
4	3.93	5.04	5.76	6.29	6.71	7.05	7.35	7.60	7.83	8.03	8.21	8.37	8.52	8.66	8.79	8.91	9.03	9.13	9.23
5	3.64	4.60	5.22	5.67	6.03	6.33	6.58	6.80	6.99	7.17	7.32	7.47	7.60	7.72	7.83	7.93	8.03	8.12	8.21
6	3.46	4.34	4.90	5.31	5.63	5.89	6.12	6.32	6.49	6.65	6.79	6.92	7.03	7.14	7.24	7.34	7.43	7.51	7.59
7	3.34	4.16	4.68	5.06	5.36	5.61	5.82	6.00	6.16	6.30	6.43	6.55	6.66	6.76	6.85	6.94	7.02	7.09	7.17
8	3.26	4.04	4.53	4.89	5.17	5.40	5.60	5.77	5.92	6.05	6.18	6.29	6.39	6.48	6.57	6.65	6.73	6.80	6.87
9	3.20	3.95	4.42	4.76	5.02	5.24	5.43	5.60	5.74	5.87	5.98	6.09	6.19	6.28	6.36	6.44	6.51	6.58	6.64
10	3.15	3.88	4.33	4.65	4.91	5.12	5.30	5.46	5.60	5.72	5.83	5.93	6.03	6.11	6.20	6.27	6.34	6.40	6.47
11	3.11	3.82	4.26	4.57	4.82	5.03	5.20	5.35	5.49	5.61	5.71	5.81	5.90	5.99	6.06	6.14	6.20	6.26	6.33
12	3.08	3.77	4.20	4.51	4.75	4.95	5.12	5.27	5.40	5.51	5.62	5.71	5.80	5.88	5.95	6.03	6.09	6.15	6.21
13	3.06	3.73	4.15	4.45	4.69	4.88	5.05	5.19	5.32	5.43	5.53	5.63	5.71	5.79	5.86	5.93	6.00	6.05	6.11
14	3.03	3.70	4.11	4.41	4.64	4.83	4.99	5.13	5.25	5.36	5.46	5.55	5.64	5.72	5.79	5.85	5.92	5.97	6.03
15	3.01	3.67	4.08	4.37	4.60	4.78	4.94	5.08	5.20	5.31	5.40	5.49	5.58	5.65	5.72	5.79	5.85	5.90	5.96
16	3.00	3.65	4.05	4.33	4.56	4.74	4.90	5.03	5.15	5.26	5.35	5.44	5.52	5.59	5.66	5.72	5.79	5.84	5.90
17	2.98	3.63	4.02	4.30	4.52	4.71	4.86	4.99	5.11	5.21	5.31	5.39	5.47	5.55	5.61	5.68	5.74	5.79	5.84
18	2.97	3.61	4.00	4.28	4.49	4.67	4.82	4.96	5.07	5.17	5.27	5.35	5.43	5.50	5.57	5.63	5.69	5.74	5.79
19	2.96	3.59	3.98	4.25	4.47	4.65	4.79	4.92	5.04	5.14	5.23	5.32	5.39	5.46	5.53	5.59	5.65	5.70	5.75
20	2.95	3.58	3.96	4.23	4.45	4.62	4.77	4.90	5.01	5.11	5.20	5.28	5.36	5.43	5.49	5.55	5.61	5.66	5.71
24	2.92	3.53	3.90	4.17	4.37	4.54	4.68	4.81	4.92	5.01	5.10	5.18	5.25	5.32	5.38	5.44	5.50	5.54	5.59
30	2.89	3.49	3.84	4.10	4.30	4.46	4.60	4.72	4.83	4.92	5.00	5.08	5.15	5.21	5.27	5.33	5.38	5.43	5.48
40	2.86	3.44	3.79	4.04	4.23	4.39	4.52	4.63	4.74	4.82	4.91	4.98	5.05	5.11	5.16	5.22	5.27	5.31	5.36
60	2.83	3.40	3.74	3.98	4.16	4.31	4.44	4.55	4.65	4.73	4.81	4.88	4.94	5.00	5.06	5.11	5.16	5.20	5.24
120	2.80	3.36	3.69	3.92	4.10	4.24	4.36	4.48	4.56	4.64	4.72	4.78	4.84	4.90	4.95	5.00	5.05	5.09	5.13
∞	2.77	3.31	3.63	3.86	4.03	4.17	4.29	4.39	4.47	4.55	4.62	4.68	4.74	4.80	4.85	4.89	4.93	4.97	5.01

(Continued)

Table B.6 (Continued)

q Value When Alpha = .01

df (within)	k=2	3	4	5	6	7	8	9	10	11	12	13	14	15	16	17	18	19	20
1	90.0	135	164	186	202	216	227	237	246	253	260	266	272	277	282	286	290	294	298
2	14.0	19.0	22.3	24.7	26.6	28.2	29.5	30.7	31.7	32.6	33.4	34.1	34.8	35.4	36.0	36.5	37.0	37.5	37.9
3	8.26	10.6	12.2	13.3	14.2	15.0	15.6	16.2	16.7	17.1	17.5	17.9	18.2	18.5	18.8	19.1	19.3	19.5	19.8
4	6.51	8.12	9.17	9.96	10.6	11.1	11.5	11.9	12.3	12.6	12.8	13.1	13.3	13.5	13.7	13.9	14.1	14.2	14.4
5	5.70	6.97	7.80	8.42	8.91	9.32	9.67	9.97	10.24	10.48	10.70	10.89	11.08	11.24	11.40	11.55	11.68	11.81	11.93
6	5.24	6.33	7.03	7.56	7.97	8.32	8.61	8.87	9.10	9.30	9.49	9.65	9.81	9.95	10.08	10.21	10.32	10.43	10.54
7	4.95	5.92	6.54	7.01	7.37	7.68	7.94	8.17	8.37	8.55	8.71	8.86	9.00	9.12	9.24	9.35	9.46	9.55	9.65
8	4.74	5.63	6.20	6.63	6.96	7.24	7.47	7.68	7.87	8.03	8.18	8.31	8.44	8.55	8.66	8.76	8.85	8.94	9.03
9	4.60	5.43	5.96	6.35	6.66	6.91	7.13	7.32	7.49	7.65	7.78	7.91	8.03	8.13	8.23	8.32	8.41	8.49	8.57
10	4.48	5.27	5.77	6.14	6.43	6.67	6.87	7.05	7.21	7.36	7.48	7.60	7.71	7.81	7.91	7.99	8.07	8.15	8.22
11	4.39	5.14	5.62	5.97	6.25	6.48	6.67	6.84	6.99	7.13	7.25	7.36	7.46	7.56	7.65	7.73	7.81	7.88	7.95
12	4.32	5.04	5.50	5.84	6.10	6.32	6.51	6.67	6.81	6.94	7.06	7.17	7.26	7.36	7.44	7.52	7.59	7.66	7.73
13	4.26	4.96	5.40	5.73	5.98	6.19	6.37	6.53	6.67	6.79	6.90	7.01	7.10	7.19	7.27	7.34	7.42	7.48	7.55
14	4.21	4.89	5.32	5.63	5.88	6.08	6.26	6.41	6.54	6.66	6.77	6.87	6.96	7.05	7.12	7.20	7.27	7.33	7.39
15	4.17	4.83	5.25	5.56	5.80	5.99	6.16	6.31	6.44	6.55	6.66	6.76	6.84	6.93	7.00	7.07	7.14	7.20	7.26
16	4.13	4.78	5.19	5.49	5.72	5.92	6.08	6.22	6.35	6.46	6.56	6.66	6.74	6.82	6.90	6.97	7.03	7.09	7.15
17	4.10	4.74	5.14	5.43	5.66	5.85	6.01	6.15	6.27	6.38	6.48	6.57	6.66	6.73	6.80	6.87	6.94	7.00	7.05
18	4.07	4.70	5.09	5.38	5.60	5.79	5.94	6.08	6.20	6.31	6.41	6.50	6.58	6.65	6.72	6.79	6.85	6.91	6.96
19	4.05	4.67	5.05	5.33	5.55	5.73	5.89	6.02	6.14	6.25	6.34	6.43	6.51	6.58	6.65	6.72	6.78	6.84	6.89
24	3.96	4.54	4.91	5.17	5.37	5.54	5.69	5.81	5.92	6.02	6.11	6.19	6.26	6.33	6.39	6.45	6.51	6.56	6.61
30	3.89	4.45	4.80	5.05	5.24	5.40	5.54	5.65	5.76	5.85	5.93	6.01	6.08	6.14	6.20	6.26	6.31	6.36	6.41
40	3.82	4.37	4.70	4.93	5.11	5.27	5.39	5.50	5.60	5.69	5.77	5.84	5.90	5.96	6.02	6.07	6.12	6.17	6.21
60	3.76	4.28	4.60	4.82	4.99	5.13	5.25	5.36	5.45	5.53	5.60	5.67	5.73	5.79	5.84	5.89	5.93	5.98	6.02
120	3.70	4.20	4.50	4.71	4.87	5.01	5.12	5.21	5.30	5.38	5.44	5.51	5.56	5.61	5.66	5.71	5.75	5.79	5.83
∞	3.64	4.12	4.40	4.60	4.76	4.88	4.99	5.08	5.16	5.23	5.29	5.35	5.40	5.45	5.49	5.54	5.57	5.61	5.65

Appendix C

Solutions to Odd-Numbered Practice Problems

🔲 CHAPTER 1

1. Researchers engage in descriptive research when the goal is simply to describe phenomena; however, when research attempts to explain something by examining the relationships between phenomena, they are typically engaging in explanatory research. Evaluation research is undertaken when the goal is to determine whether a program or policy was implemented as planned and/or whether it had the intended outcomes or impacts.

3. a. Quantitative; interval/ratio.
   b. Quantitative; interval/ratio.
   c. Quantitative; interval/ratio.
   d. Qualitative; nominal.
   e. Qualitative; nominal.
   f. Quantitative; interval/ratio.

5. Arrest is the independent variable, and future drunk driving behavior is the dependent variable.

7. The numerator would be the number of victimizations against people 14 to 18 years old, and the denominator would be the total population of people 14 to 18 years old.

9.

	f	Proportion	%
Less than $10	16	.029	2.9
$10–$49	39	.072	7.2
$50–$99	48	.088	8.8
$100–$249	86	.159	15.9
$250–$999	102	.188	18.8
$1,000 or more	251	.463	46.3
	$n = 542$		

11. The units of analysis are states. The independent variable would likely be unemployment, and the dependent variable would be crime.

🔲 CHAPTER 2

1. The first grouped frequency distribution is not a very good one for a number of reasons. First, the interval widths are not all the same size. Second, the class intervals are not mutually exclusive. A score of 7 could go into either the

first or second interval, and a score of 10 could go into either the second or third class interval. Third, the first class interval is empty; it has a frequency of zero. Fourth, there are too few class intervals; the data are "bunched up" into only three intervals, and you do not get a very good sense of the distribution of these scores. The second grouped frequency distribution avoids all of these four problems.

3. a. "Self-reported drug use" is measured at the ordinal level because our values consist of rank-ordered categories. We do not have interval/ratio-level measurement because although we can state that someone who reported using drugs "a lot" used drugs more frequently than someone who reported "never" using drugs, we do not know exactly how much more frequently.

   b. Since there were 30 students who reported "never" using, 150 – 30, or 120 students, must have been using drugs at some level of frequency. The ratio of users to non-users, then, is 120/30, or 4 to 1.

   c. 35/10, or 3.5 to 1.

   d. The first thing we would want to do is arrange the data in some order. Since we have ordinal-level data, we can order the categories in ascending or descending order.

Value	f	p	%
Never	30	.2000	20.00
A few times	75	.5000	50.00
More than a few times	35	.2333	23.33
A lot	10	.0667	6.67

   e. Since the proportion of non-users ("never") was .20, the proportion of respondents who reported using drugs must be 1 – .20, or .80. Another way to determine this is to determine the relative frequency of users (75 + 35 + 10) / 150 = 120/150 = .80.

   f. .0667 of the respondents reported using drugs "a lot."

5. a.

Value	f	cf	p	cp	%	c%
10	5	5	.20	.20	20	20
11	3	8	.12	.32	12	32
12	0	8	.00	.32	0	32
13	2	10	.08	.40	8	40
14	2	12	.08	.48	8	48
15	7	19	.28	.76	28	76
16	3	22	.12	.88	12	88
17	0	22	.00	.88	0	88
18	0	22	.00	.88	0	88
19	1	23	.04	.92	4	92
20	2	25	.08	1.00	8	100

   b.

Value	f	p	%
Male	16	.64	64
Female	9	.36	36

   c. Using the cumulative frequency column, we can determine that 10 recruits scored 13 or lower on the exam. That means that 25 – 10, or 15 recruits, must have scored 14 or higher, so 15 recruits passed the exam. Since 15 / 25 = .60, we can calculate that 60% of the recruits passed the test. We could also have used the cumulative percentage column to find this answer. Using the cumulative percentage column, we can determine that 40% of the recruits scored 13 or lower on the exam. This means that 100% – 40%, or 60%, of the recruits must have scored 14 or higher and passed the exam.

   d. Of the 25 recruits, 3, or .12 (3/25), received a score of 18 or higher on the exam and "passed with honors."

Distribution of Test Scores for Recruit Class

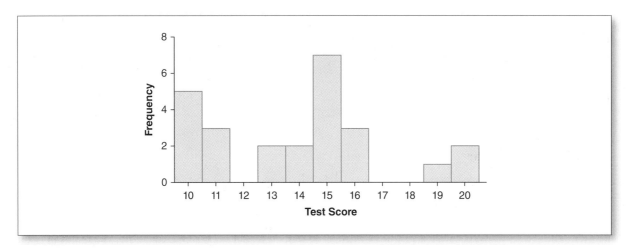

e. Using the cumulative frequency column, we can easily see that 10 recruits received a score of 13 or lower on the exam.

f. In this class of recruits, 64% were male and 36% were female.

g. The test scores would have to be graphed with a histogram since the data are quantitative.

A pie chart of the percentages for the gender data is at right.

Gender Distribution of Recruit Class

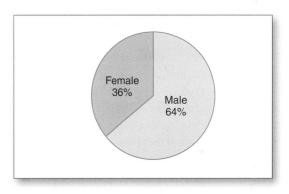

h. A cumulative frequency distribution for the test scores would look like this:

Cumulative Frequency Line Graph for Test Score Data

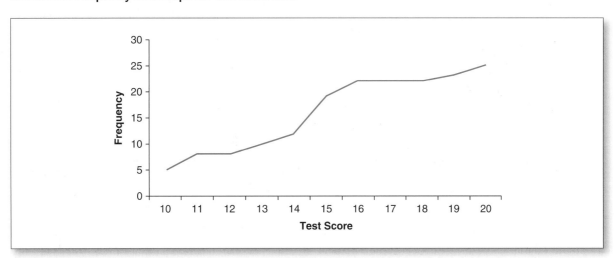

Time Plot of NCVS Property Crime Victimization Rates per 1,000 Households

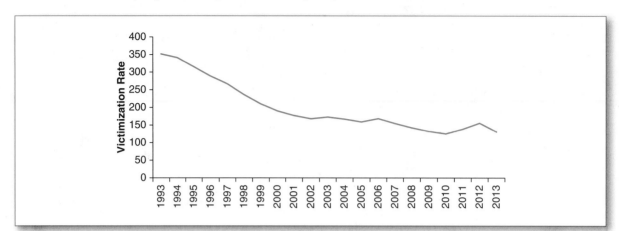

7. A time plot of the property crime victimization data from the National Crime Victimization Survey (NCVS) over the time period 1973–2013 would look like the time plot above.

The time plot shows a fairly consistent downward trend in the property crime victimization rate for the duration of the period. The sharpest decline is during the 1990s. Beginning in 2001, there was a leveling off in the rate of property victimizations until 2006, after which there was another consistent decline in the property victimization rate until 2010, when there was a short increase before a final drop resulted in a property victimization rate in 2013 that was approximately 37% of what it was in 1993.

🔲 CHAPTER 3

1. The mode for these data is "some friends" because this value appears more often than any other value ($f = 85$). The mode tells us that in our sample, more youths reported having "some" delinquent friends than any other possible response. We could not calculate a mean with these data because this variable is measured at the ordinal level and the mean requires data measured at the interval/ratio level. For example, although we can say that a person with "some" delinquent friends has more delinquent friends than a person with "none," we do not know exactly how many more (e.g., 1? 2? 10?). Without this knowledge, we cannot calculate the mean as a measure of central tendency.

3. The best measure of central tendency for these data is probably the median. The mean would not be the best in

this case because it would be inflated by the presence of a positive outlier. New Orleans, Louisiana, with a homicide rate of 43.3 per 100,000, has a homicide rate substantially higher than the other cities. When New Orleans is included in the data, the mean is equal to 10.62 homicides per 100,000, and the median is 7.25.

5. The most appropriate measure of central tendency for these data is the mode because the data are measured at the nominal level. The modal, or most frequent, reason for requesting the police when the subject was without mental illness was for a "potential offense."

7. Mean number of executions:

$$\bar{X} = \frac{(42 + 37 + 52 + 46 + 43 + 43 + 39 + 35)}{8}$$

$$\bar{X} = 42.125 \text{ exeutions per year}$$

The median is the average of the fourth and fifth years in the rank-ordered frequency distribution.

$$\text{Median} = \frac{42 + 43}{2}$$

$$\text{Median} = 42.5 \text{ executions per year}$$

When executions for the year 2006 (53) are added to the data, the mean becomes

$$\bar{X} = \frac{390}{9} = 43.33 \text{ exeutions per year}$$

The median becomes 43 executions. Either the mean or the median would be appropriate here because 53 executions in 2006 is not such a large outlier.

9. The mean is equal to

$$\bar{X} = \frac{1200}{20}$$

$$\bar{X} = 60 \text{ beats per minute}$$

The median is equal to 60.5 beats per minute.

The mean and the median are very comparable to one another. This suggests that there are no or few extreme (outlying) scores in the data and that the data are not skewed.

🔲 CHAPTER 4

1. Measures of central tendency capture the most "typical" score in a distribution of scores (the most common, the score in the middle of the ranked distribution, or the average), whereas measures of dispersion capture the variability in our scores, or how they are different from each other or different from the central tendency. It is important to report both central tendency and dispersion measures for our variables because two groups of scores may be very similar in terms of their central tendency but very different in terms of how dispersed the scores are.

3. The first thing we need to do is calculate the mean. This problem will give you experience in calculating a mean for grouped data. You should find the mean equal to 8.6 prior thefts. We are now ready to do the calculations necessary to find the variance and standard deviation.

m_i	$m_i - \bar{X}$	$(m_i - \bar{X})^2$	f	$f(m_i - \bar{X})^2$
2	2 − 8.6 = −6.6	43.56	76	3,310.56
7	7 − 8.6 = −1.6	2.56	52	133.12
12	12 − 8.6 = − 3.4	11.56	38	439.28
17	17 − 8.6 = 8.4	70.56	21	1,481.76
22	22 − 8.6 = 13.4	179.56	10	1,795.60
27	27 − 8.6 = 18.4	338.56	8	2,708.48
				Σ = 9,868.80

$$s^2 = \frac{9,868.80}{204}$$

$$s^2 = 48.38$$

The variance is equal to 48.38.

$$s = \sqrt{\frac{9,868.80}{204}}$$

$$s = 6.95$$

The standard deviation is equal to 6.95.

5. Let's calculate the variation ratio for each of the 3 years:

$$VR_{1980} = 1 - \frac{852}{1,723}$$

$$VR_{1980} = .50$$

$$VR_{1990} = 1 - \frac{979}{2,161}$$

$$VR_{1990} = .55$$

$$VR_{2000} = 1 - \frac{1,211}{3,202}$$

$$VR_{2000} = .62$$

$$VR_{2010} = 1 - \frac{1,300}{3,612}$$

$$VR_{2010} = .64$$

The variation ratio is consistently increasing from 1980 to 2010, which tells us that the dispersion in the nominal-level data is increasing. Practically, this says that the racial heterogeneity of the penitentiary is increasing over time.

🔲 CHAPTER 5

1. a. $P(x = \$30,000) = 16/110 = .145$

 b. $P(x = \$35,000) = 7/110 = .064$

 c. Yes, they are mutually exclusive events because a person cannot simultaneously have a starting salary of both $30,000 and $35,000. There is no joint probability of these two events.

 d. $P(x \geq \$31,000) = (19/110) + (12/110) + (15/110) + (8/110) + (7/110) = (61/110) = .555$

e. There are two ways to calculate this probability. First: $P(x \le \$30,000) = (16/110) + (10/110) + (9/110) + (8/110) + (6/110) = (49/110) = .445$. Or you can recognize that this event is the complement of the event in part d above and calculate the probability as $1 - .555 = .445$.

f. $P(x = \$28,000$ or $\$30,000$ or $\$31,500$ or $\$32,000$ or $\$32,500) = (10/110) + (16/110) + (19/110) + (12/110) + (15/110) = (72/110) = .655$

g. $P(x < \$25,000) = 0$

h. $P(x = \$28,000$ or $\$32,000$ or $\$35,000) = (10/110) + (12/110) + (7/110) = (29/110) = .264$

3. a. $z = 1.5$

b. $z = -1.7$

c. $z = -3.0$

d. .0548, or slightly more than 5%, of the cases have an IQ score above 115.

e. .6832

f. A raw score of 70 corresponds to a z score of -3.0. The probability of a z score less than or equal to -3.0 is .001.

g. A raw score of 125 corresponds to a z score of 2.5. The probability of a z score greater than or equal to 2.5 is .006.

5. a. A raw score of 95 is better than .9332, or 93%, of the scores. It is not in the top 5%, however, so this candidate would not be accepted.

b. A raw score of 110 is better than .9986, or 99%, of the scores. It is in the top 5%, and this candidate would be accepted.

c. A z score of 1.65 or higher is better than 95% of the scores. The z score of 1.65 corresponds to a raw score of 96.5, and that is the minimum score you need to get accepted.

7. a. The area to the right of a z score of 1.65 is equal to .0495.

b. The area to the left of a z score of -1.65 is equal to .0495.

c. The area either to the left of a z score of -1.65 or to the right of a z score of 1.65 is equal to .099.

d. The area to the right of a z score of 2.33 is .0099.

9. a. To see how unusual 9 prior arrests are in this population, let's transform the raw score into a z score:

$$z = \frac{9-6}{2} = 1.50.$$

Taking a z score of 1.50 to the z table, we can see that the area to the right of this score comprises approximately 7% of the area of the normal curve. Those who have 9 prior arrests, then, are in the top 7% of this population. Since they are not in the top 5%, we would not consider them unusual.

b. A raw score of 11 prior arrests corresponds to a z score of:

$$z = \frac{11-6}{2} = 2.50.$$

A z score of 2.50 is way at the right or upper end of the distribution. z scores of 2.50 or greater are greater than approximately 99% of all the other scores. This person does have an unusually large number of prior arrests since they are in the top 5%.

c. A raw score of 2 prior arrests corresponds to a z score of:

$$z = \frac{2-6}{2} = -2.0.$$

A z score of -2.0 falls lower than almost 98% of all the other scores. The person with only 2 prior arrests, then, does have an unusually low number for this population since he or she is in the bottom 5%.

CHAPTER 6

1. The purpose of confidence intervals is to give us a range of values for our estimated population parameter rather than a single value or a point estimate. The estimated confidence interval gives us a range of values within which we believe, with varying degrees of confidence, that the true population value falls. The advantage of providing a range of values for our estimate is that we will be more likely to include the population parameter. Think of trying to estimate your final exam score in this class. You are more likely to be accurate if you are able to estimate an interval within which your actual score will fall, such as "somewhere between 85 and 95," than if you have to give a single value as your estimate, such as "it will be an 89." Note that the wider you make your interval (consider "somewhere between 40 and 95"), the more accurate you are likely to be in that your exam score will probably fall

within that very large interval. However, the price of this accuracy is precision; you are not being very precise in estimating that your final exam score will be between 40 and 95. In this case, you will be very confident but not very precise. Note also that the more narrow or precise your interval is, the less confident you may be about it. If you predicted that your final exam score would be between 90 and 95, you would be very precise. You would probably also be far less confident of this prediction than of the one where you stated your score would fall between 40 and 95. Other things (such as sample size) being equal, there is a trade-off between precision and confidence.

3.

$$95\% \text{ c.i.} = 4.5 \pm 1.96\left(\frac{3.2}{\sqrt{110-1}}\right)$$

$$95\% \text{ c.i.} = 4.5 \pm 1.96\left(\frac{3.2}{10.44}\right)$$

$$95\% \text{ c.i.} = 4.5 \pm 1.96(.31)$$

$$95\% \text{ c.i.} = 4.5 \pm .61$$

$$3.89 \leq \mu \leq 5.11$$

We are 95% confident that the mean level of marijuana use in our population of teenagers is between 3.89 and 5.11 times per year. This means that if we were to take an infinite number of samples of size 110 from this population and estimate a confidence interval around the mean for each sample, 95% of those confidence intervals would contain the true population mean.

5. The standard deviation of the sampling distribution is the standard deviation of an infinite number of sample estimates [means (X) or proportions (p)], each drawn from a sample with sample size equal to n. It is also called the standard error. The sample size affects the value of the standard error (see problems 3 and 4 above). At a fixed confidence level, increasing the sample size will reduce the size of the standard error and, consequently, the width of the confidence interval.

7. To find a 95% confidence interval around a sample mean of 560 with a standard deviation of 45 and a sample size of 15, you would have to go to the t table. With $n = 15$, there are 14 degrees of freedom. Since confidence intervals are two-tailed problems, the value of t you should obtain is 2.145. Now you can construct the confidence interval:

$$95\% \text{ c.i.} = 560 \pm 2.145\left(\frac{4.5}{\sqrt{15-1}}\right)$$

$$95\% \text{ c.i.} = 560 \pm 2.145\left(\frac{45}{3.74}\right)$$

$$95\% \text{ c.i.} = 560 \pm 2.145(12.03)$$

$$95\% \text{ c.i.} = 560 \pm 25.8$$

$$534.2 \leq \mu \leq 585.8$$

You can say that you are 95% confident that the true police response time is between 534 seconds (almost 9 minutes) and 586 seconds (almost 10 minutes).

9. When we increased the confidence interval from 95% to 99%, we would see that the width of the confidence interval would also increase. This is because being more confident that our estimated interval contains the true population parameter (99% confident as opposed to 95% confident) comes at the price of a wider interval (all other things being equal). You should remember, from the discussion in this chapter, that you can increase the level of your confidence without expanding the width of the interval by increasing your sample size.

▣ CHAPTER 7

1. The z test and z distribution may be used for making one-sample hypothesis tests involving a population mean under two conditions: (1) if the population standard deviation (σ) is known and (2) if the sample size is large enough $(n > 30)$ so that the sample standard deviation (s) can be used as an unbiased estimate of the population standard deviation. If either of these two conditions is not met, hypothesis tests about one population mean must be conducted with the t test and t distribution.

3. The null and alternative hypotheses are

$$H_0: \mu = 4.6$$

$$H_1: \mu < 4.6$$

Since our sample size is large $(n > 30)$, we should use the z test and z distribution. With an alpha of .01 and a one-tailed test, our critical value of z is 2.33. Our decision rule is to reject the null hypothesis if our obtained value of z is 2.33 or greater (reject H_0 if $z_{obt} > 2.33$). The value of z_{obt} is

$$z_{obt} = \frac{6.3 - 4.6}{1.9/\sqrt{64}}$$

$$z_{obt} = \frac{1.7}{.2375}$$

$$z_{obt} = 7.16$$

Because 7.16 is greater than the critical value of 2.33 and falls in the critical region, we will reject the null hypothesis that the population mean is equal to 4.6 times.

5. The null and alternative hypotheses are

$$H_0: \mu = 25.9$$

$$H_1: \mu \neq 25.9$$

The critical value of z is ± 2.58. The value of z_{obt} is

$$z_{obt} = \frac{27.3 - 25.9}{6.5/\sqrt{175}}$$

$$z_{obt} = \frac{1.40}{6.5/13.23}$$

$$z_{obt} = \frac{1.40}{.49}$$

$$z_{obt} = 2.86$$

Because this value is greater than the critical value of 2.58 and falls in the critical region, we will reject the null hypothesis that the population mean is equal to 25.9 months.

7. The null and alternative hypotheses are

$$H_0: \mu = 4$$

$$H_1: \mu > 4$$

With 11 degrees of freedom, an alpha of .01, and a one-tailed test, our critical value of t is 2.718. Our decision rule is to reject the null hypothesis if our obtained value of $t > 2.718$. The value of t_{obt} is

$$t_{obt} = \frac{6.3 - 4}{1.5/\sqrt{12}}$$

$$t_{obt} = \frac{2.30}{1.5/3.46}$$

$$t_{obt} = \frac{2.30}{.43}$$

$$t_{obt} = 5.35$$

Because this value is greater than the critical value of 2.718 and falls in the critical region, we decide to reject the null hypothesis that the population mean is equal to 4 arrests.

9. The null and alternative hypotheses are

$$H_0: P = .45$$

$$H_1: P < .45$$

Because this is a problem involving a population proportion with a large sample size ($n = 200$), we can use the z test and the z distribution. Our decision rule is to reject the null hypothesis if our obtained value of z is -2.33 or less. The value of z_{obt} is

$$z_{obt} = \frac{.23 - .45}{\sqrt{\dfrac{.45(.55)}{200}}} = -6.25$$

Because our obtained value of z is less than the critical value of -2.33 and falls in the critical region, we will reject the null hypothesis that the population proportion is equal to .45, or 45%.

11. The null and alternative hypotheses are

$$H_0: P = .31$$

$$H_1: P > .31$$

Because this is a problem involving a population proportion with a large sample size ($n = 110$), we can use the z test and the z distribution. Our decision rule is to reject the null hypothesis if our obtained value of z is 1.65 or greater. The value of z_{obt} is

$$z_{obt} = \frac{.46 - .31}{\sqrt{\dfrac{.31(.69)}{110}}} = -3.40$$

Because this is greater than the critical value of 1.65 and falls in the critical region, we will reject the null hypothesis that the population proportion is equal to .31, or 31%.

□ CHAPTER 8

1. a. The type of institution is the independent variable, and satisfaction with one's job is the dependent variable.

   b. There are a total of 185 observations.

   c. There are 115 persons who reported that they were not satisfied with their jobs and 70 persons who were satisfied with their jobs.

   d. There were 45 people working in medium-security institutions and 140 people employed in maximum-security institutions.

   e. This is a 2 × 2 contingency table.

   f. A total of 30 correctional officers are in medium-security institutions and like their jobs.

   g. A total of 100 correctional officers are in maximum-security institutions and do not like their jobs.

   h. There is (2 – 1) (2 – 1) or 1 degree of freedom.

   i. The risk of not being satisfied with your job is

$$.33\left(\frac{15}{45}\right)$$

in medium-security institutions and

$$.71\left(\frac{100}{140}\right)$$

in maximum-security institutions.

It looks as if the type of institution one works in is related to one's job satisfaction. Officers are far more likely to be dissatisfied with their jobs if they work in a maximum-security facility than if they work in a medium-security facility.

   j. **Step 1:**

   H_0: Type of institution and level of job satisfaction are independent.

   H_1: Type of institution and level of job satisfaction are not independent.

   Step 2: Our test statistic is a chi-square test of independence, which has a chi-square distribution.

   Step 3: With 1 degree of freedom and an alpha of .05, our $\chi^2_{crit} = 3.841$. The critical region is any obtained chi-square to the right of this. Our decision rule is to reject the null hypothesis when $\chi^2_{obt} \geq 3.841$.

   Step 4: When we calculate our obtained chi-square, we find that it is $\chi^2_{obt} = 21.11$.

Step 5: With a critical value of 3.841 and an obtained chi-square statistic of 21.11, our decision is to reject the null hypothesis. Our conclusion is that type of institution employed at and job satisfaction for a correctional officer are not independent; there is a relationship between these two variables in the population.

We could use several different measures of association for a 2 × 2 contingency table. Our estimated value of Yule's Q would be –.67, which would tell us that there is a strong negative relationship between type of institution and job satisfaction. More specifically, we would conclude that those who work in a maximum-security facility have less job satisfaction. Since we have a 2 × 2 table, we could also have used the phi coefficient as our measure of association. Our estimated value of phi is .34. Phi indicates that there is a moderate association or correlation between type of institution and job satisfaction (remember that the phi coefficient is always positive).

3. a. The independent variable is the jurisdiction where a defendant was tried, and the dependent variable is the type of sentence the defendant received.

   b. There are a total of 425 observations.

   c. There are 80 defendants from rural jurisdictions, 125 from suburban courts, and 220 who were tried in urban courts.

   d. There are 142 defendants who received jail time only, 95 who were fined and sent to jail, 112 who were sentenced to less than 60 days of jail time, and 76 who were sentenced to 60 or more days of jail.

   e. This is a 4 × 3 contingency table.

   f. There are 38 defendants from suburban courts who received less than 60 days of jail time as their sentence.

   g. There are 22 defendants tried in rural courts who received a sentence of a fine and jail.

   h. There are (4 – 1) × (3 – 1) or 6 degrees of freedom.

   i. The risk of 60 or more days of jail time is .20 for those tried in rural courts, .16 for those tried in suburban courts, and .18 for those tried in urban courts. There seems to be a slight relationship here, with those tried in rural courts more likely to be sentenced to more than 60 days of jail time.

   j. **Step 1:**

   H_0: Place where tried and type of sentence are independent.

   H_1: Place where tried and type of sentence are not independent.

Step 2: Our test statistic is a chi-square test of independence, which has a chi-square distribution.

Step 3: With 6 degrees of freedom and an alpha of .01 our $\chi^2_{crit} = 16.812$. The critical region is any obtained chi-square to the right of this. Our decision rule is to reject the null hypothesis when $\chi^2_{obt} \geq 16.812$.

Step 4: When we calculate our obtained chi-square, we find that it is $\chi^2_{crit} = 21.85$.

Step 5: With a critical value of 16.812 and an obtained chi-square statistic of 21.85, our decision is to reject the null hypothesis. Our conclusion is there is a relationship between where in the state a defendant was tried and the type of sentence the defendant received. Location of the trial and type of sentence are both nominal-level variables.

5. a. Employment is the independent variable, and the number of arrests within 3 years after release is the dependent variable.

   b. There are 115 observations or cases.

   c. There are 45 persons who reported having stable employment, 30 who reported having sporadic employment, and 40 who reported being unemployed.

   d. There are 54 persons who had no arrests within 3 years and 61 who had one or more arrests.

   e. This is a 2×3 contingency table.

   f. A total of 16 persons who were sporadically employed had one or more arrests.

   g. A total of 10 unemployed persons had no arrests.

   h. There are $(2-1) \times (3-1) = 2$ degrees of freedom.

   i. For those with stable employment, the risk of having one or more arrests is .33; for those with sporadic employment, it is .53; and for the unemployed, it is .75. The relative risk of at least one arrest increases as the individual's employment situation becomes worse.

   j. **Step 1:**

   H_0: Employment status and the number of arrests within 3 years are independent.

   H_1: Employment status and the number of arrests within 3 years are not independent.

   Step 2: Our test statistic is a chi-square test of independence, which has a chi-square distribution.

   Step 3: With 2 degrees of freedom and an alpha of .05, our $\chi^2_{obt} = 5.991$. The critical region is any obtained chi-square to the right of this. Our decision rule is to reject the null hypothesis when $\chi^2_{obt} \geq 5.991$.

Step 4: When we calculate our obtained chi-square, we find that it is $\chi^2_{obt} = 15.33$.

Step 5: With a critical value of 5.991 and an obtained chi-square statistic of 15.33, our decision is to reject the null hypothesis. Our conclusion is that employment status and the number of arrests after release are not independent. There is a relationship between the two variables in the population.

Since both employment status and the number of arrests within 3 years are ordinal-level variables, we will use gamma as our measure of association. The value of gamma is

$$\gamma = \frac{1,800 - 520}{1,800 + 520}$$

$$\gamma = .55$$

There is a moderately strong positive association between employment status and the number of arrests. More specifically, as one moves from stable employment to sporadic employment to unemployed, the risk of having one or more arrests increases.

🔲 CHAPTER 9

1. An independent variable is the variable whose effect or influence on the dependent variable is what you want to measure. In causal terms, the independent variable is the cause, and the dependent variable is the effect. Low self-control is taken to affect one's involvement in crime, so self-control is the independent variable and involvement in crime is the dependent variable.

3. The null and alternative hypotheses are

$$H_0: \mu = \mu_2$$

$$H_1: \mu_1 < \mu_2$$

The correct test is the pooled variance independent-samples t test, and our sampling distribution is Student's t distribution. We reject the null hypothesis if $t_{obt} \leq -2.390$. The obtained value of t is

$$t_{obt} = \frac{2.1 - 8.2}{\sqrt{\frac{[(40-1)(1.8)^2] + [(25-1)(1.9)^2]}{40+25-2}} \sqrt{\frac{40+25}{(40)(25)}}}$$

$$t_{obt} = -13.01$$

Because our obtained value of t is less than the critical value and falls in the critical region, we decide to reject the null hypothesis of equal means. We conclude that those whose peers would disapprove of their driving drunk actually drive drunk less frequently than those whose coworkers are more tolerant of driving drunk.

5. The null and alternative hypotheses are

$$H_0: \mu_1 = \mu_2$$
$$H_1: \mu_1 < \mu_2$$

The problem instructs you not to presume that the population standard deviations are equal ($\sigma_1 \neq \sigma_2$), so the correct statistical test is the separate variance t test, and the sampling distribution is Student's t distribution. With approximately 60 degrees of freedom and an alpha of .05 for a one-tailed test, the critical value of t is -1.671. The value for t_{obt} is

$$t_{obt} = \frac{18.8 - 21.3}{\sqrt{\dfrac{(4.5)^2}{50-1} + \dfrac{(3.0)^2}{25-1}}}$$
$$t_{obt} = -2.82$$

Because $t_{obt} \leq t_{crit}$, we reject the null hypothesis of equal population means. Our conclusion is that the mean score on the domestic disturbance scale is significantly lower for males than for females. In other words, males are less likely to see the fair handling of domestic disturbances as an important part of police work.

7. The null and alternative hypotheses are

$$H_0: P_1 = P_2$$
$$H_1: P_1 > P_2$$

Because this is a difference of proportions problem, the correct test statistic is the z test, and our sampling distribution is the z or standard normal distribution. Our decision rule is to reject the null hypothesis if $z_{obt} \geq 2.33$.
The value of z_{obt} is

$$z_{obt} = \frac{.43 - .17}{\sqrt{(.32)(.68)}\sqrt{\dfrac{100 + 75}{(100)(75)}}}$$
$$z_{obt} = 3.65$$

Because our obtained z is greater than the critical value of z (2.33) and z_{obt} falls in the critical region, we reject the null hypothesis. Delinquent children have a significantly higher proportion of criminal parents than do non-delinquent children.

▣ CHAPTER 10

1. An analysis of variance can be performed whenever we have a continuous (interval- or ratio-level) dependent variable and a categorical variable with three or more levels or categories and we are interested in testing hypotheses about the equality of our population means.

3. It is called the analysis of variance because we make inferences about the differences among population means based on a comparison of the *variance* that exists within each sample relative to the variance that exists between the samples. More specifically, we examine the ratio of variance between the samples to the variance within the samples. The greater this ratio, the more between-samples variance there is relative to within-sample variance. Therefore, as this ratio becomes greater than 1, we are more inclined to believe that the samples were drawn from different populations with different population means.

5. The formulas for the three degrees of freedom are

$$df_{total} = n - 1$$
$$df_{between} = k - 1$$
$$df_{within} = n - k$$

To check your arithmetic, make sure that $df_{total} = df_{between} + df_{within}$.

7. a. The independent variable is the state's general policy with respect to drunk driving ("get tough," make a "moral appeal," or not do much), and the dependent variable is the drunk driving rate in the state.

   b. The correct degrees of freedom for this table are

$$df_{between} = k - 1 = 3 - 1 = 2$$
$$df_{within} = n - k = 45 - 3 = 42$$
$$df_{total} = n - 1 = 45 - 1 = 44$$

You can see that $df_{between} + df_{within} = df_{total}$.

The ratio of sum of squares to degrees of freedom can now be determined:

$$SS_{between} / df_{between} = 475.3 / 2 = 237.65$$

$$SS_{within} / df_{within} = 204.5 / 42 = 4.87$$

The F ratio is $F_{obt} = 237.65 / 4.87 = 48.80$.

c. The null and alternative hypotheses are

$$H_0: \mu_{get\,tough} = \mu_{moral\,appeal} = \mu_{control}$$

$$H_1: \mu_{get\,tough} \neq \mu_{moral\,appeal} \neq \mu_{control}$$

Our decision rule will be to reject the null hypothesis if $F_{obt} \geq 5.18$.

$F_{obt} = 48.80$. Since our obtained value of F is greater than the critical value, our decision is to reject the null hypothesis. We conclude that the population means are not equal.

d. Going to the studentized table, you find the value of q to be equal to 4.37. To find the critical difference, you plug these values into your formula:

$$CD = 4.37\sqrt{\frac{4.87}{15}}$$

$$CD = 2.49$$

The critical difference for the mean comparisons, then, is 2.49. Find the absolute value of the difference between each pair of sample means and test each null hypothesis:

$$H_0: \mu_{get\,tough} = \mu_{moral\,appeal}$$

$$H_1: \mu_{get\,tough} \neq \mu_{moral\,appeal}$$

"Get Tough"	125.2
"Moral Appeal"	-119.7
	$\lvert 5.5 \rvert$

Since the absolute value of the difference in sample means is greater than the critical difference score of 2.49, we would reject the null hypothesis. States that make a "moral appeal" have significantly lower levels of drunk driving on average than do states that "get tough."

$$H_0: \mu_{get\,tough} = \mu_{control}$$

$$H_1: \mu_{get\,tough} \neq \mu_{control}$$

"Get Tough"	125.2
"Control"	-145.3
	$\lvert 20.1 \rvert$

Since the absolute value of the difference in sample means is greater than the critical difference score of 2.49, we would reject the null hypothesis. States that "get tough" with drunk driving by increasing the penalties have significantly lower levels of drunk driving on average than do states that do nothing.

$$H_0: \mu_{moral\,appeal} = \mu_{control}$$

$$H_1: \mu_{moral\,appeal} \neq \mu_{control}$$

"Moral Appeal"	119.7
"Conrol"	-145.3
	$\lvert 25.6 \rvert$

The "moral appeal" states have significantly lower levels of drunk driving than do the "control" states. It appears, then, that doing *something* about drunk driving is better than doing little or nothing.

e. Eta squared is

$$\eta^2 = \frac{475.3}{679.8}$$

$$\eta^2 = .70$$

This tells us that there is a moderately strong relationship between the state's response to drunk driving and the rate of drunk driving in that state. Specifically, about 70% of the variability in levels of drunk driving is explained by the state's public policy.

9. a. The independent variable is the number of friends each girl has, and the dependent variable is the number of delinquent acts each girl is encouraged to commit.

   b. The total sum of squares = 154

   The between-groups sum of squares = 98

   The within-group sum of square = 56

   c. The correct degrees of freedom for this table are

$$df_{between} = k - 1 = 3 - 1 = 2$$

$$df_{within} = n - k = 21 - 3 = 18$$

$$df_{total} = n - 1 = 21 - 1 = 20$$

You can see that $df_{between} + df_{within} = df_{total}$.

The ratio of sum of squares to degrees of freedom can now be determined:

$$SS_{between} / df_{between} = 98 / 2 = 49$$

$$SS_{within} / df_{within} = 56 / 18 = 3.11$$

The F ratio is

$$F_{obt} = \frac{49}{3.11} = 15.75$$

d. The null and alternative hypotheses are

$$H_0 : \mu_{a\,lot} = \mu_{some} = \mu_{a\,few}$$

$$H_1 : \mu_{a\,lot} \neq \mu_{some} \neq \mu_{a\,few}$$

With an alpha of .05 and 2 between-groups and 18 within-group degrees of freedom, our critical value of F is 3.55. Our decision rule is to reject the null hypothesis when $F_{obt} \geq 3.55$. The obtained F is 15.75; $F_{obt} > F_{crit}$, so our decision is to reject the null hypothesis and conclude that some of the population means are different from each other.

e. The value of the critical difference score is

$$CD = 3.61\sqrt{\frac{3.11}{7}}$$

$$CD = 2.41$$

A sample mean difference equal to or greater than an absolute value of 2.41 will lead us to reject the null hypothesis. We will now conduct a hypothesis test for each pair of population means.

$$H_0 : \mu_{a\,lot} = \mu_{some}$$

$$H_1 : \mu_{a\,lot} \neq \mu_{some}$$

"a lot"	7
"some"	−6
	|1|

Since this difference is less than the critical difference score of 2.41, we will fail to reject the null hypothesis. Girls who have a lot of friends are no different in the number of delinquent acts they are encouraged to commit than girls who have some friends.

$$H_0 : \mu_{a\,lot} = \mu_{a\,few}$$

$$H_1 : \mu_{a\,lot} \neq \mu_{a\,few}$$

"a lot"	7
"a few"	−2
	|5|

Since this difference is greater than the critical difference score of 2.41, we will reject the null hypothesis. Girls who have a lot of friends are encouraged to commit significantly more delinquent acts than girls who have a few friends.

$$H_0 : \mu_{some} = \mu_{a\,few}$$

$$H_1 : \mu_{some} \neq \mu_{a\,few}$$

"some"	6
"a few"	−2
	|4|

Since this difference is greater than the critical difference score of 2.41, we will reject the null hypothesis. Girls who have some friends are encouraged to commit significantly more delinquent acts than girls who have a few friends.

It would appear that Chapple and colleagues' (2014) hypothesis is correct. The presence of more friends in a friendship network puts females at higher risk of being encouraged to commit delinquent behavior.

f. Eta squared is

$$\eta^2 = \frac{98}{154}$$

$$\eta^2 = .64$$

There is a moderately strong relationship between the number of friends in a girl's friendship group and the number of delinquent acts she is encouraged to commit.

▣ CHAPTER 11

1. a. There is a moderate negative linear relationship between the median income level in a neighborhood and its rate of crime. As the median income level in a community increases, its rate of crime decreases.

   b. There is a weak positive linear relationship between the number of hours spent working after school and self-reported delinquency. As the number of hours spent working after school increases, the number of self-reported delinquent acts increases.

   c. There is a strong positive linear relationship between the number of prior arrests and the length of the current sentence. As the number of prior arrests increases, the length of the sentence received for the last offense increases.

   d. There is a weak negative linear relationship between the number of jobs held between the ages of 15 and 17 and the number of arrests as an adult.

   e. There is no linear relationship between a state's divorce rate and its rate of violent crime.

3. a. A $1 increase in the fine imposed decreases the number of price-fixing citations by .017.

   b. A 1% increase in unemployment increases the rate of property crime by .715.

   c. An increase of 1 year in education increases a police officer's salary by $1,444.53.

5. a. Scatterplot:

b. The value of the regression coefficient is

$$b = \frac{10(4{,}491.4) - 74(541.1)}{10(664) - (74)^2}$$

$$b = \frac{4{,}872.6}{1{,}164}$$

$$b = 4.19$$

The value of the slope coefficient is 4.19. This tells us that a 1-minute increase in police response time increases the crime rate by 4.19 per 1,000. The longer the response time, the higher the crime rate. Stated conversely, the shorter the response time, the lower the crime rate.

c. The value of the y intercept is

$$54.11 = a + 4.19(7.4)$$

$$54.11 = a + 31.01$$

$$54.11 - 31.01 = a$$

$$a = 23.1$$

Thus, the value of the y intercept, or a, is equal to 23.1.

d. The predicted community rate of crime when the police response time is 11 minutes can now be determined from our regression prediction equation:

$$\hat{y} = 23.1 + 4.19(11)$$

$$\hat{y} = 23.1 + 46.09$$

$$\hat{y} = 69.19$$

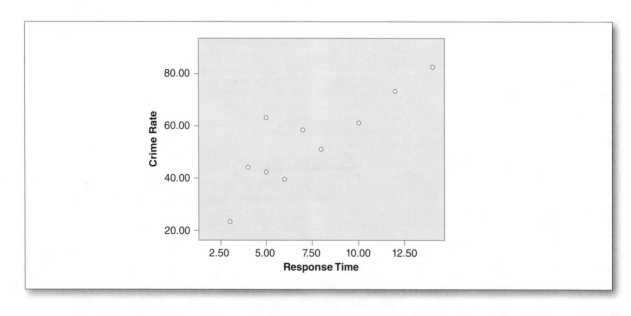

The predicted crime rate, therefore, is 69.19 crimes per 1,000 population.

e. The value of r is

$$r = \frac{10(4,491.4) - 74(541.1)}{\sqrt{\left[10(664) - (74)^2\right]\left[10(32,011.3) - (541.1)^2\right]}}$$

$$r = \frac{4,872.6}{5,639.6}$$

$$r = .86$$

There is a strong positive correlation between the time it takes the police to respond and the crime rate.

We now want to conduct a hypothesis test about r. Our null hypothesis is that $r = 0$, and our alternative hypothesis is that $r > 0$. We predict direction because we have reason to believe that there is a positive correlation between the number of minutes it takes the police to respond and the community's rate of crime (the longer the response time, the higher the crime rate). To determine whether this estimated r value is significantly different from zero with an alpha level of .05, we calculate a t statistic with $n - 2$ degrees of freedom. We go to the t table to find our critical value of t with $10 - 2 = 8$ degrees of freedom, an alpha level of .05, and a one-tailed test. The critical value of t is 1.86. Our decision rule is to reject the null hypothesis if $t_{obt} \geq 1.86$. Now we calculate our t_{obt}:

$$t = .86\sqrt{\frac{10 - 2}{1 - (.86)^2}}$$

$$t = .86(5.54)$$

$$t = 4.76$$

We have a t_{obt} of 4.76. Since $4.76 > 1.86$, we decide to reject the null hypothesis. There is a significant positive correlation between the length of police response time and community crime rate.

f. Our r was .86; $(.86)^2 = .74$, so 74% of the variation in community crime rates is explained by police response time.

g. Based on our results, we would conclude that there is a significant positive linear relationship between police response time and community crime rate.

🔲 CHAPTER 12

1. a. The least-squares regression equation for this problem is

$$y = a + b_1 x_1 + b_2 x_2$$

$$y = 19.642 + (.871)(\text{divorce rate}) + (-.146)(\text{age})$$

b. The partial slope coefficient for the variable "divorce" indicates that as the divorce rate per 100,000 population increases by 1, the rate of violent crime per 100,000 increases by .871 when controlling for the mean age of the state's population. The partial slope coefficient for the variable "age" indicates that as the mean age of the state's population increases by 1 year, the rate of violent crime per 100,000 decreases by .146 when controlling for the divorce rate. The intercept is equal to 19.642. This tells us that when both the divorce rate and the mean age are equal to zero, the rate of violent crime is 19.642 per 100,000.

c. The standardized regression coefficient for divorce is .594, and that for age is −.133. Based on this, we would conclude that the divorce rate is more influential in explaining state violent crime rates than is the mean age of the population. A second way to look at the relative strength of the independent variables is to compare the absolute values of their respective t ratios. The t ratio for divorce is 4.268, and that for age is −3.110. Based on this, we would conclude that the divorce rate is more influential in explaining rates of violence than is the mean age of a state's population.

d. The divorce rate and mean age together explain approximately 63% of the variance in rates of violent crime. The adjusted R^2 value is .61, indicating that 61% of the variance is explained.

e. The null and alternative hypotheses are

$$H_0 : \beta_1, \beta_2 = 0; \text{ or } R^2 = 0$$
$$H_1 : \beta_1, \text{ or } \beta_2 \neq 0; \text{ or } R^2 \neq 0$$

$F_{obt} = 27.531$. The probability of obtaining an F of 27.531 if the null hypothesis were true is .00001. Since this probability is less than our alpha of .01, our decision is to reject the null hypothesis that all the slope coefficients are equal to zero.

$$H_0 : \beta_{\text{divorce}} = 0$$
$$H_1 : \beta_{\text{divorce}} \neq 0$$

$t_{obt} = 4.268$. The probability of obtaining a t this size if the null hypothesis were true is equal to .0001. Since this probability is less than our alpha level of .01, we decide to reject the null hypothesis. We conclude that the population partial slope coefficient for the effect of the divorce rate on the rate of violent crime is significantly different from 0.

$$H_0 : \beta_{age} = 0$$
$$H_1 : \beta_{age} \neq 0$$

$t_{obt} = -3.110$. The probability of obtaining a t statistic this low if the null hypothesis is true is equal to .0011. Since this is less than .01, we will reject the null hypothesis that there is no relationship in the population between the mean age of a state and its rate of violent crime.

3. a. The least-squares regression equation from the supplied output would be

$$\hat{y} = 16.245 + (-1.467)(ENV) + (1.076)(REL)$$

b. The partial slope coefficient for the environmental factors variable is –1.467. This tells us that as a person's score on the environmental causes of crime scale increases by 1, his or her score on the punitiveness scale decreases by 1.467 when controlling for religious fundamentalism. The partial slope coefficient for the religious fundamentalism scale is 1.076. As a person's score on religious fundamentalism increases by 1 unit, his or her score on the punitiveness scale increases by 1.076 when controlling for score on the environmental scale. The value of the intercept is 16.245. When both independent variables are zero, a person's score on the punitiveness scale is 16.245.

c. The beta weight for ENV is –.609. The beta weight for REL is .346. A 1-unit change in the ENV variable produces almost twice as much change in the dependent variable as the REL variable. Comparing these beta weights would lead us to conclude that the environmental factors scale is more important in explaining punitiveness scores than is the religious fundamentalism variable.

The t ratio for ENV is –3.312, whereas that for REL is only 1.884. We would again conclude that ENV has the greater influence on the dependent variable.

d. The adjusted R^2 coefficient indicates that the environmental factors and religious fundamentalism scales together explain approximately 60% of the variance in the punitiveness measure.

e. The null and alternative hypotheses are

$$H_0 : \beta_{ENV}, \beta_{REL} = 0; \ or \ R^2 = 0$$
$$H_1 : \beta_{ENV}, or \beta_{REL} \neq 0; \ or \ R^2 \neq 0$$

The probability of an F of 11.59 if the null hypothesis were true is .0016. Since this probability is less than our chosen alpha of .01, our decision is to reject the null hypothesis that all the slope coefficients are equal to zero.

$$H_0 : \beta_{ENV} = 0$$
$$H_1 : \beta_{ENV} < 0$$

The output gives you a t_{obt} of –3.312, and the probability of obtaining a t this size if the null hypothesis were true is equal to .0062. Since this probability is less than our chosen alpha level of .01, we decide to reject the null hypothesis. We conclude that the population partial slope coefficient is less than 0.

$$H_0 : \beta_{REL} = 0$$
$$H_1 : \beta_{REL} > 0$$

The t ratio for the variable ENV is $t_{obt} = 1.884$. The probability of obtaining a t statistic of this magnitude if the null hypothesis were true is equal to .0840. Since this probability is greater than .01, our decision is to fail to reject the null hypothesis. The partial slope coefficient between religious fundamentalism and punitiveness toward criminal offenders is not significantly different from zero in the population once we control for a belief in environmental causes of crime.

$$\hat{y} = 16.245 + (-1.467)(ENV) + (1.076)(REL)$$
$$\hat{y} = 16.245 + (-1.467)(2) + (1.076)(8)$$
$$\hat{y} = 16.245 + (-2.934) + 8.608$$
$$\hat{y} = 21.919$$

Glossary

Alphanumeric data: Values of a variable that are represented by letters rather than by numbers.

Analysis of variance (ANOVA): Statistical model used to test the differences between three or more group means.

Beta weight: Standardized slope coefficient in an ordinary least-squares (OLS) regression model.

Between-groups sum of squares: Measures the variability between groups for an analysis of variance (ANOVA).

Bimodal distribution: Distribution that contains two distinct modes with the greatest frequency even if the frequencies are not exactly equal.

Binary variable: Two-category variable coded 1 or 0. It is also called a dichotomous variable.

Binomial distribution: Probability distribution for which there are just two possible outcomes with fixed probabilities that sum to 1.0.

Bivariate correlation: Measures the linear relationship between two variables.

Bounding rule of probabilities: The probability of any event can never be less than zero or greater than $0 \leq P(A) \leq 1.0$.

Central limit theorem: Statistical theorem stating that the sampling distribution of any statistic will approximate normality as the sample size increases.

Chi-square test of independence: Tests the null hypothesis that two nominal- or ordinal-level variables are independent.

Class interval: In creating a grouped frequency distribution, the class interval defines the range of values that are included in each interval.

Coefficient of determination (r^2): Percentage of the variation in the dependent variable (y) that is explained by the independent variable (x).

Column marginal or column frequency: Total frequencies for the variable displayed on the column of a cross-tabulation table.

Complement of an event: Complement of event A is the set of all outcomes of a sample space that are not A. It is calculated as $1 - P(A)$.

Conditional mean of y: Mean of y calculated for every value of x.

Conditional probability: Probability of one event occurring (A) given that another event has occurred (B), written as $P(A|B)$.

Confidence interval: Statistical interval around a point estimate (e.g., mean) that we can provide a level of confidence to for capturing the true population parameter.

Confidence level: Level of confidence (e.g., 95% or 99%) that is set for a statistical inference from the sample to the population.

Confidence limits: Numerical lower and upper values that correspond to any given confidence interval around a point estimate from the sample.

Contingency table: Shows the joint distribution of two categorical variables. A contingency table is defined by the number of rows and the number of columns it has. A contingency table with three rows and two columns is a "3×2" contingency table. It is also called a cross-tabulation table.

Continuous measure: Measure with numbers indicating the values of variables as points on a continuum.

Count or frequency: Number of units in the sample that has a particular value in a variable distribution.

Cramer's V: Statistical measure of association that quantifies the strength or magnitude of a relationship between two nominal-level variables.

Critical difference (CD) score: Calculated by Tukey's honest significant difference (HSD) test to determine the significant difference between a series of group mean combinations after the null hypothesis from an analysis of variance (ANOVA) has been rejected.

Critical region of a probability distribution: Defines the entire class of outcomes that will lead us to reject the null hypothesis. If the event we observe falls into the critical region, our decision will be to reject the null hypothesis.

Cumulative frequency distribution: Frequency distribution reserved for ordinal or interval/ratio-level data made by starting with the lowest value of the variable (or the highest value) and cumulating (keeping a running tally or sum) the frequencies in each adjacent value until the highest value is reached (or the lowest value is reached). The sum of a cumulative frequency distribution should be equal to the total number of cases (n).

Cumulative percentages: Identical to a cumulative frequency distribution except that what is cumulated is the percentage at each value. The cumulative summing of percentages can go either from the lowest to highest score or from the highest to lowest score. The sum of a cumulative percentage distribution should be 100%.

Cumulative proportions: Identical to a cumulative frequency distribution except that what is cumulated is the proportion at each value. The cumulative summing of proportions can go either from the lowest to highest score or from the highest to lowest score. The sum of a cumulative percentage distribution should be 1.0.

Degrees of freedom (*df*): Value necessary along with a given alpha value to determine the critical value and region for a null hypothesis test or for a confidence interval.

Dependent variable: Variable that is expected to change or vary depending on the variation in the independent variable.

Descriptive research: Research in which phenomena are defined and described.

Descriptive statistics: Statistics used to describe the distribution of a sample or population.

Dichotomy: Variable having only two values.

Directional hypothesis test: When a research/alternative hypothesis states the directional difference that is expected.

Eta squared: Ratio of variance explained in the dependent variable by an independent variable.

Evaluation research: Research about social programs or interventions.

Exhaustive intervals: Class intervals must provide a place to count all original values of the variable distribution.

Expected frequencies: Joint frequency distribution we would expect to see if the two categorical variables were independent of each other. The expected frequencies, therefore, are calculated under the assumption of the null hypothesis—or no relationship between the two variables.

Explanatory research: Research that seeks to identify causes and/or effects of social phenomena.

General addition rule of probabilities (Rule 2b): If two events are not mutually exclusive, the probability of event *A* occurring or event *B* occurring is equal to the sum of their separate probabilities minus their joint probability: $P(A \text{ or } B) = P(A) + P(B) - P(A \text{ and } B)$.

General multiplication rule of probabilities (Rule 3b): If two events are not independent of each other, the probability of event *A* occurring and event *B* occurring is equal to the product of the unconditional probability of event *A* and the conditional probability of event *B* given *A*: $P(A \text{ and } B) = P(A) \times P(B|A)$.

Generalizability: Extent to which information from a sample can be used to inform us about persons, places, or events that were not studied in the entire population from which the sample was taken.

Goodman and Kruskal's gamma: Statistical measure of association that quantifies the strength or magnitude of a relationship between two ordinal-level variables. It is also called Yule's *Q* with a 2×2 table.

Grouped frequency distribution: Reports the values of a quantitative continuous variable in intervals or a range of values, rather than reporting every distinct value.

Histogram: Method of graphing the distribution of an interval/ratio-level variable. It consists of a series of bars at each value of a variable, where the height of the bar reflects the frequency of a value, its proportion, or its percentage.

Homoscedasticity: Assumption in ordinary least-squares (OLS) regression that the error terms are constant across all values of *x*.

Hypothesis: Tentative statement about empirical reality involving the relationship between two or more variables.

Independent events: Two events, *A* and *B*, are independent when the unconditional probability of *A* is equal to the conditional probability of *A* given *B*: $P(A) = P(A|B)$. When two events are independent, knowledge of one event does not help to predict the probability of the other event occurring.

Independent random samples: Samples that are randomly and independently selected.

Independent variable: Variable that is expected to cause or lead to variation or change in the dependent variable.

Inferential statistics: Statistical tools for estimating how likely it is that a statistical result based on data from a random sample is representative of the population from which the sample has been selected.

Interquartile range: Measure of dispersion appropriate for interval/ratio-level data. It measures the range of scores in the middle 50% of a distribution of continuous scores and is calculated as the difference between the score at the third quartile (the 75th percentile) and the score at the first quartile (the 25th percentile).

Interval width: Number of different values that are contained within the class interval. For example, for the given interval 0–5 arrests, the width is 6 because the interval contains the values 0, 1, 2, 3, 4, and 5 arrests.

Interval-level variable: In addition to an inherent rank order, a value's relationship to other values is known. There is an equal and constant distance between adjacent values. Therefore, the values can be added and subtracted.

Interval-ratio level of measurement: Variables that we assume can be added and subtracted, as well as multiplied and divided, regardless of whether they have true zero points.

Joint frequency distribution: For two categorical variables, the intersection of two values or categories.

Least-squares regression line: Regression line based on the least-squares function to calculate an equation that characterizes the best-fitting line between two interval/ratio variables.

Level of measurement: Mathematical nature of the values for a variable.

Line graph (polygon): Method of graphing interval/ratio-level data.

Matched or dependent samples: Samples in which individuals are dependent or matched on several characteristics (e.g., age, race, gender) or before-and-after samples of the same people.

Mean: Arithmetic average of a group of scores calculated as the sum of the scores divided by the total number of scores. The mean is an appropriate measure of central tendency for interval/ratio-level data.

Mean deviation score: Distance between a score and the mean of the group of scores $(x_i - \overline{X})$.

Measures of association: Statistics that inform us about the strength or magnitude, as well as the direction, of the relationship between two variables.

Measures of central tendency: Summary statistics that capture the "typical," "average," and "most likely" scores or values in a variable distribution.

Measures of dispersion: Capture how different the values of a variable are. The more dispersion there is in a variable, the more different the values are from each other or from some central tendency and the more heterogeneity in the data.

Median: Score at the 50th percentile in a rank-ordered distribution of scores. Thus, one half of a variable's values are less than the median and one half are greater than the median.

Midpoint: Exact middle value in an interval of a grouped distribution. The midpoint is found by summing the lower and upper limits (stated or real) and dividing by 2.

Mode: Value of a variable that occurs more often than any other value.

Multicollinearity: Occurs whenever the independent variables in a regression equation are too highly correlated with one another.

Multiple coefficient of determination (R^2): Value of R^2 when there are two or more independent variables predicting a dependent variable.

Multiple regression equation: Equation estimated with two or more independent variables predicting one dependent variable.

Multivariate regression model: A regression model predicting one dependent variable with two or more independent variables.

Mutually exclusive events: Events that cannot occur at the same time. In other words, there is no intersection of mutually exclusive events, so their joint probability is equal to zero.

Mutually exclusive intervals: Class intervals must not overlap.

National Incident-Based Reporting System (NIBRS): Official reports about crime incidents that are reported to police departments across the United States and then voluntarily reported to the Federal Bureau of Investigation (FBI), which compiles them for statistics purposes. This system is slowly replacing the older Uniform Crime Reports (UCR) program.

Negative correlation: As the independent variable increases, the dependent variable decreases.

Negative relationship: An increase in one variable is related to a decrease in the other variable.

Negatively skewed distribution: Long "tail" is found on the left side of the distribution (toward the negative numbers).

Nominal-level variables: Values that represent categories or qualities of a case only.

Non-directional hypothesis test: When a research/alternative hypothesis does not state the direction of difference; it states only that there is a relationship between the independent and dependent variables.

Nonprobability sampling methods: These methods are not based on random selection and do not allow us to know in advance the likelihood of any element of a population being selected for the sample.

Nonspuriousness: When a relationship between two variables is not explained by a third variable.

Normal distribution: Symmetrical distribution that has the greatest frequency of its cases in the middle of the distribution, with fewer cases at each end or "tail" of the distribution. A normal distribution looks like a bell when drawn and it is often referred to as a "bell-shaped" distribution.

Null hypothesis: In a hypothesis test, the null hypothesis is the hypothesis that is initially assumed to be true. It is called the null hypothesis because it presumes that there is no relationship (null) between the variables being tested.

Numeric data: Values of a variable that represent numerical qualities.

Observed frequencies: Joint distribution of two categorical variables that we actually observed in our sample data.

Ordinal-level variables: Values that not only represent categories but also have a logical order.

Outlier: Unusually high or low value or score for a variable.

Partial correlation coefficient: Correlation between two variables after controlling for a third variable.

Partial slope coefficient: Effect of an independent variable on the dependent variable after controlling for one or more other independent variables.

Pearson correlation coefficient: Statistic that quantifies the direction and strength of the relationship between two interval/ratio-level variables.

Percent change score: Score that quantifies the percent change of a score between two different time periods or other units.

Percentage: Number of some value in a variable distribution that is divided by total possible scores and then is multiplied by 100.

Percentage differences: One way to examine the bivariate relationship in a contingency table. The rule is to calculate the percentages based on the marginals of the independent variable and to compare different levels of the independent variable at the same level or category of the dependent variable.

Phi coefficient: A measure of association used to measure the strength of the relationship between two nominal-level variables in a 2 × 2 contingency table.

Pie chart and bar chart: Graphical ways to display nominal- or ordinal-level variables. These charts can include frequencies, proportions, or percentages. Pie charts represent quantities as slices, and bar charts represent quantities as bars.

Point estimates: Sample statistics such as the mean and proportion that are sample estimates of the same values in the population.

Police reports: Data used to measure crime based on incidents that become known to police departments.

Population: Larger set of cases or aggregate number of people that a researcher is actually interested in or wishes to know something about.

Population parameter: Statistic (e.g., mean, proportion) obtained from a population. Since we rarely have entire population data, we typically estimate population parameters using sample statistics.

Positive correlation: As the independent variable increases, the dependent variable also increases.

Positive relationship: An increase in one variable is related to an increase in the other variable.

Positively skewed distribution: Long "tail" is found on the right side of the distribution (toward the positive numbers).

Predicted value of y ($\hat{y}$): Value of the dependent variable predicted by a regression equation.

Probability distribution: Distribution of all possible outcomes of a trial and the associated probability of each outcome.

Probability sampling methods: These methods rely on random selection or chance and allow us to know in advance how likely it

is that any element of a population is selected for the sample.

Proportion: Number of some value in a variable distribution that is divided by total possible scores.

Q_1, Q_2, Q_3, and Q_4: The interquartile range depends on finding the values for Q_1 and Q_3. Q_1 is the 25th percentile, and Q_3 is the 75th percentile. When a percentage distribution is divided into quartiles, there are four of them: Q_1, the 25th percentile; Q_2, the 50th percentile or median; Q_3, the 75th percentile; and Q_4, the 100th percentile.

Qualitative or categorical variables: Values that refer to qualities or categories. They tell us what kind, what group, or what type a value is referring to.

Quantitative or continuous variables: Values that refer to quantities or different measurements. They tell us how much or how many a variable has.

R^2 change: Reflects the change in the amount of variance explained when a second variable is entered into a regression model.

Random sample: A sample that was obtained through probability sampling methods.

Random selection: The fundamental aspect of probability sampling. The essential characteristic of random selection is that every element of the population has a known and independent chance of being selected for the sample.

Range: Measure of dispersion appropriate for interval/ratio-level data. It is calculated as the difference between the highest and lowest values or scores: Range = Highest value – Lowest value.

Rate: Number of a phenomenon divided by the total possible, which is then multiplied by a constant such as 1,000, 10,000, or 100,000.

Ratio: Expresses the relationship between two numbers and indicates their relative size.

Ratio-level variables: Variable that we assume can be added and subtracted as well

as multiplied and divided and that have true zero points.

Real class limits: Real limits in a grouped distribution take into account the space between the adjacent intervals. For example, for an interval with stated limits of 0–5 and 6–11 prior arrests, the real limits are .5–5.5 and 5.5–11.5.

Regression line: Line depicting the relationship between independent and dependent variables determined by an ordinary least-squares (OLS) regression equation.

Relative frequency: See *Proportion*.

Residual: Difference between the predicted value of y from the regression equation and the observed value at a given x score.

Restricted addition rule of probabilities (Rule 2a): If two events are mutually exclusive, the probability of event A occurring *or* event B occurring is equal to the sum of their separate probabilities: $P(A \text{ or } B) = P(A) + P(B)$.

Restricted multiplication rule of probabilities (Rule 3a): If two events are independent of each other, the probability of event A occurring and event B occurring is equal to the product of their separate probabilities: $P(A \text{ and } B) = P(A) \times P(B)$.

Row marginal or row frequency: Total frequencies for the categories of a variable displayed in the rows of a cross-tabulation table.

Sample: Subset of the population that a researcher must often use to make generalizations about the larger population.

Sample statistic: Statistic (e.g., mean or proportion) obtained from a sample of the population.

Sampling distribution: Probability distribution of a sample statistic (e.g., mean or proportion) drawn from a very large number of samples from some given population.

Sampling distribution of sample mean differences: Theoretical distribution of the difference between an infinite number of sample means.

Sampling error: The difference between a sample estimate (called a sample statistic) and the population value it is estimating (called a population parameter).

Sampling variation: Differences between the sample and the population that are due to chance or sample variation.

Scatterplot: Graphical display of the linear relationship between two interval/ratio-level variables. It is also called a scattergram.

Science: Set of logical, systematic, documented methods with which to investigate nature and natural processes; the knowledge produced by these investigations.

Significance or alpha level (α): Risk we are willing to take in rejecting a true null hypothesis. For example, if we select an alpha level of .05, we are willing to be incorrect 5% of the time.

Skewed distribution: Non-normal (non-symmetrical) distribution.

Slope: Term in an ordinary least-squares (OLS) regression equation that indicates the change in y associated with a 1-unit change in x.

Standard deviation: Square root of the squared deviation about the mean.

Standard error of the mean: Standard deviation of the sampling distribution of the mean.

Standard error of the proportion: Standard deviation of the sampling distribution of the proportion.

Standard score (z score): Score from the standard normal probability distribution that indicates how many standard deviation units a score is from the mean of 0.

Stated class limits: Lowest value that is included in an interval and highest value that is included in an interval.

Survey: Research method used to measure the prevalence of behavior, attitudes, or any other phenomenon by asking a sample of people to fill out a questionnaire either in person, through the mail or Internet, or on the telephone.

***t* Distribution (Student's *t* distribution):** Statistical sampling distribution used in many statistical tests, including for the construction of confidence intervals and the difference between two means.

***t* Test:** Statistical test used to test several null hypotheses, including the difference between two means.

Theory: Logically interrelated set of propositions about empirical reality that can be tested.

Total sum of squares: Measures the total variability in the sample for an analysis of variance (ANOVA).

Tukey's honest significant difference (HSD) test: Tests the difference between a series of group mean combinations after the null hypothesis from an analysis of variance (ANOVA) has been rejected.

Ungrouped frequency distribution: Every value of a variable is displayed in contrast to a grouped frequency distribution that displays intervals that correspond to the data values.

Uniform Crime Reports (UCR): Official reports about crime incidents that are reported to police departments across the United States and then voluntarily reported to the Federal Bureau of Investigation (FBI), which compiles them for statistics purposes.

Units of analysis: Particular units or aggregations (e.g., people and cities) that constitute an observation in a data set.

Univariate analysis: Examining the distribution of one variable.

Variable: Characteristic or property that can vary or take on different values or attributes.

Variance: Measures the average squared deviations from the mean for an interval/ratio variable.

Variation ratio: Appropriate measure of dispersion to use when variables are measured at the nominal or purely ordinal level. It measures the proportion of cases of a variable that are not in the modal value. The greater the magnitude of the variation ratio, the more dispersion or variability there is in the nominal or ordinal variable.

Within-group sum of squares: Measures the variability within a group for an analysis of variance (ANOVA).

***y* Intercept:** Value of y in an ordinary least-squares (OLS) regression equation when x is equal to 0.

***z* Distribution:** Statistical sampling distribution used in many statistical tests, including for the construction of confidence intervals, for determining the difference between two means, and for calculating the number of standard deviations an observation is above or below the mean.

***z* Test:** Statistical test used to test several null hypotheses, including the difference between two means.

References

Agnew, R. (1992). Foundation for a general strain theory of crime and delinquency. *Criminology, 30,* 47–87.

Andreescu, V., Shutt, J. E., & Vito, G. F. (2011). The violent South: Culture of honor, social disorganization, and murder in Appalachia. *Criminal Justice Review, 36*(1), 76–103.

Bierie, D. M. (2012). Is tougher better? The impact of physical prison conditions on inmate violence. *International Journal of Offender Therapy and Comparative Criminology, 56,* 338–355.

Blalock, H. (1979). *Social statistics* (2nd ed.). New York: McGraw–Hill.

Braga, A. A., Weisburd, D. L., Waring, E. J., Mazerolle, L. G., Spelman, W., & Gajewski, F. (1999). Problem-oriented policing in violent crime places: A randomized controlled experiment. *Criminology, 37,* 541–580.

Bureau of Justice Statistics. (1993–2013). *National Crime Victimization Survey property crime trends, 1993–2013.* Retrieved from http://www.ojp.usdoj.gov/bjs/

Burt, C. H., Sweeten, G., & Simons, R. L. (2014). Self-control through emerging adulthood: Instability, multidimensionality, and criminological significance. *Criminology, 52,* 450–487.

Buss, A. H., & Warren, W. L. (2000). *The Aggression Questionnaire.* Los Angeles: Western Psychological Services.

Caplan, J. M., Kennedy, L. W., & Piza, E. L. (2013). Joint utility of event-dependent and environmental crime analysis techniques for violent crime forecasting. *Crime & Delinquency, 59,* 243–270.

Chapple, C., Vaske, J., & Worthen, M. G. F. (2014). Gender differences in associations with deviant peer groups: Examining individual, interactional, and compositional factors. *Deviant Behavior, 35,* 394–411.

Charette, Y., Crocker, A. G., & Billette, I. (2014). Police encounters involving citizens with mental illness: Use of resources and outcomes. *Psychiatric Services, 65*(4), 511–516.

Choi, K-S., Librett, M., & Collins, T. J. (2014). An empirical evaluation: Gunshot detection system and its effectiveness on police practices. *Police Practice and Research, 15*(1), 48–61.

Cohn, D., Taylor, P., Lopez, M. H., Gallagher, C. A., Parker, K., & Maass, K. T. (2013). *Gun homicide rate down 49% since 1993 peak: Public unaware.* Washington, DC: Pew Research Center.

Copes, H., Kovandzic, T. V., Miller, J. M., & Williamson, L. (2014). The lost cause? Examining the southern culture of honor through defensive gun use. *Crime & Delinquency, 60,* 356–378.

Core Institute. (2015). *Core Alcohol and Drug Survey: Long form.* Carbondale, IL: FIPSE Core Analysis Grantee Group, Core Institute, Student Health Programs, Southern Illinois University.

Daly, K. (1987). Discrimination in the criminal courts: Family, gender, and the problem of equal treatment. *Social Forces, 66,* 152–175.

Daly, K. (1994). *Gender, crime, and punishment.* New Haven, CT: Yale University Press.

DeCoster, S., & Zito, R. C. (2010). Gender and general strain theory: The gendering of emotional experiences and expressions. *Journal of Contemporary Criminal Justice, 26,* 224–245.

Durose, M. R., Cooper, A. D., & Snyder, H. N. (2014). *Recidivism of prisoners released in 30 states in 2005: Patterns from 2005 to 2010* [special report]. Washington, DC: Department of Justice, Office of Justice Programs, Bureau of Justice Statistics.

Duxbury, L., Higgins, C., & Halinski, M. (2015). Identifying the antecedents of work-role overload in police organizations. *Criminal Justice and Behavior, 42,* 361–381.

Engen, R. L., Gainey, R. R., Crutchfield, R. D., & Weis, J. G. (2003). Discretion and disparity under sentencing guidelines: The role of departures and structured sentencing alternatives. *Criminology, 41,* 99–130.

Esbensen, F. A., Osgood, D. W., Peterson, D., Taylor, T. J., & Carson, D. C. (2013). Short-and long-term outcome results from a multisite evaluation of the G.R.E.A.T. program. *Criminology & Public Policy, 12,* 375–411.

Federal Bureau of Investigation. (2013a). *Crime in the United States.* Washington, DC: Author.

Federal Bureau of Investigation. (2013b). *Hate crime statistics—2013.* Washington, DC: Author.

Federal Bureau of Investigation. (various dates). *Uniform Crime Reports: Crime in the United States:* [*1990, 1995, 2000,* and *2005–2014*]. Washington, DC: Author.

Francis, K. A. (2014). General strain theory, gender, and the conditioning influence of negative internalizing emotions on youth risk behaviors. *Youth Violence and Juvenile Justice, 12,* 58–76.

Gallup. (2014a, October 27). *Hacking tops list of crimes Americans worry about most.* Retrieved from http://www.gallup.com/poll/178856/hacking-tops-list-crimes-americans-worry.aspx

Gallup. (2014b, October 31). *Less than half of Americans support stricter gun laws.* Retrieved from http://www.gallup.com/poll/179045/less-half-americans-support-stricter-gun-laws.aspx?g_source=gun%20laws&g_medium=search&g_campaign=tiles

Glueck, S., & Glueck, E. (1950). *Unraveling juvenile delinquency.* Cambridge, MA: Harvard University Press.

Gottfredson, M. R., & Hirschi, T. (1990). *A general theory of crime.* Stanford, CA: Stanford University Press.

Harlan, C., Brown, D. L., & Fisher, M. (2015, June 19). Night of S.C. killings started with prayers and a plot against humanity. *The Washington Post.* Retrieved from https://www.washingtonpost.com/politics/roof-friend-i-dont-think-he-hated-blacks-i-think-he-hated-humans/2015/06/19/75d697f4-15da-11e5-9518-f9e0a8959f32_story.html

Hays, W. L. (1994). *Statistics.* Belmont, CA: Wadsworth.

Hirschi, T. (1969). *Causes of delinquency.* Berkeley: University of California Press.

Holtfreter, K. (2013). Gender and "other people's money": An analysis of white-collar offender sentencing. *Women & Criminal Justice, 23,* 326–344.

Ingram, J. R., & Terrill, W. (2014). Relational demography and officer occupational attitudes: The influence of workgroup context. *Journal of Criminal Justice, 42,* 309–320.

Jennings, W. G., Hahn Fox, B., & Farrington, D. P. (2014). Inked into crime? An examination of the causal relationship between tattoos and life-course offending among males from the Cambridge Study in Delinquent Development. *Journal of Criminal Justice, 42,* 77–84.

Jennings, W. G., Piquero, N. L., Gover, A. R., & Perez, D. M. (2009). Gender and general strain theory: A replication and exploration of Broidy and Agnew's gender/strain hypothesis among a sample of southwestern Mexican American adolescents. *Journal of Criminal Justice, 37,* 404–417.

Kennedy, L., Caplan, J., & Piza, E. (2013). Risk clusters, hotspots, and spatial intelligence: Risk terrain modeling as an algorithm for police allocation strategies. *Journal of Quantitative Criminology, 27,* 339–362.

Kim, R. H., & Clark, D. (2013). The effect of prison-based college education programs on recidivism: Propensity score matching approach. *Journal of Criminal Justice, 41,* 196–204.

Lane, J., & Fox, K. A. (2013). Fear of property, violent, and gang crime: Examining the shadow of sexual assault thesis among male and female offenders. *Criminal Justice and Behavior, 40,* 472–496.

Loughran, T. A., Pogarsky, G., Piquero, A. R., & Paternoster, R. (2012). Re-examining the functional form of the certainty effect in deterrence theory. *Justice Quarterly, 29,* 712–741.

MacDonald, J. M., Piquero, A. R., Valois, R. F., & Zullig, K. J. (2005). The relationship between life satisfaction, risk-taking behaviors, and youth violence. *Journal of Interpersonal Violence, 20,* 1495–1518.

MacKenzie, D. L. (2013). First do no harm: A look at correctional policies and programs today. *Journal of Experimental Criminology, 9*(1), 1–17.

McCarthy, T., & Gambino, L. (2015, June 20). Charleston shootings: NRA blames victims as reactions echo Newtown. *The Guardian.* Retrieved from https://www.theguardian.com/us-news/2015/jun/19/nra-mass-shootings-south-carolina-church

McCuish, E. C., Corrado, R., Lussier, P., & Hart, S. D. (2014). Psychopathic traits and offending trajectories from early adolescence to adulthood. *Journal of Criminal Justice, 42,* 66–76.

Mears, D. P., Wang, X., & Bales, W. D. (2014). Does a rising tide lift all boats? Labor market changes and their effects on the recidivism of released prisoners. *Justice Quarterly, 31,* 822–851.

Megargee, E. I. (1972). Standardized reports of work performance and inmate adjustment for use in correctional settings. *Correctional Psychologist, 5,* 48–58.

Meldrum, R., Barnes, J. C., & Hay, C. (2015). Sleep deprivation, low self-control, and delinquency: A test of the strength model of self-control. *Journal of Youth and Adolescence, 44,* 465–477.

Miller, J. (2015). Contemporary modes of probation officer supervision: The triumph of the "synthetic" officer. *Justice Quarterly, 32,* 314–336.

Miller, M. K., Maskaly, J., Peoples, C. D., & Sigillo, A. E. (2014). The relationship between mock jurors' religious characteristics and their verdicts and sentencing decisions. *Psychology of Religion and Spirituality, 6,* 188–197.

Motavalli, J. (2012, May 16). *Flying vs. driving: It's complicated.* Retrieved from Cartalk.com (archives).

Nisbett, R. E., & Cohen, D. (1996). *The culture of honor.* Boulder, CO: Westview.

Nisbett, R. E., & Cohen, D. (2014). The lost cause? Examining the southern subculture of violence through defensive gun use. *Crime & Delinquency, 60,* 356–380.

Pew Research Center. (2015, January 9). *A public opinion trend that matters: Priorities for gun policy.* Retrieved from http://www.pewresearch.org/fact-tank/2015/01/09/a-public-opinion-trend-that-matters-priorities-for-gun-policy/

Piquero, N. L., Fox, K., Piquero, A., Capowich, G., & Mazerolle, P. (2010). Gender, general strain theory, negative emotions, and disordered eating. *Journal of Youth and Adolescence, 39,* 380–382.

Puzzanchera, C., & Kang, W. (2014). *Easy access to FBI arrest statistics 1994–2012.* Retrieved from http://www.ojjdp.gov/ojstatbb/ezaucr/

Raine, A. (1994). *The psychopathology of crime: Criminal behavior as a clinical disorder.* New York: Academic Press.

Raine, A., Fung, A. L. C., Portnoy, J., Choy, O., & Spring, V. L. (2014). Low heart rate as a risk factor for child and adolescent proactive aggressive and impulsive psychopathic behavior. *Aggressive Behavior, 40,* 290–299.

Rapaport, E. (1991). The death penalty and gender discrimination. *Law and Society Review, 25,* 367–383.

Riedel, M. (2012). *Research strategies for secondary data.* Thousand Oaks, CA: Sage.

Rydberg, J., & Pizarro, J. M. (2014). Victim lifestyle as a correlate of homicide clearance. *Homicide Studies, 18,* 342–362.

Schnapp, P. (2015). Identifying the effect of immigration on homicide rates in U.S. cities: An instrumental variables approach. *Homicide Studies, 19,* 103–122.

Sherman, L. W., & Berk, R. A. (1984a). The specific deterrent effects of arrest for domestic assault. *American Sociological Review, 49,* 261–272.

Sherman, L. W., & Berk, R. A. (1984b). *The Minneapolis Domestic Violence Experiment.* Washington, DC: The Police Foundation.

Sherman, L. W., Gartin, P., & Buerger, M. (1989). Hot spots of predatory crime: Routine activities and the criminology of place. *Criminology, 27,* 27–56.

Sherman, L. W., & Harris, H. M. (2015). Increased death rates of domestic violence victims from arresting vs. warning suspects in the Milwaukee Domestic Violence Experiment (MilDVE). *Journal of Experimental Criminology, 11,* 1–20.

Spohn, C. C., & Spears, J. W. (1997). Gender and case processing decisions: A comparison of case outcomes for male and female defendants charged with violent felonies. *Women & Criminal Justice, 8,* 29–45.

Starr, S. (2015). Estimating gender disparities in federal criminal cases. *American Law and Economics Review, 17,* 127–159.

Steffensmeier, D., Kramer, J., & Streifel, C. (1993). Gender and punishment. *Criminology, 31,* 411–446.

Steinmetz, N. M., & Austin, D. M. (2014). Fear of criminal victimization on a college campus: A visual and survey analysis of location and demographic factors. *American Journal of Criminal Justice, 39,* 511–537.

Sutherland, R., Sindicich, N., Barrett, E., Whittaker, E., Peacock, A., Hickey, S., & Burns, L. (2015). Motivations, substance use, and other correlates amongst property and violent offenders who regularly inject drugs. *Addictive Behaviors, 45,* 207–213.

Thornberry, T. P., Krohn, M., Lizotte, A., & Bushway, S. (2008). *The Rochester Youth Development Survey.* Albany, NY: Hindelang Criminal Justice Research Center, University of Albany. Retrieved from http://www.albany.edu/hindelang/youth_study.html

Truman, J. L., & Langton, L. (2014). *Criminal victimization, 2013.* Washington, DC: Bureau of Justice Statistics, Department of Justice.

Tucker, M. C., & Rodriguez, C. M. (2014). Family dysfunction and social isolation as moderators between stress and child physical abuse risk. *Journal of Family Violence, 29,* 175–186.

U.S. Bureau of the Census. (2014). *Population by age and sex.* Retrieved from http://www.census.gov/population/age/

Vera Institute of Justice. (2012). *The cost of prisons: What incarceration costs taxpayers*. New York: Author.

Welsh, W. N., Zajac, G., & Bucklen, K. (2014). For whom does prison based drug treatment work? Results from a randomized experiment. *Journal of Experimental Criminology, 10,* 151–177.

Worrall, J., Els, N., Piquero, A., & TenEyck, M. (2014). The moderating effects of informal social control in the sanctions–compliance nexus. *American Journal of Criminal Justice, 39,* 341–357.

Zajac, G., Lattimore, P. K., Dawes, D., & Winger, L. (2015). An implementation is local: Initial findings from the process evaluation of the Honest Opportunity Probation and Enforcement (HOPE) demonstration field experiment. *Federal Probation, 79*(1), 31–36.

Zhao, J., & Ren, L. (2015). Exploring the dimensions of public attitudes toward the police. *Police Quarterly, 18,* 3–26.

Index